THROUGH THE EYES OF A SLAVE

WRITTEN ACCOUNTS OF AMERICAN SLAVERY

By

VARIOUS

Read & Co.

Copyright © 2020 Read & Co. History

This edition is published by Read & Co. History,
an imprint of Read & Co.

This book is copyright and may not be reproduced or copied in any
way without the express permission of the publisher in writing.

British Library Cataloguing-in-Publication Data
A catalogue record for this book is available
from the British Library.

Read & Co. is part of Read Books Ltd.
For more information visit
www.readandcobooks.co.uk

CONTENTS

THIRTY YEARS A SLAVE
BY LOUIS HUGHES

NARRATIVE OF THE LIFE
OF FREDERICK DOUGLASS
BY FREDERICK DOUGLASS

TWELVE YEARS A SLAVE

BY SOLOMON NORTHUP

RUNNING A
THOUSAND MILES FOR FREEDOM
BY WILLIAM CRAFT AND ELLEN CRAFT

TWENTY-TWO YEARS A SLAVE,
AND FORTY YEARS A FREEMAN
BY AUSTIN STEWARD

ON BEING BROUGHT FROM AFRICA TO AMERICA

'Twas mercy brought me from my *Pagan* land,
Taught my benighted soul to understand
That there's a God, that there's a *Saviour* too:
Once I redemption neither sought nor knew.
Some view our sable race with scornful eye,
"Their colour is a diabolic die."
Remember, *Christians, Negros*, black as *Cain*,
May be refin'd, and join th' angelic train.

—PHILLIS WHEATLEY

THIRTY
YEARS A SLAVE

BY LOUIS HUGHES

First Published in 1896

CHAPTER I

LIFE ON A COTTON PLANTATION

BIRTH—SOLD IN A RICHMOND SLAVE PEN

I was born in Virginia, in 1832, near Charlottesville, in the beautiful valley of the Rivanna river. My father was a white man and my mother a negress, the slave of one John Martin. I was a mere child, probably not more than six years of age, as I remember, when my mother, two brothers and myself were sold to Dr. Louis, a practicing physician in the village of Scottsville. We remained with him about five years, when he died, and, in the settlement of his estate, I was sold to one Washington Fitzpatrick, a merchant of the village. He kept me a short time when he took me to Richmond, by way of canal-boat, expecting to sell me; but as the market was dull, he brought me back and kept me some three months longer, when he told me he had hired me out to work on a canal-boat running to Richmond, and to go to my mother and get my clothes ready to start on the trip. I went to her as directed, and, when she had made ready my bundle, she bade me good-by with tears in her eyes, saying: "My son, be a good boy; be polite to every one, and always behave yourself properly." It was sad to her to part with me, though she did not know that she was never to see me again, for my master had said nothing to her regarding his purpose and she only thought, as I did, that I was hired to work on the canal-boat, and that she should see me occasionally. But alas! We never met again. I can see her form still as when she bade me good-bye. That parting I can never forget. I ran off from her as quickly as I could after her parting words, for I did not want her to see me crying. I went to my master at the store, and he again told me that he had hired me to work on the canal-boat, and to go aboard immediately. Of the boat and the trip and the scenes along the route I remember little—I only thought of my mother and my leaving her.

When we arrived at Richmond, George Pullan, a "nigger-trader," as he was called, came to the boat and began to question me, asking me first if I could remember having had the chickenpox, measles or whooping-cough. I answered, yes. Then he asked me if I did not want to take a little walk with him. I said, no. "Well," said he, "you have got to go. Your master sent you down here to be sold, and told me to come and get you and take you to the trader's yard, ready to be sold." I saw that to hesitate was useless; so I at once obeyed him and went.

A SLAVE MARKET

The trader's establishment consisted of an office, a large show-room and a yard in the rear enclosed with a wall of brick fifteen feet high. The principal men of the establishment were the proprietor and the foreman. When slaves were to be exhibited for sale, the foreman was called to the office by means of a bell, and an order given him to bring into the show-room all the slaves in the establishment. This was the work of but a few minutes, and the women were placed in a row on one side of the room and the men on the other. Persons desirous of purchasing them passed up and down between the lines looking the poor creatures over, and questioning them in about the following manner: "What can you do?" "Are you a good cook? seamstress? dairymaid?"—this to the women, while the men would be questioned as to their line of work: "Can you plow? Are you a blacksmith? Have you ever cared for horses? Can you pick cotton rapidly?" Sometimes the slave would be required to open his mouth that the purchaser might examine the teeth and form some opinion as to his age and physical soundness; and if it was suspected that a slave had been beaten a good deal he would be required to step into another room and undress. If the person desiring to buy found the slave badly scarred by the common usage of whipping, he would say at once to the foreman; "Why! this slave is not worth much, he is all scarred up. No, I don't want him; bring me in another to look at." Slaves without scars from whipping and looking well physically always sold readily. They were never left long in the yard. It was expected that all the slaves in the yard for sale would be neatly dressed and clean before being brought into the show-room. It was the foreman's business to see that each one was presentable.

SLAVE WHIPPING AS A BUSINESS

Whipping was done at these markets, or trader's yards, all the time. People who lived in the city of Richmond would send their slaves here for punishment. When any one wanted a slave whipped he would send a note to that effect with the servant to the trader. Any petty offense on the part of a slave was sufficient to subject the offender to this brutal treatment. Owners who affected culture and refinement preferred to send a servant to the yard for punishment to inflicting it themselves. It saved them trouble, they said, and possibly a slight wear and tear of feeling. For this service the owner was charged a certain sum for each slave, and the earnings of the traders from this source formed a very large part of the profits of his business. The yard I was in had a regular whipping post to which they tied the slave, and gave him "nine-and-thirty," as it was called, meaning thirty-nine lashes as hard as they could lay it on. Men were stripped of their shirts in preparation for the whipping, and women had to take off their dresses from the shoulders to the waist. These whippings were not so severe as when the slaves were stripped entirely of their clothes, as was generally the case on the plantations where slaves were owned by the dozen. I saw many cases of whipping while I was in the yard. Sometimes I was so frightened that I trembled violently, for I had never seen anything like it before.

SOLD IN THE MARKET

I was only in the yard a short time before I was bought by one George Reid who lived in Richmond. He had no wife, but an old lady kept house for him and his three sons. At this time he had a place in the postoffice, but soon after I came there he lost it. He then moved into the country upon a farm of about one thousand acres, enclosed by a cedar hedge. The house was a plain frame structure upon a stone basement and contained four rooms. It was surrounded with shrubbery, and was a pleasant country seat. But I did not like it here. I grieved continually about my mother. It came to me, more and more plainly, that I would never see her again. Young and lonely as I was, I could not help crying, oftentimes for hours together. It was hard to get used to being away from my mother. I remember well "Aunt Sylvia," who was the cook in the Reid household. She was very kind to me and always spoke consolingly to me, especially if I had been blue, and had had one of my fits of crying. At these times she would always bake me an ash cake for supper, saying to me; "My child, don't cry; 'Aunt Sylvia' will look after you." This ash cake was made of corn meal and water, a little salt to make it palatable, and was baked by putting it between cabbage leaves and covering it with hot ashes. A sweeter or more delicious cake one could not desire, and it was common upon the tables of all the Virginia farmers. I always considered it a great treat to get one of these cakes from "Aunt Sylvia."

The appellations of "aunt" and "uncle" for the older slaves

14

were not only common among the blacks, but the whites also addressed them in the same way.

ON THE AUCTION BLOCK

I was sick a great deal—in fact, I had suffered with chills and fever ever since Mr. Reid bought me. He, therefore, concluded to sell me, and, in November, 1844, he took me back to Richmond, placing me in the Exchange building, or auction rooms, for the sale of slaves. The sales were carried on in a large hall where those interested in the business sat around a large block or stand, upon which the slave to be sold was placed, the auctioneer standing beside him. When I was placed upon the block, a Mr. McGee came up and felt of me and asked me what I could do. "You look like a right smart nigger," said he, "Virginia always produces good darkies." Virginia was the mother of slavery, and it was held by many that she had the best slaves. So when Mr. McGee found I was born and bred in that state he seemed satisfied. The bidding commenced, and I remember well when the auctioneer said; "Three hundred eighty dollars—once, twice and sold to Mr. Edward McGee." He was a rich cotton planter of Pontotoc, Miss. As near as I can recollect, I was not more than twelve years of age, so did not sell for very much.

PRICE OF SLAVES

Servant women sold for $500 to $700, and sometimes as high as $800 when possessing extra qualifications. A house maid, bright in looks, strong and well formed, would sell for $1,000 to $1,200. Bright mulatto girls, well versed in sewing and knitting, would sometimes bring as high as $1,800, especially if a Virginian or a Kentuckian. Good blacksmiths sold for $1,600 to $1,800. When the slaves were put upon the block they were always sold to the highest bidder. Mr. McGee, or "Boss," as I soon learned to call him, bought sixty other slaves before he bought me, and they were started in a herd for Atlanta, Ga., on foot.

STARTED FOR A COTTON PLANTATION

Boss, myself and ten others met them there. We then started for Pontotoc, Miss. On our way we stopped at Edenton, Ga., where Boss sold twenty-one of the sixty slaves. We then proceeded on our way, Boss by rail and we on foot, or in the wagon. We went about twenty miles a day. I remember, as we passed along, every white man we met was yelling, "Hurrah for Polk and Dallas!" They were feeling good, for election had given them the men that they wanted. The man who had us in charge joined with those we met in the hurrahing. We were afraid to ask them the reason for their yelling, as that would have been regarded as an impertinence, and probably would have caused us all to be whipped.

MY MISSISSIPPI HOME

At length, after a long and wearisome journey, we reached Pontotoc, McGee's home, on Christmas eve. Boss took me into the house and into the sitting room, where all the family were assembled, and presented me as a Christmas gift to the madam, his wife.

My boss, as I remember him, was a tall, raw-boned man, but rather distinguished in looks, with a fine carriage, brilliant in intellect, and considered one of the wealthiest and most successful planters of his time. Mrs. McGee was a handsome, stately lady, about thirty years of age, brunette in complexion, faultless in figure and imperious in manner. I think that they were of Scotch descent. There were four children, Emma, Willie,

Johnnie and Jimmie. All looked at me, and thought I was "a spry little fellow." I was very shy and did not say much, as everything was strange to me. I was put to sleep that night on a pallet on the floor in the dining room, using an old quilt as a covering. The next morning was Christmas, and it seemed to be a custom to have egg-nog before breakfast. The process of making this was new and interesting to me. I saw them whip the whites of eggs, on a platter, to a stiff froth; the yolks were thoroughly beaten in a large bowl, sugar and plenty of good brandy were added, and the whites of the eggs and cream were then stirred in, a little nutmeg grated on top of each glass when filled for serving. This was a delicious drink, and the best of all was, there was plenty of it. I served this to all the family, and, as there were also visiting relatives present, many glasses were required, and I found the tray so heavy I could hardly carry it. I helped myself, after the service was finished, and I was delighted, for I had never tasted anything so fine before.

My boss told me I was to wait on the madam, do any errand necessary, attend to the dining room—in fact I was installed as general utility boy. It was different from the quiet manner of life I had seen before coming here—it kept my spirits up for some time. I thought of my mother often, but I was gradually growing to the idea that it was useless to cry, and I tried hard to overcome my feelings.

PLANTATION LIFE

As already stated, it was Christmas morning, and, after breakfast, I saw the cook hurrying, and when I went out into the yard, everywhere I looked slaves met my view. I never saw so many slaves at one time before. In Virginia we did not have such large farms. There were no extensive cotton plantations, as in Mississippi. I shall never forget the dinner that day—it was a feast fit for a king, so varied and lavish was the bill of fare.

17

The next attraction for me was the farm hands getting their Christmas rations. Each was given a pint of flour of which they made biscuit, which were called "Billy Seldom," because biscuit were very rare with them. Their daily food was corn bread, which they called "Johnny Constant," as they had it constantly. In addition to the flour each received a piece of bacon or fat meat, from which they got the shortening for their biscuit. The cracklings from the rendering of lard were also used by the slaves for shortening. The hands were allowed four days off at Christmas, and if they worked on these days, as some of them did, they got fifty cents a day for chopping. It was not common to have chopping done during the holidays; some planters, however, found it convenient thus to get it out of the way for the work which came after Christmas.

THE GREAT HOUSE

I soon became familiar with my work in the house and with the neighborhood, as I often had to carry notes for Boss to neighboring farmers, as well as to carry the mail to and from the postoffice. The "great house," as the dwelling of the master was called, was two stories high, built of huge logs, chinked and daubed and whitewashed. It was divided, from front to rear, by a hall twenty-five feet long and twelve feet wide, and on each side of the hall, in each story, was one large room with a large fire-place. There were but four rooms in all, yet these were so large that they were equal to at least six of our modern rooms. The kitchen was not attached to the main building, but was about thirty feet to the rear. This was the common mode of building in the south in those days. The two bedrooms upstairs were very plain in furnishings, but neat and comfortable, judged by the standard of the times. A wing was added to the main building for dining room. In rear of the kitchen was the milk or dairy house, and beyond this the smoke house for curing

18

the meat. In line with these buildings, and still further to the rear, was the overseer's house. Near the milk house was a large tree, and attached to the trunk was a lever; and here was where the churning was done, in which I had always to assist. This establishment will serve as a sample of many of those on the large plantations in the south. The main road from Pontotoc to Holly Springs, one of the great thoroughfares of the state and a stage route, passed near the house, and through the center of the farm. On each side of this road was a fence, and in the corners of both fences, extending for a mile, were planted peach trees, which bore excellent fruit in great profusion.

HOUSE SERVANT AND ERRAND BOY

My first work in the morning was to dust the parlor and hall and arrange the dining room. It came awkward to me at first, but, after the madam told me how, I soon learned to do it satisfactorily. Then I had to wait on the table, sweep the large yard every morning with a brush broom and go for the mail once a week. I used to get very tired, for I was young and consequently not strong. Aside from these things which came regularly, I had to help the madam in warping the cloth. I dreaded this work, for I always got my ears boxed if I did not or could not do the work to suit her. She always made the warp herself and put it in, and I had to hand her the thread as she put it through the harness. I would get very tired at this work and, like any child, wanted to be at play, but I could not remember that the madam ever gave me that privilege. Saddling the horse at first was troublesome to me, but Boss was constant in his efforts to teach me, and, after many trials, I learned the task satisfactorily to the master and to bring the horse to the door when he wished to go out for business or pleasure. Riding horseback was common for both ladies and gentlemen, and sometimes I would have to saddle three or more horses when Boss, the madam, a friend or friends

19

desired a ride. Bird hunting parties were common and were greatly enjoyed, by the young people especially. Boss always invited some of the young people of the neighborhood to these parties and they never failed to put in an appearance. Williams, Bradford and Freeman were the sons of rich planters, and were always participants in this sport, and their young lady friends joined in it as on-lookers. The young men singing and whistling to the birds, I in the meantime setting the net. As soon as I had got the net in order they would approach the birds slowly, driving them into it. There was great laughter and excitement if they were successful in catching a fine flock.

CRUEL TREATMENT

I was but a lad, yet I can remember well the cruel treatment I received. Some weeks it seemed I was whipped for nothing, just to please my mistress' fancy. Once, when I was sent to town for the mail and had started back, it was so dark and rainy my horse got away from me and I had to stay all night in town. The next morning when I got back home I had a severe whipping, because the master was expecting a letter containing money and was disappointed in not receiving it that night, as he was going to Panola to spend Christmas. However, the day came and all the family went except me. During the time they were gone the overseer whipped a man so terribly with the "bull whip" that I had to go for the doctor, and when Dr. Heningford, the regular family physician, came, he said it was awful—such cruel treatment, and he complained about it. It was common for a slave to get an "over-threshing," that is, to be whipped too much. The poor man was cut up so badly all over that the doctor made a bran poultice and wrapped his entire body in it. This was done to draw out the inflammation. It seems the slave had been sick, and had killed a little pig when he became well enough to go to work, as his appetite craved hearty food, and he needed it to give him strength for his tasks. For this one act, comparatively trivial, he was almost killed. The idea never seemed to occur to the slave holders that these slaves were getting no wages for their work and, therefore, had nothing with which to procure what, at times, was necessary for their health and strength—palatable and nourishing food. When the slaves took anything the masters called it stealing, yet they were stealing the slaves' time year after year. When Boss came home he was called on by the town officials, for the case had been reported to them. Boss, however, got out of it by saying that he was not at home when the trouble occurred. The poor slave was sick from his ill treatment some four or five months, and when he recovered there was a running sore left on his body, from the deep cuts of the whip, which never healed. I can not forget how he looked, the sore was a sickening sight; yet, when he was able to walk he had to return to work in the field.

I had not been at Pontotoc very long when I saw the hounds run a slave, by name Ben Lyon. "Old Ben," as he was called, ran away and had been gone a week when he was seen by a woman who "told on him," and then I was sent to get the man who had trained dogs, or hounds as they were called. The dogs ran the slave about ten miles when they lost track at a creek, but he was caught that night in a farmer's house getting something to eat.

INSTRUCTIONS IN MEDICINE

After some time, Boss began to tell me the names of medicines and their properties. I liked this and seemed to grasp the idea very well. After giving me a number of names he would make me repeat them. Then he would tell me the properties of each medicine named, how it was used and for what purpose and how much constituted a dose. He would drill me in all this until I knew it and, in a short time, he would add other names to the list. He always showed me each medicine named and had

21

me smell and carefully examine it that I might know it when seen again. I liked this, and used to wish that I was as wise as my master. He was very precise, steady and gentle in any case of sickness, and, although he had long retired from the medical world, all recognized his merit wherever he went. I used to go to the woods and gather slippery elm, alum root and the roots of wild cherry and poplar, for we used all these in compounding medicines for the servants.

THE OVERSEER—
WHIPPINGS AND OTHER CRUELTIES

The overseer was a man hired to look after the farm and whip the slaves. Very often they were not only cruel, but barbarous. Every farmer or planter considered an overseer a necessity. As a rule, there was also on each plantation, a foreman—one of the brighter slaves, who was held responsible for the slaves under him, and whipped if they did not come up to the required task. There was, too, a forewoman, who, in like manner, had charge of the female slaves, and also the boys and girls from twelve to sixteen years of age, and all the old people that were feeble. This was called the trash gang. Ah! it would make one's heart ache to see those children and how they were worked. Cold, frosty mornings, the little ones would be crying from cold; but they had to keep on. Aunt Polly, our forewoman, was afraid to allow them to run to get warm, for fear the overseer would see them. Then she would be whipped, and he would make her whip all of the gang. At length, I became used to severe treatment of the slaves; but, every little while something would happen to make me wish I were dead. Everything was in a bustle—always there was slashing and whipping. I remember when Boss made a change in our overseer. It was the beginning of the year. Riley, one of the slaves, who was a principal plower, was not on hand for work one Monday morning, having been delayed in fixing

22

THROUGH THE EYES OF A SLAVE

the bridle of his mule, which the animal, for lack of something better, perhaps, had been vigorously chewing and rendered nearly useless. He was, therefore, considerably behind time, when he reached the field. Without waiting to learn what was the reason for the delay, the overseer sprang upon him with his bull whip, which was about seven feet long, lashing him with all his strength, every stroke leaving its mark upon the poor man's body, and finally the knot at the end of the whip buried itself in the fleshy part of the arm, and there came around it a festering sore. He suffered greatly with it, until one night his brother took out the knot, when the poor fellow was asleep, for he could not bear any one to touch it when he was awake. It was awful to hear the cracking of that whip as it was laid about Riley—one would have thought that an ox team had gotten into the mire, and was being whipped out, so loud and sharp was the noise!

I usually slept in the dining room on the floor. Early one morning an old slave, by name of "Uncle Jim," came and knocked at the window, and upon my jumping up and going to him, he told me to tell Boss that Uncle Jim was there. He had run away, some time before, and, for some reason, had returned. Boss, upon hearing the news, got up and sent me to tell the overseer to come at once. He came, and, taking the bull whip, a cowhide and a lot of peach-tree switches, he and Boss led Uncle Jim back into the cow lot, on the side of the hill, where they drove four stakes in the ground, and, laying him flat on his face, tied his hands and feet to these stakes. After whipping him, in this position, all they wanted to, a pail of strong salt and water was brought, and the poor fellow was "washed down." This washing was customary, after whippings, as the planters claimed it drew out all the soreness, and healed the lacerated flesh.

Upon one occasion, the family being away, I was left extra work to do, being set to help three fellow slaves lay off the rows for planting corn. We did not get them quite straight. The deviation we made from the line was very little, and could scarcely be seen, even by an expert; but the least thing wrong about the work would cause any slave to be whipped, and so all four of us were flogged.

THE SLAVE CABIN

There was a section of the plantation known as "the quarters," where were situated the cabins of the slaves. These cabins were built of rough logs, and daubed with the red clay or mud of the region. No attempt was made to give them a neat appearance—they were not even whitewashed. Each cabin was about fourteen feet square, containing but one room, and was covered with oak boards, three feet in length, split out of logs by hand. These boards were not nailed on, but held in their places by what were termed weight-poles laid across them at right angles. There were in each room two windows, a door and a large, rude fireplace. The door and window frames, or facings, were held in their places by wooden pins, nails being used only in putting the doors together. The interior of the cabins had nothing more attractive than the outside—there was no plastering and only a dirt floor. The furniture consisted of one bed, a plain board table and some benches made by the slaves themselves. Sometimes a cabin was occupied by two or more families, in which case the number of beds was increased proportionately. For light a grease lamp was used, which was made of iron, bowl shaped, by a blacksmith. The bowl was filled with grease and a rag or wick placed in it, one end resting on the edge for lighting. These lamps gave a good light, and were in general use among the slaves. Tallow candles were a luxury, never seen except in the "great houses" of the planters. The only light for outdoors used by the slaves was a torch made by binding together a bundle of small sticks or splinters.

COTTON RAISING

After the selection of the soil most suitable for cotton, the preparation of it was of vital importance. The land was deeply plowed, long enough before the time for planting to allow the spring rains to settle it. Then it was thrown into beds or ridges by turning furrows both ways toward a given center. The seed was planted at the rate of one hundred pounds per acre. The plant made its appearance in about ten days after planting, if the weather was favorable. Early planting, however, followed by cold, stormy weather frequently caused the seed to rot. As soon as the third leaf appeared the process of scraping commenced, which consisted of cleaning the ridge with hoes of all superfluous plants and all weeds and grass. After this a narrow plow known as a "bull tongue," was used to turn the loose earth around the plant and cover up any grass not totally destroyed by the hoes. If the surface was very rough the hoes followed, instead of preceding, the plow to unearth those plants that may have been partially covered. The slaves often acquired great skill in these operations, running plows within two inches of the stalks, and striking down weeds within half an inch with their hoes, rarely touching a leaf of the cotton. Subsequent plowing, alternating with hoeing, usually occurred once in twenty days. There was danger in deep plowing of injuring the roots, and this was avoided, except in the middle of rows in wet seasons when it was necessary to bury and more effectually kill the grass. The implements used in the culture of cotton were shovels, hoes, sweeps, cultivators, harrows and two kinds of plows. It required four months, under the most favorable circumstances, for cotton to attain its full growth. It was usually planted about the 1st of April, or from March 20th to April 10th, bloomed about the 1st of June and the first balls opened about August 15th, when picking commenced. The blooms come out in the morning and are fully developed by noon, when they are a pure white. Soon after meridian they begin to exhibit reddish streaks, and next morning are a clear pink. They fall off by noon of the second day.

THE COTTON WORM

A cut worm was troublesome sometimes; but the plants were watched very carefully, and as soon as any signs of worms were seen work for their destruction was commenced. The majority of the eggs were laid upon the calyx and involucre. The worm, after gnawing through its enclosed shell, makes its first meal upon the part of the plant upon which the egg was laid, be it leaf, stem or involucre. If it were laid upon the leaf, as was usually the case, it might be three days before the worm reached the boll; but were the eggs laid upon the involucre the worm pierced through within twenty-four hours after hatching. The newly hatched boll worm walks like a geometrical larva or looper, a measuring worm as it was called. This is easily explained by the fact that while in the full grown worm the abdominal legs, or pro legs, are nearly equal in length, in the newly hatched worm the second pair are slightly shorter than the third, and the first pair are shorter and slenderer than the second—a state of things approaching that in the full grown cotton worm, though the difference in size in the former case is not nearly so marked as in the latter. This method of walking is lost with the first or second molt. There is nothing remarkable about these young larvae. They seem to be thicker in proportion to their length than the young cotton worms, and they have not so delicate and transparent an appearance. Their heads are black and their bodies seem already to have begun to vary in color. The body above is furnished with sparse, stiff hairs, each arising from a tubercle. I have often watched the newly hatched boll while in the cotton fields. When hatched from an egg which had been deposited upon a leaf, they invariably made their first meal on the substance of the leaf, and then wandered about for a longer or shorter space of time, evidently seeking a boll or flower bud. It was always interesting to watch this seemingly aimless search of the young worm, crawling first down the leaf stem and then back, then dropping a few inches by a silken thread and then painfully working its way back again, until, at last, it found the object of its search, or fell to the ground where it was destroyed by ants. As the boll worms increase in size a most wonderful diversity of color and marking becomes apparent. In color different worms will vary from a brilliant green to a deep pink or dark brown, exhibiting almost every conceivable intermediate stage from an immaculate, unstriped specimen to one with regular spots and many stripes. The green worms were more common than those of any other color—a common variety was a very light green. When these worms put in an appearance it raised a great excitement among the planters. We did not use any poison to destroy them, as I learn is the method now employed.

THE COTTON HARVEST

The cotton harvest, or picking season, began about the latter part of August or first of September, and lasted till Christmas or after, but in the latter part of July picking commenced for "the first bale" to go into the market at Memphis. This picking was done by children from nine to twelve years of age and by women who were known as "sucklers," that is, women with infants. The pickers would pass through the rows getting very little, as the cotton was not yet in full bloom. From the lower part of the stalk where it opened first is where they got the first pickings. The season of first picking was always a great time, for the planter who brought the first bale of cotton into market at Memphis was presented with a basket of champagne by the commission merchants. This was a custom established throughout Mississippi. After the first pickings were secured

27

the cotton developed very fast, continuing to bud and bloom all over the stalk until the frost falls. The season of picking was exciting to all planters, every one was zealous in pushing his slaves in order that he might reap the greatest possible harvest. The planters talked about their prospects, discussed the cotton markets, just as the farmers of the north discuss the markets for their products. I often saw Boss so excited and nervous during the season he scarcely ate. The daily task of each able-bodied slave during the cotton picking season war 250 pounds or more, and all those who did not come up to the required amount would get a whipping. When the planter wanted more cotton picked than usual, the overseer would arrange a race. The slaves would be divided into two parties, with, a leader for each party. The first leader would choose a slave for his side, then the second leader one for his, and so on alternately until all were chosen. Each leader tried to get the best on his side. They would all work like good fellows for the prize, which was a tin cup of sugar for each slave on the winning side. The contest was kept up for three days whenever the planter desired an extra amount picked. The slaves were just as interested in the races as if they were going to get a five dollar bill.

PREPARING COTTON FOR MARKET

The gin-house was situated about four hundred yards from "the great house" on the main road. It was a large shed built upon square timbers, and was similar to a barn, only it stood some six feet from the ground, and underneath was located the machinery for running the gin. The cotton was put into the loft after it was dried, ready for ginning. In this process the cotton was dropped from the loft to the man who fed the machine. As it was ginned the lint would go into the lint room, and the seed would drop at the feeder's feet. The baskets used for holding lint were twice as large as those used in the picking process, and they were never taken from the gin house. These lint baskets were used in removing the lint from the lint room to the place where the cotton was baled. A bale contained 250 pounds, and the man who did the treading of the cotton into the bales would not vary ten pounds in the bale, so accustomed was he to the packing. Generally from fourteen to fifteen bales of cotton were in the lint room at a time.

OTHER FARM PRODUCTS

Cotton was the chief product of the Mississippi farms and nothing else was raised to sell. Wheat, oats and rye were raised in limited quantities, but only for the slaves and the stock. All the fine flour for the master's family was bought in St. Louis. Corn was raised in abundance, as it was a staple article of food for the slaves. It was planted about the 1st of March, or about a month earlier than the cotton. It was, therefore, up and partially worked before the cotton was planted and fully tilled before the cotton was ready for cultivation. Peas were planted between the rows of corn, and hundreds of bushels were raised. These peas after being harvested, dried and beaten out of the shell, were of a reddish brown tint, not like those raised for the master's family, but they were considered a wholesome and nutritious food for the slaves. Cabbage and yams, a large sweet potato, coarser than the kind generally used by the whites and not so delicate in flavor, were also raised for the servants in liberal quantities. No hay was raised, but the leaves of the corn, stripped from the stalks while yet green, cured and bound in bundles, were used as a substitute for it in feeding horses.

FARM IMPLEMENTS

Almost all the implements used on the plantation were made by the slaves. Very few things were bought. Boss had a skilled blacksmith, uncle Ben, for whom he paid $1,800, and there were slaves who were carpenters and workers in wood who could turn their hands to almost anything. Wagons, plows, harrows, grubbing hoes, hames, collars, baskets, bridle bits and hoe handles were all made on the farm and from the material which it produced, except the iron. The timber used in these implements was generally white or red oak, and was cut and thoroughly seasoned long before it was needed. The articles thus manufactured were not fine in form or finish, but they were durable, and answered the purposes of a rude method of agriculture. Horse collars were made from corn husks and from poplar bark which was stripped from the tree, in the spring, when the sap was up and it was soft and pliable, and separated into narrow strips which were plaited together. These collars were easy for the horse, and served the purpose of the more costly leather collar. Every season at least 200 cotton baskets were made. One man usually worked at this all the year round, but in the spring he had three assistants. The baskets were made from oak timber, grown in the home forests and prepared by the slaves. It was no small part of the work of the blacksmith and his assistant to keep the farm implements in good repair, and much of this work was done at night. All the plank used was sawed by hand from timber grown on the master's land, as there were no saw mills in that region. Almost the only things not made on the farm which were in general use there were axes, trace chains and the hoes used in cultivating the cotton.

THROUGH THE EYES OF A SLAVE
THE CLEARING OF NEW LAND

When additional land was required for cultivation the first step was to go into the forest in summer and "deaden" or girdle the trees on a given tract. This was cutting through the bark all around the trunk about thirty inches from the ground. The trees so treated soon died and in a year or two were in condition to be removed. The season selected for clearing the land was winter, beginning with January. The trees, except the larger ones, were cut down, cut into lengths convenient for handling and piled into great heaps, called "log heaps," and burned. The undergrowth was grubbed out and also piled and burned. The burning was done at night and the sight was often weird and grand. The chopping was done by the men slaves and the grubbing by women. All the trees that blew down during the summer were left as they fell till winter when they were removed. This went on, year after year, until all the trees were cleared out. The first year after the new land was cleared corn was put in, the next season cotton. As a rule corn and cotton were planted alternately, especially if the land was poor, if not, cotton would be continued year after year on the same land. Old corn stalks were always plowed under for the next year's crop and they served as an excellent fertilizer. Cotton was seldom planted on newly cleared land, as the roots and stumps rendered it difficult to cultivate the land without injury to the growing plant.

I never saw women put to the hard work of grubbing until I went to McGee's and I greatly wondered at it. Such work was not done by women slaves in Virginia. Children were required to do some work, it mattered not how many grown people were working. There were always tasks set for the boys and girls ranging in age from nine to thirteen years, beyond these ages they worked with the older slaves. After I had been in Pontotoc two years I had to help plant and hoe, and work in the cotton during the seasons, and soon learned to do everything pertaining to the farm.

31

COOKING FOR THE SLAVES

In summer time the cooking for the slaves was done out of doors. A large fire was built under a tree, two wooden forks were driven into the ground on opposite sides of the fire, a pole laid on the forks and on this kettles were hung over the fire for the preparation of the food. Cabbage and meat, boiled, alternated with meat and peas, were the staple for summer. Bread was furnished with the meals and corn meal dumplings, that is, little balls made of meal and grease from the boiled bacon and dropped into boiling water, were also provided and considered quite palatable, especially if cooked in the water in which the bacon was boiled. In winter the cooking was done in a cabin, and sweet potatoes, dried peas and meat were the principal diet. This bill of fare was for dinner or the mid-day meal. For supper each slave received two pieces of meat and two slices of bread, but these slices were very large, as the loaves were about six inches thick and baked in an old fashioned oven. This bread was made from corn meal for, as I have said, only on holidays and special occasions did the slaves have white bread of any kind. Part of the meat and bread received at supper time was saved for the "morning bite." The slaves never had any breakfast, but went to the field at daylight and after working till the sun was well up, all would stop for their morning bite. Very often some young fellow ate his morning bite the evening before at supper and would have nothing for the morning, going without eating until noon. The stop for morning bite was very short; then all would plunge into work until mid-day, when all hands were summoned to their principal meal.

CARDING AND SPINNING

Through the winter and on rainy days in summer, the women of the field had to card the wool and spin it into yarn. They generally worked in pairs, a spinning wheel and cards being assigned to each pair, and while one carded the wool into rolls, the other spun it into yarn suitable for weaving into cloth, or a coarse, heavy thread used in making bridles and lines for the mules that were used in the fields. This work was done in the cabins, and the women working together alternated in the carding and spinning. Four cuts were considered a task or day's work, and if any one failed to complete her task she received a whipping from the madam. At night when the spinners brought their work to the big house I would have it to reel. The reel was a contrivance consisting of a sort of wheel, turned on an axis, used to transfer the yarn from the spools or spindles of the spinning wheels into cuts or hunks. It was turned by hand and when enough yarn had been reeled to make a cut the reel signaled it with a snap. This process was continued until four cuts were reeled which made a hunk, and this was taken off and was ready for use. So the work went on until all was reeled. I often got very weary of this work and would almost fall asleep at it, as it was generally done at night after I had had a long day's toil at something else.

WEAVING—CLOTHES OF THE SLAVES

One woman did the weaving and it was her task to weave from nine to ten yards a day. Aunt Liza was our weaver and she was taught the work by the madam. At first she did not get on so well with it and many times I have seen the madam jump at her, pinch and choke her because she was dull in understanding how to do it. The madam made the unreasonable demand that she should do the full task at first, and because she failed she was punished, as was the custom in all cases of failure, no matter how unreasonable the demand. Liza finally became equal to her task and accomplished it each day. But the trouble and worry to me was when I had to assist the madam in warping—getting the work ready for the weaver. She would warp the thread herself and place it in the loom, then I would have to hand her the threads, as she put them through the hames. For any failure in quickly comprehending or doing my work, I did not fail to receive the customary blow, or blows, from her hand.

Each piece of cloth contained forty yards, and this cloth was used in making clothes for the servants. About half of the whole amount required was thus made at home; the remainder was bought, and as it was heavier it was used for winter clothing. Each man was allowed for summer two pairs of pants and two shirts, but no coat. The women had two dresses and two chemises each for summer. For winter the men had each two pairs of pants, one coat, one hat and one pair of coarse shoes. These shoes before being worn had to be greased with tallow, with a little tar in it. It was always a happy time when the men got these winter goods—it brought many a smile to their faces, though the supply was meager and the articles of the cheapest. The women's dresses for winter were made of the heavier wool-cloth used for the men. They also had one pair of shoes each and a turban. The women who could utilize old clothes, made for themselves what were called pantalets. They had no stockings or undergarments to protect their limbs—these were never given them. The pantalets were made like a pant-leg, came just above the knee, and were caught and tied. Sometimes they looked well and comfortable. The men's old pant-legs were sometimes used.

I remember once when Boss went to Memphis and brought back a bolt of gingham for turbans for the female slaves. It was a red and yellow check, and the turbans made from it were only to be worn on Sunday. The old women were so glad that they sang and prayed. A little gift from the master was greatly appreciated by them. I always came in for my share each year, but my clothes were somewhat different. I wore pants made of Boss's old ones, and all his old coats were utilized for me. They rounded them off at the tail just a little and called them jackets. My shoes were not brogans, but made of lighter leather, and made suitable for in the house. I only worked on the farm in busy seasons, and did not have the regular wear of the farm hands. On Monday morning it was a great sight to see all the hands marching to the field. The cotton clothes worn by both men and women, and the turbans of the latter, were snowy white, as were the wool hats of the men—all contrasted with the dark faces of the wearers in a strange and striking manner.

SLAVE MOTHERS—CARE OF THE CHILDREN

The women who had young babies were assigned to what was considered "light work," such as hoeing potatoes, cutting weeds from the fence corners, and any other work of like character. About nine o'clock in the forenoon, at noon, and three o'clock in the afternoon, these women, known on the farms as "the sucklers," could be seen going from work to nurse their babies. Many were the heart-sighs of these sorrowing mothers as they went to minister to their infants. Sometimes the little things would seem starved, for the mothers could only stop their toil three times a day to care for them. When old enough to receive it, the babies had milk, the liquor from boiled cabbage, and bread and milk together. A woman who was too old to do much of anything was assigned to the charge of these babies in the absence of their mothers. It was rare that she had any one to help her. The cries of these little ones, who were cut off almost entirely from motherly care and protection, were heart-rending.

The cabin used for the infants during the day was a double one, that is, double the usual size, and was located near the great house. The cradles used were made of boards, and were not more than two by three feet in size. The women carried their babies in the cradles to the baby cabin in the morning, taking them to their own cabins at night. The children ranging in age from one to seven years were numerous, and the old woman had them to look after as well as the babies. This was indeed a task,

35

and might well have taxed the strength of a younger woman. They were always from eight to a dozen infants in the cabin. The summer season was trying on the babies and young children. Often they would drink too much liquor from cabbage, or too much buttermilk, and would be taken with a severe colic. I was always called on these occasions to go with Boss to administer medicine. I remember on one occasion a little boy had eaten too much cabbage, and was taken with cramp colic. In a few minutes his stomach was swollen as tight and hard as a balloon, and his teeth clenched. He was given an emetic, put in a mustard bath and was soon relieved. The food was too heavy for these children, and they were nearly always in need of some medical attendance. Excessive heat, with improper food, often brought on cholera infantum, from which the infants sometimes died rapidly and in considerable numbers.

METHODS OF PUNISHMENT

The methods of punishment were barbarous in the extreme, and so numerous that I will not attempt to describe them all. One method was to tie the slave to a tree, strip off his clothes, and then whip him with a rawhide, or long, limber switches, or the terrible bull whip. Another was to put the slave in stocks, or to buck him, that is, fasten his feet together, draw up his knees to his chin, tie his hands together, draw them down over the knees, and put a stick under the latter and over the arms. In either of these ways the slave was entirely at the mercy of his tormentors, and the whipping could proceed at their pleasure. After these whippings the slave was often left helpless and bleeding upon the ground, until the master, or overseer, saw fit to let him up. The most common method of punishment was to have the servants form a ring, called the "bull ring," into which the one to be punished was led naked. The slaves were then each given a switch, rawhide, strap or whip, and each one was compelled to cut at the poor victim as he ran around the ring. The ring was composed of men, women and children; and, as they numbered from forty to fifty, each circuit of the ring would result in that number of lashes, and by the time the victim had made two or three rounds his condition can be readily imagined. The overseer was always one of the ring, vigorously using the whip, and seeing that all the slaves did the same. Some of the victims fainted before they had passed once around the ring. Women slaves were punished in the same manner as the men. The salt water bath was given after each punishment. Runaway slaves were usually caught by means of hounds, trained for the purpose by men who made it a business and a source of revenue, notwithstanding its brutal features and degrading influence.

FOURTH OF JULY BARBECUE

Barbecue originally meant to dress and roast a hog whole, but has come to mean the cooking of a food animal in this manner for the feeding of a great company. A feast of this kind was always given to us, by Boss, on the 4th of July. The anticipation of it acted as a stimulant through the entire year. Each one looked forward to this great day of recreation with pleasure. Even the older slaves would join in the discussion of the coming event. It mattered not what trouble or hardship the year had brought, this feast and its attendant pleasure would dissipate all gloom. Some, probably, would be punished on the morning of the 4th, but this did not matter; the men thought of the good things in store for them, and that made them forget that they had been punished. All the week previous to the great day, the slaves were in high spirits, the young girls and boys, each evening, congregating, in front of the cabins, to talk of the feast, while others would sing and dance. The older slaves were not less happy, but would only say; "Ah! God has blessed us in permitting us to see another feast day." The day before

37

the 4th was a busy one. The slaves worked with all their might. The children who were large enough were engaged in bringing wood and bark to the spot where the barbecue was to take place. They worked eagerly, all day long; and, by the time the sun was setting, a huge pile of fuel was beside the trench, ready for use in the morning. At an early hour of the great day, the servants were up, and the men whom Boss had appointed to look after the killing of the hogs and sheep were quickly at their work, and, by the time they had the meat dressed and ready, most of the slaves had arrived at the center of attraction. They gathered in groups, talking, laughing, telling tales that they had from their grandfather, or relating practical jokes that they had played or seen played by others. These tales were received with peals of laughter. But however much they seemed to enjoy these stories and social interchanges, they never lost sight of the trench or the spot where the sweetmeats were to be cooked.

The method of cooking the meat was to dig a trench in the ground about six feet long and eighteen inches deep. This trench was filled with wood and bark which was set on fire, and, when it was burned to a great bed of coals, the hog was split through the back bone, and laid on poles which had been placed across the trench. The sheep were treated in the same way, and both were turned from side to side as they cooked. During the process of roasting the cooks basted the carcasses with a preparation furnished from the great house, consisting of butter, pepper, salt and vinegar, and this was continued until the meat was ready to serve. Not far from this trench were the iron ovens, where the sweetmeats were cooked. Three or four women were assigned to this work. Peach cobbler and apple dumpling were the two dishes that made old slaves smile for joy and the young fairly dance. The crust or pastry of the cobbler was prepared in large earthen bowls, then rolled out like any pie crust, only it was almost twice as thick. A layer of this crust was laid in the oven, then a half peck of peaches poured, in, followed by a layer of sugar; then a covering of pastry was laid over all and smoothed around with a knife. The oven was then put over a bed of coals, the cover put on and coals thrown on it, and the process of baking began. Four of these ovens were usually in use at these feasts, so that enough of the pastry might be baked to supply all. The ovens were filled and refilled until there was no doubt about the quantity. The apple dumplings were made in the usual way, only larger, and served with sauce made from brown sugar. It lacked flavoring, such as cinnamon or lemon, yet it was a dish highly relished by all the slaves. I know that these feasts made me so excited, I could scarcely do my house duties, and I would never fail to stop and look out of the window from the dining room down into the quarters. I was eager to get through with my work and be with the feasters. About noon everything was ready to serve. The table was set in a grove near the quarters, a place set aside for these occasions. The tableware was not fine, being of tin, but it served the purpose, and did not detract from the slaves' relish for the feast. The drinks were strictly temperance drinks—buttermilk and water. Some of the nicest portions of the meat were sliced off and put on a platter to send to the great house for Boss and his family. It was a pleasure for the slaves to do this, for Boss always enjoyed it. It was said that the slaves could barbecue meats best, and when the whites had barbecues slaves always did the cooking. When dinner was all on the table, the invitation was given for all to come; and when all were in a good way eating, Boss and the madam would go out to witness the progress of the feast, and seemed pleased to see the servants so happy. Everything was in abundance, so all could have plenty—Boss always insisted on this. The slaves had the whole day off, and could do as they liked. After dinner some of the women would wash, sew or iron. It was a day of harmless riot for all the slaves, and I can not express the happiness it brought them. Old and young, for months, would rejoice in the memory of the day and its festivities, and "bless" Boss for this ray of sunlight in their darkened lives.

ATTENDANCE AT CHURCH

There was an observance of religious forms at least by the occupants of both the great house and the cabins. The McGee family were church-going people, and, except in very inclement weather, never failed to attend service on Sunday. They were Methodists, and their church was four miles from their residence. The Baptist church was but two miles distant, and the family usually alternated in their attendance between the two places of worship. I always attended them to church, generally riding behind while the Boss drove. Upon reaching church, my first duty was to run to a spring for a pitcher of fresh water, which I passed not only to the members of our party, but to any others desiring drink. Whatever may be thought of the religious professions of the slave-holders, there can be no question that many of the slaves were sincere believers in the Christian religion, and endeavored to obey the precepts according to their light.

RELIGIOUS MEETINGS OF THE SLAVES

Saturday evening on the farm was always hailed with delight. The air was filled with happy shouts from men and boys, so glad were they that Sunday, their only day of rest, was near. In the cabins the women were washing and fixing garments for Sunday, that they might honor the Lord in cleanliness and decency. It was astonishing how they utilized what they had, and with what skill and industry they performed these self-imposed tasks. Where the family was large it was often after midnight before this work was done. While this preparation for the Sabbath was in progress in most of the cabins, the old men would gather in one for a prayer-meeting. As they began to sing some familiar hymn, the air would ring with their voices, and it was not long before the cabin was filled with both old and young, who came in their

40

simple yet sincere way to give praise to God. It was common to have one or two exhorters on the plantation who claimed to be called to do service for God, by teaching their fellow men the principles of religion. God certainly must have revealed himself to these poor souls, for they were very ignorant—they did not know a letter of the Bible. But when they opened their mouths they were filled, and the plan of Salvation was explained in a way that all could receive it. It was always a mystery to the white brethren how the slaves could line out hymns, preach Christ and redemption, yet have no knowledge even of how the name of Christ was spelled. They were illiterate to the last degree, so there is but one theory, they were inspired. God revealed unto them just what they should teach their flock, the same as he did to Moses. I remember very well that there was always a solemnity about the services—a certain harmony, which had a peculiar effect—a certain pathetic tone which quickened the emotions as they sang those old plantation hymns. It mattered not what their troubles had been during the week—how much they had been lashed, the prayer-meeting on Saturday evening never failed to be held. Their faith was tried and true. On Sunday afternoons, they would all congregate again to praise God, and the congregation was enthusiastic. It was pathetic to hear them pray, from the depths of their hearts, for them who "despitefully used them and persecuted them." This injunction of our Saviour was strictly adhered to. The words that came from the minister were always of a consolatory kind. He knew the crosses of his fellow slaves and their hardships, for he had shared them himself. I was always touched in hearing him give out the hymns. I can hear old Uncle Ben now, as he solemnly worded out the following lines:

> Must I be carried to the skies,
> On flowery beds of ease,
> While others fought to win the prize,
> And sailed through bloody seas?

After singing he would always speak to them of the necessity for patience in bearing the crosses, urging them to endure "as good soldiers." Many tears were shed, and many glad shouts of praise would burst forth during the sermon. A hymn usually followed the sermon, then all retired. Their faces seemed to shine with a happy light—their very countenance showed that their souls had been refreshed and that it had been "good for them to be there." These meetings were the joy and comfort of the slaves, and even those who did not profess Christianity were calm and thoughtful while in attendance.

A NEIGHBORHOOD QUARREL

Opposite our farm was one owned by a Mr. Juval, and adjoining that was another belonging to one White. The McGees and the Whites were very fast friends, visiting each other regularly—indeed they had grown up together, and Mr. White at one time was the lover of the madam, and engaged to be married to her. This friendship had existed for years, when McGee bought the Juval farm, for which White had also been negotiating, but which he failed to get on account of McGee having out-bid him. From this circumstance ill feeling was engendered between the two men, and they soon became bitter enemies. McGee had decided to build a fence between the farm he had purchased and that of White, and, during the winter, his teamsters were set to hauling the rails; and, in unloading them, they accidentally threw some of them over the line on to White's land. The latter said nothing about the matter until spring, when he wrote McGee a letter, asking him to remove the rails from his land. McGee paid no attention to the request, and he soon received a second note, when he said to his wife: "That fellow is about to turn himself a fool—I'll give him a cow-hiding." A third and more emphatic note followed, in which White told the Boss that the rails must be removed within twenty-four

42

hours. He grew indignant, and, in true Southern style, he went immediately to town and bought arms, and prepared himself for the fray. When he returned he had every hand on the plantation stop regular work, and put them all to building the fence. I was of the number. Boss and the overseer came out to overlook the work and hurry it on. About four o'clock in the afternoon White put in an appearance, and came face to face with McGee, sitting on his horse and having a double barreled shot gun lying across the pummel of his saddle. White passed on without saying a word, but Boss yelled at him; "Hello! I see you are about to turn yourself a d—d fool." White checked up and began to swear, saying: "You are a coward to attack an unarmed man." He grew furious, took off his hat, ran his fingers through his hair, saying: "Here I am, blow me to h—l, and I'll have some one blow you there before night." During White's rage he said: "I'll fight you anywhere—bowie-knife fight, shot gun fight or any other." He called, in his excitement, for his nephew, who was working on his farm, to come, and immediately sent him to Billy Duncan's to get him a double barreled shot gun. Meantime, Mrs. McGee appeared on the scene, and began to cry, begging White to stop and allow her to speak to him. But he replied: "Go off, go off, I don't want to speak to you." Boss grew weak and sick, and through his excitement, was taken violently ill, vomiting as if he had taken an emetic. He said to White; "I'll return as soon as I take my wife home," but he never came back. As Boss and the madam rode off, White came galloping back, and said to Brooks, our overseer: "If I am shot down on foul play would you speak of it?" Brooks replied: "No, I don't care to interfere—I don't wish to have anything to do with it." White was bloodthirsty, and came back at intervals during the entire night, where we were working, to see if he could find Boss. It is quite probable that White may have long cherished a secret grudge against Boss, because he had robbed him of his first love; and, brooding over these offenses, he became so excited as to be almost insane. Had McGee returned that night, White would certainly have shot him. Boss became so uneasy over the situation that he sent one of his slaves, a foreman, to Panola county, some seventy-five miles distant, to Mrs. McGee's father, to get her brother, a lawyer, to come and endeavor to effect a settlement. He came, but all his efforts were unavailing. The men met at a magistrate's office, but they came to no understanding. Our folks became dissatisfied, and did not care to remain longer in the place, so they began to look out for other quarters. Boss finally decided to buy a farm in Bolivar, Miss., and to remove his family to Memphis, where he secured a fine place, just outside of the city.

CHAPTER II

SOCIAL AND OTHER ASPECTS OF SLAVERY

REMOVAL TO MEMPHIS, TENNESSEE

McGee had decided to build a new house upon the property which he had purchased at Memphis; and, in August 1850, he sent twenty-five of his slaves to the city, to make brick for the structure, and I went along as cook. After the bricks were burned, the work of clearing the ground for the buildings was commenced. There were many large and beautiful trees that had to be taken up and removed; and, when this work was completed, the excavations for the foundations and the cellar were undertaken. All of this work was done by the slaves. The site was a beautiful one, embracing fourteen acres, situated two miles southeast from the city, on the Memphis and Charleston railroad. The road ran in front of the place and the Boss built a flag-station there, for the accommodation of himself and his neighbors, which was named McGee Station.

A NEW AND SPLENDID HOUSE

The house was one of the most pretentious in that region, and was a year and a half in building. It was two stories in height, and built of brick, the exterior surface being coated with cement and marked off in blocks, about two feet square, to represent stone. It was then whitewashed. There was a veranda in front

45

with six large columns, and, above, a balcony. On the back there were also a veranda and a balcony, extending across that end to the servants' wing. A large hall led from front to rear, on one side of which were double parlors, and on the other a sitting room, a bedroom and a dining room. In the second story were a hall and four rooms, similar in all respects to those below, and above these was a large attic. The interior woodwork was of black walnut. The walls were white, and the centerpieces in the ceilings of all the rooms were very fine, being the work of an English artisan, who had been only a short time in this country. This work was so superior, in design and finish, to anything before seen in that region that local artisans were much excited over it; and some offered to purchase the right to reproduce it, but Boss refused the offer. However, some one, while the house was finishing, helped himself to the design, and it was reproduced, in whole or in part, in other buildings in the city. This employment of a foreign artist was unusual there and caused much comment. The parlors were furnished with mahogany sets, the upholstering being in red brocade satin. The dining room was also furnished in mahogany. The bedrooms had mahogany bedsteads of the old-fashioned pattern with canopies. Costly bric-a-brac, which Boss and the madam had purchased while traveling in foreign countries, was in great profusion. Money was no object to Edmund McGee, and he added every modern improvement and luxury to his home; the decorations and furnishings were throughout of the most costly and elegant; and in the whole of Tennessee there was not a mansion more sumptuously complete in all its appointments, or more palatial in its general appearance. When all was finished— pictures, bric-a-brac, statuary and flowers all in their places, Mrs. McGee was brought home.

In this new house Boss opened up in grand style; everything was changed, and the family entered upon a new, more formal and more pretentious manner of living. I was known no longer as errand boy, but installed as butler and body-servant to my master. I had the same routine of morning work, only it was more extensive. There was a great deal to be done in so spacious a mansion. Looking after the parlors, halls and dining rooms, arranging flowers in the rooms, waiting on the table, and going after the mail was my regular morning work, the year round. Then there were my duties to perform, night and morning, for my master; these were to brush his clothes, black his shoes, assist him to arrange his toilet, and do any little thing that he wanted me to. Aside from these regular duties, there were windows to wash, silver to polish and steps to stone on certain days in the week. I was called to do any errand necessary, and sometimes to assist in the garden. A new staff of house servants was installed, as follows: Aunt Delia, cook; Louisa, chambermaid; Puss, lady's maid to wait on the madam; Celia, nurse; Lethia, wet nurse; Sarah, dairymaid; Julia, laundress; Uncle Gooden, gardener; Thomas, coachman.

THE NEW STYLE OF LIVING

The servants, at first, were dazed with the splendor of the new house, and laughed and chuckled to themselves a good deal about mars' fine house, and really seemed pleased; for, strange to say, the slaves of rich people always rejoiced in that fact. A servant owned by a man in moderate circumstances was hooted at by rich men's slaves. It was common for them to say: "Oh! don't mind that darkey, he belongs to po'r white trash." So, as I said, our slaves rejoiced in master's good luck. Each of the women servants wore a new, gay colored turban, which was tied differently from that of the ordinary servant, in some fancy knot. Their frocks and aprons were new, and really the servants themselves looked new. My outfit was a new cloth suit, and my aprons for wearing when waiting on the table were of snowy white linen, the style being copied from that of the New York waiters. I felt big, for I never knew what a white bosom shirt was before; and even though the grief at the separation from my dear mother was almost unbearable at times, and my sense of loneliness in having no relative near me often made me sad, there was consolation, if not compensation, in this little change. I had known no comforts, and had been so cowed and broken in spirits, by cruel lashings, that I really felt light-hearted at this improvement in my personal appearance, although it was merely for the gratification of my master's pride; and I thought I would do all I could to please Boss.

THE ADORNMENT OF THE GROUNDS

For some time before all the appointments of the new home were completed, a great number of mechanics and workmen, besides our own servants, were employed; and there was much bustle and stir about the premises. Considerable out-door work was yet to be done—fences to be made, gardens and orchards to be arranged and planted, and the grounds about the house to be laid out and adorned with shrubbery and flower beds. When this work was finally accomplished, the grounds were indeed beautiful. The walks were graveled, and led through a profusion of shrubbery and flower beds. There was almost every variety of roses; while, scattered over the grounds, there were spruce, pine and juniper trees, and some rare varieties, seldom seen in this northern climate. Around the grounds was set a cedar hedge, and, in time, the place became noted for the beauty of its shrubbery; the roses especially were marvelous in the richness and variety of their colors, their fragrance and the luxuriousness of their growth. People who have never traveled in the South have little idea of the richness and profusion of its flowers, especially of its roses. Among the climbing plants, which adorned the house, the most beautiful and fragrant was the African honeysuckle—its odor was indeed delightful.

THE GARDEN

One of the institutions of the place was the vegetable garden. This was established not only for the convenience and comfort of the family, but to furnish employment for the slaves. Under the care of Uncle Gooden, the gardener, it flourished greatly; and there was so much more produced than the family could use, Boss concluded to sell the surplus. The gardener, therefore, went to the city, every morning, with a load of vegetables, which brought from eight to ten dollars daily, and this the madam took for "pin money." In the spring I had always to help the gardener in setting out plants and preparing beds; and, as this was in connection with my other work, I became so tired sometimes that I could hardly stand. All the vegetables raised were fine, and at that time brought a good price. The first cabbage that we sold in the markets brought twenty-five cents a head. The first sweet potatoes marketed always brought a dollar a peck, or four dollars a bushel. The Memphis market regulations required that all vegetables be washed before being exposed for sale. Corn was husked, and everything was clean and inviting. Any one found guilty of selling, or exhibiting for sale, vegetables of a previous day was fined, at once, by the market master. This rule was carried out to the letter. Nothing stale could be sold, or even come into market. The rules required that all poultry be dressed before being brought to market. The entrails were cleaned and strung and sold separately—usually for about ten cents a string.

PROFUSION OF FLOWERS

Flowers grew in profusion everywhere through the south, and it has, properly, been called the land of flowers. But flowers had no such sale there as have our flowers here in the north. The pansy and many of our highly prized plants and flowers grew wild in the south. The people there did not seem to care for

49

flowers as we do. I have sold many bouquets for a dime, and very beautiful ones for fifteen and twenty cents, that would sell in the north for fifty to seventy-five cents.

THE FRUIT ORCHARD

The new place had an orchard of about four acres, consisting of a variety of apple, peach, pear and plum trees. Boss hired an expert gardener to teach me the art of grafting, and, after some practice, I became quite skilled in this work. Some of the pear trees that had been grafted had three different kinds of fruit on them, and others had three kinds of apples on them besides the pears. This grafting I did myself, and the trees were considered very fine by Boss. Another part of my work was the trimming of the hedge and the care of all the shrubbery.

I PRACTICE MEDICINE AMONG THE SLAVES

McGee had a medicine chest built into the wall of the new house. The shelves for medicine were of wood, and the arrangement was very convenient. It was really a small drug store. It contained everything in the way of drugs that was necessary to use in doctoring the slaves. We had quinine, castor-oil, alcohol and ipecac in great quantities, as these were the principal drugs used in the limited practice in the home establishment. If a servant came from the field to the house with a chill, which was frequent, the first thing we did was to give him a dose of ipecac to vomit him. On the evening after, we would give him two or three of Cook's pills. These pills we made at home, I always had to prepare the medicines, and give the dose, the Boss standing by dictating. Working with medicine, giving it and caring for the sick were the parts of my work that I liked best. Boss used Dr. Gunn's book altogether for recipes in putting up medicines. He read me the recipe, while I compounded it.

A SWELL RECEPTION

In celebration of the opening of the new house, McGee gave an elaborate reception and dinner. The menu embraced nearly everything that one could think of or desire, and all in the greatest profusion. It was a custom, not only with the McGees but among the southern people generally, to make much of eating—it was one of their hobbies. Everything was cooked well, and highly seasoned. Scarcity was foreign to the homes of the wealthy southerners.

RELATIVES VISIT AT THE MANSION

After the family had been settled about a month in the new home, their relatives in Panola Co., Miss., Mr. Jack McGee, known among the servants as "Old Jack," Mrs. Melinda McGee, his wife, Mrs. Farrington, their daughter who was a widow, and their other children Louisa, Ella and William, all came up for a visit, and to see the wonderful house. Mr. Jack McGee was the father of madam and the uncle of Boss. My master and mistress were therefore first cousins, and Boss sometimes called the old man father and at other times, uncle. Old Master Jack, as he alighted, said to those behind him: "Now be careful, step lightly, Louisa, this is the finest house you ever set foot in." When all had come into the house, and the old man had begun to look around, he said: "I don't know what Edmund is thinking about-out to build such a house-house." He was very old, and had never lost all of his Scotch dialect, and he had a habit of repeating a part or all of some words, as in the foregoing quotation. The other members of the visiting family were well pleased with the

51

house, and said it was grand. They laughed and talked merrily over the many novel things which they saw. Mrs. Farrington, who was a gay widow, was naturally interested in everything. I busied myself waiting upon them, and it was late that night before I was through. So many made extra work for me.

ONE OF THE VISITORS DISTRUSTS ME

The next morning, after breakfast, Boss and old Master Jack went out to view the grounds. They took me along so that if anything was wanted I could do it. Boss would have me drive a stake in some place to mark where he desired to put something, perhaps some flowers, or a tree. He went on through the grounds, showing his father how everything was to be arranged. The old man shook his head, and said: "Well, it's good, but I am afraid you'll spoil these niggers-niggers. Keep you eye on that boy Lou, (meaning me) he is slippery-slippery, too smart-art." "Oh! I'll manage that, Father," said Boss. "Well, see that you do-oo, for I see running away in his eyes." One of the things that interested old Master Jack was the ringing of the dinner bell. "Well, I do think," said the old man, "that boy can ring a bell better than anybody I ever heard. Why, its got a regular tune." I used to try to see how near I could come to making it say, come to dinner.

THE MADAM IN A RAGE

The four days soon passed, and all the company gone, we were once more at our regular work. Delia, the cook, seemingly had not pleased the madam in her cooking while the company were there; so, the morning after they left, she went toward the kitchen, calling: "Delia, Delia." Delia said: "Dah! I wonder what she wants now." By this time she was in the kitchen, confronting Delia. Her face was flushed as she screamed out: "What kind of biscuits were those you baked this week?" "I think they were all right, Mis Sarh." "Hush!" screamed out the madam, stamping her foot to make it more emphatic. "You did not half cook them," said she; "they were not beat enough. Those waffles were ridiculous," said the madam. "Well, Mis Sarh, I tried." "Stop!" cried Madam in a rage, "I'll give you thunder if you dictate to me." Not a very elegant display in language or manner for a great lady! Old Aunt Delia, who was used to these occurrences, said: "My Lord! dat woman dunno what she wants. Ah! Lou, there is nothing but the devil up here, (meaning the new home); can't do nothin to please her up here in dis fine house. I tell you Satan neber git his own til he git her." They did not use baking powder, as we do now, but the biscuits were beaten until light enough. Twenty minutes was the time allotted for this work; but when company came there was so much to be done—so many more dishes to prepare, that Delia would, perhaps, not have so much time for each meal. But there was no allowance made. It was never thought reasonable that a servant should make a mistake—things must always be the same. I was listening to this quarrel between madam and Delia, supposing my time would come next; but for that once she said nothing to me.

THE MADAM'S SEVERITY

Mrs. McGee was naturally irritable. Servants always got an extra whipping when she had any personal trouble, as though they could help it. Every morning little Kate, Aunt Delia's little girl, would have to go with the madam on her rounds to the different buildings of the establishment, to carry the key basket. So many were the keys that they were kept in a basket especially provided for them, and the child was its regular bearer. The madam, with this little attendant, was everywhere— in the barn, in the hennery, in the smokehouse—and she always made trouble with the servants wherever she went. Indeed, she rarely returned to the house from these rounds without having whipped two or three servants, whether there was really any cause for the punishment or not. She seldom let a day pass without beating some poor woman unmercifully. The number and severity of these whippings depended more upon the humor of the madam than upon the conduct of the slaves. Of course, I always came in for a share in this brutal treatment. She continued her old habit of boxing my jaws, pinching my ears: no day ever passing without her indulging in this exercise of her physical powers. So long had I endured this, I came to expect it, no matter how well I did my duties; and it had its natural effect upon me, making me a coward, even though I was now growing into manhood. I remember once, in particular, when I had tried to please her by arranging the parlor, I overheard her say: "They soon get spirit—it don't do to praise servants." My heart sank within me. What good was it for me to try to please? She would find fault anyway. Her usual morning greeting was: "Well, Lou, have you dusted the parlors?" "Oh, yes," I would answer. "Have the flowers been arranged?" "Yes, all is in readiness," I would say. Once I had stoned the steps as usual, but the madam grew angry as soon as she saw them. I had labored hard, and thought she would be pleased. The result, however, was very far from that. She took me out, stripped me of my shirt and began thrashing me, saying I was spoiled. I was no longer a child, but old enough to be treated differently. I began to cry, for it seemed to me my heart would break. But, after the first burst of tears, the feeling came over me that I was a man, and it was an outrage to treat me so—to keep me under the lash day after day.

A SHOCKING ACCIDENT

Not long after Mrs. Farrington had made her first visit to our house, she came there to live. Celia had been acting as her maid. When Mrs. Farrington had been up some months, it was decided that all the family should go down to old Master Jack's for a visit. Celia, the maid, had been so hurried in the preparations for this visit that she had done nothing for herself. The night before the family was to leave, therefore, she was getting ready a garment for herself to wear on the trip; and it was supposed that she sewed until midnight, or after, when she fell asleep, letting the goods fall into the candle. All at once, a little after twelve o'clock, I heard a scream, then a cry of "fire! fire!" and Boss yelling: "Louis! Louis!" I jumped up, throwing an old coat over me, and ran up stairs, in the direction of Mrs. Farrington's room, I encountered Boss in the hall; and, as it was dark and the smoke stifling, I could hardly make any headway. At this moment Mrs. Farrington threw her door open, and screamed for "Cousin Eddie," meaning McGee. He hurriedly called to me to get a pitcher of water quick. I grasped the pitcher from the stand, and he attempted to throw the water on Celia, who was all in a blaze, running around like a mad woman; but the pitcher slipped from his hand and broke, very little of the water reaching her. She was at last wrapped in an old blanket, to extinguish the flames; but she was burned too badly to recover. Boss, being a physician, said at once: "Poor girl, poor girl! she is burned to death." He did all he could for her, wrapped her in linen sheets, and endeavored to relieve her sufferings, but all was of no avail—she had inhaled the flame, injuring her internally, and lived only a few days.

MASTER'S NEW COTTON PLANTATION

Shortly after Boss bought his home in Memphis, he bought a large farm in Bolivar, Miss. It was a regular cotton farm, on the Mississippi river, embracing 200 acres. The houses built for the slaves were frame, eighteen in number, each to contain three or four families, and arranged on each side of a street that ran through the farm. This street was all grassed over, but there were

55

no sidewalks. All the buildings—the barn, gin-house, slaves' quarters and overseers' house—were whitewashed, and on this grass-grown street they made a neat and pretty appearance. The house where the Boss and the madam staid, when they went down to the farm, was about two hundred yards from the slaves' quarters. It was arranged in two apartments, one for the overseer and wife, and the other for the master and mistress upon the occasion of their visits. This building was separated from the other buildings by a fence. There was what was called the cook house, where was cooked all the food for the hands. Aunt Matilda was cook in charge. Besides the buildings already named, there were stables, a blacksmith shop and sawmill; and the general order of arrangement was carried out with respect to all—the appearance was that of a village. Everything was raised in abundance, to last from one crop to the next. Vegetables and meat were provided from the farm, and a dairy of fifty cows furnished all the milk and butter needed.

The cane brakes were so heavy that it was common for bears to hide there, and, at night, come out and carry off hogs. Wolves were plenty in the woods behind the farm, and could be heard at any time. The cane was so thick that when they were clearing up new ground, it would have to be set on fire, and the cracking that would ensue was like the continuous explosion of small fire crackers.

About one hundred and sixty slaves, besides children, all owned by McGee, were worked on the farm. Instead of ginning two or three bales of cotton a day, as at Pontotoc, they ginned six to seven bales here.

INCIDENTS

I remember well the time when the great Swedish singer, Jenny Lind, came to Memphis. It was during her famous tour through America, in 1851. Our folks were all enthused over her. Boss went in and secured tickets to her concert, and I was summoned to drive them to the hall. It was a great event. People swarmed the streets like bees. The carriages and hacks were stacked back from the hall as far as the eye could reach.

On another occasion, when the great prodigy, Blind Tom, came to Memphis, there was a similar stir among the people. Tom was very young then, and he was called the Blind Boy. People came from far and near to hear him. Those coming from the villages and small towns, who could not get passage on the regular trains, came in freight or on flat bottom cars. The tickets were $5.00 each, as I remember, Boss said it was expensive, but all must hear this boy pianist. Many were the comments on this boy of such wonderful talents. As I drove our people home they seemed to talk of nothing else. They declared that he was indeed a wonder.

LONGING FOR FREEDOM

Sometimes when the farm hands were at work, peddlers would come along; and, as they were treated badly by the rich planters, they hated them, and talked to the slaves in a way to excite them and set them thinking of freedom. They would say encouragingly to them: "Ah! You will be free some day." But the down-trodden slaves, some of whom were bowed with age, with frosted hair and furrowed cheek, would answer, looking up from their work: "We don't blieve dat; my grandfather said we was to be free, but we aint free yet." It had been talked of (this freedom) from generation to generation. Perhaps they would not have thought of freedom, if their owners had not been so cruel. Had my mistress been more kind to me, I should have thought less of liberty. I know the cruel treatment which I received was the main thing that made me wish to be free. Besides this, it was inhuman to separate families as they did. Think of a mother being sold from all her children—separated for life! This separation was common, and many died heart-broken, by reason of it. Ah! I cannot forget the cruel separation from my mother. I know not what became of her, but I have always believed her dead many years ago. Hundreds were separated, as my mother and I were, and never met again. Though freedom was yearned for by some because the treatment was so bad, others, who were bright and had looked into the matter, knew it was a curse to be held a slave—they longed to stand out in true manhood—allowed to express their opinions as were white men. Others still desired freedom, thinking they could then reclaim a wife, or husband, or children. The mother would again see her child. All these promptings of the heart made them yearn for freedom. New Year's was always a heart-rending time, for it was then the slaves were bought and sold; and they stood in constant fear of losing some one dear to them—a child, a husband, or wife.

MY FIRST BREAK FOR FREEDOM

In the new home my duties were harder than ever. The McGees held me with tighter grip, and it was nothing but cruel abuse, from morning till night. So I made up my mind to try and run away to a free country. I used to hear Boss read sometimes, in the papers, about runaway slaves who had gone to Canada, and it always made me long to go; yet I never appeared as if I paid the slightest attention to what the family read or said on such matters; but I felt that I could be like others, and try at least to get away. One morning, when Boss had gone to town, Madam had threatened to whip me, and told me to come to the house. When she called me I did not go, but went off down through the garden and through the woods, and made my way for the city. When I got into Memphis, I found at the landing a boat called the Statesman, and I sneaked aboard. It was not expected that the boat would stay more than a few hours, but, for some reason, it stayed all night. The boat was loaded with sugar, and

I hid myself behind four hogsheads. I could see both engineers, one each side of me. When night came on, I crept out from my hiding place, and went forward to search for food and water, for I was thirsty and very hungry. I found the table where the deck hands had been eating, and managed to get a little food, left from their meal, and some water. This was by no means enough, but I had to be content, and went back to my place of concealment. I had been on board the boat three days; and, on the third night, when I came out to hunt food, the second mate saw me. In a minute he eyed me over and said: "Why, I have a reward for you." In a second he had me go up stairs to the captain. This raised a great excitement among the passengers; and, in a minute, I was besieged with numerous questions. Some spoke as if they were sorry for me, and said if they had known I was a poor runaway slave they would have slipped me ashore. The whole boat was in alarm. It seemed to me they were consulting slips of paper. One said: "Yes, he is the same. Listen how this reads:"

"Ran away from Edmund McGee, my mulatto boy Louis, 5 feet 6 inches in height, black hair, is very bright and intelligent. Will give $500 for him alive, and half of this amount for knowledge that he has been killed."

My heart sprang into my throat when I heard two men read this advertisement. I knew, at once, what it all meant, remembering how often I had heard Boss read such articles from the papers and from the handbills that were distributed through the city. The captain asked me if I could dance. It seemed he felt sorry for me, for he said: "That's a bright boy to be a slave." Then turning to me he said: "Come, give us a dance." I was young and nimble, so I danced a few of the old southern clog dances, and sang one or two songs, like this:

"Come along, Sam, the fifer's son,
Aint you mighty glad your day's work's done?"

59

After I finished singing and dancing, the captain took up a collection for me and got about two dollars. This cheered me a good deal. I knew that I would need money if I should ever succeed in getting on.

On the following evening, when we reached West Franklin, Indiana, while the passengers were at tea, another boat pushed into port right after ours. Immediately a gentleman passenger came to me hurriedly, and whispered to me to go down stairs, jump out on the bow of the other boat, and go ashore. I was alarmed, but obeyed, for I felt that he was a friend to slaves. I went out as quietly as I could, and was not missed until I had gotten on shore. Then I heard the alarm given that the boy was gone—that the runaway was gone. But I sped on, and did not stop until I had run through the village, and had come to a road that led right into the country. I took this road and went on until I had gone four or five miles, when I came to a farm house. Before reaching it, however, I met two men on horseback, on their way to the village. They passed on without specially noticing me, and I kept on my way until reaching the farmhouse. I was so hungry, I went in and asked for food. While I was eating, the men whom I had met rode up. They had been to the village, and, learning that a runaway slave was wanted, and remembering meeting me, they returned in hot haste, in hope of finding me and securing the reward. They hallooed to the people in the house, an old woman and her daughter, whom they seemed to know, saying: "There is a runaway nigger out, who stole off a boat this evening." The old lady said, "Come," becoming frightened at once. When they came in they began to question me. I trembled all over but answered them. They said: "You are the fellow we want, who ran off the boat." I was too scared to deny it; so I owned I was on the boat, and stole off. They did not tarry long, but, taking me with them, they went, about a mile and a half, to their house. They planned and talked all the way, and one said: "We are good for $75.00 for him any way." The next morning they took me into the village. They soon found out that the engineer, by order of the captain, had stayed over to search for me. A lawsuit followed, and I was taken before the magistrate before the engineer could get possession of me. There was a legal course that had to be gone through with. A lawyer, Fox by name, furnished the $75.00 for the men who had caught me. That part of the case being settled, Fox and the engineer started for Evansville, Ind., that same night. Upon arriving there, Fox received from the captain of the boat the money he had advanced to the men who caught me; and we went on, arriving at Louisville, Ky., the next day. I was then taken again before a magistrate, by the captain, when the following statement was read by that official:

"Captain Montgomery brought forth a boy, and said he is the property of Edmund McGee, of Memphis, Tenn. Come forth owner, and prove property, for after the boy shall remain in jail six months he shall be sold to pay jail feed."

Mr. McGee was informed of my whereabouts, and it was not long before he and his cousin came to get me. When they came, I was called up by the nickname they had given me, "Memphis." "Come out here, 'Memphis,'" said the turnkey, "your master has come for you." I went down stairs to the office, and found Boss waiting for me. "Hello, Lou!" said he, "what are you doing here, you dog?" I was so frightened I said nothing. Of course, some few words were passed between him and the officers. I heard him say that I was a smart fellow, and he could not tell why I had run away; that he had always treated me well. This was to impress the officers with the idea that he was not unkind to his slaves. The slave-holders all hated to be classed as bad taskmasters. Yet nearly all of them were. The clothes I wore were jail property, and he could not take me away in them; so we started to go up town to get others. As we passed out the jailer, Buckhanon, said: "Ain't you going to put hand-cuffs on him?" "Oh, no!" said Boss. After I was taken to the store and fitted with a new suit of clothes, he brought me back to the jail, where I washed myself and put on the new garments. When all was complete, and I seemed to suit master's fastidious eye, he took me to the Gault House, where he was stopping. In the evening we started for home, and reached Memphis the following day. Boss did not flog me, as I expected, but sent me to my regular routine work. We had been in this new home so short a time he did not want it to be rumored that he whipped his slaves, he was so stylish and rich. But the madam was filled with rage, although she did not say much. I think they saw that I was no longer a child—they feared I would go again. But after I had been home some three or four weeks, Madam Sarah commenced her old tricks—attempting to whip me, box my jaws and pinch me. If any little thing was not pleasing to her at meal time, it was a special delight for her to reach out, when I drew near to her to pass something, and give me a blow with her hand. Truly it was a monstrous domestic institution that not only tolerated, but fostered, such an exhibition of table manners by a would-be fine lady—such vulgar spite and cruelty!

MY SECOND RUNAWAY TRIP

About three months after my first attempt to get away, I thought I would try it again. I went to Memphis, and saw a boat at the landing, called the John Lirozey, a Cincinnati packet. This boat carried the mail. She had come into port in the morning, and was being unloaded. I went aboard in the afternoon and jumped down into the hull. Boss had been there in the fore part of the afternoon inquiring for me, but I did not know it then. After I had been in the boat some time, the men commenced loading it. I crept up in the corner and hid myself. At first two or three hundred dry and green hides were thrown in, and these hid me; but later on two or three tiers of cotton bales were put in the center of the hull, and, when the boat started, I got upon the top of these, and lay there. I could hear the people talking above me, but it was so dark I could not see anything—it was dark as a dungeon. I had lain there two nights and began to get so weak and faint I could stand it no longer. For some reason the

62

boat did not start the day I went aboard, consequently, I had not gotten as far from home as I expected, and my privations had largely been in vain. Despairing and hungry, on the third day, I commenced howling and screaming, hoping that some one would hear me, and come to my relief, for almost anything else would have been preferable to the privation and hunger from which I was suffering. But I could make no one hear, at least no one paid any attention to my screams, if they did hear. In the evening, however, one of the deck hands came in with a lantern to look around and see everything was all right. I saw the light and followed him out, but I had been out of my hiding only a short time when I was discovered by a man who took me up stairs to the captain. It was an effort for me to walk up stairs, as I was weak and faint, having neither eaten nor drank anything for three days. This boat was crowded with passengers, and it was soon a scene of confusion. I was placed in the pilot's room for safety, until we arrived at a small town in Kentucky called Monroe. I was put off here to be kept until the packet came back from Cincinnati. Then I was carried back to Memphis, arriving about one o'clock at night, and, for safe keeping, was put into what was called the calaboose. This was especially for the keeping of slaves who had run away and been caught. Word was sent to Boss of my capture; and the next morning Thomas Bland, a fellow servant of mine, was sent to take me home. I can not tell how I felt, for the only thought that came to me was that I should get killed. The madam met us as we drove into the yard. "Ah!" she said to me, "you put up at the wrong hotel, sir." I was taken to the barn where stocks had been prepared, beside which were a cowhide and a pail of salt water, all prepared for me. It was terrible, but there was no escape. I was fastened in the stocks, my clothing removed, and the whipping began. Boss whipped me a while, then he sat down and read his paper, after which the whipping was resumed. This continued for two hours. Fastened as I was in the stocks, I could only stand and take lash after lash, as long as he desired, the terrible rawhide cutting

63

into my flesh at every stroke. Then he used peach tree switches, which cracked the flesh so the blood oozed out. After this came the paddle, two and a half feet long and three inches wide. Salt and water was at once applied to wash the wounds, and the smarting was maddening. This torture was common among the southern planters. God only knows what I suffered under it all, and He alone gave me strength to endure it. I could hardly move after the terrible ordeal was finished, and could scarcely bear my clothes to touch me at first, so sore was my whole body, and it was weeks before I was myself again.

PREACHING TO THE SLAVES

As an offset, probably, to such diabolical cruelties as those which were practiced upon me in common with nearly all the slaves in the cotton region of the south, it was the custom in the section of country where I lived to have the white minister preach to the servants Sunday afternoon, after the morning service for the whites. The white people hired the minister by the year to preach for them at their church. Then he had to preach to each master's slaves in turn. The circuit was made once a month, but there was service of some kind every Sunday. The slaves on some places gathered in the yard, at others in the white folks' school houses, and they all seemed pleased and eager to hear the word of God. It was a strong evidence of their native intelligence and discrimination that they could discern the difference between the truths of the "word" and the professed practice of those truths by their masters. My Boss took pride in having all his slaves look clean and tidy at the Sabbath service; but how would he have liked to have the slaves, with backs lacerated with the lash, appear in those assemblies with their wounds uncovered? The question can never be answered. The master and most of his victims have gone where professions of righteousness will not avail to cover the barbarities practised here.

A FAMILY OF FREE
PERSONS SOLD INTO SLAVERY

My wife Matilda was born in Fayette county, Kentucky, June 17th, 1830. It seems that her mother and her seven children were to have been free according to the old Pennsylvania law. There were two uncles of the family who were also to have been free, but who had been kept over time; so they sued for their freedom, and gained it. The lawyers in the case were abolitionists and friends to the slaves, and saw that these men had justice. After they had secured their freedom, they entered suit for my wife's mother, their sister, and her seven children. But as soon as the brothers entered this suit, Robert Logan, who claimed my wife's mother and her children as his slaves, put them into a trader's yard in Lexington; and, when he saw that there was a possibility of their being successful in securing their freedom, he put them in jail, to be "sold down the river." This was a deliberate attempt to keep them from their rights, for he knew that they were to have been set free, many years before; and this fact was known to all the neighborhood. My wife's mother was born free, her mother, having passed the allotted time under a law, had been free for many years. Yet they kept her children as slaves, in plain violation of law as well as justice. The children of free persons under southern laws were free—this was always admitted. The course of Logan in putting the family in jail, for safe keeping until they could be sent to the southern market, was a tacit admission that he had no legal hold upon them. Woods and Collins, a couple of "nigger traders," were collecting a "drove" of slaves for Memphis, about this time, and, when they were ready to start, all the family were sent off with the gang; and, when they arrived in Memphis, they were put in the traders' yard of Nathan Bedford Forrest. This Forrest afterward became a general in the rebel army, and commanded at the capture of Fort Pillow; and, in harmony with the debasing influences of his early business, he was responsible for the fiendish massacre of negroes after the capture of the fort—an act which will make his name forever infamous. None of this family were sold to the same person except my wife and one sister. All the rest were sold to different persons. The elder daughter was sold seven times in one day. The reason of this was that the parties that bought her, finding that she was not legally a slave, and that they could get no written guarantee that she was, got rid of her as soon as possible. It seems that those who bought the other members of the family were not so particular, and were willing to run the risk. They knew that such things—such outrages upon law and justice—were common. Among these was my Boss, who bought two of the girls, Matilda and her sister Mary Ellen. Matilda was bought for a cook; her sister was a present to Mrs. Farrington, his wife's sister, to act as her maid and seamstress. Aunt Delia, who had been cook, was given another branch of work to do, and Matilda was installed as cook. I remember well the day she came. The madam greeted her, and said: "Well, what can you do, girl? Have you ever done any cooking? Where are you from?" Matilda was, as I remember her, a sad picture to look at. She had been a slave, it is true, but had seen good days to what the slaves down the river saw. Any one could see she was almost heart-broken—she never seemed happy. Days grew into weeks and weeks into months, but the same routine of work went on.

MY MARRIAGE—BIRTH OF TWINS

Matilda had been there three years when I married her. The Boss had always promised that he would give me a nice wedding, and he kept his word. He was very proud, and liked praise. The wedding that he gave us was indeed a pleasant one. All the slaves from their neighbor acquaintances were invited. One thing Boss did was a credit to him, but it was rare among slave-holders—he had me married by their parish minister. It was a beautiful evening, the 30th of November, 1858, when Matilda and I stood in the parlor of the McGee house and were solemnly made man and wife. Old Master Jack came up from Panola at that time, and was there when the ceremony was performed. As he looked through his fingers at us, he was overheard saying: "It will ruin them, givin wedins-wedins." Things went on as usual after this. The madam grew more irritable and exacting, always finding fault with the servants, whipping them, or threatening to do so, upon the slightest provocation, or none at all. There was something in my wife's manner, however, which kept the madam from whipping her—an open or implied threat perhaps that such treatment would not be endured without resistance or protest of some kind. This the madam regarded as a great indignity, and she hated my wife for it, and, at times, was ready to crush her, so great was her anger. In a year there were born to us twin babies; and the madam now thought she had my wife tied, as the babies would be a barrier to anything like resistance on her part, and there would be no danger of her running away. She, therefore, thought that she could enjoy, without hindrance, the privilege of beating the woman of whose womanhood she had theretofore stood somewhat in fear.

MADAM'S CRUELTY
TO MY WIFE AND CHILDREN

Boss said from the first that I should give my wife assistance, as she needed time to care for the babies. Really he was not as bad as the madam at heart, for she tried to see how hard she could be on us. She gave me all the extra work to do that she could think of, apparently to keep me from helping my wife in the kitchen. She had all the cooking to do for three heavy meals each day, all the washing and ironing of the finest clothes, besides caring for the babies between times. In the morning she would nurse the babies, then hurry off to the kitchen to get breakfast while they were left in charge of a little girl. Again at noon she repeated her visit to the babies, after cooking the dinner, then in the evening, after supper, she would go to nurse them again. After supper was over, dishes all washed and kitchen in order, she would then go to the little ones for the night. One can see that she had very little time with the children. My heart was sore and heavy, for my wife was almost run to death with work. The children grew puny and sickly for want of proper care. The doctor said it was because the milk the mother nursed to them was so heated by her constant and excessive labors as to be unwholesome, and she never had time to cool before ministering to them. So the little things, instead of thriving and developing, as was their right, dwindled toward the inevitable end. Oh! we were wretched— our hearts ached for a day which we could call our own. My wife was a Christian, and had learned to know the worth of prayer, so would always speak consolingly. "God will help us," she said: "let us try and be patient." Our trial went on, until one morning I heard a great fuss in the house, the madam calling for the yard man to come and tie my wife, as she could not manage her. My wife had always refused to allow the madam to whip her; but now, as the babies were here, mistress thought she would try it once more. Matilda resisted, and madam called for Boss. In a minute he came, and, grabbing my wife, commenced choking her, saying to her: "What do you mean? Is that the way you talk to ladies?" My wife had only said to her mistress: "You shall not whip me." This made her furious, hence her call for Boss. I was in the dining room, and could hear everything. My blood boiled in my veins to see my wife so abused; yet I dare not open my mouth. After the fuss, my wife went straight to the laundry. I followed her there, and found her bundling up her babies' clothes, which were washed but not ironed. I knew at a glance that she was going away. Boss had just gone to the city; and I did not know what to say, but I told her to do the best she could. Often when company came and I held the horses, or did an errand for them, they would tip me to a quarter or half a dollar. This money I always saved, and so had a little change, which I now gave to Matilda, for her use in her effort to get away from her cruel treatment. She started at once for Forrest's trader's yards, with the babies in her arms and, after she got into Memphis, she stopped outside the yard to rest. While she was sitting on the curb stone, Forrest came out of the yard by the back gate and saw her. Coming up to her he said: "My God! Matilda, what are you doing here? You have changed so I would not have known you. Why have you come here?" Matilda said: "I came back here to be sold again." He stepped back and called another "nigger trader," Collins by name, from Kentucky. "Look here," said Forrest, pointing to my wife. Collins took in the situation at once and said he would buy her and the children. "That woman is of a good family," said he, "and was only sold to prevent her from getting her freedom." She was then taken into the yard. "Oh!" said Forrest, "I know these McGees, they are hard colts." Word was then sent McGee that his cook was in the yard and had come to be sold. He went in haste to the yard. Collins offered to buy her, but McGee said no man's money could buy that woman and her children. I raised her husband and I would not separate them. She was brought back, and as they rode along in the rockaway, Boss said: "When I am through with you I guess you won't run away again." As they drove up I saw the madam go running out to meet them. She shouted to Matilda: "Ah! madam, you put up at the wrong hotel." They at once went to the barn where my wife was tied to the joist, and Boss and the madam beat her by turns. After they had finished the whipping, Boss said, tauntingly: "Now I am buying you and selling you—I want you to know that I never shall sell you while my head and yours is hot." I was trembling from head to foot, for I was powerless to do anything for her. My twin babies lived only six months after that, not having had the care they needed, and which it was impossible for their mother to give them while performing the almost endless labor required of her, under threats of cruel beatings. One day not long after our babies were buried the madam followed my wife to the smoke house and said: "I am tempted to take that knife from

69

you, Matilda, and cut you in two. You and old Ruben (one of the slaves) went all around the neighborhood and told the people that I killed your babies, and almost whipped you to death." Of course, when the slaves were accused falsely, as in this case, they were not allowed to make any reply—they just had to endure in silence whatever was said.

EFFORTS TO LEARN TO READ AND WRITE

Thomas, the coachman, and I were fast friends. We used to get together every time we had a chance and talk about freedom. "Oh!" Tom would say, "if I could only write." I remember when Tom first began to take lessons at night from some plasterers, workmen of the neighborhood. They saw that he was so anxious to learn that they promised to teach him every evening if he would slip out to their house. I, too, was eager to learn to read and write, but did not have the opportunity which Tom had of getting out at night. I had to sleep in the house where the folks were, and could not go out without being observed, while Tom had quarters in another part of the establishment, and could slip out unobserved. Tom, however, consoled me by saying that he would teach me as soon as he knew how. So Tom one night put a copy of some figures on the side of the barn for me to practice from. I took the chalk and imitated him as near as I could, but my work was poor beside his, as he had been learning for some months, and could make the figures quite well and write a little. Still I kept trying. Tom encouraging me and telling me that I would learn in time. "Just keep trying," said he. When this first lesson was over, I forgot to rub out the marks on the barn, and the next morning when Old Master Jack, who happened to be at our home just at that time, went out there and saw the copy and my imitation of it, he at once raised great excitement by calling attention to the rude characters and wanting to know who had done that. I was afraid to own that I had done it; but

70

old Master Jack somehow surmised that it was Tom or I, for he said to Boss: "Edmund, you must watch those fellows, Louis and Thomas, if you don't they will get spoilt—spoilt. They are pretty close to town here—here." Tom and I laughed over this a good deal and how easily we slipped out of it, but concluded not to stop trying to learn all we could. Tom always said: "Lou, I am going to be a free man yet, then we will need some education; no, let us never stop trying to learn." Tom was a Virginian, as I was, and was sold from his parents when a mere lad. Boss used to write to his parents (owners) occasionally, that his people might hear from him. The letters were to his mother, but sent in care of the white folks. Tom had progressed very fast in his secret studies, and could write enough to frame a letter. It seems it had been over a year since Boss had written for him, but nothing was said until one morning I heard Boss telling Tom to come to the barn to be whipped. He showed Tom three letters which he had written to his mother, and this so startled him that he said nothing. I listened breathlessly to each word Boss said: "Where did you learn to write?" asked he, "and when did you learn? How long have you been writing to your mother?" At that moment he produced the three letters which Tom had written. Boss, it seems, had mistrusted something, and spoke to the postmaster, telling him to stop any letters which Tom might mail for Virginia to his mother. The postmaster did as directed, for slaves had no rights which postmasters were bound to respect; hence, the letters fell into the master's hands instead of going to their destination. Tom, not hearing from his first letter, wrote a second, then a third, never dreaming that they had been intercepted. Boss raged and Tom was severely whipped. After this nothing Tom did pleased any of the family—it was a continual pick on him. Everything was wrong with both of us, for they were equally hard on me. They mistrusted, I think, that I could write; yet I could not find out just what they did think.

TOM STRIKES
FOR LIBERTY AND GAINS IT

Tom stayed only a few weeks after this. He said to me, one morning: "Lou, I am going away. If I can get a boat to-night that is starting off, why, I am gone from this place." I was sad to see him go, for he was like a brother to me—he was my companion and friend. He went, and was just in time to catch the boat at the Memphis dock. He succeeded in getting on, and made an application to the captain to work on the boat. The captain did not hesitate to employ him, as it was common for slaves to be permitted to hire themselves out for wages which they were required to return, in whole or in part, to their masters. Of course all such slaves carried a written pass to this effect. Tom was shrewd; and, having learned to write fairly well, he wrote himself a pass, which was of the usual kind, stating his name, to whom he belonged, and that he was privileged to hire himself out wherever he could, coming and going as he pleased. Where the slave was an exceptional one, and where the owner had only two or three slaves, a pass would readily be given to hire himself out, or hire his own time, as it was generally called, he being required to turn over to his master a certain amount of his earnings, each month or week, and to make a report to his master of his whereabouts and receipts. Sometimes the slave would be required to turn in to his master a certain sum, as, for instance, fifty or one hundred dollars a year; and he would have to earn that before he could use any of his earnings for himself. If he was a mechanic he would have little trouble in doing this, as the wages of such were often quite liberal. This kind of a pass was rarely, if ever, given by the planters having large numbers of slaves. Another kind of pass read something like this: "Pass my boy or my girl," as the case might be, the name being attached. These were only given to permit the slave to go from the farm of his own master to that of another. Some men had wives or children belonging on neighboring farms, and would be given passes to visit them. Without such a pass they were liable to be stopped and turned back to their homes. There was, however, a good deal of visiting without passes, but it was against the general rule which required them; and any slave leaving home without a pass was liable to punishment if discovered. On our plantation passes were never given, but the slaves did visit in the neighborhood, notwithstanding, and would sometimes slip into town at night. Tom had in this way seen the pass of a neighboring slave to hire out; and it was from this he learned the form from which he wrote his, and which opened his way to freedom. Upon reading Tom's pass, the captain did not hesitate, but hired him at once; and Tom worked his way to New Orleans, to which city the boat was bound. In the meantime Boss took me and we drove to numerous stations, where he telegraphed ahead for his run-away boy Tom. But Tom reached New Orleans without hindrance, and there fell in with the steward of a Boston steamer, and, getting aboard of it, was soon on the ocean, on his way to that city where were so many friends of the slave. Arriving there he made his way to Canada; which was, for so many generations, the only land of freedom attainable to American slaves.

NEWS OF TOM'S REACHING CANADA

Now that Tom was gone, excitement prevailed at the house among the white folks—nothing had been heard of him or the method of his escape. All the servants expected that he would be caught, and I was alarmed every time Boss came from the city, fearing that he had news that Tom was caught. He had been gone about six months, when, one morning, I went to the postoffice and brought back a letter. It seemed to me that I felt that it contained something unusual, but I did not know what it was. It proved to be a letter from Tom to Boss. They did not intend that the servants should know it was from Tom, but one of the house maids heard them reading it, and came out and told us. She whispered: "Tom is free; he has gone to Canada; Boss read it in the letter Lou brought." This news cheered me, and made me eager to get away; but I never heard from him any more until after the rebellion. Tom gone made my duties more. I now had to drive the carriage, but Uncle Madison was kept at the barn to do the work there, and hitch up the team—I only had to drive when the family went out.

M'GEE EXPECTS TO CAPTURE TOM

In the summer the McGees made up their minds to go down east, and come around by Niagara Falls, for this was the place from which Tom had written them. Boss had great confidence in himself, and did not doubt his ability to take Tom home with him if he should meet him, even though it should be in Canada. So he took a pair of handcuffs with him as a preparation for the enterprise. His young nephew had been to Niagara Falls, and seen and talked with Tom; but Boss said if he had seen him anywhere he would have laid hands on him, at once, and taken him home, at all hazards.

MAKING CLOTHES

When the family went on this visit down east I was left in charge of the house, and was expected to keep everything in order, and also to make the winter clothes for the farm hands. The madam and I had cut out these clothes before she left, and it was my principal duty to run the sewing machine in their manufacture. Many whole days I spent in this work. My wife made the button holes and sewed on the buttons. I made hundreds of sacks for use in picking cotton. This work was always done in summer. When the garments were all finished they were shipped to the farm at Bolivar, to be ready for the fall and winter wear. In like manner the clothes for summer use were made in winter.

A SUPERSTITION

It was the custom in those days for slaves to carry voo-doo bags. It was handed down from generation to generation; and, though it was one of the superstitions of a barbarous ancestry, it was still very generally and tenaciously held to by all classes. I carried a little bag, which I got from an old slave who claimed that it had power to prevent any one who carried it from being whipped. It was made of leather, and contained roots, nuts, pins and some other things. The claim that it would prevent the folks from whipping me so much, I found, was not sustained by my experience—my whippings came just the same. Many of the servants were thorough believers in it, though, and carried these bags all the time.

MEMPHIS AND
ITS COMMERCIAL IMPORTANCE

The city of Memphis, from its high bluff on the Mississippi, overlooks the surrounding country for a long distance. The muddy waters of the river, when at a low stage, lap the ever crumbling banks that yearly change, yielding to new deflections of the current. For hundreds of miles below there is a highly interesting and rarely broken series of forests, cane brakes and sand bars, covered with masses of willows and poplars which, in the spring, when the floods come down, are overflowed for many miles back. It was found necessary to run embankments practically parallel with the current, in order to confine the waters of the river in its channel. Memphis was and is the most important city of Tennessee, indeed, the most important between St. Louis and New Orleans, particularly from the commercial point of view. Cotton was the principal product of the territory tributary to it. The street running along the bluff was called Front Row, and was filled with stores and business houses. This street was the principal cotton market, and here the article which, in those days, was personified as the commercial "king," was bought and sold, and whence it was shipped, or stored, awaiting an advancing price. The completion of the Memphis and Charleston railroad was a great event in the history of the city. It was termed the marriage of the Mississippi and the Atlantic, and was celebrated with a great popular demonstration, people coming from the surrounding country for many miles. Water was brought from the Atlantic ocean and poured into the river; and water taken from the river and poured into the Atlantic at Charleston. It was anticipated that this railroad connection between the two cities would make of Charleston the great shipping port, and of Memphis the principal cotton market of the southwest. The expectation in neither of these cases has been fully realized. Boss, in common with planters and business men throughout that whole region, was greatly excited. I attended him and thus had the opportunity of witnessing this notable celebration.

CHAPTER III

SLAVERY AND
THE WAR OF THE REBELLION

BEGINNING OF THE WAR

I remember well when Abraham Lincoln was elected. Boss and the madam had been reading the papers, when he broke out with the exclamation: "The very idea of electing an old rail splitter to the presidency of the United States! Well he'll never take his seat." When Lincoln was inaugurated, Boss, old Master Jack and a great company of men met at our house to discuss the matter, and they were wild with excitement. Was not this excitement an admission that their confidence in their ability to whip the Yankees, five or six to one, was not so strong as they pretended?

The war had been talked of for some time, but at last it came. When the rebels fired upon Fort Sumter, then great excitement arose. The next day when I drove Boss to town, he went into the store of one Williams, a merchant, and when he came out, he stepped to the carriage, and said: "What do you think? Old Abraham Lincoln has called for four hundred thousand men to come to Washington immediately. Well, let them come; we will make a breakfast of them. I can whip a half dozen Yankees with my pocket knife." This was the chief topic everywhere. Soon after this Boss bought himself a six shooter. I had to mould the bullets for him, and every afternoon he would go out to practice. By his direction, I fixed a large piece of white paper on the back fence, and in the center of it put a large black dot. At this mark he would fire away, expecting to hit it; but he did not succeed well. He would sometimes miss the fence entirely, the ball going out into the woods beyond. Each time he would shoot I would have to run down to the fence to see how near he came to the mark. When he came very near to it—within an inch or so, he would say laughingly: "Ah! I would have got him that time." (Meaning a Yankee soldier.) There was something very ludicrous in this pistol practice of a man who boasted that he could whip half a dozen Yankees with a jackknife. Every day for a month this business, so tiresome to me, went on. Boss was very brave until it came time for him to go to war, when his courage oozed out, and he sent a substitute; he remaining at home as a "home guard." One day when I came back with the papers from the city, the house was soon ringing with cries of victory. Boss said: "Why, that was a great battle at Bull Run. If our men had only known, at first, what they afterwords found out, they would have wiped all the Yankees out, and succeeded in taking Washington."

PETTY DISRESPECT TO
THE EMBLEM OF THE UNION

Right after the bombardment of Fort Sumter, they brought to Memphis the Union flag that floated over the fort. There was a great jubilee in celebration of this. Portions of the flag, no larger than a half dollar in paper money, were given out to the wealthy-people, and these evidences of their treason were long preserved as precious treasures. Boss had one of these pieces which he kept a long time; but, as the rebel cause waned these reminders of its beginning were less and less seen, and if any of them are now in existence, it is not likely that their possessors will take any pride in exposing them to view.

As the war continued we would, now and then, hear of some

slave of our neighborhood running away to the Yankees. It was common when the message of a Union victory came to see the slaves whispering to each other: "We will be free." I tried to catch everything I could about the war, I was so eager for the success of the Union cause. These things went on until

THE BATTLE OF SHILOH, APRIL 9, 1862

Boss came hurrying in one morning, right after breakfast, calling to me: "Lou, Lou, come; we have a great victory! I want to go up and carry the boys something to eat. I want you and Matilda to get something ready as quickly as you can." A barrel of flour was rolled into the kitchen, and my wife and I "pitched in" to work. Biscuit, bread, hoe-cake, ham, tongue—all kinds of meat and bread were rapidly cooked; and, though the task was a heavy one for my wife and me, we worked steadily; and, about five o'clock in the afternoon the things were ready. One of the large baskets used to hold cotton was packed full of these provisions. Our limbs ached from the strain of the work, for we had little help. One reason for the anxiety of the Boss for the preparation of this provision for the soldiers was that he knew so many in one of the companies, which was known as the "Como Avengers," and he had a son, a nephew and a brother of his wife connected with it; the latter a major on Gen. Martin's staff. On the following morning I got up early, and hurried with my work to get through, as I had to go to the postoffice. Madam hurried me off, as she expected a letter from her husband, who had promised to write, at the earliest moment, of their friends and relatives. I rushed into the city, at full speed, got some letters and a morning paper, and, returning as rapidly as possible, gave them to her. She grasped them eagerly, and commenced reading the paper. In a short time I heard her calling me to come to her. I went in, and she said, in great excitement: "Louis, we want to have you drive us into town, to see the Yankee prisoners, who

79

are coming through, at noon, from Shiloh." I went and told Madison to hitch up, as soon as he could. In the meantime I got myself ready, and it was not long before we were off for the city. The madam was accompanied by a friend of hers, a Mrs. Oliver. We were at the station in plenty of time. About twelve o'clock the train from Shiloh drew into the station; but the prisoners that were reported to be on board were missing—it proved to be a false report. While they were looking for the prisoners, Mrs. Oliver saw Jack, a servant of Edward McGee, brother of madam. "Oh! Look," said Mrs. Oliver, "there is Edward's Jack. Lou, run and call him." In a minute I was off the carriage, leaving the reins in madam's hands. Jack came up to the carriage, and the women began to question him: "Where is your Master, Ed," asked both of them. "He is in the car, Missis—he is shot in the ankle," said Jack. In a minute the women were crying. "I was going to get a hack," said Jack, "to—" "No, No!" said both of them. "Go, Lou, and help Jack to bring him to our carriage. You can drive him more steadily than the hackman." Jack and I went to the car, and helped him out, and after some effort, got him into our carriage. Then I went and got a livery hack to take the women and his baggage home. When we reached home, we found there old Mrs. Jack McGee, mother of the madam, Mrs. Charles Dandridge, Mrs. Farrington, sisters of madam, and Fanny, a colored woman, Edward's housekeeper and mistress—a wife in all but name. All of these had come to hear the news of the great battle, for all had near relatives in it. Mrs. Jack McGee and Mrs. Dr. Charles Dandridge had each a son in the terrible conflict.

MOURNING IN MASTER'S FAMILY

In the afternoon, when all were seated in the library reading, and I was in the dining room, finishing up my work, I happened to look out of the window, and saw a messenger coming up the graveled walk. I went out to meet him. "Telegram for Mrs.

McGee," he said. I took it to her; and, reading it without a word, she passed it to the next member of the family, and so it was passed around until all had read it except Mrs. Dandridge. When it was handed to her, I saw, at a glance, that it contained for her the most sorrowful tidings. As she read she became livid, and when she had finished she covered her face with her handkerchief, giving a great, heavy sob. By this time the whole family was crying and screaming: "Oh! our Mack is killed." "Mars, Mack is killed," was echoed by the servants, in tones of heart-felt sorrow, for he was an exceptional young man. Every one loved him—both whites and blacks. The affection of the slaves for him bordered on reverence, and this was true not alone of his father's slaves, but of all those who knew him. This telegram was from Boss, and announced that he would be home the next day with the remains. Mrs. Farrington at once wrote to old Master Jack and to Dr. Dandridge, telling them of Mack's death and to come at once. After I mailed those letters nothing unusual happened during the afternoon, and the house was wrapped in silence and gloom. On the following morning I went for the mail as usual, but there was nothing new. At noon, the remains of the much loved young man arrived at our station, accompanied by Boss and Dr. Henry Dandridge, brother of the father of the deceased, who was a surgeon in the rebel army. I went to the station with another servant, to assist in bringing the body to the house. We carried it into the back parlor, and, after all had been made ready, we proceeded to wash and dress it. He had lain on the battlefield two days before he was found, and his face was black as a piece of coal; but Dr. Henry Dandridge, with his ready tact, suggested the idea of painting it. I was there to assist in whatever way they needed me. After the body was all dressed, and the face painted, cheeks tinted with a rosy hue, to appear as he always did in life, the look was natural and handsome. We were all the afternoon employed in this sad work, and it was not until late in the evening that his father and mother came down to view the body for the first time. I remember, as they came down the broad stairs together, the sorrow-stricken yet calm look of those two people. Mrs. Dandridge was very calm—her grief was too great for her to scream as the others did when they went in. She stood and looked at her Mack; then turning to Boss, she said: "Cousin Eddie, how brave he was! He died for his country." Poor, sorrowing, misguided woman! It was not for his country he died, but for the perpetuation of the cruel, the infamous system of human slavery. All the servants were allowed to come in and view the body. Many sad tears were shed by them. Some of the older slaves clasped their hands, as if in mute prayer, and exclaimed, as they passed by the coffin: "He was a lovin boy." It seems that all his company but five or six were killed. At an early hour next morning the funeral party started for the home in Panola, where the body of the lamented young man, sacrificed to an unholy cause, was buried, at the close of the same day.

Edward stayed at our house some six weeks, his ankle was so slow in getting well. At the end of that time, he could walk with the aid of crutches, and he took Fanny and went home.

ALARM OF THE MEMPHIS REBELS

Not long after this the people were very much worked up over the military situation. The Yankees had taken Nashville, and had begun to bombard Fort Pillow. The officials of the Memphis and Ohio railroad company became alarmed at the condition of things, fearing for the safety of their stock. The officers, therefore, set about devising some plan by which they might get the cars down on the Memphis and Jackson road, where they imagined their property would be safe from the now terrible Yankees. The railroad officials at once set to work to buy the right of way through Main street, to give them the connection with the southern road named. At first it was refused by the city authorities, but finally the right of way was granted. When, however, the railroad men began to lay the ties and rails, the people grew furious. Some fled at once, for they imagined that this act of the railroad officials indicated that the Yankees must be coming pretty near. Boss became so excited, at this time, that he almost felt like going away too. The family grew more and more uneasy; and it was the continual talk: "We must get away from Memphis. The companies are already moving their rolling stock, fearing the Yankees may come at any time and destroy everything; we must get away," said Boss, speaking to the madam.

THE FAMILY FLEE FROM MEMPHIS

Things continued in this way until about June, 1862. The Union troops had taken Fort Pillow. We had heard the firing of cannon, and did not know what it meant. One morning I was in the city after the mail, and I learned that a transient boat had just come down the river, which had lost a part of her wheelhouse. She was fired on from Fort Pillow, sustaining this serious damage from the shot. This increased the excitement among the people; and our folks became alarmed right away, and commenced talking of moving and running the servants away from the Yankees, to a place of safety. McGee was trying for some time to get some one to take the house, that is, to live in and care for it until after the war, while the family were gone. They never thought that slavery would be abolished, and so hoped to come back again. After some search, they found a widow, a Mrs. Hancock. She was to have full charge of the house and continue keeping boarders, as she had been doing in Memphis. The vaunted courage of this man seems to have early disappeared, and his thought was chiefly devoted to getting his family and his slaves into some obscure place, as far away as possible from the Yankees, that were to be so easily whipped. We were about two weeks getting ready to leave, stowing away some of the things they did not want to move. The Boss and his family, my wife and I, and all the house servants were to go to Panola, to his father's. The family went by rail, but I had to drive through in a wagon.

I AM TAKEN TO BOLIVAR FARM

Soon after the family all reached Master Jack's, Boss took me to his own farm in Bolivar county. This separated me for a time from my wife, for she remained with the family. I had to look after the house, at the farm, attend the dining room, and, between meals, sew every day, making clothes for the hands. I could run on the machine eighteen to twenty pairs of pants a day, but two women made the button holes and did the basting for me, getting the goods all ready for the machine.

CAPTURE OF A UNION TRADING BOAT

The Yankees had made a raid through Bolivar, before I came, and the excitement had not abated, as they were spreading themselves all through the state. There was a Union trading boat, the Lake City, that had been successful in exchanging her goods for cotton that came from Memphis. She usually stopped at Helena, Fryer's Point and other small towns; but on a trip at this time she came about fifty miles farther down the river, to Carson's Landing, right at Boss' farm. She was loaded with all kinds of merchandise—sugar, tobacco, liquor, etc. She had a crew of about forty men, but they were not well prepared for a vigorous defense. The rebel soldiers stationed in the vicinity saw her as she dropped her anchor near the landing, and they determined to make an effort for her capture. They put out pickets just above our farm, and allowed no one to pass, or stop to communicate with the boat. Every one that sought to pass was held prisoner, and every precaution taken to prevent those on the boat from learning of the purposes of the rebels, knowing that the boat would land in the morning, if not informed of the danger, and then it was anticipated that they could easily make her a prize. There was a small ferry boat behind the steamer, and as the latter dropped down stream, and then steamed up to the landing, the former stood off for a few moments. As the steamer touched shore, the rebels charged on her, and captured her without a struggle. In the meantime the ferry boat, seeing what had happened, sped away up stream, the soldiers firing at her, but doing little damage, except the breaking of the glass in the pilot house. The rebels, seeing that the ferry boat had escaped them, turned their attention to the unloading of the steamer. They sent out for help in this work, and the summons was answered by the neighbors far and near. Wagons were brought, two of which were from our farm, and loaded with goods, which were taken to Deer Creek, forty miles from Carson Landing. What goods they found themselves unable to carry away were packed in the warehouse. The steamer was then burned. McGee was present, and the rebel captain gave him a written statement of the affair to the effect that the residents were not responsible for it, and that this should be a protection for them against the Union forces. The officers and crew of the steamer to the number of forty were made prisoners, and taken to Deer Creek, the rebel headquarters of that region, and put in the jail there. The ferry boat that escaped went to Helena, Arkansas, and carried the news of the affair to the Union forces there.

BOSS TAKEN PRISONER

I was told by Boss to take my stand on our veranda, and keep watch on the river, and if I saw any boat coming down to let him know at once. I kept a close watch the next morning until

85

about eight o'clock, when I saw a boat, but she had almost gone past our house before I discovered her. I ran into the house and told Boss. He ordered me to get his horse at once, which I did; and he mounted and went down to the landing as fast as he could. Upon reaching there, he was taken prisoner by the Union soldiers, who had just landed from the boat. All who came near were captured. The Union soldiers went to work and transferred all the goods which the rebels had put into the warehouse from the boat which they had captured, then setting fire to the warehouse and the postoffice, they pushed off yelling and shouting with glee. Among those captured by the Union soldiers were three other rich planters besides Boss, all of whom were taken to Helena. After they had been there about a week, the planters offered to secure the release of the Unionists captured on the boat which the rebels had burned at Carson Landing, and who had been sent to the rebel jail at Deer Creek, if they were guaranteed their own release in exchange. They offered to bear the expense of a messenger to the rebel officer, at Deer Creek, with this proposition. The Union officer at Helena accepted the proposition, and the messenger was sent off. It was arranged that he should stop over at our house, both on his way down and back. Upon his return, he stopped over night, and the next morning proceeded on his way. When he had gone about five miles, he saw a flat-boat at a landing, on which were people drinking and having a merry time. He stopped, and went aboard; and, in joining the carousal, he soon became so intoxicated that he was unable to go on with his journey. Among those present was one Gilcrease, a cousin of the McGees, who recognized the man as the messenger in this important business, went to him and asked him for the letters he carried. The fellow refusing to give them up, Gilcrease took them from him, and at once sent to our overseer for a reliable man by whom to forward them to the commandant at Helena. The overseer called me up from the cabin to his room, and told me that I was to go to Helena to carry some important papers, and to come to him for them in the morning, and make an early start. I left him and went back to my cabin.

MY THIRD EFFORT FOR FREEDOM

I made up my mind that this would be a good chance for me to run away. I got my clothes, and put them in an old pair of saddle bags—two bags made of leather, connected with a strip of leather, and used when traveling horseback for the same purpose as a satchel is used in traveling in the cars. I took these bags, carried them about a half mile up the road, and hid them in a fence corner, where I could get them in the morning when I had started on my trip. Fryer's Point, the place to which I was to go, was about fifty miles from the farm. I started early in the morning, and, after I had gone twenty-five miles, I came to the farm of William McGee, a brother of the madam, and stopped to change horses. I found that William McGee was going, in the morning, down to old Master Jack's; so I took one of their horses, leaving mine to use in its place, went right to Fryer's Point, delivered the letters to a man there to carry to Helena, and got back to William McGee's farm that night. I made up my mind to go with William down to Panola, where madam was, to tell her about Boss being captured. The next morning, he started, and Gibson, his overseer and myself accompanied him. He questioned me about the capture of Boss, what the soldiers had done, etc., and I told him all I knew of the matter. "Well, Lou," he said, "why did you not bring us some whisky?" "I did bring a little with me," I said. He laughed, saying: "Oh, well, when we come to some clear water we will stop and have a drink." Then I said: "Mr. Smith will look for me to-night, but he wont see me. I am going to tell the madam that Boss is captured." "Hey, ho!" he said, "then you are running away." I replied: "Well I know Miss Sarah don't know Boss is in prison." We traveled on, all three of us, stopping at intervals to be refreshed. After

87

two days, we arrived at Panola. Our journey was a tedious one. The streams were so swollen in places that we could hardly pass. The Tallehatchie we had to swim, and one of the men came near losing his horse and his life. The horses became tangled in a prep vine, as we were nearing the shore at which we aimed, and, the current being very swift, we were carried below the landing place; but, finally, we got safely ashore, McGee landing, and we following. Reaching Panola, wet and weary, I conveyed to madam the story of her husband's capture and imprisonment, a rumor of which had already reached her.

The next morning was Christmas, and a number of the family had come to spend it together. They had heard that McGee was captured and in prison; but, now, as I told them every feature of the affair in detail, they grew excited and talked wildly about it. Among those who came were Dr. Dandridge and his wife, Blanton McGee and his wife, Tim Oliver and his wife. All these women were daughters of old Master Jack McGee, and sisters to the madam. Mrs. Farrington and old lady McGee were already there. These re-unions on Christmas were a long established custom with them, but the pleasure of this one was sadly marred by the vicissitudes and calamities of the war. A shadow hung over all the family group. They asked me many questions about Boss, and, of course, I related all I knew.

After I had been there three days, they started me back with letters for Boss. When I left it was near night, and I was to stop over at Master Jack's farm fifteen miles away. It was expected that I would reach Fryer's Point on the third morning, thus allowing me three days to go sixty miles; but I could not make much headway, as the roads were so heavy. The understanding was that I was to deliver the letters to the same gentleman, at Fryer's, to whom I delivered the others, for forwarding to Boss at Helena. I was then to go straight to the farm at Boliver, and report to Smith, the overseer. But after I had got about four miles away, I concluded that I would not go back to the farm, but try to get to the Yankees. I knew I had disobeyed Smith by going down

88

to the madam's to tell her about Boss, because he told me not to go when I spoke to him about it. And now if I went back I feared he would kill me; for I knew there would be no escape for me from being run into the bull ring, and that torture I could not think of enduring. I, therefore, stopped, and, taking the bridle and saddle from the horse, hid them in the corner of a fence in a cornfield. Then I went into the woods. The papers which I had were in the saddlebag safe. The place where I stayed in the daytime was in a large shuck-pen—a pen built in the field to feed stock from, in the winter time. This pen was on Dr. Dandridge's farm; and the second night I worked my way up near the house. Knowing all the servants, I was watching a chance to send word to the coachman, Alfred Dandridge, that I wanted him to tell my wife that I was not gone. I went down to his cabin, in the quarters; and, after a short time he came. I was badly scared, and my heart was heavy and sore; but he spoke comfortingly to me, and I was cheered, somewhat, especially when he promised to see Matilda, and tell her of my whereabouts. He gave me some food, and hid me away for the night in his house. I kept close all the next day; and, at night, when all was still, Alfred and I crept out, and went to old Master Jack's. The distance was not great, and we soon covered it. Alfred went in and told my wife that I was outside and wanted to see her. She came out, and was so frightened and nervous that she commenced sobbing and crying, and almost fainted when I told her, in low tones, that I was going to try to get to Memphis, and that Alfred was helping to plan a way to this end. The rebels occupied both roads leading to Memphis, and I was puzzled to know how to reach the city without coming in contact with them. Two days after I had talked with my wife, the rebel troops who were camped on the Holly Springs road left for some other point. My friend Alfred found this out, and came and told me the encouraging news. The following night I went to old Master Jack's and told my wife that the way now seemed clear, and that I was going at once. I was bent on freedom, and would try for it again. I urged my wife not to grieve, and endeavored to encourage her by saying that I would return for her, as soon as possible, should I succeed in getting to a land of freedom. After many tears and blessings, we parted, and I left, Uncle Alfred going with me some three miles, as I was not acquainted with the road. When he left me I went on alone with gloomy forebodings, but resolved to do my best in this hazardous undertaking, whatever might happen. The road passed over hills and through swamps, and I found the traveling very wearisome. I had traveled some hours, and thought I was doing well; when, about one o'clock in the night, I came up out of a long swamp, and, reaching the top of a hill, I stopped for a moment's rest, raising myself to an erect position from that of walking, inclined by reason of weariness and the weight of the saddle-bags thrown across my shoulders. The weather was bad, a heavy mist had come up, and was so dark that I could hardly see my way. As I started on, a soldier yelled at me from the mist: "Halt! advance and give the countersign." I stopped immediately, almost scared out of my wits. "Come right up here," said the soldier, "or I'll blow you into eternity." I saw at once he was a rebel soldier. I knew not what to do. This place where I was halted was Nelson's farm, and the house was held as headquarters for a company of rebel soldiers, known as bushwhackers. While they belonged to the rebel army, they were, in a measure, independent of its regulations and discipline, kept back in the woods, ready for any depredation upon the property of unionists—any outrage upon their persons. The soldier who had halted me took me up to the house, and all began to question me. I told them that I had been sent on an errand, and that I had lost my way. The next morning I was taken about a mile away down in the swamp, over hills and through winding paths, till at last we came to the regular rebel camp. I was in great fear and thought my end had come. Here they began to question me again—the captain taking the lead; but I still stuck to my story that I had been sent on an errand, and had lost my way. I knew that this was my only chance. They tried to make me say that I had come from the Yankees, as they were in camp near Holly Springs. They thought the Yankees had sent me out as a spy; but I said the same as at first—that I had lost my way. A soldier standing by said: "Oh! we will make you talk better than that;" and stepping back to his horse, he took a sea-grass halter, and said: "I'll hang you." There was a law or regulation of the rebel government directing or authorizing the hanging of any slave caught running away; and this fellow was going to carry it out to the letter. I talked and pleaded for my life. My feelings were indescribable. God only knows what they were. Dr. Carter, one of the soldiers, who knew me and the entire McGee family, spoke up and said: "You had better let me go and tell Mr. Jack McGee about him." The captain agreed to this, and the doctor went. The following day, Old Jack came, and steadily refused to consent to my being hung. He said: "I know Edmund would not have him hung-ung. He is too valuable-aluable. No, no! we will put him in jail and feed him on bread and water—too valuable a nigger to be hung-ung."

They tried again to make me say that I was with the Yankees. They whipped me a while, then questioned me again. The dog-wood switches that they used stung me terribly. They were commonly used in Mississippi for flogging slaves—one of the refinements of the cruelty of the institution of slavery. I refused to say anything different from what I had said; but when they had finished whipping me I was so sore I could hardly move. They made up their minds to put me in jail at Panola, twenty-two miles away, to be fed on bread and water. The next day was Sunday, and all arrangements having been made for taking me to the place appointed for those whose crime was a too great love for personal freedom, they started with me, passing on the way Old Master Jack's, where they halted to let him know that his advice respecting me was to be carried out. The old man called to my wife: "Come out and see Louis." Some one had told her that they were going to hang me; and I shall never forget her looks as she came out in the road to bid me good-by. One of the

91

soldiers was softened by her agony, and whispered to her: "Don't cry, aunty, we are not going to hang him—we will only put him in jail." I saw this changed my wife's looks in a minute. I said a few words to her, and, with a prayer for God's blessing on us both, we parted, and they moved on. After we had gone about seven miles, we met two soldiers, who belonged to the regiment at Nelson. They said: "Hello! where you going with that nigger?" The two men in charge of me replied: "We are going to take him to Panola jail." "Why," said one of the soldiers, "there is no jail there; the Yanks passed through and pulled down the doors and windows of the jail, and let all the prisoners out." This caused a stop; and a council of war was held in the fence corner, the result of which was a decision to take me back to old Jack McGee's. After we had gotten back there, they took me and gave me another flogging to satisfy the madam. I was never so lacerated before. I could hardly walk, so sore and weak was I. The law was given me that if ever I was caught out in the public road again, by any soldier, I was to be shot. Monday morning I was sent to the field to plow; and, though I was very stiff and my flesh seemed sore to the bone, my skin drawn and shriveled as if dead, I had, at least, to make the attempt to work. To have said: "Master, I am too sore to work," would only have gotten me another whipping. So I obeyed without a word.

REBELS BURN THEIR COTTON

The capture of Memphis by the Union troops closed the principal cotton market of the country, and there was, as a consequence, an immense accumulation of the product in the hands of the farmers of that region. They were, therefore, compelled to resort to temporary expedients for its protection from the elements. Old Master Jack had his piled up in a long rick, and shelters built over it. Other farmers did the same. As cotton was almost the only source of revenue for the farmers, and as there was now no opportunity of getting it to market, there was such a dearth of money as had seldom, if ever, been known, and a corresponding dearth of those necessaries of life which money was the only means of procuring. The accumulations of our family in this product were very great. While the rebel farmers were waiting for a time when they could turn their stores of this valuable article into money, a proclamation was issued by the rebel government that all the owners of cotton that had it stored on their farms must prepare to have it burned. Hundreds of rebel soldiers marched to every section of Mississippi that they could reach, and applied the torch to these cotton ricks. The destruction was enormous. This was to prevent the cotton from falling into the hands of the Unionists. Jeff Davis said to his deluded followers that it was better for them to destroy this property than to risk its coming into the possession of their enemies, since that would equally impoverish themselves, while it might result to the pecuniary advantage of those with whom they were at war. I know that it was a terrible sight when our cotton was burned. Hundreds of bales were consumed, and it seemed like a wholly unnecessary destruction of property, and, therefore, unwise as a war measure. Many were sorry that they had acquiesced in the policy, as it cost them thousands of dollars, and made many poor. They thought that possibly their farms might have escaped the visits of the Union soldiers, and the property, so much needed, been saved in whole or in part. They reasoned, and reasoned correctly, that their condition would in no sense have been worse if their cotton had not been burned by their own soldiers, but might have been much better in many cases, without any real detriment to the rebel cause. The sacrifice of the property of their own people, by the rebel authorities, was evidence of the desperation of the condition of the rebellion, and was so regarded by not a few at that time. Those were terrible days. One could see anxiety written on every face among the whites. The slaves even looked worried at times, though the war meant so much to them, as they were always looking forward to freedom, at its close, if the Union troops were successful.

MY FOURTH RUNAWAY TRIP

After I had been working on the farm about two months, and had thoroughly talked the matter over with Alfred Dandridge, we planned to make a careful and persistent effort to escape from the land of bondage. We thought that as others, here and there, all through the neighborhood, were going, we would make trial of it. My wife and I were at old Master Jacks; and, after we had consulted with Alfred and Lydia, his wife, we all concluded to go at once. Alfred had been a teamster for Dandridge for many years, and was familiar with the road, as he had hauled cotton into Memphis for his master for so long a time he could hardly tell when he began. Matt Dandridge was a fellow servant, belonging to the same man, and both had, as was not unusual, taken their master's name, or, rather, were known by it. Matt had learned of our purpose to run away, and concluded to join our party. So one night, when all was still, we started. Uncle Alfred, as I always called him, was to be our leader. He was older than any of the rest of us, and had had a good deal of experience; we, therefore, all looked to him—in fact, we relied entirely upon him. After we had traveled about twelve miles, we came to a swamp, called Hicke-Halley. Here we stopped, as day was dawning, and settled down for the day, as we could travel only in the night, lest we should be seen and caught. We were wet—our clothes soaked through from the heavy dew. We had to travel through corn fields, cotton patches, oat fields and underbrush, not daring to take the main road. This is why we were so wet. Uncle Alfred traveled wholly by the stars—they were his guide. He knew by looking at them the four cardinal points of the compass. Many old slaves were guided in this way when traveling in the night, and some could tell the time of night by the position of the stars.

We stayed in Hicke-Halley all day, and in the evening, when it was dark enough, we started on again, Uncle Alfred offering up a prayer to God to guide us safely through. Cold Water was our next stopping place, and here a difficulty rose before us that made us fearful. We had nothing to wear but what we had on, and not much of that, so had small space for carrying anything, and, therefore, had brought with us only a little bite to eat. As we had lived on this small provision for a day, there was now but little left for our increasing wants; and the difficulty of securing anything from the houses without danger of detection was almost insurmountable. But we felt encouraged as we thought of what we were striving for, and sped on our way. But the way was hard, for sometimes we got completely stuck in brier patches, and had to turn and go back, in order to find a way out. Old logs and driftwood, that had been piled up year after year, were other obstacles in our way; and one can imagine how hard it was to make our way through such a mass of brush and forest by the dim light of the stars as they struggled through the dense branches of the trees. We stumbled on, however, as best we could, each fearful, yet silently praying for guidance and help. When within four or five miles of Cold Water, Uncle Alfred stopped, and cautioned us not to speak above a whisper, as the rebel troops were camped on both sides of us. We were in a swamp between the two roads, gradually working our way through to the river, as we could not go on either of the roads for fear of detection. At the bridges, where these roads crossed the river, there were rebel camps, and it was useless for us to think of crossing either. We, therefore, worked our way carefully through the thicket that we were in until we came within sight of the river. Then Uncle Alfred went ahead, creeping a few steps, then stopping to see if the river was clear of soldiers. From this point it was some two and a half miles to the bridges, each way; and it was our idea that if we could cross here without being seen by the soldiers, we would be all right. Uncle Alfred came back to us and told us that he thought the way was clear. "I can not hear a sound," said he, "so let us go on." We followed the river down until we came to a place where we could cross. Here we found some drift-wood—an old tree had been blown down, nearly across the river, leaving a space of about twenty feet. Over this natural bridge we crept to the open space which we waded, the water being up to our knees; but we did not mind this. There was no talking above a whisper, for fear of being heard by the soldiers. Daylight had begun to dawn, and we felt good that we had succeeded thus far. We went on quietly until we got entirely out of the swamp and reached some hills. The woods were on each side of us and still thick; so we stopped here, on the side of a hill, where the sun shone brightly on us, expecting to rest for the day. Our clothes had already become quite dry from the sunshine; and, so far, we felt all right. Alfred and I had made a turn around the place, listening to see if we could hear any noise, or see any trace of soldiers; but we discovered no trace of them, and went back to our stopping place. I had been asleep and some of the others were still asleep, when suddenly I heard the yelp of blood hounds in the distance. It seemed quite far away at first, but the sound came nearer and nearer, and then we heard men yelling. We knew now that they were on our trail, and became so frightened that we all leaped to our feet, and were about to run, when Uncle Alfred said: "Stop children, let me oil you feet." He had with him a bottle of ointment made of turpentine and onions, a preparation used to throw hounds off a trail. All stopped; and the women, having their feet anointed first, started off, Uncle Alfred telling them to run in different directions. He and I were the last to start. Alfred said: "Don't let the bushes touch you;" at the same time he ran through the bushes with such a rattling noise one could have heard him a great distance. He wore one of those old fashioned oil cloth coats made in Virginia; and, as he ran, the bushes, striking against the coat, made a noise like the beating of a tin board with sticks. The funny part of it was that, having cautioned us to be careful about noise, he made more than all of us. By this time the woods were resounding with the yelping of the hounds and the cries of their masters. The hounds numbered some fourteen. The men howled and cheered in concert with the brutes, for they knew that they were on the right trail, and it would be but a short time before they caught us all. I had gotten further away than any of them. Having run about a mile, I came to a farm, and started across an open field, hoping to reach a wood beyond, where I might conceal myself. Before I was half way across the field, on looking back, I saw the dogs coming over the fence, and knowing there was no chance of my getting to the woods, I turned around, and ran back to a persimmon tree, and just had time to run up one of the branches when the dogs came upon the ground. I looked and saw the men, Williams the nigger-catcher, and Dr. Henry and Charles Dandridge. As soon as Williams rode up, he told me to come down, but I was so frightened I began to cry, yet came down trembling. The dogs laid hold of me at once, tearing my clothes and biting my flesh. Dr. Dandridge was just riding up, and seeing what was happening, yelled out to Williams: "I thought your dogs didn't bite." "Oh! well," said Williams, "he aint hurt—we've got to let 'em bite a little."

They took us all back to the fence where I crossed over, all the others having been caught. Our hearts were filled with dismay. All looked as if they were condemned to be hung. We knew not what was to be done with us. The women were pitiful to see, crying and moaning—all courage utterly gone. They started back with us to Old Master Jack's, at Panola, and we stopped for the night at a small farm house. The old woman who kept it said, tauntingly: "You niggers going to the Yankees? You all ought to be killed." We started on the following morning, and got back home at one o'clock in the afternoon. All of us were whipped. All the members of the family were very angry. Old Lady Jack McGee was so enraged that she said to my wife: "I thought you were a Christian. You'll never see your God." She seemed to think that because Matilda had sought freedom she had committed a great sin.

INCIDENTS

Ever since the beginning of the war, and the slaves had heard that possibly they might some time be free, they seemed unspeakably happy. They were afraid to let the masters know that they ever thought of such a thing, and they never dreamed of speaking about it except among themselves. They were a happy race, poor souls! notwithstanding their down-trodden condition. They would laugh and chat about freedom in their cabins; and many a little rhyme about it originated among them, and was softly sung over their work. I remember a song that Aunt Kitty, the cook at Master Jack's, used to sing. It ran something like this:

> There'll be no more talk about Monday, by and by,
> But every day will be Sunday, by and by.

The old woman was singing, or rather humming, it one day, and old lady McGee heard her. She was busy getting her dinner, and I suppose never realized she was singing such an incendiary piece, when old Mrs. McGee broke in upon her: "Don't think you are going to be free; you darkies were made by God and ordained to wait upon us." Those passages of Scripture which refer to master and servants were always cited to us when we heard the Word preached; and they were interpreted as meaning that the relation of master and slave was right and proper—that they were rightly the masters and we the slaves.

I remember, not long after Jeff Davis had been elected president of the Confederacy, that I happened to hear old Master Jack talking to some of the members of the family about the war, etc. All at once the old man broke out: "And what do you think! that rascal, Abraham Lincoln, has called for 300,000 more men. What is Jeff Davis doin'-doin'?" He talked on, and seemed so angry that he gave no one a chance to answer: "Jeff Davis is a grand rascal-rascal," said he, "he ought to go into the field himself." At first all the Southerners were jubilant over Davis; but as they were losing so, and the Unionists gaining, they grew angry and denounced him oftentimes in unsparing terms.

UNION RAID AT MASTER'S FARM

During the time the Union headquarters were at Helena, a Union gun-boat came down the river as far as Boliva, and stopped at Miles McGee's. The soldiers made a raid through the farm, taking chickens, turkeys, meat and everything that they could lay hands on. During this raid Miles McGee came out of the house with a gun, and shot the commanding officer of the party. He became alarmed over what he had done, and hid in the cabin of one of the servants. He never came near the house. The Union soldiers came three different times to catch him, but never succeeded. The last time they came, he made for the canebrake, and hid himself there until they were gone. But though he had escaped their righteous vengeance, he became so nervous that he left his hiding place in the canebraker, and went to Atlanta, Ga., and staid there among friends until things became more quiet. At last wearying of this, he determined to return to old Master Jack's, but not to his own home. Word had been received of his coming, and great preparations were made for his reception. After he had started on his return, he was taken ill on the train, and was left at a small town called Jackson, where he soon died. I drove the family to the depot upon the day of his expected arrival, and as the train came in, the women waved their handkerchiefs; and, when the conductor stepped off, they asked him if Mr. McGee was aboard. He said no—"I have his remains." The scene that followed, I can not describe—such wailing and screaming! I could not but feel sad, even though they had treated me so meanly, causing the death of my children, and separating me from my wife. Their grief was indeed great. The sad news was conveyed to his mother, old Mrs. Jack McGee, at the house by an advance messenger, and we soon followed with the body. He was the favorite son of his mother, and her grief was very great. But for his wanton shooting of the Union officer, he would probably not have met his death as he did.

UNION SOLDIERS
PASS THE PANOLA HOME

One winter night, while I was at old Master Jack's, I was awakened by a rumbling noise like that of heavy wagons, which continued steadily and so long a time that I finally concluded it must be an army passing, and such I found to be the case, upon getting up and venturing out, the rumbling which had awakened me being caused by the passing artillery. I was afraid to go out straight to the soldiers, but would take a few steps at a time, then stop and listen behind a tree or the shrubbery. All seemed quiet—there was no talking. I had listened about twenty minutes when there seemed to be a halt at the creek, some distance from the house. Soon afterwords I heard the command given: "Forward!" I at once made up my mind that they were Yankee soldiers. I got on my knees and crawled to the fence, not daring to go openly, fearing that they might hear or see me and shoot, supposing me to be a spy. I went back into the house and told my wife that they were Yankees who had just passed. "Uncle George," said I, "this would be a good time for us to go." "Oh, no," said he, "we are not quite ready." Uncle George's cabin was where my wife and I stayed while at old Master Jack's. In the morning I was to carry a parcel to Como, a place not far from home, to Mr. James McGee, who was in the rebel army. It was not quite daylight when I made ready to go on my trip, for I was anxious to find out more about the soldiers. Going to the stable and saddling my horse, I mounted and rode out to the big gate leading to the main road, just as day was dawning. As I dismounted to open the gate, some soldiers were passing and an officer sung out to me, "Hello! which way are you going." I said "to Como, to carry this parcel of clothing to my young master in the war." "You have a fine horse," said the officer, "I guess I will exchange horses with you." He took my package of clothing and some letters which I had to mail and my horse, leaving me his, which was a very poor animal. I was badly scared at this performance, fearing that I would be severely whipped for the loss of the horse and package. Yet how could I help it? We knew nothing but to serve a white man, no matter what he asked or commanded. As a matter of course, I did not go to Como, as I had nothing to take—the officer had everything, but went back to the cabin. I supposed that the soldiers had all passed; but in about half an hour Aunt Kitty, on looking out of her cabin window, exclaimed: "My God! just look at the soldiers!" The yard was covered with the blue coats. Another venerable slave said: "My Lord! de year of jubilee am come." During the excitement I ran to the big house, and told the madam that the Yankees were there, and had taken my horse and every thing I had. Old Master Jack had heard the news, but was not able to come out. He had arisen, but, when he knew of the presence of the Yankees, he went back to bed, calling for Kitty to get him a mush poultice. "Tell Kitty-ity-ity to get me a mush poultice-oltice." It was customary, after the beginning of the war, for him to take sick, and call for a poultice to be put upon his stomach whenever he heard of the Yankees being near. He and many like him were especially valorous only when the blue coats were far away. The soldiers went into the dairy and drank all the milk, helped themselves to butter, cheese, meat, bread and everything in sight which they wanted. Nothing was said to them by the white folks, but the slaves were glad, and whispered to each other: "Ah! we's goin' to be free." Old Master Jack, lying on his couch would ask every little while: "Where are they? Are they gone?" After they had all left the premises, he said; "My God! I can't stand it. Them devils-evils are just goin' through the country destroyin' everything." I was sent down to get Uncle Peter for old master, and when Peter came up the old man asked: "Well, did any of the servants go away? And, sir, them devils took Louis' horse and the clothes he had for his young master."

HIDING VALUABLES
FROM THE YANKEES

Right after this the McGees commenced planning to put away their valuables, to keep them from the Union soldiers. All the servants had to fill up their bed-ticks with fine gin cotton—the lint part—for safe keeping. Great boxes and barrels were packed full of their best things, and put into the cellar, under the house. It was not exactly a cellar, but a large shallow excavation, which held a great deal. We put all the solid silver ware, such as cake baskets, trays, spoons, forks, dishes, etc., in boxes, and buried them under the hen house. Great packages of the finest clothing I had to make up, and these were given in charge of certain servants whose duty it was to run into the big house and get them, whenever they heard that the Yankees were coming, and take them to their cabins. This was a shrewd arrangement, for the soldiers never went into the cabins to get anything. When the soldiers had passed, these packages were taken back to the house. It speaks well for the honesty and faithfulness of the slaves that such trusts could be devolved upon them, notwithstanding all the cruelties inflicted upon them by their masters.

DEATH TO RUNAWAY SLAVES

It was about this time, that the law or regulation of the rebel government was promulgated, authorizing or directing the shooting or hanging of any slave caught trying to get away to the Union army. This barbarous law was carried out in many cases, for every little while we would hear of some slave who

102

was caught running away, and hung or shot. A slave belonging to Boss, ran away, and got safely within the Union lines; but he returned to get his sister. They both got away from the house, but had gone only a few miles, when William McGee overtook them, and shot the man dead. William boasted of this, but told Uncle Peter, the foreman, that he never wanted it mentioned.

SLAVES HUNG
AND LEFT TO ROT AS A WARNING

Two slaves belonging to one Wallace, one of our nearest neighbors, had tried to escape to the Union soldiers, but were caught, brought back and hung. All of our servants were called up, told every detail of the runaway and capture of the poor creatures and their shocking murder, and then compelled to go and see them where they hung. I never shall forget the horror of the scene—it was sickening. The bodies hung at the roadside, where the execution took place, until the blue flies literally swarmed around them, and the stench was fearful. This barbarous spectacle was for the purpose of showing the passing slaves what would be the fate of those caught in the attempt to escape, and to secure the circulation of the details of the awful affair among them, throughout all the neighborhood. It is difficult at this day for those not familiar with the atrocities of the institution of slavery to believe that such scenes could ever have been witnessed in this or any other civilized land, as a result simply of a human being's effort to reach a portion of the country, where the freedom of which it was said to be the home, could be enjoyed without molestation. Yet such was the horrible truth in not one case alone, but in many, as I know only too well.

RUNAWAY SLAVE
CAUGHT AND WHIPPED

One day while I was waiting at dinner, some of the children from the slave quarters came running into the house, and said to old Master Jack: "Uncle John is going away—he is down to the creek." He had been put in the carpenter shop, fastened in the stocks, but by some means he had gotten the stocks off his feet, and got loose. All in the house immediately got up and ran out. Old master told me to run and catch the runaway. I did not like to do it, but had to obey. Old master and I ran in pursuit, and soon overtook him. He could not run, as the stocks were still on his arms and neck. We brought him back, and he was "staked out"—that is, four stakes were driven into the ground, the arms tied to two and the legs to the other two. He was then paddled with the whipping paddle upon the bottom of his feet, by old Master Jack, until blood blisters arose, when he took his knife and opened them. I was then sent for salt and water, and the bruises of the suffering chattel were washed as usual in the stinging brine.

A HOME GUARD
ACCIDENTALLY SHOOTS HIMSELF

After the capture of Memphis by the Union forces, the soldiers were in the habit of making raids into the surrounding country. These were a source of alarm and anxiety among the people, and they were constantly on the watch to defend their property and themselves, as best they could. One day Dr. Charles Dandridge went over to one of our neighbors, Mr. Bobor's, to practice shooting, and to see if he had heard anything new about the war. It was the custom of the home-guards to meet weekly, and practice with their fire-arms, in order to be the better prepared, as they pretended, for any sudden incursion of the now dreaded Yankee. Mr. Bobor had gotten a Yankee pistol from some friend, who was in the army, and Dr. Charles wanted to see and try it. It was shown him, and its workings explained. He took it and began shooting, and in showing the other men how quickly he could shoot a Yankee, and mount his horse, he accidentally shot himself under the short rib near his heart, and fell to the ground. All the men came running to him, picked him up and carried him into the house, immediately sending word to Mrs. Dandridge and Master Jack McGee, his father-in-law. The boys came hurrying in, and told us what had happened. I hitched up and drove Boss over to Mr. Bobor's. We found the wounded man rapidly sinking; and when, a little later, his wife came, he could not speak—only clasped her hand. He died that night, and we carried his body to the home, which so short a time before, he had left in health and high spirits. No casket was to be had—everything of that kind had been consumed or shut out by the war. Accordingly two slaves were ordered to make a coffin, which they did, using plain boards. It was then covered with black alpaca from a dress of the madam, and lined with the cloth from Mrs. Dandridge's opera cloak. The regular material used for these purposes was not to be had. By the time the coffin was ready, the body was so bloated, that it could not be got into it. Resort was then had to a plain box, and in this the body of another of the stricken family group was laid away. At the suggestion of old Master Jack, the coffin, was put up in the carriage house, for safe keeping, he saying it would do for him to be buried in. Sorrow had come to this family with such crushing force, that their former pride and boastful spirit had given place to utter dejection.

SUBSTITUTES FOR COFFEE

During the war everything was scarce and dear, and substitutes were devised for many of those things which had formerly been regarded as the necessaries of life. Sweet potatoes were peeled, then cut in small pieces and put out in the sun to dry. They were then used as a substitute for coffee, when that article became so scarce, toward the close of the war. Great quantities of this preparation were used. Okra was another substitute for coffee. It was dried in the pod, then the seeds shelled out, and these were dried again and prepared something as the coffee is. This made a delicious drink when served with cream, being very rich and pleasant to the taste. Quinine was a medicine that had been of almost universal use in the south; yet it became so scarce that it was sold at seven dollars a bottle, and could not often be had at that price. Lemon leaves were used as a substitute in cases of chills and fever. The leaves were made into a tea, and given to the patient hot, to produce perspiration. During an attack of chills, I was treated in this manner to some advantage. At any rate I got well, which can not always be said of all methods of treatment.

CHAPTER IV

REBELLION WEAKENING,
SLAVES' HOPES STRENGTHENING

M'GEES SLAVES TAKEN TO ALABAMA

While I was absent on my last runaway trip, the Yankees had made a raid through Panola; and our people had become greatly frightened. As soon as they had got back with me and my fellow runaways, they assembled a gang of slaves for the purpose of taking them to Atlanta, Ga., to get them out of the reach of the Union soldiers. Among the slaves selected for the transfer were myself, my wife Matilda, and the seamstress. The others all belonged to Dr. Dandridge and Blanton McGee. Both the Drs. Dandridge went with us to Atlanta. We traveled across the country until we came to Demopolis, Alabama, where we found Boss camped on the bank of the Tombigbee river with all the farm slaves from Bolivar county. This was the first time I had seen Boss since he was captured and taken to Helena. As my wife and I were the only ones in the gang who belonged to Boss, we left those with whom we had come and joined his gang. We all then went aboard a boat and were taken to the salt works, situated on the Tombigbee, ninety miles from Mobile. These salt works belonged to the rebel government. The first president of the works was Mr. Woolsey, of Salem, Alabama. During Mr. Woolsey's term, the first part of 1864, when we had been there some time, he wrote to Boss asking if he would sell myself and wife, and offering $3,000 for both of us. Boss was indignant at this and curtly refused. My wife acted as cook at the salt works, in the headquarters for the president, managers and clerks. Mr. Woolsey was delighted with her cooking; her bread and rolls, he said, could not be surpassed.

M'GEE'S GREAT SCHEME

When the election of officers of the works came off in the fall, Mr. Gallatin McGee was chosen president. Boss then hired us all, about 100 in number, to labor in these works, but he, of course, received all the revenue. The work assigned me was that of butler at headquarters, and my wife was cook. Both women and children, as well as men, were employed in these works. After some months labor here, soon after Gallatin McGee became president, Matilda and I were removed to the Montgomery headquarters, where we remained until nearly Christmas. A few days before that time, Boss came to Montgomery and arranged for us to meet him in Mobile. We started at the appointed time, reached the city in the morning, and I went directly to the hotel where he told me he would be. I found him at once, and he informed me all about his plans for the future, and what he expected to accomplish. He had purchased an island in the bay, a little way from Mobile, where he had decided to establish salt works of his own. All the brick and lumber for the buildings had been carried there, and work upon them was to be commenced immediately after Christmas. He intended to make a home for the family on the island; and, as soon as he could complete the works, to remove all his hands from the government works to his own. He was very enthusiastic over this scheme, claiming that he would make far more money by it than he was then receiving from hiring out his slaves. He told me that he would remain in Mobile two or three days and would go to Panola to spend the holidays, after which he intended to bring all the family to Mobile, and remain there until the island was in readiness to be occupied. There was to be a general break up of the old home, and the beginning of a new manner of life. I stayed in his room at the hotel all the forenoon, listening to his plans; then I went back where my wife was stopping. As I left his room, he said: "Lou," as he always called me, "I will see you and Matilda at the boat this evening." We went to the boat at the appointed time and saw the Boss, but he did not come near us. As the boat was about to put off, I looked and saw him walking up and down the levee, apparently much excited, running his hands nervously through his hair—a habit common to him when he was worried. He seemed greatly distressed. The military situation troubled him, for the Union army had conquered nearly everything; and the fact now stared him in the face that he would soon lose his slaves. He never dreamed in the beginning of the war that the Unionists would conquer, and that the slaves would be freed; but now he saw that not only all his wealth in the bodies and souls of men was slipping away from him, but that much, if not all of the gain which these chattels had brought him was likely to "take wings and fly away."

M'GEE'S DEATH

We returned to the salt works the morning after leaving Mobile. Boss remained two days in Mobile, and then started for Panola, the home of his father-in-law; but, on his way, he was taken sick, having contracted a heavy cold which ran into pneumonia, and he lasted only a short time, dying on New Year's day. He had taken cold in bringing the slaves from Bolivar over the river on barges. The river was overflowed about fifty miles out, and the only way he could get the slaves across was by using large barges made of logs. They were several days floating down in this way, before he could get out to the railroad at Jackson, Miss., where he transferred them to the cars. This was too much of an exposure and it killed him.

After Boss died all the plans were changed. Col. Hunting, son-in-law of old Master Jack, came down to the salt works and hired us all out there for another year. This was the beginning of the year 1865. Of master's plans concerning the island and his proposed salt works the family knew little, for they questioned me close as to what he told me of the matter. What he spent on the island in lumber, brick, etc., was lost, as they knew nothing of the particulars of the expenditure. The madam remained at her fathers, and the slaves at the works.

I MAKE SOME MONEY

As I was here for another year, acting as butler, I thought I would try and see if I could not make some money for myself. I asked Mr. Brooks, the manager of the works, if he could get me some tobacco by sending to Mobile for it. He said he could; and on the fourth day thereafter, in the evening, it came. I was anxious to get it the same evening, but Mr. Brooks said: "Oh! I guess you had better wait until morning, then when you finish your work come down to the office and get it—you will then have more time to see the boys in the works." In the morning I was up early, and after doing my morning work I was off to Brooks' office. When I went in he said: "There it is under the table." The package was so small I felt disappointed—a hundred dollars worth ought to be more, said I to myself; but I took it, and went out among the men. I thought I would try to sell it at five dollars a plug, and if I could not sell it at that I would take four dollars. I must make something, for I had borrowed the money to buy it with; and I saw that to clear anything on it, I must at least get four dollars a plug. The money which I had borrowed was from three fellow servants, who had been fortunate in earning some little time and had saved their money. The first man I met in the works bought two plugs, at five dollars each; and after I had been there about an hour all was sold. So

I went back with a light heart. Mr. Brooks said to me at dinner: "Well, how did you get along with your tobacco?" "I did very well," I said, "the only trouble was I did not have enough. I sold it for $180." "Well," said he, "if you did, you made more clear money than the works here. How much a plug did you sell it for?" at the same time drawing out his pencil and commencing to figure it up. "I had thirty-six plugs," said I, "and I sold them for five dollars a plug." Nothing more was said just then, but after dinner Brooks and two of the clerks went out on the veranda to smoke. When they were in a good way smoking, Brooks slipped into the dining room, and said: "Well, that was fine; you got five dollars a plug for the tobacco?" "Oh, yes!" I said, "tobacco is scarce, and they were hungry for it; it went like hot cakes—the price was not questioned, I sold at once." "What is the prospect for selling more?" he asked. "Will you sell it for half the profit if I furnish the tobacco?" I said "yes." So he sent the same day for a box of tobacco—about five hundred plugs. When the tobacco came the box was sawed in two and one-half sent up to my room. I put some fellows out as agents to sell for me—Uncle Hudson, who took care of the horses and mules at the works; John at the hospital; William, head chopper, among the 100 men in the woods. Each brought in from $40.00 to $50.00 every two or three days, and took another supply. Sometimes, when I had finished my work in the afternoon, I would get an old pony and go around through the neighborhood and sell four or five plugs. It was a mystery to the servants how I got the tobacco; but I did not let on that Brooks was backing me. In two weeks we had taken in $1,600.00, and I was happy as I could be. Brooks was a fine fellow—a northerner by birth, and did just what he said he would. I received one-half of the money. Of course this was all rebel money, but I was sharp, and bought up all the silver I could find. Just as we got on the other half of the box, Brooks received word that the Yankees were coming, and to send all the hands to their masters. I was glad that I had made some money, knowing that I would need it if I gained my freedom, which I now knew was quite probable, as the Union forces were gaining ground everywhere. But the message ended my money-making, and I prepared to go home to Panola.

GOING BACK TO PANOLA

Mr. Brooks fixed the return papers so that my wife and I could leave the party of slaves at Demopolis, and go on thence to Panola by rail, to convey the news to madam that all hands were coming home; that the Yankees were expected to capture the salt works within a short time. At Jackson, some seven miles from the salt works, we were delayed over night by reason of lack of facilities for crossing the Tombigbee river. The report that the Yankees were coming through had created a panic among the white people; and hundreds, fleeing from their homes, had gathered at the river, waiting and clamoring for an opportunity to cross. Though slaves were property, and valuable on that account, the whites seemed to think that their own lives were in danger, and to be protected first. They therefore took precedence of us. In the morning about seven o'clock a steamer was seen coming at a distance; but it could not be discovered at once just what the character of it was. The whites became alarmed. Some said: "The Yankees are coming." Other said: "It is a gun boat—they will surely fire on us." But as the boat drew near the people saw that there was nothing to fear—it was only the regular passenger boat. Besides the hundreds of people, there were scores of wagons, filled with household goods to go over, and the passage was slow and tedious. We finally got across and traveled as far as Demopolis, where Matilda and I left the other slaves, and took a train and went on to Panola. I delivered the papers to the madam from Brooks, which told her all the particulars concerning the break up at the salt works. She sent wagons right away after the other slaves who were coming back on foot. They were not brought back to Panola; but were

112

hired out to different farmers along the road home—some in Jackson, some in Granda and others in Panola town. These were all small towns in Mississippi. My wife and I went to work at old Master Jack's, I on the farm and my wife at her old duties in the house. We longed for freedom, but were content for the time with hoping and praying for the coming of the day when it should be realized. It was sad to see the changes that had come to the white folks. Sorrow had left its impress upon all and we felt it, notwithstanding all that we had suffered at their hands. Boss had willed the homestead in Memphis to Mrs. Farrington, and she was getting ready to take possession. He had borrowed a great amount of money from her when he bought the island at Mobile; and the rapid coming on of the end of the rebellion destroyed all prospect of the success of his salt works scheme, even before his death, and really rendered him bankrupt. Hence the transfer of the Memphis property to her was the only way he could make good what he owed her. The madam now had no home, but was compelled to stay with her father, old Master Jack. She was sadly changed—did not appear like the same person. Her troubles and sorrows had crushed her former cruel and haughty spirit. Her mother had died a few months before, and then her husband had followed, dying suddenly and away from home. Then much of her property had been lost, and social pleasures and distinction were gone forever. Who shall say that the wrongs done her poor, helpless slaves were not avenged in this life? The last I knew of her she was still at her father's.

INCIDENTS

A servant who belonged to Dr. Dandridge ran away and got to Memphis just after it was captured by the Union soldiers. He was put into the army and was stationed at one of the entrances to the city. He was to halt all persons passing to or from the city, no difference who they were, and learn their names and their business. Young William McGee and his sister, Miss Cherry, one day went up to Memphis and, to their surprise, were halted by this former servant of their uncle. When they came home they were speaking of it to their father, and old Master Jack said: "And you halted, did you?" "Why, yes," replied William, "we had to do it." "Well," said the old man, "I would have died-died before I would have done it. To think that a servant should have halted you, and one who has belonged to the family like Anderson!" This old man, notwithstanding all his boasting in the absence of immediate danger, was the veriest coward when danger was present; and if he had been in the place of young William, he would have halted with the greatest alacrity.

While at the salt works I had a little experience at nursing. A fellow slave was taken ill, and I was called on to care for him at night. I always liked this work; it was a pleasure to me to be in the sick room. Typhoid fever was a new case to me, but I remembered what instructions Boss had given me about it. I "pitched in" to do what I could; but the fever was so great he lasted only a few days.

MY FIFTH STRIKE
FOR FREEDOM IS A SUCCESS

We had remained at old Jack's until June, 1865, and had tried to be content. The Union soldiers were still raiding all through that section. Every day some town would be taken, and the slaves would secretly rejoice. After we came back from Alabama we were held with a tighter rein than ever. We were not allowed to go outside of the premises. George Washington, a fellow servant, and Kitty, his wife, and I had talked considerably about the Yankees, and how we might get away. We knew it was our right to be free, for the proclamation had long been issued—yet they still held us. I did not talk much to my wife about going away, as she was always so afraid I would be killed, and did not

114

want me to try any more to escape. But George, his wife and I continued to discuss the matter, whenever we had a chance. We knew that Memphis was headquarters for the Union troops, but how to reach it was the great question.

It was Sunday, and I had driven one portion of the family to church, and George the other. The family was now very large, as the madam and her family were there, in addition to Old Master Jack's, and all could not go in one carriage. On the way back, young William McGee came up through the farm, on horseback, a nearer way home from church, and encountered several servants belonging to some of the neighbors. He asked them what they were doing there, and if they had passes. To this last question all answered no. "Well," said he, "never come here again without having passes, all of you." At this they all quickly disappeared. When Old Jack came home, Will told him what had passed; and he immediately called for George and Uncle Peter, the foreman, and told them that no one not belonging there was to come into the quarters without a pass; and any servant with a pass should be brought to the house, that the pass might be inspected. They thought, or feared, that if the servants were permitted to come together freely they might plan ways of escape, and communicate to each other what they knew about the war and the Yankees. George came out, and finding me, told me what they had said. "No slave from outside is to be allowed on the place," said he. I replied: "If we listen to them we shall be here until Christmas comes again." "What do you mean?" asked George. "I mean that now, today, is the time to make a start." So, late in the afternoon, during the servants' prayer meeting, of which I have heretofore spoken, we thought would be a good time to get away, as no one would be likely to see us. We talked with John Smith, another servant, and told him all about our plan, asking him not to say a word about our being gone until he was through feeding the stock. This would give us another hour to advance on our journey, as the feeding usually took about that time—from six o'clock until seven. Our fear was that we might

115

be overtaken by the bloodhounds; and, therefore, we wished to get as far away as possible before the white people knew we were gone. It was Sunday afternoon, June 26th, 1865, when George and I, having made ready for the start for the Union lines, went to bid our wives good-bye. I told my wife to cheer up, as I was coming again to get her. I said to Kitty, George's wife: "We are going, but look for us again. It will not be with us as with so many others, who have gone away, leaving their families and never returning for them. We will be here again." She looked up at me, smiling, and with a look of resolution, said: "I'll be ready." She was of a firm, daring nature—I did not fear to tell her all my plans. As my wife was so timid, I said as little as possible to her. George and I hurriedly said our farewells to our wives. The parting was heartrending, for we knew the dangers were great, and the chances were almost even that we should not meet again. I could hardly leave my wife, her agitation and grief were so great. But we were off in a few moments. We crept through the orchard, passing through farm after farm until we struck the railroad, about seven miles from home. We followed this road until we reached Senatobia, about half past seven in the evening. We felt good, and, stopping all night, we started the next morning for Hernando, Miss., another small town, and reached there at two o'clock in the afternoon. The most of the bridges had been burned, by the troops, and there were no regular railroad trains. Fortunately, however, flat cars, drawn by horses were run over the road; and on a train of this kind we took passage. On several occasions, the passengers had to get out, and push the car over a bridge, as it was not made so horses could cross on it, the horses meantime being driven or led through the stream, and then hitched to the car again. After we had gone through this process repeatedly, we at last reached Memphis, arriving about seven o'clock Monday evening. The city was filled with slaves, from all over the south, who cheered and gave us a welcome. I could scarcely recognize Memphis, things were so changed. We met numbers of our fellow servants who had run

116

away before us, when the war began. Tuesday and Wednesday we spent in making inquiries; and I visited our old home at McGee's station. But how different it was from what it had been when the McGees were there. All was changed. Thursday we went to see Col. Walker, a Union officer, who looked after the colored folks, and saw that they had their rights. When we reached his office we found it so filled with people, waiting to see him, that we were delayed about two hours, before we had an opportunity of speaking with him. When our turn came, we went in, and told him that we were citizens of Memphis until the fall of Fort Pillow and Donelson, when our master had run us off, with a hundred other slaves, into Mississippi, and thence to the salt works in Alabama. He questioned us as to where we lived in Memphis. I answered: "What is now headquarters of the Union forces was the home of master, Mr. Edmund McGee, who is now dead." After a few minutes, I said: "Colonel, we want protection to go back to Mississippi after our wives, who are still held as slaves." He replied: "You are both free men to go and come as you please." "Why," said I, "Colonel, if we go back to Mississippi they will shoot the gizzards out of us." "Well," said he, "I can not grant your request. I would be overrun with similar applications; but I will tell you what you can do. There are hundreds of just such men as you want, who would be glad of such a scout." We thanked him and left.

GOING BACK FOR OUR WIVES

After carefully considering the matter, we concluded to go back to Senatobia and see the captain of the Union troops there. The next day, Friday, we hired a two horse wagon, and made preparations to start on our perilous undertaking Saturday morning. It was our hope to find some one at Senatobia to go with us to Panola, and protect us in the effort to bring away our wives. So, early in the morning, we set out. Our first stop was at Big Springs camping ground, where we made preparations for refreshing ourselves and spending the night. Just as we had finished building a fire, for cooking and keeping off the mosquitoes, two soldiers came riding up to the spring. "Hello," said one, "which way are you traveling?" "We are just from Memphis," said George. "Have you any whisky?" asked one of them. We replied "yes." "Will you give a fellow a horn?" We answered the question by handing them the bottle. While they were drinking, George and I stepped aside, and, after a few moments talk, we decided to put the question to them of going with us to get our wives. I asked: "Where are you from?" "Senatobia," replied one. We at once laid our cause before them, telling them what Col. Walker had said regarding our getting some one to go with us on our enterprise. They listened attentively, and when we had finished, one of them asked: "How much whisky have you?" George answered: "Two bottles." "What do you intend to do when you see the captain at Senatobia?" "Lay our complaint before him," said I. "Now my friend," said one of the soldiers, "I am afraid if you go to the captain you will be defeated. But I'll tell you what I'll do. Give my comrade and me one of your bottles of whisky, and we will put you on a straight track. The reason why I say this is that our captain has been sweetened by the rebel farmers. He is invited out to tea by them every evening. I know he will put you off. But I will write a note to some comrades of mine who, I know, will bring you out safe." We agreed at once to this proposition, and gave them the whisky. He wrote the note, and gave it to us, telling us to go to the last tent on the line in the camp, where we would find two boys to whom we should give it. "They are brave," said he, "and the only two I know of that can help you. If they are not there don't give the note to any one else, but wait till they come back, on Tuesday night. I feel satisfied that they will go and help you out." With these words, they rode off. George and I felt good over our prospects.

A HAZARDOUS TRIP

The next morning was Sunday, and we started on, reaching
Senatobia about eleven o'clock. We went into the camp, following
the directions given us, to go to the last tent in the line; but, when
we reached there, the soldiers were out. We lingered around the
grounds a short time, then went back, and found them there.
We gave them the note; and, after reading it, they simply asked
us where we had stopped our wagon. I told them outside the
village. "Go there," said one of them, "and remain until we come
out to see you." Shortly they came out; and, after we had told
them what we wanted, the distance to McGee's, which was about
nineteen miles from Senatobia, and had given them such other
information as they desired, they concluded that they would go.
"We want to be back," said I, "before daylight Monday morning,
because we must not be seen on the road; for we are well known
in that section, and, if discovered, would be captured and
killed." "Well," said one of the soldiers, "we will have to go back
to camp, and arrange to be excused from roll call this evening,
before we can make the trip." They went back to camp; and, in
about ten minutes they came out again saying: "All is right; we
will go." We gave them each ten dollars; and promised, if they
brought us out safely, to give each ten dollars more. It was now
about half-past eleven o'clock. They had to go to camp, and slip
their horses out cautiously, so as not to be seen by the captain.
In half an hour we were on our way; and, after we had ridden
some two miles, we were overtaken by the two soldiers. It was
Sunday afternoon; and our having a wagon attracted much
attention from the farmers as we passed along. They looked at us
so sharply that George and I felt decidedly uneasy; yet we kept
up courage and pressed steadily on. After a long and weary ride
we reached old Master Jack's a little after sundown. The soldiers
rode into the yard ahead of us, and the first person they met was
a servant (Frank) at the woodpile. They said to him: "Go in and
tell your master, Mr. McGee, to come out, we want to see him,"

119

at the same time asking for Louis' and George's wives. Young William McGee came out and the soldiers said to him: "We want feed for seventy-five head of horses." McGee said: "We have not got it." Just then George and I were coming up. We drove in at the gate, through the grove, and passed the woodpile where McGee and the soldiers were talking. McGee had just replied: "We have not got that much feed to spare—we are almost out." "Well," said the soldiers, "we must have it," and they followed on right after the wagons. As we drove past them, young McGee went running into the house, saying to his mother: "It is Louis and George, and I'll kill one of them to-night." This raised quite an alarm, and the members of the family told him not to do that, as it would ruin them. As soon as George and I drove up to the first cabin, which was my wife's and Kitty's, we ran in. Kitty met us at the door and said: "I am all ready." She was looking for us. We commenced loading our wagon with our few things. Meanwhile the soldiers had ridden around a few rods and came upon old Master Jack and the minister of the parish, who were watching as guards to keep the slaves from running away to the Yankees. Just think of the outrage upon those poor creatures in forcibly retaining them in slavery long after the proclamation making them free had gone into effect beyond all question! As the soldiers rode up to the two men they said: "Hello! what are you doing here? Why have you not told these two men, Louis and George, that they are free men—that they can go and come as they like?" By this time all the family were aroused, and great excitement prevailed. The soldier's presence drew all the servants near. George and I hurried to fill up our wagon, telling our wives to get in, as there was no time to lose—we must go at once. In twenty minutes we were all loaded. My wife, Aunt Kitty and nine other servants followed the wagon. I waited for a few moments for Mary Ellen, sister of my wife; and as she came running out of the white folks' house, she said to her mistress, Mrs. Farrington: "Good-bye; I wish you good luck." "I wish you all the bad luck," said she in a rage. But Mary did not stop to notice her mistress further; and joining me, we were soon on the road following the wagon.

TWO BRAVE MEN

Those soldiers were brave indeed. Think of the courage and daring involved in this scheme—only two soldiers going into a country of which they knew nothing except that every white man living in it was their enemy. The demand which they made for food for seventy-five horses was a clever ruse, invented by them to alarm the McGees, and make them think that there was a troop of horses near by, and that it would not be safe for them to offer any resistance to our going away with our wives. Had they thought that there were but two soldiers, it is certain that they would have endeavored to prevent us getting away again, and one or more of us would undoubtedly have been killed.

As already stated, nine other slaves followed our wagon, as it moved off. They had no hats on; some were bare-footed,— they had not stopped to get anything; but, as soon as they saw a chance to get away, they went just as they were at the moment. Aunt Kitty was brave and forethoughtful, for during the week we were gone she had baked and cooked a large amount of substantial food that would keep us from starving while on our journey.

At the first road crossing, the two soldiers thought they saw a large troop of soldiers in the distance, and they galloped ahead of us at full speed; but, on arriving at the spot, they found that what they had thought soldiers were only a herd of cattle. They rode on to the next crossing, we following as we conveniently could. Each poor slave was busy with his thoughts and his prayers. Now and then one would hear a moan or a word from some of the party. All were scared, even though the soldiers were with us. We came to the next cross road, and passed that safely. Our fear was that the McGees might get the neighborhood to

121

join them and pursue us, or send the home guards after us; but Providence was seemingly smiling upon us at last, for no one followed or molested us. We moved on all night, until we came to a creek, at four o'clock in the morning of Monday. The banks of the creek were very steep, and as the horses and wagon went down into the stream, the mattress on top of the wagon, upon which my wife and her sister's children were sitting, was thrown off into the water. Immediately the horses stopped, and became balky. It was such a warm night that they did not want to move on out of the water, and would not start, either, until they got ready. As soon as the soldiers saw the mattress slide off with my wife and the children, one of them plunged into the water with his horse, and, in a minute, brought them all out. All had a good ducking—indeed it seemed like a baptism by immersion. The drenched ones were wrapped in old blankets; and, after an hour's delay, we were again on our way. The soldiers said: "Now we must leave you; the time is coming when we must be in camp for roll call. If you are not at our camp when roll call is over, we will come back and see about you." We gave them each the second ten dollars, as agreed upon, and just as they rode to the top of the hill they left us. We had a clear sweep from this point, and we came into Senatobia about nine o'clock in the forenoon. Our two soldier friends, who had brought us out so safely, came out of camp to see us. They cheered us, and seemed glad that they had rendered us service. We stopped at the camp until we had dried our clothes and had some breakfast; and, then, we made our way to Memphis.

OUT OF BONDAGE AT LAST

My wife and her sister were shoeless, and the latter had no hat on—she had hurried out of the house in such excitement that she thought of nothing but getting away. Having to walk some of the way, as all could not ride in the wagon at the same time, we were all tired, dirty and rest-broken, and, on the whole, a pitiful crowd to look at, as we came into the city. One venerable old man, bent with age, whose ebony face shone with delight, came running out into the road as we appeared, exclaiming: "Oh! here dey come, God bless 'em! Poor chil'en! they come fannin." We used large palm leaves to fan ourselves with, as we were so warm. Those nine souls that followed us walked the whole distance, arriving shortly after we did. Thousands of others, in search of the freedom of which they had so long dreamed, flocked into the city of refuge, some having walked hundreds of miles.

It was appropriately the 4th of July when we arrived; and, aside from the citizens of Memphis, hundreds of colored refugees thronged the streets. Everywhere you looked you could see soldiers. Such a day I don't believe Memphis will ever see again—when so large and so motley a crowd will come together. Our two soldier rescuers looked us up after we were in Memphis, and seemed truly glad that we had attained our freedom, and that they had been instrumental in it. Only one thing we regret, and that is that we did not learn their names; but we were in so much trouble, and so absorbed in the business which we had in hand—so excited by the perils of our undertaking, that we never thought to ask them their names, or to what regiment they belonged. Then, after we got to Memphis, though we were most grateful for the service which they had rendered us, we were still so excited by our new condition and surroundings that we thought of little else, and forgot that we had no means of establishing, at a later time, the identity of those to whom we owed so much. Freedom, that we had so long looked for, had come at last; and we gave praise to God, blessing the day when we met those two heroes. It is true that we should have been free, sooner or later; still, but for their assistance, my wife and I might never have met again. If I could not have gone back, which I could never have done alone, until long after, such changes might have occurred as would have separated us for years, if not forever. Thousands were separated in this manner—men escaping to the Union lines, hoping to make a way to return for their families; but, failing in this, and not daring to return alone, never saw their wives or children more. Thanks to God, we were guided to these brave soldiers, and so escaped from so cruel a fate.

A WORD FOR MY OLD MASTER

In closing this account of my years of bondage, it is, perhaps, but justice to say of my old master that he was in some respects kinder and more humane than many other slaveholders. He fed well, and all had enough to wear, such as it was. It is true that the material was coarse, but it was suited to the season, and, therefore, comfortable, which could not truthfully be said of the clothing of the slaves of other planters. Not a few of these did not have sufficient clothes to keep them warm in winter; nor did they have sufficient nourishing and wholesome food. But while my master showed these virtues, similar to those which a provident farmer would show in the care of his dumb brutes, he lacked in that humane feeling which should have kept him from buying and selling human beings and parting kindred— which should have made it impossible for him to have permitted the lashing, beating and lacerating of his slaves, much more the hiring of an irresponsible brute, by the year, to perform this barbarous service for him. The McGees were charitable— as they interpreted the word—were always ready to contribute to educational and missionary funds, while denying, under the severest penalties, all education to those most needing it, and all true missionary effort—the spiritual enlightenment for which they were famishing. Then our masters lacked that fervent charity, the love of Christ in the heart, which if they had possessed they could not have treated us as they did. They would have remembered the golden rule: "Do unto others as ye would that men should do to you." Possessing absolute power over the bodies and souls of their slaves, and grown rich from their unrequited toil, they became possessed by the demon of avarice and pride, and lost sight of the most vital of the Christly qualities.

CHAPTER V

FREEDOM AFTER SLAVERY

COMING NORTH

As before stated, we arrived in Memphis on the Fourth of July, 1865. My first effort as a freeman was to get something to do to sustain myself and wife and a babe of a few months, that was born at the salt works. I succeeded in getting a room for us, and went to work the second day driving a public carriage. I made enough to keep us and pay our room rent. By our economy we managed to get on very well. I worked on, hoping to go further north, feeling somehow that it would be better for us there; when, one day I ran across a man who knew my wife's mother. He said to me: "Why, your wife's mother went back up the river to Cincinnati. I knew her well and the people to whom she belonged." This information made us eager to take steps to find her. My wife was naturally anxious to follow the clue thus obtained, in hopes of finding her mother, whom she had not seen since the separation at Memphis years before. We, therefore, concluded to go as far as Cincinnati, at any rate, and endeavor to get some further information of mother. My wife seemed to gather new strength in learning this news of her mother, meager though it was. After a stay in Memphis of six weeks we went on to Cincinnati, hopeful of meeting some, at least, of the family that, though free, in defiance of justice, had been consigned to cruel and hopeless bondage—bondage in violation of civil as well as moral law. We felt it was almost impossible that we

126

should see any one that we ever knew; but the man had spoken so earnestly and positively regarding my mother-in-law that we were not without hope. On arriving at Cincinnati, our first inquiry was about her, my wife giving her name and description; and, fortunately, we came upon a colored man who said he knew of a woman answering to the name and description which my wife gave of her mother, and he directed us to the house where she was stopping. When we reached the place to which we had been directed, my wife not only found her mother but one of her sisters. The meeting was a joyful one to us all. No mortal who has not experienced it can imagine the feeling of those who meet again after long years of enforced separation and hardship and utter ignorance of one another's condition and place of habitation. I questioned them as to when and where they had met, and how it happened that they were now together. My mother-in-law then began the following narrative:

"When I was sold from the Memphis trader's yard I was bought by a man who lived not far from Memphis. I never heard of any of the children, and knew nothing as to what had become of them. After the capture of Memphis by the Union army, the people to whom I belonged fled from their home, leaving their slaves; and the other slaveholders of the neighborhood did the same. The slaves, left to themselves, at once departed for Memphis, and I among the number. When I had been there but a short time a call was made for nurses to go into the hospital; and, after thinking of it for a few minutes, I concluded to answer the call, and was speedily installed in the work. When I had been there a short time I found, to my great surprise and delight, my eldest daughter was also employed there. She had come to Memphis as I had, because her master's family had fled; and, hearing the call for nurses, had entered the service at once. I can not tell my pleasure in meeting one of my children, for I had never expected to see any of them again. We continued our work in the hospital until Generals Sheridan and Grant said the city was getting too crowded with colored people—there was not room for them; some must be removed. So, large numbers of them were sent to Cincinnati, and my daughter and I were among them. This is why you see us here together."

When she had finished telling this story my wife and I were shedding tears of joy. My sister-in-law, Mary Ellen, whom Boss bought at the same time that he bought my wife, was with us; thus the mother and three daughters had met again most unexpectedly, and in a way almost miraculous. This meeting again of mother and daughters, after years of separation and many vicissitudes, was an occasion of the profoundest joy, although all were almost wholly destitute of the necessaries of life. This first evening we spent together can never be forgotten. I can see the old woman now, with bowed form and gray locks, as she gave thanks in joyful tones yet reverent manner, for such a wonderful blessing.

IN CANADA

We did not remain long in Cincinnati, as houses were so scarce we could not get a place to stop in. My wife's mother had but one room, and we could not stay there. We went on to Hamilton, but stayed there only two months. I worked at whatever I could get to do—whitewashing and odd jobs of any kind. The women managed to get washing to do, so that we got on very well. Our aim was when we left Memphis to get to Canada, as we regarded that as the safest place for refugees from slavery. We did not know what might come again for our injury. So, now, as we had found some of my wife's people, we were more eager to go; and, as I could not get any steady work in Hamilton, we made ready to move on. We went straight to Detroit, and crossed over the river to Windsor, Canada, arriving there on Christmas 1865. I succeeded in getting work as a porter at the Iron House, a hotel situated near the landing. Here my wife also was employed, and here we remained until spring; when, as the wages were so small in Windsor, I went over to Detroit to seek for more profitable employment. After some effort, I succeeded in securing a situation, as waiter, in the Biddle House, and remained there two years, when the manager died, and it changed hands; and, much as I disliked to make a change in my work, I found it necessary. An opportunity soon offered of a position as sailor on the steamer Saginaw, which ran from Green Bay to Escanaba, in connection with the railroad.

A CLEW TO MY BROTHER WILLIAM

While I was on this boat, one of the men who worked with me said to me, one day: "Have you a brother, Hughes?" I said, "Yes, but I don't know anything about him. We were sold from each other when boys." "Well," said he, "I used to sail with a man whose name was Billy Hughes, and he looked just like you." I told him there were three boys of us; that we were sold to different parties, and that I had never seen either of my brothers since. One brother was named William, but went by the nickname of Billy. "Has this man had his forefinger cut off," asked I. "Oh!" replied he, "I don't know, Hughes, about that." "Well," said I, "this is all I remember about Billy. I accidentally chopped off his forefinger one day, when we were small boys in Virginia. This is the only thing by which I could identify my brother William." Nothing more was said upon the matter, and it dropped out of my mind. I did not realize how important were the words of this man. It never occurred to me that he held the clew that might bring us together again.

WORK IN CHICAGO

When the sailing season had ended, the steamer tied up at Chicago for the winter. Upon going ashore, I at once tried to get something else to do, for I could not afford to be idle a day. One of the first men I met in Chicago was my old friend and fellow-servant Thomas Bland. He was glad to see me, and told me all about his escape to Canada, and how he had met Will McGee, at Niagara Falls. He was working at the Sherman House, having charge of the coat room. I told him that I had been sailing during the summer, but that the boat was now laid up, and that I was anxious for another job. He said he would try and see what he could do for me. He went to the proprietor of the hotel, Mr. Rice; and, to my surprise and delight, he was so fortunate as to secure me a position as porter and general utility man. My family were still at Windsor, Canada; and, when I had secured this place, I got leave of absence to make them a visit, and went there at once. Two babies had been born only a day before my arrival. I had hoped to be there on the interesting occasion, but was too late. However, I was pleased to find two bright little girls to aid in the family greeting, which was delightful after the months of separation. My wife, her sister Mary and her two children, her mother and the sister we found at Cincinnati were all still here living together.

ATTENDING NIGHT SCHOOL

After a visit of two weeks with my family, I returned to Chicago, and began my work at the Sherman House. I was full of energy and hope, and resolved to put forth every effort to make a man of myself, and to earn an honest living. I saw that I needed education, and it was one of the bitterest remembrances of my servitude that I had been cheated out of this inalienable right—this immeasurable blessing. I, therefore, determined to do what was in my power to gain something of that of which I had been cruelly defrauded. Hence I entered the night-school for freedmen, which had been established in the city, and faithfully attended its sessions during the months it was kept open.

I SETTLE IN MILWAUKEE

I worked at the Sherman House until August 1868, and, during this time, saw many travelers and business men, and made some lasting friends among them. Among these was Mr. Plankinton. He seemed to take a fancy to me, and offered me a situation in the Plankinton House, soon to be opened in Milwaukee. I readily accepted it for I was not getting a large salary, and the position which he offered promised more. The Plankinton House was opened in September, and I was placed in full charge of the coat room; and, after I had been there some time, I had, in connection with my coat room duties, charge of the bell stand. My wife had charge of the waiter's rooms, a lodging house situated on Second street, one door from Grand Avenue. This was a brick building that stood where the west portion of the Plankinton now stands. The second floor was used as our living rooms; the third and fourth floors constituted the sleeping apartments of the hotel waiters. My wife looked after these apartments, saw that they were clean, and had a general supervision of them.

BEGIN BUSINESS
FOR MYSELF IN A SMALL WAY

After the hotel had been running a little over a year, I saw there was a chance for me to make something at laundry work. I was allowed to take washing from any of the guests who desired their work done privately. In this way I worked up quite a business. I still continued my coat room duties, as my wife managed the laundry work. Our laundry business increased so rapidly I deemed it best to change our quarters from Second street to 216 Grand avenue, which seemed better suited for our purpose. Here the business continued to grow until it reached proportions of which we had little idea when we began it.

MEETING RELATIVES OF MY OLD MASTER

One day while I was at the Plankinton I happened to be coming through the hall, when whom should I meet but Col. Hunting, son-in-law of old Master Jack McGee, of Mississippi. We came face to face, and I knew him at once, but he only partially recognized me. He said: "I know your face, but can not recall your name." I said: "Don't you know Louis McGee?" He then remembered me at once. "Why," said he, "my wife, my brother and all his family are here. There is a party of us on a pleasure trip through the north." I soon learned that they had visited at Waukesha springs, and had been at the hotel only a few hours, waiting for the boat for Grand Haven. I hastened to bring my wife to see them and got back with her just in time. They were already in the 'bus, but waited for us. We very cordially shook hands with them. They asked me why I had come so far north, and I replied that we kept traveling until we found a place where we could make a good living. They wished us success and the 'bus rolled away.

FINDING MY BROTHER WILLIAM

While I was at the Plankinton House many of the traveling men seemingly liked to talk with me when they came to the coat room to check their things. I remember one day when conversing with one of these gentlemen, he asked, all of a sudden: "Say, Hughes, have you a brother?" I answered: "Yes, I had two, but I think they are dead. I was sold from them when a mere lad." "Well," said he, "if you have a brother he is in Cleveland. There is a fellow there who is chief cook at the Forest City Hotel who looks just like you." I grew eager at these words, and put the same question to him that I did to the man on the steamer when I was sailing: "Has he one fore-finger cut off?" He laughed and answered: "Well, I don't know, Hughes, about that; but I do know this: His name is Billy and he resembles you very much. I'll tell you what I'll do, when I go back to Cleveland on my next trip I'll look and see if that fore-finger is off." Now that the second person had called my attention to the fact that there was a man in Cleveland who looked very much like me, I became deeply interested—in fact, I was so excited I could hardly do my work. I awaited the agents return with what of patience I could command; and, at last, one day, when I was least expecting him, I was greeted with these words: "Hello, Hughes! I have good news for you." I grew so excited I could hardly stand still. "Well," he said, "you told me that you had a brother whose name was William, but called Billy for short?" "Yes," I said. "Did your brother Billy have his fore-finger chopped off by his brother Louis, when, as boys, they were one day playing together?" "Yes," I replied. "Then I have found your brother," he said. "I have seen the man in Cleveland, and he corroborates your story in every particular. He says that he was born in Virginia, near Charlottesville, and was owned by one John Martin." I knew now, beyond question, that this was my brother William. Words failed me to express my feelings at this news. The prospect of seeing my brother, lost so many years before, made me almost wild with joy. I thanked the agent for the interest he had taken in me, and for the invaluable and comprehensive information he had brought. He could hardly have done me a greater favor, or bound me to him by a more lasting obligation.

My first step was to arrange for a leave of absence from my work, which I found no difficulty in accomplishing, and by night I was aboard the express going to Cleveland. My excitement did not diminish as I sped on my journey, and the speed of the express was too slow for my eager anticipations. Upon reaching Cleveland I went directly to the hotel where I was told my brother was employed, and inquired at the office for Billy Hughes. A bell boy was summoned to take me around to the department where he was. When we met neither of us spoke for some moments— speech is not for such occasions, but silence rather, and the rush

133

of thoughts. When the first flash of feeling had passed I spoke, calling him by name, and he addressed me as brother. There seemed to be no doubt on either side as to our true relationship, though the features of each had long since faded forever from the memory of the other. He took me to his house; and each of us related his story with such feelings as few can fully appreciate. He told me that he had never heard anything of our mother or brother. He went back to the old home in Virginia, after the close of the rebellion, but could get no trace of her.

As we related our varied experiences—the hardships, the wrongs and sorrows which we endured and at last the coming of brighter days, we were sad, then happy. It seemed, and indeed was, wonderful that we should have met again after so long a separation. The time allotted to my visit with him passed most pleasantly, and all too quickly; and, as I looked into the faces of his wife and children, I seemed to have entered a new and broader life, and one in which the joys of social intercourse had marvelously expanded. When I came to saying good-bye to him, so close did I feel to him, the tie between us seemed never to have been broken. That week, so full of new experiences and emotions can never be erased from my memory. After many promises of the maintenance of the social relations thus renewed, we parted, to take up again the burdens of life, but with new inspiration and deeper feeling.

I came back to my work with renewed vigor, and I could not but rejoice and give praise to God for the blessings that I had experienced in the years since my bondage, and especially for this partial restoration of the broken tie of kindred. I had long since learned to love Christ, and my faith in him was so firmly established that I gave him praise for each and every ray of happiness that came into my life.

GROWTH OF
THE LAUNDRY BUSINESS

I continued the laundry work, in connection with that at the hotel, until 1874. I had been in the Plankinton House then six years and a half. The laundry business had increased to such an extent that my wife could not manage it all alone. I, therefore, gave up my position at the hotel, and went into the laundry work on a somewhat larger scale than that upon which we had been conducting it. We were still doing business at 216 Grand avenue, and there we remained until 1876; when we removed to more commodious quarters at 713 on the avenue. But we remained there only a few mouths, when we removed to 134 Fourth street in the rear. The establishment here was fitted up with all modern appliances; but I was not so successful as I anticipated. My losses were heavy; and though the facilities for doing the work were much better than those which we had before possessed, the location was not so accessible or inviting. We, therefore, went back to our former location at 713 on the avenue.

EMPLOYED AS A NURSE

Not long after this, Dr. Douglas, a prominent physician of the city at that time, was in failing health, and, wishing a nurse, I was recommended to him for this service by a friend. I served the doctor in this capacity every night for three months. I then went with him to McComb, a village in southern Mississippi, which had been, in the days of slavery, a somewhat famous resort, but which had lost its prestige, and entered upon a general decline; the hotel and all its surroundings presenting the appearance of general dilapidation. I remained here with the doctor for two weeks—until they succeeded in getting another person to care for him. I then took a run down to New Orleans.

A TRIP SOUTH

On this southern trip I had the opportunity of observing the condition of the country through which we passed. Many of the farms seemed neglected, the houses dilapidated, or abandoned, the fields either uncultivated and overgrown with bushes, or the crops struggling with grass and weeds for the mastery, and presenting but little promise of a paying harvest. In some places the bushes and other undergrowth were fifteen feet high, and the landscape was peculiar and by no means inviting. I could remember the appearance of the cotton farms in slavery days; but how changed were things I now saw! They did not look at all like those which I had been accustomed to see. Everything was dismal and uninviting. The entire country passed through in Mississippi looked like a wilderness. This deterioration was the natural result of the devastating war which had swept the country, and to the industrial revolution which followed and to which affairs had not been adjusted.

When I arrived at New Orleans I found the levee filled with fruit. Oranges and bananas were piled in masses like coal, and the scenes in this portion of the city were very different from anything one sees in the north. Among the many places of interest in the city were the cemeteries. Owing to the low level of the ground and its saturation with water, burials are seldom made in graves, but instead in tombs built of brick or marble or other stone, in which are constructed cells running back from the front and of a size and shape sufficient to admit a coffin. Then, as soon as filled, they are sealed up. These tombs contain from two to six or eight, or even more of these cells, and their general appearance from the front is not unlike that of a section of mail boxes in a postoffice. Other places of interest were the old French market, the public squares and gardens, the old Catholic churches, and some of the relics of slavery days in the shape of pens where slaves were exposed for sale. One of these was in the basement of the Hotel Royal, which would contain several hundred at once, and from which hundreds went to a bondage bitterer than death, and from which death was the only relief.

I MAKE NURSING
MY REGULAR BUSINESS

I came back to Milwaukee with a new idea. I liked nursing—it was my choice from childhood. Even though I had been deprived of a course of training, I felt that I was not too old to try, at least, to learn the art, or to add to what I already knew. Dr. Douglas gave me a splendid recommendation, and had some cards printed, bearing my name and address. These I distributed, and thus began the business which I have followed steadily since that time. Dr. Marks very kindly recommended me to well known men needing the service of a nurse, and to his professional associates; and through this means, and through his continued kindness and interest, I have been almost constantly engaged in this work. I am also indebted to Drs. Fox and Spearman and other prominent physicians for recommendations which have resulted in securing me employment which has proved remunerative to me, and which seemed to give entire satisfaction to the sick and their friends. This is no small part of the compensation in the difficult, often wearing, and always delicate duties of the nurse in the sick room. To every true man or woman it is one of the greatest satisfactions to have the consciousness of having been useful to his fellow beings. My duties as nurse have taken me to different parts of the state, to Chicago, to California and to Florida; and I have thus gained no little experience, not only in my business, but in many other directions.

I have endeavored, in the foregoing sketch, to give a clear and correct idea of the institution of human slavery, as I witnessed and experienced it—its brutality, its degrading influence upon both master and slave, and its utter incompatibility with industrial improvement and general educational progress.

Nothing has been exaggerated or set down in malice, although in the scars which I still bear upon my person, and in the wounds of spirit which will never wholly heal, there might be found a seeming excuse for such a course. Whatever of kindness was shown me during the years of my bondage, I still gratefully remember, whether it came from white master or fellow slave; and for the recognition which has been so generously accorded me since the badge of servitude was removed, I am profoundly and devoutly thankful.

NARRATIVE
OF THE LIFE OF
FREDERICK DOUGLASS

BY FREDERICK DOUGLASS

First Published in 1845

CHAPTER I

I was born in Tuckahoe, near Hillsborough, and about twelve miles from Easton, in Talbot county, Maryland. I have no accurate knowledge of my age, never having seen any authentic record containing it. By far the larger part of the slaves know as little of their ages as horses know of theirs, and it is the wish of most masters within my knowledge to keep their slaves thus ignorant. I do not remember to have ever met a slave who could tell of his birthday. They seldom come nearer to it than planting-time, harvest-time, cherry-time, spring-time, or fall-time. A want of information concerning my own was a source of unhappiness to me even during childhood. The white children could tell their ages. I could not tell why I ought to be deprived of the same privilege. I was not allowed to make any inquiries of my master concerning it. He deemed all such inquiries on the part of a slave improper and impertinent, and evidence of a restless spirit. The nearest estimate I can give makes me now between twenty-seven and twenty-eight years of age. I come to this, from hearing my master say, some time during 1835, I was about seventeen years old.

My mother was named Harriet Bailey. She was the daughter of Isaac and Betsey Bailey, both colored, and quite dark. My mother was of a darker complexion than either my grandmother or grandfather.

My father was a white man. He was admitted to be such by all I ever heard speak of my parentage. The opinion was also whispered that my master was my father; but of the correctness of this opinion, I know nothing; the means of knowing was withheld from me. My mother and I were separated when I was but an infant—before I knew her as my mother. It is a common custom, in the part of Maryland from which I ran away, to part children from their mothers at a very early age. Frequently, before the child has reached its twelfth month, its mother is taken from it, and hired out on some farm a considerable distance off, and the child is placed under the care of an old woman, too old for field labor. For what this separation is done, I do not know, unless it be to hinder the development of the child's affection toward its mother, and to blunt and destroy the natural affection of the mother for the child. This is the inevitable result.

I never saw my mother, to know her as such, more than four or five times in my life; and each of these times was very short in duration, and at night. She was hired by a Mr. Stewart, who lived about twelve miles from my home. She made her journeys to see me in the night, travelling the whole distance on foot, after the performance of her day's work. She was a field hand, and a whipping is the penalty of not being in the field at sunrise, unless a slave has special permission from his or her master to the contrary—a permission which they seldom get, and one that gives to him that gives it the proud name of being a kind master. I do not recollect of ever seeing my mother by the light of day. She was with me in the night. She would lie down with me, and get me to sleep, but long before I waked she was gone. Very little communication ever took place between us. Death soon ended what little we could have while she lived, and with it her hardships and suffering. She died when I was about seven years old, on one of my master's farms, near Lee's Mill. I was not allowed to be present during her illness, at her death, or burial. She was gone long before I knew any thing about it. Never having enjoyed, to any considerable extent, her soothing presence, her tender and watchful care, I received the tidings of her death with much the same emotions I should have probably felt at the death of a stranger.

Called thus suddenly away, she left me without the slightest intimation of who my father was. The whisper that my master was my father, may or may not be true; and, true or false, it is of but little consequence to my purpose whilst the fact remains, in all its glaring odiousness, that slaveholders have ordained, and by law established, that the children of slave women shall in all cases follow the condition of their mothers; and this is done too obviously to administer to their own lusts, and make a gratification of their wicked desires profitable as well as pleasurable; for by this cunning arrangement, the slaveholder, in cases not a few, sustains to his slaves the double relation of master and father.

I know of such cases; and it is worthy of remark that such slaves invariably suffer greater hardships, and have more to contend with, than others. They are, in the first place, a constant offence to their mistress. She is ever disposed to find fault with them; they can seldom do any thing to please her; she is never better pleased than when she sees them under the lash, especially when she suspects her husband of showing to his mulatto children favors which he withholds from his black slaves. The master is frequently compelled to sell this class of his slaves, out of deference to the feelings of his white wife; and, cruel as the deed may strike any one to be, for a man to sell his own children to human flesh-mongers, it is often the dictate of humanity for him to do so; for, unless he does this, he must not only whip them himself, but must stand by and see one white son tie up his brother, of but few shades darker complexion than himself, and ply the gory lash to his naked back; and if he lisp one word of disapproval, it is set down to his parental partiality, and only makes a bad matter worse, both for himself and the slave whom he would protect and defend.

Every year brings with it multitudes of this class of slaves. It was doubtless in consequence of a knowledge of this fact, that one great statesman of the south predicted the downfall of slavery by the inevitable laws of population. Whether this prophecy is ever fulfilled or not, it is nevertheless plain that a very different-looking class of people are springing up at the south, and are now held in slavery, from those originally brought to this country from Africa; and if their increase do no other good, it will do away the force of the argument, that God cursed Ham, and therefore American slavery is right. If the lineal descendants of Ham are alone to be scripturally enslaved, it is certain that slavery at the south must soon become unscriptural; for thousands are ushered into the world, annually, who, like myself, owe their existence to white fathers, and those fathers most frequently their own masters.

I have had two masters. My first master's name was Anthony. I do not remember his first name. He was generally called Captain Anthony—a title which, I presume, he acquired by sailing a craft on the Chesapeake Bay. He was not considered a rich slaveholder. He owned two or three farms, and about thirty slaves. His farms and slaves were under the care of an overseer. The overseer's name was Plummer. Mr. Plummer was a miserable drunkard, a profane swearer, and a savage monster. He always went armed with a cowskin and a heavy cudgel. I have known him to cut and slash the women's heads so horribly, that even master would be enraged at his cruelty, and would threaten to whip him if he did not mind himself. Master, however, was not a humane slaveholder. It required extraordinary barbarity on the part of an overseer to affect him. He was a cruel man, hardened by a long life of slaveholding. He would at times seem to take great pleasure in whipping a slave. I have often been awakened at the dawn of day by the most heart-rending shrieks of an own aunt of mine, whom he used to tie up to a joist, and whip upon her naked back till she was literally covered with blood. No words, no tears, no prayers, from his gory victim, seemed to move his iron heart from its bloody purpose. The louder she screamed, the harder he whipped; and where the blood ran fastest, there he whipped longest. He would whip her to make her scream, and whip her to make her hush; and not until overcome by fatigue, would he cease to swing the blood-clotted cowskin. I remember the first time I ever witnessed this horrible exhibition. I was quite a child, but I well remember it. I never shall forget it whilst I remember any thing. It was the first of a long series of such outrages, of which I was doomed to be a witness and a participant. It struck me with awful force. It was the blood-stained gate, the entrance to the hell of slavery, through which I was about to pass. It was a most terrible spectacle. I wish I could commit to paper the feelings with which I beheld it.

This occurrence took place very soon after I went to live with my old master, and under the following circumstances. Aunt Hester went out one night,—where or for what I do not know,—and happened to be absent when my master desired her presence. He had ordered her not to go out evenings, and warned her that she must never let him catch her in company with a young man, who was paying attention to her belonging to Colonel Lloyd. The young man's name was Ned Roberts, generally called Lloyd's Ned. Why master was so careful of her, may be safely left to conjecture. She was a woman of noble form, and of graceful proportions, having very few equals, and fewer superiors, in personal appearance, among the colored or white women of our neighborhood.

Aunt Hester had not only disobeyed his orders in going out, but had been found in company with Lloyd's Ned; which circumstance, I found, from what he said while whipping her, was the chief offence. Had he been a man of pure morals himself, he might have been thought interested in protecting the innocence of my aunt; but those who knew him will not suspect him of any such virtue. Before he commenced whipping Aunt Hester, he took her into the kitchen, and stripped her from neck to waist, leaving her neck, shoulders, and back, entirely naked. He then told her to cross her hands, calling her at the same time a d——d b—-h. After crossing her hands, he tied them with a strong rope, and led her to a stool under a large hook in the joist, put in for the purpose. He made her get upon the stool, and tied her hands to the hook. She now stood fair for his infernal purpose. Her arms were stretched up at their full length, so that she stood upon the ends of her toes. He then said to her, "Now, you d——d b—-h, I'll learn you how to disobey my orders!" and after rolling up his sleeves, he commenced to lay on the heavy cowskin, and soon the warm, red blood (amid heart-rending shrieks from her, and horrid oaths from him) came dripping to the floor. I was so terrified and horror-stricken at the sight, that I hid myself in a closet, and dared not venture out till long after the bloody transaction was over. I expected it would be my turn next. It was all new to me. I had never seen any thing like it before. I had always lived with my grandmother on the outskirts of the plantation, where she was put to raise the children of the younger women. I had therefore been, until now, out of the way of the bloody scenes that often occurred on the plantation.

CHAPTER II

My master's family consisted of two sons, Andrew and Richard; one daughter, Lucretia, and her husband, Captain Thomas Auld. They lived in one house, upon the home plantation of Colonel Edward Lloyd. My master was Colonel Lloyd's clerk and superintendent. He was what might be called the overseer of the overseers. I spent two years of childhood on this plantation in my old master's family. It was here that I witnessed the bloody transaction recorded in the first chapter; and as I received my first impressions of slavery on this plantation, I will give some description of it, and of slavery as it there existed. The plantation is about twelve miles north of Easton, in Talbot county, and is situated on the border of Miles River. The principal products raised upon it were tobacco, corn, and wheat. These were raised in great abundance; so that, with the products of this and the other farms belonging to him, he was able to keep in almost constant employment a large sloop, in carrying them to market at Baltimore. This sloop was named Sally Lloyd, in honor of one of the colonel's daughters. My master's son-in-law, Captain Auld, was master of the vessel; she was otherwise manned by the colonel's own slaves. Their names were Peter, Isaac, Rich, and Jake. These were esteemed very highly by the other slaves, and looked upon as the privileged ones of the plantation; for it was no small affair, in the eyes of the slaves, to be allowed to see Baltimore.

Colonel Lloyd kept from three to four hundred slaves on his home plantation, and owned a large number more on the neighboring farms belonging to him. The names of the farms nearest to the home plantation were Wye Town and New Design. "Wye Town" was under the overseership of a man

147

named Noah Willis. New Design was under the overseership of a Mr. Townsend. The overseers of these, and all the rest of the farms, numbering over twenty, received advice and direction from the managers of the home plantation. This was the great business place. It was the seat of government for the whole twenty farms. All disputes among the overseers were settled here. If a slave was convicted of any high misdemeanor, became unmanageable, or evinced a determination to run away, he was brought immediately here, severely whipped, put on board the sloop, carried to Baltimore, and sold to Austin Woolfolk, or some other slave-trader, as a warning to the slaves remaining.

Here, too, the slaves of all the other farms received their monthly allowance of food, and their yearly clothing. The men and women slaves received, as their monthly allowance of food, eight pounds of pork, or its equivalent in fish, and one bushel of corn meal. Their yearly clothing consisted of two coarse linen shirts, one pair of linen trousers, like the shirts, one jacket, one pair of trousers for winter, made of coarse negro cloth, one pair of stockings, and one pair of shoes; the whole of which could not have cost more than seven dollars. The allowance of the slave children was given to their mothers, or the old women having the care of them. The children unable to work in the field had neither shoes, stockings, jackets, nor trousers, given to them; their clothing consisted of two coarse linen shirts per year. When these failed them, they went naked until the next allowance-day. Children from seven to ten years old, of both sexes, almost naked, might be seen at all seasons of the year.

There were no beds given the slaves, unless one coarse blanket be considered such, and none but the men and women had these. This, however, is not considered a very great privation. They find less difficulty from the want of beds, than from the want of time to sleep; for when their day's work in the field is done, the most of them having their washing, mending, and cooking to do, and having few or none of the ordinary facilities for doing either of these, very many of their sleeping hours are consumed in preparing for the field the coming day; and when this is done, old and young, male and female, married and single, drop down side by side, on one common bed,—the cold, damp floor,—each covering himself or herself with their miserable blankets; and here they sleep till they are summoned to the field by the driver's horn. At the sound of this, all must rise, and be off to the field. There must be no halting; every one must be at his or her post; and woe betides them who hear not this morning summons to the field; for if they are not awakened by the sense of hearing, they are by the sense of feeling: no age nor sex finds any favor. Mr. Severe, the overseer, used to stand by the door of the quarter, armed with a large hickory stick and heavy cowskin, ready to whip any one who was so unfortunate as not to hear, or, from any other cause, was prevented from being ready to start for the field at the sound of the horn.

Mr. Severe was rightly named: he was a cruel man. I have seen him whip a woman, causing the blood to run half an hour at the time; and this, too, in the midst of her crying children, pleading for their mother's release. He seemed to take pleasure in manifesting his fiendish barbarity. Added to his cruelty, he was a profane swearer. It was enough to chill the blood and stiffen the hair of an ordinary man to hear him talk. Scarce a sentence escaped him but that was commenced or concluded by some horrid oath. The field was the place to witness his cruelty and profanity. His presence made it both the field of blood and of blasphemy. From the rising till the going down of the sun, he was cursing, raving, cutting, and slashing among the slaves of the field, in the most frightful manner. His career was short. He died very soon after I went to Colonel Lloyd's; and he died as he lived, uttering, with his dying groans, bitter curses and horrid oaths. His death was regarded by the slaves as the result of a merciful providence.

Mr. Severe's place was filled by a Mr. Hopkins. He was a very different man. He was less cruel, less profane, and made less noise, than Mr. Severe. His course was characterized by no extraordinary demonstrations of cruelty. He whipped, but seemed to take no pleasure in it. He was called by the slaves a good overseer.

The home plantation of Colonel Lloyd wore the appearance of a country village. All the mechanical operations for all the farms were performed here. The shoemaking and mending, the blacksmithing, cartwrighting, coopering, weaving, and grain-grinding, were all performed by the slaves on the home plantation. The whole place wore a business-like aspect very unlike the neighboring farms. The number of houses, too, conspired to give it advantage over the neighboring farms. It was called by the slaves the Great House Farm. Few privileges were esteemed higher, by the slaves of the out-farms, than that of being selected to do errands at the Great House Farm. It was associated in their minds with greatness. A representative could not be prouder of his election to a seat in the American Congress, than a slave on one of the out-farms would be of his election to do errands at the Great House Farm. They regarded it as evidence of great confidence reposed in them by their overseers; and it was on this account, as well as a constant desire to be out of the field from under the driver's lash, that they esteemed it a high privilege, one worth careful living for. He was called the smartest and most trusty fellow, who had this honor conferred upon him the most frequently. The competitors for this office sought as diligently to please their overseers, as the office-seekers in the political parties seek to please and deceive the people. The same traits of character might be seen in Colonel Lloyd's slaves, as are seen in the slaves of the political parties.

The slaves selected to go to the Great House Farm, for the monthly allowance for themselves and their fellow-slaves, were peculiarly enthusiastic. While on their way, they would make the dense old woods, for miles around, reverberate with their wild songs, revealing at once the highest joy and the deepest sadness. They would compose and sing as they went along, consulting neither time nor tune. The thought that came up, came out—

if not in the word, in the sound;—and as frequently in the one as in the other. They would sometimes sing the most pathetic sentiment in the most rapturous tone, and the most rapturous sentiment in the most pathetic tone. Into all of their songs they would manage to weave something of the Great House Farm. Especially would they do this, when leaving home. They would then sing most exultingly the following words:—

"I am going away to the Great House Farm!
O, yea! O, yea! O!"

This they would sing, as a chorus, to words which to many would seem unmeaning jargon, but which, nevertheless, were full of meaning to themselves. I have sometimes thought that the mere hearing of those songs would do more to impress some minds with the horrible character of slavery, than the reading of whole volumes of philosophy on the subject could do.

I did not, when a slave, understand the deep meaning of those rude and apparently incoherent songs. I was myself within the circle; so that I neither saw nor heard as those without might see and hear. They told a tale of woe which was then altogether beyond my feeble comprehension; they were tones loud, long, and deep; they breathed the prayer and complaint of souls boiling over with the bitterest anguish. Every tone was a testimony against slavery, and a prayer to God for deliverance from chains. The hearing of those wild notes always depressed my spirit, and filled me with ineffable sadness. I have frequently found myself in tears while hearing them. The mere recurrence to those songs, even now, afflicts me; and while I am writing these lines, an expression of feeling has already found its way down my cheek. To those songs I trace my first glimmering conception of the dehumanizing character of slavery. I can never get rid of that conception. Those songs still follow me, to deepen my hatred of slavery, and quicken my sympathies for my brethren in bonds. If any one wishes to be impressed with

151

the soul-killing effects of slavery, let him go to Colonel Lloyd's plantation, and, on allowance-day, place himself in the deep pine woods, and there let him, in silence, analyze the sounds that shall pass through the chambers of his soul,—and if he is not thus impressed, it will only be because "there is no flesh in his obdurate heart."

I have often been utterly astonished, since I came to the north, to find persons who could speak of the singing, among slaves, as evidence of their contentment and happiness. It is impossible to conceive of a greater mistake. Slaves sing most when they are most unhappy. The songs of the slave represent the sorrows of his heart; and he is relieved by them, only as an aching heart is relieved by its tears. At least, such is my experience. I have often sung to drown my sorrow, but seldom to express my happiness. Crying for joy, and singing for joy, were alike uncommon to me while in the jaws of slavery. The singing of a man cast away upon a desolate island might be as appropriately considered as evidence of contentment and happiness, as the singing of a slave; the songs of the one and of the other are prompted by the same emotion.

CHAPTER III

Colonel Lloyd kept a large and finely cultivated garden, which afforded almost constant employment for four men, besides the chief gardener, (Mr. M'Durmond.) This garden was probably the greatest attraction of the place. During the summer months, people came from far and near—from Baltimore, Easton, and Annapolis—to see it. It abounded in fruits of almost every description, from the hardy apple of the north to the delicate orange of the south. This garden was not the least source of trouble on the plantation. Its excellent fruit was quite a temptation to the hungry swarms of boys, as well as the older slaves, belonging to the colonel, few of whom had the virtue or the vice to resist it. Scarcely a day passed, during the summer, but that some slave had to take the lash for stealing fruit. The colonel had to resort to all kinds of stratagems to keep his slaves out of the garden. The last and most successful one was that of tarring his fence all around; after which, if a slave was caught with any tar upon his person, it was deemed sufficient proof that he had either been into the garden, or had tried to get in. In either case, he was severely whipped by the chief gardener. This plan worked well; the slaves became as fearful of tar as of the lash. They seemed to realize the impossibility of touching tar without being defiled.

The colonel also kept a splendid riding equipage. His stable and carriage-house presented the appearance of some of our large city livery establishments. His horses were of the finest form and noblest blood. His carriage-house contained three splendid coaches, three or four gigs, besides dearborns and barouches of the most fashionable style.

This establishment was under the care of two slaves—old

153

Barney and young Barney—father and son. To attend to this establishment was their sole work. But it was by no means an easy employment; for in nothing was Colonel Lloyd more particular than in the management of his horses. The slightest inattention to these was unpardonable, and was visited upon those, under whose care they were placed, with the severest punishment; no excuse could shield them, if the colonel only suspected any want of attention to his horses—a supposition which he frequently indulged, and one which, of course, made the office of old and young Barney a very trying one. They never knew when they were safe from punishment. They were frequently whipped when least deserving, and escaped whipping when most deserving it. Every thing depended upon the looks of the horses, and the state of Colonel Lloyd's own mind when his horses were brought to him for use. If a horse did not move fast enough, or hold his head high enough, it was owing to some fault of his keepers. It was painful to stand near the stable-door, and hear the various complaints against the keepers when a horse was taken out for use. "This horse has not had proper attention. He has not been sufficiently rubbed and curried, or he has not been properly fed; his food was too wet or too dry; he got it too soon or too late; he was too hot or too cold; he had too much hay, and not enough of grain; or he had too much grain, and not enough of hay; instead of old Barney's attending to the horse, he had very improperly left it to his son." To all these complaints, no matter how unjust, the slave must answer never a word. Colonel Lloyd could not brook any contradiction from a slave. When he spoke, a slave must stand, listen, and tremble; and such was literally the case. I have seen Colonel Lloyd make old Barney, a man between fifty and sixty years of age, uncover his bald head, kneel down upon the cold, damp ground, and receive upon his naked and toil-worn shoulders more than thirty lashes at the time. Colonel Lloyd had three sons—Edward, Murray, and Daniel,—and three sons-in-law, Mr. Winder, Mr. Nicholson, and Mr. Lowndes. All of these lived at the Great House Farm, and enjoyed the luxury of whipping the servants when they pleased, from old Barney down to William Wilkes, the coach-driver. I have seen Winder make one of the house-servants stand off from him a suitable distance to be touched with the end of his whip, and at every stroke raise great ridges upon his back.

To describe the wealth of Colonel Lloyd would be almost equal to describing the riches of Job. He kept from ten to fifteen house-servants. He was said to own a thousand slaves, and I think this estimate quite within the truth. Colonel Lloyd owned so many that he did not know them when he saw them; nor did all the slaves of the out-farms know him. It is reported of him, that, while riding along the road one day, he met a colored man, and addressed him in the usual manner of speaking to colored people on the public highways of the south: "Well, boy, whom do you belong to?" "To Colonel Lloyd," replied the slave. "Well, does the colonel treat you well?" "No, sir," was the ready reply. "What, does he work you too hard?" "Yes, sir." "Well, don't he give you enough to eat?" "Yes, sir, he gives me enough, such as it is."

The colonel, after ascertaining where the slave belonged, rode on; the man also went on about his business, not dreaming that he had been conversing with his master. He thought, said, and heard nothing more of the matter, until two or three weeks afterwards. The poor man was then informed by his overseer that, for having found fault with his master, he was now to be sold to a Georgia trader. He was immediately chained and handcuffed; and thus, without a moment's warning, he was snatched away, and forever sundered, from his family and friends, by a hand more unrelenting than death. This is the penalty of telling the truth, of telling the simple truth, in answer to a series of plain questions.

It is partly in consequence of such facts, that slaves, when inquired of as to their condition and the character of their masters, almost universally say they are contented, and that their masters are kind. The slaveholders have been known to send in spies among their slaves, to ascertain their views and feelings

155

in regard to their condition. The frequency of this has had the effect to establish among the slaves the maxim, that a still tongue makes a wise head. They suppress the truth rather than take the consequences of telling it, and in so doing prove themselves a part of the human family. If they have any thing to say of their masters, it is generally in their masters' favor, especially when speaking to an untried man. I have been frequently asked, when a slave, if I had a kind master, and do not remember ever to have given a negative answer; nor did I, in pursuing this course, consider myself as uttering what was absolutely false; for I always measured the kindness of my master by the standard of kindness set up among slaveholders around us. Moreover, slaves are like other people, and imbibe prejudices quite common to others. They think their own better than that of others. Many, under the influence of this prejudice, think their own masters are better than the masters of other slaves; and this, too, in some cases, when the very reverse is true. Indeed, it is not uncommon for slaves even to fall out and quarrel among themselves about the relative goodness of their masters, each contending for the superior goodness of his own over that of the others. At the very same time, they mutually execrate their masters when viewed separately. It was so on our plantation. When Colonel Lloyd's slaves met the slaves of Jacob Jepson, they seldom parted without a quarrel about their masters; Colonel Lloyd's slaves contending that he was the richest, and Mr. Jepson's slaves that he was the smartest, and most of a man. Colonel Lloyd's slaves would boast his ability to buy and sell Jacob Jepson. Mr. Jepson's slaves would boast his ability to whip Colonel Lloyd. These quarrels would almost always end in a fight between the parties, and those that whipped were supposed to have gained the point at issue. They seemed to think that the greatness of their masters was transferable to themselves. It was considered as being bad enough to be a slave; but to be a poor man's slave was deemed a disgrace indeed!

CHAPTER IV

Mr. Hopkins remained but a short time in the office of overseer. Why his career was so short, I do not know, but suppose he lacked the necessary severity to suit Colonel Lloyd. Mr. Hopkins was succeeded by Mr. Austin Gore, a man possessing, in an eminent degree, all those traits of character indispensable to what is called a first-rate overseer. Mr. Gore had served Colonel Lloyd, in the capacity of overseer, upon one of the out-farms, and had shown himself worthy of the high station of overseer upon the home or Great House Farm.

Mr. Gore was proud, ambitious, and persevering. He was artful, cruel, and obdurate. He was just the man for such a place, and it was just the place for such a man. It afforded scope for the full exercise of all his powers, and he seemed to be perfectly at home in it. He was one of those who could torture the slightest look, word, or gesture, on the part of the slave, into impudence, and would treat it accordingly. There must be no answering back to him; no explanation was allowed a slave, showing himself to have been wrongfully accused. Mr. Gore acted fully up to the maxim laid down by slaveholders,—"It is better that a dozen slaves should suffer under the lash, than that the overseer should be convicted, in the presence of the slaves, of having been at fault." No matter how innocent a slave might be—it availed him nothing, when accused by Mr. Gore of any misdemeanor. To be accused was to be convicted, and to be convicted was to be punished; the one always following the other with immutable certainty. To escape punishment was to escape accusation; and few slaves had the fortune to do either, under the overseership of Mr. Gore. He was just proud enough to demand the most debasing homage of the slave, and quite

157

servile enough to crouch, himself, at the feet of the master. He was ambitious enough to be contented with nothing short of the highest rank of overseers, and persevering enough to reach the height of his ambition. He was cruel enough to inflict the severest punishment, artful enough to descend to the lowest trickery, and obdurate enough to be insensible to the voice of a reproving conscience. He was, of all the overseers, the most dreaded by the slaves. His presence was painful; his eye flashed confusion; and seldom was his sharp, shrill voice heard, without producing horror and trembling in their ranks.

Mr. Gore was a grave man, and, though a young man, he indulged in no jokes, said no funny words, seldom smiled. His words were in perfect keeping with his looks, and his looks were in perfect keeping with his words. Overseers will sometimes indulge in a witty word, even with the slaves; not so with Mr. Gore. He spoke but to command, and commanded but to be obeyed; he dealt sparingly with his words, and bountifully with his whip, never using the former where the latter would answer as well. When he whipped, he seemed to do so from a sense of duty, and feared no consequences. He did nothing reluctantly, no matter how disagreeable; always at his post, never inconsistent. He never promised but to fulfil. He was, in a word, a man of the most inflexible firmness and stone-like coolness.

His savage barbarity was equalled only by the consummate coolness with which he committed the grossest and most savage deeds upon the slaves under his charge. Mr. Gore once undertook to whip one of Colonel Lloyd's slaves, by the name of Demby. He had given Demby but few stripes, when, to get rid of the scourging, he ran and plunged himself into a creek, and stood there at the depth of his shoulders, refusing to come out. Mr. Gore told him that he would give him three calls, and that, if he did not come out at the third call, he would shoot him. The first call was given. Demby made no response, but stood his ground. The second and third calls were given with the same result. Mr. Gore then, without consultation or deliberation with any one, not even giving Demby an additional call, raised his musket to his face, taking deadly aim at his standing victim, and in an instant poor Demby was no more. His mangled body sank out of sight, and blood and brains marked the water where he had stood.

A thrill of horror flashed through every soul upon the plantation, excepting Mr. Gore. He alone seemed cool and collected. He was asked by Colonel Lloyd and my old master, why he resorted to this extraordinary expedient. His reply was, (as well as I can remember,) that Demby had become unmanageable. He was setting a dangerous example to the other slaves,—one which, if suffered to pass without some such demonstration on his part, would finally lead to the total subversion of all rule and order upon the plantation. He argued that if one slave refused to be corrected, and escaped with his life, the other slaves would soon copy the example; the result of which would be, the freedom of the slaves, and the enslavement of the whites. Mr. Gore's defence was satisfactory. He was continued in his station as overseer upon the home plantation. His fame as an overseer went abroad. His horrid crime was not even submitted to judicial investigation. It was committed in the presence of slaves, and they of course could neither institute a suit, nor testify against him; and thus the guilty perpetrator of one of the bloodiest and most foul murders goes unwhipped of justice, and uncensured by the community in which he lives. Mr. Gore lived in St. Michael's, Talbot county, Maryland, when I left there; and if he is still alive, he very probably lives there now; and if so, he is now, as he was then, as highly esteemed and as much respected as though his guilty soul had not been stained with his brother's blood.

I speak advisedly when I say this,—that killing a slave, or any colored person, in Talbot county, Maryland, is not treated as a crime, either by the courts or the community. Mr. Thomas Lanman, of St. Michael's, killed two slaves, one of whom he killed with a hatchet, by knocking his brains out. He used to boast of the commission of the awful and bloody deed. I have heard him do so laughingly, saying, among other things, that he was the only benefactor of his country in the company, and that when others would do as much as he had done, we should be relieved of "the d——d niggers."

The wife of Mr. Giles Hicks, living but a short distance from where I used to live, murdered my wife's cousin, a young girl between fifteen and sixteen years of age, mangling her person in the most horrible manner, breaking her nose and breastbone with a stick, so that the poor girl expired in a few hours afterward. She was immediately buried, but had not been in her untimely grave but a few hours before she was taken up and examined by the coroner, who decided that she had come to her death by severe beating. The offence for which this girl was thus murdered was this:—She had been set that night to mind Mrs. Hicks's baby, and during the night she fell asleep, and the baby cried. She, having lost her rest for several nights previous, did not hear the crying. They were both in the room with Mrs. Hicks. Mrs. Hicks, finding the girl slow to move, jumped from her bed, seized an oak stick of wood by the fireplace, and with it broke the girl's nose and breastbone, and thus ended her life. I will not say that this most horrid murder produced no sensation in the community. It did produce sensation, but not enough to bring the murderess to punishment. There was a warrant issued for her arrest, but it was never served. Thus she escaped not only punishment, but even the pain of being arraigned before a court for her horrid crime.

Whilst I am detailing bloody deeds which took place during my stay on Colonel Lloyd's plantation, I will briefly narrate another, which occurred about the same time as the murder of Demby by Mr. Gore.

Colonel Lloyd's slaves were in the habit of spending a part of their nights and Sundays in fishing for oysters, and in this way made up the deficiency of their scanty allowance. An old man belonging to Colonel Lloyd, while thus engaged, happened to get beyond the limits of Colonel Lloyd's, and on the premises of Mr. Beal Bondly. At this trespass, Mr. Bondly took offence, and with his musket came down to the shore, and blew its deadly contents into the poor old man.

Mr. Bondly came over to see Colonel Lloyd the next day, whether to pay him for his property, or to justify himself in what he had done, I know not. At any rate, this whole fiendish transaction was soon hushed up. There was very little said about it at all, and nothing done. It was a common saying, even among little white boys, that it was worth a half-cent to kill a "nigger," and a half-cent to bury one.

CHAPTER V

As to my own treatment while I lived on Colonel Lloyd's plantation, it was very similar to that of the other slave children. I was not old enough to work in the field, and there being little else than field work to do, I had a great deal of leisure time. The most I had to do was to drive up the cows at evening, keep the fowls out of the garden, keep the front yard clean, and run of errands for my old master's daughter, Mrs. Lucretia Auld. The most of my leisure time I spent in helping Master Daniel Lloyd in finding his birds, after he had shot them. My connection with Master Daniel was of some advantage to me. He became quite attached to me, and was a sort of protector of me. He would not allow the older boys to impose upon me, and would divide his cakes with me.

I was seldom whipped by my old master, and suffered little from any thing else than hunger and cold. I suffered much from hunger, but much more from cold. In hottest summer and coldest winter, I was kept almost naked—no shoes, no stockings, no jacket, no trousers, nothing on but a coarse tow linen shirt, reaching only to my knees. I had no bed. I must have perished with cold, but that, the coldest nights, I used to steal a bag which was used for carrying corn to the mill. I would crawl into this bag, and there sleep on the cold, damp, clay floor, with my head in and feet out. My feet have been so cracked with the frost, that the pen with which I am writing might be laid in the gashes.

We were not regularly allowanced. Our food was coarse corn meal boiled. This was called mush. It was put into a large wooden tray or trough, and set down upon the ground. The children were then called, like so many pigs, and like so many pigs they would come and devour the mush; some with oyster-shells, others with pieces of shingle, some with naked hands, and none with spoons. He that ate fastest got most; he that was strongest secured the best place; and few left the trough satisfied.

I was probably between seven and eight years old when I left Colonel Lloyd's plantation. I left it with joy. I shall never forget the ecstasy with which I received the intelligence that my old master (Anthony) had determined to let me go to Baltimore, to live with Mr. Hugh Auld, brother to my old master's son-in-law, Captain Thomas Auld. I received this information about three days before my departure. They were three of the happiest days I ever enjoyed. I spent the most part of all these three days in the creek, washing off the plantation scurf, and preparing myself for my departure.

The pride of appearance which this would indicate was not my own. I spent the time in washing, not so much because I wished to, but because Mrs. Lucretia had told me I must get all the dead skin off my feet and knees before I could go to Baltimore; for the people in Baltimore were very cleanly, and would laugh at me if I looked dirty. Besides, she was going to give me a pair of trousers, which I should not put on unless I got all the dirt off me. The thought of owning a pair of trousers was great indeed! It was almost a sufficient motive, not only to make me take off what would be called by pig-drovers the mange, but the skin itself. I went at it in good earnest, working for the first time with the hope of reward.

The ties that ordinarily bind children to their homes were all suspended in my case. I found no severe trial in my departure. My home was charmless; it was not home to me; on parting from it, I could not feel that I was leaving any thing which I could have enjoyed by staying. My mother was dead, my grandmother lived far off, so that I seldom saw her. I had two sisters and one brother, that lived in the same house with me; but the early separation of us from our mother had well nigh blotted the fact of our relationship from our memories. I looked for home elsewhere, and was confident of finding none which I should relish less than the one which I was leaving. If, however, I found in my new home hardship, hunger, whipping, and nakedness, I had the consolation that I should not have escaped any one of them by staying. Having already had more than a taste of them in the house of my old master, and having endured them there, I very naturally inferred my ability to endure them elsewhere, and especially at Baltimore; for I had something of the feeling about Baltimore that is expressed in the proverb, that "being hanged in England is preferable to dying a natural death in Ireland." I had the strongest desire to see Baltimore. Cousin Tom, though not fluent in speech, had inspired me with that desire by his eloquent description of the place. I could never point out any thing at the Great House, no matter how beautiful or powerful, but that he had seen something at Baltimore far exceeding, both in beauty and strength, the object which I pointed out to him. Even the Great House itself, with all its pictures, was far inferior to many buildings in Baltimore. So strong was my desire, that I thought a gratification of it would fully compensate for whatever loss of comforts I should sustain by the exchange. I left without a regret, and with the highest hopes of future happiness.

We sailed out of Miles River for Baltimore on a Saturday morning. I remember only the day of the week, for at that time I had no knowledge of the days of the month, nor the months of the year. On setting sail, I walked aft, and gave to Colonel Lloyd's plantation what I hoped would be the last look. I then placed myself in the bows of the sloop, and there spent the remainder of the day in looking ahead, interesting myself in what was in the distance rather than in things near by or behind.

In the afternoon of that day, we reached Annapolis, the capital of the State. We stopped but a few moments, so that I had no time to go on shore. It was the first large town that I had ever seen, and though it would look small compared with some of our New England factory villages, I thought it a wonderful place for its size—more imposing even than the Great House Farm!

We arrived at Baltimore early on Sunday morning, landing at

Smith's Wharf, not far from Bowley's Wharf. We had on board the sloop a large flock of sheep; and after aiding in driving them to the slaughterhouse of Mr. Curtis on Louden Slater's Hill, I was conducted by Rich, one of the hands belonging on board of the sloop, to my new home in Alliciana Street, near Mr. Gardner's ship-yard, on Fells Point.

Mr. and Mrs. Auld were both at home, and met me at the door with their little son Thomas, to take care of whom I had been given. And here I saw what I had never seen before; it was a white face beaming with the most kindly emotions; it was the face of my new mistress, Sophia Auld. I wish I could describe the rapture that flashed through my soul as I beheld it. It was a new and strange sight to me, brightening up my pathway with the light of happiness. Little Thomas was told, there was his Freddy,—and I was told to take care of little Thomas; and thus I entered upon the duties of my new home with the most cheering prospect ahead.

I look upon my departure from Colonel Lloyd's plantation as one of the most interesting events of my life. It is possible, and even quite probable, that but for the mere circumstance of being removed from that plantation to Baltimore, I should have to-day, instead of being here seated by my own table, in the enjoyment of freedom and the happiness of home, writing this Narrative, been confined in the galling chains of slavery. Going to live at Baltimore laid the foundation, and opened the gateway, to all my subsequent prosperity. I have ever regarded it as the first plain manifestation of that kind providence which has ever since attended me, and marked my life with so many favors. I regarded the selection of myself as being somewhat remarkable. There were a number of slave children that might have been sent from the plantation to Baltimore. There were those younger, those older, and those of the same age. I was chosen from among them all, and was the first, last, and only choice.

I may be deemed superstitious, and even egotistical, in regarding this event as a special interposition of divine

Providence in my favor. But I should be false to the earliest sentiments of my soul, if I suppressed the opinion. I prefer to be true to myself, even at the hazard of incurring the ridicule of others, rather than to be false, and incur my own abhorrence. From my earliest recollection, I date the entertainment of a deep conviction that slavery would not always be able to hold me within its foul embrace; and in the darkest hours of my career in slavery, this living word of faith and spirit of hope departed not from me, but remained like ministering angels to cheer me through the gloom. This good spirit was from God, and to him I offer thanksgiving and praise.

CHAPTER VI

My new mistress proved to be all she appeared when I first met her at the door,—a woman of the kindest heart and finest feelings. She had never had a slave under her control previously to myself, and prior to her marriage she had been dependent upon her own industry for a living. She was by trade a weaver; and by constant application to her business, she had been in a good degree preserved from the blighting and dehumanizing effects of slavery. I was utterly astonished at her goodness. I scarcely knew how to behave towards her. She was entirely unlike any other white woman I had ever seen. I could not approach her as I was accustomed to approach other white ladies. My early instruction was all out of place. The crouching servility, usually so acceptable a quality in a slave, did not answer when manifested toward her. Her favor was not gained by it; she seemed to be disturbed by it. She did not deem it impudent or unmannerly for a slave to look her in the face. The meanest slave was put fully at ease in her presence, and none left without feeling better for having seen her. Her face was made of heavenly smiles, and her voice of tranquil music.

But, alas! this kind heart had but a short time to remain such. The fatal poison of irresponsible power was already in her hands, and soon commenced its infernal work. That cheerful eye, under the influence of slavery, soon became red with rage; that voice, made all of sweet accord, changed to one of harsh and horrid discord; and that angelic face gave place to that of a demon.

Very soon after I went to live with Mr. and Mrs. Auld, she very kindly commenced to teach me the A, B, C. After I had learned this, she assisted me in learning to spell words of three or four letters. Just at this point of my progress, Mr. Auld found out what was going on, and at once forbade Mrs. Auld to instruct me further, telling her, among other things, that it was unlawful, as well as unsafe, to teach a slave to read. To use his own words, further, he said, "If you give a nigger an inch, he will take an ell. A nigger should know nothing but to obey his master—to do as he is told to do. Learning would spoil the best nigger in the world. Now," said he, "if you teach that nigger (speaking of myself) how to read, there would be no keeping him. It would forever unfit him to be a slave. He would at once become unmanageable, and of no value to his master. As to himself, it could do him no good, but a great deal of harm. It would make him discontented and unhappy." These words sank deep into my heart, stirred up sentiments within that lay slumbering, and called into existence an entirely new train of thought. It was a new and special revelation, explaining dark and mysterious things, with which my youthful understanding had struggled, but struggled in vain. I now understood what had been to me a most perplexing difficulty—to wit, the white man's power to enslave the black man. It was a grand achievement, and I prized it highly. From that moment, I understood the pathway from slavery to freedom. It was just what I wanted, and I got it at a time when I the least expected it. Whilst I was saddened by the thought of losing the aid of my kind mistress, I was gladdened by the invaluable instruction which, by the merest accident, I had gained from my master. Though conscious of the difficulty of learning without a teacher, I set out with high hope, and a fixed purpose, at whatever cost of trouble, to learn how to read. The very decided manner with which he spoke, and strove to impress his wife with the evil consequences of giving me instruction, served to convince me that he was deeply sensible of the truths he was uttering. It gave me the best assurance that I might rely with the utmost confidence on the results which, he said, would flow from teaching me to read. What he most dreaded, that I most desired. What he most loved, that I most hated. That which to him was a great evil, to be carefully shunned, was to me a great good, to be diligently sought; and the argument which he so warmly urged, against my learning to read, only served to inspire me with a desire and determination to learn. In learning to read, I owe almost as much to the bitter opposition of my master, as to the kindly aid of my mistress. I acknowledge the benefit of both.

I had resided but a short time in Baltimore before I observed a marked difference, in the treatment of slaves, from that which I had witnessed in the country. A city slave is almost a freeman, compared with a slave on the plantation. He is much better fed and clothed, and enjoys privileges altogether unknown to the slave on the plantation. There is a vestige of decency, a sense of shame, that does much to curb and check those outbreaks of atrocious cruelty so commonly enacted upon the plantation. He is a desperate slaveholder, who will shock the humanity of his non-slaveholding neighbors with the cries of his lacerated slave. Few are willing to incur the odium attaching to the reputation of being a cruel master; and above all things, they would not be known as not giving a slave enough to eat. Every city slaveholder is anxious to have it known of him, that he feeds his slaves well; and it is due to them to say, that most of them do give their slaves enough to eat. There are, however, some painful exceptions to this rule. Directly opposite to us, on Philpot Street, lived Mr. Thomas Hamilton. He owned two slaves. Their names were Henrietta and Mary. Henrietta was about twenty-two years of age, Mary was about fourteen; and of all the mangled and emaciated creatures I ever looked upon, these two were the most so. His heart must be harder than stone, that could look upon these unmoved. The head, neck, and shoulders of Mary were literally cut to pieces. I have frequently felt her head, and found it nearly covered with festering sores, caused by the lash of her cruel mistress. I do not know that her master ever whipped her, but I have been an eye-witness to the cruelty of Mrs. Hamilton. I used to be in Mr. Hamilton's house nearly every day. Mrs. Hamilton used to sit in a large chair in the middle of the room, with a heavy cowskin always by her side, and scarce an hour passed during the day but was marked by the blood of one of these slaves. The girls seldom passed her without her saying, "Move faster, you black gip!" at the same time giving them a blow with the cowskin over the head or shoulders, often drawing the blood. She would then say, "Take that, you black gip!" continuing, "If you don't move faster, I'll move you!" Added to the cruel lashings to which these slaves were subjected, they were kept nearly half-starved. They seldom knew what it was to eat a full meal. I have seen Mary contending with the pigs for the offal thrown into the street. So much was Mary kicked and cut to pieces, that she was oftener called "pecked" than by her name.

THROUGH THE EYES OF A SLAVE

CHAPTER VII

I lived in Master Hugh's family about seven years. During this time, I succeeded in learning to read and write. In accomplishing this, I was compelled to resort to various stratagems. I had no regular teacher. My mistress, who had kindly commenced to instruct me, had, in compliance with the advice and direction of her husband, not only ceased to instruct, but had set her face against my being instructed by any one else. It is due, however, to my mistress to say of her, that she did not adopt this course of treatment immediately. She at first lacked the depravity indispensable to shutting me up in mental darkness. It was at least necessary for her to have some training in the exercise of irresponsible power, to make her equal to the task of treating me as though I were a brute.

My mistress was, as I have said, a kind and tender-hearted woman; and in the simplicity of her soul she commenced, when I first went to live with her, to treat me as she supposed one human being ought to treat another. In entering upon the duties of a slaveholder, she did not seem to perceive that I sustained to her the relation of a mere chattel, and that for her to treat me as a human being was not only wrong, but dangerously so. Slavery proved as injurious to her as it did to me. When I went there, she was a pious, warm, and tender-hearted woman. There was no sorrow or suffering for which she had not a tear. She had bread for the hungry, clothes for the naked, and comfort for every mourner that came within her reach. Slavery soon proved its ability to divest her of these heavenly qualities. Under its influence, the tender heart became stone, and the lamblike disposition gave way to one of tiger-like fierceness. The first step in her downward course was in her ceasing to instruct me. She

171

now commenced to practise her husband's precepts. She finally became even more violent in her opposition than her husband himself. She was not satisfied with simply doing as well as he had commanded; she seemed anxious to do better. Nothing seemed to make her more angry than to see me with a newspaper. She seemed to think that here lay the danger. I have had her rush at me with a face made all up of fury, and snatch from me a newspaper, in a manner that fully revealed her apprehension. She was an apt woman; and a little experience soon demonstrated, to her satisfaction, that education and slavery were incompatible with each other.

From this time I was most narrowly watched. If I was in a separate room any considerable length of time, I was sure to be suspected of having a book, and was at once called to give an account of myself. All this, however, was too late. The first step had been taken. Mistress, in teaching me the alphabet, had given me the inch, and no precaution could prevent me from taking the ell.

The plan which I adopted, and the one by which I was most successful, was that of making friends of all the little white boys whom I met in the street. As many of these as I could, I converted into teachers. With their kindly aid, obtained at different times and in different places, I finally succeeded in learning to read. When I was sent of errands, I always took my book with me, and by going one part of my errand quickly, I found time to get a lesson before my return. I used also to carry bread with me, enough of which was always in the house, and to which I was always welcome; for I was much better off in this regard than many of the poor white children in our neighborhood. This bread I used to bestow upon the hungry little urchins, who, in return, would give me that more valuable bread of knowledge. I am strongly tempted to give the names of two or three of those little boys, as a testimonial of the gratitude and affection I bear them; but prudence forbids;—not that it would injure me, but it might embarrass them; for it is almost an unpardonable offence

172

to teach slaves to read in this Christian country. It is enough to say of the dear little fellows, that they lived on Philpot Street, very near Durgin and Bailey's ship-yard. I used to talk this matter of slavery over with them. I would sometimes say to them, I wished I could be as free as they would be when they got to be men. "You will be free as soon as you are twenty-one, but I am a slave for life! Have not I as good a right to be free as you have?" These words used to trouble them; they would express for me the liveliest sympathy, and console me with the hope that something would occur by which I might be free.

I was now about twelve years old, and the thought of being a slave for life began to bear heavily upon my heart. Just about this time, I got hold of a book entitled "The Columbian Orator." Every opportunity I got, I used to read this book. Among much of other interesting matter, I found in it a dialogue between a master and his slave. The slave was represented as having run away from his master three times. The dialogue represented the conversation which took place between them, when the slave was retaken the third time. In this dialogue, the whole argument in behalf of slavery was brought forward by the master, all of which was disposed of by the slave. The slave was made to say some very smart as well as impressive things in reply to his master— things which had the desired though unexpected effect; for the conversation resulted in the voluntary emancipation of the slave on the part of the master.

In the same book, I met with one of Sheridan's mighty speeches on and in behalf of Catholic emancipation. These were choice documents to me. I read them over and over again with unabated interest. They gave tongue to interesting thoughts of my own soul, which had frequently flashed through my mind, and died away for want of utterance. The moral which I gained from the dialogue was the power of truth over the conscience of even a slaveholder. What I got from Sheridan was a bold denunciation of slavery, and a powerful vindication of human rights. The reading of these documents enabled me to utter my thoughts, and to meet the arguments brought forward to sustain slavery; but while they relieved me of one difficulty, they brought on another even more painful than the one of which I was relieved. The more I read, the more I was led to abhor and detest my enslavers. I could regard them in no other light than a band of successful robbers, who had left their homes, and gone to Africa, and stolen us from our homes, and in a strange land reduced us to slavery. I loathed them as being the meanest as well as the most wicked of men. As I read and contemplated the subject, behold! that very discontentment which Master Hugh had predicted would follow my learning to read had already come, to torment and sting my soul to unutterable anguish. As I writhed under it, I would at times feel that learning to read had been a curse rather than a blessing. It had given me a view of my wretched condition, without the remedy. It opened my eyes to the horrible pit, but to no ladder upon which to get out. In moments of agony, I envied my fellow-slaves for their stupidity. I have often wished myself a beast. I preferred the condition of the meanest reptile to my own. Any thing, no matter what, to get rid of thinking! It was this everlasting thinking of my condition that tormented me. There was no getting rid of it. It was pressed upon me by every object within sight or hearing, animate or inanimate. The silver trump of freedom had roused my soul to eternal wakefulness. Freedom now appeared, to disappear no more forever. It was heard in every sound, and seen in every thing. It was ever present to torment me with a sense of my wretched condition. I saw nothing without seeing it, I heard nothing without hearing it, and felt nothing without feeling it. It looked from every star, it smiled in every calm, breathed in every wind, and moved in every storm.

I often found myself regretting my own existence, and wishing myself dead; and but for the hope of being free, I have no doubt but that I should have killed myself, or done something for which I should have been killed. While in this state of mind, I was eager to hear any one speak of slavery. I was a ready listener. Every little while, I could hear something about the abolitionists. It was some time before I found what the word meant. It was always used in such connections as to make it an interesting word to me. If a slave ran away and succeeded in getting clear, or if a slave killed his master, set fire to a barn, or did any thing very wrong in the mind of a slaveholder, it was spoken of as the fruit of abolition. Hearing the word in this connection very often, I set about learning what it meant. The dictionary afforded me little or no help. I found it was "the act of abolishing;" but then I did not know what was to be abolished. Here I was perplexed. I did not dare to ask any one about its meaning, for I was satisfied that it was something they wanted me to know very little about. After a patient waiting, I got one of our city papers, containing an account of the number of petitions from the north, praying for the abolition of slavery in the District of Columbia, and of the slave trade between the States. From this time I understood the words abolition and abolitionist, and always drew near when that word was spoken, expecting to hear something of importance to myself and fellow-slaves. The light broke in upon me by degrees. I went one day down on the wharf of Mr. Waters; and seeing two Irishmen unloading a scow of stone, I went, unasked, and helped them. When we had finished, one of them came to me and asked me if I were a slave. I told him I was. He asked, "Are ye a slave for life?" I told him that I was. The good Irishman seemed to be deeply affected by the statement. He said to the other that it was a pity so fine a little fellow as myself should be a slave for life. He said it was a shame to hold me. They both advised me to run away to the north; that I should find friends there, and that I should be free. I pretended not to be interested in what they said, and treated them as if I did not understand them; for I feared they might be treacherous. White men have been known to encourage slaves to escape, and then, to get the reward, catch them and return them to their masters. I was afraid that these seemingly good men might use me so; but I nevertheless remembered their advice, and from that time I resolved to run away. I looked forward to a time at which it would be safe for me to escape. I was too young to think of doing so immediately; besides, I wished to learn how to write, as I might have occasion to write my own pass. I consoled myself with the hope that I should one day find a good chance. Meanwhile, I would learn to write.

The idea as to how I might learn to write was suggested to me by being in Durgin and Bailey's ship-yard, and frequently seeing the ship carpenters, after hewing, and getting a piece of timber ready for use, write on the timber the name of that part of the ship for which it was intended. When a piece of timber was intended for the larboard side, it would be marked thus—"L." When a piece was for the starboard side, it would be marked thus—"S." A piece for the larboard side forward, would be marked thus— "L. F." When a piece was for starboard side forward, it would be marked thus—"S. F." For larboard aft, it would be marked thus—"L. A." For starboard aft, it would be marked thus—"S. A." I soon learned the names of these letters, and for what they were intended when placed upon a piece of timber in the ship-yard. I immediately commenced copying them, and in a short time was able to make the four letters named. After that, when I met with any boy who I knew could write, I would tell him I could write as well as he. The next word would be, "I don't believe you. Let me see you try it." I would then make the letters which I had been so fortunate as to learn, and ask him to beat that. In this way I got a good many lessons in writing, which it is quite possible I should never have gotten in any other way. During this time, my copy-book was the board fence, brick wall, and pavement; my pen and ink was a lump of chalk. With these, I learned mainly how to write. I then commenced and continued copying the Italics in Webster's Spelling Book, until I could make them all without looking on the book. By this time, my little Master Thomas had gone to school, and learned how to write, and had written over a number of copy-books. These had been brought home, and shown to some of our near neighbors, and then laid aside. My mistress used to go to class meeting at the Wilk Street meetinghouse every Monday afternoon, and leave me to take care of the house. When left thus, I used to spend the time in writing in the spaces left in Master Thomas's copy-book, copying what he had written. I continued to do this until I could write a hand very similar to that of Master Thomas. Thus, after a long, tedious effort for years, I finally succeeded in learning how to write.

CHAPTER VIII

In a very short time after I went to live at Baltimore, my old master's youngest son Richard died; and in about three years and six months after his death, my old master, Captain Anthony, died, leaving only his son, Andrew, and daughter, Lucretia, to share his estate. He died while on a visit to see his daughter at Hillsborough. Cut off thus unexpectedly, he left no will as to the disposal of his property. It was therefore necessary to have a valuation of the property, that it might be equally divided between Mrs. Lucretia and Master Andrew. I was immediately sent for, to be valued with the other property. Here again my feelings rose up in detestation of slavery. I had now a new conception of my degraded condition. Prior to this, I had become, if not insensible to my lot, at least partly so. I left Baltimore with a young heart overborne with sadness, and a soul full of apprehension. I took passage with Captain Rowe, in the schooner Wild Cat, and, after a sail of about twenty-four hours, I found myself near the place of my birth. I had now been absent from it almost, if not quite, five years. I, however, remembered the place very well. I was only about five years old when I left it, to go and live with my old master on Colonel Lloyd's plantation; so that I was now between ten and eleven years old.

We were all ranked together at the valuation. Men and women, old and young, married and single, were ranked with horses, sheep, and swine. There were horses and men, cattle and women, pigs and children, all holding the same rank in the scale of being, and were all subjected to the same narrow examination. Silvery-headed age and sprightly youth, maids and matrons, had to undergo the same indelicate inspection. At this moment, I saw more clearly than ever the brutalizing effects of slavery upon both slave and slaveholder.

After the valuation, then came the division. I have no language to express the high excitement and deep anxiety which were felt among us poor slaves during this time. Our fate for life was now to be decided. we had no more voice in that decision than the brutes among whom we were ranked. A single word from the white men was enough—against all our wishes, prayers, and entreaties—to sunder forever the dearest friends, dearest kindred, and strongest ties known to human beings. In addition to the pain of separation, there was the horrid dread of falling into the hands of Master Andrew. He was known to us all as being a most cruel wretch,—a common drunkard, who had, by his reckless mismanagement and profligate dissipation, already wasted a large portion of his father's property. We all felt that we might as well be sold at once to the Georgia traders, as to pass into his hands; for we knew that that would be our inevitable condition,—a condition held by us all in the utmost horror and dread.

I suffered more anxiety than most of my fellow-slaves. I had known what it was to be kindly treated; they had known nothing of the kind. They had seen little or nothing of the world. They were in very deed men and women of sorrow, and acquainted with grief. Their backs had been made familiar with the bloody lash, so that they had become callous; mine was yet tender; for while at Baltimore I got few whippings, and few slaves could boast of a kinder master and mistress than myself; and the thought of passing out of their hands into those of Master Andrew—a man who, but a few days before, to give me a sample of his bloody disposition, took my little brother by the throat, threw him on the ground, and with the heel of his boot stamped upon his head till the blood gushed from his nose and ears—was well calculated to make me anxious as to my fate. After he had committed this savage outrage upon my brother, he turned to me, and said that was the way he meant to serve me one of these days,—meaning, I suppose, when I came into his possession.

Thanks to a kind Providence, I fell to the portion of Mrs. Lucretia, and was sent immediately back to Baltimore, to live again in the family of Master Hugh. Their joy at my return equalled their sorrow at my departure. It was a glad day to me. I had escaped a worse than lion's jaws. I was absent from Baltimore, for the purpose of valuation and division, just about one month, and it seemed to have been six.

Very soon after my return to Baltimore, my mistress, Lucretia, died, leaving her husband and one child, Amanda; and in a very short time after her death, Master Andrew died. Now all the property of my old master, slaves included, was in the hands of strangers,—strangers who had had nothing to do with accumulating it. Not a slave was left free. All remained slaves, from the youngest to the oldest. If any one thing in my experience, more than another, served to deepen my conviction of the infernal character of slavery, and to fill me with unutterable loathing of slaveholders, it was their base ingratitude to my poor old grandmother. She had served my old master faithfully from youth to old age. She had been the source of all his wealth; she had peopled his plantation with slaves; she had become a great grandmother in his service. She had rocked him in infancy, attended him in childhood, served him through life, and at his death wiped from his icy brow the cold death-sweat, and closed his eyes forever. She was nevertheless left a slave—a slave for life—a slave in the hands of strangers; and in their hands she saw her children, her grandchildren, and her great-grandchildren, divided, like so many sheep, without being gratified with the small privilege of a single word, as to their or her own destiny. And, to cap the climax of their base ingratitude and fiendish barbarity, my grandmother, who was now very old, having outlived my old master and all his children, having seen the beginning and end of all of them, and her present owners finding she was of but little value, her frame already racked with the pains of old age, and complete helplessness fast stealing over her once active limbs, they took her to the woods, built her a little hut, put up a little mud-chimney, and then made her welcome to the privilege of supporting herself there in perfect loneliness; thus virtually turning her out to die! If my poor old grandmother now lives, she lives to suffer in utter loneliness; she lives to remember and mourn over the loss of children, the loss of grandchildren, and the loss of great-grandchildren. They are, in the language of the slave's poet, Whittier,—

"Gone, gone, sold and gone
To the rice swamp dank and lone,
Where the slave-whip ceaseless swings,
Where the noisome insect stings,
Where the fever-demon strews
Poison with the falling dews,
Where the sickly sunbeams glare
Through the hot and misty air:—
    Gone, gone, sold and gone
    To the rice swamp dank and lone,
    From Virginia hills and waters—
    Woe is me, my stolen daughters!"

The hearth is desolate. The children, the unconscious children, who once sang and danced in her presence, are gone. She gropes her way, in the darkness of age, for a drink of water. Instead of the voices of her children, she hears by day the moans of the dove, and by night the screams of the hideous owl. All is gloom. The grave is at the door. And now, when weighed down by the pains and aches of old age, when the head inclines to the feet, when the beginning and ending of human existence meet, and helpless infancy and painful old age combine together—at this time, this most needful time, the time for the exercise of that tenderness and affection which children only can exercise towards a declining parent—my poor old grandmother, the devoted mother of twelve children, is left all alone, in yonder little hut, before a few dim embers. She stands—she sits—

181

she staggers—she falls—she groans—she dies—and there are none of her children or grandchildren present, to wipe from her wrinkled brow the cold sweat of death, or to place beneath the sod her fallen remains. Will not a righteous God visit for these things?

In about two years after the death of Mrs. Lucretia, Master Thomas married his second wife. Her name was Rowena Hamilton. She was the eldest daughter of Mr. William Hamilton. Master now lived in St. Michael's. Not long after his marriage, a misunderstanding took place between himself and Master Hugh; and as a means of punishing his brother, he took me from him to live with himself at St. Michael's. Here I underwent another most painful separation. It, however, was not so severe as the one I dreaded at the division of property; for, during this interval, a great change had taken place in Master Hugh and his once kind and affectionate wife. The influence of brandy upon him, and of slavery upon her, had effected a disastrous change in the characters of both; so that, as far as they were concerned, I thought I had little to lose by the change. But it was not to them that I was attached. It was to those little Baltimore boys that I felt the strongest attachment. I had received many good lessons from them, and was still receiving them, and the thought of leaving them was painful indeed. I was leaving, too, without the hope of ever being allowed to return. Master Thomas had said he would never let me return again. The barrier betwixt himself and brother he considered impassable.

I then had to regret that I did not at least make the attempt to carry out my resolution to run away; for the chances of success are tenfold greater from the city than from the country.

I sailed from Baltimore for St. Michael's in the sloop Amanda, Captain Edward Dodson. On my passage, I paid particular attention to the direction which the steamboats took to go to Philadelphia. I found, instead of going down, on reaching North Point they went up the bay, in a north-easterly direction. I deemed this knowledge of the utmost importance.

My determination to run away was again revived. I resolved to wait only so long as the offering of a favorable opportunity. When that came, I was determined to be off.

CHAPTER IX

I have now reached a period of my life when I can give dates. I left Baltimore, and went to live with Master Thomas Auld, at St. Michael's, in March, 1832. It was now more than seven years since I lived with him in the family of my old master, on Colonel Lloyd's plantation. We of course were now almost entire strangers to each other. He was to me a new master, and I to him a new slave. I was ignorant of his temper and disposition; he was equally so of mine. A very short time, however, brought us into full acquaintance with each other. I was made acquainted with his wife not less than with himself. They were well matched, being equally mean and cruel. I was now, for the first time during a space of more than seven years, made to feel the painful gnawings of hunger—a something which I had not experienced before since I left Colonel Lloyd's plantation. It went hard enough with me then, when I could look back to no period at which I had enjoyed a sufficiency. It was tenfold harder after living in Master Hugh's family, where I had always had enough to eat, and of that which was good. I have said Master Thomas was a mean man. He was so. Not to give a slave enough to eat, is regarded as the most aggravated development of meanness even among slaveholders. The rule is, no matter how coarse the food, only let there be enough of it. This is the theory; and in the part of Maryland from which I came, it is the general practice,—though there are many exceptions. Master Thomas gave us enough of neither coarse nor fine food. There were four slaves of us in the kitchen—my sister Eliza, my aunt Priscilla, Henny, and myself; and we were allowed less than a half of a bushel of corn-meal per week, and very little else, either in the shape of meat or vegetables. It was not enough for us to subsist upon. We were therefore reduced to the wretched necessity of living at the expense of our neighbors. This we did by begging and stealing, whichever came handy in the time of need, the one being considered as legitimate as the other. A great many times have we poor creatures been nearly perishing with hunger, when food in abundance lay mouldering in the safe and smoke-house, and our pious mistress was aware of the fact; and yet that mistress and her husband would kneel every morning, and pray that God would bless them in basket and store!

Bad as all slaveholders are, we seldom meet one destitute of every element of character commanding respect. My master was one of this rare sort. I do not know of one single noble act ever performed by him. The leading trait in his character was meanness; and if there were any other element in his nature, it was made subject to this. He was mean; and, like most other mean men, he lacked the ability to conceal his meanness. Captain Auld was not born a slaveholder. He had been a poor man, master only of a Bay craft. He came into possession of all his slaves by marriage; and of all men, adopted slaveholders are the worst. He was cruel, but cowardly. He commanded without firmness. In the enforcement of his rules, he was at times rigid, and at times lax. At times, he spoke to his slaves with the firmness of Napoleon and the fury of a demon; at other times, he might well be mistaken for an inquirer who had lost his way. He did nothing of himself. He might have passed for a lion, but for his ears. In all things noble which he attempted, his own meanness shone most conspicuous. His airs, words, and actions, were the airs, words, and actions of born slaveholders, and, being assumed, were awkward enough. He was not even a good imitator. He possessed all the disposition to deceive, but wanted the power. Having no resources within himself, he was compelled to be the copyist of many, and being such, he was forever the victim of inconsistency; and of consequence he was an object of contempt, and was held as such even by his slaves. The luxury of having slaves of his own to wait upon him

185

was something new and unprepared for. He was a slaveholder without the ability to hold slaves. He found himself incapable of managing his slaves either by force, fear, or fraud. We seldom called him "master;" we generally called him "Captain Auld," and were hardly disposed to title him at all. I doubt not that our conduct had much to do with making him appear awkward, and of consequence fretful. Our want of reverence for him must have perplexed him greatly. He wished to have us call him master, but lacked the firmness necessary to command us to do so. His wife used to insist upon our calling him so, but to no purpose. In August, 1832, my master attended a Methodist camp-meeting held in the Bay-side, Talbot county, and there experienced religion. I indulged a faint hope that his conversion would lead him to emancipate his slaves, and that, if he did not do this, it would, at any rate, make him more kind and humane. I was disappointed in both these respects. It neither made him to be humane to his slaves, nor to emancipate them. If it had any effect on his character, it made him more cruel and hateful in all his ways; for I believe him to have been a much worse man after his conversion than before. Prior to his conversion, he relied upon his own depravity to shield and sustain him in his savage barbarity; but after his conversion, he found religious sanction and support for his slaveholding cruelty. He made the greatest pretensions to piety. His house was the house of prayer. He prayed morning, noon, and night. He very soon distinguished himself among his brethren, and was soon made a class-leader and exhorter. His activity in revivals was great, and he proved himself an instrument in the hands of the church in converting many souls. His house was the preachers' home. They used to take great pleasure in coming there to put up; for while he starved us, he stuffed them. We have had three or four preachers there at a time. The names of those who used to come most frequently while I lived there, were Mr. Storks, Mr. Ewery, Mr. Humphry, and Mr. Hickey. I have also seen Mr. George Cookman at our house. We slaves loved Mr. Cookman. We believed him to be a good man. We thought him instrumental in getting Mr. Samuel Harrison, a very rich slaveholder, to emancipate his slaves; and by some means got the impression that he was laboring to effect the emancipation of all the slaves. When he was at our house, we were sure to be called in to prayers. When the others were there, we were sometimes called in and sometimes not. Mr. Cookman took more notice of us than either of the other ministers. He could not come among us without betraying his sympathy for us, and, stupid as we were, we had the sagacity to see it.

While I lived with my master in St. Michael's, there was a white young man, a Mr. Wilson, who proposed to keep a Sabbath school for the instruction of such slaves as might be disposed to learn to read the New Testament. We met but three times, when Mr. West and Mr. Fairbanks, both class-leaders, with many others, came upon us with sticks and other missiles, drove us off, and forbade us to meet again. Thus ended our little Sabbath school in the pious town of St. Michael's.

I have said my master found religious sanction for his cruelty. As an example, I will state one of many facts going to prove the charge. I have seen him tie up a lame young woman, and whip her with a heavy cowskin upon her naked shoulders, causing the warm red blood to drip; and, in justification of the bloody deed, he would quote this passage of Scripture—"He that knoweth his master's will, and doeth it not, shall be beaten with many stripes."

Master would keep this lacerated young woman tied up in this horrid situation four or five hours at a time. I have known him to tie her up early in the morning, and whip her before breakfast; leave her, go to his store, return at dinner, and whip her again, cutting her in the places already made raw with his cruel lash. The secret of master's cruelty toward "Henny" is found in the fact of her being almost helpless. When quite a child, she fell into the fire, and burned herself horribly. Her hands were so burnt that she never got the use of them. She could do very little but bear heavy burdens. She was to master a bill of expense; and

187

as he was a mean man, she was a constant offence to him. He seemed desirous of getting the poor girl out of existence. He gave her away once to his sister; but, being a poor gift, she was not disposed to keep her. Finally, my benevolent master, to use his own words, "set her adrift to take care of herself." Here was a recently-converted man, holding on upon the mother, and at the same time turning out her helpless child, to starve and die! Master Thomas was one of the many pious slaveholders who hold slaves for the very charitable purpose of taking care of them.

My master and myself had quite a number of differences. He found me unsuitable to his purpose. My city life, he said, had had a very pernicious effect upon me. It had almost ruined me for every good purpose, and fitted me for every thing which was bad. One of my greatest faults was that of letting his horse run away, and go down to his father-inlaw's farm, which was about five miles from St. Michael's. I would then have to go after it. My reason for this kind of carelessness, or carefulness, was, that I could always get something to eat when I went there. Master William Hamilton, my master's father-in-law, always gave his slaves enough to eat. I never left there hungry, no matter how great the need of my speedy return. Master Thomas at length said he would stand it no longer. I had lived with him nine months, during which time he had given me a number of severe whippings, all to no good purpose. He resolved to put me out, as he said, to be broken; and, for this purpose, he let me for one year to a man named Edward Covey. Mr. Covey was a poor man, a farm-renter. He rented the place upon which he lived, as also the hands with which he tilled it. Mr. Covey had acquired a very high reputation for breaking young slaves, and this reputation was of immense value to him. It enabled him to get his farm tilled with much less expense to himself than he could have had it done without such a reputation. Some slaveholders thought it not much loss to allow Mr. Covey to have their slaves one year, for the sake of the training to which they were subjected, without any other compensation. He could hire young help with great ease, in consequence of this reputation. Added to the natural good qualities of Mr. Covey, he was a professor of religion—a pious soul—a member and a class-leader in the Methodist church. All of this added weight to his reputation as a "nigger-breaker." I was aware of all the facts, having been made acquainted with them by a young man who had lived there. I nevertheless made the change gladly; for I was sure of getting enough to eat, which is not the smallest consideration to a hungry man.

CHAPTER X

I had left Master Thomas's house, and went to live with Mr. Covey, on the 1st of January, 1833. I was now, for the first time in my life, a field hand. In my new employment, I found myself even more awkward than a country boy appeared to be in a large city. I had been at my new home but one week before Mr. Covey gave me a very severe whipping, cutting my back, causing the blood to run, and raising ridges on my flesh as large as my little finger. The details of this affair are as follows: Mr. Covey sent me, very early in the morning of one of our coldest days in the month of January, to the woods, to get a load of wood. He gave me a team of unbroken oxen. He told me which was the in-hand ox, and which the off-hand one. He then tied the end of a large rope around the horns of the in-hand ox, and gave me the other end of it, and told me, if the oxen started to run, that I must hold on upon the rope. I had never driven oxen before, and of course I was very awkward. I, however, succeeded in getting to the edge of the woods with little difficulty; but I had got a very few rods into the woods, when the oxen took fright, and started full tilt, carrying the cart against trees, and over stumps, in the most frightful manner. I expected every moment that my brains would be dashed out against the trees. After running thus for a considerable distance, they finally upset the cart, dashing it with great force against a tree, and threw themselves into a dense thicket. How I escaped death, I do not know. There I was, entirely alone, in a thick wood, in a place new to me. My cart was upset and shattered, my oxen were entangled among the young trees, and there was none to help me. After a long spell of effort, I succeeded in getting my cart righted, my oxen disentangled, and again yoked to the cart. I now proceeded with my team to the place where I had, the day before, been chopping wood, and loaded my cart pretty heavily, thinking in this way to tame my oxen. I then proceeded on my way home. I had now consumed one half of the day. I got out of the woods safely, and now felt out of danger. I stopped my oxen to open the woods gate; and just as I did so, before I could get hold of my ox-rope, the oxen again started, rushed through the gate, catching it between the wheel and the body of the cart, tearing it to pieces, and coming within a few inches of crushing me against the gate-post. Thus twice, in one short day, I escaped death by the merest chance. On my return, I told Mr. Covey what had happened, and how it happened. He ordered me to return to the woods again immediately. I did so, and he followed on after me. Just as I got into the woods, he came up and told me to stop my cart, and that he would teach me how to trifle away my time, and break gates. He then went to a large gum-tree, and with his axe cut three large switches, and, after trimming them up neatly with his pocketknife, he ordered me to take off my clothes. I made him no answer, but stood with my clothes on. He repeated his order. I still made him no answer, nor did I move to strip myself. Upon this he rushed at me with the fierceness of a tiger, tore off my clothes, and lashed me till he had worn out his switches, cutting me so savagely as to leave the marks visible for a long time after. This whipping was the first of a number just like it, and for similar offences.

I lived with Mr. Covey one year. During the first six months, of that year, scarce a week passed without his whipping me. I was seldom free from a sore back. My awkwardness was almost always his excuse for whipping me. We were worked fully up to the point of endurance. Long before day we were up, our horses fed, and by the first approach of day we were off to the field with our hoes and ploughing teams. Mr. Covey gave us enough to eat, but scarce time to eat it. We were often less than five minutes taking our meals. We were often in the field from the first approach of day till its last lingering ray had left us;

and at saving-fodder time, midnight often caught us in the field binding blades.

Covey would be out with us. The way he used to stand it, was this. He would spend the most of his afternoons in bed. He would then come out fresh in the evening, ready to urge us on with his words, example, and frequently with the whip. Mr. Covey was one of the few slaveholders who could and did work with his hands. He was a hard-working man. He knew by himself just what a man or a boy could do. There was no deceiving him. His work went on in his absence almost as well as in his presence; and he had the faculty of making us feel that he was ever present with us. This he did by surprising us. He seldom approached the spot where we were at work openly, if he could do it secretly. He always aimed at taking us by surprise. Such was his cunning, that we used to call him, among ourselves, "the snake." When we were at work in the cornfield, he would sometimes crawl on his hands and knees to avoid detection, and all at once he would rise nearly in our midst, and scream out, "Ha, ha! Come, come! Dash on, dash on!" This being his mode of attack, it was never safe to stop a single minute. His comings were like a thief in the night. He appeared to us as being ever at hand. He was under every tree, behind every stump, in every bush, and at every window, on the plantation. He would sometimes mount his horse, as if bound to St. Michael's, a distance of seven miles, and in half an hour afterwards you would see him coiled up in the corner of the wood-fence, watching every motion of the slaves. He would, for this purpose, leave his horse tied up in the woods. Again, he would sometimes walk up to us, and give us orders as though he was upon the point of starting on a long journey, turn his back upon us, and make as though he was going to the house to get ready; and, before he would get half way thither, he would turn short and crawl into a fence-corner, or behind some tree, and there watch us till the going down of the sun.

Mr. Covey's forte consisted in his power to deceive. His life was devoted to planning and perpetrating the grossest deceptions.

Every thing he possessed in the shape of learning or religion, he made conform to his disposition to deceive. He seemed to think himself equal to deceiving the Almighty. He would make a short prayer in the morning, and a long prayer at night; and, strange as it may seem, few men would at times appear more devotional than he. The exercises of his family devotions were always commenced with singing; and, as he was a very poor singer himself, the duty of raising the hymn generally came upon me. He would read his hymn, and nod at me to commence. I would at times do so; at others, I would not. My non-compliance would almost always produce much confusion. To show himself independent of me, he would start and stagger through with his hymn in the most discordant manner. In this state of mind, he prayed with more than ordinary spirit. Poor man! such was his disposition, and success at deceiving, I do verily believe that he sometimes deceived himself into the solemn belief, that he was a sincere worshipper of the most high God; and this, too, at a time when he may be said to have been guilty of compelling his woman slave to commit the sin of adultery. The facts in the case are these: Mr. Covey was a poor man; he was just commencing in life; he was only able to buy one slave; and, shocking as is the fact, he bought her, as he said, for a breeder. This woman was named Caroline. Mr. Covey bought her from Mr. Thomas Lowe, about six miles from St. Michael's. She was a large, able-bodied woman, about twenty years old. She had already given birth to one child, which proved her to be just what he wanted. After buying her, he hired a married man of Mr. Samuel Harrison, to live with him one year; and him he used to fasten up with her every night! The result was, that, at the end of the year, the miserable woman gave birth to twins. At this result Mr. Covey seemed to be highly pleased, both with the man and the wretched woman. Such was his joy, and that of his wife, that nothing they could do for Caroline during her confinement was too good, or too hard, to be done. The children were regarded as being quite an addition to his wealth.

If at any one time of my life more than another, I was made to drink the bitterest dregs of slavery, that time was during the first six months of my stay with Mr. Covey. We were worked in all weathers. It was never too hot or too cold; it could never rain, blow, hail, or snow, too hard for us to work in the field. Work, work, work, was scarcely more the order of the day than of the night. The longest days were too short for him, and the shortest nights too long for him. I was somewhat unmanageable when I first went there, but a few months of this discipline tamed me. Mr. Covey succeeded in breaking me. I was broken in body, soul, and spirit. My natural elasticity was crushed, my intellect languished, the disposition to read departed, the cheerful spark that lingered about my eye died; the dark night of slavery closed in upon me; and behold a man transformed into a brute!

Sunday was my only leisure time. I spent this in a sort of beast-like stupor, between sleep and wake, under some large tree. At times I would rise up, a flash of energetic freedom would dart through my soul, accompanied with a faint beam of hope, that flickered for a moment, and then vanished. I sank down again, mourning over my wretched condition. I was sometimes prompted to take my life, and that of Covey, but was prevented by a combination of hope and fear. My sufferings on this plantation seem now like a dream rather than a stern reality.

Our house stood within a few rods of the Chesapeake Bay, whose broad bosom was ever white with sails from every quarter of the habitable globe. Those beautiful vessels, robed in purest white, so delightful to the eye of freemen, were to me so many shrouded ghosts, to terrify and torment me with thoughts of my wretched condition. I have often, in the deep stillness of a summer's Sabbath, stood all alone upon the lofty banks of that noble bay, and traced, with saddened heart and tearful eye, the countless number of sails moving off to the mighty ocean. The sight of these always affected me powerfully. My thoughts would compel utterance; and there, with no audience but the Almighty, I would pour out my soul's complaint, in my rude way, with an apostrophe to the moving multitude of ships:—

"You are loosed from your moorings, and are free; I am fast in my chains, and am a slave! You move merrily before the gentle gale, and I sadly before the bloody whip! You are freedom's swift-winged angels, that fly round the world; I am confined in bands of iron! O that I were free! O, that I were on one of your gallant decks, and under your protecting wing! Alas! betwixt me and you, the turbid waters roll. Go on, go on. O that I could also go! Could I but swim! If I could fly! O, why was I born a man, of whom to make a brute! The glad ship is gone; she hides in the dim distance. I am left in the hottest hell of unending slavery. O God, save me! God, deliver me! Let me be free! Is there any God? Why am I a slave? I will run away. I will not stand it. Get caught, or get clear, I'll try it. I had as well die with ague as the fever. I have only one life to lose. I had as well be killed running as die standing. Only think of it; one hundred miles straight north, and I am free! Try it? Yes! God helping me, I will. It cannot be that I shall live and die a slave. I will take to the water. This very bay shall yet bear me into freedom. The steamboats steered in a north-east course from North Point. I will do the same; and when I get to the head of the bay, I will turn my canoe adrift, and walk straight through Delaware into Pennsylvania. When I get there, I shall not be required to have a pass; I can travel without being disturbed. Let but the first opportunity offer, and, come what will, I am off. Meanwhile, I will try to bear up under the yoke. I am not the only slave in the world. Why should I fret? I can bear as much as any of them. Besides, I am but a boy, and all boys are bound to some one. It may be that my misery in slavery will only increase my happiness when I get free. There is a better day coming."

Thus I used to think, and thus I used to speak to myself; goaded almost to madness at one moment, and at the next reconciling myself to my wretched lot.

I have already intimated that my condition was much worse, during the first six months of my stay at Mr. Covey's, than in

195

the last six. The circumstances leading to the change in Mr. Covey's course toward me form an epoch in my humble history. You have seen how a man was made a slave; you shall see how a slave was made a man. On one of the hottest days of the month of August, 1833, Bill Smith, William Hughes, a slave named Eli, and myself, were engaged in fanning wheat. Hughes was clearing the fanned wheat from before the fan. Eli was turning, Smith was feeding, and I was carrying wheat to the fan. The work was simple, requiring strength rather than intellect; yet, to one entirely unused to such work, it came very hard. About three o'clock of that day, I broke down; my strength failed me; I was seized with a violent aching of the head, attended with extreme dizziness; I trembled in every limb. Finding what was coming, I nerved myself up, feeling it would never do to stop work. I stood as long as I could stagger to the hopper with grain. When I could stand no longer, I fell, and felt as if held down by an immense weight. The fan of course stopped; every one had his own work to do; and no one could do the work of the other, and have his own go on at the same time.

Mr. Covey was at the house, about one hundred yards from the treading-yard where we were fanning. On hearing the fan stop, he left immediately, and came to the spot where we were. He hastily inquired what the matter was. Bill answered that I was sick, and there was no one to bring wheat to the fan. I had by this time crawled away under the side of the post and rail-fence by which the yard was enclosed, hoping to find relief by getting out of the sun. He then asked where I was. He was told by one of the hands. He came to the spot, and, after looking at me awhile, asked me what was the matter. I told him as well as I could, for I scarce had strength to speak. He then gave me a savage kick in the side, and told me to get up. I tried to do so, but fell back in the attempt. He gave me another kick, and again told me to rise. I again tried, and succeeded in gaining my feet; but, stooping to get the tub with which I was feeding the fan, I again staggered and fell. While down in this situation, Mr. Covey took up the hickory slat with which Hughes had been striking off the half-bushel measure, and with it gave me a heavy blow upon the head, making a large wound, and the blood ran freely; and with this again told me to get up. I made no effort to comply, having now made up my mind to let him do his worst. In a short time after receiving this blow, my head grew better. Mr. Covey had now left me to my fate. At this moment I resolved, for the first time, to go to my master, enter a complaint, and ask his protection. In order to do this, I must that afternoon walk seven miles; and this, under the circumstances, was truly a severe undertaking. I was exceedingly feeble; made so as much by the kicks and blows which I received, as by the severe fit of sickness to which I had been subjected. I, however, watched my chance, while Covey was looking in an opposite direction, and started for St. Michael's. I succeeded in getting a considerable distance on my way to the woods, when Covey discovered me, and called after me to come back, threatening what he would do if I did not come. I disregarded both his calls and his threats, and made my way to the woods as fast as my feeble state would allow; and thinking I might be overhauled by him if I kept the road, I walked through the woods, keeping far enough from the road to avoid detection, and near enough to prevent losing my way. I had not gone far before my little strength again failed me. I could go no farther. I fell down, and lay for a considerable time. The blood was yet oozing from the wound on my head. For a time I thought I should bleed to death; and think now that I should have done so, but that the blood so matted my hair as to stop the wound. After lying there about three quarters of an hour, I nerved myself up again, and started on my way, through bogs and briers, barefooted and bareheaded, tearing my feet sometimes at nearly every step; and after a journey of about seven miles, occupying some five hours to perform it, I arrived at master's store. I then presented an appearance enough to affect any but a heart of iron. From the crown of my head to my feet, I was covered with blood. My hair was all clotted with dust and blood; my shirt was stiff with blood. I suppose I looked like a man who had escaped a den of wild beasts, and barely escaped them. In this state I appeared before my master, humbly entreating him to interpose his authority for my protection. I told him all the circumstances as well as I could, and it seemed, as I spoke, at times to affect him. He would then walk the floor, and seek to justify Covey by saying he expected I deserved it. He asked me what I wanted. I told him, to let me get a new home; that as sure as I lived with Mr. Covey again, I should live with but to die with him; that Covey would surely kill me; he was in a fair way for it. Master Thomas ridiculed the idea that there was any danger of Mr. Covey's killing me, and said that he knew Mr. Covey; that he was a good man, and that he could not think of taking me from him; that, should he do so, he would lose the whole year's wages; that I belonged to Mr. Covey for one year, and that I must go back to him, come what might; and that I must not trouble him with any more stories, or that he would himself get hold of me. After threatening me thus, he gave me a very large dose of salts, telling me that I might remain in St. Michael's that night, (it being quite late,) but that I must be off back to Mr. Covey's early in the morning; and that if I did not, he would get hold of me, which meant that he would whip me. I remained all night, and, according to his orders, I started off to Covey's in the morning, (Saturday morning,) wearied in body and broken in spirit. I got no supper that night, or breakfast that morning. I reached Covey's about nine o'clock; and just as I was getting over the fence that divided Mrs. Kemp's fields from ours, out ran Covey with his cowskin, to give me another whipping. Before he could reach me, I succeeded in getting to the cornfield; and as the corn was very high, it afforded me the means of hiding. He seemed very angry, and searched for me a long time. My behavior was altogether unaccountable. He finally gave up the chase, thinking, I suppose, that I must come home for something to eat; he would give himself no further trouble in looking for me. I spent that day mostly in the woods, having the alternative before me,—to go home and be whipped to death, or stay in the woods and be starved to death. That night, I fell in with Sandy Jenkins, a slave with whom I was somewhat acquainted. Sandy had a free wife who lived about four miles from Mr. Covey's; and it being Saturday, he was on his way to see her. I told him my circumstances, and he very kindly invited me to go home with him. I went home with him, and talked this whole matter over, and got his advice as to what course it was best for me to pursue. I found Sandy an old adviser. He told me, with great solemnity, I must go back to Covey; but that before I went, I must go with him into another part of the woods, where there was a certain root, which, if I would take some of it with me, carrying it always on my right side, would render it impossible for Mr. Covey, or any other white man, to whip me. He said he had carried it for years; and since he had done so, he had never received a blow, and never expected to while he carried it. I at first rejected the idea, that the simple carrying of a root in my pocket would have any such effect as he had said, and was not disposed to take it; but Sandy impressed the necessity with much earnestness, telling me it could do no harm, if it did no good. To please him, I at length took the root, and, according to his direction, carried it upon my right side. This was Sunday morning. I immediately started for home; and upon entering the yard gate, out came Mr. Covey on his way to meeting. He spoke to me very kindly, bade me drive the pigs from a lot near by, and passed on towards the church. Now, this singular conduct of Mr. Covey really made me begin to think that there was something in the root which Sandy had given me; and had it been on any other day than Sunday, I could have attributed the conduct to no other cause than the influence of that root; and as it was, I was half inclined to think the root to be something more than I at first had taken it to be. All went well till Monday morning. On this morning, the virtue of the root was fully tested. Long before daylight, I was called to go and rub, curry, and feed, the horses. I obeyed, and was glad to obey. But whilst thus engaged, whilst in the act of throwing down some blades from the loft, Mr. Covey entered the stable with a long rope; and just as I was half out of the loft, he caught hold of my legs, and was about tying me. As soon as I found what he was up to, I gave a sudden spring, and as I did so, he holding to my legs, I was brought sprawling on the stable floor. Mr. Covey seemed now to think he had me, and could do what he pleased; but at this moment—from whence came the spirit I don't know—I resolved to fight; and, suiting my action to the resolution, I seized Covey hard by the throat; and as I did so, I rose. He held on to me, and I to him. My resistance was so entirely unexpected that Covey seemed taken all aback. He trembled like a leaf. This gave me assurance, and I held him uneasy, causing the blood to run where I touched him with the ends of my fingers. Mr. Covey soon called out to Hughes for help. Hughes came, and, while Covey held me, attempted to tie my right hand. While he was in the act of doing so, I watched my chance, and gave him a heavy kick close under the ribs. This kick fairly sickened Hughes, so that he left me in the hands of Mr. Covey. This kick had the effect of not only weakening Hughes, but Covey also. When he saw Hughes bending over with pain, his courage quailed. He asked me if I meant to persist in my resistance. I told him I did, come what might; that he had used me like a brute for six months, and that I was determined to be used so no longer. With that, he strove to drag me to a stick that was lying just out of the stable door. He meant to knock me down. But just as he was leaning over to get the stick, I seized him with both hands by his collar, and brought him by a sudden snatch to the ground. By this time, Bill came. Covey called upon him for assistance. Bill wanted to know what he could do. Covey said, "Take hold of him, take hold of him!" Bill said his master hired him out to work, and not to help to whip me; so he left Covey and myself to fight our own battle out. We were at it for nearly two hours. Covey at length let me go, puffing and blowing at a great rate, saying that if I had not resisted, he would not have whipped me half so much. The truth was, that he had not whipped me at all. I considered him as getting entirely the worst end of the bargain; for he had drawn no blood from me, but I had from him. The whole six months afterwards, that I spent with Mr. Covey, he never laid the weight of his finger upon me in anger. He would occasionally say, he didn't want to get hold of me again. "No," thought I, "you need not; for you will come off worse than you did before."

This battle with Mr. Covey was the turning-point in my career as a slave. It rekindled the few expiring embers of freedom, and revived within me a sense of my own manhood. It recalled the departed self-confidence, and inspired me again with a determination to be free. The gratification afforded by the triumph was a full compensation for whatever else might follow, even death itself. He only can understand the deep satisfaction which I experienced, who has himself repelled by force the bloody arm of slavery. I felt as I never felt before. It was a glorious resurrection, from the tomb of slavery, to the heaven of freedom. My long-crushed spirit rose, cowardice departed, bold defiance took its place; and I now resolved that, however long I might remain a slave in form, the day had passed forever when I could be a slave in fact. I did not hesitate to let it be known of me, that the white man who expected to succeed in whipping, must also succeed in killing me.

From this time I was never again what might be called fairly whipped, though I remained a slave four years afterwards. I had several fights, but was never whipped.

It was for a long time a matter of surprise to me why Mr. Covey did not immediately have me taken by the constable to the whipping-post, and there regularly whipped for the crime of raising my hand against a white man in defence of myself. And the only explanation I can now think of does not entirely satisfy me; but such as it is, I will give it. Mr. Covey enjoyed the most unbounded reputation for being a first-rate overseer and negro-breaker. It was of considerable importance to him.

That reputation was at stake; and had he sent me—a boy about sixteen years old—to the public whipping-post, his reputation would have been lost; so, to save his reputation, he suffered me to go unpunished.

My term of actual service to Mr. Edward Covey ended on Christmas day, 1833. The days between Christmas and New Year's day are allowed as holidays; and, accordingly, we were not required to perform any labor, more than to feed and take care of the stock. This time we regarded as our own, by the grace of our masters; and we therefore used or abused it nearly as we pleased. Those of us who had families at a distance, were generally allowed to spend the whole six days in their society. This time, however, was spent in various ways. The staid, sober, thinking and industrious ones of our number would employ themselves in making corn-brooms, mats, horse-collars, and baskets; and another class of us would spend the time in hunting opossums, hares, and coons. But by far the larger part engaged in such sports and merriments as playing ball, wrestling, running foot-races, fiddling, dancing, and drinking whisky; and this latter mode of spending the time was by far the most agreeable to the feelings of our masters. A slave who would work during the holidays was considered by our masters as scarcely deserving them. He was regarded as one who rejected the favor of his master. It was deemed a disgrace not to get drunk at Christmas; and he was regarded as lazy indeed, who had not provided himself with the necessary means, during the year, to get whisky enough to last him through Christmas.

From what I know of the effect of these holidays upon the slave, I believe them to be among the most effective means in the hands of the slaveholder in keeping down the spirit of insurrection. Were the slaveholders at once to abandon this practice, I have not the slightest doubt it would lead to an immediate insurrection among the slaves. These holidays serve as conductors, or safety-valves, to carry off the rebellious spirit of enslaved humanity. But for these, the slave would be forced up to the wildest desperation; and woe betide the slaveholder, the day he ventures to remove or hinder the operation of those conductors! I warn him that, in such an event, a spirit will go forth in their midst, more to be dreaded than the most appalling earthquake.

The holidays are part and parcel of the gross fraud, wrong, and inhumanity of slavery. They are professedly a custom established by the benevolence of the slaveholders; but I undertake to say, it is the result of selfishness, and one of the grossest frauds committed upon the down-trodden slave. They do not give the slaves this time because they would not like to have their work during its continuance, but because they know it would be unsafe to deprive them of it. This will be seen by the fact, that the slaveholders like to have their slaves spend those days just in such a manner as to make them as glad of their ending as of their beginning. Their object seems to be, to disgust their slaves with freedom, by plunging them into the lowest depths of dissipation. For instance, the slaveholders not only like to see the slave drink of his own accord, but will adopt various plans to make him drunk. One plan is, to make bets on their slaves, as to who can drink the most whisky without getting drunk; and in this way they succeed in getting whole multitudes to drink to excess. Thus, when the slave asks for virtuous freedom, the cunning slaveholder, knowing his ignorance, cheats him with a dose of vicious dissipation, artfully labelled with the name of liberty. The most of us used to drink it down, and the result was just what might be supposed; many of us were led to think that there was little to choose between liberty and slavery. We felt, and very properly too, that we had almost as well be slaves to man as to rum. So, when the holidays ended, we staggered up from the filth of our wallowing, took a long breath, and marched to the field,—feeling, upon the whole, rather glad to go, from what our master had deceived us into a belief was freedom, back to the arms of slavery.

I have said that this mode of treatment is a part of the whole

203

system of fraud and inhumanity of slavery. It is so. The mode here adopted to disgust the slave with freedom, by allowing him to see only the abuse of it, is carried out in other things. For instance, a slave loves molasses; he steals some. His master, in many cases, goes off to town, and buys a large quantity; he returns, takes his whip, and commands the slave to eat the molasses, until the poor fellow is made sick at the very mention of it. The same mode is sometimes adopted to make the slaves refrain from asking for more food than their regular allowance. A slave runs through his allowance, and applies for more. His master is enraged at him; but, not willing to send him off without food, gives him more than is necessary, and compels him to eat it within a given time. Then, if he complains that he cannot eat it, he is said to be satisfied neither full nor fasting, and is whipped for being hard to please! I have an abundance of such illustrations of the same principle, drawn from my own observation, but think the cases I have cited sufficient. The practice is a very common one.

On the first of January, 1834, I left Mr. Covey, and went to live with Mr. William Freeland, who lived about three miles from St. Michael's. I soon found Mr. Freeland a very different man from Mr. Covey. Though not rich, he was what would be called an educated southern gentleman. Mr. Covey, as I have shown, was a well-trained negro-breaker and slave-driver. The former (slaveholder though he was) seemed to possess some regard for honor, some reverence for justice, and some respect for humanity. The latter seemed totally insensible to all such sentiments. Mr. Freeland had many of the faults peculiar to slaveholders, such as being very passionate and fretful; but I must do him the justice to say, that he was exceedingly free from those degrading vices to which Mr. Covey was constantly addicted. The one was open and frank, and we always knew where to find him. The other was a most artful deceiver, and could be understood only by such as were skilful enough to detect his cunningly-devised frauds. Another advantage I gained in my new master was, he made no pretensions to, or profession of, religion; and this, in my opinion, was truly a great advantage. I assert most unhesitatingly, that the religion of the south is a mere covering for the most horrid crimes,—a justifier of the most appalling barbarity,—a sanctifier of the most hateful frauds,—and a dark shelter under, which the darkest, foulest, grossest, and most infernal deeds of slaveholders find the strongest protection. Were I to be again reduced to the chains of slavery, next to that enslavement, I should regard being the slave of a religious master the greatest calamity that could befall me. For of all slaveholders with whom I have ever met, religious slaveholders are the worst. I have ever found them the meanest and basest, the most cruel and cowardly, of all others. It was my unhappy lot not only to belong to a religious slaveholder, but to live in a community of such religionists. Very near Mr. Freeland lived the Rev. Daniel Weeden, and in the same neighborhood lived the Rev. Rigby Hopkins. These were members and ministers in the Reformed Methodist Church. Mr. Weeden owned, among others, a woman slave, whose name I have forgotten. This woman's back, for weeks, was kept literally raw, made so by the lash of this merciless, religious wretch. He used to hire hands. His maxim was, Behave well or behave ill, it is the duty of a master occasionally to whip a slave, to remind him of his master's authority. Such was his theory, and such his practice.

Mr. Hopkins was even worse than Mr. Weeden. His chief boast was his ability to manage slaves. The peculiar feature of his government was that of whipping slaves in advance of deserving it. He always managed to have one or more of his slaves to whip every Monday morning. He did this to alarm their fears, and strike terror into those who escaped. His plan was to whip for the smallest offences, to prevent the commission of large ones. Mr. Hopkins could always find some excuse for whipping a slave. It would astonish one, unaccustomed to a slaveholding life, to see with what wonderful ease a slaveholder can find things, of which to make occasion to whip a slave. A mere look, word, or motion,—a mistake, accident, or want of power,—are all matters for which a slave may be whipped at any time. Does a slave look dissatisfied? It is said, he has the devil in him, and it must be whipped out. Does he speak loudly when spoken to by his master? Then he is getting high-minded, and should be taken down a button-hole lower. Does he forget to pull off his hat at the approach of a white person? Then he is wanting in reverence, and should be whipped for it. Does he ever venture to vindicate his conduct, when censured for it? Then he is guilty of impudence,—one of the greatest crimes of which a slave can be guilty. Does he ever venture to suggest a different mode of doing things from that pointed out by his master? He is indeed presumptuous, and getting above himself; and nothing less than a flogging will do for him. Does he, while ploughing, break a plough,—or, while hoeing, break a hoe? It is owing to his carelessness, and for it a slave must always be whipped. Mr. Hopkins could always find something of this sort to justify the use of the lash, and he seldom failed to embrace such opportunities. There was not a man in the whole county, with whom the slaves who had the getting their own home, would not prefer to live, rather than with this Rev. Mr. Hopkins. And yet there was not a man any where round, who made higher professions of religion, or was more active in revivals,—more attentive to the class, love-feast, prayer and preaching meetings, or more devotional in his family,—that prayed earlier, later, louder, and longer,—than this same reverend slave-driver, Rigby Hopkins.

But to return to Mr. Freeland, and to my experience while in his employment. He, like Mr. Covey, gave us enough to eat; but, unlike Mr. Covey, he also gave us sufficient time to take our meals. He worked us hard, but always between sunrise and sunset. He required a good deal of work to be done, but gave us good tools with which to work. His farm was large, but he employed hands enough to work it, and with ease, compared with many of his neighbors. My treatment, while in his employment, was heavenly, compared with what I experienced at the hands of Mr. Edward Covey.

Mr. Freeland was himself the owner of but two slaves. Their names were Henry Harris and John Harris. The rest of his hands he hired. These consisted of myself, Sandy Jenkins,[1] and Handy Caldwell.

Henry and John were quite intelligent, and in a very little while after I went there, I succeeded in creating in them a strong desire to learn how to read. This desire soon sprang up in the others also. They very soon mustered up some old spelling-books, and nothing would do but that I must keep a Sabbath school. I agreed to do so, and accordingly devoted my Sundays to teaching these my loved fellow-slaves how to read. Neither of them knew his letters when I went there. Some of the slaves of the neighboring farms found what was going on, and also availed themselves of this little opportunity to learn to read. It was understood, among all who came, that there must be as little display about it as possible. It was necessary to keep our religious masters at St. Michael's unacquainted with the fact, that, instead of spending the Sabbath in wrestling, boxing, and drinking whisky, we were trying to learn how to read the will of God; for they had much rather see us engaged in those degrading sports, than to see us behaving like intellectual, moral, and accountable beings. My blood boils as I think of the bloody manner in which Messrs. Wright Fairbanks and Garrison West, both class-leaders, in connection with many others, rushed in upon us with sticks and stones, and broke up our virtuous little Sabbath school, at St.

---

1 This is the same man who gave me the roots to prevent my being whipped by Mr. Covey. He was "a clever soul." We used frequently to talk about the fight with Covey, and as often as we did so, he would claim my success as the result of the roots which he gave me. This superstition is very common among the more ignorant slaves. A slave seldom dies but that his death is attributed to trickery.

Michael's—all calling themselves Christians! humble followers of the Lord Jesus Christ! But I am again digressing.

I held my Sabbath school at the house of a free colored man, whose name I deem it imprudent to mention; for should it be known, it might embarrass him greatly, though the crime of holding the school was committed ten years ago. I had at one time over forty scholars, and those of the right sort, ardently desiring to learn. They were of all ages, though mostly men and women. I look back to those Sundays with an amount of pleasure not to be expressed. They were great days to my soul. The work of instructing my dear fellow-slaves was the sweetest engagement with which I was ever blessed. We loved each other, and to leave them at the close of the Sabbath was a severe cross indeed. When I think that these precious souls are to-day shut up in the prison-house of slavery, my feelings overcome me, and I am almost ready to ask, "Does a righteous God govern the universe? and for what does he hold the thunders in his right hand, if not to smite the oppressor, and deliver the spoiled out of the hand of the spoiler?" These dear souls came not to Sabbath school because it was popular to do so, nor did I teach them because it was reputable to be thus engaged. Every moment they spent in that school, they were liable to be taken up, and given thirty-nine lashes. They came because they wished to learn. Their minds had been starved by their cruel masters. They had been shut up in mental darkness. I taught them, because it was the delight of my soul to be doing something that looked like bettering the condition of my race. I kept up my school nearly the whole year I lived with Mr. Freeland; and, beside my Sabbath school, I devoted three evenings in the week, during the winter, to teaching the slaves at home. And I have the happiness to know, that several of those who came to Sabbath school learned how to read; and that one, at least, is now free through my agency.

The year passed off smoothly. It seemed only about half as long as the year which preceded it. I went through it without receiving a single blow. I will give Mr. Freeland the credit of being the best master I ever had, till I became my own master. For the ease with which I passed the year, I was, however, somewhat indebted to the society of my fellow-slaves. They were noble souls; they not only possessed loving hearts, but brave ones. We were linked and interlinked with each other. I loved them with a love stronger than any thing I have experienced since. It is sometimes said that we slaves do not love and confide in each other. In answer to this assertion, I can say, I never loved any or confided in any people more than my fellow-slaves, and especially those with whom I lived at Mr. Freeland's. I believe we would have died for each other. We never undertook to do any thing, of any importance, without a mutual consultation. We never moved separately. We were one; and as much so by our tempers and dispositions, as by the mutual hardships to which we were necessarily subjected by our condition as slaves.

At the close of the year 1834, Mr. Freeland again hired me of my master, for the year 1835. But, by this time, I began to want to live upon free land as well as with Freeland; and I was no longer content, therefore, to live with him or any other slaveholder. I began, with the commencement of the year, to prepare myself for a final struggle, which should decide my fate one way or the other. My tendency was upward. I was fast approaching manhood, and year after year had passed, and I was still a slave. These thoughts roused me—I must do something. I therefore resolved that 1835 should not pass without witnessing an attempt, on my part, to secure my liberty. But I was not willing to cherish this determination alone. My fellow-slaves were dear to me. I was anxious to have them participate with me in this, my life-giving determination. I therefore, though with great prudence, commenced early to ascertain their views and feelings in regard to their condition, and to imbue their minds with thoughts of freedom. I bent myself to devising ways and means for our escape, and meanwhile strove, on all fitting occasions, to impress them with the gross fraud and inhumanity of slavery. I went first to Henry, next to John, then to the others. I found, in them all, warm hearts and noble spirits. They were ready to hear, and ready to act when a feasible plan should be proposed. This was what I wanted. I talked to them of our want of manhood, if we submitted to our enslavement without at least one noble effort to be free. We met often, and consulted frequently, and told our hopes and fears, recounted the difficulties, real and imagined, which we should be called on to meet. At times we were almost disposed to give up, and try to content ourselves with our wretched lot; at others, we were firm and unbending in our determination to go. Whenever we suggested any plan, there was shrinking—the odds were fearful. Our path was beset with the greatest obstacles; and if we succeeded in gaining the end of it, our right to be free was yet questionable—we were yet liable to be returned to bondage. We could see no spot, this side of the ocean, where we could be free. We knew nothing about Canada. Our knowledge of the north did not extend farther than New York; and to go there, and be forever harassed with the frightful liability of being returned to slavery—with the certainty of being treated tenfold worse than before—the thought was truly a horrible one, and one which it was not easy to overcome. The case sometimes stood thus: At every gate through which we were to pass, we saw a watchman—at every ferry a guard—on every bridge a sentinel—and in every wood a patrol. We were hemmed in upon every side. Here were the difficulties, real or imagined— the good to be sought, and the evil to be shunned. On the one hand, there stood slavery, a stern reality, glaring frightfully upon us,—its robes already crimsoned with the blood of millions, and even now feasting itself greedily upon our own flesh. On the other hand, away back in the dim distance, under the flickering light of the north star, behind some craggy hill or snow-covered mountain, stood a doubtful freedom—half frozen—beckoning us to come and share its hospitality. This in itself was sometimes enough to stagger us; but when we permitted ourselves to survey the road, we were frequently appalled. Upon either side we saw grim death, assuming the most horrid shapes. Now it was starvation, causing us to eat our own flesh;—now we were contending with the waves, and were drowned;—now we were overtaken, and torn to pieces by the fangs of the terrible bloodhound. We were stung by scorpions, chased by wild beasts, bitten by snakes, and finally, after having nearly reached the desired spot,—after swimming rivers, encountering wild beasts, sleeping in the woods, suffering hunger and nakedness,—we were overtaken by our pursuers, and, in our resistance, we were shot dead upon the spot! I say, this picture sometimes appalled us, and made us

"rather bear those ills we had,
Than fly to others, that we knew not of."

In coming to a fixed determination to run away, we did more than Patrick Henry, when he resolved upon liberty or death. With us it was a doubtful liberty at most, and almost certain death if we failed. For my part, I should prefer death to hopeless bondage.

Sandy, one of our number, gave up the notion, but still encouraged us. Our company then consisted of Henry Harris, John Harris, Henry Bailey, Charles Roberts, and myself. Henry Bailey was my uncle, and belonged to my master. Charles married my aunt: he belonged to my master's father-in-law, Mr. William Hamilton.

The plan we finally concluded upon was, to get a large canoe belonging to Mr. Hamilton, and upon the Saturday night previous to Easter holidays, paddle directly up the Chesapeake Bay. On our arrival at the head of the bay, a distance of seventy or eighty miles from where we lived, it was our purpose to turn our canoe adrift, and follow the guidance of the north star till we got beyond the limits of Maryland. Our reason for taking the water route was, that we were less liable to be suspected as runaways; we hoped to be regarded as fishermen; whereas, if we should take the land route, we should be subjected to interruptions of almost every kind. Any one having a white face, and being so disposed, could stop us, and subject us to examination.

The week before our intended start, I wrote several protections, one for each of us. As well as I can remember, they were in the following words, to wit:—

> "This is to certify that I, the undersigned, have given the bearer, my servant, full liberty to go to Baltimore, and spend the Easter holidays. Written with mine own hand, &c., 1835.
>
> "WILLIAM HAMILTON,
> "Near St. Michael's, in Talbot county, Maryland."

We were not going to Baltimore; but, in going up the bay, we went toward Baltimore, and these protections were only intended to protect us while on the bay.

As the time drew near for our departure, our anxiety became more and more intense. It was truly a matter of life and death with us. The strength of our determination was about to be fully tested. At this time, I was very active in explaining every difficulty, removing every doubt, dispelling every fear, and inspiring all with the firmness indispensable to success in our undertaking; assuring them that half was gained the instant we made the move; we had talked long enough; we were now ready to move; if not now, we never should be; and if we did not intend to move now, we had as well fold our arms, sit down, and acknowledge ourselves fit only to be slaves. This, none of us were prepared to acknowledge. Every man stood firm; and at our last meeting, we pledged ourselves afresh, in the most solemn manner, that, at the time appointed, we would certainly start in pursuit of freedom. This was in the middle of the week, at the end of which we were to be off. We went, as usual, to our several fields of labor, but with bosoms highly agitated with thoughts of our truly hazardous undertaking. We tried to conceal our feelings as much as possible; and I think we succeeded very well.

After a painful waiting, the Saturday morning, whose night was to witness our departure, came. I hailed it with joy, bring what of sadness it might. Friday night was a sleepless one for me. I probably felt more anxious than the rest, because I was, by common consent, at the head of the whole affair. The responsibility of success or failure lay heavily upon me. The glory of the one, and the confusion of the other, were alike mine. The first two hours of that morning were such as I never experienced before, and hope never to again. Early in the morning, we went, as usual, to the field. We were spreading manure; and all at once, while thus engaged, I was overwhelmed with an indescribable feeling, in the fulness of which I turned to Sandy, who was near by, and said, "We are betrayed!" "Well," said he, "that thought has this moment struck me." We said no more. I was never more certain of any thing.

The horn was blown as usual, and we went up from the field to the house for breakfast. I went for the form, more than for want of any thing to eat that morning. Just as I got to the house, in looking out at the lane gate, I saw four white men, with two colored men. The white men were on horseback, and the colored ones were walking behind, as if tied. I watched them a few moments till they got up to our lane gate. Here they halted, and tied the colored men to the gate-post. I was not yet certain as to what the matter was. In a few moments, in rode Mr. Hamilton, with a speed betokening great excitement. He came to the door, and inquired if Master William was in. He was told he was at the barn. Mr. Hamilton, without dismounting, rode up to the barn with extraordinary speed. In a few moments, he and Mr. Freeland returned to the house. By this time, the three constables rode up, and in great haste dismounted, tied their horses, and met Master William and Mr. Hamilton returning from the barn; and after talking awhile, they all walked up to the kitchen door. There was no one in the kitchen but myself and John. Henry and Sandy were up at the barn. Mr. Freeland put his head in at the door, and called me by name, saying, there were some gentlemen at the door who wished to see me. I stepped to the door, and inquired what they wanted. They at once seized me, and, without giving me any satisfaction, tied me—lashing my hands closely together. I insisted upon knowing what the matter was. They at length said, that they had learned I had been in a "scrape," and that I was to be examined before my master; and if their information proved false, I should not be hurt.

In a few moments, they succeeded in tying John. They then turned to Henry, who had by this time returned, and commanded him to cross his hands. "I won't!" said Henry, in a firm tone, indicating his readiness to meet the consequences of his refusal. "Won't you?" said Tom Graham, the constable. "No, I won't!" said Henry, in a still stronger tone. With this, two of the constables pulled out their shining pistols, and swore, by their Creator, that they would make him cross his hands or kill him. Each cocked his pistol, and, with fingers on the trigger, walked up to Henry, saying, at the same time, if he did not cross his hands, they would blow his damned heart out. "Shoot me, shoot me!" said Henry; "you can't kill me but once. Shoot, shoot,—and be damned! I won't be tied!" This he said in a tone of loud defiance; and at the same time, with a motion as quick as lightning, he with one single stroke dashed the pistols from the hand of each constable. As he did this, all hands fell upon him, and, after beating him some time, they finally overpowered him, and got him tied.

During the scuffle, I managed, I know not how, to get my pass out, and, without being discovered, put it into the fire. We were all now tied; and just as we were to leave for Easton jail, Betsy Freeland, mother of William Freeland, came to the door with her hands full of biscuits, and divided them between Henry and John. She then delivered herself of a speech, to the following effect:—addressing herself to me, she said, "You devil! You yellow devil! it was you that put it into the heads of Henry and John to run away. But for you, you long-legged mulatto devil! Henry nor John would never have thought of such a thing." I made no reply, and was immediately hurried off towards St. Michael's. Just a moment previous to the scuffle with Henry, Mr. Hamilton suggested the propriety of making a search for the protections which he had understood Frederick had written for himself and the rest. But, just at the moment he was about carrying his proposal into effect, his aid was needed in helping to tie Henry; and the excitement attending the scuffle caused them either to forget, or to deem it unsafe, under the circumstances, to search. So we were not yet convicted of the intention to run away.

When we got about half way to St. Michael's, while the constables having us in charge were looking ahead, Henry inquired of me what he should do with his pass. I told him to eat it with his biscuit, and own nothing; and we passed the word around, "Own nothing;" and "Own nothing!" said we all. Our confidence in each other was unshaken. We were resolved to succeed or fail together, after the calamity had befallen us as much as before. We were now prepared for any thing. We were to be dragged that morning fifteen miles behind horses, and then to be placed in the Easton jail. When we reached St. Michael's, we underwent a sort of examination. We all denied that we ever intended to run away. We did this more to bring out the evidence against us, than from any hope of getting clear of being sold; for, as I have said, we were ready for that. The fact was, we cared but little where we went, so we went together. Our greatest concern was about separation. We dreaded that more than any thing this side of death. We found the evidence against us to be the testimony of one person; our master would not tell who it was; but we came to a unanimous decision among ourselves as to who their informant was. We were sent off to the jail at Easton. When we got there, we were delivered up to the sheriff, Mr. Joseph Graham, and by him placed in jail. Henry, John, and myself, were placed in one room together—Charles, and Henry Bailey, in another. Their object in separating us was to hinder concert.

We had been in jail scarcely twenty minutes, when a swarm of slave traders, and agents for slave traders, flocked into jail to look at us, and to ascertain if we were for sale. Such a set of beings I never saw before! I felt myself surrounded by so many fiends from perdition. A band of pirates never looked more like their father, the devil. They laughed and grinned over us, saying, "Ah, my boys! we have got you, haven't we?" And after taunting us in various ways, they one by one went into an examination of us, with intent to ascertain our value. They would impudently ask us if we would not like to have them for our masters. We would make them no answer, and leave them to find out as best they could. Then they would curse and swear at us, telling us that they could take the devil out of us in a very little while, if we were only in their hands.

While in jail, we found ourselves in much more comfortable quarters than we expected when we went there. We did not get much to eat, nor that which was very good; but we had a good clean room, from the windows of which we could see what was going on in the street, which was very much better than though we had been placed in one of the dark, damp cells. Upon the whole, we got along very well, so far as the jail and its keeper were concerned. Immediately after the holidays were over, contrary to all our expectations, Mr. Hamilton and Mr. Freeland came up to Easton, and took Charles, the two Henrys, and John, out of jail, and carried them home, leaving me alone. I regarded this separation as a final one. It caused me more pain than any thing else in the whole transaction. I was ready for any thing rather than separation. I supposed that they had consulted together, and had decided that, as I was the whole cause of the intention of the others to run away, it was hard to make the innocent suffer with the guilty; and that they had, therefore, concluded to take the others home, and sell me, as a warning to the others that remained. It is due to the noble Henry to say, he seemed almost as reluctant at leaving the prison as at leaving home to come to the prison. But we knew we should, in all probability, be separated, if we were sold; and since he was in their hands, he concluded to go peaceably home.

I was now left to my fate. I was all alone, and within the walls of a stone prison. But a few days before, and I was full of hope. I expected to have been safe in a land of freedom; but now I was covered with gloom, sunk down to the utmost despair. I thought the possibility of freedom was gone. I was kept in this way about one week, at the end of which, Captain Auld, my master, to my surprise and utter astonishment, came up, and took me out, with the intention of sending me, with a gentleman of his acquaintance, into Alabama. But, from some cause or other, he did not send me to Alabama, but concluded to send me back to Baltimore, to live again with his brother Hugh, and to learn a trade.

Thus, after an absence of three years and one month, I was once more permitted to return to my old home at Baltimore. My master sent me away, because there existed against me a very great prejudice in the community, and he feared I might be killed.

In a few weeks after I went to Baltimore, Master Hugh hired me to Mr. William Gardner, an extensive ship-builder, on Fell's Point. I was put there to learn how to calk. It, however, proved a very unfavorable place for the accomplishment of this object. Mr. Gardner was engaged that spring in building two large man-of-war brigs, professedly for the Mexican government. The vessels were to be launched in the July of that year, and in failure thereof, Mr. Gardner was to lose a considerable sum; so that when I entered, all was hurry. There was no time to learn any thing. Every man had to do that which he knew how to do. In entering the shipyard, my orders from Mr. Gardner were, to do whatever the carpenters commanded me to do. This was placing me at the beck and call of about seventy-five men. I was to regard all these as masters. Their word was to be my law. My situation was a most trying one. At times I needed a dozen pair of hands. I was called a dozen ways in the space of

217

a single minute. Three or four voices would strike my ear at the same moment. It was—"Fred., come help me to cant this timber here."—"Fred., come carry this timber yonder."—"Fred., bring that roller here."—"Fred., go get a fresh can of water."—"Fred., come help saw off the end of this timber."—"Fred., go quick, and get the crowbar."—"Fred., hold on the end of this fall."—"Fred., go to the blacksmith's shop, and get a new punch."—"Hurra, Fred! run and bring me a cold chisel."—"I say, Fred., bear a hand, and get up a fire as quick as lightning under that steam-box."—"Halloo, nigger! come, turn this grindstone."—"Come, come! move, move! and bowse this timber forward."—"I say, darky, blast your eyes, why don't you heat up some pitch?"—"Halloo! halloo! halloo!" (Three voices at the same time.) "Come here!—Go there!—Hold on where you are! Damn you, if you move, I'll knock your brains out!"

This was my school for eight months; and I might have remained there longer, but for a most horrid fight I had with four of the white apprentices, in which my left eye was nearly knocked out, and I was horribly mangled in other respects. The facts in the case were these: Until a very little while after I went there, white and black ship-carpenters worked side by side, and no one seemed to see any impropriety in it. All hands seemed to be very well satisfied. Many of the black carpenters were freemen. Things seemed to be going on very well. All at once, the white carpenters knocked off, and said they would not work with free colored workmen. Their reason for this, as alleged, was, that if free colored carpenters were encouraged, they would soon take the trade into their own hands, and poor white men would be thrown out of employment. They therefore felt called upon at once to put a stop to it. And, taking advantage of Mr. Gardner's necessities, they broke off, swearing they would work no longer, unless he would discharge his black carpenters. Now, though this did not extend to me in form, it did reach me in fact. My fellow-apprentices very soon began to feel it degrading to them to work with me. They began to put on airs, and talk

218

about the "niggers" taking the country, saying we all ought to be killed; and, being encouraged by the journeymen, they commenced making my condition as hard as they could, by hectoring me around, and sometimes striking me. I, of course, kept the vow I made after the fight with Mr. Covey, and struck back again, regardless of consequences; and while I kept them from combining, I succeeded very well; for I could whip the whole of them, taking them separately. They, however, at length combined, and came upon me, armed with sticks, stones, and heavy handspikes. One came in front with a half brick. There was one at each side of me, and one behind me. While I was attending to those in front, and on either side, the one behind ran up with the handspike, and struck me a heavy blow upon the head. It stunned me. I fell, and with this they all ran upon me, and fell to beating me with their fists. I let them lay on for a while, gathering strength. In an instant, I gave a sudden surge, and rose to my hands and knees. Just as I did that, one of their number gave me, with his heavy boot, a powerful kick in the left eye. My eyeball seemed to have burst. When they saw my eye closed, and badly swollen, they left me. With this I seized the handspike, and for a time pursued them. But here the carpenters interfered, and I thought I might as well give it up. It was impossible to stand my hand against so many. All this took place in sight of not less than fifty white ship-carpenters, and not one interposed a friendly word; but some cried, "Kill the damned nigger! Kill him! kill him! He struck a white person." I found my only chance for life was in flight. I succeeded in getting away without an additional blow, and barely so; for to strike a white man is death by Lynch law,—and that was the law in Mr. Gardner's ship-yard; nor is there much of any other out of Mr. Gardner's ship-yard.

I went directly home, and told the story of my wrongs to Master Hugh; and I am happy to say of him, irreligious as he was, his conduct was heavenly, compared with that of his brother Thomas under similar circumstances. He listened attentively to

219

my narration of the circumstances leading to the savage outrage, and gave many proofs of his strong indignation at it. The heart of my once overkind mistress was again melted into pity. My puffed-out eye and blood-covered face moved her to tears. She took a chair by me, washed the blood from my face, and, with a mother's tenderness, bound up my head, covering the wounded eye with a lean piece of fresh beef. It was almost compensation for my suffering to witness, once more, a manifestation of kindness from this, my once affectionate old mistress. Master Hugh was very much enraged. He gave expression to his feelings by pouring out curses upon the heads of those who did the deed. As soon as I got a little the better of my bruises, he took me with him to Esquire Watson's, on Bond Street, to see what could be done about the matter. Mr. Watson inquired who saw the assault committed. Master Hugh told him it was done in Mr. Gardner's ship-yard at midday, where there were a large company of men at work. "As to that," he said, "the deed was done, and there was no question as to who did it." His answer was, he could do nothing in the case, unless some white man would come forward and testify. He could issue no warrant on my word. If I had been killed in the presence of a thousand colored people, their testimony combined would have been insufficient to have arrested one of the murderers. Master Hugh, for once, was compelled to say this state of things was too bad. Of course, it was impossible to get any white man to volunteer his testimony in my behalf, and against the white young men. Even those who may have sympathized with me were not prepared to do this. It required a degree of courage unknown to them to do so; for just at that time, the slightest manifestation of humanity toward a colored person was denounced as abolitionism, and that name subjected its bearer to frightful liabilities. The watchwords of the bloody-minded in that region, and in those days, were, "Damn the abolitionists!" and "Damn the niggers!" There was nothing done, and probably nothing would have been done if I had been killed. Such was, and such remains, the state of things in the

Christian city of Baltimore.

Master Hugh, finding he could get no redress, refused to let me go back again to Mr. Gardner. He kept me himself, and his wife dressed my wound till I was again restored to health. He then took me into the ship-yard of which he was foreman, in the employment of Mr. Walter Price. There I was immediately set to calking, and very soon learned the art of using my mallet and irons. In the course of one year from the time I left Mr. Gardner's, I was able to command the highest wages given to the most experienced calkers. I was now of some importance to my master. I was bringing him from six to seven dollars per week. I sometimes brought him nine dollars per week: my wages were a dollar and a half a day. After learning how to calk, I sought my own employment, made my own contracts, and collected the money which I earned. My pathway became much more smooth than before; my condition was now much more comfortable. When I could get no calking to do, I did nothing. During these leisure times, those old notions about freedom would steal over me again. When in Mr. Gardner's employment, I was kept in such a perpetual whirl of excitement, I could think of nothing, scarcely, but my life; and in thinking of my life, I almost forgot my liberty. I have observed this in my experience of slavery,— that whenever my condition was improved, instead of its increasing my contentment, it only increased my desire to be free, and set me to thinking of plans to gain my freedom. I have found that, to make a contented slave, it is necessary to make a thoughtless one. It is necessary to darken his moral and mental vision, and, as far as possible, to annihilate the power of reason. He must be able to detect no inconsistencies in slavery; he must be made to feel that slavery is right; and he can be brought to that only when he ceases to be a man.

I was now getting, as I have said, one dollar and fifty cents per day. I contracted for it; I earned it; it was paid to me; it was rightfully my own; yet, upon each returning Saturday night, I was compelled to deliver every cent of that money to Master

Hugh. And why? Not because he earned it,—not because he had any hand in earning it,—not because I owed it to him,—nor because he possessed the slightest shadow of a right to it; but solely because he had the power to compel me to give it up. The right of the grim-visaged pirate upon the high seas is exactly the same.

CHAPTER XI

I now come to that part of my life during which I planned, and finally succeeded in making, my escape from slavery. But before narrating any of the peculiar circumstances, I deem it proper to make known my intention not to state all the facts connected with the transaction. My reasons for pursuing this course may be understood from the following: First, were I to give a minute statement of all the facts, it is not only possible, but quite probable, that others would thereby be involved in the most embarrassing difficulties. Secondly, such a statement would most undoubtedly induce greater vigilance on the part of slaveholders than has existed heretofore among them; which would, of course, be the means of guarding a door whereby some dear brother bondman might escape his galling chains. I deeply regret the necessity that impels me to suppress any thing of importance connected with my experience in slavery. It would afford me great pleasure indeed, as well as materially add to the interest of my narrative, were I at liberty to gratify a curiosity, which I know exists in the minds of many, by an accurate statement of all the facts pertaining to my most fortunate escape. But I must deprive myself of this pleasure, and the curious of the gratification which such a statement would afford. I would allow myself to suffer under the greatest imputations which evil-minded men might suggest, rather than exculpate myself, and thereby run the hazard of closing the slightest avenue by which a brother slave might clear himself of the chains and fetters of slavery.

I have never approved of the very public manner in which some of our western friends have conducted what they call the underground railroad, but which I think, by their open declarations, has been made most emphatically the upper-ground railroad. I honor those good men and women for their noble daring, and applaud them for willingly subjecting themselves to bloody persecution, by openly avowing their participation in the escape of slaves. I, however, can see very little good resulting from such a course, either to themselves or the slaves escaping; while, upon the other hand, I see and feel assured that those open declarations are a positive evil to the slaves remaining, who are seeking to escape. They do nothing towards enlightening the slave, whilst they do much towards enlightening the master. They stimulate him to greater watchfulness, and enhance his power to capture his slave. We owe something to the slave south of the line as well as to those north of it; and in aiding the latter on their way to freedom, we should be careful to do nothing which would be likely to hinder the former from escaping from slavery. I would keep the merciless slaveholder profoundly ignorant of the means of flight adopted by the slave. I would leave him to imagine himself surrounded by myriads of invisible tormentors, ever ready to snatch from his infernal grasp his trembling prey. Let him be left to feel his way in the dark; let darkness commensurate with his crime hover over him; and let him feel that at every step he takes, in pursuit of the flying bondman, he is running the frightful risk of having his hot brains dashed out by an invisible agency. Let us render the tyrant no aid; let us not hold the light by which he can trace the footprints of our flying brother. But enough of this. I will now proceed to the statement of those facts, connected with my escape, for which I am alone responsible, and for which no one can be made to suffer but myself.

In the early part of the year 1838, I became quite restless. I could see no reason why I should, at the end of each week, pour the reward of my toil into the purse of my master. When I carried to him my weekly wages, he would, after counting the money, look me in the face with a robber-like fierceness, and ask, "Is this all?" He was satisfied with nothing less than the last cent.

He would, however, when I made him six dollars, sometimes give me six cents, to encourage me. It had the opposite effect. I regarded it as a sort of admission of my right to the whole. The fact that he gave me any part of my wages was proof, to my mind, that he believed me entitled to the whole of them. I always felt worse for having received any thing; for I feared that the giving me a few cents would ease his conscience, and make him feel himself to be a pretty honorable sort of robber. My discontent grew upon me. I was ever on the look-out for means of escape; and, finding no direct means, I determined to try to hire my time, with a view of getting money with which to make my escape. In the spring of 1838, when Master Thomas came to Baltimore to purchase his spring goods, I got an opportunity, and applied to him to allow me to hire my time. He unhesitatingly refused my request, and told me this was another stratagem by which to escape. He told me I could go nowhere but that he could get me; and that, in the event of my running away, he should spare no pains in his efforts to catch me. He exhorted me to content myself, and be obedient. He told me, if I would be happy, I must lay out no plans for the future. He said, if I behaved myself properly, he would take care of me. Indeed, he advised me to complete thoughtlessness of the future, and taught me to depend solely upon him for happiness. He seemed to see fully the pressing necessity of setting aside my intellectual nature, in order to contentment in slavery. But in spite of him, and even in spite of myself, I continued to think, and to think about the injustice of my enslavement, and the means of escape.

About two months after this, I applied to Master Hugh for the privilege of hiring my time. He was not acquainted with the fact that I had applied to Master Thomas, and had been refused. He too, at first, seemed disposed to refuse; but, after some reflection, he granted me the privilege, and proposed the following terms: I was to be allowed all my time, make all contracts with those for whom I worked, and find my own employment; and, in return for this liberty, I was to pay him three dollars at the end of each week; find myself in calking tools, and in board and clothing. My board was two dollars and a half per week. This, with the wear and tear of clothing and calking tools, made my regular expenses about six dollars per week. This amount I was compelled to make up, or relinquish the privilege of hiring my time. Rain or shine, work or no work, at the end of each week the money must be forthcoming, or I must give up my privilege. This arrangement, it will be perceived, was decidedly in my master's favor. It relieved him of all need of looking after me. His money was sure. He received all the benefits of slaveholding without its evils; while I endured all the evils of a slave, and suffered all the care and anxiety of a freeman. I found it a hard bargain. But, hard as it was, I thought it better than the old mode of getting along. It was a step towards freedom to be allowed to bear the responsibilities of a freeman, and I was determined to hold on upon it. I bent myself to the work of making money. I was ready to work at night as well as day, and by the most untiring perseverance and industry, I made enough to meet my expenses, and lay up a little money every week. I went on thus from May till August. Master Hugh then refused to allow me to hire my time longer. The ground for his refusal was a failure on my part, one Saturday night, to pay him for my week's time. This failure was occasioned by my attending a camp meeting about ten miles from Baltimore. During the week, I had entered into an engagement with a number of young friends to start from Baltimore to the camp ground early Saturday evening; and being detained by my employer, I was unable to get down to Master Hugh's without disappointing the company. I knew that Master Hugh was in no special need of the money that night. I therefore decided to go to camp meeting, and upon my return pay him the three dollars. I staid at the camp meeting one day longer than I intended when I left. But as soon as I returned, I called upon him to pay him what he considered his due. I found him very angry; he could scarce restrain his wrath. He said he had a great mind to give me a severe whipping. He wished to know how I dared go out of the city without asking his permission. I told him I hired my time and while I paid him the price which he asked for it, I did not know that I was bound to ask him when and where I should go. This reply troubled him; and, after reflecting a few moments, he turned to me, and said I should hire my time no longer; that the next thing he should know of, I would be running away. Upon the same plea, he told me to bring my tools and clothing home forthwith. I did so; but instead of seeking work, as I had been accustomed to do previously to hiring my time, I spent the whole week without the performance of a single stroke of work. I did this in retaliation. Saturday night, he called upon me as usual for my week's wages. I told him I had no wages; I had done no work that week. Here we were upon the point of coming to blows. He raved, and swore his determination to get hold of me. I did not allow myself a single word; but was resolved, if he laid the weight of his hand upon me, it should be blow for blow. He did not strike me, but told me that he would find me in constant employment in future. I thought the matter over during the next day, Sunday, and finally resolved upon the third day of September, as the day upon which I would make a second attempt to secure my freedom. I now had three weeks during which to prepare for my journey. Early on Monday morning, before Master Hugh had time to make any engagement for me, I went out and got employment of Mr. Butler, at his ship-yard near the drawbridge, upon what is called the City Block, thus making it unnecessary for him to seek employment for me. At the end of the week, I brought him between eight and nine dollars. He seemed very well pleased, and asked why I did not do the same the week before. He little knew what my plans were. My object in working steadily was to remove any suspicion he might entertain of my intent to run away; and in this I succeeded admirably. I suppose he thought I was never better satisfied with my condition than at the very time during which I was planning my escape. The second week passed, and again I carried him my full wages; and

227

so well pleased was he, that he gave me twenty-five cents, (quite a large sum for a slaveholder to give a slave,) and bade me to make a good use of it. I told him I would.

Things went on without very smoothly indeed, but within there was trouble. It is impossible for me to describe my feelings as the time of my contemplated start drew near. I had a number of warmhearted friends in Baltimore,—friends that I loved almost as I did my life,—and the thought of being separated from them forever was painful beyond expression. It is my opinion that thousands would escape from slavery, who now remain, but for the strong cords of affection that bind them to their friends. The thought of leaving my friends was decidedly the most painful thought with which I had to contend. The love of them was my tender point, and shook my decision more than all things else. Besides the pain of separation, the dread and apprehension of a failure exceeded what I had experienced at my first attempt. The appalling defeat I then sustained returned to torment me. I felt assured that, if I failed in this attempt, my case would be a hopeless one—it would seal my fate as a slave forever. I could not hope to get off with any thing less than the severest punishment, and being placed beyond the means of escape. It required no very vivid imagination to depict the most frightful scenes through which I should have to pass, in case I failed. The wretchedness of slavery, and the blessedness of freedom, were perpetually before me. It was life and death with me. But I remained firm, and, according to my resolution, on the third day of September, 1838, I left my chains, and succeeded in reaching New York without the slightest interruption of any kind. How I did so,—what means I adopted,—what direction I travelled, and by what mode of conveyance,—I must leave unexplained, for the reasons before mentioned.

I have been frequently asked how I felt when I found myself in a free State. I have never been able to answer the question with any satisfaction to myself. It was a moment of the highest excitement I ever experienced. I suppose I felt as one may imagine the unarmed mariner to feel when he is rescued by a friendly man-of-war from the pursuit of a pirate. In writing to a dear friend, immediately after my arrival at New York, I said I felt like one who had escaped a den of hungry lions. This state of mind, however, very soon subsided; and I was again seized with a feeling of great insecurity and loneliness. I was yet liable to be taken back, and subjected to all the tortures of slavery. This in itself was enough to damp the ardor of my enthusiasm. But the loneliness overcame me. There I was in the midst of thousands, and yet a perfect stranger; without home and without friends, in the midst of thousands of my own brethren—children of a common Father, and yet I dared not to unfold to any one of them my sad condition. I was afraid to speak to any one for fear of speaking to the wrong one, and thereby falling into the hands of money-loving kidnappers, whose business it was to lie in wait for the panting fugitive, as the ferocious beasts of the forest lie in wait for their prey. The motto which I adopted when I started from slavery was this—"Trust no man!" I saw in every white man an enemy, and in almost every colored man cause for distrust. It was a most painful situation; and, to understand it, one must needs experience it, or imagine himself in similar circumstances. Let him be a fugitive slave in a strange land—a land given up to be the hunting-ground for slaveholders— whose inhabitants are legalized kidnappers—where he is every moment subjected to the terrible liability of being seized upon by his fellowmen, as the hideous crocodile seizes upon his prey!—I say, let him place himself in my situation—without home or friends—without money or credit—wanting shelter, and no one to give it—wanting bread, and no money to buy it,—and at the same time let him feel that he is pursued by merciless men-hunters, and in total darkness as to what to do, where to go, or where to stay,—perfectly helpless both as to the means of defence and means of escape,—in the midst of plenty, yet suffering the terrible gnawings of hunger,—in the midst of houses, yet having no home,—among fellow-men, yet feeling as if in the midst of wild beasts, whose greediness to swallow up the trembling and half-famished fugitive is only equalled by that with which the monsters of the deep swallow up the helpless fish upon which they subsist,—I say, let him be placed in this most trying situation,—the situation in which I was placed,—then, and not till then, will he fully appreciate the hardships of, and know how to sympathize with, the toil-worn and whip-scarred fugitive slave.

Thank Heaven, I remained but a short time in this distressed situation. I was relieved from it by the humane hand of Mr. David Ruggles, whose vigilance, kindness, and perseverance, I shall never forget. I am glad of an opportunity to express, as far as words can, the love and gratitude I bear him. Mr. Ruggles is now afflicted with blindness, and is himself in need of the same kind offices which he was once so forward in the performance of toward others. I had been in New York but a few days, when Mr. Ruggles sought me out, and very kindly took me to his boarding-house at the corner of Church and Lespenard Streets. Mr. Ruggles was then very deeply engaged in the memorable Darg case, as well as attending to a number of other fugitive slaves, devising ways and means for their successful escape; and, though watched and hemmed in on almost every side, he seemed to be more than a match for his enemies.

Very soon after I went to Mr. Ruggles, he wished to know of me where I wanted to go; as he deemed it unsafe for me to remain in New York. I told him I was a calker, and should like to go where I could get work. I thought of going to Canada; but he decided against it, and in favor of my going to New Bedford, thinking I should be able to get work there at my trade. At this time, Anna,[2] my intended wife, came on; for I wrote to her immediately after my arrival at New York, (notwithstanding my homeless, houseless, and helpless condition,) informing her of my successful flight, and wishing her to come on forthwith. In a

2 She was free.

few days after her arrival, Mr. Ruggles called in the Rev. J. W. C. Pennington, who, in the presence of Mr. Ruggles, Mrs. Michaels, and two or three others, performed the marriage ceremony, and gave us a certificate, of which the following is an exact copy:—

"This may certify, that I joined together in holy matrimony Frederick Johnson[3] and Anna Murray, as man and wife, in the presence of Mr. David Ruggles and Mrs. Michaels.

"JAMES W. C. PENNINGTON
"*New York, Sept.* 15, 1838"

Upon receiving this certificate, and a five-dollar bill from Mr. Ruggles, I shouldered one part of our baggage, and Anna took up the other, and we set out forthwith to take passage on board of the steamboat John W. Richmond for Newport, on our way to New Bedford. Mr. Ruggles gave me a letter to a Mr. Shaw in Newport, and told me, in case my money did not serve me to New Bedford, to stop in Newport and obtain further assistance; but upon our arrival at Newport, we were so anxious to get to a place of safety, that, notwithstanding we lacked the necessary money to pay our fare, we decided to take seats in the stage, and promise to pay when we got to New Bedford. We were encouraged to do this by two excellent gentlemen, residents of New Bedford, whose names I afterward ascertained to be Joseph Ricketson and William C. Taber. They seemed at once to understand our circumstances, and gave us such assurance of their friendliness as put us fully at ease in their presence.

It was good indeed to meet with such friends, at such a time. Upon reaching New Bedford, we were directed to the house of Mr. Nathan Johnson, by whom we were kindly received, and hospitably provided for. Both Mr. and Mrs. Johnson took a deep

---

3 I had changed my name from Frederick Bailey to that of Johnson.

and lively interest in our welfare. They proved themselves quite worthy of the name of abolitionists. When the stage-driver found us unable to pay our fare, he held on upon our baggage as security for the debt. I had but to mention the fact to Mr. Johnson, and he forthwith advanced the money.

We now began to feel a degree of safety, and to prepare ourselves for the duties and responsibilities of a life of freedom. On the morning after our arrival at New Bedford, while at the breakfast-table, the question arose as to what name I should be called by. The name given me by my mother was, "Frederick Augustus Washington Bailey." I, however, had dispensed with the two middle names long before I left Maryland so that I was generally known by the name of "Frederick Bailey." I started from Baltimore bearing the name of "Stanley." When I got to New York, I again changed my name to "Frederick Johnson," and thought that would be the last change. But when I got to New Bedford, I found it necessary again to change my name. The reason of this necessity was, that there were so many Johnsons in New Bedford, it was already quite difficult to distinguish between them. I gave Mr. Johnson the privilege of choosing me a name, but told him he must not take from me the name of "Frederick." I must hold on to that, to preserve a sense of my identity. Mr. Johnson had just been reading the "Lady of the Lake," and at once suggested that my name be "Douglass." From that time until now I have been called "Frederick Douglass;" and as I am more widely known by that name than by either of the others, I shall continue to use it as my own.

I was quite disappointed at the general appearance of things in New Bedford. The impression which I had received respecting the character and condition of the people of the north, I found to be singularly erroneous. I had very strangely supposed, while in slavery, that few of the comforts, and scarcely any of the luxuries, of life were enjoyed at the north, compared with what were enjoyed by the slaveholders of the south. I probably came to this conclusion from the fact that northern people owned no slaves. I supposed that they were about upon a level with the non-slaveholding population of the south. I knew they were exceedingly poor, and I had been accustomed to regard their poverty as the necessary consequence of their being non-slaveholders. I had somehow imbibed the opinion that, in the absence of slaves, there could be no wealth, and very little refinement. And upon coming to the north, I expected to meet with a rough, hard-handed, and uncultivated population, living in the most Spartan-like simplicity, knowing nothing of the ease, luxury, pomp, and grandeur of southern slaveholders. Such being my conjectures, any one acquainted with the appearance of New Bedford may very readily infer how palpably I must have seen my mistake.

In the afternoon of the day when I reached New Bedford, I visited the wharves, to take a view of the shipping. Here I found myself surrounded with the strongest proofs of wealth. Lying at the wharves, and riding in the stream, I saw many ships of the finest model, in the best order, and of the largest size. Upon the right and left, I was walled in by granite warehouses of the widest dimensions, stowed to their utmost capacity with the necessaries and comforts of life. Added to this, almost every body seemed to be at work, but noiselessly so, compared with what I had been accustomed to in Baltimore. There were no loud songs heard from those engaged in loading and unloading ships. I heard no deep oaths or horrid curses on the laborer. I saw no whipping of men; but all seemed to go smoothly on. Every man appeared to understand his work, and went at it with a sober, yet cheerful earnestness, which betokened the deep interest which he felt in what he was doing, as well as a sense of his own dignity as a man. To me this looked exceedingly strange. From the wharves I strolled around and over the town, gazing with wonder and admiration at the splendid churches, beautiful dwellings, and finely-cultivated gardens; evincing an amount of wealth, comfort, taste, and refinement, such as I had never seen in any part of slaveholding Maryland.

Every thing looked clean, new, and beautiful. I saw few or no dilapidated houses, with poverty-stricken inmates; no half-naked children and barefooted women, such as I had been accustomed to see in Hillsborough, Easton, St. Michael's, and Baltimore. The people looked more able, stronger, healthier, and happier, than those of Maryland. I was for once made glad by a view of extreme wealth, without being saddened by seeing extreme poverty. But the most astonishing as well as the most interesting thing to me was the condition of the colored people, a great many of whom, like myself, had escaped thither as a refuge from the hunters of men. I found many, who had not been seven years out of their chains, living in finer houses, and evidently enjoying more of the comforts of life, than the average of slaveholders in Maryland. I will venture to assert, that my friend Mr. Nathan Johnson (of whom I can say with a grateful heart, "I was hungry, and he gave me meat; I was thirsty, and he gave me drink; I was a stranger, and he took me in") lived in a neater house; dined at a better table; took, paid for, and read, more newspapers; better understood the moral, religious, and political character of the nation,—than nine tenths of the slaveholders in Talbot county Maryland. Yet Mr. Johnson was a working man. His hands were hardened by toil, and not his alone, but those also of Mrs. Johnson. I found the colored people much more spirited than I had supposed they would be. I found among them a determination to protect each other from the blood-thirsty kidnapper, at all hazards. Soon after my arrival, I was told of a circumstance which illustrated their spirit. A colored man and a fugitive slave were on unfriendly terms. The former was heard to threaten the latter with informing his master of his whereabouts. Straightway a meeting was called among the colored people, under the stereotyped notice, "Business of importance!" The betrayer was invited to attend. The people came at the appointed hour, and organized the meeting by appointing a very religious old gentleman as president, who, I believe, made a prayer, after which he addressed the meeting as follows: "Friends, we have got him here, and I would recommend that you young men just take him outside the door, and kill him!" With this, a number of them bolted at him; but they were intercepted by some more timid than themselves, and the betrayer escaped their vengeance, and has not been seen in New Bedford since. I believe there have been no more such threats, and should there be hereafter, I doubt not that death would be the consequence.

I found employment, the third day after my arrival, in stowing a sloop with a load of oil. It was new, dirty, and hard work for me; but I went at it with a glad heart and a willing hand. I was now my own master. It was a happy moment, the rapture of which can be understood only by those who have been slaves. It was the first work, the reward of which was to be entirely my own. There was no Master Hugh standing ready, the moment I earned the money, to rob me of it. I worked that day with a pleasure I had never before experienced. I was at work for myself and newly-married wife. It was to me the starting-point of a new existence. When I got through with that job, I went in pursuit of a job of calking; but such was the strength of prejudice against color, among the white calkers, that they refused to work with me, and of course I could get no employment.[4]

Finding my trade of no immediate benefit, I threw off my calking habiliments, and prepared myself to do any kind of work I could get to do. Mr. Johnson kindly let me have his wood-horse and saw, and I very soon found myself a plenty of work. There was no work too hard—none too dirty. I was ready to saw wood, shovel coal, carry wood, sweep the chimney, or roll oil casks,—all of which I did for nearly three years in New Bedford, before I became known to the anti-slavery world.

In about four months after I went to New Bedford, there came a young man to me, and inquired if I did not wish to take

---

4 I am told that colored persons can now get employment at
   calking in New Bedford—a result of anti-slavery effort.

the "Liberator." I told him I did; but, just having made my escape from slavery, I remarked that I was unable to pay for it then. I, however, finally became a subscriber to it. The paper came, and I read it from week to week with such feelings as it would be quite idle for me to attempt to describe. The paper became my meat and my drink. My soul was set all on fire. Its sympathy for my brethren in bonds—its scathing denunciations of slaveholders—its faithful exposures of slavery—and its powerful attacks upon the upholders of the institution—sent a thrill of joy through my soul, such as I had never felt before!

I had not long been a reader of the "Liberator," before I got a pretty correct idea of the principles, measures and spirit of the anti-slavery reform. I took right hold of the cause. I could do but little; but what I could, I did with a joyful heart, and never felt happier than when in an anti-slavery meeting. I seldom had much to say at the meetings, because what I wanted to say was said so much better by others. But, while attending an anti-slavery convention at Nantucket, on the 11th of August, 1841, I felt strongly moved to speak, and was at the same time much urged to do so by Mr. William C. Coffin, a gentleman who had heard me speak in the colored people's meeting at New Bedford. It was a severe cross, and I took it up reluctantly. The truth was, I felt myself a slave, and the idea of speaking to white people weighed me down. I spoke but a few moments, when I felt a degree of freedom, and said what I desired with considerable ease. From that time until now, I have been engaged in pleading the cause of my brethren—with what success, and with what devotion, I leave those acquainted with my labors to decide.

TWELVE
YEARS A SLAVE

BY SOLOMON NORTHUP

A Citizen of New-York,
Kidnapped in Washington City in 1841,
and Rescued in 1853, from a Cotton Plantation
Near the Red River, in Louisiana.

First Published in 1853

CHAPTER I

Having been born a freeman, and for more than thirty years enjoyed the blessings of liberty in a free State—and having at the end of that time been kidnapped and sold into Slavery, where I remained, until happily rescued in the month of January, 1853, after a bondage of twelve years—it has been suggested that an account of my life and fortunes would not be uninteresting to the public.

Since my return to liberty, I have not failed to perceive the increasing interest throughout the Northern States, in regard to the subject of Slavery. Works of fiction, professing to portray its features in their more pleasing as well as more repugnant aspects, have been circulated to an extent unprecedented, and, as I understand, have created a fruitful topic of comment and discussion.

I can speak of Slavery only so far as it came under my own observation—only so far as I have known and experienced it in my own person. My object is, to give a candid and truthful statement of facts: to repeat the story of my life, without exaggeration, leaving it for others to determine, whether even the pages of fiction present a picture of more cruel wrong or a severer bondage.

As far back as I have been able to ascertain, my ancestors on the paternal side were slaves in Rhode Island. They belonged to a family by the name of Northup, one of whom, removing to the State of New-York, settled at Hoosic, in Rensselaer county. He brought with him Mintus Northup, my father. On the death of this gentleman, which must have occurred some fifty years ago, my father became free, having been emancipated by a direction in his will.

Henry B. Northup, Esq., of Sandy Hill, a distinguished counselor at law, and the man to whom, under Providence, I am indebted for my present liberty, and my return to the society of my wife and children, is a relative of the family in which my forefathers were thus held to service, and from which they took the name I bear. To this fact may be attributed the persevering interest he has taken in my behalf.

Sometime after my father's liberation, he removed to the town of Minerva, Essex county, N. Y., where I was born, in the month of July, 1808. How long he remained in the latter place I have not the means of definitely ascertaining. From thence he removed to Granville, Washington county, near a place known as Slyborough, where, for some years, he labored on the farm of Clark Northup, also a relative of his old master; from thence he removed to the Alden farm, at Moss Street, a short distance north of the village of Sandy Hill; and from thence to the farm now owned by Russel Pratt, situated on the road leading from Fort Edward to Argyle, where he continued to reside until his death, which took place on the 22d day of November, 1829. He left a widow and two children—myself, and Joseph, an elder brother. The latter is still living in the county of Oswego, near the city of that name; my mother died during the period of my captivity.

Though born a slave, and laboring under the disadvantages to which my unfortunate race is subjected, my father was a man respected for his industry and integrity, as many now living, who well remember him, are ready to testify. His whole life was passed in the peaceful pursuits of agriculture, never seeking employment in those more menial positions, which seem to be especially allotted to the children of Africa. Besides giving us an education surpassing that ordinarily bestowed upon children in our condition, he acquired, by his diligence and economy, a sufficient property qualification to entitle him to the right of suffrage. He was accustomed to speak to us of his early life; and although at all times cherishing the warmest emotions of kindness, and even of affection towards the family, in whose house he had been a bondsman, he nevertheless comprehended the system of Slavery, and dwelt with sorrow on the degradation of his race. He endeavored to imbue our minds with sentiments of morality, and to teach us to place our trust and confidence in Him who regards the humblest as well as the highest of his creatures. How often since that time has the recollection of his paternal counsels occurred to me, while lying in a slave hut in the distant and sickly regions of Louisiana, smarting with the undeserved wounds which an inhuman master had inflicted, and longing only for the grave which had covered him, to shield me also from the lash of the oppressor. In the church-yard at Sandy Hill, an humble stone marks the spot where he reposes, after having worthily performed the duties appertaining to the lowly sphere wherein God had appointed him to walk.

Up to this period I had been principally engaged with my father in the labors of the farm. The leisure hours allowed me were generally either employed over my books, or playing on the violin—an amusement which was the ruling passion of my youth. It has also been the source of consolation since, affording pleasure to the simple beings with whom my lot was cast, and beguiling my own thoughts, for many hours, from the painful contemplation of my fate.

On Christmas day, 1829, I was married to Anne Hampton, a colored girl then living in the vicinity of our residence. The ceremony was performed at Fort Edward, by Timothy Eddy, Esq., a magistrate of that town, and still a prominent citizen of the place. She had resided a long time at Sandy Hill, with Mr. Baird, proprietor of the Eagle Tavern, and also in the family of Rev. Alexander Proudfit, of Salem. This gentleman for many years had presided over the Presbyterian society at the latter place, and was widely distinguished for his learning and piety. Anne still holds in grateful remembrance the exceeding kindness and the excellent counsels of that good man. She is not able to determine the exact line of her descent, but the blood of three races mingles in her veins. It is difficult to tell whether the red, white, or black predominates. The union of them all, however, in her origin, has given her a singular but pleasing expression, such as is rarely to be seen. Though somewhat resembling, yet she cannot properly be styled a quadroon, a class to which, I have omitted to mention, my mother belonged.

I had just now passed the period of my minority, having reached the age of twenty-one years in the month of July previous. Deprived of the advice and assistance of my father, with a wife dependent upon me for support, I resolved to enter upon a life of industry; and notwithstanding the obstacle of color, and the consciousness of my lowly state, indulged in pleasant dreams of a good time coming, when the possession of some humble habitation, with a few surrounding acres, should reward my labors, and bring me the means of happiness and comfort.

From the time of my marriage to this day the love I have borne my wife has been sincere and unabated; and only those who have felt the glowing tenderness a father cherishes for his offspring, can appreciate my affection for the beloved children which have since been born to us. This much I deem appropriate and necessary to say, in order that those who read these pages, may comprehend the poignancy of those sufferings I have been doomed to bear.

Immediately upon our marriage we commenced house-keeping, in the old yellow building then standing at the southern extremity of Fort Edward village, and which has since been transformed into a modern mansion, and lately occupied by Captain Lathrop. It is known as the Fort House. In this building the courts were sometime held after the organization of the county. It was also occupied by Burgoyne in 1777, being situated near the old Fort on the left bank of the Hudson.

During the winter I was employed with others repairing the Champlain Canal, on that section over which William Van Nortwick was superintendent. David McEachron had the immediate charge of the men in whose company I labored. By the time the canal opened in the spring, I was enabled, from the savings of my wages, to purchase a pair of horses, and other things necessarily required in the business of navigation.

Having hired several efficient hands to assist me, I entered into contracts for the transportation of large rafts of timber from Lake Champlain to Troy. Dyer Beckwith and a Mr. Bartemy, of Whitehall, accompanied me on several trips. During the season I became perfectly familiar with the art and mysteries of rafting—a knowledge which afterwards enabled me to render profitable service to a worthy master, and to astonish the simple-witted lumbermen on the banks of the Bayou Bœuf.

In one of my voyages down Lake Champlain, I was induced to make a visit to Canada. Repairing to Montreal, I visited the cathedral and other places of interest in that city, from whence I continued my excursion to Kingston and other towns, obtaining a knowledge of localities, which was also of service to me afterwards, as will appear towards the close of this narrative.

Having completed my contracts on the canal satisfactorily to myself and to my employer, and not wishing to remain idle, now that the navigation of the canal was again suspended, I entered into another contract with Medad Gunn, to cut a large quantity of wood. In this business I was engaged during the winter of 1831-32.

With the return of spring, Anne and myself conceived the project of taking a farm in the neighborhood. I had been accustomed from earliest youth to agricultural labors, and it was an occupation congenial to my tastes. I accordingly entered into arrangements for a part of the old Alden farm, on which my father formerly resided. With one cow, one swine, a yoke of fine oxen I had lately purchased of Lewis Brown, in Hartford, and other personal property and effects, we proceeded to our new home in Kingsbury. That year I planted twenty-five acres of corn, sowed large fields of oats, and commenced farming upon as large a scale as my utmost means would permit. Anne

243

was diligent about the house affairs, while I toiled laboriously in the field.

On this place we continued to reside until 1834. In the winter season I had numerous calls to play on the violin. Wherever the young people assembled to dance, I was almost invariably there. Throughout the surrounding villages my fiddle was notorious. Anne, also, during her long residence at the Eagle Tavern, had become somewhat famous as a cook. During court weeks, and on public occasions, she was employed at high wages in the kitchen at Sherrill's Coffee House.

We always returned home from the performance of these services with money in our pockets; so that, with fiddling, cooking, and farming, we soon found ourselves in the possession of abundance, and, in fact, leading a happy and prosperous life. Well, indeed, would it have been for us had we remained on the farm at Kingsbury; but the time came when the next step was to be taken towards the cruel destiny that awaited me.

In March, 1834, we removed to Saratoga Springs. We occupied a house belonging to Daniel O'Brien, on the north side of Washington street. At that time Isaac Taylor kept a large boarding house, known as Washington Hall, at the north end of Broadway. He employed me to drive a hack, in which capacity I worked for him two years. After this time I was generally employed through the visiting season, as also was Anne, in the United States Hotel, and other public houses of the place. In winter seasons I relied upon my violin, though during the construction of the Troy and Saratoga railroad, I performed many hard days' labor upon it.

I was in the habit, at Saratoga, of purchasing articles necessary for my family at the stores of Mr. Cephas Parker and Mr. William Perry, gentlemen towards whom, for many acts of kindness, I entertained feelings of strong regard. It was for this reason that, twelve years afterwards, I caused to be directed to them the letter, which is hereinafter inserted, and which was the means, in the hands of Mr. Northup, of my fortunate deliverance.

While living at the United States Hotel, I frequently met with slaves, who had accompanied their masters from the South. They were always well dressed and well provided for, leading apparently an easy life, with but few of its ordinary troubles to perplex them. Many times they entered into conversation with me on the subject of Slavery. Almost uniformly I found they cherished a secret desire for liberty. Some of them expressed the most ardent anxiety to escape, and consulted me on the best method of effecting it. The fear of punishment, however, which they knew was certain to attend their re-capture and return, in all cases proved sufficient to deter them from the experiment. Having all my life breathed the free air of the North, and conscious that I possessed the same feelings and affections that find a place in the white man's breast; conscious, moreover, of an intelligence equal to that of some men, at least, with a fairer skin, I was too ignorant, perhaps too independent, to conceive how any one could be content to live in the abject condition of a slave. I could not comprehend the justice of that law, or that religion, which upholds or recognizes the principle of Slavery; and never once, I am proud to say, did I fail to counsel any one who came to me, to watch his opportunity, and strike for freedom.

I continued to reside at Saratoga until the spring of 1841. The flattering anticipations which, seven years before, had seduced us from the quiet farm-house, on the east side of the Hudson, had not been realized. Though always in comfortable circumstances, we had not prospered. The society and associations at that world-renowned watering place, were not calculated to preserve the simple habits of industry and economy to which I had been accustomed, but, on the contrary, to substitute others in their stead, tending to shiftlessness and extravagance.

At this time we were the parents of three children—

Elizabeth, Margaret, and Alonzo. Elizabeth, the eldest, was in her tenth year; Margaret was two years younger, and little Alonzo had just passed his fifth birth-day. They filled our house with gladness. Their young voices were music in our ears. Many an airy castle did their mother and myself build for the little innocents. When not at labor I was always walking with them, clad in their best attire, through the streets and groves of Saratoga. Their presence was my delight; and I clasped them to my bosom with as warm and tender love as if their clouded skins had been as white as snow.

Thus far the history of my life presents nothing whatever unusual—nothing but the common hopes, and loves, and labors of an obscure colored man, making his humble progress in the world. But now I had reached a turning point in my existence— reached the threshold of unutterable wrong, and sorrow, and despair. Now had I approached within the shadow of the cloud, into the thick darkness whereof I was soon to disappear, thenceforward to be hidden from the eyes of all my kindred, and shut out from the sweet light of liberty, for many a weary year.

CHAPTER II

One morning, towards the latter part of the month of March, 1841, having at that time no particular business to engage my attention, I was walking about the village of Saratoga Springs, thinking to myself where I might obtain some present employment, until the busy season should arrive. Anne, as was her usual custom, had gone over to Sandy Hill, a distance of some twenty miles, to take charge of the culinary department at Sherrill's Coffee House, during the session of the court. Elizabeth, I think, had accompanied her. Margaret and Alonzo were with their aunt at Saratoga.

On the corner of Congress street and Broadway, near the tavern, then, and for aught I know to the contrary, still kept by Mr. Moon, I was met by two gentlemen of respectable appearance, both of whom were entirely unknown to me. I have the impression that they were introduced to me by some one of my acquaintances, but who, I have in vain endeavored to recall, with the remark that I was an expert player on the violin.

At any rate, they immediately entered into conversation on that subject, making numerous inquiries touching my proficiency in that respect. My responses being to all appearances satisfactory, they proposed to engage my services for a short period, stating, at the same time, I was just such a person as their business required. Their names, as they afterwards gave them to me, were Merrill Brown and Abram Hamilton, though whether these were their true appellations, I have strong reasons to doubt. The former was a man apparently forty years of age, somewhat short and thick-set, with a countenance indicating shrewdness and intelligence. He wore a black frock coat and black hat, and said he resided either at Rochester or at Syracuse.

The latter was a young man of fair complexion and light eyes, and, I should judge, had not passed the age of twenty-five. He was tall and slender, dressed in a snuff-colored coat, with glossy hat, and vest of elegant pattern. His whole apparel was in the extreme of fashion. His appearance was somewhat effeminate, but prepossessing, and there was about him an easy air, that showed he had mingled with the world. They were connected, as they informed me, with a circus company, then in the city of Washington; that they were on their way thither to rejoin it, having left it for a short time to make an excursion northward, for the purpose of seeing the country, and were paying their expenses by an occasional exhibition. They also remarked that they had found much difficulty in procuring music for their entertainments, and that if I would accompany them as far as New-York, they would give me one dollar for each day's services, and three dollars in addition for every night I played at their performances, besides sufficient to pay the expenses of my return from New-York to Saratoga.

I at once accepted the tempting offer, both for the reward it promised, and from a desire to visit the metropolis. They were anxious to leave immediately. Thinking my absence would be brief, I did not deem it necessary to write to Anne whither I had gone; in fact supposing that my return, perhaps, would be as soon as hers. So taking a change of linen and my violin, I was ready to depart. The carriage was brought round—a covered one, drawn by a pair of noble bays, altogether forming an elegant establishment. Their baggage, consisting of three large trunks, was fastened on the rack, and mounting to the driver's seat, while they took their places in the rear, I drove away from Saratoga on the road to Albany, elated with my new position, and happy as I had ever been, on any day in all my life.

We passed through Ballston, and striking the ridge road, as it is called, if my memory correctly serves me, followed it direct to Albany. We reached that city before dark, and stopped at a hotel southward from the Museum.

248

This night I had an opportunity of witnessing one of their performances—the only one, during the whole period I was with them. Hamilton was stationed at the door; I formed the orchestra, while Brown provided the entertainment. It consisted in throwing balls, dancing on the rope, frying pancakes in a hat, causing invisible pigs to squeal, and other like feats of ventriloquism and legerdemain. The audience was extraordinarily sparse, and not of the selectest character at that, and Hamilton's report of the proceeds presented but a "beggarly account of empty boxes."

Early next morning we renewed our journey. The burden of their conversation now was the expression of an anxiety to reach the circus without delay. They hurried forward, without again stopping to exhibit, and in due course of time, we reached New-York, taking lodgings at a house on the west side of the city, in a street running from Broadway to the river. I supposed my journey was at an end, and expected in a day or two at least, to return to my friends and family at Saratoga. Brown and Hamilton, however, began to importune me to continue with them to Washington. They alleged that immediately on their arrival, now that the summer season was approaching, the circus would set out for the north. They promised me a situation and high wages if I would accompany them. Largely did they expatiate on the advantages that would result to me, and such were the flattering representations they made, that I finally concluded to accept the offer.

The next morning they suggested that, inasmuch as we were about entering a slave State, it would be well, before leaving New-York, to procure free papers. The idea struck me as a prudent one, though I think it would scarcely have occurred to me, had they not proposed it. We proceeded at once to what I understood to be the Custom House. They made oath to certain facts showing I was a free man. A paper was drawn up and handed us, with the direction to take it to the clerk's office. We did so, and the clerk having added something to it, for which he was paid six shillings, we returned again to the Custom House. Some further formalities were gone through with before it was completed, when, paying the officer two dollars, I placed the papers in my pocket, and started with my two friends to our hotel. I thought at the time, I must confess, that the papers were scarcely worth the cost of obtaining them—the apprehension of danger to my personal safety never having suggested itself to me in the remotest manner. The clerk, to whom we were directed, I remember, made a memorandum in a large book, which, I presume, is in the office yet. A reference to the entries during the latter part of March, or first of April, 1841, I have no doubt will satisfy the incredulous, at least so far as this particular transaction is concerned.

With the evidence of freedom in my possession, the next day after our arrival in New-York, we crossed the ferry to Jersey City, and took the road to Philadelphia. Here we remained one night, continuing our journey towards Baltimore early in the morning. In due time, we arrived in the latter city, and stopped at a hotel near the railroad depot, either kept by a Mr. Rathbone, or known as the Rathbone House. All the way from New-York, their anxiety to reach the circus seemed to grow more and more intense. We left the carriage at Baltimore, and entering the cars, proceeded to Washington, at which place we arrived just at nightfall, the evening previous to the funeral of General Harrison, and stopped at Gadsby's Hotel, on Pennsylvania Avenue.

After supper they called me to their apartments, and paid me forty-three dollars, a sum greater than my wages amounted to, which act of generosity was in consequence, they said, of their not having exhibited as often as they had given me to anticipate, during our trip from Saratoga. They moreover informed me that it had been the intention of the circus company to leave Washington the next morning, but that on account of the funeral, they had concluded to remain another day. They were then, as they had been from the time of our first meeting, extremely kind. No opportunity was omitted of addressing me in the language of approbation; while, on the other hand, I was certainly much prepossessed in their favor. I gave them my confidence without reserve, and would freely have trusted them to almost any extent. Their constant conversation and manner towards me—their foresight in suggesting the idea of free papers, and a hundred other little acts, unnecessary to be repeated—all indicated that they were friends indeed, sincerely solicitous for my welfare. I know not but they were. I know not but they were innocent of the great wickedness of which I now believe them guilty. Whether they were accessory to my misfortunes—subtle and inhuman monsters in the shape of men—designedly luring me away from home and family, and liberty, for the sake of gold—those who read these pages will have the same means of determining as myself. If they were innocent, my sudden disappearance must have been unaccountable indeed; but revolving in my mind all the attending circumstances, I never yet could indulge, towards them, so charitable a supposition.

After receiving the money from them, of which they appeared to have an abundance, they advised me not to go into the streets that night, inasmuch as I was unacquainted with the customs of the city. Promising to remember their advice, I left them together, and soon after was shown by a colored servant to a sleeping room in the back part of the hotel, on the ground floor. I laid down to rest, thinking of home and wife, and children, and the long distance that stretched between us, until I fell asleep. But no good angel of pity came to my bedside, bidding me to fly—no voice of mercy forewarned me in my dreams of the trials that were just at hand.

The next day there was a great pageant in Washington. The roar of cannon and the tolling of bells filled the air, while many houses were shrouded with crape, and the streets were black with people. As the day advanced, the procession made its appearance, coming slowly through the Avenue, carriage after carriage, in long succession, while thousands upon thousands

251

followed on foot—all moving to the sound of melancholy music. They were bearing the dead body of Harrison to the grave.

From early in the morning, I was constantly in the company of Hamilton and Brown. They were the only persons I knew in Washington. We stood together as the funeral pomp passed by. I remember distinctly how the window glass would break and rattle to the ground, after each report of the cannon they were firing in the burial ground. We went to the Capitol, and walked a long time about the grounds. In the afternoon, they strolled towards the President's House, all the time keeping me near to them, and pointing out various places of interest. As yet, I had seen nothing of the circus. In fact, I had thought of it but little, if at all, amidst the excitement of the day.

My friends, several times during the afternoon, entered drinking saloons, and called for liquor. They were by no means in the habit, however, so far as I knew them, of indulging to excess. On these occasions, after serving themselves, they would pour out a glass and hand it to me. I did not become intoxicated, as may be inferred from what subsequently occurred. Towards evening, and soon after partaking of one of these potations, I began to experience most unpleasant sensations. I felt extremely ill. My head commenced aching—a dull, heavy pain, inexpressibly disagreeable. At the supper table, I was without appetite; the sight and flavor of food was nauseous. About dark the same servant conducted me to the room I had occupied the previous night. Brown and Hamilton advised me to retire, commiserating me kindly, and expressing hopes that I would be better in the morning. Divesting myself of coat and boots merely, I threw myself upon the bed. It was impossible to sleep. The pain in my head continued to increase, until it became almost unbearable. In a short time I became thirsty. My lips were parched. I could think of nothing but water—of lakes and flowing rivers, of brooks where I had stooped to drink, and of the dripping bucket, rising with its cool and overflowing nectar, from the bottom of the well. Towards midnight, as near as I could judge, I arose, unable longer to bear such intensity of thirst. I was a stranger in the house, and knew nothing of its apartments. There was no one up, as I could observe. Groping about at random, I knew not where, I found the way at last to a kitchen in the basement. Two or three colored servants were moving through it, one of whom, a woman, gave me two glasses of water. It afforded momentary relief, but by the time I had reached my room again, the same burning desire of drink, the same tormenting thirst, had again returned. It was even more torturing than before, as was also the wild pain in my head, if such a thing could be. I was in sore distress—in most excruciating agony! I seemed to stand on the brink of madness! The memory of that night of horrible suffering will follow me to the grave.

In the course of an hour or more after my return from the kitchen, I was conscious of some one entering my room. There seemed to be several—a mingling of various voices,—but how many, or who they were, I cannot tell. Whether Brown and Hamilton were among them, is a mere matter of conjecture. I only remember, with any degree of distinctness, that I was told it was necessary to go to a physician and procure medicine, and that pulling on my boots, without coat or hat, I followed them through a long passage-way, or alley, into the open street. It ran out at right angles from Pennsylvania Avenue. On the opposite side there was a light burning in a window. My impression is there were then three persons with me, but it is altogether indefinite and vague, and like the memory of a painful dream. Going towards the light, which I imagined proceeded from a physician's office, and which seemed to recede as I advanced, is the last glimmering recollection I can now recall. From that moment I was insensible. How long I remained in that condition—whether only that night, or many days and nights—I do not know; but when consciousness returned, I found myself alone, in utter darkness, and in chains.

The pain in my head had subsided in a measure, but I was very faint and weak. I was sitting upon a low bench, made of rough boards, and without coat or hat. I was hand-cuffed. Around my ankles also were a pair of heavy fetters. One end of a chain was fastened to a large ring in the floor, the other to the fetters on my ankles. I tried in vain to stand upon my feet. Waking from such a painful trance, it was some time before I could collect my thoughts. Where was I? What was the meaning of these chains? Where were Brown and Hamilton? What had I done to deserve imprisonment in such a dungeon? I could not comprehend. There was a blank of some indefinite period, preceding my awakening in that lonely place, the events of which the utmost stretch of memory was unable to recall. I listened intently for some sign or sound of life, but nothing broke the oppressive silence, save the clinking of my chains, whenever I chanced to move. I spoke aloud, but the sound of my voice startled me. I felt of my pockets, so far as the fetters would allow—far enough, indeed, to ascertain that I had not only been robbed of liberty, but that my money and free papers were also gone! Then did the idea begin to break upon my mind, at first dim and confused, that I had been kidnapped. But that I thought was incredible. There must have been some misapprehension— some unfortunate mistake. It could not be that a free citizen of New-York, who had wronged no man, nor violated any law, should be dealt with thus inhumanly. The more I contemplated my situation, however, the more I became confirmed in my suspicions. It was a desolate thought, indeed. I felt there was no trust or mercy in unfeeling man; and commending myself to the God of the oppressed, bowed my head upon my fettered hands, and wept most bitterly.

CHAPTER III

Some three hours elapsed, during which time I remained seated on the low bench, absorbed in painful meditations. At length I heard the crowing of a cock, and soon a distant rumbling sound, as of carriages hurrying through the streets, came to my ears, and I knew that it was day. No ray of light, however, penetrated my prison. Finally, I heard footsteps immediately overhead, as of some one walking to and fro. It occurred to me then that I must be in an underground apartment, and the damp, mouldy odors of the place confirmed the supposition. The noise above continued for at least an hour, when, at last, I heard footsteps approaching from without. A key rattled in the lock—a strong door swung back upon its hinges, admitting a flood of light, and two men entered and stood before me. One of them was a large, powerful man, forty years of age, perhaps, with dark, chestnut-colored hair, slightly interspersed with gray. His face was full, his complexion flush, his features grossly coarse, expressive of nothing but cruelty and cunning. He was about five feet ten inches high, of full habit, and, without prejudice, I must be allowed to say, was a man whose whole appearance was sinister and repugnant. His name was James H. Burch, as I learned afterwards—a well-known slave-dealer in Washington; and then, or lately, connected in business, as a partner, with Theophilus Freeman, of New-Orleans. The person who accompanied him was a simple lackey, named Ebenezer Radburn, who acted merely in the capacity of turnkey. Both of these men still live in Washington, or did, at the time of my return through that city from slavery in January last.

The light admitted through the open door enabled me to observe the room in which I was confined. It was about twelve

255

feet square—the walls of solid masonry. The floor was of heavy plank. There was one small window, crossed with great iron bars, with an outside shutter, securely fastened.

An iron-bound door led into an adjoining cell, or vault, wholly destitute of windows, or any means of admitting light. The furniture of the room in which I was, consisted of the wooden bench on which I sat, an old-fashioned, dirty box stove, and besides these, in either cell, there was neither bed, nor blanket, nor any other thing whatever. The door, through which Burch and Radburn entered, led through a small passage, up a flight of steps into a yard, surrounded by a brick wall ten or twelve feet high, immediately in rear of a building of the same width as itself. The yard extended rearward from the house about thirty feet. In one part of the wall there was a strongly ironed door, opening into a narrow, covered passage, leading along one side of the house into the street. The doom of the colored man, upon whom the door leading out of that narrow passage closed, was sealed. The top of the wall supported one end of a roof, which ascended inwards, forming a kind of open shed. Underneath the roof there was a crazy loft all round, where slaves, if so disposed, might sleep at night, or in inclement weather seek shelter from the storm. It was like a farmer's barnyard in most respects, save it was so constructed that the outside world could never see the human cattle that were herded there.

The building to which the yard was attached, was two stories high, fronting on one of the public streets of Washington. Its outside presented only the appearance of a quiet private residence. A stranger looking at it, would never have dreamed of its execrable uses. Strange as it may seem, within plain sight of this same house, looking down from its commanding height upon it, was the Capitol. The voices of patriotic representatives boasting of freedom and equality, and the rattling of the poor slave's chains, almost commingled. A slave pen within the very shadow of the Capitol!

Such is a correct description as it was in 1841, of Williams' slave pen in Washington, in one of the cellars of which I found myself so unaccountably confined.

"Well, my boy, how do you feel now?" said Burch, as he entered through the open door. I replied that I was sick, and inquired the cause of my imprisonment. He answered that I was his slave—that he had bought me, and that he was about to send me to New-Orleans. I asserted, aloud and boldly, that I was a free man—a resident of Saratoga, where I had a wife and children, who were also free, and that my name was Northup. I complained bitterly of the strange treatment I had received, and threatened, upon my liberation, to have satisfaction for the wrong. He denied that I was free, and with an emphatic oath, declared that I came from Georgia. Again and again I asserted I was no man's slave, and insisted upon his taking off my chains at once. He endeavored to hush me, as if he feared my voice would be overheard. But I would not be silent, and denounced the authors of my imprisonment, whoever they might be, as unmitigated villains. Finding he could not quiet me, he flew into a towering passion. With blasphemous oaths, he called me a black liar, a runaway from Georgia, and every other profane and vulgar epithet that the most indecent fancy could conceive.

During this time Radburn was standing silently by. His business was, to oversee this human, or rather inhuman stable, receiving slaves, feeding and whipping them, at the rate of two shillings a head per day. Turning to him, Burch ordered the paddle and cat-o'-ninetails to be brought in. He disappeared, and in a few moments returned with these instruments of torture. The paddle, as it is termed in slave-beating parlance, or at least the one with which I first became acquainted, and of which I now speak, was a piece of hard-wood board, eighteen or twenty inches long, moulded to the shape of an old-fashioned pudding stick, or ordinary oar. The flattened portion, which was about the size in circumference of two open hands, was bored with a small auger in numerous places. The cat was a large rope of many strands—the strands unraveled, and a knot tied at the extremity of each.

As soon as these formidable whips appeared, I was seized by both of them, and roughly divested of my clothing. My feet, as has been stated, were fastened to the floor. Drawing me over the bench, face downwards, Radburn placed his heavy foot upon the fetters, between my wrists, holding them painfully to the floor. With the paddle, Burch commenced beating me. Blow after blow was inflicted upon my naked body. When his unrelenting arm grew tired, he stopped and asked if I still insisted I was a free man. I did insist upon it, and then the blows were renewed, faster and more energetically, if possible, than before. When again tired, he would repeat the same question, and receiving the same answer, continue his cruel labor. All this time, the incarnate devil was uttering most fiendish oaths. At length the paddle broke, leaving the useless handle in his hand. Still I would not yield. All his brutal blows could not force from my lips the foul lie that I was a slave. Casting madly on the floor the handle of the broken paddle, he seized the rope. This was far more painful than the other. I struggled with all my power, but it was in vain. I prayed for mercy, but my prayer was only answered with imprecations and with stripes. I thought I must die beneath the lashes of the accursed brute. Even now the flesh crawls upon my bones, as I recall the scene. I was all on fire. My sufferings I can compare to nothing else than the burning agonies of hell!

At last I became silent to his repeated questions. I would make no reply. In fact, I was becoming almost unable to speak. Still he plied the lash without stint upon my poor body, until it seemed that the lacerated flesh was stripped from my bones at every stroke. A man with a particle of mercy in his soul would not have beaten even a dog so cruelly. At length Radburn said that it was useless to whip me any more—that I would be sore enough. Thereupon, Burch desisted, saying, with an admonitory shake of his fist in my face, and hissing the words through his firm-set teeth, that if ever I dared to utter again that I was entitled to my freedom, that I had been kidnapped, or any thing whatever of the kind, the castigation I had just received was nothing in comparison with what would follow.

He swore that he would either conquer or kill me. With these consolatory words, the fetters were taken from my wrists, my feet still remaining fastened to the ring; the shutter of the little barred window, which had been opened, was again closed, and going out, locking the great door behind them, I was left in darkness as before.

In an hour, perhaps two, my heart leaped to my throat, as the key rattled in the door again. I, who had been so lonely, and who had longed so ardently to see some one, I cared not who, now shuddered at the thought of man's approach. A human face was fearful to me, especially a white one. Radburn entered, bringing with him, on a tin plate, a piece of shriveled fried pork, a slice of bread and a cup of water. He asked me how I felt, and remarked that I had received a pretty severe flogging. He remonstrated with me against the propriety of asserting my freedom. In rather a patronizing and confidential manner, he gave it to me as his advice, that the less I said on that subject the better it would be for me. The man evidently endeavored to appear kind—whether touched at the sight of my sad condition, or with the view of silencing, on my part, any further expression of my rights, it is not necessary now to conjecture. He unlocked the fetters from my ankles, opened the shutters of the little window, and departed, leaving me again alone.

By this time I had become stiff and sore; my body was covered with blisters, and it was with great pain and difficulty that I could move. From the window I could observe nothing but the roof resting on the adjacent wall. At night I laid down upon the damp, hard floor, without any pillow or covering whatever. Punctually, twice a day, Radburn came in, with his pork, and bread, and water. I had but little appetite, though I was tormented with continual thirst. My wounds would not permit me to remain but a few minutes in any one position; so, sitting, or standing, or moving slowly round, I passed the days and nights. I was heart sick and discouraged. Thoughts of my family, of my wife and children, continually occupied my mind. When sleep overpowered me I dreamed of them—dreamed I was again in Saratoga—that I could see their faces, and hear their voices calling me. Awakening from the pleasant phantasms of sleep to the bitter realities around me, I could but groan and weep. Still my spirit was not broken. I indulged the anticipation of escape, and that speedily. It was impossible, I reasoned, that men could be so unjust as to detain me as a slave, when the truth of my case was known. Burch, ascertaining I was no runaway from Georgia, would certainly let me go. Though suspicions of Brown and Hamilton were not unfrequent, I could not reconcile myself to the idea that they were instrumental to my imprisonment. Surely they would seek me out—they would deliver me from thraldom. Alas! I had not then learned the measure of "man's inhumanity to man," nor to what limitless extent of wickedness he will go for the love of gain.

In the course of several days the outer door was thrown open, allowing me the liberty of the yard. There I found three slaves—one of them a lad of ten years, the others young men of about twenty and twenty-five. I was not long in forming an acquaintance, and learning their names and the particulars of their history.

The eldest was a colored man named Clemens Ray. He had lived in Washington; had driven a hack, and worked in a livery stable there for a long time. He was very intelligent, and fully comprehended his situation. The thought of going south overwhelmed him with grief. Burch had purchased him a few days before, and had placed him there until such time as he was ready to send him to the New-Orleans market. From him I learned for the first time that I was in William's Slave Pen, a place I had never heard of previously. He described to me the uses for which it was designed. I repeated to him the particulars of my unhappy story, but he could only give me the consolation of his sympathy. He also advised me to be silent henceforth on the subject of my freedom; for, knowing the character of Burch, he assured me that it would only be attended with renewed whipping. The next eldest was named John Williams. He was raised in Virginia, not far from Washington. Burch had taken him in payment of a debt, and he constantly entertained the hope that his master would redeem him—a hope that was subsequently realized. The lad was a sprightly child, that answered to the name of Randall. Most of the time he was playing about the yard, but occasionally would cry, calling for his mother, and wondering when she would come. His mother's absence seemed to be the great and only grief in his little heart. He was too young to realize his condition, and when the memory of his mother was not in his mind, he amused us with his pleasant pranks.

At night, Ray, Williams, and the boy, slept in the loft of the shed, while I was locked in the cell. Finally we were each provided with blankets, such as are used upon horses—the only bedding I was allowed to have for twelve years afterwards. Ray and Williams asked me many questions about New-York—how colored people were treated there; how they could have homes and families of their own, with none to disturb and oppress them; and Ray, especially, sighed continually for freedom. Such conversations, however, were not in the hearing of Burch, or the keeper Radburn. Aspirations such as these would have brought down the lash upon our backs.

It is necessary in this narrative, in order to present a full and truthful statement of all the principal events in the history of my life, and to portray the institution of Slavery as I have seen and known it, to speak of well-known places, and of many persons who are yet living. I am, and always was, an entire stranger in Washington and its vicinity—aside from Burch and Radburn, knowing no man there, except as I have heard of them through my enslaved companions. What I am about to say, if false, can be easily contradicted.

261

I remained in Williams' slave pen about two weeks. The night previous to my departure a woman was brought in, weeping bitterly, and leading by the hand a little child. They were Randall's mother and half-sister. On meeting them he was overjoyed, clinging to her dress, kissing the child, and exhibiting every demonstration of delight. The mother also clasped him in her arms, embraced him tenderly, and gazed at him fondly through her tears, calling him by many an endearing name.

Emily, the child, was seven or eight years old, of light complexion, and with a face of admirable beauty. Her hair fell in curls around her neck, while the style and richness of her dress, and the neatness of her whole appearance indicated she had been brought up in the midst of wealth. She was a sweet child indeed. The woman also was arrayed in silk, with rings upon her fingers, and golden ornaments suspended from her ears. Her air and manners, the correctness and propriety of her language—all showed, evidently, that she had sometime stood above the common level of a slave. She seemed to be amazed at finding herself in such a place as that. It was plainly a sudden and unexpected turn of fortune that had brought her there. Filling the air with her complainings, she was hustled, with the children and myself, into the cell. Language can convey but an inadequate impression of the lamentations to which she gave incessant utterance. Throwing herself upon the floor, and encircling the children in her arms, she poured forth such touching words as only maternal love and kindness can suggest. They nestled closely to her, as if *there* only was there any safety or protection. At last they slept, their heads resting upon her lap. While they slumbered, she smoothed the hair back from their little foreheads, and talked to them all night long. She called them her darlings—her sweet babes—poor innocent things, that knew not the misery they were destined to endure. Soon they would have no mother to comfort them—they would be taken from her. What would become of them? Oh! she could not live away from her little Emmy and her dear boy. They had always

262

been good children, and had such loving ways. It would break her heart, God knew, she said, if they were taken from her; and yet she knew they meant to sell them, and, may be, they would be separated, and could never see each other any more. It was enough to melt a heart of stone to listen to the pitiful expressions of that desolate and distracted mother. Her name was Eliza; and this was the story of her life, as she afterwards related it:

She was the slave of Elisha Berry, a rich man, living in the neighborhood of Washington. She was born, I think she said, on his plantation. Years before, he had fallen into dissipated habits, and quarreled with his wife. In fact, soon after the birth of Randall, they separated. Leaving his wife and daughter in the house they had always occupied, he erected a new one near by, on the estate. Into this house he brought Eliza; and, on condition of her living with him, she and her children were to be emancipated. She resided with him there nine years, with servants to attend upon her, and provided with every comfort and luxury of life. Emily was his child! Finally, her young mistress, who had always remained with her mother at the homestead, married a Mr. Jacob Brooks. At length, for some cause, (as I gathered from her relation,) beyond Berry's control, a division of his property was made. She and her children fell to the share of Mr. Brooks. During the nine years she had lived with Berry, in consequence of the position she was compelled to occupy, she and Emily had become the object of Mrs. Berry and her daughter's hatred and dislike. Berry himself she represented as a man of naturally a kind heart, who always promised her that she should have her freedom, and who, she had no doubt, would grant it to her then, if it were only in his power. As soon as they thus came into the possession and control of the daughter, it became very manifest they would not live long together. The sight of Eliza seemed to be odious to Mrs. Brooks; neither could she bear to look upon the child, half-sister, and beautiful as she was!

The day she was led into the pen, Brooks had brought her from the estate into the city, under pretence that the time had

263

come when her free papers were to be executed, in fulfillment of her master's promise. Elated at the prospect of immediate liberty, she decked herself and little Emmy in their best apparel, and accompanied him with a joyful heart. On their arrival in the city, instead of being baptized into the family of freemen, she was delivered to the trader Burch. The paper that was executed was a bill of sale. The hope of years was blasted in a moment. From the height of most exulting happiness to the utmost depths of wretchedness, she had that day descended. No wonder that she wept, and filled the pen with wailings and expressions of heart-rending woe.

Eliza is now dead. Far up the Red River, where it pours its waters sluggishly through the unhealthy low lands of Louisiana, she rests in the grave at last—the only resting place of the poor slave! How all her fears were realized—how she mourned day and night, and never would be comforted—how, as she predicted, her heart did indeed break, with the burden of maternal sorrow, will be seen as the narrative proceeds.

CHAPTER IV

At intervals during the first night of Eliza's incarceration in the pen, she complained bitterly of Jacob Brooks, her young mistress' husband. She declared that had she been aware of the deception he intended to practice upon her, he never would have brought her there alive. They had chosen the opportunity of getting her away when Master Berry was absent from the plantation. He had always been kind to her. She wished that she could see him; but she knew that even he was unable now to rescue her. Then would she commence weeping again—kissing the sleeping children—talking first to one, then to the other, as they lay in their unconscious slumbers, with their heads upon her lap. So wore the long night away; and when the morning dawned, and night had come again, still she kept mourning on, and would not be consoled.

About midnight following, the cell door opened, and Burch and Radburn entered, with lanterns in their hands. Burch, with an oath, ordered us to roll up our blankets without delay, and get ready to go on board the boat. He swore we would be left unless we hurried fast. He aroused the children from their slumbers with a rough shake, and said they were d—d sleepy, it appeared. Going out into the yard, he called Clem Ray, ordering him to leave the loft and come into the cell, and bring his blanket with him. When Clem appeared, he placed us side by side, and fastened us together with hand-cuffs—my left hand to his right. John Williams had been taken out a day or two before, his master having redeemed him, greatly to his delight. Clem and I were ordered to march, Eliza and the children following. We were conducted into the yard, from thence into the covered passage, and up a flight of steps through a side door into the upper room, where I had heard the walking to and fro. Its furniture was a stove, a few old chairs, and a long table, covered with papers. It was a white-washed room, without any carpet on the floor, and seemed a sort of office. By one of the windows, I remember, hung a rusty sword, which attracted my attention. Burch's trunk was there. In obedience to his orders, I took hold of one of its handles with my unfettered hand, while he taking hold of the other, we proceeded out of the front door into the street in the same order as we had left the cell.

It was a dark night. All was quiet. I could see lights, or the reflection of them, over towards Pennsylvania Avenue, but there was no one, not even a straggler, to be seen. I was almost resolved to attempt to break away. Had I not been hand-cuffed the attempt would certainly have been made, whatever consequence might have followed. Radburn was in the rear, carrying a large stick, and hurrying up the children as fast as the little ones could walk. So we passed, hand-cuffed and in silence, through the streets of Washington—through the Capital of a nation, whose theory of government, we are told, rests on the foundation of man's inalienable right to life, liberty, and the pursuit of happiness! Hail! Columbia, happy land, indeed!

Reaching the steamboat, we were quickly hustled into the hold, among barrels and boxes of freight. A colored servant brought a light, the bell rung, and soon the vessel started down the Potomac, carrying us we knew not where. The bell tolled as we passed the tomb of Washington! Burch, no doubt, with uncovered head, bowed reverently before the sacred ashes of the man who devoted his illustrious life to the liberty of his country.

None of us slept that night but Randall and little Emmy. For the first time Clem Ray was wholly overcome. To him the idea of going south was terrible in the extreme. He was leaving the friends and associations of his youth—every thing that was dear and precious to his heart—in all probability never to return. He and Eliza mingled their tears together, bemoaning their cruel fate. For my own part, difficult as it was, I endeavored to keep up my spirits. I resolved in my mind a hundred plans of escape, and fully determined to make the attempt the first desperate chance that offered. I had by this time become satisfied, however, that my true policy was to say nothing further on the subject of my having been born a freeman. It would but expose me to mal-treatment, and diminish the chances of liberation.

After sunrise in the morning we were called up on deck to breakfast. Burch took our hand-cuffs off, and we sat down to table. He asked Eliza if she would take a dram. She declined, thanking him politely. During the meal we were all silent—not a word passed between us. A mulatto woman who served at table seemed to take an interest in our behalf—told us to cheer up, and not to be so cast down. Breakfast over, the hand-cuffs were restored, and Burch ordered us out on the stern deck. We sat down together on some boxes, still saying nothing in Burch's presence. Occasionally a passenger would walk out to where we were, look at us for a while, then silently return.

It was a very pleasant morning. The fields along the river were covered with verdure, far in advance of what I had been accustomed to see at that season of the year. The sun shone out warmly; the birds were singing in the trees. The happy birds—I envied them. I wished for wings like them, that I might cleave the air to where my birdlings waited vainly for their father's coming, in the cooler region of the North.

In the forenoon the steamer reached Aquia Creek. There the passengers took stages—Burch and his five slaves occupying one exclusively. He laughed with the children, and at one stopping place went so far as to purchase them a piece of gingerbread. He told me to hold up my head and look smart. That I might, perhaps, get a good master if I behaved myself. I made him no reply. His face was hateful to me, and I could not bear to look upon it. I sat in the corner, cherishing in my heart the hope, not yet extinct, of some day meeting the tyrant on the soil of my native State.

At Fredericksburgh we were transferred from the stage coach

to a car, and before dark arrived in Richmond, the chief city of Virginia. At this city we were taken from the cars, and driven through the street to a slave pen, between the railroad depot and the river, kept by a Mr. Goodin. This pen is similar to Williams' in Washington, except it is somewhat larger; and besides, there were two small houses standing at opposite corners within the yard. These houses are usually found within slave yards, being used as rooms for the examination of human chattels by purchasers before concluding a bargain. Unsoundness in a slave, as well as in a horse, detracts materially from his value. If no warranty is given, a close examination is a matter of particular importance to the negro jockey.

We were met at the door of Goodin's yard by that gentleman himself—a short, fat man, with a round, plump face, black hair and whiskers, and a complexion almost as dark as some of his own negroes. He had a hard, stern look, and was perhaps about fifty years of age. Burch and he met with great cordiality. They were evidently old friends. Shaking each other warmly by the hand, Burch remarked he had brought some company, inquired at what time the brig would leave, and was answered that it would probably leave the next day at such an hour. Goodin then turned to me, took hold of my arm, turned me partly round, looked at me sharply with the air of one who considered himself a good judge of property, and as if estimating in his own mind about how much I was worth.

"Well, boy, where did you come from?"

Forgetting myself, for a moment, I answered, "From New-York."

"New-York! H—l! what have you been doing up there?" was his astonished interrogatory.

Observing Burch at this moment looking at me with an angry expression that conveyed a meaning it was not difficult to understand, I immediately said, "O, I have only been up that way a piece," in a manner intended to imply that although I might have been as far as New-York, yet I wished it distinctly

268

understood that I did not belong to that free State, nor to any other.

Goodin then turned to Clem, and then to Eliza and the children, examining them severally, and asking various questions. He was pleased with Emily, as was every one who saw the child's sweet countenance. She was not as tidy as when I first beheld her; her hair was now somewhat disheveled; but through its unkempt and soft profusion there still beamed a little face of most surpassing loveliness. "Altogether we were a fair lot—a devilish good lot," he said, enforcing that opinion with more than one emphatic adjective not found in the Christian vocabulary. Thereupon we passed into the yard. Quite a number of slaves, as many as thirty I should say, were moving about, or sitting on benches under the shed. They were all cleanly dressed—the men with hats, the women with handkerchiefs tied about their heads.

Burch and Goodin, after separating from us, walked up the steps at the back part of the main building, and sat down upon the door sill. They entered into conversation, but the subject of it I could not hear. Presently Burch came down into the yard, unfettered me, and led me into one of the small houses.

"You told that man you came from New-York," said he.

I replied, "I told him I had been up as far as New-York, to be sure, but did not tell him I belonged there, nor that I was a freeman. I meant no harm at all, Master Burch. I would not have said it had I thought."

He looked at me a moment as if he was ready to devour me, then turning round went out. In a few minutes he returned. "If ever I hear you say a word about New-York, or about your freedom, I will be the death of you—I will kill you; you may rely on that," he ejaculated fiercely.

I doubt not he understood then better than I did, the danger and the penalty of selling a free man into slavery. He felt the necessity of closing my mouth against the crime he knew he was committing. Of course, my life would not have weighed a feather, in any emergency requiring such a sacrifice. Undoubtedly, he meant precisely what he said.

Under the shed on one side of the yard, there was constructed a rough table, while overhead were sleeping lofts—the same as in the pen at Washington. After partaking at this table of our supper of pork and bread, I was hand-cuffed to a large yellow man, quite stout and fleshy, with a countenance expressive of the utmost melancholy. He was a man of intelligence and information. Chained together, it was not long before we became acquainted with each other's history. His name was Robert. Like myself, he had been born free, and had a wife and two children in Cincinnati. He said he had come south with two men, who had hired him in the city of his residence. Without free papers, he had been seized at Fredericksburgh, placed in confinement, and beaten until he had learned, as I had, the necessity and the policy of silence. He had been in Goodin's pen about three weeks. To this man I became much attached. We could sympathize with, and understand each other. It was with tears and a heavy heart, not many days subsequently, that I saw him die, and looked for the last time upon his lifeless form!

Robert and myself, with Clem, Eliza and her children, slept that night upon our blankets, in one of the small houses in the yard. There were four others, all from the same plantation, who had been sold, and were now on their way south, who also occupied it with us. David and his wife, Caroline, both mulattoes, were exceedingly affected. They dreaded the thought of being put into the cane and cotton fields; but their greatest source of anxiety was the apprehension of being separated. Mary, a tall, lithe girl, of a most jetty black, was listless and apparently indifferent. Like many of the class, she scarcely knew there was such a word as freedom. Brought up in the ignorance of a brute, she possessed but little more than a brute's intelligence. She was one of those, and there are very many, who fear nothing but their master's lash, and know no further duty than to obey his voice. The other was Lethe. She was of an entirely different character. She had long, straight hair, and bore more the appearance of an Indian than a negro woman. She had sharp and spiteful eyes, and continually gave utterance to the language of hatred and revenge. Her husband had been sold. She knew not where she was. An exchange of masters, she was sure, could not be for the worse. She cared not whither they might carry her. Pointing to the scars upon her face, the desperate creature wished that she might see the day when she could wipe them off in some man's blood!

While we were thus learning the history of each other's wretchedness, Eliza was seated in a corner by herself, singing hymns and praying for her children. Wearied from the loss of so much sleep, I could no longer bear up against the advances of that "sweet restorer," and laying down by the side of Robert, on the floor, soon forgot my troubles, and slept until the dawn of day.

In the morning, having swept the yard, and washed ourselves, under Goodin's superintendence, we were ordered to roll up our blankets, and make ready for the continuance of our journey. Clem Ray was informed that he would go no further, Burch, for some cause, having concluded to carry him back to Washington. He was much rejoiced. Shaking hands, we parted in the slave pen at Richmond, and I have not seen him since. But, much to my surprise, since my return, I learned that he had escaped from bondage, and on his way to the free soil of Canada, lodged one night at the house of my brother-in-law in Saratoga, informing my family of the place and the condition in which he left me.

In the afternoon we were drawn up, two abreast, Robert and myself in advance, and in this order, driven by Burch and Goodin from the yard, through the streets of Richmond to the brig Orleans. She was a vessel of respectable size, full rigged, and freighted principally with tobacco. We were all on board by five o'clock. Burch brought us each a tin cup and a spoon. There were forty of us in the brig, being all, except Clem, that were in the pen.

With a small pocket knife that had not been taken from me,

271

I began cutting the initials of my name upon the tin cup. The others immediately flocked round me, requesting me to mark theirs in a similar manner. In time, I gratified them all, of which they did not appear to be forgetful.

We were all stowed away in the hold at night, and the hatch barred down. We laid on boxes, or where-ever there was room enough to stretch our blankets on the floor.

Burch accompanied us no farther than Richmond, returning from that point to the capital with Clem. Not until the lapse of almost twelve years, to wit, in January last, in the Washington police office, did I set my eyes upon his face again.

James H. Burch was a slave-trader—buying men, women and children at low prices, and selling them at an advance. He was a speculator in human flesh—a disreputable calling—and so considered at the South. For the present he disappears from the scenes recorded in this narrative, but he will appear again before its close, not in the character of a man-whipping tyrant, but as an arrested, cringing criminal in a court of law, that failed to do him justice.

CHAPTER V

After we were all on board, the brig Orleans proceeded down James River. Passing into Chesapeake Bay, we arrived next day opposite the city of Norfolk. While lying at anchor, a lighter approached us from the town, bringing four more slaves. Frederick, a boy of eighteen, had been born a slave, as also had Henry, who was some years older. They had both been house servants in the city. Maria was a rather genteel looking colored girl, with a faultless form, but ignorant and extremely vain. The idea of going to New-Orleans was pleasing to her. She entertained an extravagantly high opinion of her own attractions. Assuming a haughty mien, she declared to her companions, that immediately on our arrival in New-Orleans, she had no doubt, some wealthy single gentleman of good taste would purchase her at once!

But the most prominent of the four, was a man named Arthur. As the lighter approached, he struggled stoutly with his keepers. It was with main force that he was dragged aboard the brig. He protested, in a loud voice, against the treatment he was receiving, and demanded to be released. His face was swollen, and covered with wounds and bruises, and, indeed, one side of it was a complete raw sore. He was forced, with all haste, down the hatchway into the hold. I caught an outline of his story as he was borne struggling along, of which he afterwards gave me a more full relation, and it was as follows: He had long resided in the city of Norfolk, and was a free man. He had a family living there, and was a mason by trade. Having been unusually detained, he was returning late one night to his house in the suburbs of the city, when he was attacked by a gang of persons in an unfrequented street. He fought until his strength failed him.

273

Overpowered at last, he was gagged and bound with ropes, and beaten, until he became insensible. For several days they secreted him in the slave pen at Norfolk—a very common establishment, it appears, in the cities of the South. The night before, he had been taken out and put on board the lighter, which, pushing out from shore, had awaited our arrival. For some time he continued his protestations, and was altogether irreconcilable. At length, however, he became silent. He sank into a gloomy and thoughtful mood, and appeared to be counseling with himself. There was in the man's determined face, something that suggested the thought of desperation.

After leaving Norfolk the hand-cuffs were taken off, and during the day we were allowed to remain on deck. The captain selected Robert as his waiter, and I was appointed to superintend the cooking department, and the distribution of food and water. I had three assistants, Jim, Cuffee and Jenny. Jenny's business was to prepare the coffee, which consisted of corn meal scorched in a kettle, boiled and sweetened with molasses. Jim and Cuffee baked the hoe-cake and boiled the bacon.

Standing by a table, formed of a wide board resting on the heads of the barrels, I cut and handed to each a slice of meat and a "dodger" of the bread, and from Jenny's kettle also dipped out for each a cup of the coffee. The use of plates was dispensed with, and their sable fingers took the place of knives and forks. Jim and Cuffee were very demure and attentive to business, somewhat inflated with their situation as second cooks, and without doubt feeling that there was a great responsibility resting on them. I was called steward—a name given me by the captain.

The slaves were fed twice a day, at ten and five o'clock—always receiving the same kind and quantity of fare, and in the same manner as above described. At night we were driven into the hold, and securely fastened down.

Scarcely were we out of sight of land before we were overtaken by a violent storm. The brig rolled and plunged until we feared she would go down. Some were sea-sick, others on their knees praying, while some were fast holding to each other, paralyzed with fear. The sea-sickness rendered the place of our confinement loathsome and disgusting. It would have been a happy thing for most of us—it would have saved the agony of many hundred lashes, and miserable deaths at last—had the compassionate sea snatched us that day from the clutches of remorseless men. The thought of Randall and little Emmy sinking down among the monsters of the deep, is a more pleasant contemplation than to think of them as they are now, perhaps, dragging out lives of unrequited toil.

When in sight of the Bahama Banks, at a place called Old Point Compass, or the Hole in the Wall, we were becalmed three days. There was scarcely a breath of air. The waters of the gulf presented a singularly white appearance, like lime water.

In the order of events, I come now to the relation of an occurrence, which I never call to mind but with sensations of regret. I thank God, who has since permitted me to escape from the thralldom of slavery, that through his merciful interposition I was prevented from imbruing my hands in the blood of his creatures. Let not those who have never been placed in like circumstances, judge me harshly. Until they have been chained and beaten—until they find themselves in the situation I was, borne away from home and family towards a land of bondage— let them refrain from saying what they would not do for liberty. How far I should have been justified in the sight of God and man, it is unnecessary now to speculate upon. It is enough to say that I am able to congratulate myself upon the harmless termination of an affair which threatened, for a time, to be attended with serious results.

Towards evening, on the first day of the calm, Arthur and myself were in the bow of the vessel, seated on the windlass. We were conversing together of the probable destiny that awaited us, and mourning together over our misfortunes. Arthur said, and I agreed with him, that death was far less terrible than the living prospect that was before us. For a long time we talked of our children, our past lives, and of the probabilities of escape. Obtaining possession of the brig was suggested by one of us. We discussed the possibility of our being able, in such an event, to make our way to the harbor of New-York. I knew little of the compass; but the idea of risking the experiment was eagerly entertained. The chances, for and against us, in an encounter with the crew, was canvassed. Who could be relied upon, and who could not, the proper time and manner of the attack, were all talked over and over again. From the moment the plot suggested itself I began to hope. I revolved it constantly in my mind. As difficulty after difficulty arose, some ready conceit was at hand, demonstrating how it could be overcome. While others slept, Arthur and I were maturing our plans. At length, with much caution, Robert was gradually made acquainted with our intentions. He approved of them at once, and entered into the conspiracy with a zealous spirit. There was not another slave we dared to trust. Brought up in fear and ignorance as they are, it can scarcely be conceived how servilely they will cringe before a white man's look. It was not safe to deposit so bold a secret with any of them, and finally we three resolved to take upon ourselves alone the fearful responsibility of the attempt.

At night, as has been said, we were driven into the hold, and the hatch barred down. How to reach the deck was the first difficulty that presented itself. On the bow of the brig, however, I had observed the small boat lying bottom upwards. It occurred to me that by secreting ourselves underneath it, we would not be missed from the crowd, as they were hurried down into the hold at night. I was selected to make the experiment, in order to satisfy ourselves of its feasibility. The next evening, accordingly, after supper, watching my opportunity, I hastily concealed myself beneath it. Lying close upon the deck, I could see what was going on around me, while wholly unperceived myself. In the morning, as they came up, I slipped from my hiding place without being observed. The result was entirely satisfactory.

The captain and mate slept in the cabin of the former. From

Robert, who had frequent occasion, in his capacity of waiter, to make observations in that quarter, we ascertained the exact position of their respective berths. He further informed us that there were always two pistols and a cutlass lying on the table. The crew's cook slept in the cook galley on deck, a sort of vehicle on wheels, that could be moved about as convenience required, while the sailors, numbering only six, either slept in the forecastle, or in hammocks swung among the rigging.

Finally our arrangements were all completed. Arthur and I were to steal silently to the captain's cabin, seize the pistols and cutlass, and as quickly as possible despatch him and the mate. Robert, with a club, was to stand by the door leading from the deck down into the cabin, and, in case of necessity, beat back the sailors, until we could hurry to his assistance. We were to proceed then as circumstances might require. Should the attack be so sudden and successful as to prevent resistance, the hatch was to remain barred down; otherwise the slaves were to be called up, and in the crowd, and hurry, and confusion of the time, we resolved to regain our liberty or lose our lives. I was then to assume the unaccustomed place of pilot, and, steering northward, we trusted that some lucky wind might bear us to the soil of freedom.

The mate's name was Biddee, the captain's I cannot now recall, though I rarely ever forget a name once heard. The captain was a small, genteel man, erect and prompt, with a proud bearing, and looked the personification of courage. If he is still living, and these pages should chance to meet his eye, he will learn a fact connected with the voyage of the brig, from Richmond to New-Orleans, in 1841, not entered on his log-book.

We were all prepared, and impatiently waiting an opportunity of putting our designs into execution, when they were frustrated by a sad and unforeseen event. Robert was taken ill. It was soon announced that he had the small-pox. He continued to grow worse, and four days previous to our arrival in New-Orleans he died. One of the sailors sewed him in his blanket, with

277

a large stone from the ballast at his feet, and then laying him on a hatchway, and elevating it with tackles above the railing, the inanimate body of poor Robert was consigned to the white waters of the gulf.

We were all panic-stricken by the appearance of the small-pox. The captain ordered lime to be scattered through the hold, and other prudent precautions to be taken. The death of Robert, however, and the presence of the malady, oppressed me sadly, and I gazed out over the great waste of waters with a spirit that was indeed disconsolate.

An evening or two after Robert's burial, I was leaning on the hatchway near the forecastle, full of desponding thoughts, when a sailor in a kind voice asked me why I was so down-hearted. The tone and manner of the man assured me, and I answered, because I was a freeman, and had been kidnapped. He remarked that it was enough to make any one down-hearted, and continued to interrogate me until he learned the particulars of my whole history. He was evidently much interested in my behalf, and, in the blunt speech of a sailor, swore he would aid me all he could, if it "split his timbers." I requested him to furnish me pen, ink and paper, in order that I might write to some of my friends. He promised to obtain them—but how I could use them undiscovered was a difficulty. If I could only get into the forecastle while his watch was off, and the other sailors asleep, the thing could be accomplished. The small boat instantly occurred to me. He thought we were not far from the Balize, at the mouth of the Mississippi, and it was necessary that the letter be written soon, or the opportunity would be lost. Accordingly, by arrangement, I managed the next night to secret myself again under the long-boat. His watch was off at twelve. I saw him pass into the forecastle, and in about an hour followed him. He was nodding over a table, half asleep, on which a sickly light was flickering, and on which also was a pen and sheet of paper. As I entered he aroused, beckoned me to a seat beside him, and pointed to the paper. I directed the letter to Henry B. Northup, of Sandy Hill—stating that I had been kidnapped, was then on board the brig Orleans, bound for New-Orleans; that it was then impossible for me to conjecture my ultimate destination, and requesting he would take measures to rescue me. The letter was sealed and directed, and Manning, having read it, promised to deposit it in the New-Orleans post-office. I hastened back to my place under the long-boat, and in the morning, as the slaves came up and were walking round, crept out unnoticed and mingled with them.

My good friend, whose name was John Manning, was an Englishman by birth, and a noble-hearted, generous sailor as ever walked a deck. He had lived in Boston—was a tall, well-built man, about twenty-four years old, with a face somewhat pock-marked, but full of benevolent expression.

Nothing to vary the monotony of our daily life occurred, until we reached New-Orleans. On coming to the levee, and before the vessel was made fast, I saw Manning leap on shore and hurry away into the city. As he started off he looked back over his shoulder significantly, giving me to understand the object of his errand. Presently he returned, and passing close by me, hunched me with his elbow, with a peculiar wink, as much as to say, "it is all right."

The letter, as I have since learned, reached Sandy Hill. Mr. Northup visited Albany and laid it before Governor Seward, but inasmuch as it gave no definite information as to my probable locality, it was not, at that time, deemed advisable to institute measures for my liberation. It was concluded to delay, trusting that a knowledge of where I was might eventually be obtained.

A happy and touching scene was witnessed immediately upon our reaching the levee. Just as Manning left the brig, on his way to the post-office, two men came up and called aloud for Arthur. The latter, as he recognized them, was almost crazy with delight. He could hardly be restrained from leaping over the brig's side; and when they met soon after, he grasped them by the hand, and clung to them a long, long time. They were men from Norfolk, who had come on to New-Orleans to rescue him. His kidnappers, they informed him, had been arrested, and were then confined in the Norfolk prison. They conversed a few moments with the captain, and then departed with the rejoicing Arthur.

But in all the crowd that thronged the wharf, there was no one who knew or cared for me. Not one. No familiar voice greeted my ears, nor was there a single face that I had ever seen. Soon Arthur would rejoin his family, and have the satisfaction of seeing his wrongs avenged: my family, alas, should I ever see them more? There was a feeling of utter desolation in my heart, filling it with a despairing and regretful sense, that I had not gone down with Robert to the bottom of the sea.

Very soon traders and consignees came on board. One, a tall, thin-faced man, with light complexion and a little bent, made his appearance, with a paper in his hand. Burch's gang, consisting of myself, Eliza and her children, Harry, Lethe, and some others, who had joined us at Richmond, were consigned to him. This gentleman was Mr. Theophilus Freeman. Reading from his paper, he called, "Platt." No one answered. The name was called again and again, but still there was no reply. Then Lethe was called, then Eliza, then Harry, until the list was finished, each one stepping forward as his or her name was called.

"Captain, where's Platt?" demanded Theophilus Freeman.

The captain was unable to inform him, no one being on board answering to that name.

"Who shipped *that* nigger?" he again inquired of the captain, pointing to me.

"Burch," replied the captain.

"Your name is Platt—you answer my description. Why don't you come forward?" he demanded of me, in an angry tone.

I informed him that was not my name; that I had never been called by it, but that I had no objection to it as I knew of.

"Well, I will learn you your name," said he; "and so you won't forget it either, by ——," he added.

Mr. Theophilus Freeman, by the way, was not a whit behind his partner, Burch, in the matter of blasphemy. On the vessel I had gone by the name of "Steward," and this was the first time I had ever been designated as Platt—the name forwarded by Burch to his consignee. From the vessel I observed the chain-gang at work on the levee. We passed near them as we were driven to Freeman's slave pen. This pen is very similar to Goodin's in Richmond, except the yard was enclosed by plank, standing upright, with ends sharpened, instead of brick walls.

Including us, there were now at least fifty in this pen. Depositing our blankets in one of the small buildings in the yard, and having been called up and fed, we were allowed to saunter about the enclosure until night, when we wrapped our blankets round us and laid down under the shed, or in the loft, or in the open yard, just as each one preferred.

It was but a short time I closed my eyes that night. Thought was busy in my brain. Could it be possible that I was thousands of miles from home—that I had been driven through the streets like a dumb beast—that I had been chained and beaten without mercy—that I was even then herded with a drove of slaves, a slave myself? Were the events of the last few weeks realities indeed?—or was I passing only through the dismal phases of a long, protracted dream? It was no illusion. My cup of sorrow was full to overflowing. Then I lifted up my hands to God, and in the still watches of the night, surrounded by the sleeping forms of my companions, begged for mercy on the poor, forsaken captive. To the Almighty Father of us all—the freeman and the slave—I poured forth the supplications of a broken spirit, imploring strength from on high to bear up against the burden of my troubles, until the morning light aroused the slumberers, ushering in another day of bondage.

CHAPTER VI

The very amiable, pious-hearted Mr. Theophilus Freeman, partner or consignee of James H. Burch, and keeper of the slave pen in New-Orleans, was out among his animals early in the morning. With an occasional kick of the older men and women, and many a sharp crack of the whip about the ears of the younger slaves, it was not long before they were all astir, and wide awake. Mr. Theophilus Freeman bustled about in a very industrious manner, getting his property ready for the sales-room, intending, no doubt, to do that day a rousing business.

In the first place we were required to wash thoroughly, and those with beards, to shave. We were then furnished with a new suit each, cheap, but clean. The men had hat, coat, shirt, pants and shoes; the women frocks of calico, and handkerchiefs to bind about their heads. We were now conducted into a large room in the front part of the building to which the yard was attached, in order to be properly trained, before the admission of customers. The men were arranged on one side of the room, the women on the other. The tallest was placed at the head of the row, then the next tallest, and so on in the order of their respective heights. Emily was at the foot of the line of women. Freeman charged us to remember our places; exhorted us to appear smart and lively,—sometimes threatening, and again, holding out various inducements. During the day he exercised us in the art of "looking smart," and of moving to our places with exact precision.

After being fed, in the afternoon, we were again paraded and made to dance. Bob, a colored boy, who had some time belonged to Freeman, played on the violin. Standing near him, I made bold to inquire if he could play the "Virginia Reel." He answered he could not, and asked me if I could play. Replying in the affirmative, he handed me the violin. I struck up a tune, and finished it. Freeman ordered me to continue playing, and seemed well pleased, telling Bob that I far excelled him—a remark that seemed to grieve my musical companion very much.

Next day many customers called to examine Freeman's "new lot." The latter gentleman was very loquacious, dwelling at much length upon our several good points and qualities. He would make us hold up our heads, walk briskly back and forth, while customers would feel of our hands and arms and bodies, turn us about, ask us what we could do, make us open our mouths and show our teeth, precisely as a jockey examines a horse which he is about to barter for or purchase. Sometimes a man or woman was taken back to the small house in the yard, stripped, and inspected more minutely. Scars upon a slave's back were considered evidence of a rebellious or unruly spirit, and hurt his sale.

One old gentleman, who said he wanted a coachman, appeared to take a fancy to me. From his conversation with Burch, I learned he was a resident in the city. I very much desired that he would buy me, because I conceived it would not be difficult to make my escape from New-Orleans on some northern vessel. Freeman asked him fifteen hundred dollars for me. The old gentleman insisted it was too much, as times were very hard. Freeman, however, declared that I was sound and healthy, of a good constitution, and intelligent. He made it a point to enlarge upon my musical attainments. The old gentleman argued quite adroitly that there was nothing extraordinary about the nigger, and finally, to my regret, went out, saying he would call again. During the day, however, a number of sales were made. David and Caroline were purchased together by a Natchez planter. They left us, grinning broadly, and in the most happy state of mind, caused by the fact of their not being separated. Lethe was sold to a planter of Baton Rouge, her eyes flashing with anger as she was led away.

The same man also purchased Randall. The little fellow was made to jump, and run across the floor, and perform many other feats, exhibiting his activity and condition. All the time the trade was going on, Eliza was crying aloud, and wringing her hands. She besought the man not to buy him, unless he also bought herself and Emily. She promised, in that case, to be the most faithful slave that ever lived. The man answered that he could not afford it, and then Eliza burst into a paroxysm of grief, weeping plaintively. Freeman turned round to her, savagely, with his whip in his uplifted hand, ordering her to stop her noise, or he would flog her. He would not have such work—such snivelling; and unless she ceased that minute, he would take her to the yard and give her a hundred lashes. Yes, he would take the nonsense out of her pretty quick—if he didn't, might he be d—d. Eliza shrunk before him, and tried to wipe away her tears, but it was all in vain. She wanted to be with her children, she said, the little time she had to live. All the frowns and threats of Freeman, could not wholly silence the afflicted mother. She kept on begging and beseeching them, most piteously, not to separate the three. Over and over again she told them how she loved her boy. A great many times she repeated her former promises—how very faithful and obedient she would be; how hard she would labor day and night, to the last moment of her life, if he would only buy them all together. But it was of no avail; the man could not afford it. The bargain was agreed upon, and Randall must go alone. Then Eliza ran to him; embraced him passionately; kissed him again and again; told him to remember her—all the while her tears falling in the boy's face like rain.

Freeman damned her, calling her a blubbering, bawling wench, and ordered her to go to her place, and behave herself, and be somebody. He swore he wouldn't stand such stuff but a little longer. He would soon give her something to cry about, if she was not mighty careful, and *that* she might depend upon.

The planter from Baton Rouge, with his new purchases, was ready to depart.

"Don't cry, mama. I will be a good boy. Don't cry," said Randall, looking back, as they passed out of the door.

What has become of the lad, God knows. It was a mournful scene indeed. I would have cried myself if I had dared.

That night, nearly all who came in on the brig Orleans, were taken ill. They complained of violent pain in the head and back. Little Emily—a thing unusual with her—cried constantly. In the morning a physician was called in, but was unable to determine the nature of our complaint. While examining me, and asking questions touching my symptoms, I gave it as my opinion that it was an attack of small-pox—mentioning the fact of Robert's death as the reason of my belief. It might be so indeed, he thought, and he would send for the head physician of the hospital. Shortly, the head physician came—a small, light-haired man, whom they called Dr. Carr. He pronounced it small-pox, whereupon there was much alarm throughout the yard. Soon after Dr. Carr left, Eliza, Emmy, Harry and myself were put into a hack and driven to the hospital—a large white marble building, standing on the outskirts of the city. Harry and I were placed in a room in one of the upper stories. I became very sick. For three days I was entirely blind. While lying in this state one day, Bob came in, saying to Dr. Carr that Freeman had sent him over to inquire how we were getting on. Tell him, said the doctor, that Platt is very bad, but that if he survives until nine o'clock, he may recover.

I expected to die. Though there was little in the prospect before me worth living for, the near approach of death appalled me. I thought I could have been resigned to yield up my life in the bosom of my family, but to expire in the midst of strangers, under such circumstances, was a bitter reflection.

There were a great number in the hospital, of both sexes, and of all ages. In the rear of the building coffins were manufactured. When one died, the bell tolled—a signal to the undertaker to come and bear away the body to the potter's field. Many times, each day and night, the tolling bell sent forth its melancholy voice, announcing another death. But my time had not yet come. The crisis having passed, I began to revive, and at the end of two weeks and two days, returned with Harry to the pen, bearing upon my face the effects of the malady, which to this day continues to disfigure it. Eliza and Emily were also brought back next day in a hack, and again were we paraded in the sales-room, for the inspection and examination of purchasers. I still indulged the hope that the old gentleman in search of a coachman would call again, as he had promised, and purchase me. In that event I felt an abiding confidence that I would soon regain my liberty. Customer after customer entered, but the old gentleman never made his appearance.

At length, one day, while we were in the yard, Freeman came out and ordered us to our places, in the great room. A gentleman was waiting for us as we entered, and inasmuch as he will be often mentioned in the progress of this narrative, a description of his personal appearance, and my estimation of his character, at first sight, may not be out of place.

He was a man above the ordinary height, somewhat bent and stooping forward. He was a good-looking man, and appeared to have reached about the middle age of life. There was nothing repulsive in his presence; but on the other hand, there was something cheerful and attractive in his face, and in his tone of voice. The finer elements were all kindly mingled in his breast, as any one could see. He moved about among us, asking many questions, as to what we could do, and what labor we had been accustomed to; if we thought we would like to live with him, and would be good boys if he would buy us, and other interrogatories of like character.

After some further inspection, and conversation touching prices, he finally offered Freeman one thousand dollars for me, nine hundred for Harry, and seven hundred for Eliza. Whether the small-pox had depreciated our value, or from what cause Freeman had concluded to fall five hundred dollars from the price I was before held at, I cannot say. At any rate, after a little shrewd reflection, he announced his acceptance of the offer.

As soon as Eliza heard it, she was in an agony again. By this time she had become haggard and hollow-eyed with sickness and with sorrow. It would be a relief if I could consistently pass over in silence the scene that now ensued. It recalls memories more mournful and affecting than any language can portray. I have seen mothers kissing for the last time the faces of their dead offspring; I have seen them looking down into the grave, as the earth fell with a dull sound upon their coffins, hiding them from their eyes forever; but never have I seen such an exhibition of intense, unmeasured, and unbounded grief, as when Eliza was parted from her child. She broke from her place in the line of women, and rushing down where Emily was standing, caught her in her arms. The child, sensible of some impending danger, instinctively fastened her hands around her mother's neck, and nestled her little head upon her bosom. Freeman sternly ordered her to be quiet, but she did not heed him. He caught her by the arm and pulled her rudely, but she only clung the closer to the child. Then, with a volley of great oaths, he struck her such a heartless blow, that she staggered backward, and was like to fall. Oh! how piteously then did she beseech and beg and pray that they might not be separated. Why could they not be purchased together? Why not let her have one of her dear children? "Mercy, mercy, master!" she cried, falling on her knees. "Please, master, buy Emily. I can never work any if she is taken from me: I will die."

Freeman interfered again, but, disregarding him, she still plead most earnestly, telling how Randall had been taken from her—how she never would see him again, and now it was too bad—oh, God! it was too bad, too cruel, to take her away from Emily—her pride—her only darling, that could not live, it was so young, without its mother!

Finally, after much more of supplication, the purchaser of Eliza stepped forward, evidently affected, and said to Freeman he would buy Emily, and asked him what her price was.

287

"What is her *price*? *Buy* her?" was the responsive interrogatory of Theophilus Freeman. And instantly answering his own inquiry, he added, "I won't sell her. She's not for sale."

The man remarked he was not in need of one so young—that it would be of no profit to him, but since the mother was so fond of her, rather than see them separated, he would pay a reasonable price. But to this humane proposal Freeman was entirely deaf. He would not sell her then on any account whatever. There were heaps and piles of money to be made of her, he said, when she was a few years older. There were men enough in New-Orleans who would give five thousand dollars for such an extra, handsome, fancy piece as Emily would be, rather than not get her. No, no, he would not sell her then. She was a beauty—a picture—a doll—one of the regular bloods—none of your thick-lipped, bullet-headed, cotton-picking niggers—if she was might he be d—d.

When Eliza heard Freeman's determination not to part with Emily, she became absolutely frantic.

"I will *not* go without her. They shall *not* take her from me," she fairly shrieked, her shrieks commingling with the loud and angry voice of Freeman, commanding her to be silent.

Meantime Harry and myself had been to the yard and returned with our blankets, and were at the front door ready to leave. Our purchaser stood near us, gazing at Eliza with an expression indicative of regret at having bought her at the expense of so much sorrow. We waited some time, when, finally, Freeman, out of patience, tore Emily from her mother by main force, the two clinging to each other with all their might.

"Don't leave me, mama—don't leave me," screamed the child, as its mother was pushed harshly forward; "Don't leave me—come back, mama," she still cried, stretching forth her little arms imploringly. But she cried in vain. Out of the door and into the street we were quickly hurried. Still we could hear her calling to her mother, "Come back—don't leave me—come back, mama," until her infant voice grew faint and still more faint, and gradually died away, as distance intervened, and finally was wholly lost.

Eliza never after saw or heard of Emily or Randall. Day nor night, however, were they ever absent from her memory. In the cotton field, in the cabin, always and everywhere, she was talking of them—often *to* them, as if they were actually present. Only when absorbed in that illusion, or asleep, did she ever have a moment's comfort afterwards.

She was no common slave, as has been said. To a large share of natural intelligence which she possessed, was added a general knowledge and information on most subjects. She had enjoyed opportunities such as are afforded to very few of her oppressed class. She had been lifted up into the regions of a higher life. Freedom—freedom for herself and for her offspring, for many years had been her cloud by day, her pillar of fire by night. In her pilgrimage through the wilderness of bondage, with eyes fixed upon that hope-inspiring beacon, she had at length ascended to "the top of Pisgah," and beheld "the land of promise." In an unexpected moment she was utterly overwhelmed with disappointment and despair. The glorious vision of liberty faded from her sight as they led her away into captivity. Now "she weepeth sore in the night, and tears are on her cheeks: all her friends have dealt treacherously with her: they have become her enemies."

CHAPTER VII

On leaving the New-Orleans slave pen, Harry and I followed our new master through the streets, while Eliza, crying and turning back, was forced along by Freeman and his minions, until we found ourselves on board the steamboat Rodolph, then lying at the levee. In the course of half an hour we were moving briskly up the Mississippi, bound for some point on Red River. There were quite a number of slaves on board beside ourselves, just purchased in the New-Orleans market. I remember a Mr. Kelsow, who was said to be a well known and extensive planter, had in charge a gang of women.

Our master's name was William Ford. He resided then in the "Great Pine Woods," in the parish of Avoyelles, situated on the right bank of Red River, in the heart of Louisiana. He is now a Baptist preacher. Throughout the whole parish of Avoyelles, and especially along both shores of Bayou Bœuf, where he is more intimately known, he is accounted by his fellow-citizens as a worthy minister of God. In many northern minds, perhaps, the idea of a man holding his brother man in servitude, and the traffic in human flesh, may seem altogether incompatible with their conceptions of a moral or religious life. From descriptions of such men as Burch and Freeman, and others hereinafter mentioned, they are led to despise and execrate the whole class of slaveholders, indiscriminately. But I was sometime his slave, and had an opportunity of learning well his character and disposition, and it is but simple justice to him when I say, in my opinion, there never was a more kind, noble, candid, Christian man than William Ford. The influences and associations that had always surrounded him, blinded him to the inherent wrong at the bottom of the system of Slavery. He never doubted the moral right of one man holding another in subjection. Looking through the same medium with his fathers before him, he saw things in the same light. Brought up under other circumstances and other influences, his notions would undoubtedly have been different. Nevertheless, he was a model master, walking uprightly, according to the light of his understanding, and fortunate was the slave who came to his possession. Were all men such as he, Slavery would be deprived of more than half its bitterness.

We were two days and three nights on board the steamboat Rodolph, during which time nothing of particular interest occurred. I was now known as Platt, the name given me by Burch, and by which I was designated through the whole period of my servitude. Eliza was sold by the name of "Dradey." She was so distinguished in the conveyance to Ford, now on record in the recorder's office in New-Orleans.

On our passage I was constantly reflecting on my situation, and consulting with myself on the best course to pursue in order to effect my ultimate escape. Sometimes, not only then, but afterwards, I was almost on the point of disclosing fully to Ford the facts of my history. I am inclined now to the opinion it would have resulted in my benefit. This course was often considered, but through fear of its miscarriage, never put into execution, until eventually my transfer and his pecuniary embarrassments rendered it evidently unsafe. Afterwards, under other masters, unlike William Ford, I knew well enough the slightest knowledge of my real character would consign me at once to the remoter depths of Slavery. I was too costly a chattel to be lost, and was well aware that I would be taken farther on, into some by-place, over the Texan border, perhaps, and sold; that I would be disposed of as the thief disposes of his stolen horse, if my right to freedom was even whispered. So I resolved to lock the secret closely in my heart—never to utter one word or syllable as to who or what I was—trusting in Providence and my own shrewdness for deliverance.

At length we left the steamboat Rodolph at a place called Alexandria, several hundred miles from New-Orleans. It is a small town on the southern shore of Red River. Having remained there over night, we entered the morning train of cars, and were soon at Bayou Lamourie, a still smaller place, distant eighteen miles from Alexandria. At that time it was the termination of the railroad. Ford's plantation was situated on the Texas road, twelve miles from Lamourie, in the Great Pine Woods. This distance, it was announced to us, must be traveled on foot, there being public conveyances no farther. Accordingly we all set out in the company of Ford. It was an excessively hot day. Harry, Eliza, and myself were yet weak, and the bottoms of our feet were very tender from the effects of the small-pox. We proceeded slowly, Ford telling us to take our time and sit down and rest whenever we desired—a privilege that was taken advantage of quite frequently. After leaving Lamourie and crossing two plantations, one belonging to Mr. Carnell, the other to a Mr. Flint, we reached the Pine Woods, a wilderness that stretches to the Sabine River.

The whole country about Red River is low and marshy. The Pine Woods, as they are called, is comparatively upland, with frequent small intervals, however, running through them. This upland is covered with numerous trees—the white oak, the chincopin, resembling chestnut, but principally the yellow pine. They are of great size, running up sixty feet, and perfectly straight. The woods were full of cattle, very shy and wild, dashing away in herds, with a loud snuff, at our approach. Some of them were marked or branded, the rest appeared to be in their wild and untamed state. They are much smaller than northern breeds, and the peculiarity about them that most attracted my attention was their horns. They stand out from the sides of the head precisely straight, like two iron spikes.

At noon we reached a cleared piece of ground containing three or four acres. Upon it was a small, unpainted, wooden house, a corn crib, or, as we would say, a barn, and a log kitchen, standing about a rod from the house. It was the summer residence of Mr. Martin. Rich planters, having large establishments on Bayou Bœuf, are accustomed to spend the warmer season in these woods. Here they find clear water and delightful shades. In fact, these retreats are to the planters of that section of the country what Newport and Saratoga are to the wealthier inhabitants of northern cities.

We were sent around into the kitchen, and supplied with sweet potatoes, corn-bread, and bacon, while Master Ford dined with Martin in the house. There were several slaves about the premises. Martin came out and took a look at us, asking Ford the price of each, if we were green hands, and so forth, and making inquiries in relation to the slave market generally.

After a long rest we set forth again, following the Texas road, which had the appearance of being very rarely traveled. For five miles we passed through continuous woods without observing a single habitation. At length, just as the sun was sinking in the west, we entered another opening, containing some twelve or fifteen acres.

In this opening stood a house much larger than Mr. Martin's. It was two stories high, with a piazza in front. In the rear of it was also a log kitchen, poultry house, corncribs, and several negro cabins. Near the house was a peach orchard, and gardens of orange and pomegranate trees. The space was entirely surrounded by woods, and covered with a carpet of rich, rank verdure. It was a quiet, lonely, pleasant place—literally a green spot in the wilderness. It was the residence of my master, William Ford.

As we approached, a yellow girl—her name was Rose— was standing on the piazza. Going to the door, she called her mistress, who presently came running out to meet her lord. She kissed him, and laughingly demanded if he had bought "those niggers." Ford said he had, and told us to go round to Sally's cabin and rest ourselves. Turning the corner of the house, we discovered Sally washing—her two baby children near her, rolling on the grass. They jumped up and toddled towards us, looked at us a moment like a brace of rabbits, then ran back to their mother as if afraid of us.

Sally conducted us into the cabin, told us to lay down our bundles and be seated, for she was sure that we were tired. Just then John, the cook, a boy some sixteen years of age, and blacker than any crow, came running in, looked steadily in our faces, then turning round, without saying as much as "how d'ye do," ran back to the kitchen, laughing loudly, as if our coming was a great joke indeed.

Much wearied with our walk, as soon as it was dark, Harry and I wrapped our blankets round us, and laid down upon the cabin floor. My thoughts, as usual, wandered back to my wife and children. The consciousness of my real situation; the hopelessness of any effort to escape through the wide forests of Avoyelles, pressed heavily upon me, yet my heart was at home in Saratoga.

I was awakened early in the morning by the voice of Master Ford, calling Rose. She hastened into the house to dress the children, Sally to the field to milk the cows, while John was busy in the kitchen preparing breakfast. In the meantime Harry and I were strolling about the yard, looking at our new quarters. Just after breakfast a colored man, driving three yoke of oxen, attached to a wagon load of lumber, drove into the opening. He was a slave of Ford's, named Walton, the husband of Rose. By the way, Rose was a native of Washington, and had been brought from thence five years before. She had never seen Eliza, but she had heard of Berry, and they knew the same streets, and the same people, either personally, or by reputation. They became fast friends immediately, and talked a great deal together of old times, and of friends they had left behind.

Ford was at that time a wealthy man. Besides his seat in the Pine Woods, he owned a large lumbering establishment on Indian Creek, four miles distant, and also, in his wife's right, an extensive plantation and many slaves on Bayou Bœuf.

Walton had come with his load of lumber from the mills on Indian Creek. Ford directed us to return with him, saying he would follow us as soon as possible. Before leaving, Mistress Ford called me into the store-room, and handed me, as it is there termed, a tin bucket of molasses for Harry and myself.

Eliza was still ringing her hands and deploring the loss of her children. Ford tried as much as possible to console her—told her she need not work very hard; that she might remain with Rose, and assist the madam in the house affairs.

Riding with Walton in the wagon, Harry and I became quite well acquainted with him long before reaching Indian Creek. He was a "born thrall" of Ford's, and spoke kindly and affectionately of him, as a child would speak of his own father. In answer to his inquiries from whence I came, I told him from Washington. Of that city, he had heard much from his wife, Rose, and all the way plied me with many extravagant and absurd questions.

On reaching the mills at Indian Creek, we found two more of Ford's slaves, Sam and Antony. Sam, also, was a Washingtonian, having been brought out in the same gang with Rose. He had worked on a farm near Georgetown. Antony was a blacksmith, from Kentucky, who had been in his present master's service about ten years. Sam knew Burch, and when informed that he was the trader who had sent me on from Washington, it was remarkable how well we agreed upon the subject of his superlative rascality. He had forwarded Sam, also.

On Ford's arrival at the mill, we were employed in piling lumber, and chopping logs, which occupation we continued during the remainder of the summer.

We usually spent our Sabbaths at the opening, on which days our master would gather all his slaves about him, and read and expound the Scriptures. He sought to inculcate in our minds feelings of kindness towards each other, of dependence upon God—setting forth the rewards promised unto those who lead an upright and prayerful life. Seated in the doorway of his house, surrounded by his man-servants and his maid-servants, who looked earnestly into the good man's face, he spoke of the loving kindness of the Creator, and of the life that is to come. Often did the voice of prayer ascend from his lips to heaven, the only sound that broke the solitude of the place.

In the course of the summer Sam became deeply convicted, his mind dwelling intensely on the subject of religion. His mistress gave him a Bible, which he carried with him to his work. Whatever leisure time was allowed him, he spent in perusing it, though it was only with great difficulty that he could master any part of it. I often read to him, a favor which he well repaid me by many expressions of gratitude. Sam's piety was frequently observed by white men who came to the mill, and the remark it most generally provoked was, that a man like Ford, who allowed his slaves to have Bibles, was "not fit to own a nigger."

He, however, lost nothing by his kindness. It is a fact I have more than once observed, that those who treated their slaves most leniently, were rewarded by the greatest amount of labor. I know it from my own experience. It was a source of pleasure to surprise Master Ford with a greater day's work than was required, while, under subsequent masters, there was no prompter to extra effort but the overseer's lash.

It was the desire of Ford's approving voice that suggested to me an idea that resulted to his profit. The lumber we were manufacturing was contracted to be delivered at Lamourie. It had hitherto been transported by land, and was an important item of expense. Indian Creek, upon which the mills were situated, was a narrow but deep stream emptying into Bayou Bœuf. In some places it was not more than twelve feet wide, and much obstructed with trunks of trees. Bayou Bœuf was connected with Bayou Lamourie. I ascertained the distance from the mills to the point on the latter bayou, where our lumber was to be delivered, was but a few miles less by land than by water. Provided the creek could be made navigable for rafts, it occurred to me that the expense of transportation would be materially diminished.

Adam Taydem, a little white man, who had been a soldier in Florida, and had strolled into that distant region, was foreman and superintendent of the mills. He scouted the idea; but Ford, when I laid it before him, received it favorably, and permitted me to try the experiment.

Having removed the obstructions, I made up a narrow raft, consisting of twelve cribs. At this business I think I was quite skillful, not having forgotten my experience years before on the Champlain canal. I labored hard, being extremely anxious to succeed, both from a desire to please my master, and to show Adam Taydem that my scheme was not such a visionary one as he incessantly pronounced it. One hand could manage three cribs. I took charge of the forward three, and commenced poling down the creek. In due time we entered the first bayou, and finally reached our destination in a shorter period of time than I had anticipated.

The arrival of the raft at Lamourie created a sensation, while Mr. Ford loaded me with commendations. On all sides I heard Ford's Platt pronounced the "smartest nigger in the Pine Woods"—in fact I was the Fulton of Indian Creek. I was not insensible to the praise bestowed upon me, and enjoyed, especially, my triumph over Taydem, whose half-malicious ridicule had stung my pride. From this time the entire control of bringing the lumber to Lamourie was placed in my hands until the contract was fulfilled.

Indian Creek, in its whole length, flows through a magnificent forest. There dwells on its shore a tribe of Indians, a remnant of the Chickasaws or Chickopees, if I remember rightly. They live in simple huts, ten or twelve feet square, constructed of pine poles and covered with bark. They subsist principally on the flesh of the deer, the coon, and opossum, all of which are plenty in these woods. Sometimes they exchange venison for a little corn and whisky with the planters on the bayous. Their usual dress is buckskin breeches and calico hunting shirts of fantastic colors, buttoned from belt to chin. They wear brass rings on their wrists, and in their ears and noses. The dress of the squaws is very similar. They are fond of dogs and horses—owning many of the latter, of a small, tough breed—and are skillful riders. Their bridles, girths and saddles were made of raw skins of animals; their stirrups of a certain kind of wood. Mounted astride their ponies, men and women, I have seen them dash out into the woods at the utmost of their speed, following narrow winding paths, and dodging trees, in a manner that eclipsed the most miraculous feats of civilized equestrianism. Circling away in various directions, the forest echoing and re-echoing with their whoops, they would presently return at the same dashing, headlong speed with which they started. Their village was on Indian Creek, known as Indian Castle, but their range extended to the Sabine River. Occasionally a tribe from Texas would come over on a visit, and then there was indeed a carnival in the "Great Pine Woods." Chief of the tribe was Cascalla; second in rank, John Baltese, his son-in-law; with both of whom, as with many others of the tribe, I became acquainted during my frequent voyages down the creek with rafts. Sam and myself would often visit them when the day's task was done. They were obedient to the chief; the word of Cascalla was their law. They were a rude but harmless people, and enjoyed their wild mode of life. They had little fancy for the open country, the cleared lands on the shores of the bayous, but preferred to hide themselves within the shadows of the forest. They worshiped the Great Spirit, loved whisky, and were happy.

On one occasion I was present at a dance, when a roving herd from Texas had encamped in their village. The entire carcass of a deer was roasting before a large fire, which threw its light a long distance among the trees under which they were assembled. When they had formed in a ring, men and squaws alternately, a sort of Indian fiddle set up an indescribable tune. It was a continuous, melancholy kind of wavy sound, with the slightest possible variation. At the first note, if indeed there was more than one note in the whole tune, they circled around, trotting

298

after each other, and giving utterance to a guttural, sing-song noise, equally as nondescript as the music of the fiddle. At the end of the third circuit, they would stop suddenly, whoop as if their lungs would crack, then break from the ring, forming in couples, man and squaw, each jumping backwards as far as possible from the other, then forwards—which graceful feat having been twice or thrice accomplished, they would form in a ring, and go trotting round again. The best dancer appeared to be considered the one who could whoop the loudest, jump the farthest, and utter the most excruciating noise. At intervals, one or more would leave the dancing circle, and going to the fire, cut from the roasting carcass a slice of venison.

In a hole, shaped like a mortar, cut in the trunk of a fallen tree, they pounded corn with a wooden pestle, and of the meal made cake. Alternately they danced and ate. Thus were the visitors from Texas entertained by the dusky sons and daughters of the Chicopees, and such is a description, as I saw it, of an Indian ball in the Pine Woods of Avoyelles.

In the autumn, I left the mills, and was employed at the opening. One day the mistress was urging Ford to procure a loom, in order that Sally might commence weaving cloth for the winter garments of the slaves. He could not imagine where one was to be found, when I suggested that the easiest way to get one would be to make it, informing him at the same time, that I was a sort of "Jack at all trades," and would attempt it, with his permission. It was granted very readily, and I was allowed to go to a neighboring planter's to inspect one before commencing the undertaking. At length it was finished and pronounced by Sally to be perfect. She could easily weave her task of fourteen yards, milk the cows, and have leisure time besides each day. It worked so well, I was continued in the employment of making looms, which were taken down to the plantation on the bayou.

At this time one John M. Tibeats, a carpenter, came to the opening to do some work on master's house. I was directed to quit the looms and assist him. For two weeks I was in his

299

company, planning and matching boards for ceiling, a plastered room being a rare thing in the parish of Avoyelles.

John M. Tibeats was the opposite of Ford in all respects. He was a small, crabbed, quick-tempered, spiteful man. He had no fixed residence that I ever heard of, but passed from one plantation to another, wherever he could find employment. He was without standing in the community, not esteemed by white men, nor even respected by slaves. He was ignorant, withal, and of a revengeful disposition. He left the parish long before I did, and I know not whether he is at present alive or dead. Certain it is, it was a most unlucky day for me that brought us together. During my residence with Master Ford I had seen only the bright side of slavery. His was no heavy hand crushing us to the earth. *He* pointed upwards, and with benign and cheering words addressed us as his fellow-mortals, accountable, like himself, to the Maker of us all. I think of him with affection, and had my family been with me, could have borne his gentle servitude, without murmuring, all my days. But clouds were gathering in the horizon—forerunners of a pitiless storm that was soon to break over me. I was doomed to endure such bitter trials as the poor slave only knows, and to lead no more the comparatively happy life which I had led in the "Great Pine Woods."

CHAPTER VIII

William Ford unfortunately became embarrassed in his pecuniary affairs. A heavy judgment was rendered against him in consequence of his having become security for his brother, Franklin Ford, residing on Red River, above Alexandria, and who had failed to meet his liabilities. He was also indebted to John M. Tibeats to a considerable amount in consideration of his services in building the mills on Indian Creek, and also a weaving-house, corn-mill and other erections on the plantation at Bayou Bœuf, not yet completed. It was therefore necessary, in order to meet these demands, to dispose of eighteen slaves, myself among the number. Seventeen of them, including Sam and Harry, were purchased by Peter Compton, a planter also residing on Red River.

I was sold to Tibeats, in consequence, undoubtedly, of my slight skill as a carpenter. This was in the winter of 1842. The deed of myself from Freeman to Ford, as I ascertained from the public records in New-Orleans on my return, was dated June 23d, 1841. At the time of my sale to Tibeats, the price agreed to be given for me being more than the debt, Ford took a chattel mortgage of four hundred dollars. I am indebted for my life, as will hereafter be seen, to that mortgage.

I bade farewell to my good friends at the opening, and departed with my new master Tibeats. We went down to the plantation on Bayou Bœuf, distant twenty-seven miles from the Pine Woods, to complete the unfinished contract. Bayou Bœuf is a sluggish, winding stream—one of those stagnant bodies of water common in that region, setting back from Red River. It stretches from a point not far from Alexandria, in a south-easterly direction, and following its tortuous course, is more than fifty miles in length. Large cotton and sugar plantations line each shore, extending back to the borders of interminable swamps. It is alive with alligators, rendering it unsafe for swine, or unthinking slave children to stroll along its banks. Upon a bend in this bayou, a short distance from Cheneyville, was situated the plantation of Madam Ford—her brother, Peter Tanner, a great landholder, living on the opposite side.

On my arrival at Bayou Bœuf, I had the pleasure of meeting Eliza, whom I had not seen for several months. She had not pleased Mrs. Ford, being more occupied in brooding over her sorrows than in attending to her business, and had, in consequence, been sent down to work in the field on the plantation. She had grown feeble and emaciated, and was still mourning for her children. She asked me if I had forgotten them, and a great many times inquired if I still remembered how handsome little Emily was—how much Randall loved her—and wondered if they were living still, and where the darlings could then be. She had sunk beneath the weight of an excessive grief. Her drooping form and hollow cheeks too plainly indicated that she had well nigh reached the end of her weary road.

Ford's overseer on this plantation, and who had the exclusive charge of it, was a Mr. Chapin, a kindly-disposed man, and a native of Pennsylvania. In common with others, he held Tibeats in light estimation, which fact, in connection with the four hundred dollar mortgage, was fortunate for me.

I was now compelled to labor very hard. From earliest dawn until late at night, I was not allowed to be a moment idle. Notwithstanding which, Tibeats was never satisfied. He was continually cursing and complaining. He never spoke to me a kind word. I was his faithful slave, and earned him large wages every day, and yet I went to my cabin nightly, loaded with abuse and stinging epithets.

We had completed the corn mill, the kitchen, and so forth, and were at work upon the weaving-house, when I was guilty of an act, in that State punishable with death. It was my first fight with Tibeats. The weaving-house we were erecting stood in the orchard a few rods from the residence of Chapin, or the "great house," as it was called. One night, having worked until it was too dark to see, I was ordered by Tibeats to rise very early in the morning, procure a keg of nails from Chapin, and commence putting on the clapboards. I retired to the cabin extremely tired, and having cooked a supper of bacon and corn cake, and conversed a while with Eliza, who occupied the same cabin, as also did Lawson and his wife Mary, and a slave named Bristol, laid down upon the ground floor, little dreaming of the sufferings that awaited me on the morrow. Before daylight I was on the piazza of the "great house," awaiting the appearance of overseer Chapin. To have aroused him from his slumbers and stated my errand, would have been an unpardonable boldness. At length he came out. Taking off my hat, I informed him Master Tibeats had directed me to call upon him for a keg of nails. Going into the store-room, he rolled it out, at the same time saying, if Tibeats preferred a different size, he would endeavor to furnish them, but that I might use those until further directed. Then mounting his horse, which stood saddled and bridled at the door, he rode away into the field, whither the slaves had preceded him, while I took the keg on my shoulder, and proceeding to the weaving-house, broke in the head, and commenced nailing on the clapboards.

As the day began to open, Tibeats came out of the house to where I was, hard at work. He seemed to be that morning even more morose and disagreeable than usual. He was my master, entitled by law to my flesh and blood, and to exercise over me such tyrannical control as his mean nature prompted; but there was no law that could prevent my looking upon him with intense contempt. I despised both his disposition and his intellect. I had just come round to the keg for a further supply of nails, as he reached the weaving-house.

"I thought I told you to commence putting on weather-boards this morning," he remarked.

"Yes, master, and I am about it," I replied.

"Where?" he demanded.

"On the other side," was my answer.

He walked round to the other side, examined my work for a while, muttering to himself in a fault-finding tone.

"Didn't I tell you last night to get a keg of nails of Chapin?" he broke forth again.

"Yes, master, and so I did; and overseer said he would get another size for you, if you wanted them, when he came back from the field."

Tibeats walked to the keg, looked a moment at the contents, then kicked it violently. Coming towards me in a great passion, he exclaimed,

"G—d d—n you! I thought you *knowed* something."

I made answer: "I tried to do as you told me, master. I didn't mean anything wrong. Overseer said—" But he interrupted me with such a flood of curses that I was unable to finish the sentence. At length he ran towards the house, and going to the piazza, took down one of the overseer's whips. The whip had a short wooden stock, braided over with leather, and was loaded at the butt. The lash was three feet long, or thereabouts, and made of raw-hide strands.

At first I was somewhat frightened, and my impulse was to run. There was no one about except Rachel, the cook, and Chapin's wife, and neither of them were to be seen. The rest were in the field. I knew he intended to whip me, and it was the first time any one had attempted it since my arrival at Avoyelles. I felt, moreover, that I had been faithful—that I was guilty of no wrong whatever, and deserved commendation rather than punishment. My fear changed to anger, and before he reached me I had made up my mind fully not to be whipped, let the result be life or death.

Winding the lash around his hand, and taking hold of the small end of the stock, he walked up to me, and with a malignant look, ordered me to strip.

"Master Tibeats" said I, looking him boldly in the face, "I will *not*." I was about to say something further in justification, but with concentrated vengeance, he sprang upon me, seizing me by the throat with one hand, raising the whip with the other, in the act of striking. Before the blow descended, however, I had caught him by the collar of the coat, and drawn him closely to me. Reaching down, I seized him by the ankle, and pushing him back with the other hand, he fell over on the ground. Putting one arm around his leg, and holding it to my breast, so that his head and shoulders only touched the ground, I placed my foot upon his neck. He was completely in my power. My blood was up. It seemed to course through my veins like fire. In the frenzy of my madness I snatched the whip from his hand. He struggled with all his power; swore that I should not live to see another day; and that he would tear out my heart. But his struggles and his threats were alike in vain. I cannot tell how many times I struck him. Blow after blow fell fast and heavy upon his wriggling form. At length he screamed—cried murder—and at last the blasphemous tyrant called on God for mercy. But he who had never shown mercy did not receive it. The stiff stock of the whip warped round his cringing body until my right arm ached.

Until this time I had been too busy to look about me. Desisting for a moment, I saw Mrs. Chapin looking from the window, and Rachel standing in the kitchen door. Their attitudes expressed the utmost excitement and alarm. His screams had been heard in the field. Chapin was coming as fast as he could ride. I struck him a blow or two more, then pushed him from me with such a well-directed kick that he went rolling over on the ground.

Rising to his feet, and brushing the dirt from his hair, he stood looking at me, pale with rage. We gazed at each other in silence. Not a word was uttered until Chapin galloped up to us.

"What is the matter?" he cried out.

"Master Tibeats wants to whip me for using the nails you gave me," I replied.

"What is the matter with the nails?" he inquired,

305

turning to Tibeats.

Tibeats answered to the effect that they were too large, paying little heed, however, to Chapin's question, but still keeping his snakish eyes fastened maliciously on me.

"I am overseer here," Chapin began. "I told Platt to take them and use them, and if they were not of the proper size I would get others on returning from the field. It is not his fault. Besides, I shall furnish such nails as I please. I hope you will understand *that*, Mr. Tibeats."

Tibeats made no reply, but, grinding his teeth and shaking his fist, swore he would have satisfaction, and that it was not half over yet. Thereupon he walked away, followed by the overseer, and entered the house, the latter talking to him all the while in a suppressed tone, and with earnest gestures.

I remained where I was, doubting whether it was better to fly or abide the result, whatever it might be. Presently Tibeats came out of the house, and, saddling his horse, the only property he possessed besides myself, departed on the road to Cheneyville.

When he was gone, Chapin came out, visibly excited, telling me not to stir, not to attempt to leave the plantation on any account whatever. He then went to the kitchen, and calling Rachel out, conversed with her some time. Coming back, he again charged me with great earnestness not to run, saying my master was a rascal; that he had left on no good errand, and that there might be trouble before night. But at all events, he insisted upon it, I must not stir.

As I stood there, feelings of unutterable agony overwhelmed me. I was conscious that I had subjected myself to unimaginable punishment. The reaction that followed my extreme ebullition of anger produced the most painful sensations of regret. An unfriended, helpless slave—what could I *do*, what could I *say*, to justify, in the remotest manner, the heinous act I had committed, of resenting a *white* man's contumely and abuse. I tried to pray—I tried to beseech my Heavenly Father to sustain me in my sore extremity, but emotion choked my utterance, and I could only bow my head upon my hands and weep. For at least an hour I remained in this situation, finding relief only in tears, when, looking up, I beheld Tibeats, accompanied by two horsemen, coming down the bayou. They rode into the yard, jumped from their horses, and approached me with large whips, one of them also carrying a coil of rope.

"Cross your hands," commanded Tibeats, with the addition of such a shuddering expression of blasphemy as is not decorous to repeat.

"You need not bind me, Master Tibeats, I am ready to go with you anywhere," said I.

One of his companions then stepped forward, swearing if I made the least resistance he would break my head—he would tear me limb from limb—he would cut my black throat—and giving wide scope to other similar expressions. Perceiving any importunity altogether vain, I crossed my hands, submitting humbly to whatever disposition they might please to make of me. Thereupon Tibeats tied my wrists, drawing the rope around them with his utmost strength. Then he bound my ankles in the same manner. In the meantime the other two had slipped a cord within my elbows, running it across my back, and tying it firmly. It was utterly impossible to move hand or foot. With a remaining piece of rope Tibeats made an awkward noose, and placed it about my neck.

"Now, then," inquired one of Tibeats' companions, "where shall we hang the nigger?"

One proposed such a limb, extending from the body of a peach tree, near the spot where we were standing. His comrade objected to it, alleging it would break, and proposed another. Finally they fixed upon the latter.

During this conversation, and all the time they were binding me, I uttered not a word. Overseer Chapin, during the progress of the scene, was walking hastily back and forth on the piazza. Rachel was crying by the kitchen door, and Mrs. Chapin was still looking from the window. Hope died within my heart.

307

Surely my time had come. I should never behold the light of another day—never behold the faces of my children—the sweet anticipation I had cherished with such fondness. I should that hour struggle through the fearful agonies of death! None would mourn for me—none revenge me. Soon my form would be mouldering in that distant soil, or, perhaps, be cast to the slimy reptiles that filled the stagnant waters of the bayou! Tears flowed down my cheeks, but they only afforded a subject of insulting comment for my executioners.

At length, as they were dragging me towards the tree, Chapin, who had momentarily disappeared from the piazza, came out of the house and walked towards us. He had a pistol in each hand, and as near as I can now recall to mind, spoke in a firm, determined manner, as follows:

"Gentlemen, I have a few words to say. You had better listen to them. Whoever moves that slave another foot from where he stands is a dead man. In the first place, he does not deserve this treatment. It is a shame to murder him in this manner. I never knew a more faithful boy than Platt. You, Tibeats, are in the fault yourself. You are pretty much of a scoundrel, and I know it, and you richly deserve the flogging you have received. In the next place, I have been overseer on this plantation seven years, and, in the absence of William Ford, am master here. My duty is to protect his interests, and that duty I shall perform. You are not responsible—you are a worthless fellow. Ford holds a mortgage on Platt of four hundred dollars. If you hang him he loses his debt. Until that is canceled you have no right to take his life. You have no right to take it any way. There is a law for the slave as well as for the white man. You are no better than a murderer.

"As for you," addressing Cook and Ramsay, a couple of overseers from neighboring plantations, "as for you—begone! If you have any regard for your own safety, I say, begone."

Cook and Ramsay, without a further word, mounted their horses and rode away.

Tibeats, in a few minutes, evidently in fear, and overawed by the decided tone of Chapin, sneaked off like a coward, as he was, and mounting his horse, followed his companions.

I remained standing where I was, still bound, with the rope around my neck. As soon as they were gone, Chapin called Rachel, ordering her to run to the field, and tell Lawson to hurry to the house without delay, and bring the brown mule with him, an animal much prized for its unusual fleetness. Presently the boy appeared.

"Lawson," said Chapin, "you must go to the Pine Woods. Tell your master Ford to come here at once—that he must not delay a single moment. Tell him they are trying to murder Platt. Now hurry, boy. Be at the Pine Woods by noon if you kill the mule."

Chapin stepped into the house and wrote a pass. When he returned, Lawson was at the door, mounted on his mule. Receiving the pass, he plied the whip right smartly to the beast, dashed out of the yard, and turning up the bayou on a hard gallop, in less time than it has taken me to describe the scene, was out of sight.

CHAPTER IX

As the sun approached the meridian that day it became insufferably warm. Its hot rays scorched the ground. The earth almost blistered the foot that stood upon it. I was without coat or hat, standing bare-headed, exposed to its burning blaze. Great drops of perspiration rolled down my face, drenching the scanty apparel wherewith I was clothed. Over the fence, a very little way off, the peach trees cast their cool, delicious shadows on the grass. I would gladly have given a long year of service to have been enabled to exchange the heated oven, as it were, wherein I stood, for a seat beneath their branches. But I was yet bound, the rope still dangling from my neck, and standing in the same tracks where Tibeats and his comrades left me. I could not move an inch, so firmly had I been bound. To have been enabled to lean against the weaving house would have been a luxury indeed. But it was far beyond my reach, though distant less than twenty feet. I wanted to lie down, but knew I could not rise again. The ground was so parched and boiling hot I was aware it would but add to the discomfort of my situation. If I could have only moved my position, however slightly, it would have been relief unspeakable. But the hot rays of a southern sun, beating all the long summer day on my bare head, produced not half the suffering I experienced from my aching limbs. My wrists and ankles, and the cords of my legs and arms began to swell, burying the rope that bound them into the swollen flesh.

All day Chapin walked back and forth upon the stoop, but not once approached me. He appeared to be in a state of great uneasiness, looking first towards me, and then up the road, as if expecting some arrival every moment. He did not go to the field, as was his custom. It was evident from his manner that he supposed Tibeats would return with more and better armed assistance, perhaps, to renew the quarrel, and it was equally evident he had prepared his mind to defend my life at whatever hazard. Why he did not relieve me—why he suffered me to remain in agony the whole weary day, I never knew. It was not for want of sympathy, I am certain. Perhaps he wished Ford to see the rope about my neck, and the brutal manner in which I had been bound; perhaps his interference with another's property in which he had no legal interest might have been a trespass, which would have subjected him to the penalty of the law. Why Tibeats was all day absent was another mystery I never could divine. He knew well enough that Chapin would not harm him unless he persisted in his design against me. Lawson told me afterwards, that, as he passed the plantation of John David Cheney, he saw the three, and that they turned and looked after him as he flew by. I think his supposition was, that Lawson had been sent out by Overseer Chapin to arouse the neighboring planters, and to call on them to come to his assistance. He, therefore, undoubtedly, acted on the principle, that "discretion is the better part of valor," and kept away.

But whatever motive may have governed the cowardly and malignant tyrant, it is of no importance. There I still stood in the noon-tide sun, groaning with pain. From long before daylight I had not eaten a morsel. I was growing faint from pain, and thirst, and hunger. Once only, in the very hottest portion of the day, Rachel, half fearful she was acting contrary to the overseer's wishes, ventured to me, and held a cup of water to my lips. The humble creature never knew, nor could she comprehend if she had heard them, the blessings I invoked upon her, for that balmy draught. She could only say, "Oh, Platt, how I do pity you," and then hastened back to her labors in the kitchen.

Never did the sun move so slowly through the heavens— never did it shower down such fervent and fiery rays, as it did that day. At least, so it appeared to me. What my meditations were—the innumerable thoughts that thronged through my distracted brain—I will not attempt to give expression to. Suffice it to say, during the whole long day I came not to the conclusion, even once, that the southern slave, fed, clothed, whipped and protected by his master, is happier than the free colored citizen of the North. To that conclusion I have never since arrived. There are many, however, even in the Northern States, benevolent and well-disposed men, who will pronounce my opinion erroneous, and gravely proceed to substantiate the assertion with an argument. Alas! they have never drunk, as I have, from the bitter cup of slavery. Just at sunset my heart leaped with unbounded joy, as Ford came riding into the yard, his horse covered with foam. Chapin met him at the door, and after conversing a short time, he walked directly to me.

"Poor Platt, you are in a bad state," was the only expression that escaped his lips.

"Thank God!" said I, "thank God, Master Ford, that you have come at last."

Drawing a knife from his pocket, he indignantly cut the cord from my wrists, arms, and ankles, and slipped the noose from my neck. I attempted to walk, but staggered like a drunken man, and fell partially to the ground.

Ford returned immediately to the house, leaving me alone again. As he reached the piazza, Tibeats and his two friends rode up. A long dialogue followed. I could hear the sound of their voices, the mild tones of Ford mingling with the angry accents of Tibeats, but was unable to distinguish what was said. Finally the three departed again, apparently not well pleased.

I endeavored to raise the hammer, thinking to show Ford how willing I was to work, by proceeding with my labors on the weaving house, but it fell from my nerveless hand. At dark I crawled into the cabin, and laid down. I was in great misery— all sore and swollen—the slightest movement producing excruciating suffering. Soon the hands came in from the field. Rachel, when she went after Lawson, had told them what had happened. Eliza and Mary broiled me a piece of bacon, but my appetite was gone. Then they scorched some corn meal and made coffee. It was all that I could take. Eliza consoled me and was very kind. It was not long before the cabin was full of slaves. They gathered round me, asking many questions about the difficulty with Tibeats in the morning—and the particulars of all the occurrences of the day. Then Rachel came in, and in her simple language, repeated it over again—dwelling emphatically on the kick that sent Tibeats rolling over on the ground—whereupon there was a general titter throughout the crowd. Then she described how Chapin walked out with his pistols and rescued me, and how Master Ford cut the ropes with his knife, just as if he was mad.

By this time Lawson had returned. He had to regale them with an account of his trip to the Pine Woods—how the brown mule bore him faster than a "streak o'lightnin"—how he astonished everybody as he flew along—how Master Ford started right away—how he said Platt was a good nigger, and they shouldn't kill him, concluding with pretty strong intimations that there was not another human being in the wide world, who could have created such a universal sensation on the road, or performed such a marvelous John Gilpin feat, as he had done that day on the brown mule.

The kind creatures loaded me with the expression of their sympathy—saying, Tibeats was a hard, cruel man, and hoping "Massa Ford" would get me back again. In this manner they passed the time, discussing, chatting, talking over and over again the exciting affair, until suddenly Chapin presented himself at the cabin door and called me.

"Platt," said he, "you will sleep on the floor in the great house to-night; bring your blanket with you."

I arose as quickly as I was able, took my blanket in my hand, and followed him. On the way he informed me that he should not wonder if Tibeats was back again before morning—that he intended to kill me—and that he did not mean he should do it without witnesses. Had he stabbed me to the heart in the

313

presence of a hundred slaves, not one of them, by the laws of Louisiana, could have given evidence against him. I laid down on the floor in the "great house"—the first and the last time such a sumptuous resting place was granted me during my twelve years of bondage—and tried to sleep. Near midnight the dog began to bark. Chapin arose, looked from the window, but could discover nothing. At length the dog was quiet. As he returned to his room, he said,

"I believe, Platt, that scoundrel is skulking about the premises somewhere. If the dog barks again, and I am sleeping, wake me."

I promised to do so. After the lapse of an hour or more, the dog re-commenced his clamor, running towards the gate, then back again, all the while barking furiously.

Chapin was out of bed without waiting to be called. On this occasion, he stepped forth upon the piazza, and remained standing there a considerable length of time. Nothing, however, was to be seen, and the dog returned to his kennel. We were not disturbed again during the night. The excessive pain that I suffered, and the dread of some impending danger, prevented any rest whatever. Whether or not Tibeats did actually return to the plantation that night, seeking an opportunity to wreak his vengeance upon me, is a secret known only to himself, perhaps. I thought then, however, and have the strong impression still, that he was there. At all events, he had the disposition of an assassin—cowering before a brave man's words, but ready to strike his helpless or unsuspecting victim in the back, as I had reason afterwards to know.

At daylight in the morning, I arose, sore and weary, having rested little. Nevertheless, after partaking breakfast, which Mary and Eliza had prepared for me in the cabin, I proceeded to the weaving house and commenced the labors of another day. It was Chapin's practice, as it is the practice of overseers generally, immediately on arising, to bestride his horse, always saddled and bridled and ready for him—the particular business of some slave—and ride into the field. This morning, on the contrary, he came to the weaving house, asking if I had seen anything of Tibeats yet. Replying in the negative, he remarked there was something not right about the fellow—there was bad blood in him—that I must keep a sharp watch of him, or he would do me wrong some day when I least expected it.

While he was yet speaking, Tibeats rode in, hitched his horse, and entered the house. I had little fear of him while Ford and Chapin were at hand, but they could not be near me always.

Oh! how heavily the weight of slavery pressed upon me then. I must toil day after day, endure abuse and taunts and scoffs, sleep on the hard ground, live on the coarsest fare, and not only this, but live the slave of a blood-seeking wretch, of whom I must stand henceforth in continued fear and dread. Why had I not died in my young years—before God had given me children to love and live for? What unhappiness and suffering and sorrow it would have prevented. I sighed for liberty; but the bondman's chain was round me, and could not be shaken off. I could only gaze wistfully towards the North, and think of the thousands of miles that stretched between me and the soil of freedom, over which a *black* freeman may not pass.

Tibeats, in the course of half an hour, walked over to the weaving-house, looked at me sharply, then returned without saying anything. Most of the forenoon he sat on the piazza, reading a newspaper and conversing with Ford. After dinner, the latter left for the Pine Woods, and it was indeed with regret that I beheld him depart from the plantation.

Once more during the day Tibeats came to me, gave me some order, and returned.

During the week the weaving-house was completed—Tibeats in the meantime making no allusion whatever to the difficulty—when I was informed he had hired me to Peter Tanner, to work under another carpenter by the name of Myers. This announcement was received with gratification, as any place was desirable that would relieve me of his hateful presence.

Peter Tanner, as the reader has already been informed, lived on the opposite shore, and was the brother of Mistress Ford. He is one of the most extensive planters on Bayou Bœuf, and owns a large number of slaves.

Over I went to Tanner's, joyfully enough. He had heard of my late difficulties—in fact, I ascertained the flogging of Tibeats was soon blazoned far and wide. This affair, together with my rafting experiment, had rendered me somewhat notorious. More than once I heard it said that Platt Ford, now Platt Tibeats—a slave's name changes with his change of master—was "a devil of a nigger." But I was destined to make a still further noise, as will presently be seen, throughout the little world of Bayou Bœuf.

Peter Tanner endeavored to impress upon me the idea that he was quite severe, though I could perceive there was a vein of good humor in the old fellow, after all.

"You're the nigger," he said to me on my arrival—"You're the nigger that flogged your master, eh? You're the nigger that kicks, and holds carpenter Tibeats by the leg, and wallops him, are ye? I'd like to see you hold me by the leg—I should. You're a 'portant character—you're a great nigger—very remarkable nigger, ain't ye? *I'd* lash you—*I'd* take the tantrums out of ye. Jest take hold of my leg, if you please. None of your pranks here, my boy, remember *that*. Now go to work, you *kickin'* rascal," concluded Peter Tanner, unable to suppress a half-comical grin at his own wit and sarcasm.

After listening to this salutation, I was taken charge of by Myers, and labored under his direction for a month, to his and my own satisfaction.

Like William Ford, his brother-in-law, Tanner was in the habit of reading the Bible to his slaves on the Sabbath, but in a somewhat different spirit. He was an impressive commentator on the New Testament. The first Sunday after my coming to the plantation, he called them together, and began to read the twelfth chapter of Luke. When he came to the 47th verse, he looked deliberately around him, and continued—"And that servant which knew his lord's *will*,"—here he paused, looking

316

around more deliberately than before, and again proceeded—"which knew his lord's *will*, and *prepared* not himself"—here was another pause—"*prepared* not himself, neither did *according* to his will, shall be beaten with many *stripes.*"

"D'ye hear that?" demanded Peter, emphatically. "*Stripes,*" he repeated, slowly and distinctly, taking off his spectacles, preparatory to making a few remarks.

"That nigger that don't take care—that don't obey his lord—that's his master—d'ye see?—that 'ere nigger shall be beaten with many stripes. Now, 'many' signifies a *great* many—forty, a hundred, a hundred and fifty lashes. *That's* Scripter!" and so Peter continued to elucidate the subject for a great length of time, much to the edification of his sable audience.

At the conclusion of the exercises, calling up three of his slaves, Warner, Will and Major, he cried out to me—

"Here, Platt, you held Tibeats by the legs; now I'll see if you can hold these rascals in the same way, till I get back from meetin'."

Thereupon he ordered them to the stocks—a common thing on plantations in the Red River country. The stocks are formed of two planks, the lower one made fast at the ends to two short posts, driven firmly into the ground. At regular distances half circles are cut in the upper edge. The other plank is fastened to one of the posts by a hinge, so that it can be opened or shut down, in the same manner as the blade of a pocket-knife is shut or opened. In the lower edge of the upper plank corresponding half circles are also cut, so that when they close, a row of holes is formed large enough to admit a negro's leg above the ankle, but not large enough to enable him to draw out his foot. The other end of the upper plank, opposite the hinge, is fastened to its post by lock and key. The slave is made to sit upon the ground, when the uppermost plank is elevated, his legs, just above the ankles, placed in the sub-half circles, and shutting it down again, and locking it, he is held secure and fast. Very often the neck instead of the ankle is enclosed. In this manner they are held during the operation of whipping.

317

Warner, Will and Major, according to Tanner's account of them, were melon-stealing, Sabbath-breaking niggers, and not approving of such wickedness, he felt it his duty to put them in the stocks. Handing me the key, himself, Myers, Mistress Tanner and the children entered the carriage and drove away to church at Cheneyville. When they were gone, the boys begged me to let them out. I felt sorry to see them sitting on the hot ground, and remembered my own sufferings in the sun. Upon their promise to return to the stocks at any moment they were required to do so, I consented to release them. Grateful for the lenity shown them, and in order in some measure to repay it, they could do no less, of course, than pilot me to the melon-patch. Shortly before Tanner's return, they were in the stocks again. Finally he drove up, and looking at the boys, said, with a chuckle,—

"Aha! ye havn't been strolling about much to-day, any way. *I'll* teach you what's what. *I'll* tire ye of eating water-melons on the Lord's day, ye Sabbath-breaking niggers."

Peter Tanner prided himself upon his strict religious observances: he was a deacon in the church.

But I have now reached a point in the progress of my narrative, when it becomes necessary to turn away from these light descriptions, to the more grave and weighty matter of the second battle with Master Tibeats, and the flight through the great Pacoudrie Swamp.

CHAPTER X

At the end of a month, my services being no longer required at Tanner's I was sent over the bayou again to my master, whom I found engaged in building the cotton press. This was situated at some distance from the great house, in a rather retired place. I commenced working once more in company with Tibeats, being entirely alone with him most part of the time. I remembered the words of Chapin, his precautions, his advice to beware, lest in some unsuspecting moment he might injure me. They were always in my mind, so that I lived in a most uneasy state of apprehension and fear. One eye was on my work, the other on my master. I determined to give him no cause of offence, to work still more diligently, if possible, than I had done, to bear whatever abuse he might heap upon me, save bodily injury, humbly and patiently, hoping thereby to soften in some degree his manner towards me, until the blessed time might come when I should be delivered from his clutches.

The third morning after my return, Chapin left the plantation for Cheneyville, to be absent until night. Tibeats, on that morning, was attacked with one of those periodical fits of spleen and ill-humor to which he was frequently subject, rendering him still more disagreeable and venomous than usual.

It was about nine o'clock in the forenoon, when I was busily employed with the jack-plane on one of the sweeps. Tibeats was standing by the work-bench, fitting a handle into the chisel, with which he had been engaged previously in cutting the thread of the screw.

"You are not planing that down enough," said he.

"It is just even with the line," I replied.

"You're a d—d liar," he exclaimed passionately.

"Oh, well, master," I said, mildly, "I will plane it down more if you say so," at the same time proceeding to do as I supposed he desired. Before one shaving had been removed, however, he cried out, saying I had now planed it too deep—it was too small—I had spoiled the sweep entirely. Then followed curses and imprecations. I had endeavored to do exactly as he directed, but nothing would satisfy the unreasonable man. In silence and in dread I stood by the sweep, holding the jack-plane in my hand, not knowing what to do, and not daring to be idle. His anger grew more and more violent, until, finally, with an oath, such a bitter, frightful oath as only Tibeats could utter, he seized a hatchet from the work-bench and darted towards me, swearing he would cut my head open.

It was a moment of life or death. The sharp, bright blade of the hatchet glittered in the sun. In another instant it would be buried in my brain, and yet in that instant—so quick will a man's thoughts come to him in such a fearful strait—I reasoned with myself. If I stood still, my doom was certain; if I fled, ten chances to one the hatchet, flying from his hand with a too-deadly and unerring aim, would strike me in the back. There was but one course to take. Springing towards him with all my power, and meeting him full half-way, before he could bring down the blow, with one hand I caught his uplifted arm, with the other seized him by the throat. We stood looking each other in the eyes. In his I could see murder. I felt as if I had a serpent by the neck, watching the slightest relaxation of my gripe, to coil itself round my body, crushing and stinging it to death. I thought to scream aloud, trusting that some ear might catch the sound—but Chapin was away; the hands were in the field; there was no living soul in sight or hearing.

The good genius, which thus far through life has saved me from the hands of violence, at that moment suggested a lucky thought. With a vigorous and sudden kick, that brought him on one knee, with a groan, I released my hold upon his throat, snatched the hatchet, and cast it beyond reach.

Frantic with rage, maddened beyond control, he seized a white oak stick, five feet long, perhaps, and as large in circumference as his hand could grasp, which was lying on the ground. Again he rushed towards me, and again I met him, seized him about the waist, and being the stronger of the two, bore him to the earth. While in that position I obtained possession of the stick, and rising, cast it from me, also.

He likewise arose and ran for the broad-axe, on the workbench. Fortunately, there was a heavy plank lying upon its broad blade, in such a manner that he could not extricate it, before I had sprung upon his back. Pressing him down closely and heavily on the plank, so that the axe was held more firmly to its place, I endeavored, but in vain, to break his grasp upon the handle. In that position we remained some minutes.

There have been hours in my unhappy life, many of them, when the contemplation of death as the end of earthly sorrow—of the grave as a resting place for the tired and worn out body—has been pleasant to dwell upon. But such contemplations vanish in the hour of peril. No man, in his full strength, can stand undismayed, in the presence of the "king of terrors." Life is dear to every living thing; the worm that crawls upon the ground will struggle for it. At that moment it was dear to me, enslaved and treated as I was.

Not able to unloose his hand, once more I seized him by the throat, and this time, with a vice-like gripe that soon relaxed his hold. He became pliant and unstrung. His face, that had been white with passion, was now black from suffocation. Those small serpent eyes that spat such venom, were now full of horror—two great white orbs starting from their sockets!

There was "a lurking devil" in my heart that prompted me to kill the human blood-hound on the spot—to retain the grip on his accursed throat till the breath of life was gone! I dared not murder him, and I dared not let him live. If I killed him, my life must pay the forfeit—if he lived, my life only would satisfy his vengeance. A voice within whispered me to fly. To be a wanderer among the swamps, a fugitive and a vagabond on the face of the earth, was preferable to the life that I was leading.

My resolution was soon formed, and swinging him from the work-bench to the ground, I leaped a fence near by, and hurried across the plantation, passing the slaves at work in the cotton field. At the end of a quarter of a mile I reached the wood-pasture, and it was a short time indeed that I had been running it. Climbing on to a high fence, I could see the cotton press, the great house, and the space between. It was a conspicuous position, from whence the whole plantation was in view. I saw Tibeats cross the field towards the house, and enter it—then he came out, carrying his saddle, and presently mounted his horse and galloped away.

I was desolate, but thankful. Thankful that my life was spared,—desolate and discouraged with the prospect before me. What would become of me? Who would befriend me? Whither should I fly? Oh, God! Thou who gavest me life, and implanted in my bosom the love of life—who filled it with emotions such as other men, thy creatures, have, do not forsake me. Have pity on the poor slave—let me not perish. If thou dost not protect me, I am lost—lost! Such supplications, silently and unuttered, ascended from my inmost heart to Heaven. But there was no answering voice—no sweet, low tone, coming down from on high, whispering to my soul, "It is I, be not afraid." I was the forsaken of God, it seemed—the despised and hated of men!

In about three-fourths of an hour several of the slaves shouted and made signs for me to run. Presently, looking up the bayou, I saw Tibeats and two others on horse-back, coming at a fast gait, followed by a troop of dogs. There were as many as eight or ten. Distant as I was, I knew them. They belonged on the adjoining plantation. The dogs used on Bayou Bœuf for hunting slaves are a kind of blood-hound, but a far more savage breed than is found in the Northern States. They will attack a negro, at their master's bidding, and cling to him as the common bull-dog will cling to a four footed animal. Frequently their loud bay is heard in the swamps, and then there is speculation as to what point the runaway will be overhauled—the same as a New-York hunter stops to listen to the hounds coursing along the hillsides, and suggests to his companion that the fox will be taken at such a place. I never knew a slave escaping with his life from Bayou Bœuf. One reason is, they are not allowed to learn the art of swimming, and are incapable of crossing the most inconsiderable stream. In their flight they can go in no direction but a little way without coming to a bayou, when the inevitable alternative is presented, of being drowned or overtaken by the dogs. In youth I had practised in the clear streams that flow through my native district, until I had become an expert swimmer, and felt at home in the watery element.

I stood upon the fence until the dogs had reached the cotton press. In an instant more, their long, savage yells announced they were on my track. Leaping down from my position, I ran towards the swamp. Fear gave me strength, and I exerted it to the utmost. Every few moments I could hear the yelpings of the dogs. They were gaining upon me. Every howl was nearer and nearer. Each moment I expected they would spring upon my back—expected to feel their long teeth sinking into my flesh. There were so many of them, I knew they would tear me to pieces, that they would worry me, at once, to death. I gasped for breath—gasped forth a half-uttered, choking prayer to the Almighty to save me—to give me strength to reach some wide, deep bayou where I could throw them off the track, or sink into its waters. Presently I reached a thick palmetto bottom. As I fled through them they made a loud rustling noise, not loud enough, however, to drown the voices of the dogs.

Continuing my course due south, as nearly as I can judge, I came at length to water just over shoe. The hounds at that moment could not have been five rods behind me. I could hear them crashing and plunging through the palmettoes, their loud, eager yells making the whole swamp clamorous with the sound. Hope revived a little as I reached the water. If it were only

323

deeper, they might lose the scent, and thus disconcerted, afford me the opportunity of evading them. Luckily, it grew deeper the farther I proceeded—now over my ankles—now half-way to my knees—now sinking a moment to my waist, and then emerging presently into more shallow places. The dogs had not gained upon me since I struck the water. Evidently they were confused. Now their savage intonations grew more and more distant, assuring me that I was leaving them. Finally I stopped to listen, but the long howl came booming on the air again, telling me I was not yet safe. From bog to bog, where I had stepped, they could still keep upon the track, though impeded by the water. At length, to my great joy, I came to a wide bayou, and plunging in, had soon stemmed its sluggish current to the other side. There, certainly, the dogs would be confounded—the current carrying down the stream all traces of that slight, mysterious scent, which enables the quick-smelling hound to follow in the track of the fugitive.

After crossing this bayou the water became so deep I could not run. I was now in what I afterwards learned was the "Great Pacoudrie Swamp." It was filled with immense trees—the sycamore, the gum, the cotton wood and cypress, and extends, I am informed, to the shore of the Calcasieu river. For thirty or forty miles it is without inhabitants, save wild beasts—the bear, the wild-cat, the tiger, and great slimy reptiles, that are crawling through it everywhere. Long before I reached the bayou, in fact, from the time I struck the water until I emerged from the swamp on my return, these reptiles surrounded me. I saw hundreds of moccasin snakes. Every log and bog—every trunk of a fallen tree, over which I was compelled to step or climb, was alive with them. They crawled away at my approach, but sometimes in my haste, I almost placed my hand or foot upon them. They are poisonous serpents—their bite more fatal than the rattlesnake's. Besides, I had lost one shoe, the sole having come entirely off, leaving the upper only dangling to my ankle.

I saw also many alligators, great and small, lying in the water, or on pieces of floodwood. The noise I made usually startled them, when they moved off and plunged into the deepest places. Sometimes, however, I would come directly upon a monster before observing it. In such cases, I would start back, run a short way round, and in that manner shun them. Straight forward, they will run a short distance rapidly, but do not possess the power of turning. In a crooked race, there is no difficulty in evading them.

About two o'clock in the afternoon, I heard the last of the hounds. Probably they did not cross the bayou. Wet and weary, but relieved from the sense of instant peril, I continued on, more cautious and afraid, however, of the snakes and alligators than I had been in the earlier portion of my flight. Now, before stepping into a muddy pool, I would strike the water with a stick. If the waters moved, I would go around it, if not, would venture through.

At length the sun went down, and gradually night's trailing mantle shrouded the great swamp in darkness. Still I staggered on, fearing every instant I should feel the dreadful sting of the moccasin, or be crushed within the jaws of some disturbed alligator. The dread of them now almost equaled the fear of the pursuing hounds. The moon arose after a time, its mild light creeping through the overspreading branches, loaded with long, pendent moss. I kept traveling forwards until after midnight, hoping all the while that I would soon emerge into some less desolate and dangerous region. But the water grew deeper and the walking more difficult than ever. I perceived it would be impossible to proceed much farther, and knew not, moreover, what hands I might fall into, should I succeed in reaching a human habitation. Not provided with a pass, any white man would be at liberty to arrest me, and place me in prison until such time as my master should "prove property, pay charges, and take me away." I was an estray, and if so unfortunate as to meet a law-abiding citizen of Louisiana, he would deem it his duty to his neighbor, perhaps, to put me forthwith in the pound.

Really, it was difficult to determine which I had most reason to fear—dogs, alligators or men!

After midnight, however, I came to a halt. Imagination cannot picture the dreariness of the scene. The swamp was resonant with the quacking of innumerable ducks! Since the foundation of the earth, in all probability, a human footstep had never before so far penetrated the recesses of the swamp. It was not silent now—silent to a degree that rendered it oppressive,— as it was when the sun was shining in the heavens. My midnight intrusion had awakened the feathered tribes, which seemed to throng the morass in hundreds of thousands, and their garrulous throats poured forth such multitudinous sounds—there was such a fluttering of wings—such sullen plunges in the water all around me—that I was affrighted and appalled. All the fowls of the air, and all the creeping things of the earth appeared to have assembled together in that particular place, for the purpose of filling it with clamor and confusion. Not by human dwellings— not in crowded cities alone, are the sights and sounds of life. The wildest places of the earth are full of them. Even in the heart of that dismal swamp, God had provided a refuge and a dwelling place for millions of living things.

The moon had now risen above the trees, when I resolved upon a new project. Thus far I had endeavored to travel as nearly south as possible. Turning about I proceeded in a north-west direction, my object being to strike the Pine Woods in the vicinity of Master Ford's. Once within the shadow of his protection, I felt I would be comparatively safe.

My clothes were in tatters, my hands, face, and body covered with scratches, received from the sharp knots of fallen trees, and in climbing over piles of brush and floodwood. My bare foot was full of thorns. I was besmeared with muck and mud, and the green slime that had collected on the surface of the dead water, in which I had been immersed to the neck many times during the day and night. Hour after hour, and tiresome indeed had they become, I continued to plod along on my north-west course. The water began to grow less deep, and the ground more firm under my feet. At last I reached the Pacoudrie, the same wide bayou I had swam while "outward bound." I swam it again, and shortly after thought I heard a cock crow, but the sound was faint, and it might have been a mockery of the ear. The water receded from my advancing footsteps—now I had left the bogs behind me— now I was on dry land that gradually ascended to the plain, and I knew I was somewhere in the "Great Pine Woods."

Just at day-break I came to an opening—a sort of small plantation—but one I had never seen before. In the edge of the woods I came upon two men, a slave and his young master, engaged in catching wild hogs. The white man I knew would demand my pass, and not able to give him one, would take me into possession. I was too wearied to run again, and too desperate to be taken, and therefore adopted a ruse that proved entirely successful. Assuming a fierce expression, I walked directly towards him, looking him steadily in the face. As I approached, he moved backwards with an air of alarm. It was plain he was much affrighted—that he looked upon me as some infernal goblin, just arisen from the bowels of the swamp!

"Where does William Ford live?" I demanded, in no gentle tone.

"He lives seven miles from here," was the reply.

"Which is the way to his place?" I again demanded, trying to look more fiercely than ever.

"Do you see those pine trees yonder?" he asked, pointing to two, a mile distant, that rose far above their fellows, like a couple of tall sentinels, overlooking the broad expanse of forest.

"I see them," was the answer.

"At the feet of those pine trees," he continued, "runs the Texas road. Turn to the left, and it will lead you to William Ford's."

Without farther parley, I hastened forward, happy as he was, no doubt, to place the widest possible distance between us. Striking the Texas road, I turned to the left hand, as directed, and soon passed a great fire, where a pile of logs were burning.

I went to it, thinking I would dry my clothes; but the gray light of the morning was fast breaking away,—some passing white man might observe me; besides, the heat overpowered me with the desire of sleep: so, lingering no longer, I continued my travels, and finally, about eight o'clock, reached the house of Master Ford.

The slaves were all absent from the quarters, at their work. Stepping on to the piazza, I knocked at the door, which was soon opened by Mistress Ford. My appearance was so changed—I was in such a wobegone and forlorn condition, she did not know me. Inquiring if Master Ford was at home, that good man made his appearance, before the question could be answered. I told him of my flight, and all the particulars connected with it. He listened attentively, and when I had concluded, spoke to me kindly and sympathetically, and taking me to the kitchen, called John, and ordered him to prepare me food. I had tasted nothing since daylight the previous morning.

When John had set the meal before me, the madam came out with a bowl of milk, and many little delicious dainties, such as rarely please the palate of a slave. I was hungry, and I was weary, but neither food nor rest afforded half the pleasure as did the blessed voices speaking kindness and consolation. It was the oil and the wine which the Good Samaritan in the "Great Pine Woods" was ready to pour into the wounded spirit of the slave, who came to him, stripped of his raiment and half-dead.

They left me in the cabin, that I might rest. Blessed be sleep! It visiteth all alike, descending as the dews of heaven on the bond and free. Soon it nestled to my bosom, driving away the troubles that oppressed it, and bearing me to that shadowy region, where I saw again the faces, and listened to the voices of my children, who, alas, for aught I knew in my waking hours, had fallen into the arms of that *other* sleep, from which they *never* would arouse.

CHAPTER XI

After a long sleep, sometime in the afternoon I awoke, refreshed, but very sore and stiff. Sally came in and talked with me, while John cooked me some dinner. Sally was in great trouble, as well as myself, one of her children being ill, and she feared it could not survive. Dinner over, after walking about the quarters for a while, visiting Sally's cabin and looking at the sick child, I strolled into the madam's garden. Though it was a season of the year when the voices of the birds are silent, and the trees are stripped of their summer glories in more frigid climes, yet the whole variety of roses were then blooming there, and the long, luxuriant vines creeping over the frames. The crimson and golden fruit hung half hidden amidst the younger and older blossoms of the peach, the orange, the plum, and the pomegranate; for, in that region of almost perpetual warmth, the leaves are falling and the buds bursting into bloom the whole year long.

I indulged the most grateful feelings towards Master and Mistress Ford, and wishing in some manner to repay their kindness, commenced trimming the vines, and afterwards weeding out the grass from among the orange and pomegranate trees. The latter grows eight or ten feet high, and its fruit, though larger, is similar in appearance to the jelly-flower. It has the luscious flavor of the strawberry. Oranges, peaches, plums, and most other fruits are indigenous to the rich, warm soil of Avoyelles; but the apple, the most common of them all in colder latitudes, is rarely to be seen.

Mistress Ford came out presently, saying it was praise-worthy in me, but I was not in a condition to labor, and might rest myself at the quarters until master should go down to

329

Bayou Bœuf, which would not be that day, and it might not be the next. I said to her—to be sure, I felt bad, and was stiff, and that my foot pained me, the stubs and thorns having so torn it, but thought such exercise would not hurt me, and that it was a great pleasure to work for so good a mistress. Thereupon she returned to the great house, and for three days I was diligent in the garden, cleaning the walks, weeding the flower beds, and pulling up the rank grass beneath the jessamine vines, which the gentle and generous hand of my protectress had taught to clamber along the walls.

The fourth morning, having become recruited and refreshed, Master Ford ordered me to make ready to accompany him to the bayou. There was but one saddle horse at the opening, all the others with the mules having been sent down to the plantation. I said I could walk, and bidding Sally and John goodbye, left the opening, trotting along by the horse's side.

That little paradise in the Great Pine Woods was the oasis in the desert, towards which my heart turned lovingly, during many years of bondage. I went forth from it now with regret and sorrow, not so overwhelming, however, as if it had then been given me to know that I should never return to it again.

Master Ford urged me to take his place occasionally on the horse, to rest me; but I said no, I was not tired, and it was better for me to walk than him. He said many kind and cheering things to me on the way, riding slowly, in order that I might keep pace with him. The goodness of God was manifest, he declared, in my miraculous escape from the swamp. As Daniel came forth unharmed from the den of lions, and as Jonah had been preserved in the whale's belly, even so had I been delivered from evil by the Almighty. He interrogated me in regard to the various fears and emotions I had experienced during the day and night, and if I had felt, at any time, a desire to pray. I felt forsaken of the whole world, I answered him, and was praying mentally all the while. At such times, said he, the heart of man turns instinctively towards his Maker. In prosperity, and when

330

there is nothing to injure or make him afraid, he remembers Him not, and is ready to defy Him; but place him in the midst of dangers, cut him off from human aid, let the grave open before him—then it is, in the time of his tribulation, that the scoffer and unbelieving man turns to God for help, feeling there is no other hope, or refuge, or safety, save in his protecting arm.

So did that benignant man speak to me of this life and of the life hereafter; of the goodness and power of God, and of the vanity of earthly things, as we journeyed along the solitary road towards Bayou Bœuf.

When within some five miles of the plantation, we discovered a horseman at a distance, galloping towards us. As he came near I saw that it was Tibeats! He looked at me a moment, but did not address me, and turning about, rode along side by side with Ford. I trotted silently at their horses' heels, listening to their conversation. Ford informed him of my arrival in the Pine Woods three days before, of the sad plight I was in, and of the difficulties and dangers I had encountered.

"Well," exclaimed Tibeats, omitting his usual oaths in the presence of Ford, "I never saw such running before. I'll bet him against a hundred dollars, he'll beat any nigger in Louisiana. I offered John David Cheney twenty-five dollars to catch him, dead or alive, but he outran his dogs in a fair race. Them Cheney dogs ain't much, after all. Dunwoodie's hounds would have had him down before he touched the palmettoes. Somehow the dogs got off the track, and we had to give up the hunt. We rode the horses as far as we could, and then kept on foot till the water was three feet deep. The boys said he was drowned, sure. I allow I wanted a shot at him mightily. Ever since, I have been riding up and down the bayou, but had'nt much hope of catching him—thought he was dead, *sartin*. Oh, he's a cuss to run— that nigger is!"

In this way Tibeats ran on, describing his search in the swamp, the wonderful speed with which I had fled before the hounds, and when he had finished, Master Ford responded by

331

saying, I had always been a willing and faithful boy with him; that he was sorry we had such trouble; that, according to Platt's story, he had been inhumanly treated, and that he, Tibeats, was himself in fault. Using hatchets and broad-axes upon slaves was shameful, and should not be allowed, he remarked. "This is no way of dealing with them, when first brought into the country. It will have a pernicious influence, and set them all running away. The swamps will be full of them. A little kindness would be far more effectual in restraining them, and rendering them obedient, than the use of such deadly weapons. Every planter on the bayou should frown upon such inhumanity. It is for the interest of all to do so. It is evident enough, Mr. Tibeats, that you and Platt cannot live together. You dislike him, and would not hesitate to kill him, and knowing it, he will run from you again through fear of his life. Now, Tibeats, you must sell him, or hire him out, at least. Unless you do so, I shall take measures to get him out of your possession."

In this spirit Ford addressed him the remainder of the distance. I opened not my mouth. On reaching the plantation they entered the great house, while I repaired to Eliza's cabin. The slaves were astonished to find me there, on returning from the field, supposing I was drowned. That night, again, they gathered about the cabin to listen to the story of my adventure. They took it for granted I would be whipped, and that it would be severe, the well-known penalty of running away being five hundred lashes.

"Poor fellow," said Eliza, taking me by the hand, "it would have been better for you if you had drowned. You have a cruel master, and he will kill you yet, I am afraid."

Lawson suggested that it might be, overseer Chapin would be appointed to inflict the punishment, in which case it would not be severe, whereupon Mary, Rachel, Bristol, and others hoped it would be Master Ford, and then it would be no whipping at all. They all pitied me and tried to console me, and were sad in view of the castigation that awaited me, except Kentucky John.

There were no bounds to his laughter; he filled the cabin with cachinnations, holding his sides to prevent an explosion, and the cause of his noisy mirth was the idea of my outstripping the hounds. Somehow, he looked at the subject in a comical light. "I *know'd* dey would'nt cotch him, when he run cross de plantation. O, de lor', did'nt Platt pick his feet right up, tho', hey? When dem dogs got whar he was, he was'nt *dar*—haw, haw, haw! O, de lor' a' mity!"—and then Kentucky John relapsed into another of his boisterous fits.

Early the next morning, Tibeats left the plantation. In the course of the forenoon, while sauntering about the gin-house, a tall, good-looking man came to me, and inquired if I was Tibeats' boy, that youthful appellation being applied indiscriminately to slaves even though they may have passed the number of three score years and ten. I took off my hat, and answered that I was.

"How would you like to work for me?" he inquired.

"Oh, I would like to, very much," said I, inspired with a sudden hope of getting away from Tibeats.

"You worked under Myers at Peter Tanner's, didn't you?"

I replied I had, adding some complimentary remarks that Myers had made concerning me.

"Well, boy," said he, "I have hired you of your master to work for me in the "Big Cane Brake," thirty-eight miles from here, down on Red River."

This man was Mr. Eldret, who lived below Ford's, on the same side of the bayou. I accompanied him to his plantation, and in the morning started with his slave Sam, and a wagon-load of provisions, drawn by four mules, for the Big Cane, Eldret and Myers having preceded us on horseback. This Sam was a native of Charleston, where he had a mother, brother and sisters. He "allowed"—a common word among both black and white—that Tibeats was a mean man, and hoped, as I most earnestly did also, that his master would buy me.

We proceeded down the south shore of the bayou, crossing it at Carey's plantation; from thence to Huff Power, passing which,

333

we came upon the Bayou Rouge road, which runs towards Red River. After passing through Bayou Rouge Swamp, and just at sunset, turning from the highway, we struck off into the "Big Cane Brake." We followed an unbeaten track, scarcely wide enough to admit the wagon. The cane, such as are used for fishing-rods, were as thick as they could stand. A person could not be seen through them the distance of a rod. The paths of wild beasts run through them in various directions—the bear and the American tiger abounding in these brakes, and wherever there is a basin of stagnant water, it is full of alligators.

We kept on our lonely course through the "Big Cane" several miles, when we entered a clearing, known as "Sutton's Field." Many years before, a man by the name of Sutton had penetrated the wilderness of cane to this solitary place. Tradition has it, that he fled thither, a fugitive, not from service, but from justice. Here he lived alone—recluse and hermit of the swamp—with his own hands planting the seed and gathering in the harvest. One day a band of Indians stole upon his solitude, and after a bloody battle, overpowered and massacred him. For miles the country round, in the slaves' quarters, and on the piazzas of "great houses," where white children listen to superstitious tales, the story goes, that that spot, in the heart of the "Big Cane," is a haunted place. For more than a quarter of a century, human voices had rarely, if ever, disturbed the silence of the clearing. Rank and noxious weeds had overspread the once cultivated field—serpents sunned themselves on the doorway of the crumbling cabin. It was indeed a dreary picture of desolation.

Passing "Sutton's Field," we followed a new-cut road two miles farther, which brought us to its termination. We had now reached the wild lands of Mr. Eldret, where he contemplated clearing up an extensive plantation. We went to work next morning with our cane-knives, and cleared a sufficient space to allow the erection of two cabins—one for Myers and Eldret, the other for Sam, myself, and the slaves that were to join us. We were now in the midst of trees of enormous growth, whose wide-spreading branches almost shut out the light of the sun, while the space between the trunks was an impervious mass of cane, with here and there an occasional palmetto.

The bay and the sycamore, the oak and the cypress, reach a growth unparalleled, in those fertile lowlands bordering the Red River. From every tree, moreover, hang long, large masses of moss, presenting to the eye unaccustomed to them, a striking and singular appearance. This moss, in large quantities, is sent north, and there used for manufacturing purposes.

We cut down oaks, split them into rails, and with these erected temporary cabins. We covered the roofs with the broad palmetto leaf, an excellent substitute for shingles, as long as they last.

The greatest annoyance I met with here were small flies, gnats and mosquitoes. They swarmed the air. They penetrated the porches of the ear, the nose, the eyes, the mouth. They sucked themselves beneath the skin. It was impossible to brush or beat them off. It seemed, indeed, as if they would devour us—carry us away piecemeal, in their small tormenting mouths.

A lonelier spot, or one more disagreeable, than the centre of the "Big Cane Brake," it would be difficult to conceive; yet to me it was a paradise, in comparison with any other place in the company of Master Tibeats. I labored hard, and oft-times was weary and fatigued, yet I could lie down at night in peace, and arise in the morning without fear.

In the course of a fortnight, four black girls came down from Eldret's plantation—Charlotte, Fanny, Cresia and Nelly. They were all large and stout. Axes were put into their hands, and they were sent out with Sam and myself to cut trees. They were excellent choppers, the largest oak or sycamore standing but a brief season before their heavy and well-directed blows. At piling logs, they were equal to any man. There are lumberwomen as well as lumbermen in the forests of the South. In fact, in the region of the Bayou Bœuf they perform their share of all the labor required on the plantation. They plough, drag, drive

335

team, clear wild lands, work on the highway, and so forth. Some planters, owning large cotton and sugar plantations, have none other than the labor of slave women. Such a one is Jim Burns, who lives on the north shore of the bayou, opposite the plantation of John Fogaman.

On our arrival in the brake, Eldret promised me, if I worked well, I might go up to visit my friends at Ford's in four weeks. On Saturday night of the fifth week, I reminded him of his promise, when he told me I had done so well, that I might go. I had set my heart upon it, and Eldret's announcement thrilled me with pleasure. I was to return in time to commence the labors of the day on Tuesday morning.

While indulging the pleasant anticipation of so soon meeting my old friends again, suddenly the hateful form of Tibeats appeared among us. He inquired how Myers and Platt got along together, and was told, very well, and that Platt was going up to Ford's plantation in the morning on a visit.

"Poh, poh!" sneered Tibeats; "it isn't worth while—the nigger will get unsteady. He can't go."

But Eldret insisted I had worked faithfully—that he had given me his promise, and that, under the circumstances, I ought not to be disappointed. They then, it being about dark, entered one cabin and I the other. I could not give up the idea of going; it was a sore disappointment. Before morning I resolved, if Eldret made no objection, to leave at all hazards. At daylight I was at his door, with my blanket rolled up into a bundle, and hanging on a stick over my shoulder, waiting for a pass. Tibeats came out presently in one of his disagreeable moods, washed his face, and going to a stump near by, sat down upon it, apparently busily thinking with himself. After standing there a long time, impelled by a sudden impulse of impatience, I started off.

"Are you going without a pass?" he cried out to me.

"Yes, master, I thought I would," I answered.

"How do you think you'll get there?" demanded he.

"Don't know," was all the reply I made him.

"You'd be taken and sent to jail, where you ought to be, before you got half-way there," he added, passing into the cabin as he said it. He came out soon with the pass in his hand, and calling me a "d—d nigger that deserved a hundred lashes," threw it on the ground. I picked it up, and hurried away right speedily.

A slave caught off his master's plantation without a pass, may be seized and whipped by any white man whom he meets. The one I now received was dated, and read as follows:

> "Platt has permission to go to Ford's plantation,
> on Bayou Bœuf, and return by Tuesday morning.
>
> JOHN M. TIBEATS."

This is the usual form. On the way, a great many demanded it, read it, and passed on. Those having the air and appearance of gentlemen, whose dress indicated the possession of wealth, frequently took no notice of me whatever; but a shabby fellow, an unmistakable loafer, never failed to hail me, and to scrutinize and examine me in the most thorough manner. Catching runaways is sometimes a money-making business. If, after advertising, no owner appears, they may be sold to the highest bidder; and certain fees are allowed the finder for his services, at all events, even if reclaimed. "A mean white," therefore,—a name applied to the species loafer—considers it a god-send to meet an unknown negro without a pass.

There are no inns along the highways in that portion of the State where I sojourned. I was wholly destitute of money, neither did I carry any provisions, on my journey from the Big Cane to Bayou Bœuf; nevertheless, with his pass in his hand, a slave need never suffer from hunger or from thirst. It is only necessary to present it to the master or overseer of a plantation, and state his wants, when he will be sent round to the kitchen and provided with food or shelter, as the case may require. The traveler stops at any house and calls for a meal with as much freedom as if it was a public tavern. It is the general custom of the country. Whatever their faults may be, it is certain the inhabitants along Red River, and around the bayous in the interior of Louisiana are not wanting in hospitality.

I arrived at Ford's plantation towards the close of the afternoon, passing the evening in Eliza's cabin, with Lawson, Rachel, and others of my acquaintance. When we left Washington Eliza's form was round and plump. She stood erect, and in her silks and jewels, presented a picture of graceful strength and elegance. Now she was but a thin shadow of her former self. Her face had become ghastly haggard, and the once straight and active form was bowed down, as if bearing the weight of a hundred years. Crouching on her cabin floor, and clad in the coarse garments of a slave, old Elisha Berry would not have recognized the mother of his child. I never saw her afterwards. Having become useless in the cotton-field, she was bartered for a trifle, to some man residing in the vicinity of Peter Compton's. Grief had gnawed remorselessly at her heart, until her strength was gone; and for that, her last master, it is said, lashed and abused her most unmercifully. But he could not whip back the departed vigor of her youth, nor straighten up that bended body to its full height, such as it was when her children were around her, and the light of freedom was shining on her path.

I learned the particulars relative to her departure from this world, from some of Compton's slaves, who had come over Red River to the bayou, to assist young Madam Tanner during the "busy season." She became at length, they said, utterly helpless, for several weeks lying on the ground floor in a dilapidated cabin, dependent upon the mercy of her fellow-thralls for an occasional drop of water, and a morsel of food. Her master did not "knock her on the head," as is sometimes done to put a suffering animal out of misery, but left her unprovided for, and unprotected, to linger through a life of pain and wretchedness to its natural close. When the hands returned from the field one night they found her dead! During the day, the Angel of the

Lord, who moveth invisibly over all the earth, gathering in his harvest of departing souls, had silently entered the cabin of the dying woman, and taken her from thence. She was *free* at last!

Next day, rolling up my blanket, I started on my return to the Big Cane. After traveling five miles, at a place called Huff Power, the ever-present Tibeats met me in the road. He inquired why I was going back so soon, and when informed I was anxious to return by the time I was directed, he said I need go no farther than the next plantation, as he had that day sold me to Edwin Epps. We walked down into the yard, where we met the latter gentleman, who examined me, and asked me the usual questions propounded by purchasers. Having been duly delivered over, I was ordered to the quarters, and at the same time directed to make a hoe and axe handle for myself.

I was now no longer the property of Tibeats—his dog, his brute, dreading his wrath and cruelty day and night; and whoever or whatever my new master might prove to be, I could not, certainly, regret the change. So it was good news when the sale was announced, and with a sigh of relief I sat down for the first time in my new abode.

Tibeats soon after disappeared from that section of the country. Once afterwards, and only once, I caught a glimpse of him. It was many miles from Bayou Bœuf. He was seated in the doorway of a low groggery. I was passing, in a drove of slaves, through St. Mary's parish.

CHAPTER XII

Edwin Epps, of whom much will be said during the remainder of this history, is a large, portly, heavy-bodied man with light hair, high cheek bones, and a Roman nose of extraordinary dimensions. He has blue eyes, a fair complexion, and is, as I should say, full six feet high. He has the sharp, inquisitive expression of a jockey. His manners are repulsive and coarse, and his language gives speedy and unequivocal evidence that he has never enjoyed the advantages of an education. He has the faculty of saying most provoking things, in that respect even excelling old Peter Tanner. At the time I came into his possession, Edwin Epps was fond of the bottle, his "sprees" sometimes extending over the space of two whole weeks. Latterly, however, he had reformed his habits, and when I left him, was as strict a specimen of temperance as could be found on Bayou Bœuf. When "in his cups," Master Epps was a roystering, blustering, noisy fellow, whose chief delight was in dancing with his "niggers," or lashing them about the yard with his long whip, just for the pleasure of hearing them screech and scream, as the great welts were planted on their backs. When sober, he was silent, reserved and cunning, not beating us indiscriminately, as in his drunken moments, but sending the end of his rawhide to some tender spot of a lagging slave, with a sly dexterity peculiar to himself.

He had been a driver and overseer in his younger years, but at this time was in possession of a plantation on Bayou Huff Power, two and a half miles from Holmesville, eighteen from Marksville, and twelve from Cheneyville. It belonged to Joseph B. Roberts, his wife's uncle, and was leased by Epps. His principal business was raising cotton, and inasmuch as some may read this book who have never seen a cotton field, a description of the

340

manner of its culture may not be out of place.

The ground is prepared by throwing up beds or ridges, with the plough—back-furrowing, it is called. Oxen and mules, the latter almost exclusively, are used in ploughing. The women as frequently as the men perform this labor, feeding, currying, and taking care of their teams, and in all respects doing the field and stable work, precisely as do the ploughboys of the North.

The beds, or ridges, are six feet wide, that is, from water furrow to water furrow. A plough drawn by one mule is then run along the top of the ridge or center of the bed, making the drill, into which a girl usually drops the seed, which she carries in a bag hung round her neck. Behind her comes a mule and harrow, covering up the seed, so that two mules, three slaves, a plough and harrow, are employed in planting a row of cotton. This is done in the months of March and April. Corn is planted in February. When there are no cold rains, the cotton usually makes its appearance in a week. In the course of eight or ten days afterwards the first hoeing is commenced. This is performed in part, also, by the aid of the plough and mule. The plough passes as near as possible to the cotton on both sides, throwing the furrow from it. Slaves follow with their hoes, cutting up the grass and cotton, leaving hills two feet and a half apart. This is called scraping cotton. In two weeks more commences the second hoeing. This time the furrow is thrown towards the cotton. Only one stalk, the largest, is now left standing in each hill. In another fortnight it is hoed the third time, throwing the furrow towards the cotton in the same manner as before, and killing all the grass between the rows. About the first of July, when it is a foot high or thereabouts, it is hoed the fourth and last time. Now the whole space between the rows is ploughed, leaving a deep water furrow in the center. During all these hoeings the overseer or driver follows the slaves on horseback with a whip, such as has been described. The fastest hoer takes the lead row. He is usually about a rod in advance of his companions. If one of them passes him, he is whipped. If one falls behind or is a moment idle, he is whipped. In fact, the lash is flying from morning until night, the whole day long. The hoeing season thus continues from April until July, a field having no sooner been finished once, than it is commenced again.

In the latter part of August begins the cotton picking season. At this time each slave is presented with a sack. A strap is fastened to it, which goes over the neck, holding the mouth of the sack breast high, while the bottom reaches nearly to the ground. Each one is also presented with a large basket that will hold about two barrels. This is to put the cotton in when the sack is filled. The baskets are carried to the field and placed at the beginning of the rows.

When a new hand, one unaccustomed to the business, is sent for the first time into the field, he is whipped up smartly, and made for that day to pick as fast as he can possibly. At night it is weighed, so that his capability in cotton picking is known. He must bring in the same weight each night following. If it falls short, it is considered evidence that he has been laggard, and a greater or less number of lashes is the penalty.

An ordinary day's work is two hundred pounds. A slave who is accustomed to picking, is punished, if he or she brings in a less quantity than that. There is a great difference among them as regards this kind of labor. Some of them seem to have a natural knack, or quickness, which enables them to pick with great celerity, and with both hands, while others, with whatever practice or industry, are utterly unable to come up to the ordinary standard. Such hands are taken from the cotton field and employed in other business. Patsey, of whom I shall have more to say, was known as the most remarkable cotton picker on Bayou Bœuf. She picked with both hands and with such surprising rapidity, that five hundred pounds a day was not unusual for her.

Each one is tasked, therefore, according to his picking abilities, none, however, to come short of two hundred weight. I, being unskillful always in that business, would have satisfied my master by bringing in the latter quantity, while on the other hand, Patsey would surely have been beaten if she failed to produce twice as much.

The cotton grows from five to seven feet high, each stalk having a great many branches, shooting out in all directions, and lapping each other above the water furrow.

There are few sights more pleasant to the eye, than a wide cotton field when it is in the bloom. It presents an appearance of purity, like an immaculate expanse of light, new-fallen snow.

Sometimes the slave picks down one side of a row, and back upon the other, but more usually, there is one on either side, gathering all that has blossomed, leaving the unopened bolls for a succeeding picking. When the sack is filled, it is emptied into the basket and trodden down. It is necessary to be extremely careful the first time going through the field, in order not to break the branches off the stalks. The cotton will not bloom upon a broken branch. Epps never failed to inflict the severest chastisement on the unlucky servant who, either carelessly or unavoidably, was guilty in the least degree in this respect.

The hands are required to be in the cotton field as soon as it is light in the morning, and, with the exception of ten or fifteen minutes, which is given them at noon to swallow their allowance of cold bacon, they are not permitted to be a moment idle until it is too dark to see, and when the moon is full, they often times labor till the middle of the night. They do not dare to stop even at dinner time, nor return to the quarters, however late it be, until the order to halt is given by the driver.

The day's work over in the field, the baskets are "toted," or in other words, carried to the gin-house, where the cotton is weighed. No matter how fatigued and weary he may be—no matter how much he longs for sleep and rest—a slave never approaches the gin-house with his basket of cotton but with fear. If it falls short in weight—if he has not performed the full task appointed him, he knows that he must suffer. And if he has exceeded it by ten or twenty pounds, in all probability his master will measure the next day's task accordingly. So, whether he has too little or too much, his approach to the gin-house is always with, fear and trembling. Most frequently they have too little, and therefore it is they are not anxious to leave the field. After weighing, follow the whippings; and then the baskets are carried to the cotton house, and their contents stored away like hay, all hands being sent in to tramp it down. If the cotton is not dry, instead of taking it to the gin-house at once, it is laid upon platforms, two feet high, and some three times as wide, covered with boards or plank, with narrow walks running between them.

This done, the labor of the day is not yet ended, by any means. Each one must then attend to his respective chores. One feeds the mules, another the swine—another cuts the wood, and so forth; besides, the packing is all done by candle light. Finally, at a late hour, they reach the quarters, sleepy and overcome with the long day's toil. Then a fire must be kindled in the cabin, the corn ground in the small hand-mill, and supper, and dinner for the next day in the field, prepared. All that is allowed them is corn and bacon, which is given out at the corncrib and smoke-house every Sunday morning. Each one receives, as his weekly, allowance, three and a half pounds of bacon, and corn enough to make a peck of meal. That is all—no tea, coffee, sugar, and with the exception of a very scanty sprinkling now and then, no salt. I can say, from a ten years' residence with Master Epps, that no slave of his is ever likely to suffer from the gout, superinduced by excessive high living. Master Epps' hogs were fed on *shelled* corn—it was thrown out to his "niggers" in the ear. The former, he thought, would fatten faster by shelling, and soaking it in the water—the latter, perhaps, if treated in the same manner, might grow too fat to labor. Master Epps was a shrewd calculator, and knew how to manage his own animals, drunk or sober.

The corn mill stands in the yard beneath a shelter. It is like a common coffee mill, the hopper holding about six quarts. There was one privilege which Master Epps granted freely to every

344

slave he had. They might grind their corn nightly, in such small quantities as their daily wants required, or they might grind the whole week's allowance at one time, on Sundays, just as they preferred. A very generous man was Master Epps!

I kept my corn in a small wooden box, the meal in a gourd; and, by the way, the gourd is one of the most convenient and necessary utensils on a plantation. Besides supplying the place of all kinds of crockery in a slave cabin, it is used for carrying water to the fields. Another, also, contains the dinner. It dispenses with the necessity of pails, dippers, basins, and such tin and wooden superfluities altogether.

When the corn is ground, and fire is made, the bacon is taken down from the nail on which it hangs, a slice cut off and thrown upon the coals to broil. The majority of slaves have no knife, much less a fork. They cut their bacon with the axe at the wood-pile. The corn meal is mixed with a little water, placed in the fire, and baked. When it is "done brown," the ashes are scraped off, and being placed upon a chip, which answers for a table, the tenant of the slave hut is ready to sit down upon the ground to supper. By this time it is usually midnight. The same fear of punishment with which they approach the gin-house, possesses them again on lying down to get a snatch of rest. It is the fear of oversleeping in the morning. Such an offence would certainly be attended with not less than twenty lashes. With a prayer that he may be on his feet and wide awake at the first sound of the horn, he sinks to his slumbers nightly.

The softest couches in the world are not to be found in the log mansion of the slave. The one whereon I reclined year after year, was a plank twelve inches wide and ten feet long. My pillow was a stick of wood. The bedding was a coarse blanket, and not a rag or shred beside. Moss might be used, were it not that it directly breeds a swarm of fleas.

The cabin is constructed of logs, without floor or window. The latter is altogether unnecessary, the crevices between the logs admitting sufficient light. In stormy weather the rain drives through them, rendering it comfortless and extremely disagreeable. The rude door hangs on great wooden hinges. In one end is constructed an awkward fire-place.

An hour before day light the horn is blown. Then the slaves arouse, prepare their breakfast, fill a gourd with water, in another deposit their dinner of cold bacon and corn cake, and hurry to the field again. It is an offence invariably followed by a flogging, to be found at the quarters after daybreak. Then the fears and labors of another day begin; and until its close there is no such thing as rest. He fears he will be caught lagging through the day; he fears to approach the gin-house with his basket-load of cotton at night; he fears, when he lies down, that he will oversleep himself in the morning. Such is a true, faithful, unexaggerated picture and description of the slave's daily life, during the time of cotton-picking, on the shores of Bayou Bœuf.

In the month of January, generally, the fourth and last picking is completed. Then commences the harvesting of corn. This is considered a secondary crop, and receives far less attention than the cotton. It is planted, as already mentioned, in February. Corn is grown in that region for the purpose of fattening hogs and feeding slaves; very little, if any, being sent to market. It is the white variety, the ear of great size, and the stalk growing to the height of eight, and often times ten feet. In August the leaves are stripped off, dried in the sun, bound in small bundles, and stored away as provender for the mules and oxen. After this the slaves go through the field, turning down the ear, for the purpose of keeping the rains from penetrating to the grain. It is left in this condition until after cotton-picking is over, whether earlier or later. Then the ears are separated from the stalks, and deposited in the corncrib with the husks on; otherwise, stripped of the husks, the weevil would destroy it. The stalks are left standing in the field.

The Carolina, or sweet potato, is also grown in that region to some extent. They are not fed, however, to hogs or cattle, and are considered but of small importance. They are preserved by placing them upon the surface of the ground, with a slight covering of earth or cornstalks. There is not a cellar on Bayou Bœuf. The ground is so low it would fill with water. Potatoes are worth from two to three "bits," or shillings a barrel; corn, except when there is an unusual scarcity, can be purchased at the same rate.

As soon as the cotton and corn crops are secured, the stalks are pulled up, thrown into piles and burned. The ploughs are started at the same time, throwing up the beds again, preparatory to another planting. The soil, in the parishes of Rapides and Avoyelles, and throughout the whole country, so far as my observation extended, is of exceeding richness and fertility. It is a kind of marl, of a brown or reddish color. It does not require those invigorating composts necessary to more barren lands, and on the same field the same crop is grown for many successive years.

Ploughing, planting, picking cotton, gathering the corn, and pulling and burning stalks, occupies the whole of the four seasons of the year. Drawing and cutting wood, pressing cotton, fattening and killing hogs, are but incidental labors.

In the month of September or October, the hogs are run out of the swamps by dogs, and confined in pens. On a cold morning, generally about New Year's day, they are slaughtered. Each carcass is cut into six parts, and piled one above the other in salt, upon large tables in the smoke-house. In this condition it remains a fortnight, when it is hung up, and a fire built, and continued more than half the time during the remainder of the year. This thorough smoking is necessary to prevent the bacon from becoming infested with worms. In so warm a climate it is difficult to preserve it, and very many times myself and my companions have received our weekly allowance of three pounds and a half, when it was full of these disgusting vermin.

Although the swamps are overrun with cattle, they are never made the source of profit, to any considerable extent. The planter cuts his mark upon the ear, or brands his initials upon the side, and turns them into the swamps, to roam unrestricted within their almost limitless confines. They are the Spanish breed, small and spike-horned. I have known of droves being taken from Bayou Bœuf, but it is of very rare occurrence. The value of the best cows is about five dollars each. Two quarts at one milking, would be considered an unusual large quantity. They furnish little tallow, and that of a soft, inferior quality. Notwithstanding the great number of cows that throng the swamps, the planters are indebted to the North for their cheese and butter, which is purchased in the New-Orleans market. Salted beef is not an article of food either in the great house, or in the cabin.

Master Epps was accustomed to attend shooting matches for the purpose of obtaining what fresh beef he required. These sports occurred weekly at the neighboring village of Holmesville. Fat beeves are driven thither and shot at, a stipulated price being demanded for the privilege. The lucky marksman divides the flesh among his fellows, and in this manner the attending planters are supplied.

The great number of tame and untamed cattle which swarm the woods and swamps of Bayou Bœuf, most probably suggested that appellation to the French, inasmuch as the term, translated, signifies the creek or river of the wild ox.

Garden products, such as cabbages, turnips and the like, are cultivated for the use of the master and his family. They have greens and vegetables at all times and seasons of the year. "The grass withereth and the flower fadeth" before the desolating winds of autumn in the chill northern latitudes, but perpetual verdure overspreads the hot lowlands, and flowers bloom in the heart of winter, in the region of Bayou Bœuf.

There are no meadows appropriated to the cultivation of the grasses. The leaves of the corn supply a sufficiency of food for the laboring cattle, while the rest provide for themselves all the year in the ever-growing pasture.

There are many other peculiarities of climate, habit, custom, and of the manner of living and laboring at the South, but the foregoing, it is supposed, will give the reader an insight and general idea of life on a cotton plantation in Louisiana. The mode of cultivating cane, and the process of sugar manufacturing, will be mentioned in another place.

CHAPTER XIII

On my arrival at Master Epps', in obedience to his order, the first business upon which I entered was the making of an axe-helve. The handles in use there are simply a round, straight stick. I made a crooked one, shaped like those to which I had been accustomed at the North. When finished, and presented to Epps, he looked at it with astonishment, unable to determine exactly what it was. He had never before seen such a handle, and when I explained its conveniences, he was forcibly struck with the novelty of the idea. He kept it in the house a long time, and when his friends called, was wont to exhibit it as a curiosity.

It was now the season of hoeing. I was first sent into the corn-field, and afterwards set to scraping cotton. In this employment I remained until hoeing time was nearly passed, when I began to experience the symptoms of approaching illness. I was attacked with chills, which were succeeded by a burning fever. I became weak and emaciated, and frequently so dizzy that it caused me to reel and stagger like a drunken man. Nevertheless, I was compelled to keep up my row. When in health I found little difficulty in keeping pace with my fellow-laborers, but now it seemed to be an utter impossibility. Often I fell behind, when the driver's lash was sure to greet my back, infusing into my sick and drooping body a little temporary energy. I continued to decline until at length the whip became entirely ineffectual. The sharpest sting of the rawhide could not arouse me. Finally, in September, when the busy season of cotton picking was at hand, I was unable to leave my cabin. Up to this time I had received no medicine, nor any attention from my master or mistress. The old cook visited me occasionally, preparing me corn-coffee, and sometimes boiling a bit of bacon, when I had grown too feeble to accomplish it myself.

When it was said that I would die, Master Epps, unwilling to bear the loss, which the death of an animal worth a thousand dollars would bring upon him, concluded to incur the expense of sending to Holmesville for Dr. Wines. He announced to Epps that it was the effect of the climate, and there was a probability of his losing me. He directed me to eat no meat, and to partake of no more food than was absolutely necessary to sustain life. Several weeks elapsed, during which time, under the scanty diet to which I was subjected, I had partially recovered. One morning, long before I was in a proper condition to labor, Epps appeared at the cabin door, and, presenting me a sack, ordered me to the cotton field. At this time I had had no experience whatever in cotton picking. It was an awkward business indeed. While others used both hands, snatching the cotton and depositing it in the mouth of the sack, with a precision and dexterity that was incomprehensible to me, I had to seize the boll with one hand, and deliberately draw out the white, gushing blossom with the other.

Depositing the cotton in the sack, moreover, was a difficulty that demanded the exercise of both hands and eyes. I was compelled to pick it from the ground where it would fall, nearly as often as from the stalk where it had grown. I made havoc also with the branches, loaded with the yet unbroken bolls, the long, cumbersome sack swinging from side to side in a manner not allowable in the cotton field. After a most laborious day I arrived at the gin-house with my load. When the scale determined its weight to be only ninety-five pounds, not half the quantity required of the poorest picker, Epps threatened the severest flogging, but in consideration of my being a "raw hand," concluded to pardon me on that occasion. The following day, and many days succeeding, I returned at night with no better success—I was evidently not designed for that kind of labor. I had not the gift—the dexterous fingers and quick motion of Patsey, who could fly along one side of a row of cotton, stripping

351

it of its undefiled and fleecy whiteness miraculously fast. Practice and whipping were alike unavailing, and Epps, satisfied of it at last, swore I was a disgrace—that I was not fit to associate with a cotton-picking "nigger"—that I could not pick enough in a day to pay the trouble of weighing it, and that I should go into the cotton field no more. I was now employed in cutting and hauling wood, drawing cotton from the field to the gin-house, and performed whatever other service was required. Suffice to say, I was never permitted to be idle.

It was rarely that a day passed by without one or more whippings. This occurred at the time the cotton was weighed. The delinquent, whose weight had fallen short, was taken out, stripped, made to lie upon the ground, face downwards, when he received a punishment proportioned to his offence. It is the literal, unvarnished truth, that the crack of the lash, and the shrieking of the slaves, can be heard from dark till bed time, on Epps' plantation, any day almost during the entire period of the cotton-picking season.

The number of lashes is graduated according to the nature of the case. Twenty-five are deemed a mere brush, inflicted, for instance, when a dry leaf or piece of boll is found in the cotton, or when a branch is broken in the field; fifty is the ordinary penalty following all delinquencies of the next higher grade; one hundred is called severe: it is the punishment inflicted for the serious offence of standing idle in the field; from one hundred and fifty to two hundred is bestowed upon him who quarrels with his cabin-mates, and five hundred, well laid on, besides the mangling of the dogs, perhaps, is certain to consign the poor, unpitied runaway to weeks of pain and agony.

During the two years Epps remained on the plantation at Bayou Huff Power, he was in the habit, as often as once in a fortnight at least, of coming home intoxicated from Holmesville. The shooting-matches almost invariably concluded with a debauch. At such times he was boisterous and half-crazy. Often he would break the dishes, chairs, and whatever furniture he

352

could lay his hands on. When satisfied with his amusement in the house, he would seize the whip and walk forth into the yard. Then it behooved the slaves to be watchful and exceeding wary. The first one who came within reach felt the smart of his lash. Sometimes for hours he would keep them running in all directions, dodging around the corners of the cabins. Occasionally he would come upon one unawares, and if he succeeded in inflicting a fair, round blow, it was a feat that much delighted him. The younger children, and the aged, who had become inactive, suffered then. In the midst of the confusion he would slily take his stand behind a cabin, waiting with raised whip, to dash it into the first black face that peeped cautiously around the corner.

At other times he would come home in a less brutal humor. Then there must be a merry-making. Then all must move to the measure of a tune. Then Master Epps must needs regale his melodious ears with the music of a fiddle. Then did he become buoyant, elastic, gaily "tripping the light fantastic toe" around the piazza and all through the house.

Tibeats, at the time of my sale, had informed him I could play on the violin. He had received his information from Ford. Through the importunities of Mistress Epps, her husband had been induced to purchase me one during a visit to New-Orleans. Frequently I was called into the house to play before the family, mistress being passionately fond of music.

All of us would be assembled in the large room of the great house, whenever Epps came home in one of his dancing moods. No matter how worn out and tired we were, there must be a general dance. When properly stationed on the floor, I would strike up a tune.

"Dance, you d—d niggers, dance," Epps would shout.

Then there must be no halting or delay, no slow or languid movements; all must be brisk, and lively, and alert. "Up and down, heel and toe, and away we go," was the order of the hour. Epps' portly form mingled with those of his dusky slaves,

353

moving rapidly through all the mazes of the dance.

Usually his whip was in his hand, ready to fall about the ears of the presumptuous thrall, who dared to rest a moment, or even stop to catch his breath. When he was himself exhausted, there would be a brief cessation, but it would be very brief. With a slash, and crack, and flourish of the whip, he would shout again, "Dance, niggers, dance," and away they would go once more, pell-mell, while I spurred by an occasional sharp touch of the lash, sat in a corner, extracting from my violin a marvelous quick-stepping tune. The mistress often upbraided him, declaring she would return to her father's house at Cheneyville; nevertheless, there were times she could not restrain a burst of laughter, on witnessing his uproarious pranks. Frequently, we were thus detained until almost morning. Bent with excessive toil—actually suffering for a little refreshing rest, and feeling rather as if we could cast ourselves upon the earth and weep, many a night in the house of Edwin Epps have his unhappy slaves been made to dance and laugh.

Notwithstanding these deprivations in order to gratify the whim of an unreasonable master, we had to be in the field as soon as it was light, and during the day perform the ordinary and accustomed task. Such deprivations could not be urged at the scales in extenuation of any lack of weight, or in the cornfield for not hoeing with the usual rapidity. The whippings were just as severe as if we had gone forth in the morning, strengthened and invigorated by a night's repose. Indeed, after such frantic revels, he was always more sour and savage than before, punishing for slighter causes, and using the whip with increased and more vindictive energy.

Ten years I toiled for that man without reward. Ten years of my incessant labor has contributed to increase the bulk of his possessions. Ten years I was compelled to address him with down-cast eyes and uncovered head—in the attitude and language of a slave. I am indebted to him for nothing, save undeserved abuse and stripes.

Beyond the reach of his inhuman thong, and standing on the soil of the free State where I was born, thanks be to Heaven, I can raise my head once more among men. I can speak of the wrongs I have suffered, and of those who inflicted them, with upraised eyes. But I have no desire to speak of him or any other one otherwise than truthfully. Yet to speak truthfully of Edwin Epps would be to say—he is a man in whose heart the quality of kindness or of justice is not found. A rough, rude energy, united with an uncultivated mind and an avaricious spirit, are his prominent characteristics. He is known as a "nigger breaker," distinguished for his faculty of subduing the spirit of the slave, and priding himself upon his reputation in this respect, as a jockey boasts of his skill in managing a refractory horse. He looked upon a colored man, not as a human being, responsible to his Creator for the small talent entrusted to him, but as a "chattel personal," as mere live property, no better, except in value, than his mule or dog. When the evidence, clear and indisputable, was laid before him that I was a free man, and as much entitled to my liberty as he—when, on the day I left, he was informed that I had a wife and children, as dear to me as his own babes to him, he only raved and swore, denouncing the law that tore me from him, and declaring he would find out the man who had forwarded the letter that disclosed the place of my captivity, if there was any virtue or power in money, and would take his life. He thought of nothing but his loss, and cursed me for having been born free. He could have stood unmoved and seen the tongues of his poor slaves torn out by the roots—he could have seen them burned to ashes over a slow fire, or gnawed to death by dogs, if it only brought him profit. Such a hard, cruel, unjust man is Edwin Epps.

There was but one greater savage on Bayou Bœuf than he. Jim Burns' plantation was cultivated, as already mentioned, exclusively by women. That barbarian kept their backs so sore and raw, that they could not perform the customary labor demanded daily of the slave. He boasted of his cruelty, and

THROUGH THE EYES OF A SLAVE

through all the country round was accounted a more thorough-going, energetic man than even Epps. A brute himself, Jim Burns had not a particle of mercy for his subject brutes, and like a fool, whipped and scourged away the very strength upon which depended his amount of gain.

Epps remained on Huff Power two years, when, having accumulated a considerable sum of money, he expended it in the purchase of the plantation on the east bank of Bayou Bœuf, where he still continues to reside. He took possession of it in 1845, after the holidays were passed. He carried thither with him nine slaves, all of whom, except myself, and Susan, who has since died, remain there yet. He made no addition to this force, and for eight years the following were my companions in his quarters, viz: Abram, Wiley, Phebe, Bob, Henry, Edward, and Patsey. All these, except Edward, born since, were purchased out of a drove by Epps during the time he was overseer for Archy B. Williams, whose plantation is situated on the shore of Red River, not far from Alexandria.

Abram was tall, standing a full head above any common man. He is sixty years of age, and was born in Tennessee. Twenty years ago, he was purchased by a trader, carried into South Carolina, and sold to James Buford, of Williamsburgh county, in that State. In his youth he was renowned for his great strength, but age and unremitting toil have somewhat shattered his powerful frame and enfeebled his mental faculties.

Wiley is forty-eight. He was born on the estate of William Tassle, and for many years took charge of that gentleman's ferry over the Big Black River, in South Carolina.

Phebe was a slave of Buford, Tassle's neighbor, and having married Wiley, he bought the latter, at her instigation. Buford was a kind master, sheriff of the county, and in those days a man of wealth.

Bob and Henry are Phebe's children, by a former husband, their father having been abandoned to give place to Wiley. That seductive youth had insinuated himself into Phebe's affections, and therefore the faithless spouse had gently kicked her first husband out of her cabin door. Edward had been born to them on Bayou Huff Power.

Patsey is twenty-three—also from Buford's plantation. She is in no wise connected with the others, but glories in the fact that she is the offspring of a "Guinea nigger," brought over to Cuba in a slave ship, and in the course of trade transferred to Buford, who was her mother's owner.

This, as I learned from them, is a genealogical account of my master's slaves. For years they had been together. Often they recalled the memories of other days, and sighed to retrace their steps to the old home in Carolina. Troubles came upon their master Buford, which brought far greater troubles upon them. He became involved in debt, and unable to bear up against his failing fortunes, was compelled to sell these, and others of his slaves. In a chain gang they had been driven from beyond the Mississippi to the plantation of Archy B. Williams. Edwin Epps, who, for a long while had been his driver and overseer, was about establishing himself in business on his own account, at the time of their arrival, and accepted them in payment of his wages.

Old Abram was a kind-hearted being—a sort of patriarch among us, fond of entertaining his younger brethren with grave and serious discourse. He was deeply versed in such philosophy as is taught in the cabin of the slave; but the great absorbing hobby of Uncle Abram was General Jackson, whom his young master in Tennessee had followed to the wars. He loved to wander back, in imagination, to the place where he was born, and to recount the scenes of his youth during those stirring times when the nation was in arms. He had been athletic, and more keen and powerful than the generality of his race, but now his eye had become dim, and his natural force abated. Very often, indeed, while discussing the best method of baking the hoe-cake, or expatiating at large upon the glory of Jackson, he would forget where he left his hat, or his hoe, or his basket; and then would the old man be laughed at, if Epps was absent, and whipped if he was present. So was he perplexed continually, and sighed to think that he was growing aged and going to decay. Philosophy and Jackson and forgetfulness had played the mischief with him, and it was evident that all of them combined were fast bringing down the gray hairs of Uncle Abram to the grave.

Aunt Phebe had been an excellent field hand, but latterly was put into the kitchen, where she remained, except occasionally, in a time of uncommon hurry. She was a sly old creature, and when not in the presence of her mistress or her master, was garrulous in the extreme.

Wiley, on the contrary, was silent. He performed his task without murmur or complaint, seldom indulging in the luxury of speech, except to utter a wish, that he was away from Epps, and back once more in South Carolina.

Bob and Henry had reached the ages of twenty and twenty-three, and were distinguished for nothing extraordinary or unusual, while Edward, a lad of thirteen, not yet able to maintain his row in the corn or the cotton field, was kept in the great house, to wait on the little Eppses.

Patsey was slim and straight. She stood erect as the human form is capable of standing. There was an air of loftiness in her movement, that neither labor, nor weariness, nor punishment could destroy. Truly, Patsey was a splendid animal, and were it not that bondage had enshrouded her intellect in utter and everlasting darkness, would have been chief among ten thousand of her people. She could leap the highest fences, and a fleet hound it was indeed, that could outstrip her in a race. No horse could fling her from his back. She was a skillful teamster. She turned as true a furrow as the best, and at splitting rails there were none who could excel her. When the order to halt was heard at night, she would have her mules at the crib, unharnessed, fed and curried, before uncle Abram had found his hat. Not, however, for all or any of these, was she chiefly famous. Such lightning-like motion was in her fingers as no other fingers ever possessed, and therefore it was, that in cotton picking time, Patsey was queen of the field.

She had a genial and pleasant temper, and was faithful and obedient. Naturally, she was a joyous creature, a laughing, light-hearted girl, rejoicing in the mere sense of existence. Yet Patsey wept oftener, and suffered more, than any of her companions. She had been literally excoriated. Her back bore the scars of a thousand stripes; not because she was backward in her work, nor because she was of an unmindful and rebellious spirit, but because it had fallen to her lot to be the slave of a licentious master and a jealous mistress. She shrank before the lustful eye of the one, and was in danger even of her life at the hands of the other, and between the two, she was indeed accursed. In the great house, for days together, there were high and angry words, poutings and estrangement, whereof she was the innocent cause. Nothing delighted the mistress so much as to see her suffer, and more than once, when Epps had refused to sell her, has she tempted me with bribes to put her secretly to death, and bury her body in some lonely place in the margin of the swamp. Gladly would Patsey have appeased this unforgiving spirit, if it had been in her power, but not like Joseph, dared she escape from Master Epps, leaving her garment in his hand. Patsey walked under a cloud. If she uttered a word in opposition to her master's will, the lash was resorted to at once, to bring her to subjection; if she was not watchful when about her cabin, or when walking in the yard, a billet of wood, or a broken bottle perhaps, hurled from her mistress' hand, would smite her unexpectedly in the face. The enslaved victim of lust and hate, Patsey had no comfort of her life.

These were my companions and fellow-slaves, with whom I was accustomed to be driven to the field, and with whom it has been my lot to dwell for ten years in the log cabins of Edwin Epps. They, if living, are yet toiling on the banks of Bayou Bœuf, never destined to breathe, as I now do, the blessed air of liberty, nor to shake off the heavy shackles that enthrall them, until they shall lie down forever in the dust.

CHAPTER XIV

The first year of Epps' residence on the bayou, 1845, the caterpillars almost totally destroyed the cotton crop throughout that region. There was little to be done, so that the slaves were necessarily idle half the time. However, there came a rumor to Bayou Bœuf that wages were high, and laborers in great demand on the sugar plantations in St. Mary's parish. This parish is situated on the coast of the Gulf of Mexico, about one hundred and forty miles from Avoyelles. The Rio Teche, a considerable stream, flows through St. Mary's to the gulf.

It was determined by the planters, on the receipt of this intelligence, to make up a drove of slaves to be sent down to Tuckapaw in St. Mary's, for the purpose of hiring them out in the cane fields. Accordingly, in the month of September, there were one hundred and forty-seven collected at Holmesville, Abram, Bob and myself among the number. Of these about one-half were women. Epps, Alonson Pierce, Henry Toler, and Addison Roberts, were the white men, selected to accompany, and take charge of the drove. They had a two-horse carriage and two saddle horses for their use. A large wagon, drawn by four horses, and driven by John, a boy belonging to Mr. Roberts, carried the blankets and provisions.

About 2 o'clock in the afternoon, having been fed, preparations were made to depart. The duty assigned me was, to take charge of the blankets and provisions, and see that none were lost by the way. The carriage proceeded in advance, the wagon following; behind this the slaves were arranged, while the two horsemen brought up the rear, and in this order the procession moved out of Holmesville.

That night we reached a Mr. McCrow's plantation, a distance

360

of ten or fifteen miles, when we were ordered to halt. Large fires were built, and each one spreading his blanket on the ground, laid down upon it. The white men lodged in the great house. An hour before day we were aroused by the drivers coming among us, cracking their whips and ordering us to arise. Then the blankets were rolled up, and being severally delivered to me and deposited in the wagon, the procession set forth again.

The following night it rained violently. We were all drenched, our clothes saturated with mud and water. Reaching an open shed, formerly a gin-house, we found beneath it such shelter as it afforded. There was not room for all of us to lay down. There we remained, huddled together, through the night, continuing our march, as usual, in the morning. During the journey we were fed twice a day, boiling our bacon and baking our corn-cake at the fires in the same manner as in our huts. We passed through Lafayetteville, Mountsville, New-Town, to Centreville, where Bob and Uncle Abram were hired. Our number decreased as we advanced—nearly every sugar plantation requiring the services of one or more.

On our route we passed the Grand Coteau or prairie, a vast space of level, monotonous country, without a tree, except an occasional one which had been transplanted near some dilapidated dwelling. It was once thickly populated, and under cultivation, but for some cause had been abandoned. The business of the scattered inhabitants that now dwell upon it is principally raising cattle. Immense herds were feeding upon it as we passed. In the centre of the Grand Coteau one feels as if he were on the ocean, out of sight of land. As far as the eye can see, in all directions, it is but a ruined and deserted waste.

I was hired to Judge Turner, a distinguished man and extensive planter, whose large estate is situated on Bayou Salle, within a few miles of the gulf. Bay on Salle is a small stream flowing into the bay of Atchafalaya. For some days I was employed at Turner's in repairing his sugar house, when a cane knife was put into my hand, and with thirty or forty others, I was sent into the field. I found no such difficulty in learning the art of cutting cane that I had in picking cotton. It came to me naturally and intuitively, and in a short time I was able to keep up with the fastest knife. Before the cutting was over, however, Judge Turner transferred me from the field to the sugar house, to act there in the capacity of driver. From the time of the commencement of sugar making to the close, the grinding and boiling does not cease day or night. The whip was given me with directions to use it upon any one who was caught standing idle. If I failed to obey them to the letter, there was another one for my own back. In addition to this my duty was to call on and off the different gangs at the proper time. I had no regular periods of rest, and could never snatch but a few moments of sleep at a time.

It is the custom in Louisiana, as I presume it is in other slave States, to allow the slave to retain whatever compensation he may obtain for services performed on Sundays. In this way, only, are they able to provide themselves with any luxury or convenience whatever. When a slave, purchased, or kidnapped in the North, is transported to a cabin on Bayou Bœuf he is furnished with neither knife, nor fork, nor dish, nor kettle, nor any other thing in the shape of crockery, or furniture of any nature or description. He is furnished with a blanket before he reaches there, and wrapping that around him, he can either stand up, or lie down upon the ground, or on a board, if his master has no use for it. He is at liberty to find a gourd in which to keep his meal, or he can eat his corn from the cob, just as he pleases. To ask the master for a knife, or skillet, or any small convenience of the kind, would be answered with a kick, or laughed at as a joke. Whatever necessary article of this nature is found in a cabin has been purchased with Sunday money. However injurious to the morals, it is certainly a blessing to the physical condition of the slave, to be permitted to break the Sabbath. Otherwise there would be no way to provide himself with any utensils, which seem to be indispensable to him who is compelled to be his own cook.

On cane plantations in sugar time, there is no distinction as to the days of the week. It is well understood that all hands must labor on the Sabbath, and it is equally well understood that those especially who are hired, as I was to Judge Turner, and others in succeeding years, shall receive remuneration for it. It is usual, also, in the most hurrying time of cotton-picking, to require the same extra service. From this source, slaves generally are afforded an opportunity of earning sufficient to purchase a knife, a kettle, tobacco and so forth. The females, discarding the latter luxury, are apt to expend their little revenue in the purchase of gaudy ribbons, wherewithal to deck their hair in the merry season of the holidays.

I remained in St. Mary's until the first of January, during which time my Sunday money amounted to ten dollars. I met with other good fortune, for which I was indebted to my violin, my constant companion, the source of profit, and soother of my sorrows during years of servitude. There was a grand party of whites assembled at Mr. Yarney's, in Centreville, a hamlet in the vicinity of Turner's plantation. I was employed to play for them, and so well pleased were the merry-makers with my performance, that a contribution was taken for my benefit, which amounted to seventeen dollars.

With this sum in possession, I was looked upon by my fellows as a millionaire. It afforded me great pleasure to look at it—to count it over and over again, day after day. Visions of cabin furniture, of water pails, of pocket knives, new shoes and coats and hats, floated through my fancy, and up through all rose the triumphant contemplation, that I was the wealthiest "nigger" on Bayou Bœuf.

Vessels run up the Rio Teche to Centreville. While there, I was bold enough one day to present myself before the captain of a steamer, and beg permission to hide myself among the freight. I was emboldened to risk the hazard of such a step, from overhearing a conversation, in the course of which I ascertained he was a native of the North. I did not relate to him the particulars of my history, but only expressed an ardent desire to escape from slavery to a free State. He pitied me, but said it would be impossible to avoid the vigilant custom house officers in New-Orleans, and that detection would subject him to punishment, and his vessel to confiscation. My earnest entreaties evidently excited his sympathies, and doubtless he would have yielded to them, could he have done so with any kind of safety. I was compelled to smother the sudden flame that lighted up my bosom with sweet hopes of liberation, and turn my steps once more towards the increasing darkness of despair.

Immediately after this event the drove assembled at Centreville, and several of the owners having arrived and collected the monies due for our services, we were driven back to Bayou Bœuf. It was on our return, while passing through a small village, that I caught sight of Tibeats, seated in the door of a dirty grocery, looking somewhat seedy and out of repair. Passion and poor whisky, I doubt not, have ere this laid him on the shelf.

During our absence, I learned from Aunt Phebe and Patsey, that the latter had been getting deeper and deeper into trouble. The poor girl was truly an object of pity. "Old Hogjaw," the name by which Epps was called, when the slaves were by themselves, had beaten her more severely and frequently than ever. As surely as he came from Holmesville, elated with liquor— and it was often in those days—he would whip her, merely to gratify the mistress; would punish her to an extent almost beyond endurance, for an offence of which he himself was the sole and irresistible cause. In his sober moments he could not always be prevailed upon to indulge his wife's insatiable thirst for vengeance.

To be rid of Patsey—to place her beyond sight or reach, by sale, or death, or in any other manner, of late years, seemed to be the ruling thought and passion of my mistress. Patsey had been a favorite when a child, even in the great house. She had been petted and admired for her uncommon sprightliness and pleasant disposition. She had been fed many a time, so Uncle Abram said, even on biscuit and milk, when the madam, in her younger days, was wont to call her to the piazza, and fondle her as she would a playful Kitten. But a sad change had come over the spirit of the woman. Now, only black and angry fiends ministered in the temple of her heart, until she could look on Patsey but with concentrated venom.

Mistress Epps was not naturally such an evil woman, after all. She was possessed of the devil, jealousy, it is true, but aside from that, there was much in her character to admire. Her father, Mr. Roberts, resided in Cheneyville, an influential and honorable man, and as much respected throughout the parish as any other citizen. She had been well educated at some institution this side the Mississippi; was beautiful, accomplished, and usually good-humored. She was kind to all of us but Patsey—frequently, in the absence of her husband, sending out to us some little dainty from her own table. In other situations—in a different society from that which exists on the shores of Bayou Bœuf, she would have been pronounced an elegant and fascinating woman. An ill wind it was that blew her into the arms of Epps.

He respected and loved his wife as much as a coarse nature like his is capable of loving, but supreme selfishness always overmastered conjugal affection.

> "He loved as well as baser natures can,
> But a mean heart and soul were in that man."

He was ready to gratify any whim—to grant any request she made, provided it did not cost too much. Patsey was equal to any two of his slaves in the cotton field. He could not replace her with the same money she would bring. The idea of disposing of her, therefore, could not be entertained. The mistress did not regard her at all in that light. The pride of the haughty woman was aroused; the blood of the fiery southern boiled at the sight of Patsey, and nothing less than trampling out the life of the

365

THROUGH THE EYES OF A SLAVE
helpless bondwoman would satisfy her.

Sometimes the current of her wrath turned upon him whom she had just cause to hate. But the storm of angry words would pass over at length, and there would be a season of calm again. At such times Patsey trembled with fear, and cried as if her heart would break, for she knew from painful experience, that if mistress should work herself to the red-hot pitch of rage, Epps would quiet her at last with a promise that Patsey should be flogged—a promise he was sure to keep. Thus did pride, and jealousy, and vengeance war with avarice and brute-passion in the mansion of my master, filling it with daily tumult and contention. Thus, upon the head of Patsey—the simple-minded slave, in whose heart God had implanted the seeds of virtue— the force of all these domestic tempests spent itself at last.

During the summer succeeding my return from St. Mary's parish, I conceived a plan of providing myself with food, which, though simple, succeeded beyond expectation. It has been followed by many others in my condition, up and down the bayou, and of such benefit has it become that I am almost persuaded to look upon myself as a benefactor. That summer the worms got into the bacon. Nothing but ravenous hunger could induce us to swallow it. The weekly allowance of meal scarcely sufficed to satisfy us. It was customary with us, as it is with all in that region, where the allowance is exhausted before Saturday night, or is in such a state as to render it nauseous and disgusting, to hunt in the swamps for coon and opossum. This, however, must be done at night, after the day's work is accomplished. There are planters whose slaves, for months at a time, have no other meat than such as is obtained in this manner. No objections are made to hunting, inasmuch as it dispenses with drafts upon the smoke-house, and because every marauding coon that is killed is so much saved from the standing corn. They are hunted with dogs and clubs, slaves not being allowed the use of fire-arms.

The flesh of the coon is palatable, but verily there is nothing in all butcherdom so delicious as a roasted 'possum. They are a round, rather long-bodied, little animal, of a whitish color, with nose like a pig, and caudal extremity like a rat. They burrow among the roots and in the hollows of the gum tree, and are clumsy and slow of motion. They are deceitful and cunning creatures. On receiving the slightest tap of a stick, they will roll over on the ground and feign death. If the hunter leaves him, in pursuit of another, without first taking particular pains to break his neck, the chances are, on his return, he is not to be found. The little animal has out witted the enemy—has "played 'possum"—and is off. But after a long and hard day's work, the weary slave feels little like going to the swamp for his supper, and half the time prefers throwing himself on the cabin floor without it. It is for the interest of the master that the servant should not suffer in health from starvation, and it is also for his interest that he should not become gross from over-feeding. In the estimation of the owner, a slave is the most serviceable when in rather a lean and lank condition, such a condition as the race-horse is in, when fitted for the course, and in that condition they are generally to be found on the sugar and cotton plantations along Red River.

My cabin was within a few rods of the bayou bank, and necessity being indeed the mother of invention, I resolved upon a mode of obtaining the requisite amount of food, without the trouble of resorting nightly to the woods. This was to construct a fish trap. Having, in my mind, conceived the manner in which it could be done, the next Sunday I set about putting it into practical execution. It may be impossible for me to convey to the reader a full and correct idea of its construction, but the following will serve as a general description:

A frame between two and three feet square is made, and of a greater or less height, according to the depth of water. Boards or slats are nailed on three sides of this frame, not so closely, however, as to prevent the water circulating freely through it. A door is fitted into the fourth side, in such manner that it will slide easily up and down in the grooves cut in the two posts.

A movable bottom is then so fitted that it can be raised to the top of the frame without difficulty. In the centre of the movable bottom an auger hole is bored, and into this one end of a handle or round stick is fastened on the under side so loosely that it will turn. The handle ascends from the centre of the movable bottom to the top of the frame, or as much higher as is desirable. Up and down this handle, in a great many places, are gimlet holes, through which small sticks are inserted, extending to opposite sides of the frame. So many of these small sticks are running out from the handle in all directions, that a fish of any considerable dimensions cannot pass through without hitting one of them. The frame is then placed in the water and made stationary.

The trap is "set" by sliding or drawing up the door, and kept in that position by another stick, one end of which rests in a notch on the inner side, the other end in a notch made in the handle, running up from the centre of the movable bottom. The trap is baited by rolling a handful of wet meal and cotton together until it becomes hard, and depositing it in the back part of the frame. A fish swimming through the upraised door towards the bait, necessarily strikes one of the small sticks turning the handle, which displacing the stick supporting the door, the latter falls, securing the fish within the frame. Taking hold of the top of the handle, the movable bottom is then drawn up to the surface of the water, and the fish taken out. There may have been other such traps in use before mine was constructed, but if there were I had never happened to see one. Bayou Bœuf abounds in fish of large size and excellent quality, and after this time I was very rarely in want of one for myself, or for my comrades. Thus a mine was opened—a new resource was developed, hitherto unthought of by the enslaved children of Africa, who toil and hunger along the shores of that sluggish, but prolific stream.

About the time of which I am now writing, an event occurred in our immediate neighborhood, which made a deep impression upon me, and which shows the state of society existing there, and the manner in which affronts are oftentimes avenged.

Directly opposite our quarters, on the other side of the bayou, was situated the plantation of Mr. Marshall. He belonged to a family among the most wealthy and aristocratic in the country. A gentleman from the vicinity of Natchez had been negotiating with him for the purchase of the estate. One day a messenger came in great haste to our plantation, saying that a bloody and fearful battle was going on at Marshall's—that blood had been spilled—and unless the combatants were forthwith separated, the result would be disastrous.

On repairing to Marshall's house, a scene presented itself that beggars description. On the floor of one of the rooms lay the ghastly corpse of the man from Natchez, while Marshall, enraged and covered with wounds and blood, was stalking back and forth, "breathing out threatenings and slaughter." A difficulty had arisen in the course of their negotiation, high words ensued, when drawing their weapons, the deadly strife began that ended so unfortunately. Marshall was never placed in confinement. A sort of trial or investigation was had at Marksville, when he was acquitted, and returned to his plantation, rather more respected, as I thought, than ever, from the fact that the blood of a fellow being was on his soul.

Epps interested himself in his behalf, accompanying him to Marksville, and on all occasions loudly justifying him, but his services in this respect did not afterwards deter a kinsman of this same Marshall from seeking his life also. A brawl occurred between them over a gambling-table, which terminated in a deadly feud. Riding up on horseback in front of the house one day, armed with pistols and bowie knife, Marshall challenged him to come forth and make a final settlement of the quarrel, or he would brand him as a coward, and shoot him like a dog the first opportunity. Not through cowardice, nor from any conscientious scruples, in my opinion, but through the influence of his wife, he was restrained from accepting the challenge of his enemy. A reconciliation, however, was effected afterward, since which time they have been on terms of the closest intimacy.

Such occurrences, which would bring upon the parties concerned in them merited and condign punishment in the Northern States, are frequent on the bayou, and pass without notice, and almost without comment. Every man carries his bowie knife, and when two fall out, they set to work hacking and thrusting at each other, more like savages than civilized and enlightened beings.

The existence of Slavery in its most cruel form among them, has a tendency to brutalize the humane and finer feelings of their nature. Daily witnesses of human suffering—listening to the agonizing screeches of the slave—beholding him writhing beneath the merciless lash—bitten and torn by dogs—dying without attention, and buried without shroud or coffin—it cannot otherwise be expected, than that they should become brutified and reckless of human life. It is true there are many kind-hearted and good men in the parish of Avoyelles—such men as William Ford—who can look with pity upon the sufferings of a slave, just as there are, over all the world, sensitive and sympathetic spirits, who cannot look with indifference upon the sufferings of any creature which the Almighty has endowed with life. It is not the fault of the slaveholder that he is cruel, so much as it is the fault of the system under which he lives. He cannot withstand the influence of habit and associations that surround him. Taught from earliest childhood, by all that he sees and hears, that the rod is for the slave's back, he will not be apt to change his opinions in maturer years.

There may be humane masters, as there certainly are inhuman ones—there may be slaves well-clothed, well-fed, and happy, as there surely are those half-clad, half-starved and miserable; nevertheless, the institution that tolerates such wrong and inhumanity as I have witnessed, is a cruel, unjust, and barbarous one. Men may write fictions portraying lowly life as it is, or as it is not—may expatiate with owlish gravity upon the bliss of ignorance—discourse flippantly from arm chairs of the pleasures of slave life; but let them toil with him

370

in the field—sleep with him in the cabin—feed with him on husks; let them behold him scourged, hunted, trampled on, and they will come back with another story in their mouths. Let them know the *heart* of the poor slave—learn his secret thoughts—thoughts he dare not utter in the hearing of the white man; let them sit by him in the silent watches of the night— converse with him in trustful confidence, of "life, liberty, and the pursuit of happiness," and they will find that ninety-nine out of every hundred are intelligent enough to understand their situation, and to cherish in their bosoms the love of freedom, as passionately as themselves.

CHAPTER XV

In consequence of my inability in cotton-picking, Epps was in the habit of hiring me out on sugar plantations during the season of cane-cutting and sugar-making. He received for my services a dollar a day, with the money supplying my place on his cotton plantation. Cutting cane was an employment that suited me, and for three successive years I held the lead row at Hawkins', leading a gang of from fifty to an hundred hands.

In a previous chapter the mode of cultivating cotton is described. This may be the proper place to speak of the manner of cultivating cane.

The ground is prepared in beds, the same as it is prepared for the reception of the cotton seed, except it is ploughed deeper. Drills are made in the same manner. Planting commences in January, and continues until April. It is necessary to plant a sugar field only once in three years. Three crops are taken before the seed or plant is exhausted.

Three gangs are employed in the operation. One draws the cane from the rick, or stack, cutting the top and flags from the stalk, leaving only that part which is sound and healthy. Each joint of the cane has an eye, like the eye of a potato, which sends forth a sprout when buried in the soil. Another gang lays the cane in the drill, placing two stalks side by side in such manner that joints will occur once in four or six inches. The third gang follows with hoes, drawing earth upon the stalks, and covering them to the depth, of three inches.

In four weeks, at the farthest, the sprouts appear above the ground, and from this time forward grow with great rapidity. A sugar field is hoed three times, the same as cotton, save that a greater quantity of earth is drawn to the roots. By the first of

August hoeing is usually over. About the middle of September, whatever is required for seed is cut and stacked in ricks, as they are termed. In October it is ready for the mill or sugar-house, and then the general cutting begins. The blade of a cane-knife is fifteen inches long, three inches wide in the middle, and tapering towards the point and handle. The blade is thin, and in order to be at all serviceable must be kept very sharp. Every third hand takes the lead of two others, one of whom is on each side of him. The lead hand, in the first place, with a blow of his knife shears the flags from the stalk. He next cuts off the top down as far as it is green. He must be careful to sever all the green from the ripe part, inasmuch as the juice of the former sours the molasses, and renders it unsalable. Then he severs the stalk at the root, and lays it directly behind him. His right and left hand companions lay their stalks, when cut in the same manner, upon his. To every three hands there is a cart, which follows, and the stalks are thrown into it by the younger slaves, when it is drawn to the sugar-house and ground.

If the planter apprehends a frost, the cane is winrowed. Winrowing is the cutting the stalks at an early period and throwing them lengthwise in the water furrow in such a manner that the tops will cover the butts of the stalks. They will remain in this condition three weeks or a month without souring, and secure from frost. When the proper time arrives, they are taken up, trimmed and carted to the sugar-house.

In the month of January the slaves enter the field again to prepare for another crop. The ground is now strewn with the tops, and flags cut from the past year's cane. On a dry day fire is set to this combustible refuse, which sweeps over the field, leaving it bare and clean, and ready for the hoes. The earth is loosened about the roots of the old stubble, and in process of time another crop springs up from the last year's seed. It is the same the year following; but the third year the seed has exhausted its strength, and the field must be ploughed and planted again. The second year the cane is sweeter and yields more than the first, and the third year more than the second.

During the three seasons I labored on Hawkins' plantation, I was employed a considerable portion of the time in the sugar-house. He is celebrated as the producer of the finest variety of white sugar. The following is a general description of his sugar-house and the process of manufacture:

The mill is an immense brick building, standing on the shore of the bayou. Running out from the building is an open shed, at least an hundred feet in length and forty or fifty feet in width. The boiler in which the steam is generated is situated outside the main building; the machinery and engine rest on a brick pier, fifteen feet above the floor, within the body of the building. The machinery turns two great iron rollers, between two and three feet in diameter and six or eight feet in length. They are elevated above the brick pier, and roll in towards each other. An endless carrier, made of chain and wood, like leathern belts used in small mills, extends from the iron rollers out of the main building and through the entire length of the open shed. The carts in which the cane is brought from the field as fast as it is cut, are unloaded at the sides of the shed. All along the endless carrier are ranged slave children, whose business it is to place the cane upon it, when it is conveyed through the shed into the main building, where it falls between the rollers, is crushed, and drops upon another carrier that conveys it out of the main building in an opposite direction, depositing it in the top of a chimney upon a fire beneath, which consumes it. It is necessary to burn it in this manner, because otherwise it would soon fill the building, and more especially because it would soon sour and engender disease. The juice of the cane falls into a conductor underneath the iron rollers, and is carried into a reservoir. Pipes convey it from thence into five filterers, holding several hogsheads each. These filterers are filled with bone-black, a substance resembling pulverized charcoal. It is made of bones calcinated in close vessels, and is used for the purpose of decolorizing, by filtration, the cane juice before

374

boiling. Through these five filterers it passes in succession, and then runs into a large reservoir underneath the ground floor, from whence it is carried up, by means of a steam pump, into a clarifier made of sheet iron, where it is heated by steam until it boils. From the first clarifier it is carried in pipes to a second and a third, and thence into close iron pans, through which tubes pass, filled with steam. While in a boiling state it flows through three pans in succession, and is then carried in other pipes down to the coolers on the ground floor. Coolers are wooden boxes with sieve bottoms made of the finest wire. As soon as the syrup passes into the coolers, and is met by the air, it grains, and the molasses at once escapes through the sieves into a cistern below. It is then white or loaf sugar of the finest kind—clear, clean, and as white as snow. When cool, it is taken out, packed in hogsheads, and is ready for market. The molasses is then carried from the cistern into the upper story again, and by another process converted into brown sugar.

There are larger mills, and those constructed differently from the one thus imperfectly described, but none, perhaps, more celebrated than this anywhere on Bayou Bœuf. Lambert, of New-Orleans, is a partner of Hawkins. He is a man of vast wealth, holding, as I have been told, an interest in over forty different sugar plantations in Louisiana.

The only respite from constant labor the slave has through the whole year, is during the Christmas holidays. Epps allowed us three—others allow four, five and six days, according to the measure of their generosity. It is the only time to which they look forward with any interest or pleasure. They are glad when night comes, not only because it brings them a few hours repose, but because it brings them one day nearer Christmas. It is hailed with equal delight by the old and the young; even Uncle Abram ceases to glorify Andrew Jackson, and Patsey forgets her many sorrows, amid the general hilarity of the holidays. It is the time of feasting, and frolicking, and fiddling—the carnival season with the children of bondage. They are the only days when they are allowed a little restricted liberty, and heartily indeed do they enjoy it.

It is the custom for one planter to give a "Christmas supper," inviting the slaves from neighboring plantations to join his own on the occasion; for instance, one year it is given by Epps, the next by Marshall, the next by Hawkins, and so on. Usually from three to five hundred are assembled, coming together on foot, in carts, on horseback, on mules, riding double and triple, sometimes a boy and girl, at others a girl and two boys, and at others again a boy, a girl and an old woman. Uncle Abram astride a mule, with Aunt Phebe and Patsey behind him, trotting towards a Christmas supper, would be no uncommon sight on Bayou Bœuf.

Then, too, "of all days i' the year," they array themselves in their best attire. The cotton coat has been washed clean, the stump of a tallow candle has been applied to the shoes, and if so fortunate as to possess a rimless or a crownless hat, it is placed jauntily on the head. They are welcomed with equal cordiality, however, if they come bare-headed and barefooted to the feast. As a general thing, the women wear handkerchiefs tied about their heads, but if chance has thrown in their way a fiery red ribbon, or a cast-off bonnet of their mistress' grandmother, it is sure to be worn on such occasions. Red—the deep blood red—is decidedly the favorite color among the enslaved damsels of my acquaintance. If a red ribbon does not encircle the neck, you will be certain to find all the hair of their woolly heads tied up with red strings of one sort or another.

The table is spread in the open air, and loaded with varieties of meat and piles of vegetables. Bacon and corn meal at such times are dispensed with. Sometimes the cooking is performed in the kitchen on the plantation, at others in the shade of wide branching trees. In the latter case, a ditch is dug in the ground, and wood laid in and burned until it is filled with glowing coals, over which chickens, ducks, turkeys, pigs, and not unfrequently the entire body of a wild ox, are roasted. They are furnished also with flour, of which biscuits are made, and often with peach and other preserves, with tarts, and every manner and description of pies, except the mince, that being an article of pastry as yet unknown among them. Only the slave who has lived all the years on his scanty allowance of meal and bacon, can appreciate such suppers. White people in great numbers assemble to witness the gastronomical enjoyments.

They seat themselves at the rustic table—the males on one side, the females on the other. The two between whom there may have been an exchange of tenderness, invariably manage to sit opposite; for the omnipresent Cupid disdains not to hurl his arrows into the simple hearts of slaves. Unalloyed and exulting happiness lights up the dark faces of them all. The ivory teeth, contrasting with their black complexions, exhibit two long, white streaks the whole extent of the table. All round the bountiful board a multitude of eyes roll in ecstacy. Giggling and laughter and the clattering of cutlery and crockery succeed. Cuffee's elbow hunches his neighbor's side, impelled by an involuntary impulse of delight; Nelly shakes her finger at Sambo and laughs, she knows not why, and so the fun and merriment flows on.

When the viands have disappeared, and the hungry maws of the children of toil are satisfied, then, next in the order of amusement, is the Christmas dance. My business on these gala days always was to play on the violin. The African race is a music-loving one, proverbially; and many there were among my fellow-bondsmen whose organs of tune were strikingly developed, and who could thumb the banjo with dexterity; but at the expense of appearing egotistical, I must, nevertheless, declare that I was considered the Ole Bull of Bayou Bœuf. My master often received letters, sometimes from a distance of ten miles, requesting him to send me to play at a ball or festival of the whites. He received his compensation, and usually I also returned with many picayunes jingling in my pockets—the extra contributions of those to whose delight I had administered. In this manner I became more acquainted than I otherwise would, up and down

377

the bayou. The young men and maidens of Holmesville always knew there was to be a jollification somewhere, whenever Platt Epps was seen passing through the town with his fiddle in his hand. "Where are you going now, Platt?" and "What is coming off to-night, Platt?" would be interrogatories issuing from every door and window, and many a time when there was no special hurry, yielding to pressing importunities, Platt would draw his bow, and sitting astride his mule, perhaps, discourse musically to a crowd of delighted children, gathered around him in the street.

Alas! had it not been for my beloved violin, I scarcely can conceive how I could have endured the long years of bondage. It introduced me to great houses—relieved me of many days' labor in the field—supplied me with conveniences for my cabin—with pipes and tobacco, and extra pairs of shoes, and oftentimes led me away from the presence of a hard master, to witness scenes of jollity and mirth. It was my companion—the friend of my bosom—triumphing loudly when I was joyful, and uttering its soft, melodious consolations when I was sad. Often, at midnight, when sleep had fled affrighted from the cabin, and my soul was disturbed and troubled with the contemplation of my fate, it would sing me a song of peace. On holy Sabbath days, when an hour or two of leisure was allowed, it would accompany me to some quiet place on the bayou bank, and, lifting up its voice, discourse kindly and pleasantly indeed. It heralded my name round the country—made me friends, who, otherwise would not have noticed me—gave me an honored seat at the yearly feasts, and secured the loudest and heartiest welcome of them all at the Christmas dance. The Christmas dance! Oh, ye pleasure-seeking sons and daughters of idleness, who move with measured step, listless and snail-like, through the slow-winding cotillon, if ye wish to look upon the celerity, if not the "poetry of motion"— upon genuine happiness, rampant and unrestrained—go down to Louisiana, and see the slaves dancing in the starlight of a Christmas night.

On that particular Christmas I have now in my mind, a description whereof will serve as a description of the day generally, Miss Lively and Mr. Sam, the first belonging to Stewart, the latter to Roberts, started the ball. It was well known that Sam cherished an ardent passion for Lively, as also did one of Marshall's and another of Carey's boys; for Lively was *lively* indeed, and a heart-breaking coquette withal. It was a victory for Sam Roberts, when, rising from the repast, she gave him her hand for the first "figure" in preference to either of his rivals. They were somewhat crest-fallen, and, shaking their heads angrily, rather intimated they would like to pitch into Mr. Sam and hurt him badly. But not an emotion of wrath ruffled the placid bosom of Samuel, as his legs flew like drum-sticks down the outside and up the middle, by the side of his bewitching partner. The whole company cheered them vociferously, and, excited with the applause, they continued "tearing down" after all the others had become exhausted and halted a moment to recover breath. But Sam's superhuman exertions overcame him finally, leaving Lively alone, yet whirling like a top. Thereupon one of Sam's rivals, Pete Marshall, dashed in, and, with might and main, leaped and shuffled and threw himself into every conceivable shape, as if determined to show Miss Lively and all the world that Sam Roberts was of no account.

Pete's affection, however, was greater than his discretion. Such violent exercise took the breath out of him directly, and he dropped like an empty bag. Then was the time for Harry Carey to try his hand; but Lively also soon out-winded him, amidst hurrahs and shouts, fully sustaining her well-earned reputation of being the "fastest gal" on the bayou.

One "set" off, another takes its place, he or she remaining longest on the floor receiving the most uproarious commendation, and so the dancing continues until broad daylight. It does not cease with the sound of the fiddle, but in that case they set up a music peculiar to themselves. This is called "patting," accompanied with one of those unmeaning songs, composed rather for its adaptation to a certain tune or measure, than for the purpose of expressing any distinct idea. The patting is performed by striking the hands on the knees, then striking the hands together, then striking the right shoulder with one hand, the left with the other—all the while keeping time with the feet, and singing, perhaps, this song:

> "Harper's creek and roarin' ribber,
> Thar, my dear, we'll live forebber;
> Den we'll go to de Ingin nation,
> All I want in dis creation,
> Is pretty little wife and big plantation.
> *Chorus.* Up dat oak and down dat ribber,
> Two overseers and one little nigger."

Or, if these words are not adapted to the tune called for, it may be that "Old Hog Eye" *is*—a rather solemn and startling specimen of versification, not, however, to be appreciated unless heard at the South. It runneth as follows:

> "Who's been here since I've been gone?
> Pretty little gal wid a josey on.
> > Hog Eye!
> > Old Hog Eye,
> > And Hosey too!
>
> Never see de like since I was born,
> Here come a little gal wid a josey on.
> > Hog Eye!
> > Old Hog Eye!
> > And Hosey too!"

Or, may be the following, perhaps, equally nonsensical, but full of melody, nevertheless, as it flows from the negro's mouth:

"Ebo Dick and Jurdan's Jo,
Them two niggers stole my yo'.
     Chorus. Hop Jim along,
          Walk Jim along,
          Talk Jim along," &c.

Old black Dan, as black as tar,
He dam glad he was not dar.
          Hop Jim along," &c.

During the remaining holidays succeeding Christmas, they are provided with passes, and permitted to go where they please within a limited distance, or they may remain and labor on the plantation, in which case they are paid for it. It is very rarely, however, that the latter alternative is accepted. They may be seen at these times hurrying in all directions, as happy looking mortals as can be found on the face of the earth. They are different beings from what they are in the field; the temporary relaxation, the brief deliverance from fear, and from the lash, producing an entire metamorphosis in their appearance and demeanor. In visiting, riding, renewing old friendships, or, perchance, reviving some old attachment, or pursuing whatever pleasure may suggest itself, the time is occupied. Such is "southern life as it is," *three days in the year,* as I found it—the other three hundred and sixty-two being days of weariness, and fear, and suffering, and unremitting labor.

Marriage is frequently contracted during the holidays, if such an institution may be said to exist among them. The only ceremony required before entering into that "holy estate," is to obtain the consent of the respective owners. It is usually encouraged by the masters of female slaves. Either party can have as many husbands or wives as the owner will permit, and either is at liberty to discard the other at pleasure. The law in relation to divorce, or to bigamy, and so forth, is not applicable to property, of course. If the wife does not belong on the same plantation with the husband, the latter is permitted to visit her on Saturday nights, if the distance is not too far. Uncle Abram's wife lived seven miles from Epps', on Bayou Huff Power. He had permission to visit her once a fortnight, but he was growing old, as has been said, and truth to say, had latterly well nigh forgotten her. Uncle Abram had no time to spare from his meditations on General Jackson—connubial dalliance being well enough for the young and thoughtless, but unbecoming a grave and solemn philosopher like himself.

CHAPTER XVI

With the exception of my trip to St. Mary's parish, and my absence during the cane-cutting seasons, I was constantly employed on the plantation of Master Epps. He was considered but a small planter, not having a sufficient number of hands to require the services of an overseer, acting in the latter capacity himself. Not able to increase his force, it was his custom to hire during the hurry of cotton-picking.

On larger estates, employing fifty or a hundred, or perhaps two hundred hands, an overseer is deemed indispensable. These gentlemen ride into the field on horseback, without an exception, to my knowledge, armed with pistols, bowie knife, whip, and accompanied by several dogs. They follow, equipped in this fashion, in rear of the slaves, keeping a sharp lookout upon them all. The requisite qualifications in an overseer are utter heartlessness, brutality and cruelty. It is his business to produce large crops, and if that is accomplished, no matter what amount of suffering it may have cost. The presence of the dogs are necessary to overhaul a fugitive who may take to his heels, as is sometimes the case, when faint or sick, he is unable to maintain his row, and unable, also, to endure the whip. The pistols are reserved for any dangerous emergency, there having been instances when such weapons were necessary. Goaded into uncontrollable madness, even the slave will sometimes turn upon his oppressor. The gallows were standing at Marksville last January, upon which one was executed a year ago for killing his overseer. It occurred not many miles from Epps' plantation on Red River. The slave was given his task at splitting rails. In the course of the day the overseer sent him on an errand, which occupied so much time that it was not possible for him to perform the task. The next day he was called to an account, but the loss of time occasioned by the errand was no excuse, and he was ordered to kneel and bare his back for the reception of the lash. They were in the woods alone—beyond the reach of sight or hearing. The boy submitted until maddened at such injustice, and insane with pain, he sprang to his feet, and seizing an axe, literally chopped the overseer in pieces. He made no attempt whatever at concealment, but hastening to his master, related the whole affair, and declared himself ready to expiate the wrong by the sacrifice of his life. He was led to the scaffold, and while the rope was around his neck, maintained an undismayed and fearless bearing, and with his last words justified the act.

Besides the overseer, there are drivers under him, the number being in proportion to the number of hands in the field. The drivers are black, who, in addition to the performance of their equal share of work, are compelled to do the whipping of their several gangs. Whips hang around their necks, and if they fail to use them thoroughly, are whipped themselves. They have a few privileges, however; for example, in cane-cutting the hands are not allowed to sit down long enough to eat their dinners. Carts filled with corn cake, cooked at the kitchen, are driven into the field at noon. The cake is distributed by the drivers, and must be eaten with the least possible delay.

When the slave ceases to perspire, as he often does when taxed beyond his strength, he falls to the ground and becomes entirely helpless. It is then the duty of the driver to drag him into the shade of the standing cotton or cane, or of a neighboring tree, where he dashes buckets of water upon him, and uses other means of bringing out perspiration again, when he is ordered to his place, and compelled to continue his labor.

At Huff Power, when I first came to Epps', Tom, one of Roberts' negroes, was driver. He was a burly fellow, and severe in the extreme. After Epps' removal to Bayou Bœuf, that distinguished honor was conferred upon myself. Up to the time of my departure I had to wear a whip about my neck in the field. If Epps was present, I dared not show any lenity, not having the Christian fortitude of a certain well-known Uncle Tom sufficiently to brave his wrath, by refusing to perform the office. In that way, only, I escaped the immediate martyrdom he suffered, and, withal, saved my companions much suffering, as it proved in the end. Epps, I soon found, whether actually in the field or not, had his eyes pretty generally upon us. From the piazza, from behind some adjacent tree, or other concealed point of observation, he was perpetually on the watch. If one of us had been backward or idle through the day, we were apt to be told all about it on returning to the quarters, and as it was a matter of principle with him to reprove every offence of that kind that came within his knowledge, the offender not only was certain of receiving a castigation for his tardiness, but I likewise was punished for permitting it.

If, on the other hand, he had seen me use the lash freely, the man was satisfied. "Practice makes perfect," truly; and during my eight years' experience as a driver, I learned to handle the whip with marvelous dexterity and precision, throwing the lash within a hair's breadth of the back, the ear, the nose, without, however, touching either of them. If Epps was observed at a distance, or we had reason to apprehend he was sneaking somewhere in the vicinity, I would commence plying the lash vigorously, when, according to arrangement, they would squirm and screech as if in agony, although not one of them had in fact been even grazed. Patsey would take occasion, if he made his appearance presently, to mumble in his hearing some complaints that Platt was lashing them the whole time, and Uncle Abram, with an appearance of honesty peculiar to himself, would declare roundly I had just whipped them worse than General Jackson whipped the enemy at New-Orleans. If Epps was not drunk, and in one of his beastly humors, this was, in general, satisfactory. If he was, some one or more of us must suffer, as a matter of course. Sometimes his violence assumed a dangerous form, placing the lives of his human stock in jeopardy. On one occasion the drunken madman thought to amuse himself by cutting my throat.

He had been absent at Holmesville, in attendance at a shooting-match, and none of us were aware of his return. While hoeing by the side of Patsey, she exclaimed, in a low voice, suddenly, "Platt, d'ye see old Hog-Jaw beckoning me to come to him?"

Glancing sideways, I discovered him in the edge of the field, motioning and grimacing, as was his habit when half-intoxicated. Aware of his lewd intentions, Patsey began to cry. I whispered her not to look up, and to continue at her work, as if she had not observed him. Suspecting the truth of the matter, however, he soon staggered up to me in a great rage.

"What did you say to Pats?" he demanded, with an oath. I made him some evasive answer, which only had the effect of increasing his violence.

"How long have you owned this plantation, *say*, you d——d nigger?" he inquired, with a malicious sneer, at the same time taking hold of my shirt collar with one hand, and thrusting the other into his pocket. "Now I'll cut your black throat; that's what I'll do," drawing his knife from his pocket as he said it. But with one hand he was unable to open it, until finally seizing the blade in his teeth, I saw he was about to succeed, and felt the necessity of escaping from him, for in his present reckless state, it was evident he was not joking, by any means. My shirt was open in front, and as I turned round quickly and sprang from him, while he still retained his gripe, it was stripped entirely from my back. There was no difficulty now in eluding him. He would chase me until out of breath, then stop until it was recovered, swear, and renew the chase again. Now he would command me to come to him, now endeavor to coax me, but I was careful to keep at a respectful distance. In this manner we made the circuit of the field several times, he making desperate plunges, and I always dodging them, more amused than frightened, well knowing that when his sober senses returned, he would laugh at his own drunken folly. At length I observed the mistress standing by the yard fence, watching our half-serious, half-comical manœuvres. Shooting past him, I ran directly to her. Epps, on discovering her, did not follow. He remained about the field an hour or more, during which time I stood by the mistress, having related the particulars of what had taken place. Now, *she* was aroused again, denouncing her husband and Patsey about equally. Finally, Epps came towards the house, by this time nearly sober, walking demurely, with his hands behind his back, and attempting to look as innocent as a child.

As he approached, nevertheless, Mistress Epps began to berate him roundly, heaping upon him many rather disrespectful epithets, and demanding for what reason he had attempted to cut my throat. Epps made wondrous strange of it all, and to my surprise, swore by all the saints in the calendar he had not spoken to me that day.

"Platt, you lying nigger, *have* I?" was his brazen appeal to me.

It is not safe to contradict a master, even by the assertion of a truth. So I was silent, and when he entered the house I returned to the field, and the affair was never after alluded to.

Shortly after this time a circumstance occurred that came nigh divulging the secret of my real name and history, which I had so long and carefully concealed, and upon which I was convinced depended my final escape. Soon after he purchased me, Epps asked me if I could write and read, and on being informed that I had received some instruction in those branches of education, he assured me, with emphasis, if he ever caught me with a book, or with pen and ink, he would give me a hundred lashes. He said he wanted me to understand that he bought "niggers" to work and not to educate. He never inquired a word of my past life, or from whence I came. The mistress, however, cross-examined me frequently about Washington, which she supposed was my native city, and more than once remarked that I did not talk nor act like the other "niggers," and she was sure I had seen more of the world than I admitted.

My great object always was to invent means of getting a letter secretly into the post-office, directed to some of my friends or family at the North. The difficulty of such an achievement cannot be comprehended by one unacquainted with the severe restrictions imposed upon me. In the first place, I was deprived of pen, ink, and paper. In the second place, a slave cannot leave his plantation without a pass, nor will a post-master mail a letter for one without written instructions from his owner. I was in slavery nine years, and always watchful and on the alert, before I met with the good fortune of obtaining a sheet of paper. While Epps was in New-Orleans, one winter, disposing of his cotton, the mistress sent me to Holmesville, with an order for several articles, and among the rest a quantity of foolscap. I appropriated a sheet, concealing it in the cabin, under the board on which I slept.

After various experiments I succeeded in making ink, by boiling white maple bark, and with a feather plucked from the wing of a duck, manufactured a pen. When all were asleep in the cabin, by the light of the coals, lying upon my plank couch, I managed to complete a somewhat lengthy epistle. It was directed to an old acquaintance at Sandy Hill, stating my condition, and urging him to take measures to restore me to liberty. This letter I kept a long time, contriving measures by which it could be safely deposited in the post-office. At length, a low fellow, by the name of Armsby, hitherto a stranger, came into the neighborhood, seeking a situation as overseer. He applied to Epps, and was about the plantation for several days. He next went over to Shaw's, near by, and remained with him several weeks. Shaw was generally surrounded by such worthless characters, being himself noted as a gambler and unprincipled man. He had made a wife of his slave Charlotte, and a brood of young mulattoes were growing up in his house. Armsby became so much reduced at last, that he was compelled to labor with the slaves. A white man working in the field is a rare and unusual spectacle on Bayou Bœuf. I improved every opportunity of cultivating his acquaintance privately, desiring to obtain his confidence so far as to be willing to intrust the letter to his keeping. He visited Marksville repeatedly, he informed me, a town some twenty miles distant, and there, I proposed to myself, the letter should be mailed.

Carefully deliberating on the most proper manner of approaching him on the subject, I concluded finally to ask him simply if he would deposit a letter for me in the Marksville post-office the next time he visited that place, without disclosing to him that the letter was written, or any of the particulars it contained; for I had fears that he might betray me, and knew that some inducement must be held out to him of a pecuniary nature, before it would be safe to confide in him. As late as one o'clock one night I stole noiselessly from my cabin, and, crossing the field to Shaw's, found him sleeping on the piazza. I had but a few picayunes—the proceeds of my fiddling performances, but all I had in the world I promised him if he would do me the favor required. I begged him not to expose me if he could not grant the request. He assured me, upon his honor, he would deposit it in the Marksville post-office, and that he would keep it an inviolable secret forever. Though the letter was in my pocket at the time, I dared not then deliver it to him, but stating I would have it written in a day or two, bade him good night, and returned to my cabin. It was impossible for me to expel the suspicions I entertained, and all night I lay awake, revolving in my mind the safest course to pursue. I was willing to risk a great deal to accomplish my purpose, but should the letter by any means fall into the hands of Epps, it would be a death-blow to my aspirations. I was "perplexed in the extreme."

My suspicions were well-founded, as the sequel demonstrated. The next day but one, while scraping cotton in the field, Epps seated himself on the line fence between Shaw's plantation and his own, in such a position as to overlook the scene of our labors. Presently Armsby made his appearance, and, mounting the fence, took a seat beside him. They remained two or three hours, all of which time I was in an agony of apprehension.

That night, while broiling my bacon, Epps entered the cabin with his rawhide in his hand.

"Well, boy," said he, "I understand I've got a larned nigger, that writes letters, and tries to get white fellows to mail 'em. Wonder if you know who he is?"

My worst fears were realized, and although it may not be considered entirely creditable, even under the circumstances, yet a resort to duplicity and downright falsehood was the only refuge that presented itself.

"Don't know nothing about it, Master Epps," I answered him, assuming an air of ignorance and surprise; "Don't know nothing at all about it, sir."

"Wan't you over to Shaw's night before last?" he inquired.

"No, master," was the reply.

"Hav'nt you asked that fellow, Armsby, to mail a letter for you at Marksville?"

"Why, Lord, master, I never spoke three words to him in all my life. I don't know what you mean."

"Well," he continued, "Armsby told me to-day the devil was among my niggers; that I had one that needed close watching or he would run away; and when I axed him why, he said you come over to Shaw's, and waked him up in the night, and wanted him to carry a letter to Marksville. What have you got to say to that, ha?"

"All I've got to say, master," I replied, "is, there is no truth in it. How could I write a letter without any ink or paper? There is nobody I want to write to, 'cause I haint got no friends living as I know of. That Armsby is a lying, drunken fellow, they say, and nobody believes him anyway. You know I always tell the truth, and that I never go off the plantation without a pass. Now, master, I can see what that Armsby is after, plain enough. Did'nt he want you to hire him for an overseer?"

"Yes, he wanted me to hire him," answered Epps.

"That's it," said I, "he wants to make you believe we're all going to run away, and then he thinks you'll hire an overseer to watch us. He just made that story out of whole cloth, 'cause he wants to get a situation. It's all a lie, master, you may depend on't."

Epps mused awhile, evidently impressed with the plausibility of my theory, and exclaimed,

"I'm d—d, Platt, if I don't believe you tell the truth. He must take me for a soft, to think he can come it over me with them kind of yarns, musn't he? Maybe he thinks he can fool me; maybe he thinks I don't know nothing—can't take care of my own niggers, eh! Soft soap old Epps, eh! Ha, ha, ha! D—n Armsby! Set the dogs on him, Platt," and with many other comments descriptive of Armsby's general character, and his capability of taking care of his own business, and attending to his own "niggers," Master Epps left the cabin. As soon as he was gone I threw the letter in the fire, and, with a desponding and despairing heart, beheld the epistle which had cost me so much anxiety and thought, and which I fondly hoped would have been my forerunner to the land of freedom, writhe and shrivel on its bed of coals, and dissolve into smoke and ashes. Armsby, the treacherous wretch, was driven from Shaw's plantation not long subsequently, much to my relief, for I feared he might renew his conversation, and perhaps induce Epps to credit him.

I knew not now whither to look for deliverance. Hopes sprang up in my heart only to be crushed and blighted. The summer of my life was passing away; I felt I was growing prematurely old; that a few years more, and toil, and grief, and the poisonous miasmas of the swamps would accomplish their work upon me—would consign me to the grave's embrace, to moulder and be forgotten. Repelled, betrayed, cut off from the hope of succor, I could only prostrate myself upon the earth and groan in unutterable anguish. The hope of rescue was the only light that cast a ray of comfort on my heart. That was now flickering, faint and low; another breath of disappointment would extinguish it altogether, leaving me to grope in midnight darkness to the end of life.

CHAPTER XVII

The year 1850, down to which time I have now arrived, omitting many occurrences uninteresting to the reader, was an unlucky year for my companion Wiley, the husband of Phebe, whose taciturn and retiring nature has thus far kept him in the background. Notwithstanding Wiley seldom opened his mouth, and revolved in his obscure and unpretending orbit without a grumble, nevertheless the warm elements of sociality were strong in the bosom of that silent "nigger." In the exuberance of his self-reliance, disregarding the philosophy of Uncle Abram, and setting the counsels of Aunt Phebe utterly at naught, he had the fool-hardiness to essay a nocturnal visit to a neighboring cabin without a pass.

So attractive was the society in which he found himself, that Wiley took little note of the passing hours, and the light began to break in the east before he was aware. Speeding homeward as fast as he could run, he hoped to reach the quarters before the horn would sound; but, unhappily, he was spied on the way by a company of patrollers.

How it is in other dark places of slavery, I do not know, but on Bayou Bœuf there is an organization of patrollers, as they are styled, whose business it is to seize and whip any slave they may find wandering from the plantation. They ride on horseback, headed by a captain, armed, and accompanied by dogs. They have the right, either by law, or by general consent, to inflict discretionary chastisement upon a black man caught beyond the boundaries of his master's estate without a pass, and even to shoot him, if he attempts to escape. Each company has a certain distance to ride up and down the bayou. They are compensated by the planters, who contribute in proportion to the number of slaves they own. The clatter of their horses' hoofs dashing by can be heard at all hours of the night, and frequently they may be seen driving a slave before them, or leading him by a rope fastened around his neck, to his owner's plantation.

Wiley fled before one of these companies, thinking he could reach his cabin before they could overtake him; but one of their dogs, a great ravenous hound, griped him by the leg, and held him fast. The patrollers whipped him severely, and brought him, a prisoner, to Epps. From him he received another flagellation still more severe, so that the cuts of the lash and the bites of the dog rendered him sore, stiff and miserable, insomuch he was scarcely able to move. It was impossible in such a state to keep up his row, and consequently there was not an hour in the day but Wiley felt the sting of his master's rawhide on his raw and bleeding back. His sufferings became intolerable, and finally he resolved to run away. Without disclosing his intentions to run away even to his wife Phebe, he proceeded to make arrangements for carrying his plan into execution. Having cooked his whole week's allowance, he cautiously left the cabin on a Sunday night, after the inmates of the quarters were asleep. When the horn sounded in the morning, Wiley did not make his appearance. Search was made for him in the cabins, in the corn-crib, in the cotton-house, and in every nook and corner of the premises. Each of us was examined, touching any knowledge we might have that could throw light upon his sudden disappearance or present whereabouts. Epps raved and stormed, and mounting his horse, galloped to neighboring plantations, making inquiries in all directions. The search was fruitless. Nothing whatever was elicited, going to show what had become of the missing man. The dogs were led to the swamp, but were unable to strike his trail. They would circle away through the forest, their noses to the ground, but invariably returned in a short time to the spot from whence they started.

Wiley had escaped, and so secretly and cautiously as to elude and baffle all pursuit. Days and even weeks passed away, and nothing could be heard of him. Epps did nothing but curse and swear. It was the only topic of conversation among us when alone. We indulged in a great deal of speculation in regard to him, one suggesting he might have been drowned in some bayou, inasmuch as he was a poor swimmer; another, that perhaps he might have been devoured by alligators, or stung by the venomous moccasin, whose bite is certain and sudden death. The warm and hearty sympathies of us all, however, were with poor Wiley, wherever he might be. Many an earnest prayer ascended from the lips of Uncle Abram, beseeching safety for the wanderer.

In about three weeks, when all hope of ever seeing him again was dismissed, to our surprise, he one day appeared among us. On leaving the plantation, he informed us, it was his intention to make his way back to South Carolina—to the old quarters of Master Buford. During the day he remained secreted, sometimes in the branches of a tree, and at night pressed forward through the swamps. Finally, one morning, just at dawn, he reached the shore of Red River. While standing on the bank, considering how he could cross it, a white man accosted him, and demanded a pass. Without one, and evidently a runaway, he was taken to Alexandria, the shire town of the parish of Rapides, and confined in prison. It happened several days after that Joseph B. Roberts, uncle of Mistress Epps, was in Alexandria, and going into the jail, recognized him. Wiley had worked on his plantation, when Epps resided at Huff Power. Paying the jail fee, and writing him a pass, underneath which was a note to Epps, requesting him not to whip him on his return, Wiley was sent back to Bayou Bœuf. It was the hope that hung upon this request, and which Roberts assured him would be respected by his master, that sustained him as he approached the house. The request, however, as may be readily supposed, was entirely disregarded. After being kept in suspense three days, Wiley was stripped, and compelled to endure one of those inhuman floggings to which the poor slave is so often subjected. It was the first and last attempt of Wiley to run away. The long scars upon his back, which he will carry with him to the grave, perpetually remind him of the dangers of such a step.

There was not a day throughout the ten years I belonged to Epps that I did not consult with myself upon the prospect of escape. I laid many plans, which at the time I considered excellent ones, but one after the other they were all abandoned. No man who has never been placed in such a situation, can comprehend the thousand obstacles thrown in the way of the flying slave. Every white man's hand is raised against him—the patrollers are watching for him—the hounds are ready to follow on his track, and the nature of the country is such as renders it impossible to pass through it with any safety. I thought, however, that the time might come, perhaps, when I should be running through the swamps again. I concluded, in that case, to be prepared for Epps' dogs, should they pursue me. He possessed several, one of which was a notorious slave-hunter, and the most fierce and savage of his breed. While out hunting the coon or the opossum, I never allowed an opportunity to escape, when alone, of whipping them severely. In this manner I succeeded at length in subduing them completely. They feared me, obeying my voice at once when others had no control over them whatever. Had they followed and overtaken me, I doubt not they would have shrank from attacking me.

Notwithstanding the certainty of being captured, the woods and swamps are, nevertheless, continually filled with runaways. Many of them, when sick, or so worn out as to be unable to perform their tasks, escape into the swamps, willing to suffer the punishment inflicted for such offences, in order to obtain a day or two of rest.

While I belonged to Ford, I was unwittingly the means of disclosing the hiding-place of six or eight, who had taken up their residence in the "Great Pine Woods." Adam Taydem frequently sent me from the mills over to the opening after provisions. The whole distance was then a thick pine forest.

About ten o'clock of a beautiful moonlight night, while walking along the Texas road, returning to the mills, carrying a dressed pig in a bag swung over my shoulder, I heard footsteps behind me, and turning round, beheld two black men in the dress of slaves approaching at a rapid pace. When within a short distance, one of them raised a club, as if intending to strike me; the other snatched at the bag. I managed to dodge them both, and seizing a pine knot, hurled it with such force against the head of one of them that he was prostrated apparently senseless to the ground. Just then two more made their appearance from one side of the road. Before they could grapple me, however, I succeeded in passing them, and taking to my heels, fled, much affrighted, towards the mills. When Adam was informed of the adventure, he hastened straightway to the Indian village, and arousing Cascalla and several of his tribe, started in pursuit of the highwaymen. I accompanied them to the scene of attack, when we discovered a puddle of blood in the road, where the man whom I had smitten with the pine knot had fallen. After searching carefully through the woods a long time, one of Cascalla's men discovered a smoke curling up through the branches of several prostrate pines, whose tops had fallen together. The rendezvous was cautiously surrounded, and all of them taken prisoners. They had escaped from a plantation in the vicinity of Lamourie, and had been secreted there three weeks. They had no evil design upon me, except to frighten me out of my pig. Having observed me passing towards Ford's just at night-fall, and suspecting the nature of my errand, they had followed me, seen me butcher and dress the porker, and start on my return. They had been pinched for food, and were driven to this extremity by necessity. Adam conveyed them to the parish jail, and was liberally rewarded.

Not unfrequently the runaway loses his life in the attempt to escape. Epps' premises were bounded on one side by Carey's, a very extensive sugar plantation. He cultivates annually at least fifteen hundred acres of cane, manufacturing twenty-two or twenty-three hundred hogsheads of sugar; an hogshead and a half being the usual yield of an acre. Besides this he also cultivates five or six hundred acres of corn and cotton. He owned last year one hundred and fifty three field hands, besides nearly as many children, and yearly hires a drove during the busy season from this side the Mississippi.

One of his negro drivers, a pleasant, intelligent boy, was named Augustus. During the holidays, and occasionally while at work in adjoining fields, I had an opportunity of making his acquaintance, which eventually ripened into a warm and mutual attachment. Summer before last he was so unfortunate as to incur the displeasure of the overseer, a coarse, heartless brute, who whipped him most cruelly. Augustus ran away. Reaching a cane rick on Hawkins' plantation, he secreted himself in the top of it. All Carey's dogs were put upon his track—some fifteen of them—and soon scented his footsteps to the hiding place. They surrounded the rick, baying and scratching, but could not reach him. Presently, guided by the clamor of the hounds, the pursuers rode up, when the overseer, mounting on to the rick, drew him forth. As he rolled down to the ground the whole pack plunged upon him, and before they could be beaten off, had gnawed and mutilated his body in the most shocking manner, their teeth having penetrated to the bone in an hundred places. He was taken up, tied upon a mule, and carried home. But this was Augustus' last trouble. He lingered until the next day, when death sought the unhappy boy, and kindly relieved him from his agony.

It was not unusual for slave women as well as slave men to endeavor to escape. Nelly, Eldret's girl, with whom I lumbered for a time in the "Big Cane Brake," lay concealed in Epps' corn crib three days. At night, when his family were asleep, she would steal into the quarters for food, and return to the crib again. We concluded it would no longer be safe for us to allow her to remain, and accordingly she retraced her steps to her own cabin.

But the most remarkable instance of a successful evasion of

dogs and hunters was the following: Among Carey's girls was one by the name of Celeste. She was nineteen or twenty, and far whiter than her owner, or any of his offspring. It required a close inspection to distinguish in her features the slightest trace of African blood. A stranger would never have dreamed that she was the descendant of slaves. I was sitting in my cabin late at night, playing a low air on my violin, when the door opened carefully, and Celeste stood before me. She was pale and haggard. Had an apparition arisen from the earth, I could not have been more startled.

"Who are you?" I demanded, after gazing at her a moment.

"I'm hungry; give me some bacon," was her reply.

My first impression was that she was some deranged young mistress, who, escaping from home, was wandering, she knew not whither, and had been attracted to my cabin by the sound of the violin. The coarse cotton slave dress she wore, however, soon dispelled such a supposition.

"What is your name?" I again interrogated.

"My name is Celeste," she answered. "I belong to Carey, and have been two days among the palmettoes. I am sick and can't work, and would rather die in the swamp than be whipped to death by the overseer. Carey's dogs won't follow me. They have tried to set them on. There's a secret between them and Celeste, and they wont mind the devilish orders of the overseer. Give me some meat—I'm starving."

I divided my scanty allowance with her, and while partaking of it, she related how she had managed to escape, and described the place of her concealment. In the edge of the swamp, not half a mile from Epps' house, was a large space, thousands of acres in extent, thickly covered with palmetto. Tall trees, whose long arms interlocked each other, formed a canopy above them, so dense as to exclude the beams of the sun. It was like twilight always, even in the middle of the brightest day. In the centre of this great space, which nothing but serpents very often explore—a sombre and solitary spot—Celeste had erected a rude hut of dead branches that had fallen to the ground, and covered it with the leaves of the palmetto. This was the abode she had selected. She had no fear of Carey's dogs, any more than I had of Epps'. It is a fact, which I have never been able to explain, that there are those whose tracks the hounds will absolutely refuse to follow. Celeste was one of them.

For several nights she came to my cabin for food. On one occasion our dogs barked as she approached, which aroused Epps, and induced him to reconnoitre the premises. He did not discover her, but after that it was not deemed prudent for her to come to the yard. When all was silent I carried provisions to a certain spot agreed upon, where she would find them.

In this manner Celeste passed the greater part of the summer. She regained her health, and became strong and hearty. At all seasons of the year the howlings of wild animals can be heard at night along the borders of the swamps. Several times they had made her a midnight call, awakening her from slumber with a growl. Terrified by such unpleasant salutations, she finally concluded to abandon her lonely dwelling; and, accordingly, returning to her master, was scourged, her neck meanwhile being fastened in the stocks, and sent into the field again.

The year before my arrival in the country there was a concerted movement among a number of slaves on Bayou Bœuf, that terminated tragically indeed. It was, I presume, a matter of newspaper notoriety at the time, but all the knowledge I have of it, has been derived from the relation of those living at that period in the immediate vicinity of the excitement. It has become a subject of general and unfailing interest in every slave-hut on the bayou, and will doubtless go down to succeeding generations as their chief tradition. Lew Cheney, with whom I became acquainted—a shrewd, cunning negro, more intelligent than the generality of his race, but unscrupulous and full of treachery—conceived the project of organizing a company sufficiently strong to fight their way against all opposition, to the neighboring territory of Mexico.

A remote spot, far within the depths of the swamp, back of Hawkins' plantation, was selected as the rallying point. Lew flitted from one plantation to another, in the dead of night, preaching a crusade to Mexico, and, like Peter the Hermit, creating a furor of excitement wherever he appeared. At length a large number of runaways were assembled; stolen mules, and corn gathered from the fields, and bacon filched from smoke-houses, had been conveyed into the woods. The expedition was about ready to proceed, when their hiding place was discovered. Lew Cheney, becoming convinced of the ultimate failure of his project, in order to curry favor with his master, and avoid the consequences which he foresaw would follow, deliberately determined to sacrifice all his companions. Departing secretly from the encampment, he proclaimed among the planters the number collected in the swamp, and, instead of stating truly the object they had in view, asserted their intention was to emerge from their seclusion the first favorable opportunity, and murder every white person along the bayou.

Such an announcement, exaggerated as it passed from mouth to mouth, filled the whole country with terror. The fugitives were surrounded and taken prisoners, carried in chains to Alexandria, and hung by the populace. Not only those, but many who were suspected, though entirely innocent, were taken from the field and from the cabin, and without the shadow of process or form of trial, hurried to the scaffold. The planters on Bayou Bœuf finally rebelled against such reckless destruction of property, but it was not until a regiment of soldiers had arrived from some fort on the Texan frontier, demolished the gallows, and opened the doors of the Alexandria prison, that the indiscriminate slaughter was stayed. Lew Cheney escaped, and was even rewarded for his treachery. He is still living, but his name is despised and execrated by all his race throughout the parishes of Rapides and Avoyelles.

Such an idea as insurrection, however, is not new among the enslaved population of Bayou Bœuf. More than once I have joined in serious consultation, when the subject has been discussed, and there have been times when a word from me would have placed hundreds of my fellow-bondsmen in an attitude of defiance. Without arms or ammunition, or even with them, I saw such a step would result in certain defeat, disaster and death, and always raised my voice against it.

During the Mexican war I well remember the extravagant hopes that were excited. The news of victory filled the great house with rejoicing, but produced only sorrow and disappointment in the cabin. In my opinion—and I have had opportunity to know something of the feeling of which I speak—there are not fifty slaves on the shores of Bayou Bœuf, but would hail with unmeasured delight the approach of an invading army.

They are deceived who flatter themselves that the ignorant and debased slave has no conception of the magnitude of his wrongs. They are deceived who imagine that he arises from his knees, with back lacerated and bleeding, cherishing only a spirit of meekness and forgiveness. A day may come—it *will* come, if his prayer is heard—a terrible day of vengeance, when the master in his turn will cry in vain for mercy.

CHAPTER XVIII

Wiley suffered severely at the hands of Master Epps, as has been related in the preceding chapter, but in this respect he fared no worse than his unfortunate companions. "Spare the rod," was an idea scouted by our master. He was constitutionally subject to periods of ill-humor, and at such times, however little provocation there might be, a certain amount of punishment was inflicted. The circumstances attending the last flogging but one that I received, will show how trivial a cause was sufficient with him for resorting to the whip.

A Mr. O'Niel, residing in the vicinity of the Big Pine Woods, called upon Epps for the purpose of purchasing me. He was a tanner and currier by occupation, transacting an extensive business, and intended to place me at service in some department of his establishment, provided he bought me. Aunt Phebe, while preparing the dinner-table in the great house, overheard their conversation. On returning to the yard at night, the old woman ran to meet me, designing, of course, to overwhelm me with the news. She entered into a minute repetition of all she had heard, and Aunt Phebe was one whose ears never failed to drink in every word of conversation uttered in her hearing. She enlarged upon the fact that "Massa Epps was g'wine to sell me to a tanner ober in de Pine Woods," so long and loudly as to attract the attention of the mistress, who, standing unobserved on the piazza at the time, was listening to our conversation.

"Well, Aunt Phebe," said I, "I'm glad of it. I'm tired of scraping cotton, and would rather be a tanner. I hope he'll buy me."

O'Niel did not effect a purchase, however, the parties differing as to price, and the morning following his arrival, departed homewards. He had been gone but a short time, when

402

Epps made his appearance in the field. Now nothing will more violently enrage a master, especially Epps, than the intimation of one of his servants that he would like to leave him. Mistress Epps had repeated to him my expressions to Aunt Phebe the evening previous, as I learned from the latter afterwards, the mistress having mentioned to her that she had overheard us. On entering the field, Epps walked directly to me.

"So, Platt, you're tired of scraping cotton, are you? You would like to change your master, eh? You're fond of moving round—traveler—ain't ye? Ah, yes—like to travel for your health, may be? Feel above cotton-scraping, I 'spose. So you're going into the tanning business? Good business—devilish fine business. Enterprising nigger! B'lieve I'll go into that business myself. Down on your knees, and strip that rag off your back! I'll try my hand at tanning."

I begged earnestly, and endeavored to soften him with excuses, but in vain. There was no other alternative; so kneeling down, I presented my bare back for the application of the lash.

"How do you like *tanning*?" he exclaimed, as the rawhide descended upon my flesh. "How do you like *tanning*?" he repeated at every blow. In this manner he gave me twenty or thirty lashes, incessantly giving utterance to the word "tanning," in one form of expression or another. When sufficiently "tanned," he allowed me to arise, and with a half-malicious laugh assured me, if I still fancied the business, he would give me further instruction in it whenever I desired. This time, he remarked, he had only given me a short lesson in "*tanning*"—the next time he would "curry me down."

Uncle Abram, also, was frequently treated with great brutality, although he was one of the kindest and most faithful creatures in the world. He was my cabin-mate for years. There was a benevolent expression in the old man's face, pleasant to behold. He regarded us with a kind of parental feeling, always counseling us with remarkable gravity and deliberation.

Returning from Marshall's plantation one afternoon, whither

I had been sent on some errand of the mistress, I found him lying on the cabin floor, his clothes saturated with blood. He informed me that he had been stabbed! While spreading cotton on the scaffold, Epps came home intoxicated from Holmesville. He found fault with every thing, giving many orders so directly contrary that it was impossible to execute any of them. Uncle Abram, whose faculties were growing dull, became confused, and committed some blunder of no particular consequence. Epps was so enraged thereat, that, with drunken recklessness, he flew upon the old man, and stabbed him in the back. It was a long, ugly wound, but did not happen to penetrate far enough to result fatally. It was sewed up by the mistress, who censured her husband with extreme severity, not only denouncing his inhumanity, but declaring that she expected nothing else than that he would bring the family to poverty—that he would kill all the slaves on the plantation in some of his drunken fits.

It was no uncommon thing with him to prostrate Aunt Phebe with a chair or stick of wood; but the most cruel whipping that ever I was doomed to witness—one I can never recall with any other emotion than that of horror—was inflicted on the unfortunate Patsey.

It has been seen that the jealousy and hatred of Mistress Epps made the daily life of her young and agile slave completely miserable. I am happy in the belief that on numerous occasions I was the means of averting punishment from the inoffensive girl. In Epps' absence the mistress often ordered me to whip her without the remotest provocation. I would refuse, saying that I feared my master's displeasure, and several times ventured to remonstrate with her against the treatment Patsey received. I endeavored to impress her with the truth that the latter was not responsible for the acts of which she complained, but that she being a slave, and subject entirely to her master's will, he alone was answerable.

At length "the green-eyed monster" crept into the soul of Epps also, and then it was that he joined with his wrathful wife in an

404

infernal jubilee over the girl's miseries.

On a Sabbath day in hoeing time, not long ago, we were on the bayou bank, washing our clothes, as was our usual custom. Presently Patsey was missing. Epps called aloud, but there was no answer. No one had observed her leaving the yard, and it was a wonder with us whither she had gone. In the course of a couple of hours she was seen approaching from the direction of Shaw's. This man, as has been intimated, was a notorious profligate, and withal not on the most friendly terms with Epps. Harriet, his black wife, knowing Patsey's troubles, was kind to her, in consequence of which the latter was in the habit of going over to see her every opportunity. Her visits were prompted by friendship merely, but the suspicion gradually entered the brain of Epps, that another and a baser passion led her thither—that it was not Harriet she desired to meet, but rather the unblushing libertine, his neighbor. Patsey found her master in a fearful rage on her return. His violence so alarmed her that at first she attempted to evade direct answers to his questions, which only served to increase his suspicions. She finally, however, drew herself up proudly, and in a spirit of indignation boldly denied his charges.

"Missus don't give me soap to wash with, as she does the rest," said Patsey, "and you know why. I went over to Harriet's to get a piece," and saying this, she drew it forth from a pocket in her dress and exhibited it to him. "That's what I went to Shaw's for, Massa Epps," continued she; "the Lord knows that was all."

"You lie, you black wench!" shouted Epps.

"I *don't* lie, massa. If you kill me, I'll stick to that."

"Oh! I'll fetch you down. I'll learn you to go to Shaw's. I'll take the starch out of ye," he muttered fiercely through his shut teeth.

Then turning to me, he ordered four stakes to be driven into the ground, pointing with the toe of his boot to the places where he wanted them. When the stakes were driven down, he ordered her to be stripped of every article of dress. Ropes were then brought, and the naked girl was laid upon her face, her wrists and

405

feet each tied firmly to a stake. Stepping to the piazza, he took down a heavy whip, and placing it in my hands, commanded me to lash her. Unpleasant as it was, I was compelled to obey him. Nowhere that day, on the face of the whole earth, I venture to say, was there such a demoniac exhibition witnessed as then ensued.

Mistress Epps stood on the piazza among her children, gazing on the scene with an air of heartless satisfaction. The slaves were huddled together at a little distance, their countenances indicating the sorrow of their hearts. Poor Patsey prayed piteously for mercy, but her prayers were vain. Epps ground his teeth, and stamped upon the ground, screaming at me, like a mad fiend, to strike *harder*.

"Strike harder, or *your* turn will come next, you scoundrel," he yelled.

"Oh, mercy, massa!—oh! have mercy, *do*. Oh, God! pity me," Patsey exclaimed continually, struggling fruitlessly, and the flesh quivering at every stroke.

When I had struck her as many as thirty times, I stopped, and turned round toward Epps, hoping he was satisfied; but with bitter oaths and threats, he ordered me to continue. I inflicted ten or fifteen blows more. By this time her back was covered with long welts, intersecting each other like net work. Epps was yet furious and savage as ever, demanding if she would like to go to Shaw's again, and swearing he would flog her until she wished she was in h—l. Throwing down the whip, I declared I could punish her no more. He ordered me to go on, threatening me with a severer flogging than she had received, in case of refusal. My heart revolted at the inhuman scene, and risking the consequences, I absolutely refused to raise the whip. He then seized it himself, and applied it with ten-fold greater force than I had. The painful cries and shrieks of the tortured Patsey, mingling with the loud and angry curses of Epps, loaded the air. She was terribly lacerated—I may say, without exaggeration, literally flayed. The lash was wet with blood, which flowed down her sides and dropped upon the ground. At length she ceased struggling. Her head sank listlessly on the ground. Her screams and supplications gradually decreased and died away into a low moan. She no longer writhed and shrank beneath the lash when it bit out small pieces of her flesh. I thought that she was dying!

It was the Sabbath of the Lord. The fields smiled in the warm sunlight—the birds chirped merrily amidst the foliage of the trees—peace and happiness seemed to reign everywhere, save in the bosoms of Epps and his panting victim and the silent witnesses around him. The tempestuous emotions that were raging there were little in harmony with the calm and quiet beauty of the day. I could look on Epps only with unutterable loathing and abhorrence, and thought within myself—"Thou devil, sooner or later, somewhere in the course of eternal justice, thou shalt answer for this sin!"

Finally, he ceased whipping from mere exhaustion, and ordered Phebe to bring a bucket of salt and water. After washing her thoroughly with this, I was told to take her to her cabin. Untying the ropes, I raised her in my arms. She was unable to stand, and as her head rested on my shoulder, she repeated many times, in a faint voice scarcely perceptible, "Oh, Platt—oh, Platt!" but nothing further. Her dress was replaced, but it clung to her back, and was soon stiff with blood. We laid her on some boards in the hut, where she remained a long time, with eyes closed and groaning in agony. At night Phebe applied melted tallow to her wounds, and so far as we were able, all endeavored to assist and console her. Day after day she lay in her cabin upon her face, the sores preventing her resting in any other position.

A blessed thing it would have been for her—days and weeks and months of misery it would have saved her—had she never lifted up her head in life again. Indeed, from that time forward she was not what she had been. The burden of a deep melancholy weighed heavily on her spirits. She no longer moved with that buoyant and elastic step—there was not that mirthful sparkle in her eyes that formerly distinguished her. The bounding vigor—the sprightly, laughter-loving spirit of her youth, were gone.

She fell into a mournful and desponding mood, and oftentimes would start up in her sleep, and with raised hands, plead for mercy. She became more silent than she was, toiling all day in our midst, not uttering a word. A care-worn, pitiful expression settled on her face, and it was her humor now to weep, rather than rejoice. If ever there was a broken heart—one crushed and blighted by the rude grasp of suffering and misfortune—it was Patsey's.

She had been reared no better than her master's beast—looked upon merely as a valuable and handsome animal—and consequently possessed but a limited amount of knowledge. And yet a faint light cast its rays over her intellect, so that it was not wholly dark. She had a dim perception of God and of eternity, and a still more dim perception of a Saviour who had died even for such as her. She entertained but confused notions of a future life—not comprehending the distinction between the corporeal and spiritual existence. Happiness, in her mind, was exemption from stripes—from labor—from the cruelty of masters and overseers. Her idea of the joy of heaven was simply *rest*, and is fully expressed in these lines of a melancholy bard:

"I ask no paradise on high,
    With cares on earth oppressed,
The only heaven for which I sigh,
    Is rest, eternal rest."

It is a mistaken opinion that prevails in some quarters, that the slave does not understand the term—does not comprehend the idea of freedom. Even on Bayou Bœuf, where I conceive slavery exists in its most abject and cruel form—where it exhibits features altogether unknown in more northern States—the most ignorant of them generally know full well its meaning. They understand the privileges and exemptions that belong to it—that it would bestow upon them the fruits of their own labors, and that it would secure to them the enjoyment of domestic happiness. They do not fail to observe the difference between their own condition and the meanest white man's, and to realize the injustice of the laws which place it in his power not only to appropriate the profits of their industry, but to subject them to unmerited and unprovoked punishment, without remedy, or the right to resist, or to remonstrate.

Patsey's life, especially after her whipping, was one long dream of liberty. Far away, to her fancy an immeasurable distance, she knew there was a land of freedom. A thousand times she had heard that somewhere in the distant North there were no slaves—no masters. In her imagination it was an enchanted region, the Paradise of the earth. To dwell where the black man may work for himself—live in his own cabin—till his own soil, was a blissful dream of Patsey's—a dream, alas! the fulfillment of which she can never realize.

The effect of these exhibitions of brutality on the household of the slave-holder, is apparent. Epps' oldest son is an intelligent lad of ten or twelve years of age. It is pitiable, sometimes, to see him chastising, for instance, the venerable Uncle Abram. He will call the old man to account, and if in his childish judgment it is necessary, sentence him to a certain number of lashes, which he proceeds to inflict with much gravity and deliberation. Mounted on his pony, he often rides into the field with his whip, playing the overseer, greatly to his father's delight. Without discrimination, at such times, he applies the rawhide, urging the slaves forward with shouts, and occasional expressions of profanity, while the old man laughs, and commends him as a thorough-going boy.

"The child is father to the man," and with such training, whatever may be his natural disposition, it cannot well be otherwise than that, on arriving at maturity, the sufferings and miseries of the slave will be looked upon with entire indifference. The influence of the iniquitous system necessarily fosters an unfeeling and cruel spirit, even in the bosoms of those who, among their equals, are regarded as humane and generous.

409

Young Master Epps possessed some noble qualities, yet no process of reasoning could lead him to comprehend, that in the eye of the Almighty there is no distinction of color. He looked upon the black man simply as an animal, differing in no respect from any other animal, save in the gift of speech and the possession of somewhat higher instincts, and, therefore, the more valuable. To work like his father's mules—to be whipped and kicked and scourged through life—to address the white man with hat in hand, and eyes bent servilely on the earth, in his mind, was the natural and proper destiny of the slave. Brought up with such ideas—in the notion that we stand without the pale of humanity—no wonder the oppressors of my people are a pitiless and unrelenting race.

CHAPTER XIX

In the month of June, 1852, in pursuance of a previous contract, Mr. Avery, a carpenter of Bayou Rouge, commenced the erection of a house for Master Epps. It has previously been stated that there are no cellars on Bayou Bœuf; on the other hand, such is the low and swampy nature of the ground, the great houses are usually built upon spiles. Another peculiarity is, the rooms are not plastered, but the ceiling and sides are covered with matched cypress boards, painted such color as most pleases the owner's taste. Generally the plank and boards are sawed by slaves with whip-saws, there being no waterpower upon which mills might be built within many miles. When the planter erects for himself a dwelling, therefore, there is plenty of extra work for his slaves. Having had some experience under Tibeats as a carpenter, I was taken from the field altogether, on the arrival of Avery and his hands.

Among them was one to whom I owe an immeasurable debt of gratitude. Only for him, in all probability, I should have ended my days in slavery. He was my deliverer—a man whose true heart overflowed with noble and generous emotions. To the last moment of my existence I shall remember him with feelings of thankfulness. His name was Bass, and at that time he resided in Marksville. It will be difficult to convey a correct impression of his appearance or character. He was a large man, between forty and fifty years old, of light complexion and light hair. He was very cool and self-possessed, fond of argument, but always speaking with extreme deliberation. He was that kind of person whose peculiarity of manner was such that nothing he uttered ever gave offence. What would be intolerable, coming from the lips of another, could be said by him with impunity. There was not a man on Red River, perhaps, that agreed with him on the subject of politics or religion, and not a man, I venture to say, who discussed either of those subjects half as much. It seemed to be taken for granted that he would espouse the unpopular side of every local question, and it always created amusement rather than displeasure among his auditors, to listen to the ingenious and original manner in which he maintained the controversy. He was a bachelor—an "old bachelor," according to the true acceptation of the term—having no kindred living, as he knew of, in the world. Neither had he any permanent abiding place—wandering from one State to another, as his fancy dictated. He had lived in Marksville three or four years, and in the prosecution of his business as a carpenter; and in consequence, likewise, of his peculiarities, was quite extensively known throughout the parish of Avoyelles. He was liberal to a fault; and his many acts of kindness and transparent goodness of heart rendered him popular in the community, the sentiment of which he unceasingly combated.

He was a native of Canada, from whence he had wandered in early life, and after visiting all the principal localities in the northern and western States, in the course of his peregrinations, arrived in the unhealthy region of the Red River. His last removal was from Illinois. Whither he has now gone, I regret to be obliged to say, is unknown to me. He gathered up his effects and departed quietly from Marksville the day before I did, the suspicions of his instrumentality in procuring my liberation rendering such a step necessary. For the commission of a just and righteous act he would undoubtedly have suffered death, had he remained within reach of the slave-whipping tribe on Bayou Bœuf.

One day, while working on the new house, Bass and Epps became engaged in a controversy, to which, as will be readily supposed, I listened with absorbing interest. They were discussing the subject of Slavery.

"I tell you what it is Epps," said Bass, "it's all wrong—all wrong,

412

sir—there's no justice nor righteousness in it. I wouldn't own a slave if I was rich as Crœsus, which I am not, as is perfectly well understood, more particularly among my creditors. *There's* another humbug—the credit system—humbug, sir; no credit—no debt. Credit leads a man into temptation. Cash down is the only thing that will deliver him from evil. But this question of *Slavery*; what *right* have you to your niggers when you come down to the point?"

"What right!" said Epps, laughing; "why, I bought 'em, and paid for 'em."

"Of *course* you did; the law says you have the right to hold a nigger, but begging the law's pardon, it *lies*. Yes, Epps, when the law says that it's a *liar*, and the truth is not in it. Is every thing right because the law allows it? Suppose they'd pass a law taking away your liberty and making you a slave?"

"Oh, that ain't a supposable case," said Epps, still laughing; "hope you don't compare me to a nigger, Bass."

"Well," Bass answered gravely, "no, not exactly. But I have seen niggers before now as good as I am, and I have no acquaintance with any white man in these parts that I consider a whit better than myself. Now, in the sight of God, what is the difference, Epps, between a white man and a black one?"

"All the difference in the world," replied Epps. "You might as well ask what the difference is between a white man and a baboon. Now, I've seen one of them critters in Orleans that knowed just as much as any nigger I've got. You'd call them feller citizens, I s'pose?"—and Epps indulged in a loud laugh at his own wit.

"Look here, Epps," continued his companion; "you can't laugh me down in that way. Some men are witty, and some ain't so witty as they think they are. Now let me ask you a question. Are all men created free and equal as the Declaration of Independence holds they are?"

"Yes," responded Epps, "but all men, niggers, and monkeys *ain't;*" and hereupon he broke forth into a more boisterous

413

laugh than before.

"There are monkeys among white people as well as black, when you come to that," coolly remarked Bass. "I know some white men that use arguments no sensible monkey would. But let that pass. These niggers are human beings. If they don't know as much as their masters, whose fault is it? They are not *allowed* to know anything. You have books and papers, and can go where you please, and gather intelligence in a thousand ways. But your slaves have no privileges. You'd whip one of them if caught reading a book. They are held in bondage, generation after generation, deprived of mental improvement, and who can expect them to possess much knowledge? If they are not brought down to a level with the brute creation, you slaveholders will never be blamed for it. If they are baboons, or stand no higher in the scale of intelligence than such animals, you and men like you will have to answer for it. There's a sin, a fearful sin, resting on this nation, that will not go unpunished forever. There will be a reckoning yet—yes, Epps, there's a day coming that will burn as an oven. It may be sooner or it may be later, but it's a coming as sure as the Lord is just."

"If you lived up among the Yankees in New-England," said Epps, "I expect you'd be one of them cursed fanatics that know more than the constitution, and go about peddling clocks and coaxing niggers to run away."

"If I was in New-England," returned Bass, "I would be just what I am here. I would say that Slavery was an iniquity, and ought to be abolished. I would say there was no reason nor justice in the law, or the constitution that allows one man to hold another man in bondage. It would be hard for you to lose your property, to be sure, but it wouldn't be half as hard as it would be to lose your liberty. You have no more right to your freedom, in exact justice, than Uncle Abram yonder. Talk about black skin, and black blood; why, how many slaves are there on this bayou as white as either of us? And what difference is there in the color of the soul? Pshaw! the whole system is as absurd as

414

it is cruel. You may own niggers and behanged, but I wouldn't own one for the best plantation in Louisiana."

"You like to hear yourself talk, Bass, better than any man I know of. You would argue that black was white, or white black, if any body would contradict you. Nothing suits you in this world, and I don't believe you will be satisfied with the next, if you should have your choice in them."

Conversations substantially like the foregoing were not unusual between the two after this; Epps drawing him out more for the purpose of creating a laugh at his expense, than with a view of fairly discussing the merits of the question. He looked upon Bass, as a man ready to say anything merely for the pleasure of hearing his own voice; as somewhat self-conceited, perhaps, contending against his faith and judgment, in order, simply, to exhibit his dexterity in argumentation.

He remained at Epps' through the summer, visiting Marksville generally once a fortnight. The more I saw of him, the more I became convinced he was a man in whom I could confide. Nevertheless, my previous ill-fortune had taught me to be extremely cautious. It was not my place to speak to a white man except when spoken to, but I omitted no opportunity of throwing myself in his way, and endeavored constantly in every possible manner to attract his attention. In the early part of August he and myself were at work alone in the house, the other carpenters having left, and Epps being absent in the field. Now was the time, if ever, to broach the subject, and I resolved to do it, and submit to whatever consequences might ensue. We were busily at work in the afternoon, when I stopped suddenly and said—

"Master Bass, I want to ask you what part of the country you came from?"

"Why, Platt, what put that into your head?" he answered. "You wouldn't know if I should tell you." After a moment or two he added—"I was born in Canada; now guess where that is."

"Oh, I know where Canada is," said I, "I have been

415

there myself."

"Yes, I expect you are well acquainted all through that country," he remarked, laughing incredulously.

"As sure as I live, Master Bass," I replied, "I have been there. I have been in Montreal and Kingston, and Queenston, and a great many places in Canada, and I have been in York State, too—in Buffalo, and Rochester, and Albany, and can tell you the names of the villages on the Erie canal and the Champlain canal."

Bass turned round and gazed at me a long time without uttering a syllable.

"How came you here?" he inquired, at length. "Master Bass," I answered, "if justice had been done, I never would have been here."

"Well, how's this?" said he. "Who are you? You have been in Canada sure enough; I know all the places you mention. How did you happen to get here? Come, tell me all about it."

"I have no friends here," was my reply, "that I can put confidence in. I am afraid to tell you, though I don't believe you would tell Master Epps if I should."

He assured me earnestly he would keep every word I might speak to him a profound secret, and his curiosity was evidently strongly excited. It was a long story, I informed him, and would take some time to relate it. Master Epps would be back soon, but if he would see me that night after all were asleep, I would repeat it to him. He consented readily to the arrangement, and directed me to come into the building where we were then at work, and I would find him there. About midnight, when all was still and quiet, I crept cautiously from my cabin, and silently entering the unfinished building, found him awaiting me.

After further assurances on his part that I should not be betrayed, I began a relation of the history of my life and misfortunes. He was deeply interested, asking numerous questions in reference to localities and events. Having ended my story I besought him to write to some of my friends at the North, acquainting them with my situation, and begging them to forward free papers, or take such steps as they might consider proper to secure my release. He promised to do so, but dwelt upon the danger of such an act in case of detection, and now impressed upon me the great necessity of strict silence and secresy. Before we parted our plan of operation was arranged.

We agreed to meet the next night at a specified place among the high weeds on the bank of the bayou, some distance from master's dwelling. There he was to write down on paper the names and address of several persons, old friends in the North, to whom he would direct letters during his next visit to Marksville. It was not deemed prudent to meet in the new house, inasmuch as the light it would be necessary to use might possibly be discovered. In the course of the day I managed to obtain a few matches and a piece of candle, unperceived, from the kitchen, during a temporary absence of Aunt Phebe. Bass had pencil and paper in his tool chest.

At the appointed hour we met on the bayou bank, and creeping among the high weeds, I lighted the candle, while he drew forth pencil and paper and prepared for business. I gave him the names of William Perry, Cephas Parker and Judge Marvin, all of Saratoga Springs, Saratoga county, New-York. I had been employed by the latter in the United States Hotel, and had transacted business with the former to a considerable extent, and trusted that at least one of them would be still living at that place. He carefully wrote the names, and then remarked, thoughtfully—

"It is so many years since you left Saratoga, all these men may be dead, or may have removed. You say you obtained papers at the custom house in New-York. Probably there is a record of them there, and I think it would be well to write and ascertain."

I agreed with him, and again repeated the circumstances related heretofore, connected with my visit to the custom house with Brown and Hamilton. We lingered on the bank of the bayou an hour or more, conversing upon the subject which now engrossed our thoughts. I could no longer doubt his fidelity, and

417

freely spoke to him of the many sorrows I had borne in silence, and so long. I spoke of my wife and children, mentioning their names and ages, and dwelling upon the unspeakable happiness it would be to clasp them to my heart once more before I died. I caught him by the hand, and with tears and passionate entreaties implored him to befriend me—to restore me to my kindred and to liberty—promising I would weary Heaven the remainder of my life with prayers that it would bless and prosper him. In the enjoyment of freedom—surrounded by the associations of youth, and restored to the bosom of my family—that promise is not yet forgotten, nor shall it ever be so long as I have strength to raise my imploring eyes on high.

"Oh, blessings on his kindly voice and on his silver hair,
And blessings on his whole life long, until he meet me there."

He overwhelmed me with assurances of friendship and faithfulness, saying he had never before taken so deep an interest in the fate of any one. He spoke of himself in a somewhat mournful tone, as a lonely man, a wanderer about the world— that he was growing old, and must soon reach the end of his earthly journey, and lie down to his final rest without kith or kin to mourn for him, or to remember him—that his life was of little value to himself, and henceforth should be devoted to the accomplishment of my liberty, and to an unceasing warfare against the accursed shame of Slavery.

After this time we seldom spoke to, or recognized each other. He was, moreover, less free in his conversation with Epps on the subject of Slavery. The remotest suspicion that there was any unusual intimacy—any secret understanding between us— never once entered the mind of Epps, or any other person, white or black, on the plantation.

I am often asked, with an air of incredulity, how I succeeded so many years in keeping from my daily and constant companions the knowledge of my true name and history. The terrible lesson Burch taught me, impressed indelibly upon my mind the danger and uselessness of asserting I was a freeman. There was no possibility of any slave being able to assist me, while, on the other hand, there *was* a possibility of his exposing me. When it is recollected the whole current of my thoughts, for twelve years, turned to the contemplation of escape, it will not be wondered at, that I was always cautious and on my guard. It would have been an act of folly to have proclaimed my *right* to freedom; it would only have subjected me to severer scrutiny—probably have consigned me to some more distant and inaccessible region than even Bayou Bœuf. Edwin Epps was a person utterly regardless of a black man's rights or wrongs—utterly destitute of any natural sense of justice, as I well knew. It was important, therefore, not only as regarded my hope of deliverance, but also as regarded the few personal privileges I was permitted to enjoy, to keep from him the history of my life.

The Saturday night subsequent to our interview at the water's edge, Bass went home to Marksville. The next day, being Sunday, he employed himself in his own room writing letters. One he directed to the Collector of Customs at New-York, another to Judge Marvin, and another to Messrs. Parker and Perry jointly. The latter was the one which led to my recovery. He subscribed my true name, but in the postscript intimated I was not the writer. The letter itself shows that he considered himself engaged in a dangerous undertaking—no less than running "the risk of his life, if detected." I did not see the letter before it was mailed, but have since obtained a copy, which is here inserted:

"Bayou Bœuf,
August 15, 1852

"Mr. William Perry or Mr. Cephas Parker:

"Gentlemen—It having been a long time since I have seen or heard from you, and not knowing that you are living, it is with uncertainty that I write to you, but the necessity of the case must be my excuse.

419

"Having been born free, just across the river from you, I am certain you must know me, and I am here now a slave. I wish you to obtain free papers for me, and forward them to me at Marksville, Louisiana, Parish of Avoyelles, and oblige

"Yours,

SOLOMON NORTHUP

"The way I came to be a slave, I was taken sick in Washington City, and was insensible for some time. When I recovered my reason, I was robbed of my free-papers, and in irons on my way to this State, and have never been able to get any one to write for me until now; and he that is writing for me runs the risk of his life if detected."

The allusion to myself in the work recently issued, entitled "A Key to Uncle Tom's Cabin," contains the first part of this letter, omitting the postscript. Neither are the full names of the gentlemen to whom it is directed correctly stated, there being a slight discrepancy, probably a typographical error. To the postscript more than to the body of the communication am I indebted for my liberation, as will presently be seen.

When Bass returned from Marksville he informed me of what he had done. We continued our midnight consultations, never speaking to each other through the day, excepting as it was necessary about the work. As nearly as he was able to ascertain, it would require two weeks for the letter to reach Saratoga in due course of mail, and the same length of time for an answer to return. Within six weeks, at the farthest, we concluded, an answer would arrive, if it arrived at all. A great many suggestions were now made, and a great deal of conversation took place between us, as to the most safe and proper course to pursue on receipt of the free papers. They would stand between him and harm, in case we were overtaken and arrested leaving the country altogether. It would be no infringement of law, however much it might provoke individual hostility, to assist a freeman to regain his freedom.

At the end of four weeks he was again at Marksville, but no answer had arrived. I was sorely disappointed, but still reconciled myself with the reflection that sufficient length of time had not yet elapsed—that there might have been delays—and that I could not reasonably expect one so soon. Six, seven, eight, and ten weeks passed by, however, and nothing came. I was in a fever of suspense whenever Bass visited Marksville, and could scarcely close my eyes until his return. Finally my master's house was finished, and the time came when Bass must leave me. The night before his departure I was wholly given up to despair. I had clung to him as a drowning man clings to the floating spar, knowing if it slips from his grasp he must forever sink beneath the waves. The all-glorious hope, upon which I had laid such eager hold, was crumbling to ashes in my hands. I felt as if sinking down, down, amidst the bitter waters of Slavery, from the unfathomable depths of which I should never rise again.

The generous heart of my friend and benefactor was touched with pity at the sight of my distress. He endeavored to cheer me up, promising to return the day before Christmas, and if no intelligence was received in the meantime, some further step would be undertaken to effect our design. He exhorted me to keep up my spirits—to rely upon his continued efforts in my behalf, assuring me, in most earnest and impressive language, that my liberation should, from thenceforth, be the chief object of his thoughts.

In his absence the time passed slowly indeed. I looked forward to Christmas with intense anxiety and impatience. I had about given up the expectation of receiving any answer to the letters. They might have miscarried, or might have been misdirected. Perhaps those at Saratoga, to whom they had been addressed, were all dead; perhaps, engaged in their pursuits, they did not consider the fate of an obscure, unhappy black man of sufficient importance to be noticed. My whole reliance was in Bass. The faith I had in him was continually re-assuring me, and enabled me to stand up against the tide of disappointment that had overwhelmed me.

So wholly was I absorbed in reflecting upon my situation and prospects, that the hands with whom I labored in the field often observed it. Patsey would ask me if I was sick, and Uncle Abram, and Bob, and Wiley frequently expressed a curiosity to know what I could be thinking about so steadily. But I evaded their inquiries with some light remark, and kept my thoughts locked closely in my breast.

CHAPTER XX

Faithful to his word, the day before Christmas, just at night-fall, Bass came riding into the yard.

"How are you," said Epps, shaking him by the hand, "glad to see you."

He would not have been *very* glad had he known the object of his errand.

"Quite well, quite well," answered Bass. "Had some business out on the bayou, and concluded to call and see you, and stay over night."

Epps ordered one of the slaves to take charge of his horse, and with much talk and laughter they passed into the house together; not, however, until Bass had looked at me significantly, as much as to say, "Keep dark, we understand each other." It was ten o'clock at night before the labors of the day were performed, when I entered the cabin. At that time Uncle Abram and Bob occupied it with me. I laid down upon my board and feigned I was asleep. When my companions had fallen into a profound slumber, I moved stealthily out of the door, and watched, and listened attentively for some sign or sound from Bass. There I stood until long after midnight, but nothing could be seen or heard. As I suspected, he dared not leave the house, through fear of exciting the suspicion of some of the family. I judged, correctly, he would rise earlier than was his custom, and take the opportunity of seeing me before Epps was up. Accordingly I aroused Uncle Abram an hour sooner than usual, and sent him into the house to build a fire, which, at that season of the year, is a part of Uncle Abram's duties.

I also gave Bob a violent shake, and asked him if he intended to sleep till noon, saying master would be up before the mules were fed. He knew right well the consequence that would follow such an event, and, jumping to his feet, was at the horse-pasture in a twinkling.

Presently, when both were gone, Bass slipped into the cabin.

"No letter yet, Platt," said he. The announcement fell upon my heart like lead.

"Oh, *do* write again, Master Bass," I cried; "I will give you the names of a great many I know. Surely they are not all dead. Surely some one will pity me."

"No use," Bass replied, "no use. I have made up my mind to that. I fear the Marksville post-master will mistrust something, I have inquired so often at his office. Too uncertain—too dangerous."

"Then it is all over," I exclaimed. "Oh, my God, how can I end my days here!"

"You're not going to end them here," he said, "unless you die very soon. I've thought this matter all over, and have come to a determination. There are more ways than one to manage this business, and a better and surer way than writing letters. I have a job or two on hand which can be completed by March or April. By that time I shall have a considerable sum of money, and then, Platt, I am going to Saratoga myself."

I could scarcely credit my own senses as the words fell from his lips. But he assured me, in a manner that left no doubt of the sincerity of his intention, that if his life was spared until spring, he should certainly undertake the journey.

"I have lived in this region long enough," he continued; "I may as well be in one place as another. For a long time I have been thinking of going back once more to the place where I was born. I'm tired of Slavery as well as you. If I can succeed in getting you away from here, it will be a good act that I shall like to think of all my life. And I *shall* succeed, Platt; I'm *bound* to do it. Now let me tell you what I want. Epps will be up soon, and it won't do to be caught here. Think of a great many men at Saratoga and Sandy Hill, and in that neighborhood, who once knew you. I shall make excuse to come here again in the course of the winter, when I will write down their names. I will then know who to call on when I go north. Think of all you can. Cheer up! Don't be discouraged. I'm with you, life or death. Good-bye. God bless you," and saying this he left the cabin quickly, and entered the great house.

It was Christmas morning—the happiest day in the whole year for the slave. That morning he need not hurry to the field, with his gourd and cotton-bag. Happiness sparkled in the eyes and overspread the countenances of all. The time of feasting and dancing had come. The cane and cotton fields were deserted. That day the clean dress was to be donned—the red ribbon displayed; there were to be re-unions, and joy and laughter, and hurrying to and fro. It was to be a day of *liberty* among the children of Slavery. Wherefore they were happy, and rejoiced.

After breakfast Epps and Bass sauntered about the yard, conversing upon the price of cotton, and various other topics.

"Where do your niggers hold Christmas?" Bass inquired.

"Platt is going to Tanners to-day. His fiddle is in great demand. They want him at Marshall's Monday, and Miss Mary McCoy, on the old Norwood plantation, writes me a note that she wants him to play for her niggers Tuesday."

"He is rather a smart boy, ain't he?" said Bass. "Come here, Platt," he added, looking at me as I walked up to them, as if he had never thought before to take any special notice of me.

"Yes," replied Epps, taking hold of my arm and feeling it, "there isn't a bad joint in him. There ain't a boy on the bayou worth more than he is—perfectly sound, and no bad tricks. D—n him, he isn't like other niggers; doesn't look like 'em— don't act like 'em. I was offered seventeen hundred dollars for him last week."

"And didn't take it?" Bass inquired, with an air of surprise.

"Take it—no; devilish clear of it. Why, he's a reg'lar genius; can make a plough beam, wagon tongue—anything, as well as you can. Marshall wanted to put up one of his niggers agin him and raffle for them, but I told him I would see the devil have him first."

"I don't see anything remarkable about him," Bass observed.

"Why, just feel of him, now," Epps rejoined. "You don't see a boy very often put together any closer than he is. He's a thin-skin'd cuss, and won't bear as much whipping as some; but he's got the muscle in him, and no mistake."

Bass felt of me, turned me round, and made a thorough examination, Epps all the while dwelling on my good points. But his visitor seemed to take but little interest finally in the subject, and consequently it was dropped. Bass soon departed, giving me another sly look of recognition and significance, as he trotted out of the yard.

When he was gone I obtained a pass, and started for Tanner's—not Peter Tanner's, of whom mention has previously been made, but a relative of his. I played during the day and most of the night, spending the next day, Sunday, in my cabin. Monday I crossed the bayou to Douglas Marshall's, all Epps' slaves accompanying me, and on Tuesday went to the old Norwood place, which is the third plantation above Marshall's, on the same side of the water.

This estate is now owned by Miss Mary McCoy, a lovely girl, some twenty years of age. She is the beauty and the glory of Bayou Bœuf. She owns about a hundred working hands, besides a great many house servants, yard boys, and young children. Her brother-in-law, who resides on the adjoining estate, is her general agent. She is beloved by all her slaves, and good reason indeed have they to be thankful that they have fallen into such gentle hands. Nowhere on the bayou are there such feasts, such merrymaking, as at young Madam McCoy's. Thither, more than to any other place, do the old and the young for miles around love to repair in the time of the Christmas holidays; for nowhere else can they find such delicious repasts; nowhere else can they hear a voice speaking to them so pleasantly. No one is so well beloved—no one fills so large a space in the hearts of a thousand slaves, as young Madam McCoy, the orphan mistress of the old Norwood estate.

On my arrival at her place, I found two or three hundred had assembled. The table was prepared in a long building, which she had erected expressly for her slaves to dance in. It was covered with every variety of food the country afforded, and was pronounced by general acclamation to be the rarest of dinners. Roast turkey, pig, chicken, duck, and all kinds of meat, baked, boiled, and broiled, formed a line the whole length of the extended table, while the vacant spaces were filled with tarts, jellies, and frosted cake, and pastry of many kinds. The young mistress walked around the table, smiling and saying a kind word to each one, and seemed to enjoy the scene exceedingly.

When the dinner was over the tables were removed to make room for the dancers. I tuned my violin and struck up a lively air; while some joined in a nimble reel, others patted and sang their simple but melodious songs, filling the great room with music mingled with the sound of human voices and the clatter of many feet.

In the evening the mistress returned, and stood in the door a long time, looking at us. She was magnificently arrayed. Her dark hair and eyes contrasted strongly with her clear and delicate complexion. Her form was slender but commanding, and her movement was a combination of unaffected dignity and grace. As she stood there, clad in her rich apparel, her face animated with pleasure, I thought I had never looked upon a human being half so beautiful. I dwell with delight upon the description of this fair and gentle lady, not only because she inspired me with emotions of gratitude and admiration, but because I would have the reader understand that all slave-owners on Bayou Bœuf are not like Epps, or Tibeats, or Jim Burns. Occasionally can be found, rarely it may be, indeed, a good man like William Ford, or an angel of kindness like young Mistress McCoy.

Tuesday concluded the three holidays Epps yearly allowed us. On my way home, Wednesday morning, while passing the

427

plantation of William Pierce, that gentleman hailed me, saying he had received a line from Epps, brought down by William Varnell, permitting him to detain me for the purpose of playing for his slaves that night. It was the last time I was destined to witness a slave dance on the shores of Bayou Bœuf. The party at Pierce's continued their jollification until broad daylight, when I returned to my master's house, somewhat wearied with the loss of rest, but rejoicing in the possession of numerous bits and picayunes, which the whites, who were pleased with my musical performances, had contributed.

On Saturday morning, for the first time in years, I overslept myself. I was frightened on coming out of the cabin to find the slaves were already in the field. They had preceded me some fifteen minutes. Leaving my dinner and water-gourd, I hurried after them as fast as I could move. It was not yet sunrise, but Epps was on the piazza as I left the hut, and cried out to me that it was a pretty time of day to be getting up. By extra exertion my row was up when he came out after breakfast. This, however, was no excuse for the offence of oversleeping. Bidding me strip and lie down, he gave me ten or fifteen lashes, at the conclusion of which he inquired if I thought, after that, I could get up sometime in the *morning.* I expressed myself quite positively that I *could,* and, with back stinging with pain, went about my work.

The following day, Sunday, my thoughts were upon Bass, and the probabilities and hopes which hung upon his action and determination. I considered the uncertainty of life; that if it should be the will of God that he should die, my prospect of deliverance, and all expectation of happiness in this world, would be wholly ended and destroyed. My sore back, perhaps, did not have a tendency to render me unusually cheerful. I felt down-hearted and unhappy all day long, and when I laid down upon the hard board at night, my heart was oppressed with such a load of grief, it seemed that it must break.

Monday morning, the third of January, 1853, we were in the field betimes. It was a raw, cold morning, such as is unusual in that region. I was in advance, Uncle Abram next to me, behind him Bob, Patsey and Wiley, with our cotton-bags about our necks. Epps happened (a rare thing, indeed,) to come out that morning without his whip. He swore, in a manner that would shame a pirate, that we were doing nothing. Bob ventured to say that his fingers were so numb with cold he couldn't pick fast. Epps cursed himself for not having brought his rawhide, and declared that when he came out again he would warm us well; yes, he would make us all hotter than that fiery realm in which I am sometimes compelled to believe he will himself eventually reside.

With these fervent expressions, he left us. When out of hearing, we commenced talking to each other, saying how hard it was to be compelled to keep up our tasks with numb fingers; how unreasonable master was, and speaking of him generally in no flattering terms. Our conversation was interrupted by a carriage passing rapidly towards the house. Looking up, we saw two men approaching us through the cotton-field.

* * * * *

Having now brought down this narrative to the last hour I was to spend on Bayou Bœuf—having gotten through my last cotton picking, and about to bid Master Epps farewell—I must beg the reader to go back with me to the month of August; to follow Bass' letter on its long journey to Saratoga; to learn the effect it produced—and that, while I was repining and despairing in the slave hut of Edwin Epps, through the friendship of Bass and the goodness of Providence, all things were working together for my deliverance.

CHAPTER XXI

I am indebted to Mr. Henry B. Northup and others for many of the particulars contained in this chapter.

The letter written by Bass, directed to Parker and Perry, and which was deposited in the post-office in Marksville on the 15th day of August, 1852, arrived at Saratoga in the early part of September. Some time previous to this, Anne had removed to Glens Falls, Warren county, where she had charge of the kitchen in Carpenter's Hotel. She kept house, however, lodging with our children, and was only absent from them during such time as the discharge of her duties in the hotel required.

Messrs. Parker and Perry, on receipt of the letter, forwarded it immediately to Anne. On reading it the children were all excitement, and without delay hastened to the neighboring village of Sandy Hill, to consult Henry B. Northup, and obtain his advice and assistance in the matter.

Upon examination, that gentleman found among the statutes of the State an act providing for the recovery of free citizens from slavery. It was passed May 14, 1840, and is entitled "An act more effectually to protect the free citizens of this State from being kidnapped or reduced to slavery." It provides that it shall be the duty of the Governor, upon the receipt of satisfactory information that any free citizen or inhabitant of this State, is wrongfully held in another State or Territory of the United States, upon the allegation or pretence that such person is a slave, or by color of any usage or rule of law is deemed or taken to be a slave, to take such measures to procure the restoration of such person to liberty, as he shall deem necessary. And to that end, he is authorized to appoint and employ an agent, and directed to furnish him with such credentials and instructions as will be likely to accomplish the object of his appointment. It requires the agent so appointed to proceed to collect the proper proof to establish the right of such person to his freedom; to perform such journeys, take such measures, institute such legal proceedings, &c., as may be necessary to return such person to this State, and charges all expenses incurred in carrying the act into effect, upon moneys not otherwise appropriated in the treasury.

It was necessary to establish two facts to the satisfaction of the Governor: First, that I was a free citizen of New-York; and secondly, that I was wrongfully held in bondage. As to the first point, there was no difficulty, all the older inhabitants in the vicinity being ready to testify to it. The second point rested entirely upon the letter to Parker and Perry, written in an unknown hand, and upon the letter penned on board the brig Orleans, which, unfortunately, had been mislaid or lost.

A memorial was prepared, directed to his excellency, Governor Hunt, setting forth her marriage, my departure to Washington city; the receipt of the letters; that I was a free citizen, and such other facts as were deemed important, and was signed and verified by Anne. Accompanying this memorial were several affidavits of prominent citizens of Sandy Hill and Fort Edward, corroborating fully the statements it contained, and also a request of several well known gentlemen to the Governor, that Henry B. Northup be appointed agent under the legislative act.

On reading the memorial and affidavits, his excellency took a lively interest in the matter, and on the 23d day of November, 1852, under the seal of the State, "constituted, appointed and employed Henry B. Northup, Esq., an agent, with full power to effect" my restoration, and to take such measures as would be most likely to accomplish it, and instructing him to proceed to Louisiana with all convenient dispatch.

The pressing nature of Mr. Northup's professional and political engagements delayed his departure until December.

431

On the fourteenth day of that month he left Sandy Hill, and proceeded to Washington. The Hon. Pierre Soule, Senator in Congress from Louisiana, Hon. Mr. Conrad, Secretary of War, and Judge Nelson, of the Supreme Court of the United States, upon hearing a statement of the facts, and examining his commission, and certified copies of the memorial and affidavits, furnished him with open letters to gentlemen in Louisiana, strongly urging their assistance in accomplishing the object of his appointment.

Senator Soule especially interested himself in the matter, insisting, in forcible language, that it was the duty and interest of every planter in his State to aid in restoring me to freedom, and trusted the sentiments of honor and justice in the bosom of every citizen of the commonwealth would enlist him at once in my behalf. Having obtained these valuable letters, Mr. Northup returned to Baltimore, and proceeded from thence to Pittsburgh. It was his original intention, under advice of friends at Washington, to go directly to New Orleans, and consult the authorities of that city. Providentially, however, on arriving at the mouth of Red River, he changed his mind. Had he continued on, he would not have met with Bass, in which case the search for me would probably have been fruitless.

Taking passage on the first steamer that arrived, he pursued his journey up Red River, a sluggish, winding stream, flowing through a vast region of primitive forests and impenetrable swamps, almost wholly destitute of inhabitants. About nine o'clock in the forenoon, January 1st, 1853, he left the steamboat at Marksville, and proceeded directly to Marksville Court House, a small village four miles in the interior.

From the fact that the letter to Messrs. Parker and Perry was post-marked at Marksville, it was supposed by him that I was in that place or its immediate vicinity. On reaching this town, he at once laid his business before the Hon. John P. Waddill, a legal gentleman of distinction, and a man of fine genius and most noble impulses. After reading the letters and

432

documents presented him, and listening to a representation of the circumstances under which I had been carried away into captivity, Mr. Waddill at once proffered his services, and entered into the affair with great zeal and earnestness. He, in common with others of like elevated character, looked upon the kidnapper with abhorrence. The title of his fellow parishioners and clients to the property which constituted the larger proportion of their wealth, not only depended upon the good faith in which slave sales were transacted, but he was a man in whose honorable heart emotions of indignation were aroused by such an instance of injustice.

Marksville, although occupying a prominent position, and standing out in impressive italics on the map of Louisiana, is, in fact, but a small and insignificant hamlet. Aside from the tavern, kept by a jolly and generous boniface, the court house, inhabited by lawless cows and swine in the seasons of vacation, and a high gallows, with its dissevered rope dangling in the air, there is little to attract the attention of the stranger.

Solomon Northup was a name Mr. Waddill had never heard, but he was confident that if there was a slave bearing that appellation in Marksville or vicinity, his black boy Tom would know him. Tom was accordingly called, but in all his extensive circle of acquaintances there was no such personage.

The letter to Parker and Perry was dated at Bayou Bœuf. At this place, therefore, the conclusion was, I must be sought. But here a difficulty suggested itself, of a very grave character indeed. Bayou Bœuf, at its nearest point, was twenty-three miles distant, and was the name applied to the section of country extending between fifty and a hundred miles, on both sides of that stream. Thousands and thousands of slaves resided upon its shores, the remarkable richness and fertility of the soil having attracted thither a great number of planters. The information in the letter was so vague and indefinite as to render it difficult to conclude upon any specific course of proceeding. It was finally determined, however, as the only plan that presented any prospect of success, that Northup and the brother of Waddill, a student in the office of the latter, should repair to the Bayou, and traveling up one side and down the other its whole length, inquire at each plantation for me. Mr. Waddill tendered the use of his carriage, and it was definitely arranged that they should start upon the excursion early Monday morning.

It will be seen at once that this course, in all probability, would have resulted unsuccessfully. It would have been impossible for them to have gone into the fields and examine all the gangs at work. They were not aware that I was known only as Platt; and had they inquired of Epps himself, he would have stated truly that he knew nothing of Solomon Northup.

The arrangement being adopted, however, there was nothing further to be done until Sunday had elapsed. The conversation between Messrs. Northup and Waddill, in the course of the afternoon, turned upon New-York politics.

"I can scarcely comprehend the nice distinctions and shades of political parties in your State," observed Mr. Waddill. "I read of soft-shells and hard-shells, hunkers and barnburners, woolly-heads and silver-grays, and am unable to understand the precise difference between them. Pray, what is it?"

Mr. Northup, re-filling his pipe, entered into quite an elaborate narrative of the origin of the various sections of parties, and concluded by saying there was another party in New-York, known as free-soilers or abolitionists. "You have seen none of those in this part of the country, I presume?" Mr. Northup remarked.

"Never, but one," answered Waddill, laughingly. "We have one here in Marksville, an eccentric creature, who preaches abolitionism as vehemently as any fanatic at the North. He is a generous, inoffensive man, but always maintaining the wrong side of an argument. It affords us a deal of amusement. He is an excellent mechanic, and almost indispensable in this community. He is a carpenter. His name is Bass."

Some further good-natured conversation was had at the

expense of Bass' peculiarities, when Waddill all at once fell into a reflective mood, and asked for the mysterious letter again.

"Let me see—l-e-t m-e s-e-e!" he repeated, thoughtfully to himself, running his eyes over the letter once more. "'Bayou Bœuf, August 15.' August 15—post-marked here. 'He that is writing for me—' Where did Bass work last summer?" he inquired, turning suddenly to his brother. His brother was unable to inform him, but rising, left the office, and soon returned with the intelligence that "Bass worked last summer somewhere on Bayou Bœuf."

"He is the man," bringing down his hand emphatically on the table, "who can tell us all about Solomon Northup," exclaimed Waddill.

Bass was immediately searched for, but could not be found. After some inquiry, it was ascertained he was at the landing on Red River. Procuring a conveyance, young Waddill and Northup were not long in traversing the few miles to the latter place. On their arrival, Bass was found, just on the point of leaving, to be absent a fortnight or more. After an introduction, Northup begged the privilege of speaking to him privately a moment. They walked together towards the river, when the following conversation ensued:

"Mr. Bass," said Northup, "allow me to ask you if you were on Bayou Bœuf last August?"

"Yes, sir, I was there in August," was the reply.

"Did you write a letter for a colored man at that place to some gentleman in Saratoga Springs?"

"Excuse me, sir, if I say that is none of your business," answered Bass, stopping and looking his interrogator searchingly in the face.

"Perhaps I am rather hasty, Mr. Bass; I beg your pardon; but I have come from the State of New-York to accomplish the purpose the writer of a letter dated the 15th of August, post-marked at Marksville, had in view. Circumstances have led me to think that you are perhaps the man who wrote it. I am

435

in search of Solomon Northup. If you know him, I beg you to inform me frankly where he is, and I assure you the source of any information you may give me shall not be divulged, if you desire it not to be."

A long time Bass looked his new acquaintance steadily in the eyes, without opening his lips. He seemed to be doubting in his own mind if there was not an attempt to practice some deception upon him. Finally he said, deliberately—

"I have done nothing to be ashamed of. I am the man who wrote the letter. If you have come to rescue Solomon Northup, I am glad to see you."

"When did you last see him, and where is he?" Northup inquired.

"I last saw him Christmas, a week ago to-day. He is the slave of Edwin Epps, a planter on Bayou Bœuf, near Holmesville. He is not known as Solomon Northup; he is called Platt."

The secret was out—the mystery was unraveled. Through the thick, black cloud, amid whose dark and dismal shadows I had walked twelve years, broke the star that was to light me back to liberty. All mistrust and hesitation were soon thrown aside, and the two men conversed long and freely upon the subject uppermost in their thoughts. Bass expressed the interest he had taken in my behalf—his intention of going north in the Spring, and declaring that he had resolved to accomplish my emancipation, if it were in his power. He described the commencement and progress of his acquaintance with me, and listened with eager curiosity to the account given him of my family, and the history of my early life. Before separating, he drew a map of the bayou on a strip of paper with a piece of red chalk, showing the locality of Epps' plantation, and the road leading most directly to it.

Northup and his young companion returned to Marksville, where it was determined to commence legal proceedings to test the question of my right to freedom. I was made plaintiff, Mr. Northup acting as my guardian, and Edwin Epps defendant.

The process to be issued was in the nature of replevin, directed to the sheriff of the parish, commanding him to take me into custody, and detain me until the decision of the court. By the time the papers were duly drawn up, it was twelve o'clock at night—too late to obtain the necessary signature of the Judge, who resided some distance out of town. Further business was therefore suspended until Monday morning.

Everything, apparently, was moving along swimmingly, until Sunday afternoon, when Waddill called at Northup's room to express his apprehension of difficulties they had not expected to encounter. Bass had become alarmed, and had placed his affairs in the hands of a person at the landing, communicating to him his intention of leaving the State. This person had betrayed the confidence reposed in him to a certain extent, and a rumor began to float about the town, that the stranger at the hotel, who had been observed in the company of lawyer Waddill, was after one of old Epps' slaves, over on the bayou. Epps was known at Marksville, having frequent occasion to visit that place during the session of the courts, and the fear entertained by Mr. Northup's adviser was, that intelligence would be conveyed to him in the night, giving him an opportunity of secreting me before the arrival of the sheriff.

This apprehension had the effect of expediting matters considerably. The sheriff, who lived in one direction from the village, was requested to hold himself in readiness immediately after midnight, while the Judge was informed he would be called upon at the same time. It is but justice to say, that the authorities at Marksville cheerfully rendered all the assistance in their power.

As soon after midnight as bail could be perfected, and the Judge's signature obtained, a carriage, containing Mr. Northup and the sheriff, driven by the landlord's son, rolled rapidly out of the village of Marksville, on the road towards Bayou Bœuf.

It was supposed that Epps would contest the issue involving my right to liberty, and it therefore suggested itself to Mr.

437

Northup, that the testimony of the sheriff, describing my first meeting with the former, might perhaps become material on the trial. It was accordingly arranged during the ride, that, before I had an opportunity of speaking to Mr. Northup, the sheriff should propound to me certain questions agreed upon, such as the number and names of my children, the name of my wife before marriage, of places I knew at the North, and so forth. If my answers corresponded with the statements given him, the evidence must necessarily be considered conclusive.

At length, shortly after Epps had left the field, with the consoling assurance that he would soon return and *warm* us, as was stated in the conclusion of the preceding chapter, they came in sight of the plantation, and discovered us at work. Alighting from the carriage, and directing the driver to proceed to the great house, with instructions not to mention to any one the object of their errand until they met again, Northup and the sheriff turned from the highway, and came towards us across the cotton field. We observed them, on looking up at the carriage—one several rods in advance of the other. It was a singular and unusual thing to see white men approaching us in that manner, and especially at that early hour in the morning, and Uncle Abram and Patsey made some remarks, expressive of their astonishment. Walking up to Bob, the sheriff inquired:

"Where's the boy they call Platt?"

"Thar he is, massa," answered Bob, pointing to me, and twitching off his hat.

I wondered to myself what business he could possibly have with me, and turning round, gazed at him until he had approached within a step. During my long residence on the bayou, I had become familiar with the face of every planter within many miles; but this man was an utter stranger—certainly I had never seen him before.

"Your name is Platt, is it?" he asked.

"Yes, master," I responded.

Pointing towards Northup, standing a few rods distant, he

demanded—"Do you know that man?"

I looked in the direction indicated, and as my eyes rested on his countenance, a world of images thronged my brain; a multitude of well-known faces—Anne's, and the dear children's, and my old dead father's; all the scenes and associations of childhood and youth; all the friends of other and happier days, appeared and disappeared, flitting and floating like dissolving shadows before the vision of my imagination, until at last the perfect memory of the man recurred to me, and throwing up my hands towards Heaven, I exclaimed, in a voice louder than I could utter in a less exciting moment—

"*Henry B. Northup!* Thank God—thank God!"

In an instant I comprehended the nature of his business, and felt that the hour of my deliverance was at hand. I started towards him, but the sheriff stepped before me.

"Stop a moment," said he; "have you any other name than Platt?"

"Solomon Northup is my name, master," I replied.

"Have you a family?" he inquired.

"I *had* a wife and three children."

"What were your children's names?"

"Elizabeth, Margaret and Alonzo."

"And your wife's name before her marriage?"

"Anne Hampton."

"Who married you?"

"Timothy Eddy, of Fort Edward."

"Where does that gentleman live?" again pointing to Northup, who remained standing in the same place where I had first recognized him.

"He lives in Sandy Hill, Washington county, New-York," was the reply.

He was proceeding to ask further questions, but I pushed past him, unable longer to restrain myself. I seized my old acquaintance by both hands. I could not speak. I could not refrain from tears.

439

"Sol," he said at length, "I'm glad to see you."

I essayed to make some answer, but emotion choked all utterance, and I was silent. The slaves, utterly confounded, stood gazing upon the scene, their open mouths and rolling eyes indicating the utmost wonder and astonishment. For ten years I had dwelt among them, in the field and in the cabin, borne the same hardships, partaken the same fare, mingled my griefs with theirs, participated in the same scanty joys; nevertheless, not until this hour, the last I was to remain among them, had the remotest suspicion of my true name, or the slightest knowledge of my real history, been entertained by any one of them.

Not a word was spoken for several minutes, during which time I clung fast to Northup, looking up into his face, fearful I should awake and find it all a dream.

"Throw down that sack," Northup added, finally; "your cotton-picking days are over. Come with us to the man you live with."

I obeyed him, and walking between him and the sheriff, we moved towards the great house. It was not until we had proceeded some distance that I had recovered my voice sufficiently to ask if my family were all living. He informed me he had seen Anne, Margaret and Elizabeth but a short time previously; that Alonzo was also living, and all were well. My mother, however, I could never see again. As I began to recover in some measure from the sudden and great excitement which so overwhelmed me, I grew faint and weak, insomuch it was with difficulty I could walk. The sheriff took hold of my arm and assisted me, or I think I should have fallen. As we entered the yard, Epps stood by the gate, conversing with the driver. That young man, faithful to his instructions, was entirely unable to give him the least information in answer to his repeated inquiries of what was going on. By the time we reached him he was almost as much amazed and puzzled as Bob or Uncle Abram.

Shaking hands with the sheriff, and receiving an introduction to Mr. Northup, he invited them into the house, ordering me, at the same time, to bring in some wood. It was some time before I succeeded in cutting an armful, having, somehow, unaccountably lost the power of wielding the axe with any manner of precision. When I entered with it at last, the table was strewn with papers, from one of which Northup was reading. I was probably longer than necessity required, in placing the sticks upon the fire, being particular as to the exact position of each individual one of them. I heard the words, "the said Solomon Northup," and "the deponent further says," and "free citizen of New-York," repeated frequently, and from these expressions understood that the secret I had so long retained from Master and Mistress Epps, was finally developing. I lingered as long as prudence permitted, and was about leaving the room, when Epps inquired, "Platt, do you know this gentleman?"

"Yes, master," I replied, "I have known him as long as I can remember."

"Where does he live?"

"He lives in New-York."

"Did you ever live there?"

"Yes, master—born and bred there."

"You was free, then. Now you d——d nigger," he exclaimed, "why did you not tell me that when I bought you?"

"Master Epps," I answered, in a somewhat different tone than the one in which I had been accustomed to address him— "Master Epps, you did not take the trouble to ask me; besides, I told one of my owners—the man that kidnapped me—that I was free, and was whipped almost to death for it."

"It seems there has been a letter written for you by somebody. Now, who is it?" he demanded, authoritatively. I made no reply.

"I say, who wrote that letter?" he demanded again.

"Perhaps I wrote it myself," I said.

"You haven't been to Marksville post-office and back before light, I know."

He insisted upon my informing him, and I insisted I would not.

He made many vehement threats against the man, whoever

441

he might be, and intimated the bloody and savage vengeance he would wreak upon him, when he found him out. His whole manner and language exhibited a feeling of anger towards the unknown person who had written for me, and of fretfulness at the idea of losing so much property. Addressing Mr. Northup, he swore if he had only had an hour's notice of his coming, he would have saved him the trouble of taking me back to New-York; that he would have run me into the swamp, or some other place out of the way, where all the sheriffs on earth couldn't have found me.

I walked out into the yard, and was entering the kitchen door, when something struck me in the back. Aunt Phebe, emerging from the back door of the great house with a pan of potatoes, had thrown one of them with unnecessary violence, thereby giving me to understand that she wished to speak to me a moment confidentially. Running up to me, she whispered in my ear with great earnestness,

"Lor a' mity, Platt! what d'ye think? Dem two men come after ye. Heard 'em tell massa you free—got wife and tree children back thar whar you come from. Goin' wid 'em? Fool if ye don't—wish I could go," and Aunt Phebe ran on in this manner at a rapid rate.

Presently Mistress Epps made her appearance in the kitchen. She said many things to me, and wondered why I had not told her who I was. She expressed her regret, complimenting me by saying she had rather lose any other servant on the plantation. Had Patsey that day stood in my place, the measure of my mistress' joy would have overflowed. Now there was no one left who could mend a chair or a piece of furniture—no one who was of any use about the house—no one who could play for her on the violin—and Mistress Epps was actually affected to tears.

Epps had called to Bob to bring up his saddle horse. The other slaves, also, overcoming their fear of the penalty, had left their work and come to the yard. They were standing behind the cabins, out of sight of Epps. They beckoned me to come to them, and with all the eagerness of curiosity, excited to the highest pitch, conversed with and questioned me. If I could repeat the exact words they uttered, with the same emphasis—if I could paint their several attitudes, and the expression of their countenances—it would be indeed an interesting picture. In their estimation, I had suddenly arisen to an immeasurable height—had become a being of immense importance.

The legal papers having been served, and arrangements made with Epps to meet them the next day at Marksville, Northup and the sheriff entered the carriage to return to the latter place. As I was about mounting to the driver's seat, the sheriff said I ought to bid Mr. and Mrs. Epps good bye. I ran back to the piazza where they were standing, and taking off my hat, said,

"Good-bye, missis."

"Good-bye, Platt," said Mrs. Epps, kindly.

"Good-bye, master."

"Ah! you d—d nigger," muttered Epps, in a surly, malicious tone of voice, "you needn't feel so cussed tickled—you ain't gone yet—I'll see about this business at Marksville to-morrow."

I was only a "*nigger*" and knew my place, but felt as strongly as if I had been a white man, that it would have been an inward comfort, had I dared to have given him a parting kick. On my way back to the carriage, Patsey ran from behind a cabin and threw her arms about my neck.

"Oh! Platt," she cried, tears streaming down her face, "you're goin' to be free—you're goin' way off yonder where we'll neber see ye any more. You've saved me a good many whippins, Platt; I'm glad you're goin' to be free—but oh! de Lord, de Lord! what'll become of me?"

I disengaged myself from her, and entered the carriage. The driver cracked his whip and away we rolled. I looked back and saw Patsey, with drooping head, half reclining on the ground; Mrs. Epps was on the piazza; Uncle Abram, and Bob, and Wiley, and Aunt Phebe stood by the gate, gazing after me. I waved my hand, but the carriage turned a bend of the bayou, hiding them

443

from my eyes forever.

We stopped a moment at Carey's sugar house, where a great number of slaves were at work, such an establishment being a curiosity to a Northern man. Epps dashed by us on horseback at full speed—on the way, as we learned next day, to the "Pine Woods," to see William Ford, who had brought me into the country.

Tuesday, the fourth of January, Epps and his counsel, the Hon. H. Taylor, Northup, Waddill, the Judge and sheriff of Avoyelles, and myself, met in a room in the village of Marksville. Mr. Northup stated the facts in regard to me, and presented his commission, and the affidavits accompanying it. The sheriff described the scene in the cotton field. I was also interrogated at great length. Finally, Mr. Taylor assured his client that he was satisfied, and that litigation would not only be expensive, but utterly useless. In accordance with his advice, a paper was drawn up and signed by the proper parties, wherein Epps acknowledged he was satisfied of my right to freedom, and formally surrendered me to the authorities of New-York. It was also stipulated that it be entered of record in the recorder's office of Avoyelles.

Mr. Northup and myself immediately hastened to the landing, and taking passage on the first steamer that arrived, were soon floating down Red River, up which, with such desponding thoughts, I had been borne twelve years before.

CHAPTER XXII

As the steamer glided on its way towards New-Orleans, *perhaps* I was not happy—*perhaps* there was no difficulty in restraining myself from dancing round the deck—perhaps I did not feel grateful to the man who had come so many hundred miles for me—perhaps I did not light his pipe, and wait and watch his word, and run at his slightest bidding. If I didn't— well, no matter.

We tarried at New-Orleans two days. During that time I pointed out the locality of Freeman's slave pen, and the room in which Ford purchased me. We happened to meet Theophilus in the street, but I did not think it worth while to renew acquaintance with him. From respectable citizens we ascertained he had become a low, miserable rowdy—a broken-down, disreputable man.

We also visited the recorder, Mr. Genois, to whom Senator Soule's letter was directed, and found him a man well deserving the wide and honorable reputation that he bears. He very generously furnished us with a sort of legal pass, over his signature and seal of office, and as it contains the recorder's description of my personal appearance, it may not be amiss to insert it here. The following is a copy:

> "STATE OF LOUISIANA—CITY OF NEW-ORLEANS:
> *Recorder's Office, Second District*

> "TO ALL TO WHOM THESE PRESENTS SHALL COME:—

> "This is to certify that Henry B. Northup, Esquire, of the county of Washington, New-York, has produced before me due

445

evidence of the freedom of Solomon, a mulatto man, aged about forty-two years, five feet, seven inches and six lines, woolly hair, and chestnut eyes, who is a native born of the State of New-York. That the said Northup, being about bringing the said Solomon to his native place, through the southern routes, the civil authorities are requested to let the aforesaid colored man Solomon pass unmolested, he demeaning well and properly.

"Given under my hand and the seal of the city of New-Orleans this 7th January, 1853.

"TH. GENOIS, *Recorder.*"

On the 8th we came to Lake Pontchartrain, by railroad, and, in due time, following the usual route, reached Charleston. After going on board the steamboat, and paying our passage at this city, Mr. Northup was called upon by a custom-house officer to explain why he had not registered his servant. He replied that he had no servant—that, as the agent of New-York, he was accompanying a free citizen of that State from slavery to freedom, and did not desire nor intend to make any registry whatever. I conceived from his conversation and manner, though I may perhaps be entirely mistaken, that no great pains would be taken to avoid whatever difficulty the Charleston officials might deem proper to create. At length, however, we were permitted to proceed, and, passing through Richmond, where I caught a glimpse of Goodin's pen, arrived in Washington January 17th, 1853.

We ascertained that both Burch and Radburn were still residing in that city. Immediately a complaint was entered with a police magistrate of Washington, against James H. Burch, for kidnapping and selling me into slavery. He was arrested upon a warrant issued by Justice Goddard, and returned before Justice Mansel, and held to bail in the sum of three thousand dollars. When first arrested, Burch was much excited, exhibiting the utmost fear and alarm, and before reaching the justice's office on

446

Louisiana Avenue, and before knowing the precise nature of the complaint, begged the police to permit him to consult Benjamin O. Shekels, a slave trader of seventeen years' standing, and his former partner. The latter became his bail.

At ten o'clock, the 18th of January, both parties appeared before the magistrate. Senator Chase, of Ohio, Hon. Orville Clark, of Sandy Hill, and Mr. Northup acted as counsel for the prosecution, and Joseph H. Bradley for the defence.

Gen. Orville Clark was called and sworn as a witness, and testified that he had known me from childhood, and that I was a free man, as was my father before me. Mr. Northup then testified to the same, and proved the facts connected with his mission to Avoyelles.

Ebenezer Radburn was then sworn for the prosecution, and testified he was forty-eight years old; that he was a resident of Washington, and had known Burch fourteen years; that in 1841 he was keeper of Williams' slave pen; that he remembered the fact of my confinement in the pen that year. At this point it was admitted by the defendant's counsel, that I had been placed in the pen by Burch in the spring of 1841, and hereupon the prosecution rested.

Benjamin O. Shekels was then offered as a witness by the prisoner. Benjamin is a large, coarse-featured man, and the reader may perhaps get a somewhat correct conception of him by reading the exact language he used in answer to the first question of defendant's lawyer. He was asked the place of his nativity, and his reply, uttered in a sort of rowdyish way, was in these very words—

"I was born in Ontario county, New-York, and *weighed fourteen pounds!*"

Benjamin was a prodigious baby! He further testified that he kept the Steamboat Hotel in Washington in 1841, and saw me there in the spring of that year. He was proceeding to state what he had heard two men say, when Senator Chase raised a legal objection, to wit, that the sayings of third persons, being

447

hearsay, was improper evidence. The objection was overruled by the Justice, and Shekels continued, stating that two men came to his hotel and represented they had a colored man for sale; that they had an interview with Burch; that they stated they came from Georgia, but he did not remember the county; that they gave a full history of the boy, saying he was a bricklayer, and played on the violin; that Burch remarked he would purchase if they could agree; that they went out and brought the boy in, and that I was the same person. He further testified, with as much unconcern as if it was the truth, that I represented I was born and bred in Georgia; that one of the young men with me was my master; that I exhibited a great deal of regret at parting with him, and he believed "got into tears!"—nevertheless, that I insisted my master had a right to sell me; that he *ought* to sell me; and the remarkable reason I gave was, according to Shekels, because he, my master, "had been gambling and on a spree!"

He continued, in these words, copied from the minutes taken on the examination: "Burch interrogated the boy in the usual manner, told him if he purchased him he should send him south. The boy said he had no objection, that in fact he would like to go south. Burch paid $650 for him, to my knowledge. I don't know what name was given him, but think it was not Solomon. Did not know the name of either of the two men. They were in my tavern two or three hours, during which time the boy played on the violin. The bill of sale was signed in my bar-room. It was a *printed blank, filled up by Burch.* Before 1838 Burch was my partner. Our business was buying and selling slaves. After that time he was a partner of Theophilus Freeman, of New-Orleans. Burch bought here—Freeman sold there!"

Shekels, before testifying, had heard my relation of the circumstances connected with the visit to Washington with Brown and Hamilton, and therefore, it was, undoubtedly, he spoke of "two men," and of my playing on the violin. Such was his fabrication, utterly untrue, and yet there was found in Washington a man who endeavored to corroborate him.

Benjamin A. Thorn testified he was at Shekels' in 1841, and saw a colored boy playing on a fiddle. "Shekels said he was for sale. Heard his master tell him he should sell him. The boy acknowledged to me he was a slave. I was not present when the money was paid. Will not swear positively this is the boy. The master *came near shedding tears: I think the boy did*! I have been engaged in the business of taking slaves south, off and on, for twenty years. When I can't do that I do something else."

I was then offered as a witness, but, objection being made, the court decided my evidence inadmissible. It was rejected solely on the ground that I was a colored man—the fact of my being a free citizen of New-York not being disputed.

Shekels having testified there was a bill of sale executed, Burch was called upon by the prosecution to produce it, inasmuch as such a paper would corroborate the testimony of Thorn and Shekels. The prisoner's counsel saw the necessity of exhibiting it, or giving some reasonable explanation for its non-production. To effect the latter, Burch himself was offered as a witness in his own behalf. It was contended by counsel for the people, that such testimony should not be allowed—that it was in contravention of every rule of evidence, and if permitted would defeat the ends of justice. His testimony, however, was received by the court! He made oath that such a bill of sale had been drawn up and signed, *but he had lost it, and did not know what had become of it*! Thereupon the magistrate was requested to dispatch a police officer to Burch's residence, with directions to bring his books, containing his bills of sales for the year 1841. The request was granted, and before any measure could be taken to prevent it, the officer had obtained possession of the books, and brought them into court. The sales for the year 1841 were found, and carefully examined, but no sale of myself, by any name, was discovered!

Upon this testimony the court held the fact to be established, that Burch came innocently and honestly by me, and accordingly he was discharged.

449

An attempt was then made by Burch and his satellites, to fasten upon me the charge that I had conspired with the two white men to defraud him—with what success, appears in an extract taken from an article in the New-York Times, published a day or two subsequent to the trial: "The counsel for the defendant had drawn up, before the defendant was discharged, an affidavit, signed by Burch, and had a warrant out against the colored man for a conspiracy with the two white men before referred to, to defraud Burch out of six hundred and twenty-five dollars. The warrant was served, and the colored man arrested and brought before officer Goddard. Burch and his witnesses appeared in court, and H. B. Northup appeared as counsel for the colored man, stating he was ready to proceed as counsel on the part of the defendant, and asking no delay whatever. Burch, after consulting privately a short time with Shekels, stated to the magistrate that he wished him to dismiss the complaint, as he would not proceed farther with it. Defendant's counsel stated to the magistrate that if the complaint was withdrawn, it must be without the request or consent of the defendant. Burch then asked the magistrate to let him have the complaint and the warrant, and he took them. The counsel for the defendant objected to his receiving them, and insisted they should remain as part of the records of the court, and that the court should endorse the proceedings which had been had under the process. Burch delivered them up, and the court rendered a judgment of discontinuance by the request of the prosecutor, and filed it in his office."

There may be those who will affect to believe the statement of the slave-trader—those, in whose minds his allegations will weigh heavier than mine. I am a poor colored man—one of a down-trodden and degraded race, whose humble voice may not be heeded by the oppressor—but *knowing* the truth, and with a full sense of my accountability, I do solemnly declare before men, and before God, that any charge or assertion, that I conspired directly or indirectly with any person or persons to sell myself;

that any other account of my visit to Washington, my capture and imprisonment in Williams' slave pen, than is contained in these pages, is utterly and absolutely false. I never played on the violin in Washington. I never was in the Steamboat Hotel, and never saw Thorn or Shekels, to my knowledge, in my life, until last January. The story of the trio of slave-traders is a fabrication as absurd as it is base and unfounded. Were it true, I should not have turned aside on my way back to liberty for the purpose of prosecuting Burch. I should have *avoided* rather than sought him. I should have known that such a step would have resulted in rendering me infamous. Under the circumstances—longing as I did to behold my family, and elated with the prospect of returning home—it is an outrage upon probability to suppose I would have run the hazard, not only of exposure, but of a criminal prosecution and conviction, by voluntarily placing myself in the position I did, if the statements of Burch and his confederates contain a particle of truth. I took pains to seek him out, to confront him in a court of law, charging him with the crime of kidnapping; and the only motive that impelled me to this step, was a burning sense of the wrong he had inflicted upon me, and a desire to bring him to justice. He was acquitted, in the manner, and by such means as have been described. A human tribunal has permitted him to escape; but there is another and a higher tribunal, where false testimony will not prevail, and where I am willing, so far at least as these statements are concerned, to be judged at last.

We left Washington on the 20th of January, and proceeding by the way of Philadelphia, New-York, and Albany, reached Sandy Hill in the night of the 21st. My heart overflowed with happiness as I looked around upon old familiar scenes, and found myself in the midst of friends of other days. The following morning I started, in company with several acquaintances, for Glens Falls, the residence of Anne and our children.

As I entered their comfortable cottage, Margaret was the first that met me. She did not recognize me. When I left her,

451

she was but seven years old, a little prattling girl, playing with her toys. Now she was grown to womanhood—was married, with a bright-eyed boy standing by her side. Not forgetful of his enslaved, unfortunate grand-father, she had named the child Solomon Northup Staunton. When told who I was, she was overcome with emotion, and unable to speak. Presently Elizabeth entered the room, and Anne came running from the hotel, having been informed of my arrival. They embraced me, and with tears flowing down their cheeks, hung upon my neck. But I draw a veil over a scene which can better be imagined than described.

When the violence of our emotions had subsided to a sacred joy—when the household gathered round the fire, that sent out its warm and crackling comfort through the room, we conversed of the thousand events that had occurred—the hopes and fears, the joys and sorrows, the trials and troubles we had each experienced during the long separation. Alonzo was absent in the western part of the State. The boy had written to his mother a short time previous, of the prospect of his obtaining sufficient money to purchase my freedom. From his earliest years, that had been the chief object of his thoughts and his ambition. They knew I was in bondage. The letter written on board the brig, and Clem Ray himself, had given them that information. But where I was, until the arrival of Bass' letter, was a matter of conjecture. Elizabeth and Margaret once returned from school—so Anne informed me—weeping bitterly. On inquiring the cause of the children's sorrow, it was found that, while studying geography, their attention had been attracted to the picture of slaves working in the cotton-field, and an overseer following them with his whip. It reminded them of the sufferings their father might be, and, as it happened, actually *was*, enduring in the South. Numerous incidents, such as these, were related—incidents showing they still held me in constant remembrance, but not, perhaps, of sufficient interest to the reader, to be recounted.

My narrative is at an end. I have no comments to make upon

452

the subject of Slavery. Those who read this book may form their own opinions of the "peculiar institution." What it may be in other States, I do not profess to know; what it is in the region of Red River, is truly and faithfully delineated in these pages. This is no fiction, no exaggeration. If I have failed in anything, it has been in presenting to the reader too prominently the bright side of the picture. I doubt not hundreds have been as unfortunate as myself; that hundreds of free citizens have been kidnapped and sold into slavery, and are at this moment wearing out their lives on plantations in Texas and Louisiana. But I forbear. Chastened and subdued in spirit by the sufferings I have borne, and thankful to that good Being through whose mercy I have been restored to happiness and liberty, I hope henceforward to lead an upright though lowly life, and rest at last in the church yard where my father sleeps.

RUNNING A THOUSAND MILES FOR FREEDOM

BY WILLIAM CRAFT
AND ELLEN CRAFT

First Published in 1860

PART I

MY wife and myself were born in different towns in the State of Georgia, which is one of the principal slave States. It is true, our condition as slaves was not by any means the worst; but the mere idea that we were held as chattels, and deprived of all legal rights—the thought that we had to give up our hard earnings to a tyrant, to enable him to live in idleness and luxury—the thought that we could not call the bones and sinews that God gave us our own: but above all, the fact that another man had the power to tear from our cradle the new-born babe and sell it in the shambles like a brute, and then scourge us if we dared to lift a finger to save it from such a fate, haunted us for years.

But in December, 1848, a plan suggested itself that proved quite successful, and in eight days after it was first thought of we were free from the horrible trammels of slavery, rejoicing and praising God in the glorious sunshine of liberty.

My wife's first master was her father, and her mother his slave, and the latter is still the slave of his widow.

Notwithstanding my wife being of African extraction on her mother's side, she is almost white— in fact, she is so nearly so that the tyrannical old lady to whom she first belonged became so annoyed, at finding her frequently mistaken for a child of the family, that she gave her when eleven years of age to a daughter, as a wedding present. This separated my wife from her mother, and also from several other dear friends. But the incessant cruelty of her old mistress made the change of owners or treatment so desirable, that she did not grumble much at this cruel separation.

It may be remembered that slavery in America is not at all confined to persons of any particular complexion; there are

457

a very large number of slaves as white as any one; but as the evidence of a slave is not admitted in court against a free white person, it is almost impossible for a white child, after having been kidnapped and sold into or reduced to slavery, in a part of the country where it is not known (as often is the case), ever to recover its freedom.

I have myself conversed with several slaves who told me that their parents were white and free; but that they were stolen away from them and sold when quite young. As they could not tell their address, and also as the parents did not know what had become of their lost and dear little ones, of course all traces of each other were gone.

The following facts are sufficient to prove, that he who has the power, and is inhuman enough to trample upon the sacred rights of the weak, cares nothing for race or colour:—

In March, 1818, three ships arrived at New Orleans, bringing several hundred German emigrants from the province of Alsace, on the lower Rhine. Among them were Daniel Muller and his two daughters, Dorothea and Salome, whose mother had died on the passage. Soon after his arrival, Muller, taking with him his two daughters, both young children, went up the river to Attakapas parish, to work on the plantation of John F. Miller. A few weeks later, his relatives, who had remained at New Orleans, learned that he had died of the fever of the country. They immediately sent for the two girls; but they had disappeared, and the relatives, notwithstanding repeated and persevering inquiries and researches, could find no traces of them. They were at length given up for dead. Dorothea was never again heard of; nor was any thing known of Salome from 1818 till 1843.

In the summer of that year, Madame Karl, a German woman who had come over in the same ship with the Mullers, was passing through a street in New Orleans, and accidentally saw Salome in a wine-shop, belonging to Louis Belmonte, by whom she was held as a slave. Madame Karl recognised her at once, and carried her to the house of another German woman, Mrs.

Schubert, who was Salome's cousin and godmother, and who no sooner set eyes on her than, without having any intimation that the discovery had been previously made, she unhesitatingly exclaimed, "My God! here is the long-lost Salome Muller."

The Law Reporter, in its account of this case, says:—

"As many of the German emigrants of 1818 as could be gathered together were brought to the house of Mrs. Schubert, and every one of the number who had any recollection of the little girl upon the passage, or any acquaintance with her father and mother, immediately identified the woman before them as the long-lost Salome Muller. By all these witnesses, who appeared at the trial, the identity was fully established. The family resemblance in every feature was declared to be so remarkable, that some of the witnesses did not hesitate to say that they should know her among ten thousand; that they were as certain the plaintiff was Salome Muller, the daughter of Daniel and Dorothea Muller, as of their own existence."

Among the witnesses who appeared in Court was the midwife who had assisted at the birth of Salome. She testified to the existence of certain peculiar marks upon the body of the child, which were found, exactly as described, by the surgeons who were appointed by the Court to make an examination for the purpose.

There was no trace of African descent in any feature of Salome Muller. She had long, straight, black hair, hazel eyes, thin lips, and a Roman nose. The complexion of her face and neck was as dark as that of the darkest brunette. It appears, however, that, during the twenty-five years of her servitude, she had been exposed to the sun's rays in the hot climate of Louisiana, with head and neck unsheltered, as is customary with the female slaves, while labouring in the cotton or the sugar field. Those parts of her person which had been shielded from the sun were comparatively white.

Belmonte, the pretended owner of the girl, had obtained possession of her by an act of sale from John F. Miller, the planter in whose service Salome's father died. This Miller was a man of consideration and substance, owning large sugar estates, and bearing a high reputation for honour and honesty, and for indulgent treatment of his slaves. It was testified on the trial that he had said to Belmonte, a few weeks after the sale of Salome, "that she was white, and had as much right to her freedom as any one, and was only to be retained in slavery by care and kind treatment." The broker who negotiated the sale from Miller to Belmonte, in 1838, testified in Court that he then thought, and still thought, that the girl was white!

The case was elaborately argued on both sides, but was at length decided in favour of the girl, by the Supreme Court declaring that "she was free and white, and therefore unlawfully held in bondage."

The Rev. George Bourne, of Virginia, in his Picture of Slavery, published in 1834, relates the case of a white boy who, at the age of seven, was stolen from his home in Ohio, tanned and stained in such a way that he could not be distinguished from a person of colour, and then sold as a slave in Virginia. At the age of twenty, he made his escape, by running away, and happily succeeded in rejoining his parents.

I have known worthless white people to sell their own free children into slavery; and, as there are good-for-nothing white as well as coloured persons everywhere, no one, perhaps, will wonder at such inhuman transactions: particularly in the Southern States of America, where I believe there is a greater want of humanity and high principle amongst the whites, than among any other civilized people in the world.

I know that those who are not familiar with the working of "the peculiar institution," can scarcely imagine any one so totally devoid of all natural affection as to sell his own offspring into returnless bondage. But Shakespeare, that great observer of human nature, says:—

"With caution judge of probabilities.
Things deemed unlikely, e'en impossible,
Experience often shews us to be true."

My wife's new mistress was decidedly more humane than the majority of her class. My wife has always given her credit for not exposing her to many of the worst features of slavery. For instance, it is a common practice in the slave States for ladies, when angry with their maids, to send them to the calybuce sugar-house, or to some other place established for the purpose of punishing slaves, and have them severely flogged; and I am sorry it is a fact, that the villains to whom those defenceless creatures are sent, not only flog them as they are ordered, but frequently compel them to submit to the greatest indignity. Oh! if there is any one thing under the wide canopy of heaven, horrible enough to stir a man's soul, and to make his very blood boil, it is the thought of his dear wife, his unprotected sister, or his young and virtuous daughters, struggling to save themselves from falling a prey to such demons!

It always appears strange to me that any one who was not born a slaveholder, and steeped to the very core in the demoralizing atmosphere of the Southern States, can in any way palliate slavery. It is still more surprising to see virtuous ladies looking with patience upon, and remaining indifferent to, the existence of a system that exposes nearly two millions of their own sex in the manner I have mentioned, and that too in a professedly free and Christian country. There is, however, great consolation in knowing that God is just, and will not let the oppressor of the weak, and the spoiler of the virtuous, escape unpunished here and hereafter.

I believe a similar retribution to that which destroyed Sodom is hanging over the slaveholders. My sincere prayer is that they may not provoke God, by persisting in a reckless course of wickedness, to pour out his consuming wrath upon them.

I must now return to our history.

My old master had the reputation of being a very humane and Christian man, but he thought nothing of selling my poor old father, and dear aged mother, at separate times, to different persons, to be dragged off never to behold each other again, till summoned to appear before the great tribunal of heaven. But, oh! what a happy meeting it will be on that day for those faithful souls. I say a happy meeting, because I never saw persons more devoted to the service of God than they. But how will the case stand with those reckless traffickers in human flesh and blood, who plunged the poisonous dagger of separation into those loving hearts which God had for so many years closely joined together—nay, sealed as it were with his own hands for the eternal courts of heaven? It is not for me to say what will become of those heartless tyrants. I must leave them in the hands of an all-wise and just God, who will, in his own good time, and in his own way, avenge the wrongs of his oppressed people.

My old master also sold a dear brother and a sister, in the same manner as he did my father and mother. The reason he assigned for disposing of my parents, as well as of several other aged slaves, was, that "they were getting old, and would soon become valueless in the market, and therefore he intended to sell off all the old stock, and buy in a young lot." A most disgraceful conclusion for a man to come to, who made such great professions of religion!

This shameful conduct gave me a thorough hatred, not for true Christianity, but for slaveholding piety.

My old master, then, wishing to make the most of the rest of his slaves, apprenticed a brother and myself out to learn trades: he to a blacksmith, and myself to a cabinet-maker. If a slave has a good trade, he will let or sell for more than a person without one, and many slaveholders have their slaves taught trades on this account. But before our time expired, my old master wanted money; so he sold my brother, and then mortgaged my sister, a dear girl about fourteen years of age, and myself, then about sixteen, to one of the banks, to get money to speculate in

462

cotton. This we knew nothing of at the moment; but time rolled on, the money became due, my master was unable to meet his payments; so the bank had us placed upon the auction stand and sold to the highest bidder.

My poor sister was sold first: she was knocked down to a planter who resided at some distance in the country. Then I was called upon the stand. While the auctioneer was crying the bids, I saw the man that had purchased my sister getting her into a cart, to take her to his home. I at once asked a slave friend who was standing near the platform, to run and ask the gentleman if he would please to wait till I was sold, in order that I might have an opportunity of bidding her good-bye. He sent me word back that he had some distance to go, and could not wait.

I then turned to the auctioneer, fell upon my knees, and humbly prayed him to let me just step down and bid my last sister farewell. But, instead of granting me this request, he grasped me by the neck, and in a commanding tone of voice, and with a violent oath, exclaimed, "Get up! You can do the wench no good; therefore there is no use in your seeing her."

On rising, I saw the cart in which she sat moving slowly off; and, as she clasped her hands with a grasp that indicated despair, and looked pitifully round towards me, I also saw the large silent tears trickling down her cheeks. She made a farewell bow, and buried her face in her lap. This seemed more than I could bear. It appeared to swell my aching heart to its utmost. But before I could fairly recover, the poor girl was gone;—gone, and I have never had the good fortune to see her from that day to this! Perhaps I should have never heard of her again, had it not been for the untiring efforts of my good old mother, who became free a few years ago by purchase, and, after a great deal of difficulty, found my sister residing with a family in Mississippi. My mother at once wrote to me, informing me of the fact, and requesting me to do something to get her free; and I am happy to say that, partly by lecturing occasionally, and through the sale of an engraving of my wife in the disguise in which she

463

escaped, together with the extreme kindness and generosity of Miss Burdett Coutts, Mr. George Richardson of Plymouth, and a few other friends, I have nearly accomplished this. It would be to me a great and ever-glorious achievement to restore my sister to our dear mother, from whom she was forcibly driven in early life.

I was knocked down to the cashier of the bank to which we were mortgaged, and ordered to return to the cabinet shop where I previously worked.

But the thought of the harsh auctioneer not allowing me to bid my dear sister farewell, sent red-hot indignation darting like lightning through every vein. It quenched my tears, and appeared to set my brain on fire, and made me crave for power to avenge our wrongs! But alas! we were only slaves, and had no legal rights; consequently we were compelled to smother our wounded feelings, and crouch beneath the iron heel of despotism.

I must now give the account of our escape; but, before doing so, it may be well to quote a few passages from the fundamental laws of slavery; in order to give some idea of the legal as well as the social tyranny from which we fled.

According to the law of Louisiana, "A slave is one who is in the power of a master to whom he belongs. The master may sell him, dispose of his person, his industry, and his labour; he can do nothing, possess nothing, nor acquire anything but what must belong to his master."—*Civil Code, art.* 35.

In South Carolina it is expressed in the following language:—"Slaves shall be deemed, sold, taken, reputed and judged in law to be chattels personal in the hands of their owners and possessors, and their executors, administrators, and assigns, to *all intents, constructions, and purposes whatsoever.*— 2 *Brevard's Digest,* 229.

The Constitution of Georgia has the following (Art. 4, sec. 12):—"Any person who shall maliciously dismember or deprive a slave of life, shall suffer such punishment as would be inflicted in case the like offence had been committed on a free white person, and on the like proof, except in case of insurrection of such slave, and unless SUCH DEATH SHOULD HAPPEN BY ACCIDENT IN GIVING SUCH SLAVE MODERATE CORRECTION."—*Prince's Digest*, 559.

I have known slaves to be beaten to death, but as they died under "moderate correction," it was quite lawful; and of course the murderers were not interfered with.

"If any slave, who shall be out of the house or plantation where such slave shall live, or shall be usually employed, or without some white person in company with such slave, shall *refuse to submit* to undergo the examination of *any white person*, (let him be ever so drunk or crazy), it shall be lawful for such white person to pursue, apprehend, and moderately correct such slave; and if such slave shall assault and strike such white person, such slave may be *lawfully killed.*"—2 *Brevard's Digest*, 231.

"Provided always," says the law, "that such striking be not done by the command and in the defence of the person or property of the owner, or other person having the government of such slave; in which case the slave shall be wholly excused."

According to this law, if a slave, by the direction of his overseer, strike a white person who is beating said overseer's pig, "the slave shall be wholly excused." But, should the bondman, of his own accord, fight to defend his wife, or should his terrified daughter instinctively raise her hand and strike the wretch who attempts to violate her chastity, he or she shall, saith the model republican law, suffer death.

From having been myself a slave for nearly twenty-three years, I am quite prepared to say, that the practical working of slavery is worse than the odious laws by which it is governed.

At an early age we were taken by the persons who held us as property to Macon, the largest town in the interior of the State of Georgia, at which place we became acquainted with each other for several years before our marriage; in fact, our marriage was postponed for some time simply because one of the unjust and worse than Pagan laws under which we lived compelled all children of slave mothers to follow their condition. That is to say, the father of the slave may be the President of the Republic; but if the mother should be a slave at the infant's birth, the poor child is ever legally doomed to the same cruel fate.

It is a common practice for gentlemen (if I may call them such), moving in the highest circles of society, to be the fathers of children by their slaves, whom they can and do sell with the greatest impunity; and the more pious, beautiful, and virtuous the girls are, the greater the price they bring, and that too for the most infamous purposes.

Any man with money (let him be ever such a rough brute), can buy a beautiful and virtuous girl, and force her to live with him in a criminal connexion; and as the law says a slave shall have no higher appeal than the mere will of the master, she cannot escape, unless it be by flight or death.

In endeavouring to reconcile a girl to her fate, the master sometimes says that he would marry her if it was not unlawful. [5] However, he will always consider her to be his wife, and will treat her as such; and she, on the other hand, may regard him as her lawful husband; and if they have any children, they will be free and well educated.

I am in duty bound to add, that while a great majority of such men care nothing for the happiness of the women with whom they live, nor for the children of whom they are the fathers, there are those to be found, even in that heterogeneous mass of licentious monsters, who are true to their pledges. But as the woman and her children are legally the property of the man, who stands in the anomalous relation to them of husband and

---

5 It is unlawful in the slave States for any one of purely European descent to intermarry with a person of African ex- traction; though a white man may live with as many coloured women as he pleases without materially damaging his reputa- tion in Southern society.

father, as well as master, they are liable to be seized and sold for his debts, should he become involved.

There are several cases on record where such persons have been sold and separated for life. I know of some myself, but I have only space to glance at one.

I knew a very humane and wealthy gentleman, that bought a woman, with whom he lived as his wife. They brought up a family of children, among whom were three nearly white, well educated, and beautiful girls.

On the father being suddenly killed it was found that he had not left a will; but, as the family had always heard him say that he had no surviving relatives, they felt that their liberty and property were quite secured to them, and, knowing the insults to which they were exposed, now their protector was no more, they were making preparations to leave for a free State.

But, poor creatures, they were soon sadly undeceived. A villain residing at a distance, hearing of the circumstance, came forward and swore that he was a relative of the deceased; and as this man bore, or assumed, Mr. Slator's name, the case was brought before one of those horrible tribunals, presided over by a second Judge Jeffreys, and calling itself a court of justice, but before whom no coloured person, nor an abolitionist, was ever known to get his full rights.

A verdict was given in favour of the plaintiff, whom the better portion of the community thought had wilfully conspired to cheat the family.

The heartless wretch not only took the ordinary property, but actually had the aged and friendless widow, and all her fatherless children, except Frank, a fine young man about twenty-two years of age, and Mary, a very nice girl, a little younger than her brother, brought to the auction stand and sold to the highest bidder. Mrs. Slator had cash enough, that her husband and master left, to purchase the liberty of herself and children; but on her attempting to do so, the pusillanimous scoundrel, who had robbed them of their freedom, claimed the money as his

467

property; and, poor creature, she had to give it up. According to law, as will be seen hereafter, a slave cannot own anything. The old lady never recovered from her sad affliction.

At the sale she was brought up first, and after being vulgarly criticised, in the presence of all her distressed family, was sold to a cotton planter, who said he wanted the "proud old critter to go to his plantation, to look after the little woolly heads, while their mammies were working in the field."

When the sale was over, then came the separation, and

"O, deep was the anguish of that slave mother's heart,
When called from her darlings for ever to part;
The poor mourning mother of reason bereft,
Soon ended her sorrows, and sank cold in death."

Antoinette, the flower of the family, a girl who was much beloved by all who knew her, for her Christ-like piety, dignity of manner, as well as her great talents and extreme beauty, was bought by an uneducated and drunken salve-dealer.

I cannot give a more correct description of the scene, when she was called from her brother to the stand, than will be found in the following lines—

"Why stands she near the auction stand?
    That girl so young and fair;
What brings her to this dismal place?
    Why stands she weeping there?

Why does she raise that bitter cry?
    Why hangs her head with shame,
As now the auctioneer's rough voice
    So rudely calls her name!

But see! she grasps a manly hand,
  And in a voice so low,
As scarcely to be heard, she says,
  "My brother, must I go?"

A moment's pause: then, midst a wail
  Of agonizing woe,
His answer falls upon the ear,—
  "Yes, sister, you must go!

No longer can my arm defend,
  No longer can I save
My sister from the horrid fate
  That waits her as a SLAVE!"

Blush, Christian, blush! for e'en the dark
  Untutored heathen see
Thy inconsistency, and lo!
  They scorn thy God, and thee!"

The low trader said to a kind lady who wished to purchase Antoinette out of his hands, "I reckon I'll not sell the smart critter for ten thousand dollars; I always wanted her for my own use." The lady, wishing to remonstrate with him, commenced by saying, "You should remember, Sir, that there is a just God." Hoskens not understanding Mrs. Huston, interrupted her by saying, "I does, and guess its monstrous kind an' him to send such likely niggers for our convenience." Mrs. Huston finding that a long course of reckless wickedness, drunkenness, and vice, had destroyed in Hoskens every noble impulse, left him.

Antoinette, poor girl, also seeing that there was no help for her, became frantic. I can never forget her cries of despair, when Hoskens gave the order for her to be taken to his house, and locked in an upper room. On Hoskens entering the apartment, in a state of intoxication, a fearful struggle ensued. The brave

Antoinette broke loose from him, pitched herself head foremost through the window, and fell upon the pavement below.

Her bruised but unpolluted body was soon picked up—restoratives brought—doctor called in; but, alas! it was too late: her pure and noble spirit had fled away to be at rest in those realms of endless bliss, "where the wicked cease from troubling, and the weary are at rest."

Antoinette like many other noble women who are deprived of liberty, still

"Holds something sacred, something undefiled;
Some pledge and keepsake of their higher nature.
And, like the diamond in the dark, retains
Some quenchless gleam of the celestial light."

On Hoskens fully realizing the fact that his victim was no more, he exclaimed "By thunder I am a used-up man!" The sudden disappointment, and the loss of two thousand dollars, was more than he could endure: so he drank more than ever, and in a short time died, raving mad with delirium tremens.

The villain Slator said to Mrs. Huston, the kind lady who endeavoured to purchase Antoinette from Hoskens, "Nobody needn't talk to me 'bout buying them ar likely niggers, for I'm not going to sell em." "But Mary is rather delicate," said Mrs. Huston, "and, being unaccustomed to hard work, cannot do you much service on a plantation." "I don't want her for the field," replied Slator, "but for another purpose." Mrs. Huston understood what this meant, and instantly exclaimed, "Oh, but she is your cousin!" "The devil she is!" said Slator; and added, "Do you mean to insult me, Madam, by saying that I am related to niggers?" "No," replied Mrs. Huston, "I do not wish to offend you, Sir. But wasn't Mr. Slator, Mary's father, your uncle?" "Yes, I calculate he was," said Slator; "but I want you and everybody to understand that I'm no kin to his niggers." "Oh, very well," said Mrs. Huston; adding, "Now what will you take for the poor girl?" "Nothin'," he replied; "for, as I said before, I'm not goin' to sell, so you needn't trouble yourself no more. If the critter behaves herself, I'll do as well by her as any man."

Slator spoke up boldly, but his manner and sheepish look clearly indicated that

"His heart within him was at strife
    With such accursed gains;
For he knew whose passions gave her life,
    Whose blood ran in her veins."

"The monster led her from the door,
    He led her by the hand,
To be his slave and paramour
    In a strange and distant land!"

Poor Frank and his sister were handcuffed together, and confined in prison. Their dear little twin brother and sister were sold, and taken where they knew not. But it often happens that misfortune causes those whom we counted dearest to shrink away; while it makes friends of those whom we least expected to take any interest in our affairs. Among the latter class Frank found two comparatively new but faithful friends to watch the gloomy paths of the unhappy little twins.

In a day or two after the sale, Slator had two fast horses put to a large light van, and placed in it a good many small but valuable things belonging to the distressed family. He also took with him Frank and Mary, as well as all the money for the spoil; and after treating all his low friends and bystanders, and drinking deeply himself, he started in high glee for his home in South Carolina. But they had not proceeded many miles, before Frank and his sister discovered that Slator was too drunk to drive. But he, like most tipsy men, thought he was all right; and as he had with him some of the ruined family's best brandy and wine, such as he had not been accustomed to, and being a thirsty soul, he drank till the reins fell from his fingers, and in attempting to catch them he tumbled out of the vehicle, and was unable to get up. Frank and Mary there and then contrived a plan by which to escape. As they were still handcuffed by one wrist each, they alighted, took from the drunken assassin's pocket the key, undid the iron bracelets, and placed them upon Slator, who was better fitted to wear such ornaments. As the demon lay unconscious of what was taking place, Frank and Mary took from him the large sum of money that was realized at the sale, as well as that which Slator had so very meanly obtained from their poor mother. They then dragged him into the woods, tied him to a tree, and left the inebriated robber to shift for himself, while they made good their escape to Savannah. The fugitives being white, of course no one suspected that they were slaves.

Slator was not able to call any one to his rescue till late the next day; and as there were no railroads in that part of the country at that time, it was not until late the following day that Slator was able to get a party to join him for the chase. A person informed Slator that he had met a man and woman, in a trap, answering to the description of those whom he had lost, driving furiously towards Savannah. So Slator and several slavehunters on horseback started off in full tilt, with their bloodhounds, in pursuit of Frank and Mary.

On arriving at Savannah, the hunters found that the fugitives had sold the horses and trap, and embarked as free white persons, for New York. Slator's disappointment and rascality so preyed upon his base mind, that he, like Judas, went and hanged himself.

As soon as Frank and Mary were safe, they endeavoured to redeem their good mother. But, alas! she was gone; she had passed on to the realm of spirit life.

In due time Frank learned from his friends in Georgia where his little brother and sister dwelt. So he wrote at once to purchase them, but the persons with whom they lived would not sell them. After failing in several attempts to buy them, Frank cultivated large whiskers and moustachios, cut off his hair, put on a wig and glasses, and went down as a white man, and stopped in the neighbourhood where his sister was; and after seeing her and also his little brother, arrangements were made for them to meet at a particular place on a Sunday, which they did, and got safely off.

I saw Frank myself, when he came for the little twins. Though I was then quite a lad, I well remember being highly delighted by hearing him tell how nicely he and Mary had served Slator.

Frank had so completely disguised or changed his appearance that his little sister did not know him, and would not speak till he showed their mother's likeness; the sight of which melted her to tears,—for she knew the face. Frank might have said to her

> "'O, Emma! O, my sister, speak to me!
> Dost thou not know me, that I am thy brother?
> Come to me, little Emma, thou shalt dwell
> With me henceforth, and know no care or want.'
> Emma was silent for a space, as if
> 'Twere hard to summon up a human voice."

Frank and Mary's mother was my wife's own dear aunt.

After this great diversion from our narrative, which I hope dear reader, you will excuse, I shall return at once to it.

My wife was torn from her mother's embrace in childhood, and taken to a distant part of the country. She had seen so many other children separated from their parents in this cruel manner, that the mere thought of her ever becoming the mother of a child, to linger out a miserable existence under the wretched system of American slavery, appeared to fill her very soul with horror; and as she had taken what I felt to be an important view of her condition, I did not, at first, press the marriage, but agreed to assist her in trying to devise some plan by which we might escape from our unhappy condition, and then be married.

We thought of plan after plan, but they all seemed crowded

with insurmountable difficulties. We knew it was unlawful for any public conveyance to take us as passengers, without our master's consent. We were also perfectly aware of the startling fact, that had we left without this consent the professional slave-hunters would have soon had their ferocious bloodhounds baying on our track, and in a short time we should have been dragged back to slavery, not to fill the more favourable situations which we had just left, but to be separated for life, and put to the very meanest and most laborious drudgery; or else have been tortured to death as examples, in order to strike terror into the hearts of others, and thereby prevent them from even attempting to escape from their cruel taskmasters. It is a fact worthy of remark, that nothing seems to give the slaveholders so much pleasure as the catching and torturing of fugitives. They had much rather take the keen and poisonous lash, and with it cut their poor trembling victims to atoms, than allow one of them to escape to a free country, and expose the infamous system from which he fled.

The greatest excitement prevails at a slave-hunt. The slaveholders and their hired ruffians appear to take more pleasure in this inhuman pursuit than English sportsmen do in chasing a fox or a stag. Therefore, knowing what we should have been compelled to suffer, if caught and taken back, we were more than anxious to hit upon a plan that would lead us safely to a land of liberty.

But, after puzzling our brains for years, we were reluctantly driven to the sad conclusion, that it was almost impossible to escape from slavery in Georgia, and travel 1,000 miles across the slave States. We therefore resolved to get the consent of our owners, be married, settle down in slavery, and endeavour to make ourselves as comfortable as possible under that system; but at the same time ever to keep our dim eyes steadily fixed upon the glimmering hope of liberty, and earnestly pray God mercifully to assist us to escape from our unjust thraldom.

We were married, and prayed and toiled on till December,

1848, at which time (as I have stated) a plan suggested itself that proved quite successful, and in eight days after it was first thought of we were free from the horrible trammels of slavery, and glorifying God who had brought us safely out of a land of bondage.

Knowing that slaveholders have the privilege of taking their slaves to any part of the country they think proper, it occurred to me that, as my wife was nearly white, I might get her to disguise herself as an invalid gentleman, and assume to be my master, while I could attend as his slave, and that in this manner we might effect our escape. After I thought of the plan, I suggested it to my wife, but at first she shrank from the idea. She thought it was almost impossible for her to assume that disguise, and travel a distance of 1,000 miles across the slave States. However, on the other hand, she also thought of her condition. She saw that the laws under which we lived did not recognize her to be a woman, but a mere chattel, to be bought and sold, or otherwise dealt with as her owner might see fit. Therefore the more she contemplated her helpless condition, the more anxious she was to escape from it. So she said, "I think it is almost too much for us to undertake; however, I feel that God is on our side, and with his assistance, notwithstanding all the difficulties, we shall be able to succeed. Therefore, if you will purchase the disguise, I will try to carry out the plan."

But after I concluded to purchase the disguise, I was afraid to go to any one to ask him to sell me the articles. It is unlawful in Georgia for a white man to trade with slaves without the master's consent. But, notwithstanding this, many persons will sell a slave any article that he can get the money to buy. Not that they sympathize with the slave, but merely because his testimony is not admitted in court against a free white person.

Therefore, with little difficulty I went to different parts of the town, at odd times, and purchased things piece by piece, (except the trowsers which she found necessary to make,) and took them home to the house where my wife resided. She being a ladies' maid, and a favourite slave in the family, was allowed a little room to herself; and amongst other pieces of furniture which I had made in my overtime, was a chest of drawers; so when I took the articles home, she locked them up carefully in these drawers. No one about the premises knew that she had anything of the kind. So when we fancied we had everything ready the time was fixed for the flight. But we knew it would not do to start off without first getting our master's consent to be away for a few days. Had we left without this, they would soon have had us back into slavery, and probably we should never have got another fair opportunity of even attempting to escape.

Some of the best slaveholders will sometimes give their favourite slaves a few days' holiday at Christmas time; so, after no little amount of perseverance on my wife's part, she obtained a pass from her mistress, allowing her to be away for a few days. The cabinet-maker with whom I worked gave me a similar paper, but said that he needed my services very much, and wished me to return as soon as the time granted was up. I thanked him kindly; but somehow I have not been able to make it convenient to return yet; and, as the free air of good old England agrees so well with my wife and our dear little ones, as well as with myself, it is not at all likely we shall return at present to the "peculiar institution" of chains and stripes.

On reaching my wife's cottage she handed me her pass, and I showed mine, but at that time neither of us were able to read them. It is not only unlawful for slaves to be taught to read, but in some of the States there are heavy penalties attached, such as fines and imprisonment, which will be vigorously enforced upon any one who is humane enough to violate the so-called law.

The following case will serve to show how persons are treated in the most enlightened slaveholding community.

"INDICTMENT.

COMMONWEALTH OF VIRGINIA, NORFOLK COUNTY, ss.
In the Circuit Court.

The Grand Jurors empannelled in the body of the said County on their oath present, that Margaret Douglass, being an evil disposed person, not having the fear of God before her eyes, but moved and instigated by the devil, wickedly, maliciously, and feloniously, on the fourth day of July, in the year of our Lord one thousand eight hundred and fiftyfour, at Norfolk, in said County, did teach a certain black girl named Kate to read in the Bible, to the great displeasure of Almighty God, to the pernicious example of others in like case offending, contrary to the form of the statute in such case made and provided, and against the peace and dignity of the Commonwealth of Virginia.

"VICTOR VAGABOND,
Prosecuting Attorney."

"On this indictment Mrs. Douglass was arraigned as a necessary matter of form, tried, found guilty of course; and Judge Scalaway, before whom she was tried, having consulted with Dr. Adams, ordered the sheriff to place Mrs. Douglass in the prisoner's box, when he addressed her as follows: 'Margaret Douglass, stand up. You are guilty of one of the vilest crimes that ever disgraced society; and the jury have found you so. You have taught a slave girl to read in the Bible. No enlightened society can exist where such offences go unpunished. The Court, in your case, do not feel for you one solitary ray of sympathy, and they will inflict on you the utmost penalty of the law. In any other civilized country you would have paid the forfeit of your crime with your life, and the Court have only to regret that such is not the law in this country. The sentence for your offence is, that you be imprisoned one month in the county jail, and that you pay the costs of this prosecution. Sheriff, remove the prisoner to jail.' On the publication of these proceedings, the Doctors of Divinity preached each a sermon on the necessity of obeying the laws; the New York Observer noticed with much pious gladness a revival of religion on Dr. Smith's plantation in Georgia, among his slaves; while the Journal of Commerce commended this political preaching of the Doctors of Divinity because it favoured slavery. Let us do nothing to offend our Southern brethren."

However, at first, we were highly delighted at the idea of having gained permission to be absent for a few days; but when the thought flashed across my wife's mind, that it was customary for travellers to register their names in the visitors' book at hotels, as well as in the clearance or Custom-house book at Charleston, South Carolina —it made our spirits droop within us.

So, while sitting in our little room upon the verge of despair, all at once my wife raised her head, and with a smile upon her face, which was a moment before bathed in tears, said, "I think I have it!" I asked what it was. She said, "I think I can make a poultice and bind up my right hand in a sling, and with propriety ask the officers to register my name for me." I thought that would do.

It then occurred to her that the smoothness of her face might betray her; so she decided to make another poultice, and put it in a white handkerchief to be worn under the chin, up the cheeks, and to tie over the head. This nearly hid the expression of the countenance, as well as the beardless chin.

The poultice is left off in the engraving, because the likeness could not have been taken well with it on.

My wife, knowing that she would be thrown a good deal into the company of gentlemen, fancied that she could get on better if she had something to go over the eyes; so I went to a shop and bought a pair of green spectacles. This was in the evening.

We sat up all night discussing the plan, and making preparations. Just before the time arrived, in the morning, for

478

us to leave, I cut off my wife's hair square at the back of the head, and got her to dress in the disguise and stand out on the floor. I found that she made a most respectable looking gentleman.

My wife had no ambition whatever to assume this disguise, and would not have done so had it been possible to have obtained our liberty by more simple means; but we knew it was not customary in the South for ladies to travel with male servants; and therefore, notwithstanding my wife's fair complexion, it would have been a very difficult task for her to have come off as a free white lady, with me as her slave; in fact, her not being able to write would have made this quite impossible. We knew that no public conveyance would take us, or any other slave, as a passenger, without our master's consent. This consent could never be obtained to pass into a free State. My wife's being muffled in the poultices, &c., furnished a plausible excuse for avoiding general conversation, of which most Yankee travellers are passionately fond.

There are a large number of free negroes residing in the southern States; but in Georgia (and I believe in all the slave States,) every coloured person's complexion is *prima* facie evidence of his being a slave; and the lowest villain in the country, should he be a white man, has the legal power to arrest, and question, in the most inquisitorial and insulting manner, any coloured person, male or female, that he may find at large, particularly at night and on Sundays, without a written pass, signed by the master or some one in authority; or stamped free papers, certifying that the person is the rightful owner of himself.

If the coloured person refuses to answer questions put to him, he may be beaten, and his defending himself against this attack makes him an outlaw, and if he be killed on the spot, the murderer will be exempted from all blame; but after the coloured person has answered the questions put to him, in a most humble and pointed manner, he may then be taken to prison; and should it turn out, after further examination, that he

479

was caught where he had no permission or legal right to be, and that he has not given what they term a satisfactory account of himself, the master will have to pay a fine. On his refusing to do this, the poor slave may be legally and severely flogged by public officers. Should the prisoner prove to be a free man, he is most likely to be both whipped and fined.

The great majority of slaveholders hate this class of persons with a hatred that can only be equalled by the condemned spirits of the infernal regions. They have no mercy upon, nor sympathy for, any negro whom they cannot enslave. They say that God made the black man to be a slave for the white, and act as though they really believed that all free persons of colour are in open rebellion to a direct command from heaven, and that they (the whites) are God's chosen agents to pour out upon them unlimited vengeance. For instance, a Bill has been introduced in the Tennessee Legislature to prevent free negroes from travelling on the railroads in that State. It has passed the first reading. The bill provides that the President who shall permit a free negro to travel on any road within the jurisdiction of the State under his supervision shall pay a fine of 500 dollars; any conductor permitting a violation of the Act shall pay 250 dollars; provided such free negro is not under the control of a free white citizen of Tennessee, who will vouch for the character of said free negro in a penal bond of one thousand dollars. The State of Arkansas has passed a law to banish all free negroes from its bounds, and it came into effect on the 1st day of January, 1860. Every free negro found there after that date will be liable to be sold into slavery, the crime of freedom being unpardonable. The Missouri Senate has before it a bill providing that all free negroes above the age of eighteen years who shall be found in the State after September, 1860, shall be sold into slavery; and that all such negroes as shall enter the State after September, 1861, and remain there twenty-four hours, shall also be sold into slavery for ever. Mississippi, Kentucky, and Georgia, and in fact, I believe, all the slave States, are legislating in the same manner. Thus the slaveholders make it almost impossible for free persons of colour to get out of the slave States, in order that they may sell them into slavery if they don't go. If no white persons travelled upon railroads except those who could get some one to vouch for their character in a penal bond of one thousand dollars, the railroad companies would soon go to the "wall." Such mean legislation is too low for comment; therefore I leave the villainous acts to speak for themselves.

But the Dred Scott decision is the crowning act of infamous Yankee legislation. The Supreme Court, the highest tribunal of the Republic, composed of nine Judge Jeffries's, chosen both from the free and slave States, has decided that no coloured person, or persons of African extraction, can ever become a citizen of the United States, or have any rights which white men are bound to respect. That is to say, in the opinion of this Court, robbery, rape, and murder are not crimes when committed by a white upon a coloured person.

Judges who will sneak from their high and honourable position down into the lowest depths of human depravity, and scrape up a decision like this, are wholly unworthy the confidence of any people. I believe such men would, if they had the power, and were it to their temporal interest, sell their country's independence, and barter away every man's birthright for a mess of pottage. Well may Thomas Campbell say—

> United States, your banner wears,
> Two emblems,—one of fame,
> Alas, the other that it bears
> Reminds us of your shame!
> The white man's liberty in types
> Stands blazoned by your stars;
> But what's the meaning of your stripes?
> They mean your Negro-scars.

481

When the time had arrived for us to start, we blew out the lights, knelt down, and prayed to our Heavenly Father mercifully to assist us, as he did his people of old, to escape from cruel bondage; and we shall ever feel that God heard and answered our prayer. Had we not been sustained by a kind, and I sometimes think special, providence, we could never have overcome the mountainous difficulties which I am now about to describe.

After this we rose and stood for a few moments in breathless silence,—we were afraid that some one might have been about the cottage listening and watching our movements. So I took my wife by the hand, stepped softly to the door, raised the latch, drew it open, and peeped out. Though there were trees all around the house, yet the foliage scarcely moved; in fact, everything appeared to be as still as death. I then whispered to my wife, "Come, my dear, let us make a desperate leap for liberty!" But poor thing, she shrank back, in a state of trepidation. I turned and asked what was the matter; she made no reply, but burst into violent sobs, and threw her head upon my breast. This appeared to touch my very heart, it caused me to enter into her feelings more fully than ever. We both saw the many mountainous difficulties that rose one after the other before our view, and knew far too well what our sad fate would have been, were we caught and forced back into our slavish den. Therefore on my wife's fully realizing the solemn fact that we had to take our lives, as it were, in our hands, and contest every inch of the thousand miles of slave territory over which we had to pass, it made her heart almost sink within her, and, had I known them at that time, I would have repeated the following encouraging lines, which may not be out of place here—

"The hill, though high, I covet to ascend,
The *difficulty will not me offend*;
For I perceive the way to life lies here:
Come, pluck up heart, let's neither faint nor fear;
Better, though difficult, the right way to go,—
Than wrong, though easy, where the end is woe."

However, the sobbing was soon over, and after a few moments of silent prayer she recovered her self-possession, and said, "Come, William, it is getting late, so now let us venture upon our perilous journey."

We then opened the door, and stepped as softly out as "moonlight upon the water." I locked the door with my own key, which I now have before me, and tiptoed across the yard into the street. I say tiptoed, because we were like persons near a tottering avalanche, afraid to move, or even breathe freely, for fear the sleeping tyrants should be aroused, and come down upon us with double vengeance, for daring to attempt to escape in the manner which we contemplated.

We shook hands, said farewell, and started in different directions for the railway station. I took the nearest possible way to the train, for fear I should be recognized by some one, and got into the negro car in which I knew I should have to ride; but my *master* (as I will now call my wife) took a longer way round, and only arrived there with the bulk of the passengers. He obtained a ticket for himself and one for his slave to Savannah, the first port, which was about two hundred miles off. My master then had the luggage stowed away, and stepped into one of the best carriages.

But just before the train moved off I peeped through the window, and, to my great astonishment, I saw the cabinet-maker with whom I had worked so long, on the platform. He stepped up to the ticketseller, and asked some question, and then commenced looking rapidly through the passengers, and into the carriages. Fully believing that we were caught, I shrank into a corner, turned my face from the door, and expected in a moment to be dragged out. The cabinet-maker looked into my master's carriage, but did not know him in his new attire, and, as God would have it, before he reached mine the bell rang, and the train moved off.

I have heard since that the cabinet-maker had a presentiment that we were about to "make tracks for parts unknown;" but, not seeing me, his suspicions vanished, until he received the startling intelligence that we had arrived freely in a free State.

As soon as the train had left the platform, my master looked round in the carriage, and was terror-stricken to find a Mr. Cray—an old friend of my wife's master, who dined with the family the day before, and knew my wife from childhood—sitting on the same seat.

The doors of the American railway carriages are at the ends. The passengers walk up the aisle, and take seats on either side; and as my master was engaged in looking out of the window, he did not see who came in.

My master's first impression, after seeing Mr. Cray, was, that he was there for the purpose of securing him. However, my master thought it was not wise to give any information respecting himself, and for fear that Mr. Cray might draw him into conversation and recognise his voice, my master resolved to feign deafness as the only means of self-defence.

After a little while, Mr. Cray said to my master, "It is a very fine morning, sir." The latter took no notice, but kept looking out of the window. Mr. Cray soon repeated this remark, in a little louder tone, but my master remained as before. This indifference attracted the attention of the passengers near, one of whom laughed out. This, I suppose, annoyed the old gentleman; so he said, "I will make him hear;" and in a loud tone of voice repeated, "It is a very fine morning, sir."

My master turned his head, and with a polite bow said, "Yes," and commenced looking out of the window again.

One of the gentlemen remarked that it was a very great

deprivation to be deaf. "Yes," replied Mr. Cray, "and I shall not trouble that fellow any more." This enabled my master to breathe a little easier, and to feel that Mr. Cray was not his pursuer after all.

The gentlemen then turned the conversation upon the three great topics of discussion in firstclass circles in Georgia, namely, Niggers, Cotton, and the Abolitionists.

My master had often heard of abolitionists, but in such a connection as to cause him to think that they were a fearful kind of wild animal. But he was highly delighted to learn, from the gentlemen's conversation, that the abolitionists were persons who were opposed to oppression; and therefore, in his opinion, not the lowest, but the very highest, of God's creatures.

Without the slightest objection on my master's part, the gentlemen left the carriage at Gordon, for Milledgeville (the capital of the State).

We arrived at Savannah early in the evening, and got into an omnibus, which stopped at the hotel for the passengers to take tea. I stepped into the house and brought my master something on a tray to the omnibus, which took us in due time to the steamer, which was bound for Charleston, South Carolina.

Soon after going on board, my master turned in; and as the captain and some of the passengers seemed to think this strange, and also questioned me respecting him, my master thought I had better get out the flannels and opodeldoc which we had prepared for the rheumatism, warm them quickly by the stove in the gentleman's saloon, and bring them to his berth. We did this as an excuse for my master's retiring to bed so early.

While at the stove one of the passengers said to me, "Buck, what have you got there?" "Opodeldoc, sir," I replied. "I should think it's opod*evil*," said a lanky swell, who was leaning back in a chair with his heels upon the back of another, and chewing tobacco as if for a wager; "it stinks enough to kill or cure twenty men. Away with it, or I reckon I will throw it overboard!"

It was by this time warm enough, so I took it to my master's berth, remained there a little while, and then went on deck and asked the steward where I was to sleep. He said there was no place provided for coloured passengers, whether slave or free. So I paced the deck till a late hour, then mounted some cotton bags, in a warm place near the funnel, sat there till morning, and then went and assisted my master to get ready for breakfast.

He was seated at the right hand of the captain, who, together with all the passengers, inquired very kindly after his health. As my master had one hand in a sling, it was my duty to carve his food. But when I went out the captain said, "You have a very attentive boy, sir; but you had better watch him like a hawk when you get on to the North. He seems all very well here, but he may act quite differently there. I know several gentlemen who have lost their valuable niggers among them d—d cut-throat abolitionists."

Before my master could speak, a rough slavedealer, who was sitting opposite, with both elbows on the table, and with a large piece of broiled fowl in his fingers, shook his head with emphasis, and in a deep Yankee tone, forced through his crowded mouth the words, "Sound doctrine, captain, very sound." He then dropped the chicken into the plate, leant back, placed his thumbs in the armholes of his fancy waistcoat, and continued, "I would not take a nigger to the North under no consideration. I have had a deal to do with niggers in my time, but I never saw one who ever had his heel upon free soil that was worth a d—n." "Now stranger," addressing my master, "if you have made up your mind to sell that ere nigger, I am your man; just mention your price, and if it isn't out of the way, I will pay for him on this board with hard silver dollars." This hard-featured, bristly-bearded, wire-headed, red-eyed monster, staring at my master as the serpent did at Eve, said, "What do you say, stranger?" He replied, "I don't wish to sell, sir; I cannot get on well without him."

"You will have to get on without him if you take him to the North," continued this man; "for I can tell ye, stranger, as a friend, I am an older cove than you, I have seen lots of this ere world, and I reckon I have had more dealings with niggers than any man living or dead. I was once employed by General Wade Hampton, for ten years, in doing nothing but breaking 'em in; and everybody knows that the General would not have a man that didn't understand his business. So I tell ye, stranger, again, you had better sell, and let me take him down to Orleans. He will do you no good if you take him across Mason's and Dixon's line; he is a keen nigger, and I can see from the cut of his eye that he is certain to run away." My master said, "I think not, sir; I have great confidence in his fidelity." "*FiDevil*," indignantly said the dealer, as his fist came down upon the edge of the saucer and upset a cup of hot coffee in a gentleman's lap. (As the scalded man jumped up the trader quietly said, "Don't disturb yourself, neighbour; accidents will happen in the best of families.") "It always makes me mad to hear a man talking about fidelity in niggers. There isn't a d—d one on 'em who wouldn't cut sticks, if he had half a chance."

By this time we were near Charleston; my master thanked the captain for his advice, and they all withdrew and went on deck, where the trader fancied he became quite eloquent. He drew a crowd around him, and with emphasis said, "Cap'en, if I was the President of this mighty United States of America, the greatest and freest country under the whole universe, I would never let no man, I don't care who he is, take a nigger into the North and bring him back here, filled to the brim, as he is sure to be, with d—d abolition vices, to taint all quiet niggers with the hellish spirit of running away. These air, cap'en, my flat-footed, every day, right up and down sentiments, and as this is a free country, cap'en, I don't care who hears 'em; for I am a Southern man, every inch on me to the backbone." "Good!" said an insignificant-looking individual of the slave-dealer stamp. "Three cheers for John C. Calhoun and the whole fair sunny South!" added the trader. So off went their hats, and out burst a terrific roar of irregular but continued cheering. My master took

487

no more notice of the dealer. He merely said to the captain that the air on deck was too keen for him, and he would therefore return to the cabin.

While the trader was in the zenith of his eloquence, he might as well have said, as one of his kit did, at a great Filibustering meeting, that "When the great American Eagle gets one of his mighty claws upon Canada and the other into South America, and his glorious and starry wings of liberty extending from the Atlantic to the Pacific, oh! then, where will England be, ye gentlemen? I tell ye, she will only serve as a pockethandkerchief for Jonathan to wipe his nose with."

On my master entering the cabin he found at the breakfast-table a young southern military officer, with whom he had travelled some distance the previous day.

After passing the usual compliments the conversation turned upon the old subject,—niggers.

The officer, who was also travelling with a manservant, said to my master, "You will excuse me, Sir, for saying I think you are very likely to spoil your boy by saying 'thank you' to him. I assure you, sir, nothing spoils a slave so soon as saying, 'thank you' and 'if you please' to him. The only way to make a nigger toe the mark, and to keep him in his place, is to storm at him like thunder, and keep him trembling like a leaf. Don't you see, when I speak to my Ned, he darts like lightning; and if he didn't I'd skin him."

Just then the poor dejected slave came in, and the officer swore at him fearfully, merely to teach my master what he called the proper way to treat me.

After he had gone out to get his master's luggage ready, the officer said, "That is the way to speak to them. If every nigger was drilled in this manner, they would be as humble as dogs, and never dare to run away.

The gentleman urged my master not to go to the North for the restoration of his health, but to visit the Warm Springs in Arkansas.

My master said, he thought the air of Philadelphia would suit his complaint best; and, not only so, he thought he could get better advice there.

The boat had now reached the wharf. The officer wished my master a safe and pleasant journey, and left the saloon.

There were a large number of persons on the quay waiting the arrival of the steamer: but we were afraid to venture out for fear that some one might recognize me; or that they had heard that we were gone, and had telegraphed to have us stopped. However, after remaining in the cabin till all the other passengers were gone, we had our luggage placed on a fly, and I took my master by the arm, and with a little difficulty he hobbled on shore, got in and drove off to the best hotel, which John C. Calhoun, and all the other great southern fire-eating statesmen, made their head-quarters while in Charleston.

On arriving at the house the landlord ran out and opened the door: but judging, from the poultices and green glasses, that my master was an invalid, he took him very tenderly by one arm and ordered his man to take the other.

My master then eased himself out, and with their assistance found no trouble in getting up the steps into the hotel. The proprietor made me stand on one side, while he paid my master the attention and homage he thought a gentleman of his high position merited.

My master asked for a bed-room. The servant was ordered to show a good one, into which we helped him. The servant returned. My master then handed me the bandages, I took them downstairs in great haste, and told the landlord my master wanted two hot poultices as quickly as possible. He rang the bell, the servant came in, to whom he said, "Run to the kitchen and tell the cook to make two hot poultices right off, for there is a gentleman upstairs very badly off indeed!"

In a few minutes the smoking poultices were brought in. I placed them in white handkerchiefs, and hurried upstairs, went into my master's apartment, shut the door, and laid them on the

489

mantel-piece. As he was alone for a little while, he thought he could rest a great deal better with the poultices off. However, it was necessary to have them to complete the remainder of the journey. I then ordered dinner, and took my master's boots out to polish them. While doing so I entered into conversation with one of the slaves. I may state here, that on the sea-coast of South Carolina and Georgia the slaves speak worse English than in any other part of the country. This is owing to the frequent importation, or smuggling in, of Africans, who mingle with the natives. Consequently the language cannot properly be called English or African, but a corruption of the two.

The shrewd son of African parents to whom I referred said to me, "Say, brudder, way you come from, and which side you goin day wid dat ar little don up buckra" (white man)?

I replied, "To Philadelphia."

"What!" he exclaimed, with astonishment, "to Philumadelphy?"

"Yes," I said.

"By squash! I wish I was going wid you! I hears um say dat dare's no slaves way over in dem parts; is um so?"

I quietly said, "I have heard the same thing."

"Well," continued he, as he threw down the boot and brush, and, placing his hands in his pockets, strutted across the floor with an air of independence—"Gorra Mighty, dem is de parts for Pompey; and I hope when you get dare you will stay, and nebber follow dat buckra back to dis hot quarter no more, let him be eber so good."

I thanked him; and just as I took the boots up and started off, he caught my hand between his two, and gave it a hearty shake, and, with tears streaming down his cheeks, said:—

"God bless you, broder, and may de Lord be wid you. When you gets de freedom, and sitin under your own wine and fig-tree, don't forget to pray for poor Pompey."

I was afraid to say much to him, but I shall never forget his earnest request, nor fail to do what little I can to release the millions of unhappy bondmen, of whom he was one.

At the proper time my master had the poultices placed on, came down, and seated himself at a table in a very brilliant dining-room, to have his dinner. I had to have something at the same time, in order to be ready for the boat; so they gave me my dinner in an old broken plate, with a rusty knife and fork, and said, "Here, boy, you go in the kitchen." I took it and went out, but did not stay more than a few minutes, because I was in a great hurry to get back to see how the invalid was getting on. On arriving I found two or three servants waiting on him; but as he did not feel able to make a very hearty dinner, he soon finished, paid the bill, and gave the servants each a trifle, which caused one of them to say to me, "Your massa is a big bug"—meaning a gentleman of distinction— "he is the greatest gentleman dat has been dis way for dis six months." I said, "Yes, he is some pumpkins," meaning the same as "big bug."

When we left Macon, it was our intention to take a steamer at Charleston through to Philadelphia; but on arriving there we found that the vessels did not run during the winter, and I have no doubt it was well for us they did not; for on the very last voyage the steamer made that we intended to go by, a fugitive was discovered secreted on board, and sent back to slavery. However, as we had also heard of the Overland Mail Route, we were all right. So I ordered a fly to the door, had the luggage placed on; we got in, and drove down to the Custom-house Office, which was near the wharf where we had to obtain tickets, to take a steamer for Wilmington, North Carolina. When we reached the building, I helped my master into the office, which was crowded with passengers. He asked for a ticket for himself and one for his slave to Philadelphia. This caused the principal officer—a very mean-looking, cheese-coloured fellow, who was sitting there— to look up at us very suspiciously, and in a fierce tone of voice he said to me, "Boy, do you belong to that gentleman?" I quickly replied, "Yes, sir" (which was quite correct). The tickets were handed out, and as my master was paying for them the chief man said to him, "I wish you to register your name here, sir, and also the name of your nigger, and pay a dollar duty on him."

My master paid the dollar, and pointing to the hand that was in the poultice, requested the officer to register his name for him. This seemed to offend the "high-bred" South Carolinian. He jumped up, shaking his head; and, cramming his hands almost through the bottom of his trousers pockets, with a slave-bullying air, said, "I shan't do it."

This attracted the attention of all the passengers. Just then the young military officer with whom my master travelled and conversed on the steamer from Savannah stepped in, somewhat the worse for brandy; he shook hands with my master, and pretended to know all about him. He said, "I know his kin (friends) like a book;" and as the officer was known in Charleston, and was going to stop there with friends, the recognition was very much in my master's favor.

The captain of the steamer, a good-looking, jovial fellow, seeing that the gentleman appeared to know my master, and perhaps not wishing to lose us as passengers, said in an off-hand sailor-like manner, "I will register the gentleman's name, and take the responsibility upon myself." He asked my master's name. He said, "William Johnson." The names were put down, I think, "Mr. Johnson and slave." The captain said, "It's all right now, Mr. Johnson." He thanked him kindly, and the young officer begged my master to go with him, and have something to drink and a cigar; but as he had not acquired these accomplishments, he excused himself, and we went on board and came off to Wilmington, North Carolina. When the gentleman finds out his mistake, he will, I have no doubt, be careful in future not to pretend to have an intimate acquaintance with an entire stranger. During the voyage the captain said, "It was rather sharp shooting this morning, Mr. Johnson. It was not out of any disrespect to you, sir; but they make it a rule to be very strict at Charleston. I have known families to be detained there with their slaves till reliable information could be received respecting them. If they were not very careful, any d—d abolitionist might take off a lot of valuable niggers."

My master said, "I suppose so," and thanked him again for helping him over the difficulty.

We reached Wilmington the next morning, and took the train for Richmond, Virginia. I have stated that the American railway carriages (or cars, as they are called), are constructed differently to those in England. At one end of some of them, in the South, there is a little apartment with a couch on both sides for the convenience of families and invalids; and as they thought my master was very poorly, he was allowed to enter one of these apartments at Petersburg, Virginia, where an old gentleman and two handsome young ladies, his daughters, also got in, and took seats in the same carriage. But before the train started, the gentleman stepped into my car, and questioned me respecting my master. He wished to know what was the matter with him, where he was from, and where he was going. I told him where he came from, and said that he was suffering from a complication of complaints, and was going to Philadelphia, where he thought he could get more suitable advice than in Georgia.

The gentleman said my master could obtain the very best advice in Philadelphia. Which turned out to be quite correct, though he did not receive it from physicians, but from kind abolitionists who understood his case much better. The gentleman also said, "I reckon your master's father hasn't any more such faithful and smart boys as you." "O, yes, sir, he has," I replied, "lots on 'em." Which was literally true. This seemed all he wished to know. He thanked me, gave me a ten-cent piece, and requested me to be attentive to my good master. I promised that I would do so, and have ever since endeavoured to keep my pledge. During the gentleman's absence, the ladies and my master had a little cosy chat. But on his return, he said, "You seem to be very much afflicted, sir." "Yes, sir," replied the gentleman in the poultices. "What seems to be the matter with you, sir; may I be allowed to ask?" "Inflammatory rheumatism, sir." "Oh! that is very bad, sir," said the kind gentleman: "I can sympathise with you; for I know from bitter experience what the rheumatism is." If he did, he knew a good deal more than Mr. Johnson.

The gentleman thought my master would feel better if he would lie down and rest himself; and as he was anxious to avoid conversation, he at once acted upon this suggestion. The ladies politely rose, took their extra shawls, and made a nice pillow for the invalid's head. My master wore a fashionable cloth cloak, which they took and covered him comfortably on the couch. After he had been lying a little while the ladies, I suppose, thought he was asleep; so one of them gave a long sigh, and said, in a quiet fascinating tone, "Papa, he seems to be a very nice young gentleman." But before papa could speak, the other lady quickly said, "Oh! dear me, I never felt so much for a gentleman in my life!" To use an American expression, "they fell in love with the wrong chap."

After my master had been lying a little while he got up, the gentleman assisted him in getting on his cloak, the ladies took their shawls, and soon they were all seated. They then insisted upon Mr. Johnson taking some of their refreshments, which of course he did, out of courtesy to the ladies. All went on enjoying themselves until they reached Richmond, where the ladies and their father left the train. But, before doing so, the good old Virginian gentleman, who appeared to be much pleased with my master, presented him with a recipe, which he said was a perfect cure for the inflammatory rheumatism. But the invalid not being able to read it, and fearing he should hold it upside down in pretending to do so, thanked the donor kindly, and placed it in his waistcoat pocket. My master's new friend also gave him his card, and requested him the next time he travelled that way to do him the kindness to call; adding, "I shall be pleased to see you, and so will my daughters." Mr. Johnson expressed his gratitude for the proffered hospitality, and said he should feel glad to call on his return. I have not the slightest doubt that he will fulfil the promise whenever that return takes place. After changing trains we went on a little beyond Fredericksburg, and took a steamer to Washington.

At Richmond, a stout elderly lady, whose whole demeanour indicated that she belonged (as Mrs. Stowe's Aunt Chloe expresses it) to one of the "firstest families," stepped into the carriage, and took a seat near my master. Seeing me passing quickly along the platform, she sprang up as if taken by a fit, and exclaimed, "Bless my soul! there goes my nigger, Ned!"

My master said, "No; that is my boy."

The lady paid no attention to this; she poked her head out of the window, and bawled to me, "You Ned, come to me, sir, you runaway rascal!"

On my looking round she drew her head in, and said to my master, "I beg your pardon, sir, I was sure it was my nigger; I never in my life saw two black pigs more alike than your boy and my Ned."

After the disappointed lady had resumed her seat, and the train had moved off, she closed her eyes, slightly raising her hands, and in a sanctified tone said to my master, "Oh! I hope, sir, your boy will not turn out to be so worthless as my Ned has. Oh! I was as kind to him as if he had been my own son. Oh! sir, it grieves me very much to think that after all I did for him he should go off without having any cause whatever."

"When did he leave you?" asked Mr. Johnson.

"About eighteen months ago, and I have never seen hair or hide of him since."

"Did he have a wife?" enquired a very respectable-looking young gentleman, who was sitting near my master and opposite to the lady.

"No, sir; not when he left, though he did have one a little before that. She was very unlike him; she was as good and as faithful a nigger as any one need wish to have. But, poor thing! she became so ill, that she was unable to do much work; so I thought it would be best to sell her, to go to New Orleans, where

495

the climate is nice and warm."

"I suppose she was very glad to go South for the restoration of her health?" said the gentleman.

"No; she was not," replied the lady, "for niggers never know what is best for them. She took on a great deal about leaving Ned and the little nigger; but, as she was so weakly, I let her go."

"Was she good-looking?" asked the young passenger, who was evidently not of the same opinion as the talkative lady, and therefore wished her to tell all she knew.

"Yes; she was very handsome, and much whiter than I am; and therefore will have no trouble in getting another husband. I am sure I wish her well. I asked the speculator who bought her to sell her to a good master. Poor thing! she has my prayers, and I know she prays for me. She was a good Christian, and always used to pray for my soul. It was through her earliest prayers," continued the lady, "that I was first led to seek forgiveness of my sins, before I was converted at the great camp-meeting."

This caused the lady to snuffle and to draw from her pocket a richly embroidered handkerchief, and apply it to the corner of her eyes. But my master could not see that it was at all soiled.

The silence which prevailed for a few moments was broken by the gentleman's saying, "As your 'July' was such a very good girl, and had served you so faithfully before she lost her health, don't you think it would have been better to have emancipated her?"

"No, indeed I do not!" scornfully exclaimed the lady, as she impatiently crammed the fine handkerchief into a little work-bag. "I have no patience with people who set niggers at liberty. It is the very worst thing you can do for them. My dear husband just before he died willed all his niggers free. But I and all our friends knew very well that he was too good a man to have ever thought of doing such an unkind and foolish thing, had he been in his right mind, and, therefore we had the will altered as it should have been in the first place."

"Did you mean, madam," asked my master, "that willing the slaves free was unjust to yourself, or unkind to them?"

496

"I mean that it was decidedly unkind to the servants themselves. It always seems to me such a cruel thing to turn niggers loose to shift for themselves, when there are so many good masters to take care of them. As for myself," continued the considerate lady, "I thank the Lord my dear husband left me and my son well provided for. Therefore I care nothing for the niggers, on my own account, for they are a great deal more trouble than they are worth, I sometimes wish that there was not one of them in the world; for the ungrateful wretches are always running away. I have lost no less than ten since my poor husband died. It's ruinous, sir!"

"But as you are well provided for, I suppose you do not feel the loss very much," said the passenger.

"I don't feel it at all," haughtily continued the good soul; "but that is no reason why property should be squandered. If my son and myself had the money for those valuable niggers, just see what a great deal of good we could do for the poor, and in sending missionaries abroad to the poor heathen, who have never heard the name of our blessed Redeemer. My dear son who is a good Christian minister has advised me not to worry and send my soul to hell for the sake of niggers; but to sell every blessed one of them for what they will fetch, and go and live in peace with him in New York. This I have concluded to do. I have just been to Richmond and made arrangements with my agent to make clean work of the forty that are left."

"Your son being a good Christian minister," said the gentleman, "It's strange he did not advise you to let the poor negroes have their liberty and go North."

"It's not at all strange, sir; it's not at all strange. My son knows what's best for the niggers; he has always told me that they were much better off than the free niggers in the North. In fact, I don't believe there are any white labouring people in the world who are as well off as the slaves."

"You are quite mistaken, madam," said the young man. "For instance, my own widowed mother, before she died, emancipated all her slaves, and sent them to Ohio, where they are getting along well. I saw several of them last summer myself."

"Well," replied the lady, "freedom may do for your ma's niggers, but it will never do for mine; and, plague them, they shall never have it; that is the word, with the bark on it."

"If freedom will not do for your slaves," replied the passenger, "I have no doubt your Ned and the other nine negroes will find out their mistake, and return to their old home.

"Blast them!" exclaimed the old lady, with great emphasis, "if I ever get them, I will cook their infernal hash, and tan their accursed black hides well for them! God forgive me," added the old soul, "the niggers will make me lose all my religion!"

By this time the lady had reached her destination. The gentleman got out at the next station beyond. As soon as she was gone, the young Southerner said to my master, "What a d—d shame it is for that old whining hypocritical humbug to cheat the poor negroes out of their liberty! If she has religion, may the devil prevent me from ever being converted!"

For the purpose of somewhat disguising myself, I bought and wore a very good second-hand white beaver, an article which I had never indulged in before. So just before we arrived at Washington, an uncouth planter, who had been watching me very closely, said to my master, "I reckon, stranger, you are '*spiling*' that ere nigger of yourn, by letting him wear such a devilish fine hat. Just look at the quality on it; the President couldn't wear a better. I should just like to go and kick it overboard." His friend touched him, and said, "Don't speak so to a gentleman." "Why not?" exclaimed the fellow. He grated his short teeth, which appeared to be nearly worn away by the incessant chewing of tobacco, and said, "It always makes me itch all over, from head to toe, to get hold of every d—d nigger I see dressed like a white man. Washington is run away with *spiled* and free niggers. If I had my way I would sell every d—d rascal of 'em way down South, where the devil would be whipped out on 'em."

This man's fierce manner made my master feel rather nervous, and therefore he thought the less he said the better; so he walked off without making any reply. In a few minutes we were landed at Washington, where we took a conveyance and hurried off to the train for Baltimore.

We left our cottage on Wednesday morning, the 21st of December, 1848, and arrived at Baltimore, Saturday evening, the 24th (Christmas Eve). Baltimore was the last slave port of any note at which we stopped.

On arriving there we felt more anxious than ever, because we knew not what that last dark night would bring forth. It is true we were near the goal, but our poor hearts were still as if tossed at sea; and, as there was another great and dangerous bar to pass, we were afraid our liberties would be wrecked, and, like the ill-fated Royal Charter, go down for ever just off the place we longed to reach.

They are particularly watchful at Baltimore to prevent slaves from escaping into Pennsylvania, which is a free State. After I had seen my master into one of the best carriages, and was just about to step into mine, an officer, a full-blooded Yankee of the lower order, saw me. He came quickly up, and, tapping me on the shoulder, said in his unmistakable native twang, together with no little display of his authority, "Where are you going, boy?" "To Philadelphia, sir," I humbly replied. "Well, what are you going there for?" "I am travelling with my master, who is in the next carriage, sir." "Well, I calculate you had better get him out; and be mighty quick about it, because the train will soon be starting. It is against my rules to let any man take a slave past here, unless he can satisfy them in the office that he has a right to take him along."

The officer then passed on and left me standing upon the platform, with my anxious heart apparently palpitating in the throat. At first I scarcely knew which way to turn. But it soon occurred to me that the good God, who had been with us thus far, would not forsake us at the eleventh hour. So with renewed hope I stepped into my master's carriage, to inform him of the difficulty. I found him sitting at the farther end, quite alone. As soon as he looked up and saw me, he smiled. I also tried to wear a cheerful countenance, in order to break the shock of the sad news. I knew what made him smile. He was aware that if we were fortunate we should reach our destination at five o'clock the next morning, and this made it the more painful to communicate what the officer had said; but, as there was no time to lose, I went up to him and asked him how he felt. He said "Much better," and that he thanked God we were getting on so nicely. I then said we were not getting on quite so well as we had anticipated. He anxiously and quickly asked what was the matter. I told him. He started as if struck by lightning, and exclaimed, "Good Heavens! William, is it possible that we are, after all, doomed to hopeless bondage?" I could say nothing, my heart was too full to speak, for at first I did not know what to do. However we knew it would never do to turn back to the "City of Destruction," like Bunyan's Mistrust and Timorous, because they saw lions in the narrow way after ascending the hill Difficulty; but press on, like noble Christian and Hopeful, to the great city in which dwelt a few "shining ones." So, after a few moments, I did all I could to encourage my companion, and we stepped out and made for the office; but how or where my master obtained sufficient courage to face the tyrants who had power to blast all we held dear, heaven only knows! Queen Elizabeth could not have been more terror-stricken, on being forced to land at the traitors' gate leading to the Tower, than we were on entering that office. We felt that our very existence was at stake, and that we must either sink or swim. But, as God was our present and mighty helper in this as well as in all former trials, we were able to keep our heads up and press forwards.

On entering the room we found the principal man, to whom my master said, "Do you wish to see me, sir?" "Yes," said this eagle-eyed officer; and he added, "It is against our rules, sir, to allow any person to take a slave out of Baltimore into Philadelphia, unless he can satisfy us that he has a right to take him along." "Why is that?" asked my master, with more firmness than could be expected. "Because, sir," continued he, in a voice and manner that almost chilled our blood, "if we should suffer any gentleman to take a slave past here into Philadelphia; and should the gentleman with whom the slave might be travelling turn out not to be his rightful owner; and should the proper master come and prove that his slave escaped on our road, we shall have him to pay for; and, therefore, we cannot let any slave pass here without receiving security to show, and to satisfy us, that it is all right."

This conversation attracted the attention of the large number of bustling passengers. After the officer had finished, a few of them said, "Chit, chit, chit;" not because they thought we were slaves endeavouring to escape, but merely because they thought my master was a slaveholder and invalid gentleman, and therefore it was wrong to detain him. The officer, observing that the passengers sympathised with my master, asked him if he was not acquainted with some gentleman in Baltimore that he could get to endorse for him, to show that I was his property, and that he had a right to take me off. He said, "No;" and added, "I bought tickets in Charleston to pass us through to Philadelphia, and therefore you have no right to detain us here." "Well, sir," said the man, indignantly, "right or no right, we shan't let you go." These sharp words fell upon our anxious hearts like the crack of doom, and made us feel that hope only smiles to deceive.

For a few moments perfect silence prevailed. My master looked at me, and I at him, but neither of us dared to speak a word, for fear of making some blunder that would tend to our detection. We knew that the officers had power to throw us into prison, and if they had done so we must have been detected and driven back, like the vilest felons, to a life of slavery, which we dreaded far more than sudden death.

We felt as though we had come into deep waters and were about being overwhelmed, and that the slightest mistake would clip asunder the last brittle thread of hope by which we were suspended, and let us down for ever into the dark and horrible pit of misery and degradation from which we were straining every nerve to escape. While our hearts were crying lustily unto Him who is ever ready and able to save, the conductor of the train that we had just left stepped in. The officer asked if we came by the train with him from Washington; he said we did, and left the room. Just then the bell rang for the train to leave; and had it been the sudden shock of an earthquake it could not have given us a greater thrill. The sound of the bell caused every eye to flash with apparent interest, and to be more steadily fixed upon us than before. But, as God would have it, the officer all at once thrust his fingers through his hair, and in a state of great agitation said, "I really don't know what to do; I calculate it is all right." He then told the clerk to run and tell the conductor to "let this gentleman and slave pass;" adding, "As he is not well, it is a pity to stop him here. We will let him go." My master thanked him, and stepped out and hobbled across the platform as quickly as possible. I tumbled him unceremoniously into one of the best carriages, and leaped into mine just as the train was gliding off towards our happy destination.

We thought of this plan about four days before we left Macon; and as we had our daily employment to attend to, we only saw each other at night. So we sat up the four long nights talking over the plan and making preparations.

We had also been four days on the journey; and as we travelled night and day, we got but very limited opportunities for sleeping. I believe nothing in the world could have kept us awake so long but the intense excitement, produced by the fear of being retaken on the one hand, and the bright anticipation of liberty on the other.

We left Baltimore about eight o'clock in the evening; and not being aware of a stoppingplace of any consequence between there and Philadelphia, and also knowing that if we were fortunate we should be in the latter place early the next morning, I thought I might indulge in a few minutes' sleep in the car; but I, like Bunyan's Christian in the arbour, went to sleep at the wrong time, and took too long a nap. So, when the train reached Havre de Grace, all the first-class passengers had to get out of the carriages and into a ferry-boat, to be ferried across the Susquehanna river, and take the train on the opposite side.

The road was constructed so as to be raised or lowered to suit the tide. So they rolled the luggagevans on to the boat, and off on the other side; and as I was in one of the apartments adjoining a baggage-car, they considered it unnecessary to awaken me, and tumbled me over with the luggage. But when my master was asked to leave his seat, he found it very dark, and cold, and raining. He missed me for the first time on the journey. On all previous occasions, as soon as the train stopped, I was at hand to assist him. This caused many slaveholders to praise me very much: they said they had never before seen a slave so attentive to his master: and therefore my absence filled him with terror and confusion; the children of Israel could not have felt more troubled on arriving at the Red Sea. So he asked the conductor if he had seen anything of his slave. The man being somewhat of an abolitionist, and believing that my master was really a slaveholder, thought he would tease him a little respecting me. So he said, "No, sir; I haven't seen anything of him for some time: I have no doubt he has run away, and is in Philadelphia, free, long before now." My master knew that there was nothing in this; so he asked the conductor if he would please to see if he could find me. The man indignantly replied, "I am no slave-hunter; and as far as I am concerned everybody must look after their own niggers." He went off and left the confused invalid to fancy whatever he felt inclined. My master at first thought I must have been kidnapped into slavery by some one, or left, or perhaps killed on the train. He also thought of stopping to see if he could hear anything of me, but he soon remembered that he had no money. That night all the money we had was consigned to my own pocket, because we thought, in case there were any pickpockets about, a slave's pocket would be the last

503

one they would look for. However, hoping to meet me some day in a land of liberty, and as he had the tickets, he thought it best upon the whole to enter the boat and come off to Philadelphia, and endeavour to make his way alone in this cold and hollow world as best he could. The time was now up, so he went on board and came across with feelings that can be better imagined than described.

After the train had got fairly on the way to Philadelphia, the guard came into my car and gave me a violent shake, and bawled out at the same time, "Boy, wake up!" I started, almost frightened out of my wits. He said, "Your master is scared half to death about you." That frightened me still more—I thought they had found him out; so I anxiously inquired what was the matter. The guard said, "He thinks you have run away from him." This made me feel quite at ease. I said, "No, sir; I am satisfied my good master doesn't think that." So off I started to see him. He had been fearfully nervous, but on seeing me he at once felt much better. He merely wished to know what had become of me.

On returning to my seat, I found the conductor and two or three other persons amusing themselves very much respecting my running away. So the guard said, "Boy, what did your master want?"[6] I replied, "He merely wished to know what had become of me." "No," said the man, "that was not it; he thought you had taken French leave, for parts unknown. I never saw a fellow so badly scared about losing his slave in my life. Now," continued the guard, "let me give you a little friendly advice. When you get to Philadelphia, run away and leave that cripple, and have your liberty." "No, sir," I indifferently replied, "I can't promise to do that." "Why not?" said the conductor, evidently much surprised;

---

6 I may state here that every man slave is called boy till he is very old, then the more respectable slaveholders call him uncle. The women are all girls till they are aged, then they are called aunts. This is the reason why Mrs. Stowe calls her characters Uncle Tom, Aunt Chloe, Uncle Tiff, &c.

"don't you want your liberty?" "Yes, sir," I replied; "but I shall never run away from such a good master as I have at present."

One of the men said to the guard, "Let him alone; I guess he will open his eyes when he gets to Philadelphia, and see things in another light." After giving me a good deal of information, which I afterwards found to be very useful, they left me alone.

I also met with a coloured gentleman on this train, who recommended me to a boarding-house that was kept by an abolitionist, where he thought I would be quite safe, if I wished to run away from my master. I thanked him kindly, but of course did not let him know who we were. Late at night, or rather early in the morning, I heard a fearful whistling of the steam-engine; so I opened the window and looked out, and saw a large number of flickering lights in the distance, and heard a passenger in the next carriage— who also had his head out of the window—say to his companion, "Wake up, old horse, we are at Philadelphia!"

The sight of those lights and that announcement made me feel almost as happy as Bunyan's Christian must have felt when he first caught sight of the cross. I, like him, felt that the straps that bound the heavy burden to my back began to pop, and the load to roll off. I also looked, and looked again, for it appeared very wonderful to me how the mere sight of our first city of refuge should have all at once made my hitherto sad and heavy heart become so light and happy. As the train speeded on, I rejoiced and thanked God with all my heart and soul for his great kindness and tender mercy, in watching over us, and bringing us safely through.

As soon as the train had reached the platform, before it had fairly stopped, I hurried out of my carriage to my master, whom I got at once into a cab, placed the luggage on, jumped in myself, and we drove off to the boarding-house which was so kindly recommended to me. On leaving the station, my master—or rather my wife, as I may now say— who had from the commencement of the journey borne up in a manner that much surprised us both, grasped me by the hand, and said,

"Thank God, William, we are safe!" and then burst into tears, leant upon me, and wept like a child. The reaction was fearful. So when we reached the house, she was in reality so weak and faint that she could scarcely stand alone. However, I got her into the apartments that were pointed out, and there we knelt down, on this Sabbath, and Christmas-day,—a day that will ever be memorable to us,—and poured out our heartfelt gratitude to God, for his goodness in enabling us to overcome so many perilous difficulties, in escaping out of the jaws of the wicked.

PART II

AFTER my wife had a little recovered herself, she threw off the disguise and assumed her own apparel. We then stepped into the sitting-room, and asked to see the landlord. The man came in, but he seemed thunderstruck on finding a fugitive slave and his wife, instead of a "young cotton planter and his nigger." As his eyes travelled round the room, he said to me, "Where is your master?" I pointed him out. The man gravely replied, "I am not joking, I really wish to see your master." I pointed him out again, but at first he could not believe his eyes; he said "he knew that was not the gentleman that came with me."

But, after some conversation, we satisfied him that we were fugitive slaves, and had just escaped in the manner I have described. We asked him if he thought it would be safe for us to stop in Philadelphia. He said he thought not, but he would call in some persons who knew more about the laws than himself. He then went out, and kindly brought in several of the leading abolitionists of the city, who gave us a most hearty and friendly welcome amongst them. As it was in December, and also as we had just left a very warm climate, they advised us not to go to Canada as we had intended, but to settle at Boston in the United States. It is true that the constitution of the Republic has always guaranteed the slaveholders the right to come into any of the so-called free States, and take their fugitives back to southern Egypt. But through the untiring, uncompromising, and manly efforts of Mr. Garrison, Wendell Phillips, Theodore Parker, and a host of other noble abolitionists of Boston and the neighbourhood, public opinion in Massachusetts had become so much opposed to slavery and to kidnapping, that it was almost impossible for any one to take a fugitive slave out of that State.

So we took the advice of our good Philadelphia friends, and settled at Boston. I shall have something to say about our sojourn there presently.

Among other friends we met with at Philadelphia, was Robert Purves, Esq., a well educated and wealthy coloured gentleman, who introduced us to Mr. Barkley Ivens, a member of the Society of Friends, and a noble and generous-hearted farmer, who lived at some distance in the country.

This good Samaritan at once invited us to go and stop quietly with his family, till my wife could somewhat recover from the fearful reaction of the past journey. We most gratefully accepted the invitation, and at the time appointed we took a steamer to a place up the Delaware river, where our new and dear friend met us with his snug little cart, and took us to his happy home. This was the first act of great and disinterested kindness we had ever received from a white person.

The gentleman was not of the fairest complexion, and therefore, as my wife was not in the room when I received the information respecting him and his anti-slavery character, she thought of course he was a quadroon like herself. But on arriving at the house, and finding out her mistake, she became more nervous and timid than ever.

As the cart came into the yard, the dear good old lady, and her three charming and affectionate daughters, all came to the door to meet us. We got out, and the gentleman said, "Go in, and make yourselves at home; I will see after the baggage." But my wife was afraid to approach them. She stopped in the yard, and said to me, "William, I thought we were coming among coloured people?" I replied, "It is all right; these are the same." "No," she said, "it is not all right, and I am not going to stop here; I have no confidence whatever in white people, they are only trying to get us back to slavery." She turned round and said, "I am going right off." The old lady then came out, with her sweet, soft, and winning smile, shook her heartily by the hand, and kindly said, "How art thou, my dear? We are all very glad to see thee and thy husband. Come in, to the fire; I dare say thou art cold and hungry after thy journey."

We went in, and the young ladies asked if she would like to go upstairs and "fix" herself before tea. My wife said, "No, I thank you; I shall only stop a little while." "But where art thou going this cold night?" said Mr. Ivens, who had just stepped in. "I don't know," was the reply. "Well, then," he continued, "I think thou hadst better take off thy things and sit near the fire; tea will soon be ready. "Yes, come, Ellen," said Mrs. Ivens, "let me assist thee;" (as she commenced undoing my wife's bonnet-strings;) "don't be frightened, Ellen, I shall not hurt a single hair of thy head. We have heard with much pleasure of the marvellous escape of thee and thy husband, and deeply sympathise with thee in all that thou hast undergone. I don't wonder at thee, poor thing, being timid; but thou needs not fear us; we would as soon send one of our own daughters into slavery as thee; so thou mayest make thyself quite at ease!" These soft and soothing words fell like balm upon my wife's unstrung nerves, and melted her to tears; her fears and prejudices vanished, and from that day she has firmly believed that there are good and bad persons of every shade of complexion.

After seeing Sally Ann and Jacob, two coloured domestics, my wife felt quite at home. After partaking of what Mrs. Stowe's Mose and Pete called a "busting supper," the ladies wished to know whether we could read. On learning we could not, they said if we liked they would teach us. To this kind offer, of course, there was no objection. But we looked rather knowingly at each other, as much as to say that they would have rather a hard task to cram anything into our thick and matured skulls.

However, all hands set to and quickly cleared away the tea-things, and the ladies and their good brother brought out the spelling and copy books and slates, &c., and commenced with their new and green pupils. We had, by stratagem, learned the alphabet while in slavery, but not the writing characters; and, as we had been such a time learning so little, we at first felt that it was a waste of time for any one at our ages to undertake to learn to read and write. But, as the ladies were so anxious that we should learn, and so willing to teach us, we concluded to give our whole minds to the work, and see what could be done. By so doing, at the end of the three weeks we remained with the good family we could spell and write our names quite legibly. They all begged us to stop longer; but, as we were not safe in the State of Pennsylvania, and also as we wished to commence doing something for a livelihood, we did not remain.

When the time arrived for us to leave for Boston, it was like parting with our relatives. We have since met with many very kind and hospitable friends, both in America and England; but we have never been under a roof where we were made to feel more at home, or where the inmates took a deeper interest in our well-being, than Mr. Barkley Ivens and his dear family. May God ever bless them, and preserve each one from every reverse of fortune!

We finally, as I have stated, settled at Boston, where we remained nearly two years, I employed as cabinet-maker and furniture broker, and my wife at her needle; and, as our little earnings in slavery were not all spent on the journey, we were getting on very well, and would have made money, if we had not been compelled by the General Government, at the bidding of the slaveholders, to break up business, and fly from under the Stars and Stripes to save our liberties and our lives.

In 1850, Congress passed the Fugitive Slave Bill, an enactment too infamous to have been thought of or tolerated by any people in the world, except the unprincipled and tyrannical Yankees. The following are a few of the leading features of the above law; which requires, under heavy penalties, that the inhabitants of the FREE States should not only refuse food and shelter to a starving, hunted human being, but also should assist, if called upon by the authorities, to seize the unhappy fugitive and send him back to slavery.

In no case is a person's evidence admitted in Court, in defence of his liberty, when arrested under this law.

If the judge decides that the prisoner is a slave, he gets ten dollars; but if he sets him at liberty, he only receives five.

After the prisoner has been sentenced to slavery, he is handed over to the United States Marshal, who has the power, at the expense of the General Government, to summon a sufficient force to take the poor creature back to slavery, and to the lash, from which he fled.

Our old masters sent agents to Boston after us. They took out warrants, and placed them in the hands of the United States Marshal to execute. But the following letter from our highly esteemed and faithful friend, the Rev. Samuel May, of Boston, to our equally dear and much lamented friend, Dr. Estlin of Bristol, will show why we were not taken into custody.

"21, *Cornhill, Boston,*
"*November 6th,* 1850.

"MY DEAR MR ESTLIN,

"I trust that in God's good providence this letter will be handed to you in safety by our good friends, William and Ellen Craft. They have lived amongst us about two years, and have proved themselves worthy, in all respects, of our confidence and regard. The laws of this republican and Christian land (tell it not in Moscow, nor in Constantinople) regard them only as slaves— chattels— personal property. But they nobly vindicated their title and right to freedom, two years since, by winning their way to it; at least, so they thought. But now, the slave power, with the aid of Daniel Webster and a band of lesser traitors, has enacted a law, which puts their dearly-bought liberties in the most imminent peril; holds out a strong temptation to every mercenary and unprincipled ruffian to become their kidnapper; and has stimulated the slaveholders generally to such desperate acts for the recovery of their fugitive property, as have never

511

before been enacted in the history of this government.

"Within a fortnight, two fellows from Macon, Georgia, have been in Boston for the purpose of arresting our friends William and Ellen. A writ was served against them from the United States District Court; but it was not served by the United States Marshal; why not, is not certainly known: perhaps through fear, for a general feeling of indignation, and a cool determination not to allow this young couple to be taken from Boston into slavery, was aroused, and pervaded the city. It is understood that one of the judges told the Marshal that he would not be authorised in breaking the door of Craft's house. Craft kept himself close within the house, armed himself, and awaited with remarkable composure the event. Ellen, in the meantime, had been taken to a retired place out of the city. The Vigilance Committee (appointed at a late meeting in Fanueil Hall) enlarged their numbers, held an almost permanent session, and appointed various subcommittees to act in different ways. One of these committees called repeatedly on Messrs. Hughes and Knight, the slave-catchers, and requested and advised them to leave the city. At first they peremptorily refused to do so, "till they got hold of the niggers.' On complaint of different persons, these two fellows were several times arrested, carried before one of our county courts, and held to bail on charges of 'conspiracy to kidnap,' and of 'defamation,' in calling William and Ellen 'slaves.' At length, they became so alarmed, that they left the city by an indirect route, evading the vigilance of many persons who were on the look-out for them. Hughes, at one time, was near losing his life at the hands of an infuriated coloured man. While these men remained in the city, a prominent whig gentleman sent word to William Craft, that if he would submit peaceably to an arrest, he and his wife should be bought from their owners, cost what it might. Craft replied, in effect, that he was in a measure the representative of all the other fugitives in Boston, some 200 or 300 in number; that, if he gave up, they would all be at the mercy of the slave-catchers, and must fly from the city at any sacrifice; and that, if his freedom could be bought for two cents, he would not consent to compromise the matter in such a way. This event has stirred up the slave spirit of the country, south and north; the United States government is determined to try its hand in enforcing the Fugitive Slave law; and William and Ellen Craft would be prominent objects of the slaveholders' vengeance. Under these circumstances, it is the almost unanimous opinion of their best friends, that they should quit America as speedily as possible, and seek an asylum in England! Oh! shame, shame upon us, that Americans, whose fathers fought against Great Britain, in order to be *free*, should have to acknowledge this disgraceful fact! God gave us a fair and goodly heritage in this land, but man has cursed it with his devices and crimes against human souls and human rights. Is America the 'land of the free, and the home of the brave?' God knows it is not; and we know it too. A brave young man and a virtuous young woman must fly the American shores, and seek, under the shadow of the British throne, the enjoyment of 'life, liberty, and the pursuit of happiness.'

"But I must pursue my plain, sad story. All day long, I have been busy planning a safe way for William and Ellen to leave Boston. We dare not allow them to go on board a vessel, even in the port of Boston; for the writ is yet in the Marshal's hands, and he *may* be waiting an opportunity to serve it; so I am expecting to accompany them to-morrow to Portland, Maine, which is beyond the reach of the Marshal's authority; and there I hope to see them on board a British steamer.

"This letter is written to introduce them to you. I know your infirm health; but I am sure, if you were stretched on your bed in your last illness, and could lift your hand at all, you would extend it to welcome these poor hunted fellow-creatures. Henceforth, England is their nation and their home. It is with real regret for our personal loss in their departure, as well as burning shame for the land that is not worthy of them, that we send them away, or rather allow them to go. But, with all the resolute courage they have shown in a most trying hour, they themselves see it is the part of a foolhardy rashness to attempt to stay here longer.

"I must close; and with many renewed thanks for all your kind words and deeds towards us,

"I am, very respectfully yours,

"SAMUEL MAY, JUN."

Our old masters, having heard how their agents were treated at Boston, wrote to Mr. Filmore, who was then President of the States, to know what he could do to have us sent back to slavery. Mr. Filmore said that we should be returned. He gave instructions for military force to be sent to Boston to assist the officers in making the arrest. Therefore we, as well as our friends (among whom was George Thompson, Esq., late M.P. for the Tower Hamlets—the slave's long-tried, self-sacrificing friend, and eloquent advocate) thought it best, at any sacrifice, to leave the mock-free Republic, and come to a country where we and our dear little ones can be truly free.—"No one daring to molest or make us afraid." But, as the officers were watching every vessel that left the port to prevent us from escaping, we had to take the expensive and tedious overland route to Halifax.

We shall always cherish the deepest feelings of gratitude to the Vigilance Committee of Boston (upon which were many of the leading abolitionists), and also to our numerous friends, for the very kind and noble manner in which they assisted us to preserve our liberties and to escape from Boston, as it were like Lot from Sodom, to a place of refuge, and finally to this truly free and glorious country; where no tyrant, let his power be ever so absolute over his poor trembling victims at home, dare come and lay violent hands upon us or upon our dear little boys (who had the good fortune to be born upon British soil), and reduce us to the legal level of the beast that perisheth. Oh! may God

514

bless the thousands of unflinching, disinterested abolitionists of America, who are labouring through evil as well as through good report, to cleanse their country's escutcheon from the foul and destructive blot of slavery, and to restore to every bondman his God-given rights; and may God ever smile upon England and upon England's good, much-beloved, and deservedly-honoured Queen, for the generous protection that is given to unfortunate refugees of every rank, and of every colour and clime.

On the passing of the Fugitive Slave Bill, the following learned doctors, as well as a host of lesser traitors, came out strongly in its defence.

The Rev. Dr. Gardiner Spring, an eminent Presbyterian Clergyman of New York, well known in this country by his religious publications, declared from the pulpit that, "if by one prayer he could liberate every slave in the world he would not dare to offer it."

The Rev. Dr. Joel Parker, of Philadelphia, in the course of a discussion on the nature of Slavery, says, "What, then, are the evils inseparable from slavery? There is not one that is not equally inseparable from depraved human nature in other lawful relations."

The Rev. Moses Stuart, D.D., (late Professor in the Theological College of Andover), in his vindication of this Bill, reminds his readers that "many Southern slaveholders are true *Christians*." That "sending back a fugitive to them is not like restoring one to an idolatrous people." That "though we may *pity* the fugitive, yet the Mosaic Law does not authorize the rejection of the claims of the slaveholders to their stolen or strayed *property*."

The Rev. Dr. Spencer, of Brooklyn, New York, has come forward in support of the "Fugitive Slave Bill," by publishing a sermon entitled the "Religious Duty of Obedience to the Laws," which has elicited the highest encomiums from Dr. Samuel H. Cox, the Presbyterian minister of Brooklyn (notorious both in this country and America for his sympathy with the slaveholder).

The Rev. W. M. Rogers, an orthodox minister of Boston,

515

delivered a sermon in which he says, "When the slave asks me to stand between him and his master, what does he ask? He asks me to murder a nation's life; and I will not do it, because I have a conscience,— because there is a God." He proceeds to affirm that if resistance to the carrying out of the "Fugitive Slave Law" should lead the magistracy to call the citizens to arms, their duty was to obey and "if ordered to take human life, in the name of God to take it;" and he concludes by admonishing the fugitives to "hearken to the Word of God, and to count their own masters worthy of all honour."

The Rev. William Crowell, of Waterfield, State of Maine, printed a Thanksgiving Sermon of the same kind, in which he calls upon his hearers not to allow "excessive sympathies for a few hundred fugitives to blind them so that they may risk increased suffering to the millions already in chains."

The Rev. Dr. Taylor, an Episcopal Clergyman of New Haven, Connecticut, made a speech at a Union Meeting, in which he deprecates the agitation on the law, and urges obedience to it; asking,—"Is that article in the Constitution contrary to the law of Nature, of nations, or to the will of God? Is it so? Is there a shadow of reason for saying it? I have not been able to discover it. Have I not shown you it is lawful to deliver up, in compliance with the laws, fugitive slaves, for the high, the great, the momentous interests of those [Southern] States?"

The Right Rev. Bishop Hopkins, of Vermont, in a Lecture at Lockport, says, "It was warranted by the Old Testament;" and inquires, "What effect had the Gospel in doing away with slavery? None whatever." Therefore he argues, as it is expressly permitted by the Bible, it does not in itself involve any sin; but that every Christian is authorised by the Divine Law to own slaves, provided they were not treated with unnecessary cruelty.

The Rev. Orville Dewey, D.D., of the Unitarian connexion, maintained in his lectures that the safety of the Union is not to be hazarded for the sake of the African race. He declares that, for his part, he would send his own brother or child into slavery, if needed to preserve the Union between the free and the slaveholding States; and, counselling the slave to similar magnanimity, thus exhorts him:—"*Your right to be free is not absolute, unqualified, irrespective of all consequences.* If my espousal of your claim is likely to involve your race and mine together in disasters infinitely greater than your personal servitude, then you ought not to be free. In such a case personal rights ought to be sacrificed to the general good. You yourself ought to see this, and be willing to suffer for a while — one for many."

If the Doctor is prepared, he is quite at liberty to sacrifice his "personal rights to the general good." But, as I have suffered a long time in slavery, it is hardly fair for the Doctor to advise me to go back. According to his showing, he ought rather to take my place. That would be practically carrying out his logic, as respects "suffering awhile —one for many."

In fact, so eager were they to prostrate themselves before the great idol of slavery, and, like Balaam, to curse instead of blessing the people whom God had brought out of bondage, that they in bring up obsolete passages from the Old Testament to justify their downward course, overlooked, or would not see, the following verses, which show very clearly, according to the Doctor's own textbook, that the slaves have a right to run away, and that it is unscriptural for any one to send them back.

In the 23rd chapter of Deuteronomy, 15th and 16th verses, it is thus written:—"Thou shalt not deliver unto his master the servant which is escaped from his master unto thee. He shall dwell with thee, even among you, in that place which he shall choose in one of thy gates, where it liketh him best: thou shalt not oppress him."

"Hide the outcast. Bewray not him that wandereth. Let mine outcasts dwell with thee. Be thou a covert to them from the face of the spoiler." —(Isa. xvi. 3, 4.)

The great majority of the American ministers are not content with uttering sentences similar to the above, or remaining wholly indifferent to the cries of the poor bondman; but they do all they can to blast the reputation, and to muzzle the mouths, of the few good men who dare to beseech the God of mercy "to loose the bonds of wickedness, to undo the heavy burdens, and let the oppressed go free." These reverend gentlemen pour a terrible cannonade upon "Jonah," for refusing to carry God's message against Nineveh, and tell us about the whale in which he was entombed; while they utterly overlook the existence of the whales which trouble their republican waters, and know not that they themselves are the "Jonahs" who threaten to sink their ship of state, by steering in an unrighteous direction. We are told that the whale vomited up the runaway prophet. This would not have seemed so strange, had it been one of the above lukewarm Doctors of Divinity whom he had swallowed; for even a whale might find such a morsel difficult of digestion.

"I venerate the man whose heart is warm,
  Whose hands are pure; whose doctrines and whose life
  Coincident, exhibit lucid proof
  That he is honest in the sacred cause."

"But grace abused brings forth the foulest deeds,
  As richest soil the most luxuriant weeds."

I must now leave the reverend gentlemen in the hands of Him who knows best how to deal with a recreant ministry.

I do not wish it to be understood that all the ministers of the States are of the Balaam stamp. There are those who are as uncompromising with slaveholders as Moses was with Pharaoh, and, like Daniel, will never bow down before the great false God that has been set up.

On arriving at Portland, we found that the steamer we intended to take had run into a schooner the previous night, and was lying up for repairs; so we had to wait there, in fearful suspense, for two or three days. During this time, we had the honour of being the guest of the late and much lamented Daniel Oliver, Esq., one of the best and most hospitable men in the State. By simply fulfilling the Scripture injunction, to take in the stranger, &c., he ran the risk of incurring a penalty of 2,000 dollars, and twelve months' imprisonment.

But neither the Fugitive Slave Law, nor any other Satanic enactment, can ever drive the spirit of liberty and humanity out of such noble and generous-hearted men.

May God ever bless his dear widow, and eventually unite them in His courts above!

We finally got off to St. John's, New Brunswick, where we had to wait two days for the steamer that conveyed us to Windsor, Nova Scotia.

On going into a hotel at St. John's, we met the butler in the hall, to whom I said, "We wish to stop here to-night." He turned round, scratching his head, evidently much put about. But thinking that my wife was white, he replied, "We have plenty of room for the lady, but I don't know about yourself; we never take in coloured folks." "Oh, don't trouble about me," I said; "if you have room for the lady, that will do; so please have the luggage taken to a bed-room." Which was immediately done, and my wife went upstairs into the apartment.

After taking a little walk in the town, I returned, and asked to see the "lady." On being conducted to the little sitting-room, where she then was, I entered without knocking, much to the surprise of the whole house. The "lady" then rang the bell, and ordered dinner for two. "Dinner for two, mum!" exclaimed the waiter, as he backed out of the door. "Yes, for two," said my wife. In a little while the stout, red-nosed butler, whom we first met, knocked at the door. I called out, "Come in." On entering, he rolled his whisky eyes at me, and then at my wife, and said, in a very solemn tone, "Did you order dinner for two, mum?" "Yes, for two," my wife again replied. This confused the chubby butler more than ever; and, as the landlord was not in the house, he seemed at a loss what to do.

519

When dinner was ready, the maid came in and said, "Please, mum, the Missis wishes to know whether you will have dinner up now, or wait till your friend arrives?" "I will have it up at once, if you please." "Thank you, mum," continued the maid, and out she glided.

After a good deal of giggling in the passage, some one said, "You are in for it, butler, after all; so you had better make the best of a bad job." But before dinner was sent up, the landlord returned, and having heard from the steward of the steamer by which we came that we were bound for England, the proprietor's native country, he treated us in the most respectful manner.

At the above house, the boots (whose name I forget) was a fugitive slave, a very intelligent and active man, about forty-five years of age. Soon after his marriage, while in slavery, his bride was sold away from him, and he could never learn where the poor creature dwelt. So after remaining single for many years, both before and after his escape, and never expecting to see again, nor even to hear from, his longlost partner, he finally married a woman at St. John's. But, poor fellow, as he was passing down the street one day, he met a woman; at the first glance they nearly recognized each other; they both turned round and stared, and unconsciously advanced, till she screamed and flew into his arms. Her first words were, "Dear, are you married?" On his answering in the affirmative, she shrank from his embrace, hung her head, and wept. A person who witnessed this meeting told me it was most affecting.

This couple knew nothing of each other's escape or whereabouts. The woman had escaped a few years before to the free States, by secreting herself in the hold of a vessel; but as they tried to get her back to bondage, she fled to New Brunswick for that protection which her native country was too mean to afford.

The man at once took his old wife to see his new one, who was also a fugitive slave, and as they all knew the workings of the infamous system of slavery, the could (as no one else can,) sympathise with each other's misfortune.

According to the rules of slavery, the man and his first wife were already divorced, but not morally; and therefore it was arranged between the three that he should live only with the lastly married wife, and allow the other one so much a week, as long as she requested his assistance.

After staying at St. John's two days, the steamer arrived, which took us to Windsor, where we found a coach bound for Halifax. Prejudice against colour forced me on the top in the rain. On arriving within about seven miles of the town, the coach broke down and was upset. I fell upon the big crotchety driver, whose head stuck in the mud; and as he "always objected to niggers riding inside with white folks," I was not particularly sorry to see him deeper in the mire than myself. All of us were scratched and bruised more or less. After the passengers had crawled out as best they could, we all set off, and paddled through the deep mud and cold and rain, to Halifax.

On leaving Boston, it was our intention to reach Halifax at least two or three days before the steamer from Boston touched there, en route for Liverpool; but, having been detained so long at Portland and St. John's, we had the misfortune to arrive at Halifax at dark, just two hours after the steamer had gone; consequently we had to wait there a fortnight, for the Cambria.

The coach was patched up, and reached Halifax with the luggage, soon after the passengers arrived. The only respectable hotel that was then in the town had suspended business, and was closed; so we went to the inn, opposite the market, where the coach stopped: a most miserable, dirty hole it was.

Knowing that we were still under the influence of the low Yankee prejudice, I sent my wife in with the other passengers, to engage a bed for herself and husband. I stopped outside in the rain till the coach came up. If I had gone in and asked for a bed they would have been quite full. But as they thought my wife was white, she had no difficulty in securing apartments, into which the luggage was afterwards carried. The landlady, observing that I took an interest in the baggage, became somewhat uneasy, and went into my wife's room, and said to her, "Do you know the dark man downstairs?" "Yes, he is my husband." "Oh! I mean the black man—the *nigger*?" "I quite understand you; he is my husband." "My God!" exclaimed the woman as she flounced out and banged to the door. On going upstairs, I heard what had taken place: but, as we were there, and did not mean to leave that night, we did not disturb ourselves. On our ordering tea, the landlady sent word back to say that we must take it in the kitchen, or in our bed-room, as she had no other room for "niggers." We replied that we were not particular, and that they could sent it up to our room,—which they did.

After the pro-slavery persons who were staying there heard that we were in, the whole house became agitated, and all sorts of oaths and fearful threats were heaped upon the "d—d niggers, for coming among white folks." Some of them said they would not stop there a minute if there was another house to go to.

The mistress came up the next morning to know how long we wished to stop. We said a fortnight. "Oh! dear me, it is impossible for us to accommodate you, and I think you had better go: you must understand, I have no prejudice myself; I think a good deal of the coloured people, and have always been their friend; but if you stop here we shall lose all our customers, which we can't do nohow." We said we were glad to hear that she had "no prejudice," and was such a staunch friend to the coloured people. We also informed her that we would be sorry for her "customers" to leave on our account; and as it was not our intention to interfere with anyone, it was foolish for them to be frightened away. However, if she would get us a comfortable place, we would be glad to leave. The landlady said she would go out and try. After spending the whole morning in canvassing the town, she came to our room and said, "I have been from one end of the place to the other, but everybody is full." Having a little foretaste of the vulgar prejudice of the town, we did not wonder at this result. However, the landlady gave me the address of some respectable coloured families, whom she thought, "under the circumstances," might be induced to take us. And, as we were not at all comfortable—being compelled to sit, eat and sleep, in the same small room—we were quite willing to change our quarters.

I called upon the Rev. Mr. Cannady, a truly goodhearted Christian man, who received us at a word; and both he and his kind lady treated us handsomely, and for a nominal charge.

My wife and myself were both unwell when we left Boston, and, having taken fresh cold on the journey to Halifax, we were laid up there under the doctor's care, nearly the whole fortnight. I had much worry about getting tickets, for they baffled us shamefully at the Cunard office. They at first said that they did not book till the steamer came; which was not the fact. When I called again, they said they knew the steamer would come full from Boston, and therefore we had "better try to get to Liverpool by other means." Other mean Yankee excuses were made; and it was not till an influential gentleman, to whom Mr. Francis Jackson, of Boston, kindly gave us a letter, went and rebuked them, that we were able to secure our tickets. So when we went on board my wife was very poorly, and was also so ill on the voyage that I did not believe she could live to see Liverpool.

However, I am thankful to say she arrived; and, after laying up at Liverpool very ill for two or three weeks, gradually recovered.

It was not until we stepped upon the shore at Liverpool that we were free from every slavish fear.

We raised our thankful hearts to Heaven, and could have knelt down, like the Neapolitan exiles, and kissed the soil; for we felt that from slavery

"Heaven sure had kept this spot of earth uncurs'd,
To show how all lthings were created first."

In a few days after we landed, the Rev. Francis Bishop and his lady came and invited us to be their guests; to whose unlimited kindness and watchful care my wife owes, in a great degree, her restoration to health.

We enclosed our letter from the Rev. Mr. May to Mr. Estlin, who at once wrote to invite us to his house at Bristol. On arriving there, both Mr. and Miss Estlin received us as cordially as did our first good Quaker friends in Pennsylvania. It grieves me much to have to mention that he is no more. Everyone who knew him can truthfully say—

> "Peace to the memory of a man of worth,
> A man of letters, and of manners too!
> Of manners sweet as Virtue always wears
> When gay Good-nature dresses her in smiles."

It was principally through the extreme kindness of Mr. Estlin, the Right Hon. Lady Noel Byron, Miss Harriet Martineau, Mrs. Reid, Miss Sturch, and a few other good friends, that my wife and myself were able to spend a short time at a school in this country, to acquire a little of that education which we were so shamefully deprived of while in the house of bondage. The school is under the supervision of the Misses Lushington, D.C.L. During our stay at the school we received the greatest attention from every one; and I am particularly indebted to Thomas Wilson, Esq., of Bradmore House, Chiswick, (who was then the master,) for the deep interest he took in trying to get me on in my studies. We shall ever fondly and gratefully cherish the memory of our endeared and departed friend, Mr. Estlin. We, as well as the Anti-Slavery cause, lost a good friend in him. However, if departed spirits in Heaven are conscious of the wickedness of this world, and are allowed to speak, he will never fail to plead in the presence of the angelic host, and before the great and just Judge, for downtrodden and outraged humanity.

"Therefore I cannot think thee wholly gone;
    The better part of thee is with us still;
Thy soul its hampering clay aside hath thrown,
    And only freer wrestles with the ill.

"Thou livest in the life of all good things;
    What words thou spak'st for Freedom shall not die;
Thou sleepest not, for now thy Love hath wings
    To soar where hence thy hope could hardly fly.

"And often, from that other world, on this
    Some gleams from great souls gone before may shine,
To shed on struggling hearts a clearer bliss,
    And clothe the Right with lustre more divine.

"Farewell! good man, good angel now! this hand
    Soon, like thine own, shall lose its cunning, too;
Soon shall this soul, like thine, bewildered stand,
    Then leap to thread the free unfathomed blue."

— JAMES RUSSELL LOWELL

* * * * *

In the preceding pages I have not dwelt upon the great barbarities which are practised upon the slaves; because I wish to present the system in its mildest form, and to show that the "tender mercies of the wicked are cruel." But I do now, however, most solemnly declare, that a very large majority of the American slaves are over-worked, under-fed, and frequently unmercifully flogged.

I have often seen slaves tortured in every conceivable manner. I have seen him hunted down and torn by bloodhounds. I have seen them shamefully beaten, and branded with hot irons. I have seen them hunted, and even burned alive at the stake, frequently for offences that would be applauded if committed by white persons for similar purposes.

In short, it is well known in England, if not all over the world, that the Americans, as a people, are notoriously mean and cruel towards all coloured persons, whether they are bond or free.

> "Oh, tyrant, thou who sleepest
> On a volcano, from whose pent-up wrath,
> Already some red flashes bursting up,
> Beware!"

TWENTY-TWO YEARS A SLAVE, AND FORTY YEARS A FREEMAN

BY AUSTIN STEWARD

First Published in 1857

CHAPTER I

SLAVE LIFE ON THE PLANTATION

I was born in Prince William County, Virginia. At seven years of age, I found myself a slave on the plantation of Capt. William Helm. Our family consisted of my father and mother—whose names were Robert and Susan Steward—a sister, Mary, and myself. As was the usual custom, we lived in a small cabin, built of rough boards, with a floor of earth, and small openings in the sides of the cabin were substituted for windows. The chimney was built of sticks and mud; the door, of rough boards; and the whole was put together in the rudest possible manner. As to the furniture of this rude dwelling, it was procured by the slaves themselves, who were occasionally permitted to earn a little money after their day's toil was done. I never knew Capt. H. to furnish his slaves with household utensils of any description.

The amount of provision given out on the plantation per week, was invariably one peck of corn or meal for each slave. This allowance was given in meal when it could be obtained; when it could not, they received corn, which they pounded in mortars after they returned from their labor in the field. The slaves on our plantation were provided with very little meat In addition to the peck of corn or meal, they were allowed a little salt and a few herrings. If they wished for more, they were obliged to earn it by over-work. They were permitted to cultivate small gardens, and were thereby enabled to provide themselves with many trifling conveniences. But these gardens were only allowed to some of the more industrious. Capt. Helm allowed his slaves a small quantity of meat during harvest time, but when the harvest was over they were obliged to fall back on the old allowance.

It was usual for men and women to work side by side on our plantation; and in many kinds of work, the women were compelled to do as much as the men. Capt. H. employed an overseer, whose business it was to look after each slave in the field, and see that he performed his task. The overseer always went around with a whip, about nine feet long, made of the toughest kind of cowhide, the but-end of which was loaded with lead, and was about four or five inches in circumference, running to a point at the opposite extremity. This made a dreadful instrument of torture, and, when in the hands of a cruel overseer, it was truly fearful. With it, the skin of an ox or a horse could be cut through. Hence, it was no uncommon thing to see the poor slaves with their backs mangled in a most horrible manner. Our overseer, thus armed with his cowhide, and with a large bull-dog behind him, followed the slaves all day; and, if one of them fell in the rear from any cause, this cruel weapon was plied with terrible force. He would strike the dog one blow and the slave another, in order to keep the former from tearing the delinquent slave in pieces,—such was the ferocity of his canine attendant.

It was the rule for the slaves to rise and be ready for their task by sun-rise, on the blowing of a horn or conch-shell; and woe be to the unfortunate, who was not in the field at the time appointed, which was in thirty minutes from the first sounding of the horn. I have heard the poor creatures beg as for their lives, of the inhuman overseer, to desist from his cruel punishment. Hence, they were usually found in the field "betimes in the morning," (to use an old Virginia phrase), where they worked until nine o'clock. They were then allowed thirty minutes to eat their morning meal, which consisted of a little bread. At a given signal, all hands were compelled to return to their work. They toiled until noon, when they were permitted to take their breakfast, which corresponds to our dinner.

On our plantation, it was the usual practice to have one of the old slaves set apart to do the cooking. All the field hands were required to give into the hands of the cook a certain portion of their weekly allowance, either in dough or meal, which was prepared in the following manner. The cook made a hot fire and rolled up each person's portion in some cabbage leaves, when they could be obtained, and placed it in a hole in the ashes, carefully covered with the same, where it remained until done. Bread baked in this way is very sweet and good. But cabbage leaves could not always be obtained. When this was the case, the bread was little better than a mixture of dough and ashes, which was not very palatable. The time allowed for breakfast, was one hour. At the signal, all hands were obliged to resume their toil. The overseer was always on hand to attend to all delinquents, who never failed to feel the blows of his heavy whip.

The usual mode of punishing the poor slaves was, to make them take off their clothes to the bare back, and then tie their hands before them with a rope, pass the end of the rope over a beam, and draw them up till they stood on the tips of their toes. Sometimes they tied their legs together and placed a rail between. Thus prepared, the overseer proceeded to punish the poor, helpless victim. Thirty-nine was the number of lashes ordinarily inflicted for the most trifling offence.

Who can imagine a position more painful? Oh, who, with feelings of common humanity, could look quietly on such torture? Who could remain unmoved, to see a fellow-creature thus tied, unable to move or to raise a hand in his own defence; scourged on his bare back, with a cowhide, until the blood flows in streams from his quivering flesh? And for what? Often for the most trifling fault; and, as sometimes occurs, because a mere whim or caprice of his brutal overseer demands it. Pale with passion, his eyes flashing and his stalwart frame trembling with rage, like some volcano, just ready to belch forth its fiery contents, and, in all its might and fury, spread death and destruction all around, he continues to wield the bloody lash on the broken flesh of the poor, pleading slave, until his arm

531

grows weary, or he sinks down, utterly exhausted, on the very spot where already stand the pools of blood which his cruelty has drawn from thee mangled body of his helpless victim, and within the hearing of those agonized groans and feeble cries of "Oh do, Massa! Oh do, Massa! Do, Lord, have mercy! Oh, Lord, have mercy!" &c.

Nor is this cruel punishment inflicted on the bare backs of the male portion of slaves only. Oh no! The slave husband must submit without a murmur, to see the form of his cherished, but wretched wife, not only exposed to the rude gaze of a beastly tyrant, but he must unresistingly see the heavy cowhide descend upon her shrinking flesh, and her manacled limbs writhe in inexpressible torture, while her piteous cries for help ring through his ears unanswered. The wild throbbing of his heart must be suppressed, and his righteous indignation find no voice, in the presence of the human monster who holds dominion over him.

After the infuriated and heartless overseer had satiated his thirst for vengeance, on the disobedient or delinquent slave, he was untied, and left to crawl away as best he could; sometimes on his hands and knees, to his lonely and dilapidated cabin, where, stretched upon the cold earth, he lay weak and bleeding and often faint from the loss of blood, without a friend who dare administer to his necessities, and groaning in the agony of his crushed spirit. In his cabin, which was not as good as many of our stables at the North, he might lie for weeks before recovering sufficient strength to resume the labor imposed upon him, and all this time without a bed or bed clothing, or any of the necessaries considered so essential to the sick.

Perhaps some of his fellow-slaves might come and bathe his wounds in warm water, to prevent his clothing from tearing open his flesh anew, and thus make the second suffering well nigh equal to the first; or they might from their scanty store bring him such food as they could spare, to keep him from suffering hunger, and offer their sympathy, and then drag their own weary bodies to their place of rest, after their daily task was finished.

Oh, you who have hearts to feel; you who have kind friends around you, in sickness and in sorrow, think of the sufferings of the helpless, destitute, and down-trodden slave. Has sickness laid its withering hand upon you, or disappointment blasted your fairest earthly prospects, still, the outgushings of an affectionate heart are not denied you, and you may look forward with hope to a bright future. Such a hope seldom animates the heart of the poor slave. He toils on, in his unrequited labor, looking only to the grave to find a quiet resting place, where he will be free from the oppressor.

CHAPTER II

AT THE GREAT HOUSE

When eight years of age, I was taken to the "great house," or the family mansion of my master, to serve as an errand boy, where I had to stand in the presence of my master's family all the day, and a part of the night, ready to do any thing which they commanded me to perform.

My master's family consisted of himself and wife, and seven children. His overseer, whose name was Barsly Taylor, had also a wife and five children. These constituted the white population on the plantation. Capt. Helm was the owner of about one hundred slaves, which made the residents on the plantation number about one hundred and sixteen persons in all. One hundred and seven of them, were required to labor for the benefit of the remaining nine, who possessed that vast domain; and one hundred of the number doomed to unrequited toil, under the lash of a cruel task-master during life, with no hope of release this side of the grave, and as far as the cruel oppressor is concerned, shut out from hope beyond it.

And here let me ask, why is this practice of working slaves half clad, poorly fed, with nothing or nearly so, to stimulate them to exertion, but fear of the lash? Do the best interests of our common country require it? I think not. Did the true interest of Capt. Helm demand it? Whatever may have been his opinion, I cannot think it did. Can it be for the best interest or good of the enslaved? Certainly not; for there is no real inducement for the slaveholder to make beasts of burden of his fellow men, but that which was frankly acknowledged by Gibbs and other

534

pirates: "we have the power,"—the power to rob and murder on the high seas!—which they will undoubtedly continue to hold, until overtaken by justice; which will certainly come some time, just as sure as that a righteous God reigns over the earth or rules in heaven.

Some have attempted to apologize for the enslaving of the Negro, by saying that they are inferior to the Anglo-Saxon race in every respect. This charge I deny; it is utterly false. Does not the Bible inform us that "God hath created of one blood all the nations of the earth?" And certainly in stature and physical force the colored man is quite equal to his white brother, and in many instances his superior; but were it otherwise, I can not see why the more favored class should enslave the other. True, God has given to the African a darker complexion than to his white brother; still, each have the same desires and aspirations. The food required for the sustenance of one is equally necessary for the other. Naturally or physically, they alike require to be warmed by the cheerful fire, when chilled by our northern winter's breath; and alike they welcome the cool spring and the delightful shade of summer. Hence, I have come to the conclusion that God created all men free and equal, and placed them upon this earth to do good and benefit each other, and that war and slavery should be banished from the face of the earth.

My dear reader will not understand me to say, that all nations are alike intelligent, enterprising and industrious, for we all know that it is far otherwise; but to man, and not to our Creator, should the fault be charged. But, to resume our narrative,

Capt. Helm was not a very hard master; but generally was kind and pleasant. Indulgent when in good humor, but like many of the southerners, terrible when in a passion. He was a great sportsman, and very fond of company. He generally kept one or two race horses, and a pack of hounds for fox-hunting, which at that time, was a very common and fashionable diversion in that section of country. He was not only a sportsman, but a gamester, and was in the habit of playing cards, and sometimes betting very high and losing accordingly.

I well remember an instance of the kind: it was when he played cards with a Mr. W. Graham, who won from him in one sweep, two thousand and seven hundred dollars in all, in the form of a valuable horse, prized at sixteen hundred dollars, another saddle-horse of less value, one slave, and his wife's gold watch. The company decided that all this was fairly won, but Capt. Holm demurred, and refused to give up the property until an application was made to Gen. George Washington, ("the father of his country,") who decided that Capt. Helm had lost the game, and that Mr. Graham had fairly won the property, of which Mr. G. took immediate possession, and conveyed to his own plantation.

Capt. Helm was not a good business man, unless we call horse-racing, fox-hunting, and card-playing, business. His overseer was entrusted with every thing on the plantation, and allowed to manage about as he pleased, while the Captain enjoyed himself in receiving calls from his wealthy neighbors, and in drinking what he called "grog," which was no more nor less than whisky, of which he was extremely fond, notwithstanding his cellar contained the choicest wines and liquors. To show his partiality for his favorite beverage, I will relate an incident which occurred between Capt. Helm and Col. Charles Williamson. The Colonel, believing wine to be a healthier beverage than whisky, accepted a bet made by Capt. Helm, of one thousand dollars, that he would live longer and drink whisky, than the Colonel, who drank wine. Shortly after, Col. Williamson was called home by the British government, and while on his way to England, died, and his body, preserved in a cask of brandy, was taken home. The bet Capt. Helm made considerable effort to get, but was unsuccessful.

Mrs. Helm was a very industrious woman, and generally busy in her household affairs—sewing, knitting, and looking after the servants; but she was a great scold,—continually finding fault with some of the servants, and frequently punishing the young slaves herself, by striking them over the head with a heavy iron key, until the blood ran; or else whipping them with a cowhide, which she always kept by her side when sitting in her room. The older servants she would cause to be punished by having them severely whipped by a man, which she never failed to do for every trifling fault. I have felt the weight of some of her heaviest keys on my own head, and for the slightest offences. No slave could possibly escape being punished—I care not how attentive they might be, nor how industrious—punished they must be, and punished they certainly were. Mrs. Helm appeared to be uneasy unless some of the servants were under the lash. She came into the kitchen one morning and my mother, who was cook, had just put on the dinner. Mrs. Helm took out her white cambric handkerchief, and rubbed it on the inside of the pot, and it crocked it! That was enough to invoke the wrath of my master, who came forth immediately with his horse-whip, with which he whipped my poor mother most unmercifully—far more severely than I ever knew him to whip a horse.

I once had the misfortune to break the lock of master's shot gun, and when it came to his knowledge, he came to me in a towering passion, and charged me with what he considered the *crime* of carelessness. I denied it, and told him I knew nothing about it; but I was so terribly frightened that he saw I was guilty, and told me so, foaming with rage; and then I confessed the truth. But oh, there was no escaping the lash. Its recollection is still bitter, and ever will be. I was commanded to take off my clothes, which I did, and then master put me on the back of another slave, my arms hanging down before him and my hands clasped in his, where he was obliged to hold me with a vise-like grasp. Then master gave me the most severe flogging that I ever received, and I pray God that I may never again experience such torture. And yet Capt. Helm was not the worst of masters.

These cruelties are daily occurrences, and so degrading is the whole practice of Slavery, that it not only crushes and brutalizes the wretched slave, but it hardens the heart, benumbs all the fine feelings of humanity, and deteriorates from the character of the slaveholders themselves,—whether man or woman. Otherwise, how could a gentle, and in other respects, amiable woman, look on such scenes of cruelty, without a shudder of utter abhorrence? But slaveholding ladies, can not only look on quietly, but with approbation; and what is worse, though very common, they can and do use the lash and cowhide themselves, on the backs of their slaves, and that too on those of their own sex! Far rather would I spend my life in a State's Prison, than be the slave of the best slaveholder on the earth!

When I was not employed as an errand-boy, it was my duty to stand behind my master's chair, which was sometimes the whole day, never being allowed to sit in his presence. Indeed, no slave is ever allowed to sit down in the presence of their master or mistress. If a slave is addressed when sitting, he is required to spring to his feet, and instantly remove his hat, if he has one, and answer in the most humble manner, or lay the foundation for a flogging, which will not be long delayed.

I slept in the same room with my master and mistress. This room was elegantly furnished with damask curtains, mahogany bedstead of the most expensive kind, and every thing else about it was of the most costly kind. And while Mr. and Mrs. Helm reposed on their bed of down, with a cloud of lace floating over them, like some Eastern Prince, with their slaves to fan them while they slept, and to tremble when they awoke, I always slept upon the floor, without a pillow or even a blanket, but, like a dog, lay down anywhere I could find a place.

Slaves are never allowed to leave the plantation to which they belong, without a written pass. Should any one venture to disobey this law, he will most likely be caught by the *patrol* and given thirty-nine lashes. This patrol is always on duty every Sunday, going to each plantation under their supervision, entering every slave cabin, and examining closely the conduct of the slaves; and if they find one slave from another plantation without a pass, he is immediately punished with a severe flogging.

I recollect going one Sunday with my mother, to visit my grand-mother; and while there, two or three of the patrol came and looked into the cabin, and seeing my mother, demanded her pass. She told them that she had one, but had left it in another cabin, from whence she soon brought it, which saved her a whipping but we were terribly frightened.

The reader will obtain a better knowledge of the character of a Virginia patrol, by the relation of an affair, which came off on the neighboring plantation of Col. Alexander, in which some forty of Capt. Helm's slaves were engaged, and which proved rather destructive of human life in the end.

But I must first say that it is not true, that slave owners are respected for kindness to their slaves. The more tyrannical a master is, the more will he be favorably regarded by his neighboring planters; and from the day that he acquires the reputation of a kind and indulgent master, he is looked upon with suspicion, and sometimes hatred, and his slaves are watched more closely than before.

Col. Alexander was a very wealthy planter and owned a great number of slaves, but he was very justly suspected of being a kind, humane, and indulgent master. His slaves were always better fed, better clad, and had greater privileges than any I knew in the Old Dominion; and of course, the patrol had long had an eye on them, anxious to flog some of "those pampered niggers, who were spoiled by the indulgence of a weak, inefficient, but well-meaning owner."

Col. A. gave his slaves the liberty to get up a grand dance. Invitations were sent and accepted, to a large number of slaves on other plantations, and so, for miles around, all or many of the slaves were in high anticipation of joining in the great dance, which was to come off on Easter night. In the mean time, the patrol was closely watching their movements, and evinced rather a joyful expectancy of the many they should find there without a pass, and the flogging they would give them for that, if not guilty of any other offence, and perhaps they might catch some of the Colonel's slaves doing something for which they could be taught "to know their place," by the application of the cowhide.

The slaves on Col. A.'s plantation had to provide and prepare the supper for the expected vast "turn out," which was no light matter; and as slaves like on such occasions to pattern as much as possible after their master's family, the result was, to meet the emergency of the case, they *took* without saying, "by your leave, Sir," some property belonging to their master, reasoning among themselves, as slaves often do, that it can not be *stealing*, because "it belongs to massa, and so do *we*, and we only use one part of his property to benefit another. Sure, 'tis all massa's." And if they do not get detected in this removal of "massa's property" from one location to another, they think no more of it.

Col. Alexander's slaves were hurrying on with their great preparations for the dance and feast; and as the time drew near, the old and knowing ones might be seen in groups, discussing the matter, with many a wink and nod; but it was in the valleys and by-places where the younger portion were to be found, rather secretly preparing food for the great time coming. This consisted of hogs, sheep, calves; and as to master's *poultry*, that suffered daily. Sometimes it was missed, but the disappearance was always easily accounted for, by informing "massa" that a great number of hawks had been around of late; and their preparation went on, night after night, undetected. They who repaired to a swamp or other by-place to cook by night, carefully destroyed everything likely to detect them, before they returned to their cabins in the morning.

The night for the dance *came* at last, and long before the time, the road leading to Col. Alexander's plantation presented a gay spectacle. The females were seen flocking to the place of resort, with heads adorned with gaudy bandanna turbans and new calico dresses, of the gayest colors, —their whole attire decked over with bits of gauze ribbon and other fantastic finery. The shades of night soon closed over the plantation, and then could be heard the rude music and loud laugh of the unpolished slave. It was about ten o'clock when the *aristocratic slaves* began to assemble, dressed in the cast-off finery of their master and mistress, swelling out and putting on airs in imitation of those they were forced to obey from day to day.

When they were all assembled, the dance commenced; the old fiddler struck up some favorite tune, and over the floor they went; the flying feet of the dancers were heard, pat, pat, over the apartment till the clock warned them it was twelve at midnight, or what some call "low twelve," to distinguish it from twelve o'clock at noon; then the violin ceased its discordant sounds, and the merry dancers paused to take breath.

Supper was then announced, and all began to prepare for the sumptuous feast. It being the pride of slaves to imitate the manners of their master and mistress, especially in the ceremonies of the table, all was conducted with great propriety and good order. The food was well cooked, and in a very plentiful supply. They had also managed in some way, to get a good quantity of excellent wine, which was sipped in the most approved and modern style. Every dusky face was lighted up, and every eye sparkled with joy. However ill fed they might have been, here, for once, there was plenty. Suffering and toil was forgotten, and they all seemed with one accord to give themselves up to the intoxication of pleasurable amusement.

House servants were of course, "the stars" of the party; all eyes were turned to them to see how they conducted, for they, among slaves, are what a military man would call "fugle-men." The field hands, and such of them as have generally been excluded from the dwelling of their owners, look to the house servant as a pattern of politeness and gentility. And indeed, it is often the only method of obtaining any knowledge of the manners of what is called "genteel society;" hence, they are ever regarded as a privileged class; and are sometimes greatly envied, while others are bitterly hated. And too often justly, for many of them are the most despicable tale-bearers and mischief-makers, who will, for the sake of the favor of his master or mistress, frequently betray his fellow-slave, and by tattling, get him severely whipped; and for these acts of perfidy, and sometimes downright falsehood, he is often rewarded by his master, who knows it is for his interest to keep such ones about him; though he is sometimes obliged, in addition to a reward, to send him away, for fear of the vengeance of the betrayed slaves. In the family of his master, the example of bribery and treachery is ever set before him, hence it is, that insurrections and stampedes are so generally detected. Such slaves are always treated with more affability than others, for the slaveholder is well aware that he stands over a volcano, that may at any moment rock his foundation to the center, and with one mighty burst of its long suppressed fire, sweep him and his family to destruction. When he lies down at night, he knows not but that ere another morning shall dawn, he may be left mangled and bleeding, and at the mercy of those maddened slaves whom he has so long ruled with a rod of iron.

But the supper, like other events, came to an end at last. The expensive table service, with other things, which had been secretly brought from the "great house," was hurriedly cleansed by the slaves, and carefully returned. The floor was again cleared, the violin sounded, and soon they were performing another "break down," with all the wild abandon of the African character,—in the very midst of which, the music suddenly ceased, and the old musician assumed a listening attitude. Every foot was motionless; every face terrified, and every ear listening for the cause of the alarm.

Soon the slave who was kept on the "look-out," shouted to the listeners the single word "*patrol!*" and then the tumult that followed that announcement, is beyond the power of language to describe! Many a poor slave who had stolen from his cabin, to join in the dance, now remembered that they had no pass! Many screamed in affright, as if they already felt the lash and heard the crack of the overseer's whip; others clenched their hands, and assumed an attitude of bold defiance, while a savage frown contracted the brow of all. Their unrestrained merriment

542

and delicious fare, seemed to arouse in them the natural feelings of self-defence and defiance of their oppressors. But what could be done? The patrol was nearing the building, when an athletic, powerful slave, who had been but a short time from his "fatherland," whose spirit the cowardly overseer had labored in vain to quell, said in a calm, clear voice, that we had better stand our ground, and advised the females to lose no time in useless wailing, but get their things and repair immediately to a cabin at a short distance, and there remain quiet, without a light, which they did with all possible haste. The men were terrified at this bold act of their leader; and many with dismay at the thought of resistance, began to skulk behind fences and old buildings, when he opened the door and requested every slave to leave who felt unwilling to fight. None were urged to remain, and those who stood by him did so voluntarily.

Their number was now reduced to twenty-five men, but the leader, a gigantic African, with a massive, compact frame, and an arm of great strength, looked competent to put ten common men to flight. He clenched his powerful fist, and declared that he would resist unto death, before he would be arrested by those savage men, even if they promised not to flog him. They closed the door, and agreed not to open it; and then the leader cried, "Extinguish the lights and let them come! we will meet them hand to hand!" Five of the number he stationed near the door, with orders to rush out, if the patrol entered, and seize their horses, cut the bridles, or otherwise unfit them for use. This would prevent them from giving an alarm and getting a reinforcement from surrounding plantations. In silence they awaited the approach of the enemy, and soon the tramping of horses' feet announced their approach, but when within a few yards of the house they halted, and were overheard by one of the skulking slaves, maturing their plans and mode of attack. There was great hesitancy expressed by a part of the company to engage in the affair at all.

543

"Coming events cast their shadow before."

The majority, however, seemed to think it safe enough, and uttered expressions of triumph that they had got the rascals at last.

"Are you not afraid that they will resist?" said the weaker party.

"Resist?" was the astonished answer. "This old fellow, the Colonel, has pampered and indulged his slaves, it is true, and they have slipped through our fingers whenever we have attempted to chastise them; but they are not such fools as to dare resistance! Those niggers know as well as we, that it is *death*, by the law of the State, for a slave to strike a white man."

"Very true," said the other, "but it is dark and long past midnight, and beside they have been indulging their appetites, and we cannot tell what they may attempt to do."

"Pshaw!" he answered, contemptuously, "they are unarmed, and I should not fear in the least, to go in among them *alone*, armed only with my cowhide!"

"As you please, then," he said, rather dubiously, "but look well to your weapons; are they in order?"

"In prime order, Sir." And putting spurs to their horses, were soon at the house, where they dismounted and requested one of the party to remain with the horses.

"What," said he, "are you so chicken-hearted as to suppose those d——d cowardly niggers are going to get up an insurrection?"

"Oh no," he replied, carelessly, but would not consent to have the horses left alone. "Besides," said he, "they may forget themselves at this late hour; but if they do, a few lashes of the cowhide will quicken their memory, I reckon."

The slaves were aware of their movements, and prepared to receive them.

They stepped up to the door boldly, and demanded admittance, but all was silent; they tried to open it, but it was fastened. Those inside, ranged on each side of the door, and stood perfectly still.

The patrol finding the slaves not disposed to obey, burst off the slight fastening that secured the door, and the chief of the patrol bounded into their midst, followed by several of his companions, all in total darkness!

Vain is the attempt to describe the tumultuous scene which followed. Hand to hand they fought and struggled with each other, amid the terrific explosion of firearms,—oaths and curses, mingled with the prayers of the wounded, and the groans of the dying! Two of the patrol were killed on the spot, and lay drenched in the warm blood that so lately flowed through their veins. Another with his arm broken and otherwise wounded, lay groaning and helpless, beside the fallen slaves, who had sold their lives so dearly. Another of his fellows was found at a short distance, mortally wounded and about to bid adieu to life. In the yard lay the keeper of the horses, a stiffened corpse. Six of the slaves were killed and two wounded.

It would be impossible to convey to the minds of northern people, the alarm and perfect consternation that the above circumstance occasioned in that community. The knowledge of its occurrence was carried from one plantation to another, as on the wings of the wind; exaggerated accounts were given, and prophecies of the probable result made, until the excitement became truly fearful. Every cheek was blanched and every frame trembled when listening to the tale, that "insurrection among the slaves had commenced on the plantation of Col. Alexander; that three or four of the patrol had been killed, &c." The day after, people flocked from every quarter, armed to the teeth, swearing vengeance on the defenceless slaves. Nothing can teach plainer than this, the constant and tormenting fear in which the slaveholder lives, and yet he repents not of his deeds.

The kind old Colonel was placed in the most difficult and unenviable position. His warm heart was filled with sorrow for the loss of his slaves, but not alone, as is generally the case in such instances, because he had lost so much property. He truly

regretted the death of his faithful servants, and boldly rebuked
the occasion of their sudden decease. When beset and harassed
by his neighbors to give up his slaves to be tried for insurrection
and murder, he boldly resisted, contending for the natural
right of the slaves, to act in their own defence, and especially
when on his own plantation and in their own quarters. They
contended, however, that as his slaves had got up a dance, and
had invited those of the adjoining plantations, the patrol was
only discharging their duty in looking after them; but the gallant
old Colonel defended his slaves, and told them plainly that he
should continue to do so to the extent of his ability and means.

The poor slaves were sad enough, on the morning after their
merry meeting, and they might be seen standing in groups,
conversing with a very different air from the one they had worn
the day before.

Their business was now to prepare the bodies of their late
associates for the grave. Robert, the brave African, who had so
boldly led them on the night before, and who had so judiciously
provided for their escape, was calmly sleeping in death's cold
embrace. He left a wife and five slave children. Two of the other
slaves left families, whose pitiful cries it was painful to hear.

The Colonel's family, deeply afflicted by what was passing
around them, attended the funeral. One of the slaves, who
sometimes officiated as a minister, read a portion of Scripture,
and gave out two hymns;—one of which commences with

"Hark! from the tomb a doleful sound."

Both were sung with great solemnity by the congregation,
and then the good old man offered a prayer; after which he
addressed the slaves on the shortness of human life and the
certainty of death, and more than once hinted at the hardness
of their lot, assuring, however, his fellow-slaves, that if they were
good and faithful, all would be right hereafter. His master, Col.
Alexander, was deeply affected by this simple faith and sincere

regard for the best interests of all, both master and slave.

When the last look at their fellow-servants had been taken, the procession was formed in the following manner: First, the old slave minister, then the remains of the dead, followed by their weeping relatives; then came the master and his family; next the slaves belonging to the plantation; and last, friends and strangers, black and white; all moved on solemnly to the final resting-place of those brave men, whose descendants may yet be heard from, in defence of right and freedom.

CHAPTER III

HORSE-RACING AND ITS CONSEQUENCES

Capt. Helm had a race-course on his plantation, on which he trained young horses for the fall races. One very fine horse he owned, called *Mark Anthony*, which he trained in the most careful manner for several months previous to the races. He would put him on the course every morning, sometimes covering him with a blanket, and then put him to his utmost speed, which he called "sweating him." Mark Anthony was to be put on the race-course in October following, as a competitor for the purse of ten thousand dollars, which was the amount to be lost or gained on the first day of the fall races. Capt. H. had also another young horse, called *Buffer*, under a course of training, which he designed to enter the lists for the second day. His course of training had been about the same as Mark Anthony's, but being a year or two younger, it was thought that he had not sufficient "bottom" to risk so much money on, as was at stake on the first day.

When the time for the races to commence came, all was bustle and excitement in the house and on the plantation. It was a fine October morning, and the sun shed a mellow radiance on all around, when people began to throng the race-course. Some came with magnificent equipages, attended by their numerous train of black servants, dressed in livery, —some in less splendid array,—and others on foot, all hurrying on to the exciting scene. There the noblest blood of Old Virginia, of which many are wont to boast, was fully represented, as was also the wealth and fashion of the country for many miles around.

548

All were in high spirits, and none seemed to fear that they would be the losers in the amount of money about to change hands. And for what, pray, is all this grand outlay—this vast expenditure? Merely the pleasure and gratification of witnessing the speed of a fine horse, and the vanity of prejudging concerning it.

The arrangements were at length completed,—the horses regularly entered, Mark Anthony among the rest,—and then the word "go!" was given, when each horse sprang as if for his life, each striving to take the lead. Away they go, sweeping round the course with lightning speed, while every spectator's eye is strained, and every countenance flushed with intense anxiety.

Some of the noble animals were distanced the first heat, and others were taken away by their owners.

The judges allowed twenty minutes to prepare the horses for the second trial of their speed—a trial which must enrich or empoverish many of the thousands present. Already there were sad countenances to be seen in the crowd.

The horses were again in readiness, and the word given,—away they flew with the fleetness of the wind, to come in the second time.

But who can describe the anxiety written on every face, as they prepared for the third and last trial? I cannot. Many had already lost all they had staked, and others who had bet high began to fear for the result. Soon, however, all was again prepared and those foaming steeds, after having exerted their animal power to the utmost, have accomplished their task and come in for the last time. The purse was won, *but not by Mark Anthony.* Capt. Helm was more fortunate the second day. Buffer won the smaller purse, but the Captain came from the races, a much poorer man than when they commenced. These repeated failures and heavy losses had the effect to arouse him to a sense of his pecuniary position, and he soon after began to think and talk about going to some new country.

He resolved at last to visit the far-off "Genesee Country,"

which he shortly after put in practice, and after an absence of about three weeks he returned in good health, and delighted with the country; the more so, doubtless, because he said, "the more slaves a man possessed in that country the more he would be respected, and the higher would be his position in society."

Capt. Helm finally concluded to sell his plantation and stock, except the slaves, and remove to the Genesee Country, where he designed to locate his future residence.

The plantation and stock (retaining the slaves) were advertised for sale, and on a certain day named, all would be disposed of at a public sale, or to the highest bidder.

When the day of sale arrived, there flocked from all parts of the surrounding country the largest assemblage of people I ever saw in that place. A large number of wealthy and respectable planters were present, whose gentlemanly behavior should have been an example to others.

The majority of that vast crowd, however, were a rough, quarrelsome, fighting set, just such as might be expected from slave-holding districts. There were several regularly fought battles during the first day of the sale.

One Thomas Ford, a large, muscular, ferocious-looking fellow, a good specimen of a southern bully and woman-whipper, had been victorious through the day in numerous fights and brawls; but he had to pay dear for it when night came. Some one or more of the vanquished party, took advantage of the dark night to stab him in both sides. The knife of the assassin had been thrust into his thigh, tearing the flesh upward, leaving a frightful and dangerous wound; but what is most singular, both sides were wounded in nearly the same manner, and at the same time, for so quickly was the deed committed that the offenders made their escape, before an alarm could be raised for their detection; nor have I ever heard of any one being arrested for the crime.

Ford's groans and cries were painful to hear, but his brother acted like a madman; rushing hither and thither, with a heavy bludgeon in his hand, with which he indiscriminately beat the fences and whatever came in his way, crying "Oh my brother, my poor brother! Who has murdered my poor brother?"

Physicians came to the aid of the wounded man who at first thought he might recover, but in a climate like that of Virginia it was impossible. His friends did all they could to save him, but the poor wretch lingered a few days and died. Thus ended the life of a bad man and a hard master.

And who will wonder, if his slaves rejoiced to hear of his death? If they must be sold to pay his debts, they could not fall into the hands of a more heartless tyrant. Who then can blame those feeble women and helpless children, long held as chattels in his iron grasp, if they are grateful that the man-stealer is no more?

This Ford was a fair specimen of that class, known in more modern parlance as a "Border Ruffian." Such as are at this time endeavoring, by their swaggering and bullying, to cast on the fair fields of Kansas the deep curse of Slavery—a curse which, like the poison of the deadly Upas, blights all within its influence: the colored and the white man, the slave and the master. We were thankful, however, that no more lives were lost during the vendue, which was commenced with the stock; this occupied two days.

The reader will see that we had cause to be grateful, when he takes into consideration that drinking and fighting was the order of the day, and drunkenness and carousing the order of the night.

Then too, the practice of dueling was carried on in all its hideous barbarity. If a gentleman thought himself insulted, he would immediately challenge the offender to mortal combat, and if he refused to do so, then the insulted gentleman felt bound by that barbarous code of honor, to take his life, whenever or wherever he might meet him, though it might be in a crowded assembly, where the lives of innocent persons were endangered.

A case of this kind happened in Kentucky, where the belligerent parties met in a large concourse of people, the majority of them women and children; but the combat ensued, regardless of consequences. One woman was shot through the face, but that was not worthy of notice, for she was only a *colored woman*; and in that, as in other slave States, the laws give to the white population the liberty to trample under foot the claims of all such persons to justice. Justly indignant ladies present remonstrated, but all to no purpose. The Governor of the State was there and was in danger of being wounded by their flying bullets, and it is possible that if he had been in the place of the poor African, some action would have been taken, and laws made to protect the people against such inhuman practices. But I must return to Capt. Helm and the vendue.

The sale continued for several days, during which there was no such thing as rest or sleep or one quiet moment on the premises. As was customary in that State, Capt. Helm provided the food and drink for all who came, and of course a great many came to drink and revel and not to buy; and that class generally took the night time for their hideous outbreaks, when the more respectable class had retired to their beds or to their homes. And many foul deeds and cruel outrages were committed; nor could the perpetrators be detected or brought to justice. Nothing could be done but to submit quietly to their depredations.

One peaceable old slave was killed by having his head split open with an ax. He was found in the morning lying in the yard, with the bloody instrument of death by his side. This occasioned some excitement among the slaves, but as the white people paid but little attention to it, it soon passed off, and the sorrowful slaves put the old man's remains in a rough box, and conveyed them to their last resting-place.

After the sale was over, the slaves were allowed a holiday, with permission to go and visit their friends and relatives previous to their departure for their new home in a strange land.

The slaves generally on Capt. Helm's plantation looked upon this removal as the greatest hardship they had ever met; the severest trial they had ever endured; and the separation from our old home and fellow-slaves, from our relatives and the old State of Virginia, was to us a contemplation of sorrowful interest. Those who remained, thought us the most unfortunate of human beings to be taken away off into the State of New York, and, as they believed, beyond the bounds of civilization, where we should in all probability be destroyed by wild beasts, devoured by cannibals, or scalped by the Indians. We never expected to meet again in this life, hence our parting interviews were as solemn as though we were committing our friends to the grave. But He whose tender mercies are over all his creatures, knew best what was for our good.

Little did Capt. Helm think when bringing his slaves to New York that in a few short years, they would be singing the song of deliverance from Slavery's thralldom; and as little thought he of the great and painful change, to be brought about in his own circumstances. Could any one have looked into futurity and traced the difficult path, my master was to tread,—could any one have foreseen the end to which he must soon come, and related it to him in the days of his greatness and prosperity, he would, I am certain, have turned from such a narrator of misfortune in a greater rage than did Namaan when the man of God told him "to go and dip seven times in the Jordan."

He could not have believed, nor could I, that in a few years the powerful, wealthy slaveholder, living in luxury and extravagance, would be so reduced that the *necessaries* of life even, were beyond his means, and that he must be supported by the town!

But I anticipate. Let us return to the old plantation which seems dearer than ever, now that we are about to leave it forever.

We thought Capt. Helm's prospects pretty fair, and yet we shuddered when we realized our condition as slaves. This change in our circumstances was calculated to awaken all our fears that had been slumbering, and bring all the perilous changes to which we might be subjected most vividly to mind.

We were about to leave the land of our birth, the home of

553

our childhood, and we felt that untried scenes were before us. We were slaves, it is true, but we had heart-felt emotions to suppress, when we thought of leaving all that was so familiar to us, and chose rather to "bear the ills we had, than to fly to those we knew not of." And oh, the terrible uncertainty of the future, that ever rests on the slave, even the most favored, was now felt with a crushing weight. To-day, they are in the old familiar cabin surrounded by their family, relatives and friends; to-morrow, they may be scattered, parted forever. The master's circumstances, not their own, may have assigned one to the dreadful slave-pen, and another to the distant rice-swamp; and it is this continual dread of some perilous future that holds in check every joyous emotion, every lofty aspiration, of the most favored slave at the South. They know that their owners indulge in high living, and they are well aware also that their continual indulgences engender disease, which make them very liable to sudden death; or their master may be killed in a duel, or at a horse-race, or in a drunken brawl; then his creditors are active in looking after the estate; and next, the blow of the auctioneer's hammer separates them perhaps for life.

Now, after the lapse of so many years, when my thoughts wander back, as they often do, to my native State, I confess that painful recollections drive from my mind those joyful emotions that should ever arise in the heart of man, when contemplating the familiar scenes of his youth, and especially when recurring to the venerable shades and the sheltering roof under which he was born. True, around the well-remembered spot where our childhood's years were spent, recollection still loves to linger; yet memory, ever ready with its garnered store, paints in glowing colors, Virginia's crouching slaves in the foreground. Her loathsome slave-pens and slave markets—chains, whips and instruments of torture; and back of all this is as truthfully recorded the certain doom, the retributive justice, that will sooner or later overtake her; and with a despairing sigh I turn away from the imaginary view of my native State.

What though she may have been justly styled, "The Mother of Presidents?" What avails the honor of being the birth-place of the brave and excellent Washington, while the prayers and groans of the down-trodden African daily ascend to heaven for redress? What though her soil be fertile, yielding a yearly product of wealth to its possessors? And what matter is it, that their lordly mansions are embowered in the shade of trees of a century's growth, if, through their lofty and tangled branches, we espy the rough cabin of the mangled bondman, and know that the soil on which he labors has drunk his heart's blood?

Ah! to me, life's sweetest memories are all embittered. Slavery had cast its dark and fearful shadow over my childhood, youth, and early manhood, and I went out from the land of my birth, a fettered slave. A land which I can regard only as "the house of bondage and the grave of freedom." But God forgive me for having envied my master his fair prospects at this time.

After the sale of the plantation, Capt. Helm was in possession of quite a large sum of money, and having never paid much attention to his pecuniary interests, he acted as if there could be no end of it. He realized about forty thousand dollars from the sale of his estate in Virginia, which would have been a pretty sum in the hands of a man who had been accustomed to look after his own interests; but under the management of one who had all his life lived and prospered on the unrequited toil of slaves, it was of little account. He bought largely of every thing he thought necessary for himself or the comfort of his family, for which he always paid the most extravagant prices. The Captain was not as well qualified to take care of himself and family as some of his slaves were; but he thought differently, and so the preparations for leaving the old plantation for a home in the wilds of New York, went on under his direction, and at last we bade a final adieu to our friends and all we held dear in the State of Virginia.

CHAPTER IV

JOURNEY TO OUR NEW HOME IN NEW YORK

All things having been prepared for our departure, our last "Good-bye" spoken, and our last look taken of the old plantation, we started, amid the sobs and prolonged cries of separating families, in company with our master, the overseer and another white man named Davis, who went with us to take back the five-horse "Pennsylvania team," which was provided for the conveyance of the food for the slaves, and what little baggage they might have, and also that of the overseer.

Capt. Helm had determined to leave his family until he could get his slaves settled in their future quarters, and a home provided for himself, when they were expected to join him.

We traveled northward, through Maryland, Pennsylvania, and a portion of New York, to Sodus Bay, where we halted for some time. We made about twenty miles per day, camping out every night, and reached that place after a march of twenty days. Every morning the overseer called the roll, when every slave must answer to his or her name, felling to the ground with his cowhide, any delinquent who failed to speak out in quick time.

After the roll had been called, and our scanty breakfast eaten, we marched on again, our company presenting the appearance of some numerous caravan crossing the desert of Sahara.

When we pitched our tents for the night, the slaves must immediately set about cooking not their supper only, but their breakfast, so as to be ready to start early the next morning, when the tents were struck; and we proceeded on our journey in this way to the end.

At Sodus Bay there was then one small tavern, kept by a man named Sill.

The bay is ten miles in length and from a half to two miles in breadth, and makes an excellent harbor. The surrounding country then was almost an unbroken wilderness.

After Capt. Helm had rested a few days at Sodus, he went six miles up the bay and purchased a large tract of land lying on both sides of that beautiful sheet of water, and put his slaves on to clear and cultivate it. Then came the "tug of war." Neither the overseer nor the slaves had the least knowledge of *clearing* land, and that was the first thing to be done. It was useless to consult the Captain, for he knew still less about matters of that kind. To obviate this difficulty, our master bought out a Mr. Cummings, who had some cleared land on the west side of the bay. On this he put the overseer and a part of the slaves, and then hired a Mr. Herrington to take charge of the remainder. Herrington and his gang of slaves was sent to the east side to chop down the heavy timber and clear the land for cultivation, all of which had first to be learned, for we knew nothing of felling trees, and the poor slaves had rather a hard time of it.

Provisions were scarce and could not be procured for cash in that section. There was no corn to be had, and we had but little left. We had no neighbors to assist us in this trying time, and we came near starvation. True, the wild, romantic region in which we were located abounded in game,—elk, deer, bear, panther, and wolves, roamed abroad through the dense forest, in great abundance, but the business of the slaves was not hunting or fishing, but clearing the land, preparatory to raising crops of grain the coming season.

At last Capt. Helm chartered a boat, and manned it to go to the mouth of the Genesee River to buy corn. They embarked under favorable auspices, but soon there came on such a tremendous storm, that the boat could no longer be managed, and the crew in despair threw themselves on the bottom of the boat to await their inevitable destruction, when one of their

557

number, a colored man named Dunbar, sprang to the helm, and with great difficulty succeeded in running her safely into a Canadian port, where they were obliged to part with every thing in their possession to obtain the means to return to their families in Sodus, who had given them up as lost. But, to the great joy of all, they came back at last with their lives, but with nothing for the famishing slaves. Before another boat could be sent for our relief, we were reduced to the last extremity. We became so weak we could not work, and it was difficult to drag ourselves about, as we were now obliged to do, to gather up all the old bones we could find, break them up fine and then boil them; which made a sort of broth sufficient barely to sustain life. This we drank, and merely existed, until at last, the long looked for boat returned, loaded with provision, which saved us from starvation and gave us strength to pursue our labor.

CHAPTER V

INCIDENTS AT SODUS BAY

About this time two slaves who were laboring in the forest, instead of returning to their cabin as was expected, got lost, and wandered eight days in the dense forest without provision, except what they could procure from roots and the bark of trees. Great exertion was made to find them; guns were fired, horns blown, and shouts raised, but all to no purpose. Finally, we gave them up, supposing they had starved to death or had been killed by wild beasts. One of them was an elderly man, named Benjamin Bristol, and the other, Edmund Watkins, a lad of about eighteen years of age. They wandered in an easterly direction, a distance of some sixty or seventy miles, through an unbroken wilderness, vainly trying to find their way home. On the eighth day, to their inexpressible joy, they came out on the shore of Lake Ontario, near Oswego; but young Watkins was so completely exhausted that he declared himself incapable of further exertion, and begged to be left to his fate. Bristol, however, who chewed tobacco, which it was supposed kept him from sinking so low as his companion, took him on his back, and carried him home, which they reached in a famished state and reduced to skeletons. All were thankful for the preservation of their lives, and, with the best we could do for them, they soon recruited and became strong as ever.

One day, two others and myself thought we saw some animal swimming across the bay. We got a boat and went out to see what it was. After rowing for some time we came near enough to perceive it was a large bear. Those who watched us from the

559

shore expected to see our boat upset, and all on board drowned, but it was not so to be; the, bear was struck on the nose with a blow that killed him instantly, and he was hauled ashore in great triumph.

While these things were transpiring on the east side of the bay, the overseer on the west side determined to punish one of the slaves who worked on the east side. The name of the slave was Williams; a strong, athletic man, and generally a good workman, but he had unfortunately offended the overseer, for which nothing could appease his wrath but the privilege of flogging him. The slave, however, thought as he was no longer in Virginia, he would not submit to such chastisement, and the overseer was obliged to content himself with threatening what he would do if he caught him on the west side of the bay.

A short time after, the overseer called at the cabin of one of the slaves, and was not a little surprised to find there the refractory slave, Williams, in company with three other men. He immediately walked up to him and asked him some question, to which Williams made no reply. Attended, as he always was, by his ferocious bull-dog, he flourished his cowhide in great wrath and demanded an instant reply, but he received none, whereupon he struck the slave a blow with the cowhide. Instantly Williams sprang and caught him by the throat and held him writhing in his vise-like grasp, until he succeeded in getting possession of the cowhide, with which he gave the overseer such a flogging as slaves seldom get. Williams was seized at once by the dog who endeavored to defend his brutal master, but the other slaves came to the rescue, and threw the dog into a huge fire which was near by, from which, after a singeing, he ran off, howling worse than his master when in the hands of Williams. He foamed and swore and still the blows descended; then he commanded the slaves to assist him, but as none obeyed, he commenced begging in the most humble manner, and at last entreated them as "gentlemen" to spare him; but all to no purpose. When Williams thought he had thrashed him sufficiently, he let him go and hurried to his boat and rowed down the bay, instead of crossing it. The overseer no sooner found himself at liberty than he ran out, calling to a servant girl to bring his rifle, which was loaded. The rifle was brought, but before he could get to the bay, Williams had gone beyond his reach; but unfortunately another boat was at this moment crossing the bay, which he, mad with rage, fired into. The men in the boat immediately cried out to him not to repeat the shot, but he was so angry that he swore he would shoot somebody, and sent another bullet after them. No one was hurt, however, but the brave overseer was vanquished. Crest-fallen and unrevenged, he shortly after called on Capt. Helm for a settlement, which was granted, and bidding a final adieu to the "Genesee Country," he departed for Virginia, where he could beat slaves without himself receiving a cow-hiding. No one regretted his absence, nor do I think any but the most heartless would cordially welcome his return to the land of Slavery.

CHAPTER VI

REMOVAL FROM SODUS TO BATH

Capt. Helm went to Virginia for his family, and returning with them, concluded to locate his future residence in the village of Bath, Steuben County. He purchased a large tract of land near the village, a large grist mill, and two saw mills; also, two farms; one called the "Maringo," east of the village; and the other, called "Epsam," north of it; and a fine house and lot in the village. He also kept a distillery, which in those days was well patronized, for nearly every body drank whisky; and with Capt. Helm it was a favorite beverage.

The slaves were removed to Bath, where our master was well suited, and was everywhere noted for his hospitality. He had a great deal of land to cultivate, and carried on a multiplicity of business.

Soon after we were settled at Bath, Capt. Helm's eldest daughter, Jenny, was married to Mr. John Fitzhugh, her cousin, who had come from Virginia to claim his bride.

The wedding was a splendid affair. No pains were spared to make it more imposing than any thing that had ever happened in that country. Never before had the quiet village of Bath seen such splendor. All that wealth, power and ambition could do, was done to make the event one of great brilliancy. Europe contributed her full proportion; Turkey, the Indias, East and West, were heavily taxed to produce their finest fabrics to adorn the bride and bridal guests; and contribute delicacies to add elegance to the festal scene. Two days previous to the wedding, the invited guests began to arrive with their retinue of servants, and on the evening of the marriage the large mansion was thrown open, and there was the most magnificent assemblage I ever beheld. In the drawing-room, where the ceremony took place, every thing was surpassingly elegant. Costly chandeliers shed their light on the rich tapestry, and beautiful dresses glittering with diamonds, and the large mirrors everywhere reflecting the gay concourse. While the servants were preparing supper it was announced that the hour had arrived for the ceremony to commence. The bridal pair took their place in the center of the apartment. Pearls, diamonds, and jewelry glittered on the bride with such luster, that it was almost painful to the eye to look upon her.

The minister, after asking God to bless the assembled guests, and those he was about to unite in the holy bonds of wedlock, proceeded in a very solemn and impressive manner with the marriage service. The ceremony concluded, and good wishes having been expressed over the sparkling wine, the man of God took his leave, two hundred dollars richer than when he came. The company were all very happy, or appeared so; mirth reigned supreme, and every countenance wore a smile. They were seated at tables loaded with luxuries of every description, and while partaking, a band of music enlivened the scene.

All business was suspended for several days, the wedding party making a tour of ten days to Niagara Falls. After a while, however, affairs assumed their usual aspect, and business took its regular routine.

The grist mill belonging to the Captain was the only one for many miles around, and was a source of great profit to him; the saw mills also, were turning out a large quantity of lumber, which was in good demand; and the distillery kept up a *steaming* business. It yielded, however, a handsome income to Capt. Helm, who was now, for the first time since I knew him, overseeing his affairs himself, dispensing altogether with the service of a regularly installed overseer.

The oldest son of our master had been absent from home for

sometime, nor did he return to attend his sister's grand wedding. He had sought and obtained a commission in the United States service as a Lieutenant. This had been his own choice; he had preferred the service and hardships of a soldier, to a plantation well stocked with slaves, and the quietude of domestic life. He had cheerfully given up his friends and prospects as a planter, and entered the service of his country. Frank Helm, the second son, soon followed the example of his older brother, Lina. He obtained a like commission, but he did not, like his brother, get along quietly. His prospects as an officer were soon blighted, and all hope of being serviceable to his country vanished forever.

CHAPTER VII

DUELING

Lina Helm was an easy, good-natured, clever fellow; but his brother Frank was his opposite in nearly every thing; proud, fractious and unyielding. As might be expected, Frank, soon after entering the army, got into an "affair of honor," according to the duelist's code of laws. He was not, however, the principal in the difficulty. One of his friends and a brother officer, had a quarrel with a gentleman whom he challenged to mortal combat. Frank was the bearer of his friend's challenge, and on presenting it, the gentleman refused to accept it, saying that the challenger "was no gentleman." Then, according to the rules of dueling, no alternative was left for Frank, but to take his brother officer's place, and fight. This he did and came from the bloody field disabled for life. In consequence of his lameness, he was under the necessity of resigning his commission in the army, which he did, and came home a cripple, and nearly unfitted for any kind of business whatever.

While on the subject of dueling, permit me to record some of the incidents of another "affair of honor," which occurred in the District of Columbia, between Gen. Mason and Mr. M'Carter, two antagonistic politicians.

M'Carter offered his vote to the inspectors, and Mason challenged it. M'Carter offered to swear it in, when Mason said if he did so he would perjure himself. This blew what appeared to be but a spark into an angry blaze, and a duel was momentarily expected; but their warlike propensities subsided into a newspaper combat, which was kept up for several weeks, each party supposing they had the advantage of their adversary. In this stage of the quarrel, Gen. Jackson, with one of his aid-de-camps, Dr. Bruno, visited Washington. Dr. Bruno was a friend of Gen. Mason's, and to him the General submitted the correspondence, desiring his opinion relative to the advantage one had obtained over the other. Dr. Bruno decided against his friend, which probably exasperated him still more, and the General expressed his determination to fight his antagonist. Dr. Bruno wrote to M'Carter to come to Washington, and he came immediately, and was as readily waited upon by the Doctor, who inquired if he would receive a communication from his friend, Gen. Mason. M'Carter replied, that he "would receive no communication from Gen. Mason, except a challenge to fight." The challenge was therefore sent, and accepted, and the Doctor appointed to make the necessary arrangements for the duel. He proposed the weapons to be pistols, and the distance, ten paces; to which M'Carter objected, because he said, "the General was a dead shot with the pistol, while he hardly knew how to use one." Then it was left to M'Carter to choose the mode of warfare. He proposed muskets and ten paces distance. This was agreed upon, and finally the morning arrived for the conflict, and people began to assemble in great numbers to witness this murderous scene.

The belligerent parties unflinchingly took their place, each with his loaded musket at his shoulder, and gazing in each other's face, with feelings of the most bitter hatred, while their eyes flashed vengeance.

Oh! what a state of mind was this in which to meet inevitable death? How could intelligent men, or gentlemen, if you please so to term them, look placidly on such a horrid scene? Was there no heart of humanity to interfere and arrest the murderous designs of these madmen? Alas, no! The slaveholder's "code of honor" must be acknowledged, though it outrage the laws of God and his country.

Dr. Bruno asks, "Gentlemen, are you ready?" and the duelists take their deadly aim at each other. The signal to fire is given, and both weapons are discharged, and when the smoke had cleared away, what a spectacle was there presented to the duelist and spectator? Gen. Mason, a husband, a father, a statesman, and a kind friend, lies bleeding, and gasping for breath. He is no more! Who will bear to his loving and unsuspecting wife, the sad intelligence of her sudden bereavement? Who will convey his lifeless body to his late residence, and throw grief and consternation into the bosom of his family, and drape in sadness his whole household? And yet this painful task must be performed. The family of General Mason remained entirely ignorant of what was transpiring regarding the duel, until his mangled corpse was brought into his dwelling, from which he had so recently gone forth in all the vigor of life and manhood. And here let us drop the curtain, nor intrude on that scene of domestic affliction around the deserted hearth-stone of the bereaved family of General Mason.

But where is Mr. M'Carter, the more fortunate party in the duel? Hurrying away from the frightful scene, his hands dripping with the blood of his fellow-man, he skulks about, until an opportunity is given him to step on board a vessel bound to a foreign port; he leaves home, friends and country, in the vain hope of finding peace of mind, and ridding himself of that guilt and censure which must attach itself to a crime so heinous as that of taking the life of another. I can but regard the inhuman practice of dueling as the legitimate fruit of Slavery.

Men who have been raised in the Slave States, where, if the laws do not give them the power, they do not restrain them from cruelly punishing every offender with personal violence, even unto death, if their insulted dignity seems to demand it. It is, however, encouraging to know that for a few years past the practice of dueling has somewhat fallen into disrepute among the more humane and candid class of community.

CHAPTER VIII

HORSE-RACING AND GENERAL TRAINING

After the return of the wedding party, Mr. Fitzhugh purchased a tract of land near that of Capt. Helm, on which the newly-married couple commenced keeping house. They, however, became dissatisfied with their location, and soon after sold their possessions and returned to the South.

Capt. Helm still continued to take the oversight of his slaves, and was out every day, superintending his business, just as his overseer used to do.

About this time a man named Henry Tower came to Bath to hire "slave boys," as we were called. The Captain hired to him Simon and myself, and a Mr. Baker also hired to him one slave named Vol. McKenzie. We three started for Dresden, Ontario County, where we arrived in due time.

Mr. Tower had just bought a tract of land, three miles this side of the village of Lyons, on the Canandaigua outlet. Here Mr. Tower contemplated making great improvements, building mills, opening stores &c. This tract of land was comparatively wild, there being but a small frame house for a dwelling, one for a store, and another for a blacksmith shop. Mr. Tower had two brothers; James, the eldest, who took charge of the store, and John, the younger, who took charge of the hands who worked on the farm; Henry himself superintending the building of the mills. This firm had a great number of men in their employ that year. I was kept busy helping the women about the cooking and house-work. And here, for the first time in my life, I had a comfortable bed to sleep on, and plenty of wholesome food to eat; which was something both new and strange to me.

The Towers were thorough-going business-men; they built a large grist mill, with four run of stone, and also a distillery. In those days it was customary for nearly all classes to drink spirituous liquors; hence, the distilleries were sources of great pecuniary interest to those who owned them. But having lived to see the dreadful evils which the drinking of alcoholic beverages have produced on community, I can hardly speak of distilleries in the favorable light in which they were then regarded.

The Towers, with commendable enterprise, cleared a great number of acres of land during the first year I lived with them, besides doing a heavy business in the mill, store and distillery.

It was customary then for men to assemble at some public place for the purpose of drinking whisky and racing horses.

One Saturday afternoon there was to be a race, and all was excitement. Being young, I wished to go with the rest. I hurried through my work as fast as possible, and then, with a trembling heart, set off in search of my master, fearing lest he would refuse me the simple request. But he happened to be in uncommon good humor, and readily gave his consent; and away I went, "as happy as a lark." When I reached the race-ground, they were just preparing to run the horses. Seeing me, they knew me to be a poor friendless little slave boy, helpless and unprotected, and they could therefore do with me as they pleased, and have some fine sport at my expense.

When I was asked to ride one of the fast horses, I felt proud of the honor conferred, and was assisted to mount, feeling highly elated with the lofty position I had gained.

The word "go," was shouted, and the horse whirled off, and it seemed to me as if he flew with the speed of lightning. My hat fell off the first thing; and there I was, clinging with might and main to the neck of the fiery animal, my head bare, my feet bootless, and my old stripped shirt blown from my back, and streaming out behind, and fluttering like a banner in the breeze; my ragged pants off at the knees, and my long legs dangling down some length below; and at the same time crying "Whoa! whoa!" as loud as I could. Nor was this all; frightened as I was, nearly to death, I cast a despairing look behind me, and the loud, derisive laugh of the bystanders rung in my ears.

Ludicrous as I must have appeared, this was too much,—I felt a giddiness coming over me, my brain reeled, my hold relaxed, and the next instant I had fallen to the ground, where all consciousness left me. When I came to my senses I was lying in bed, surrounded by all the appurtenances of a dying person.

The first thing I heard was Mr. Tower scolding the men who put me on the horse, and threatening them with a law-suit for presuming to do such a thing without his permission. Mr. Tower considered himself holden to Capt. Helm for my safe return, and was therefore justly indignant at their placing my life in such peril. It was indeed a narrow escape, for the horse was running with all his speed when I fell. My bones were unbroken, however, and I suppose it must have been the tremendous jar I got when I fell that rendered me unconscious; nor do I think it impossible that the fright may not have contributed somewhat to the catastrophe.

It was while I was living with that gentleman that the greatest "general training" ever known in Western New York, came off at "Oak's Corners," in the town of Phelps. It really seemed to me that the whole world were going to the training, and I, of course, felt a great curiosity to go where "all creation" appeared to be going. Mr. Tower permitted me to go, and I started off in high spirits. When I arrived within two or three miles of the place the road was almost blocked up with people, and when I got to Oak's Corners the crowd beggared all description; carriages of all sorts were there, containing eatables of all kinds, and tents of all dimensions were on the road-side, for the houses could not begin to accommodate the people. The entire brigade was to meet at that place, and Gov. Lewis was expected to review the different companies, and all were anxious to see the Governor, for, in those days, it was a rare thing to see so high a dignitary in

Western New York; the eastern portion of the State having had every thing of that kind their own way.

Nor was the means and mode of traveling brought to such perfection as now. The roads were new and rough, and our best public conveyances only the slow lumbering stage-coach; yet, notwithstanding these inconveniences, there was an innumerable crowd gathered at that place. I spent the day in walking about the encampment, and seeing what was to be seen, for it was all new to me.

Officers were riding over the ground, dressed in uniform, and mounted on their splendid steeds: their plumes waving over their cocked-hats in true military array. A band of music, as is usual, accompanied the soldiers. There was also a "sham-fight," before the breaking up of the encampment, and it was really terrifying to me, who had never seen a battle fought, to witness two columns of troops drawn up, and, at the roll of the drum, behold them engage in deadly conflict, to all appearance, and the smoke curling up in a blackened mass toward heaven; and, above all, the neighing of horses, with the feigned groans of the wounded and dying. I inwardly prayed to God that those men might ever draw their weapons in a feigned encounter.

The first night I spent at the encampment was one long to be remembered; it was like the confusion of Babel. Of all the hideous noises I ever heard none could exceed those made there that night. They fired guns, quarreled, drank, and swore, till day light. There was such a crowd at the tavern that I did not suppose I could get a bed, so I threw myself down upon a door-step, and began to compose myself to sleep, when a man came and wakened me, inquiring at the same time whose boy I was. I replied that I lived with Mr. Tower. "Follow me," said he; I arose and followed him into the house, where he procured for me a bed, to be shared with another "boy," who had already occupied it.

I had just began to doze, when the explosion of firearms startled all in the house. The keeper of the tavern ran up stairs in great alarm, and when an examination was made, we found that a drunken fellow had discharged his musket in the room below the one where we were sleeping, and that the ball had passed up through the second floor and completely through the bed on which I slept, to the roof, where, having passed through that also, rolled from thence to the ground! And yet, strange as it may appear, no one was injured, though the house was filled to overflowing with guests.

There were groups of disorderly and drunken men continually roaming over the camp-ground at night, who seemed to have no other object than to annoy others, and torment any one they might find sleeping, by shaking them, or, if soundly asleep, dragging them out of their beds by their feet. Among these thus annoyed by them was a physician from Canandaigua. Being a passionate man, they seemed to think it fine sport to arouse him from sleep and hear him scold. The first time they dragged him from his tent he merely remonstrated in a very gentlemanly manner, and quietly crept back again. The rowdies were disappointed; they had expected a "scene." As soon as he was asleep they attacked him again, dragging him out by the heels; then he was angry, and told them if they repeated the offence it would be at the peril of their lives, and a third time retired to his tent; but a third party soon came, and one, more bold than the rest, entered the tent and laid hold of the Doctor. He sprang to his feet and drew his sword, which he ran through the body of a man supposed to be that of his tormentor; but oh! what sorrow and consternation possessed him when he found he had taken the life of a quiet, unoffending person who happened to be standing by, attracted to the spot probably by the noise of the revelers. The unhappy Doctor was obliged to flee from his country for a time, but after a while the shadows which had so suddenly fallen on his fair prospects were cleared away, and he returned to his home and country.

The second day of the encampment was one of surpassing beauty. The sun shone in all its softened radiance on that vast concourse of human beings. The field presented a spectacle which must have been imposing to those of more experienced vision than mine; but to me, in my ignorant simplicity, it was superbly grand; fascinating beyond my power of resistance, and made an impression on my mind never to be effaced.

The brigade was drawn up in a line, each colonel stationed just so many paces in front of the line, and all the other officers, such as majors, quarter-masters, &c., were stationed at an equal distance in the rear. When all were paraded, the Governor of the State made his appearance, dressed in full uniform, his hat being one of the Bonaparte style, attended by his aid-de-camp, who was dressed much in the same manner as his Excellency Governor Lewis, who, after the salute, took his place at the head of the brigade, and the military exercises commenced. When the Governor issued his orders, they were first given to his aid, who passed them to the officers, and they gave the word of command to the soldiers; for instance if the Governor wished the brigade to "shoulder arms,"—the order went to the officer who commanded the first regiment, and he repeated the order, and was obeyed; then the same order passed to the next, and so on, until the whole brigade had complied with the order of his Excellency.

But this, I believe, was the first and last time that the military were ever called out on so large a scale, in the State of New York. It was supposed that the effect would be decidedly injurious to a community and the idea was abandoned. Young men were so liable to be fascinated by the magnificent spectacle, that not the rabble only were attracted by the "trappings of war," but they have a tendency to induce young, and *old men even*, of fair prospects, to neglect *their agricultural interests* for military pursuits, which, in a new country, were certainly of paramount importance, if not the greater of the two.

I know that it became very hard for me to content myself to labor as I had done, after witnessing this grand display. I was completely intoxicated with a military spirit, and sighed for the liberty to go out "on the lines" and fight the British.

The martial music, the waving plumes, and magnificent uniform, had driven from my mind entirely the bloodshed and carnage of the battle field; beside, I was sick and tired of being a slave, and felt ready to do almost any thing to get where I could act and feel like a free man.

I became acquainted with a Mr. McClure, a merchant in Bath, who, while on a journey to Philadelphia, to purchase goods, was taken suddenly ill and died; when his brother, George McClure, came on to attend to his diseased brother's business. He was a fine, persevering kind of man, and very soon got to be General McClure, and commanded the brigade in Steuben County, and, as such, was liable to be called at any time when his services were required, to go to the frontier and guard our lines from the invasion of the English army.

To him I applied for a situation as waiter, which he readily agreed to give me if I could get the consent of Captain Helm. I thought there would be no trouble about that; and oh! how I dreamed of and anticipated the happiness of being *something* beside a slave, for a *little while at least*. Almost every day I went to the store to talk to Gen. McClure of this greatest happiness imaginable, "going to the lines!" and was impatient for the chance to arrive that would send me there.

At last Gen. McClure wrote to Gen. Armstrong, to say that he was ready to obey any order that he might send him, and march to "the lines," if his services were needed; and, to *my* inexpressible joy, marching orders were returned. I nearly flew in search of Capt. Helm, never once suspecting that he would object; because I knew that he did not then require my services himself, and the pay would be quite as good as he had been receiving for my time; besides I had so completely set my heart on going, that it was impossible for me to dream of a disappointment so bitter as that of being denied going "to the lines."

Oh! how then were my high hopes fallen, and how much more hateful appeared that slavery which had blighted all my military

574

prospects? Nor was Capt. Helm's heartless and mercenary reply to my humble pleading any antidote to my disappointed feelings and desire for freedom. He said, "you shall not go; I will permit nothing of the kind, so let there be an end to it. The *pay* is all well enough, I know, but if you get killed your wages will stop; and then who, do you suppose, will indemnify me for the loss? Go about your business, and let me hear no more of such nonsense!"

There was an emergency I had not provided for; and, as I then believed, the master could make no demand on or for the slaves beyond the grave, I was silent; but both master and myself were mistaken on that point; for I have since learned numerous instances where slaves have fought and died in the service of their master's country, and the slave-owner received his wages up to the hour of his death, and then recovered of the United States the full value of his person as property!

Gen. McClure left soon after for the frontier; my saddened heart followed him, and that was all; my body was in slavery still, and painful though it was, I must quietly submit.

The General, however, reaped but few if any laurels in that campaign; he burned the small village of Newark, in Canada, for which he got very little credit on either side of the lake; so I comforted myself as well as I could with the reflection, that all who "went to the wars" did not return covered with glory and laurels of victory.

I continued to live with the Towers; and in the fall of that year, I had the misfortune to cut my foot badly. While chopping fire wood at the door, I accidentally struck my ax against a post, which glanced the blow in such a manner that it came down with sufficient force to nearly sever my great toe from my left foot, gashing upward completely through the large joint, which made a terrible wound. Dr. Taylor was immediately called, and sewed the flesh together, taking two stitches on the upper, and one on the under, side of the foot, before it began to swell; but when the swelling came on, the stitches on the upper side gave way, which occasioned the toe to fall over so much, that I have

575

been slightly lame from that day to this. For several weeks I was unable to be moved, and was regularly attended by Dr. Taylor, but as soon as it could be done without danger, I was taken back to Capt. Helm's, where I found things in much the same condition as when I left them over a year before.

On leaving the family of Mr. Tower, I endeavored to express to them as well in my power the gratitude I felt for their kindness, and the attention I had received during my lameness.

We returned to Bath in a sleigh, and arrived without accident or any great suffering. But the kind treatment I had always received from the Messrs. Tower and family, made it very hard for me to reconcile myself to my former mode of living; especially now that I was lame and weak, from sickness and long confinement; besides, it was cold weather. Oh! how hard it did seem to me, after having a good bed and plenty of bed clothes every night for so long time, to now throw myself down, like a dog, on the "*softest side*" of a rough board, without a pillow, and without a particle of bedding to cover me during the long cold nights of winter. To be reduced from a plentiful supply of good, wholesome food, to the mere pittance which the Captain allowed his slaves, seemed to me beyond endurance.

And yet I had always lived and fared thus, but I never felt so bitterly these hardships and the cruelties of Slavery as I did at that time; making a virtue of necessity, however, I turned my thoughts in another direction.

I managed to purchase a spelling book, and set about teaching myself to read, as best I could. Every spare moment I could find was devoted to that employment, and when about my work I could catch now and then a stolen glance at my book, just to refresh my memory with the simple lesson I was trying to learn. But here Slavery showed its cloven foot in all its hideous deformity. It finally reached the ears of my master that I was learning to read; and then, if he saw me with a book or a paper in my hand, oh, how he would swear at me, sending me off in a hurry, about some employment. Still I persevered, but was more careful about being seen making any attempt to learn to read. At last, however, I was discovered, and had to pay the penalty of my determination.

I had been set to work in the sugar bush, and I took my spelling book with me. When a spare moment occurred I sat down to study, and so absorbed was I in the attempt to blunder through my lesson, that I did not hear the Captain's son-in-law coming until he was fairly upon me. He sprang forward, caught my poor old spelling book, and threw it into the fire, where it was burned to ashes; and then came my turn. He gave me first a severe flogging, and then swore if he ever caught me with another book, he would "whip every inch of skin off my back," &c.

This treatment, however, instead of giving me the least idea of giving it up, only made me look upon it as a more valuable attainment. Else, why should my oppressors feel so unwilling that their slaves should possess that which they thought so essential to themselves? Even then, with my back bleeding and smarting from the punishment I had received, I determined to learn to read and write, at all hazards, if my life was only spared. About this time Capt. Helm began to sell off his slaves to different persons, as he could find opportunity, and sometimes at a great sacrifice. It became apparent that the Captain, instead of prospering in business, was getting poorer every day.

CHAPTER IX

DEATH BED AND BRIDAL SCENES

Neither Capt. Helm nor his wife made any religious pretensions. I hardly know whether or not they were avowed infidels; but they alike ridiculed all religious professions and possessed some very singular notions regarding life and death.

I have often heard the Captain say, that no person need die unless they choose to do so; and his wife was of the same belief. I have frequently heard her remark that if mankind would firmly resist death it would flee from them.

An opportunity, however, was soon after given to test the truth of this strange dogma. Mrs. Helm's health began to decline, but she would pay no attention to it, following her usual course and regular routine of household duties; but all in vain; she was taken down, alarmingly ill, and it became apparent to all, that the "king of terrors" had chosen his victim. She tried with all her natural energy of character, to baffle his pursuit and escape his steady approach, but all to no purpose. "The valley and the shadow of death" were before her, and she had no assurance that the "rod and staff" of the Almighty would sustain and comfort her through the dark passage. She shrank with perfect horror from the untried scenes of the future.

If any one had ever envied Mrs. Helm in her drawing-room, richly attired and sparkling with jewels, or as she moved with the stately step of a queen among her trembling slaves, they should have beheld her on her death bed! They should have listened to her groans and cries for help, while one piercing shriek after another rang through the princely mansion of which she had been the absolute mistress!

Surrounded as she was with every elegance and luxury that wealth could procure, she lay shrieking out her prayers for a short respite, a short lengthening out of the life she had spent so unprofitably; her eyes wandering restlessly about the apartment, and her hands continually clinching the air, as if to grasp something that would prevent her from sinking into the embrace of death! There was not a slave present, who would have exchanged places with her. Not one of those over whom she had ruled so arbitrarily would have exchanged their rough, lowly cabin and quiet conscience, for all the wealth and power she had ever possessed.

Nothing of all she had enjoyed in life, nor all that she yet called her own, could give her one hour of life or one peaceful moment in death!

Oh! what a scene was that! The wind blew, and great drops of rain fell on the casements. The room lighted only with a single taper; the wretched wife mingles her dying groans with the howling of the storm, until, as the clock struck the hour of midnight she fell back upon her pillow and expired, amid the tears and cries of her family and friends, who not only deplored the loss of a wife and mother, but were grieved by the manner in which she died.

The slaves were all deeply affected by the scene; some doubtless truly lamented the death of their mistress; others rejoiced that she was no more, and all were more or less frightened. One of them I remember went to the pump and wet his face, so as to appear to weep with the rest.

What a field was opened for reflection, by the agonizing death of Mrs. Helm? Born and reared in affluence; well educated and highly accomplished, possessed of every means to become a useful woman and an ornament to her sex; which she most likely would have been, had she been instructed in the Christian religion, and had lived under a different influence. As infidelity ever deteriorates from the female character, so Slavery transforms more than one, otherwise excellent woman, into a feminine monster. Of Mrs. Helm, with her active intellect and great force of character, it made a tyrannical demon. Her race, however, is ended; her sun gone down in darkness, and her soul we must leave in the keeping of a righteous God, to whom we must all give an account for the deeds done in the body. But in view of the transitory pleasures of this life; the unsatisfactory realization of wealth, and the certainty of death, we may well inquire, "What shall it profit a man to gain the whole world and lose his own soul?"

Some little time after the scene just recorded, there came to Bath a young physician named Henry, who commenced practice under very flattering prospects. He was an accomplished young man, well educated and very skillful in his profession. He was affable and gay in his manners, and very fond of company. An intimate acquaintance was soon formed with Capt. Helm and family, and he called almost daily to chat and drink wine with the Captain,—both being quite fond of a social glass.

One night in the depth of winter, the Doctor was called to see a patient who lived six miles down the Conhocton river. Previous, however, to the call, he had accepted an invitation to attend a party at Capt. Helm's, and there he was found. They had music and dancing, while the wine passed around very freely. None seemed to join in the dance and other amusements of the evening with more enjoyment than did Dr. Henry; but after he was sent for, it being a most bitter cold night, he asked the Captain for a horse to ride to see his patient, to which he readily assented, and had his fine *race-horse* (for the Captain had not left off all his old habits), brought out from the stable, and the Doctor sprang lightly into the saddle. Unfortunately his way led by the race-course, and when the trained animal came to it he started with such speed as to throw the Doctor to the ground, where he lay all that terrible cold night. In the morning, some person going after wood, came in sight of the Doctor as he was trying to creep away on his frozen hands and feet. He

580

was put into the sleigh and taken to the village with all possible speed. All was done for him that could be, but his feet and legs were frozen solid. His uncle, Dr. Henry, was brought as soon as possible, who decided that nothing could save his life but the amputation of both legs, just below the knee. This was done; but what a change in the prospects of this promising young man! Instead of stepping lightly about as he used to do, with a smiling countenance, he at last came forth after a tedious confinement, a cripple for life, hobbling about on his knees, sad and dejected. And what, think you, was the cause of this terrible calamity? What prevented the Doctor from an exertion to save his life? Wine, intoxicating wine, was undoubtedly the occasion of the heedless and reckless conduct of both himself and Capt. Helm. And should not this circumstance be a warning to parents and guardians, to young men and children, "to look not upon the wine when it is red," and remember that at last "it will bite like a serpent and sting like an adder?" Should it not also remind those who have guests to entertain, of the sinfulness of putting the cup to their neighbor's lips? Certainly it should. But I must resume my story.

About this time Major Thornton of Bath, died. He had long been an intimate friend and acquaintance of Capt. Helm, and as the reader is already informed of the death of Mrs. Helm, they will not be surprised to know that he began to look earnestly after the widow of his late friend. It become apparent that his solicitude for the loneliness of Madam Thornton was not so much as a disconsolate widow, as that of making her the future Mrs. Helm; nor was it less observable that the new-made widow accepted the Captain's attentions with great favor, and more as a lover than a comforter.

The result was, after the Major had been dead six weeks, Capt. Helm was married to his widow, and brought her and her servants in great triumph to his house, giving her the charge of it. His own servants were discharged, and hers took their places.

All went on pleasantly for a while; then the slaves began to grow sullen and discontented; and two of them ran away. Capt. Helm started a man named Morrison, a Scotchman, in pursuit, who hunted them ten days, and then returned without any tidings of the absconding slaves. They made good their escape and were never heard from afterwards, by those whose interest suffered by the loss.

I was one afternoon at a neighbor's house in the village, when I was suddenly taken so violently ill with pain in my head and side, that I had to be carried home. When we arrived there, I was allowed a pallet of straw to lie on, which was better than nothing. Day after day, my disease increased in violence, and my master employed a physician to attend me through my illness, which brought me very low indeed. I was constantly burning with fever, and so thirsty that I knew not what I would have given for a draught of cold water, which was denied me by the physician's direction. I daily grew weaker until I was reduced to helplessness, and was little else than "skin and bones." I really thought my time had come to die; and when I had strength to talk, I tried to arrange the few little business affairs I had, and give my father direction concerning them. And then I began to examine my own condition before God, and to determine how the case stood between Him and my poor soul. And "there was the rub." I had often excused myself, for frequent derelictions in duty, and often wild and passionate outbreaks, on account of the hardness of my lot, and the injustice with which I was treated, even in my best endeavors to do as well as I knew how. But now, with death staring me in the face, I could see that though I was a friendless "slave-boy," I had *not* always done as well as I knew how; that I had *not* served God as I knew I ought, nor had I always set a good example before my fellow-slaves, nor warned them as well as I might, "to flee the wrath to come." Then I prayed my Heavenly Father to spare me a little longer, that I might serve Him better; and in His mercy and gracious goodness, He did so; though when the fever was turning they gave me up; and I could hear them say, when they came to feel my pulse, "he is almost gone," "it will soon be over," &c., and then inquire if I knew them. I did, but was too weak to say so. I recollect with gratitude, the kindness of Mrs. H.A. Townsend, who sent me many delicacies and cooling drinks to soften the rigor of my disease; and though I suppose she has long since "passed away" and gone to her reward, may the blessing of those who are ready to perish, rest upon the descendants of that excellent woman.

Capt. Helm was driving on in his milling, distillery and farming business. He now began to see the necessity of treating his slaves better by far than he had ever done before, and granted them greater privileges than he would have dared to do at the South. Many of the slaves he had sold, were getting their liberty and doing well.

CHAPTER X

HIRED OUT TO A NEW MASTER

While I was staying with my master at Bath, he having little necessity for my services, hired me out to a man by the name of Joseph Robinson, for the purpose of learning me to drive a team. Robinson lived about three miles from the village of Bath, on a small farm, and was not only a poor man but a very mean one. He was cross and heartless in his family, as well as tyrannical and cruel to those in his employ; and having hired me as a "slave boy," he appeared to feel at full liberty to wreak his brutal passion on me at any time, whether I deserved rebuke or not; nor did his terrible outbreaks of anger vent themselves in oaths, curses and threatenings only, but he would frequently draw from the cart-tongue a heavy iron pin, and beat me over the head with it, so unmercifully that he frequently sent the blood flowing over my scanty apparel, and from that to the ground, before he could feel satisfied.

These kind of beatings were not only excessively painful, but they always reminded me of the blows I had so often received from the key, in the hand of Mrs. Helm, when I was but a little waiter lad; and in truth I must say that the effect of these heavy blows on the head, have followed me thus far through life; subjecting me to frequent and violent head-aches, from which I never expect to be entirely free. Even to this day I shudder at the thought, when I think how Robinson used to fly at me, swearing, foaming, and seeming to think there was no weapon too large or too heavy to strike me with.

He and I were at one time logging with a yoke of oxen, which

584

it was my business to drive. At that time rattle-snakes were numerous, and a great terror to the inhabitants. To be bitten by one of these poisonous reptiles was certain and almost instant death; hence, the greatest caution and constant vigilance was necessary to avoid them while at work. I had been sent with the oxen to draw a log to the pile, and when I came up to it, I observed that it appeared to be hollow; but stepping forward, with the chain in my hand, ready to attach it to the log, when, oh, horror! the warning rattle of a snake sounded like a death knell in my ears, proceeding from the log I was about to lay hold of. I was so much frightened by the sound, that I dropped the chain as though it were red hot, left my team, and ran with all the speed in my power, screaming "murder, murder!" as loud as I could.

This proceeding, which was the fearful impulse of the moment, offended Robinson, and gave him another opportunity to beat me most cruelly. He was himself as much afraid of rattle-snakes as I; but he was the master and I the "slave boy," which made a vast difference. He caught hold of me, and, with horrid oaths, beat me with his fist again and again; threatening me with awful punishment if I did not instantly return and bring the log to the desired spot. I never can forget the mortal agony I was in, while compelled by his kicks and blows to return and fasten the chain around the log containing the deadly serpent. I, however, succeeded with trembling hands, and drove the oxen, but keeping myself at the fartherest possible distance from them and the log. When I finally arrived at the pile, Mr. Robinson and some other men, cut a hole with an ax in the log, and killed the large, venomous rattle-snake that had occasioned me so much alarm and such a cruel beating. Nor was the uncontrollable and brutal passion of Robinson his only deficiency; he was mean as he was brutal.

He had, at one time, borrowed a wagon of a neighbor living two miles distant, through a dense forest. On the day of the total eclipse of the sun, it entered his head that it would be fine sport, knowing my my ignorance and superstition, to send me, just as the darkness was coming on, to return the borrowed wagon. I accordingly hitched the ox-team to it and started. As I proceeded through the wood, I saw, with astonishment and some alarm, that it was growing very dark, and thought it singular at that hour of the day. When I reached the place of my destination it was almost total darkness, and some persons, ignorant as myself, were running about, wringing their hands, and declaring that they believed the Day of Judgment had come, and such like expressions.

The effect of all this was, however, very different from what my master had expected. I thought, of course, if the judgment day had come, I should be no longer a slave in the power of a heartless tyrant. I recollect well of thinking, that if indeed all things earthly were coming to an end, I should be free from Robinson's brutal force, and as to meeting my Creator, I felt far less dread of that than of meeting my cross, unmerciful master. I felt that, sinful as I had been, and unworthy as I was, I should be far better off than I then was; driven to labor all day, without compensation; half starved and poorly clad, and above all, subjected to the whims and caprices of any heartless tyrant to whom my master might give the power to rule over me. But I had not much time for reflection, I hurried home; my mind filled with the calm anticipation that the end of all things was at hand; which greatly disappointed my expectant master, who was looking for me to return in a great fright, making some very ludicrous demonstration of fear and alarm. But after a few months more of hardship I was permitted to return to Capt. Helm's, where I was treated much better than at Robinson's, and much, better than the Captain used to treat his slaves.

Capt. Helm, not having demand for slave labor as much as formerly, was in the practice of hiring out his slaves to different persons, both in and out of the village; and among others, my only sister was hired out to a *professed* gentleman living in Bath. She had become the mother of two or three children, and was considered a good servant.

One pleasant Sabbath morning, as I was passing the house where she lived, on my way to the Presbyterian church, where I was sent to ring the bell as usual, I heard the most piteous cries and earnest pleadings issuing from the dwelling. To my horror and the astonishment of those with me, my poor sister made her appearance, weeping bitterly, and followed by her inhuman master, who was polluting the air of that clear Sabbath morning, with the most horrid imprecations and threatenings, and at the same time flourishing a large raw-hide. Very soon his bottled wrath burst forth, and the blows, aimed with all his strength, descended upon the unprotected head, shoulders and back of the helpless woman, until she was literally cut to pieces. She writhed in his powerful grasp, while shriek after shriek died away in heart-rending moanings; and yet the inhuman demon continued to beat her, though her pleading cries had ceased, until obliged to desist from the exhaustion of his own strength.

What a spectacle was that, for the sight of a brother? The God of heaven only knows the conflict of feeling I then endured; He alone witnessed the tumult of my heart, at this outrage of manhood and kindred affection. God knows that my will was good enough to have wrung his neck; or to have drained from his heartless system its last drop of blood! And yet I was obliged to turn a deaf ear to her cries for assistance, which to this day ring in my ears. Strong and athletic as I was, no hand of mine could be raised in her defence, but at the peril of both our lives;—nor could her husband, had he been a witness of the scene, be allowed any thing more than unresisting submission to any cruelty, any indignity which the master saw fit to inflict on *his wife*, but the other's *slave*.

Does any indignant reader feel that I was wanting in courage or brotherly affection, and say that he would have interfered, and, at all hazards, rescued his sister from the power of her master; let him remember that he is a *freeman*; that he has not from his infancy been taught to cower beneath the white man's frown, and bow at his bidding, or suffer all the rigor of the slave laws. Had the gentlemanly woman-whipper been seen beating his horse, or his ox, in the manner he beat my poor sister, and that too for no fault which the law could recognize as an offence, he would have been complained of most likely; but as it was, she was but a "slave girl,"—with whom the slave law allowed her master to do what he pleased.

Well, I finally passed on, with a clinched fist and contracted brow, to the church, and rung the bell, I think rather furiously, to notify the inhabitants of Bath, that it was time to assemble for the worship of that God who has declared himself to be "no respecter of persons." With my own heart beating wildly with indignation and sorrow, the kind reader may imagine my feelings when I saw the smooth-faced hypocrite, the inhuman slave-whipper, enter the church, pass quietly on to his accustomed seat, and then meekly bow his hypocritical face on the damask cushion, in the reverent acknowledgment of that religion which teaches its adherents "to do unto others as they would be done by," just as if nothing unusual had happened on that Sabbath morning. Can any one wonder that I, and other slaves, often doubted the sincerity of every white man's religion? Can it be a matter of astonishment, that slaves often feel that there is no just God for the poor African? Nay, verily; and were it not for the comforting and sustaining influence that these poor, illiterate and suffering creatures feel as coming from an unearthly source, they would in their ignorance all become infidels. To me, that beautiful Sabbath morning was clouded in midnight darkness, and I retired to ponder on what could be done.

For some reason or other, Capt. Helm had supplied every lawyer in that section of country with slaves, either by purchase or hire; so when I thought of seeking legal redress for my poor, mangled sister, I saw at once it would be all in vain. The laws were in favor of the slave owner, and besides, every legal gentleman in the village had one or more of the Captain's slaves, who were treated with more or less rigor; and of course they would do nothing toward censuring one of their own number, so nothing could be done to give the slave even the few privileges which the laws of the State allowed them.

The Captain sold my aunt Betsy Bristol to a distinguished lawyer in the village, retaining her husband, Aaron Bristol, in his own employ; and two of her children he sold to another legal gentleman named Cruger. One day Captain Helm came out where the slaves were at work, and finding Aaron was not there, he fell into a great rage and swore terribly. He finally started off to a beach tree, from which he cut a stout limb, and trimmed it so as to leave a knot on the but end of the stick, or bludgeon rather, which was about two and a half feet in length. With this formidable weapon he started for Aaron's lonely cabin. When the solitary husband saw him coming he suspected that he was angry, and went forth to meet him in the street. They had no sooner met than my master seized Aaron by the collar, and taking the limb he had prepared by the smaller end, commenced beating him with it, over the head and face, and struck him some thirty or more terrible blows in quick succession; after which Aaron begged to know for what he was so unmercifully flogged.

"Because you deserve it," was the angry reply. Aaron said that he had ever endeavored to discharge his duty, and had done so to the best of his ability; and that he thought it very hard to be treated in that manner for no offence at all. Capt. Helm was astonished at his audacity; but the reader will perceive that the slaves were not blind to the political condition of the country, and were beginning to feel that they had some rights, and meant to claim them.

Poor Aaron's face and head, however, was left in a pitiable condition after such a pummeling with a knotty stick. His face, covered with blood, was so swollen that he could hardly see for some time; but what of that? Did he not belong to Capt. Helm, soul and body; and if his brutal owner chose to destroy his own property, certainly had he not a right to do so, without let or hindrance? Of course; such is the power that Slavery gives one

589

human being over another.

And yet it must be confessed that among the poor, degraded and ignorant slaves there exists a foolish pride, which loves to boast of their master's wealth and influence. A white person, too poor to own slaves, is as often looked upon with as much disdain by the miserable slave as by his wealthy owner. This disposition seems to be instilled into the mind of every slave at the South, and indeed, I have heard slaves object to being sent in very small companies to labor in the field, lest that some passer-by should think that they belonged to a poor man, who was unable to keep a large gang. Nor is this ridiculous sentiment maintained by the slaves only; the rich planter feels such a contempt for all white persons without slaves, that he does not want them for his neighbors. I know of many instances where such persons have been under the necessity of buying or hiring slaves, just to preserve their reputation and keep up appearances; and even among a class of people who profess to be opposed to Slavery, have I known instances of the same kind, and have heard them apologize for their conduct by saying that "when in Rome, we must do as the Romans do."

Uncle Aaron Bristol was one of Capt. Helm's slaves who had a large amount of this miserable pride; and for him to be associated with a white man in the same humble occupation, seemed to give him ideas of great superiority, and full liberty to treat him with all the scorn and sarcasm he was capable of, in which my uncle was by no means deficient.

At this time the Captain owned a fine and valuable horse, by the name of *Speculator*. This horse, groomed by uncle Aaron, stood sometimes at Bath and sometimes at Geneva; and at the latter village another horse was kept, groomed by a white man. The white groom was not very well pleased with Aaron's continual disparagement of the clumsy animal which my uncle called "a great, awkward plow-horse;" and then he would fling out some of his proud nonsense about "*poor white people* who were obliged to groom their own old dumpy horses," &c.

Well, things went on in this unpleasant manner for several weeks, when at last the white groom and Aaron met at Geneva, and the horse belonging to the former, designedly or accidentally, escaped from his keeper, and came with full speed, with his mouth wide open, after Speculator. When the fiery fellow had overtaken uncle Aaron he attempted to grasp the wethers of Speculator with his teeth, instead of which he caught Aaron on the inside of his thigh, near the groin, from whence he bit a large piece of flesh, laying the bone entirely bare; at the same moment flinging Aaron to the ground, some rods off; and the next instant he kicked Speculator down a steep embankment Aaron was taken up for dead, and Dr. Henry sent for, who dressed his wounds; and after several months' confinement he finally recovered. It is probable that the biting and overthrow of Aaron saved his life, as he must have otherwise been killed in the encounter of the two horses.

A while after his recovery, uncle Aaron succeeded in procuring a team and some kind of vehicle, in which he put his wife and children, and between two days, took "French leave" of his master as well as of the lawyer to whom his wife belonged.

The lawyer, however, was far from being pleased when he missed his property, and immediately set his wits to work to reclaim her. All was kept secret as possible, but it was whispered about that it was to be done by a State's warrant, for removing the clothing and furniture they had taken, and so, being thus arrested, "Madam Bristol" would be glad to return to her work in the lawyer's kitchen. But Aaron was a smart, shrewd man, and kept out of their reach, where he soon found friends and employment, and could go where he pleased, without having an infuriated master to beat and disfigure him with a knotted stick, until his clothes were bespattered with blood. They appreciated their liberty, and lived and died in peace and freedom.

Capt. Helm continued his old manner of treating slaves, dealing out their weekly allowance of corn or meal; but living as we now did, so much more intimately with white inhabitants, our condition was materially improved. The slaves became more refined in manners and in possession of far greater opportunities to provide for themselves, than they had ever before enjoyed, and yet it was *Slavery*. Any reverse in the fortunes of our master would be disadvantageous to us. Oh, how this fearful uncertainty weighed upon us as we saw that our master was not prospering and increasing in wealth; but we had not the dismal fears of the loathsome slave-pen, rice swamps, and many other things we should have to fear in Virginia. We were still *slaves*, and yet we had so much greater chance to learn from the kind, intelligent people about us, so many things which we never knew before, that I think a slave-trader would have found it a difficult task to take any one of us to a Southern slave market, if our master had so ordered it.

The village of Bath is rather an out-of-the-way place, hemmed in on all sides by mountains of considerable height, leaving an opening on the north, through a pleasant valley, to the head of Crooked Lake. Produce of every kind, when once there, met a ready sale for the New York market.

In the first settlement of the country this was the only outlet for the country produce, which was transported in rude boats or vessels called *arks*, built during the winter season to await the spring freshet; then they loaded them with wheat or other produce, and sent them to Baltimore or elsewhere. They used also to obtain great quantities of fine lumber, and floated it through the same rivers every spring; but it was attended with great loss of life and property.

Bath assumed a warlike appearance during the last war with Great Britain; the public square was dotted all over with officers, marquees, and soldiers' tents. Some of these soldiers were unprincipled and reckless men, who seemed to care very little what they did.

One evening I was walking around the encampment in company with a Mr. James Morrison, a clerk in the land office, looking at the soldiers, until we came near a sentinel on duty.

592

He kept his gun to his shoulder until we came near enough, and then he attempted to run me through with his bayonet. Young Morrison sprang forward, and seizing the musket, told me to run; I did so, which probably saved my life.

CHAPTER XI

THOUGHTS ON FREEDOM

After living sometime in Bath, and having the privilege of more enlightened society, I began to think that it was possible for me to become a free man in some way besides going into the army or running away, as I had often thought of doing. I had listened to the conversation of others, and determined to ask legal counsel on the subject the first opportunity I could find. Very soon after, as I was drawing wood, I met on the river bridge, Mr. D. Cruger, the eminent lawyer before mentioned, and I asked him to tell me if I was not free, by the laws of New York. He started, and looked around him as if afraid to answer my question, but after a while told me I was *not* free. I passed on, but the answer to my question by no means satisfied me, especially when I remembered the hesitancy with which it was given.

I sought another opportunity to speak with Mr. Cruger, and at last found him in his office alone; then he conversed freely on the subject of Slavery, telling me that Capt. Helm could not hold me as a slave in that State, if I chose to leave him, and then directed me to D. Comstock and J. Moore; the first being at the head of a manumission society, and the last named gentleman one of its directors.

Our condition, as I have said before, was greatly improved; and yet the more we knew of freedom the more we desired it, and the less willing were we to remain in bondage. The slaves that Capt. Helm had sold or hired out, were continually leaving him and the country, for a place of freedom; and I determined to become my own possessor.

There is no one, I care not how favorable his condition, who desires to be a slave, to labor for nothing all his life for the benefit of others. I have often heard fugitive slaves say, that it was not so much the cruel beatings and floggings that they received which induced them to leave the South, as the idea of dragging out a whole life of unrequited toil to enrich their masters.

Everywhere that Slavery exists, it is nothing but *slavery*. I found it just as hard to be beaten over the head with a piece of iron in New York as it was in Virginia. Whips and chains are everywhere necessary to degrade and brutalize the slave, in order to reduce him to that abject and humble state which Slavery requires. Nor is the effect much less disastrous on the man who holds supreme control over the soul and body of his fellow beings. Such unlimited power, in almost every instance transforms the man into a tyrant; the brother into a demon.

When the first of our persecuted race were brought to this country it was to teach them to reverence the only true and living God; or such was the answer of Her Majesty Queen Elizabeth of England, when her subjects desired the liberty to bring from their native land the poor, ignorant African. "Let them," said the Queen, "be brought away only by their own consent, otherwise the act will be detestable, and bring down the vengeance of heaven upon us." A very different position truly, from the one assumed at the present day by apologists for the traffic in human flesh. But, to return to myself.

I had determined to make an effort to own myself, and as a preliminary step, I obtained permission of Capt. Helm to visit some friends living in Canandaigua and Geneva. This was in the winter of 1814. I went first to Geneva; from there to Canandaigua. Between the two villages I met a company of United States' troops, returning from Buffalo, where they had been to repel an invasion of the British.

The two villages above named, were small but very pretty, having been laid out with taste and great care. Some wealthy and enterprising gentlemen had come from the East into this great

Western country, who were making every improvement in their power. The dense forest had long since fallen under the stroke of the woodman's ax, and in that section, flourishing villages were springing up as if by magic, where so lately roamed wild beasts and rude savages, both having fallen back before the march of civilization.

I called on James Moore, as directed by Mr. Cruger, and found he was one of the directors of the "Manumission Society," as it was then called. This was an association of humane and intelligent gentlemen whose object it was to aid any one who was illegally held in bondage. The funds of the society were ample; and able counsel was employed to assist those who needed it. The late lamented John C. Spencer, one of the most eminent lawyers in Western New York, was then counsel for that society.

I soon got an interview with Mr. Moore, to whom I related the history of my life,—the story of my wrongs and hardships. I told him about my having been hired out by Capt. Helm, which he said was sufficient to insure my freedom! Oh! how my heart leaped at the thought! The tears started, my breast heaved with a mighty throb of gratitude, and I could hardly refrain from grasping his hand or falling down at his feet; and perhaps should have made some ludicrous demonstration of my feelings, had not the kind gentleman continued his conversation in another direction.

He said that indispensable business called him to Albany, where he must go immediately, but assured me that he would return in March following; then I must come to him and he would see that I had what justly belonged to me—my freedom from Slavery. He advised me to return to Bath and go on with my work as usual until March, but to say nothing of my intentions and prospects. I returned according to his directions, with a heart so light, that I could not realize that my bonds were not yet broken, nor the yoke removed from off my neck. I was already free in spirit, and I silently exulted in the bright prospect of liberty.

Could my master have felt what it was to be relieved of such a crushing weight, as the one which was but partially lifted from my mind, he would have been a happier man than he had been for a long time.

I went cheerfully back to my labor, and worked with alacrity, impatient only for March to come; and as the time drew near I began to consider what kind of an excuse I could make to get away. I could think of none, but I determined to go without one, rather than to remain.

Just before the time appointed for me to meet Mr. Moore, a slave girl named Milly, came secretly to Bath. She had been one of Capt. Helm's slaves, and he had a while before sold her to a man who lived some distance west of the village. Milly had now taken the matter into her own hands. She had left her master to take care of himself, and was in short, "running away," determined as myself, that she would be a slave no longer; resolved on death, or freedom from the power of the slaveholder.

The time I had set for my departure was so near at hand, that I concluded to accompany her in her flight. When the dark night came on, we started together, and traveled all night, and just as the day dawned we arrived at Manchester, where we stopped a short time with one Thomas Watkins.

But I was not to be let go so easily. I had been missed at Capt. Helm's, and several men started in immediate pursuit. I was weary, and so intent on getting a little rest that I did not see my pursuers until they had well nigh reached the house where I was; but I *did* see them in time to spring from the house with the agility of a deer, and to run for the woods as for life. And indeed, I so considered it. I was unarmed to be sure, and not prepared to defend myself against two or three men, armed to the teeth; but it would have gone hard with me before I surrendered myself to them, after having dreamed as I had, and anticipated the blessings of a free man. I escaped them, thank God, and reached the woods, where I concealed myself for some time, and where I had ample opportunity to reflect on the injustice and cruelty of my oppressors, and to ask myself why it was that I was obliged to fly from my home. Why was I there panting and weary, hungry and destitute—skulking in the woods like a thief, and concealing myself like a murderer? What had I done? For what fault, or for what crime was I pursued by armed men, and hunted like a beast of prey? God only knows how these inquiries harrowed up my very soul, and made me well nigh doubt the justice and mercy of the Almighty, until I remembered my narrow escape, when my doubts dissolved in grateful tears.

But why, oh why, had I been forced to flee thus from my fellow men? I was guilty of no crime; I had committed no violence; I had broken no law of the land; I was not charged even with a fault, except of *the love of liberty* and a desire to be *free*! I had claimed the right to possess my own person, and remove it from oppression. Oh my God, thought I, can the American People, who at this very hour are pouring out their blood in defence of their country's liberty; offering up as a sacrifice on the battle field their promising young men, to preserve their land and hearthstones from English oppression; can they, will they, continue to hunt the poor African slave from their soil because he desires that same liberty, so dear to the heart of every American citizen? Will they not blot out from their fair escutcheon the foul stain which Slavery has cast upon it? Will they not remember the Southern bondman, in whom the love of freedom is as inherent as in themselves; and will they not, when contending for equal rights, use their mighty forces "to break *every yoke*, and let the oppressed go free?" God grant that it may be so!

As soon as I thought it prudent, I pursued my journey, and finally came out into the open country, near the dwelling of Mr. Dennis Comstock, who, as I have said, was president of the Manumission Society. To him I freely described my situation, and found him a friend indeed. He expressed his readiness to assist me, and wrote a line for me to take to his brother, Otis Comstock, who took me into his family at once. I hired to Mr.

Comstock for the season, and from that time onward lived with him nearly four years.

When I arrived there I was about twenty-two years of age, and felt for the first time in my life, that I was my own master. I cannot describe to a free man, what a proud manly feeling came over me when I hired to Mr. C. and made my first bargain, nor when I assumed the dignity of collecting my own earnings. Notwithstanding I was very happy in my freedom from Slavery, and had a good home, where for the first time in my life I was allowed to sit at table with others, yet I found myself very deficient in almost every thing which I should have learned when a boy.

These and other recollections of the past often saddened my spirit; but *hope* ,—cheering and bright, was now mine, and it lighted up the future and gave me patience to persevere.

In the autumn when the farm work was done, I called on Mr. Comstock for some money, and the first thing I did after receiving it I went to Canandaigua where I found a book-store kept by a man named J.D. Bemis, and of him I purchased some school books.

No king on his throne could feel prouder or grander than I did that day. With my books under my arm, and money of my own earning in my pocket, I stepped loftily along toward Farmington, where I determined to attend the Academy. The thought, however, that though I was twenty-three years old, I had yet to learn what most boys of eight years knew, was rather a damper on my spirits. The school was conducted by Mr. J. Comstock, who was a pleasant young man and an excellent teacher. He showed me every kindness and consideration my position and ignorance demanded; and I attended his school three winters, with pleasure and profit to myself at least.

When I had been with Mr. Comstock about a year, we received a visit from my old master, Capt. Helm, who had spared no pains to find me, and when he learned where I was he came to claim me as "his boy," who, he said he "wanted and must have."

Mr. Comstock told him I was *not* "his boy," and as such he would not give me up; and further, that I was free by the laws of the State. He assured the Captain that his hiring me out in the first instance, to Mr. Tower, forfeited his claim to me, and gave me a right to freedom,—but if he chose to join issue, they would have the case tried in the Supreme Court; but this proposition the Captain declined: he knew well enough that it would result in my favor; and after some flattery and coaxing, he left me with my friend, Mr. Comstock, in liberty and peace!

CHAPTER XII

CAPT HELM—DIVORCE—KIDNAPPING

The business affairs of Capt. Helm had for some time been far from prosperous; and now he was quite poor. His slave property proved a bad investment, and Madam Thornton a far worse one. She had already applied for a divorce, and a good share of the estate as alimony; both of which she succeeded in getting, the Captain allowing her to take pretty much her own course. These troubles, with costs of lawsuits, bad management, &c., had now emptied the coffers of my old master almost to the last farthing; and he began to cast about him for some way to replenish his purse, and retrieve his fallen fortunes.

Had Capt. Helm been brought up to honorable industry, and accustomed to look after his own pecuniary interests, he doubtless would have sustained his position; or if reverses were unavoidable, he would have by persevering industry, regained what he had lost. But he had been raised in a slave State, and Southern principles were as deeply instilled into his mind, as Southern manners were impressed on his life and conduct.

He had no partiality for labor of any kind; horse-racing and card-playing were far more congenial to his tastes; reduced as he now was, he would deny himself no luxury that his means or credit would procure. His few remaining slaves were given into the hands of an idle, brutal overseer —while they, half fed, half clothed, grew more and more discontented, and ran away on every opportunity that offered.

The Captain at last hit upon a method of making money, which, if it had been carried into operation on the high seas,

601

would in all probability have been called by its right name, and incurred the penalty of the gallows—as piracy. Ought it then to be deemed less criminal because transpiring on the free soil of the American Republic? I think not. Nor was it less censurable on account of its failure.

The Captain's plan was to collect all the slaves he had once owned, many of whom had escaped to the surrounding villages, and when once in his grasp, to run them speedily into a slave State, and there sell them for the Southern market. To carry forward this hellish design, it was necessary to have recourse to stratagem. Some person must be found to lure the unsuspecting slaves into the net he was spreading for them. At last he found a scoundrel named Simon Watkins, who for the consideration of fifty dollars, was to collect as many of the slaves as he could at one place; and when he had done so, he was to receive the money, leaving Capt. Helm to do the rest.

Simon set immediately about the business, which was first to go to Palmyra, and in great kindness and generosity, give a large party to the colored people,—desiring that all Capt. Helm's former slaves, *in particular,* should be present to have a joyous re-union, and celebrate their freedom in having a fine time generally.

Invitations were sent to all, and extensive preparation made for a large "social party," at Palmyra, at the house of Mrs. Bristol. My parents were invited; and Simon took the pains to come to Farmington to give me a special invitation. When the time arrived for the party, I went to Palmyra with the intention of attending. I had not the least suspicion of any thing wrong; yet, by some mysterious providence, or something for which I can not account, a presentiment took possession of my mind that all was not right. I knew not what I feared, and could in no way define my apprehensions; but I grew so uneasy, that I finally gave up the party and returned home, before the guests were assembled.

Capt. Helm and his assistants came on to Palmyra in disguise, before evening, and secreted themselves in one of the hotels to await the arrival of their victims.

At the appointed hour the slaves began to assemble in large numbers and great glee, without the least suspicion of danger. They soon began their amusements, and in the midst of their mirth, Capt. Helm and party stealthily crept from their hiding place and surrounded the house; then bursting in suddenly upon the revelers, began to make arrests. Such a tumult, such an affray as ensued would be hard to describe.

The slaves fought for their lives and their liberty, and the Captain's party for their property and power. Fists, clubs, chairs, and any thing they could get hold of, was freely used with a strength and will of men who had tasted the joys of freedom. Cries and curses were mingled, while blows fell like hail on both sides. Commands from our old master were met with shouts of bold defiance on the part of the negroes, until the miserable kidnappers were glad to desist, and were driven of—not stealthily as they came, but in quick time and in the best way they could, to escape the threatened vengeance of the slaves, who drove them like "feathers before the wind." But it was a terrible battle and many were severely wounded; among them was my father. He was taken to his home, mangled and bleeding, and from the effects of that night's affray he never recovered. He lingered on in feeble health until death finally released him from suffering, and placed him beyond the reach of kidnappers and tyrants.

The Captain and his party, enraged and disappointed in their plans at Palmyra, returned to Bath to see what could be done there toward success, in getting up a gang of slaves for the Southern market. When they came among the colored people of Bath, it was like a hawk alighting among a flock of chickens at noon-day. They scattered and ran in every direction, some to the woods, some hid themselves in cellars, and others in their terror plunged into the Conhocton River. In this manner the majority of the negroes escaped, but not all; and those were so unfortunate as to get caught were instantly thrown into a large covered "Pennsylvania wagon," and hurried off, closely guarded, to Olean Point. Among those taken were Harry Lucas, his wife, Lucinda, and seven children; Mrs. Jane Cooper and four children, with some others, were also taken.

When Capt. Helm arrived at Olean Point with his stolen freight of human beings, he was unexpectedly detained until he could build a boat,—which, to his great dismay took him several days.

The sorrow and fearful apprehension of those wretched recaptured slaves can not be described nor imagined by any one except those who have experienced a like affliction. They had basked for a short season in the sunshine of liberty, and thought themselves secure from the iron grasp of Slavery, and the heel of the oppressor, when in the height of their exultation, they had been thrust down to the lowest depths of misery and despair, with the oppressor's heel again upon their necks. To be snatched without a moment's warning from their homes and friends,—hurried and crowded into the close slave wagon, regardless of age or sex, like sheep for the slaughter, to be carried they knew not whither; but, doubtless to the dismal rice swamp of the South,—was to them an agony too great for endurance. The adult portion of the miserable company determined at last to go no farther with their heartless master, but to resist unto death if need be, before they surrendered themselves to the galling chains they had so recently broken, or writhed again under the torturing lash of the slave-driver.

Harry Lucas and wife, and Jane Cooper, silently prepared themselves for the conflict, determined to sell their lives as dearly as possible. When they were nearly ready to start, Jane Cooper sent her oldest daughter and younger sister, (she who is now our worthy friend Mrs. P. of Bath), into the woods, and then when the men undertook to get Lucas and the two women on board the boat the struggle commenced. The women fought the Captain and his confederates like a lioness robbed of her whelps! They ran and dodged about, making the woods ring

604

with their screams and shouts of "Murder! Murder! Help! Help! Murder!" until the Captain's party, seeing they could do nothing to quell them, became so exceedingly alarmed lest they should be detected in their illegal proceedings, that they ran off at full speed, as if they thought an officer at their heels. In their hurry and fright they caught two of Harry's children, and throwing them into the boat, pushed off as quick as possible, amid the redoubled cries of the agonized parents and sympathizing friends, all trying in every way possible, to recover from the merciless grasp of the man-stealer, the two frightened and screaming children. Guns were fired and horns sounded, but all to no purpose—they held tightly the innocent victims of their cupidity, and made good their escape.

Mr. D. C——, a gentleman of wealth and high standing in Steuben County, became responsible for the fifty dollars which Capt. Helm promised to pay Simon Watkins for his villainy in betraying, Judas-like, those unsuspecting persons whom it should have been his pleasure to protect and defend against their common oppressor,—his own as well as theirs.

In addition to this rascality, it can not appear very creditable to the citizens of Steuben County, that Capt. Helm and Thomas McBirney should both hold high and important offices at the time, and *after* they had been tried and convicted of the crime of kidnapping. Both of these gentlemen, guilty of a State's prison offence, were judges of the common pleas. T. McBirney was first judge in the county, and Capt. Helm was side judge; and notwithstanding their participation in, and conviction of, a flagrant outrage on the laws of God and man, they managed not only to escape the penalty, but to retain their offices and their respectable standing in community for years after.

CHAPTER XIII

LOCATE IN THE VILLAGE OF ROCHESTER

I continued to labor in the employ of Mr. O. Comstock, whose son, Zeno, was married during the year 1816, and purchased a farm on the site of the present flourishing village of Lockport, to which he moved his family and effects; but from a mistaken supposition that the Erie Canal, which was then under contemplation, would take a more southern route, he was induced to sell his farm in Hartland, which has proved a mine of wealth to the more fortunate purchaser.

In the winter of that year, I was sent by my employer to Hartland with a sleigh-load of produce, and passed through the village of Rochester, which I had never before seen. It was a very small, forbidding looking place at first sight, with few inhabitants, and surrounded by a dense forest.

I recollect that while pursuing my journey, I overtook a white man driving a span of horses, who contended that I had not a right to travel the public highway as other men did, but that it was my place to keep behind him and his team. Being in haste I endeavored to pass him quietly, but he would not permit it and hindered me several hours, very much to my annoyance and indignation. This was, however, but a slight incident indicating the bitter prejudice which every man seemed to feel against the negro. No matter how industrious he might be, no matter how honorable in his dealings, or respectful in his manners,—he was a "nigger," and as such he must be treated, with a few honorable exceptions.

This year also, my father died in the village of Palmyra, where, as I have before mentioned, he received injuries from which he never entirely recovered. After about six months severe illness which he bore with commendable patience and resignation, his spirit returned to God who gave it; and his sorrowing friends and bereaved family followed his remains to their final abode, where we laid him down to rest from unrequited labor and dire oppression, until "all they who are in their graves shall hear the voice of the Son of God, and they that hear shall live forever," where the "tears shall be wiped from off all faces"—and where the righteous bondman shall no longer fear the driver's lash or master's frown, but freely join in the song of "Alleluia! The Lord God Omnipotent reigneth!"

My father had a good reputation for honesty and uprightness of character among his employers and acquaintances, and was a kind, affectionate husband and a fond, indulgent parent. His, I believe was the life and death of a good man. "Peace be to his ashes."

The following season I commenced a new business—that of peddling in the village of Rochester such articles as my employer, Mr. Comstock, desired to sell: the products of his farm,—wheat, corn, oats, butter, cheese, meat, and poultry—all of which met a ready sale, generally for cash at liberal prices. That market was then but little known to the generality of farmers, and the enterprising gentlemen of that place, were desirous of encouraging commerce with the surrounding country, offered every encouragement in their power. Hence, we found it a profitable business, which I continued in for several months.

The present flourishing city of Rochester was then, as I have said, but a village in its infancy, situated near the upper falls of the Genesee River, and about seven miles from its mouth. Here, some time previously, three gentlemen from Maryland bought a large tract of land, and as no business man could fail to observe and appreciate its rare advantages they commenced laying out a village. Sirs Fitzhugh, Carroll, and Rochester, composed the company; but the management of the business devolved almost wholly on Col. Rochester, whose wealth, enterprise, and intelligence well qualified him for the undertaking; and as it had been assigned him to cognominate the new village, I have heard it said that he jocularly gave his reason for selecting its present title, as follows: "Should he call it *Fitzhugh* or *Carroll*, the slighted gentleman would certainly feel offended with the other; but if he called it by his own name, they would most likely *both* be angry with him; so it was best to serve them alike."

There was then two grist mills,—one owned by Mr. Ely, and the other by Mr. Brown; one small building for religious worship, occupied by the Presbyterians on Carroll street (now State street); and but two stone buildings within what now comprises that beautiful city. There were then no brick buildings at all, but business was good; merchants and mechanics from the East soon began to settle there and give it a thriving aspect.

About this time another company was formed, whose moving spirit was Mr. E. Stone, a man of worth and talent; the object of which was to locate another village at the head of navigation and about half way between the mouth of the river and Rochester, which they called *Carthage*.

The company commenced building and improving the place so rapidly, that many who came to purchase residences and business stations were at a loss to decide which of the two places would finally become the center of business. It, however, was soon perceivable that the advantage of water privileges, stone, and access to both, was greatly in favor of Rochester. At Carthage the Genesee is narrow and its banks steep and abrupt, rising in many places three hundred feet above the bed of the river, which of course render the privileges and business on it far less easy of access for building purposes. I may have occasion to speak hereafter of the expensive and magnificent bridge at Carthage, which was the wonder and admiration of the times.

The following year I concluded to go into business for myself, and was as much at loss as others, whether to locate at Rochester or Carthage; but after considering the matter in all its bearings, and closely watching the progress of events, my choice preponderated in favor of Rochester, and to that place I went, designing to enter into business on my own account.

It was indeed painful to my feelings to leave the home and family of Mr. Comstock, where I had experienced so much real comfort and happiness, where I had ever been treated with uniform kindness, where resided those kind friends to whom I felt under the greatest obligation for the freedom and quietude I then enjoyed, as well as for the little knowledge of business and of the world that I then possessed. Thinking, however, that I could better my condition, I subdued, as well as I could, my rising emotions, and after sincerely thanking them for their goodness and favors—wishing them long life and prosperity,—I took my departure for the chosen place of my destination.

Soon after I left Mr. Comstock's, that gentleman, sent his hired man, named John Cline, to Rochester with a wagon load of produce to sell, as had been his custom for some time. In vain the family looked for his return at the usual hour in the evening, and began to wonder what had detained him; but what was their horror and surprise to find, when they arose the next morning, the horses standing at the door, and the poor unfortunate man lying in the wagon, *dead*! How long they had been there nobody knew; no one had heard them come in; and how the man had been killed was a matter of mere conjecture. The coroner was sent for and an inquest held, and yet it was difficult to solve the whole mystery.

The most probable explanation was, that he was sitting in the back part of the wagon, and fell over on his left side, striking his neck on the edge of the wagon box, breaking it instantly.

The verdict of the jury was, in accordance with these facts, "accidental death," &c.

When I left Mr. Comstock's I had acquired quite a knowledge of reading, writing, arithmetic, and had made a small beginning in English grammar.

It had been for some time a question which I found hard to

decide, whether or not I should pursue my studies as I had done. If I went into business as I contemplated, I knew it would end my proficiency in the sciences; and yet I felt a desire to accumulate more of the wealth that perisheth. Considering too that I was advancing in age, and had no means of support but by my own labor, I finally concluded to do what I have from that time to this deeply regretted,—give up the pursuit of an education, and turn my attention wholly to business. I do not regret having desired a competency, nor for having labored to obtain it, but I *do* regret not having spared myself sufficient leisure to pursue some regular system of reading and study; to have cultivated my mind and stored it with useful knowledge.

Truly has it been said, "knowledge is power." But it is not like the withering curse of a tyrant's power; not like the degrading and brutalizing power of the slave-driver's lash, chains, and thumb-screws; not like the beastly, demonical power of rum, nor like the brazen, shameless power of lust; but a power that elevates and refines the intellect; directs the affections; controls unholy passions; a power so God-like in its character, that it enables its possessor to feel for the oppressed of every clime, and prepares him to defend the weak and down-trodden.

What but ignorance renders the poor slave so weak and inefficient in claiming his right to liberty, and the possession of his own being! Nor will that God who is "no respecter of persons," hold him guiltless who assumes unlimited control over his fellow. The chain of Slavery which fetters every slave south of Mason and Dixon's Line, is as closely linked around the master as the slave. The time has passed by when African blood alone is enslaved. In Virginia as well as in some other slave States, there is as much European blood in the veins of the enslaved as there is African; and the increase is constantly in favor of the white population. This fact alone speaks volumes, and should remind the slave-breeding Southerner of that fearful retribution which must sooner or later overtake him.

In September, 1817, I commenced business in Rochester.

Having rented a room of Mr. A. Wakely, I established a meat market, which was supplied mostly by my former employer, Mr. Comstock, and was liberally patronized by the citizens; but there were butchers in the village who appeared to be unwilling that I should have any share in public patronage. Sometimes they tore down my sign, at others painted it black, and so continued to annoy me until after I had one of their number arrested, which put a stop to their unmanly proceedings.

The village was now rapidly increasing, and yet the surrounding country was mostly a wilderness. Mr. E. Stone, who then owned the land on the east side of the river, thought his farm a very poor one; he, however, commenced clearing it in the midst of wild beasts and rattlesnakes, both of which were abundant, and in a few years was richly rewarded for his labor, in the sale of village lots, which commanded high prices.

In the summer of 1818, I commenced teaching a Sabbath School for the neglected children of our oppressed race. For a while it was well attended, and I hoped to be able to benefit in some measure the poor and despised colored children, but the parents interested themselves very little in the undertaking, and it shortly came to naught. So strong was the prejudice then existing against the colored people, that very few of the negroes seemed to have any courage or ambition to rise from the abject degradation in which the estimation of the white man had placed him.

This year, also, I purchased a lot of land, eighteen by fifty feet, situated on Main street, for which I was to pay five hundred dollars. Having secured my land, I began making preparations for building, and soon had a good two story dwelling and store, into which I moved my effects, and commenced a more extensive business.

Some disadvantage as well as sport was occasioned on business men, who resided on the confines of Ontario and Genesee Counties. It was indeed laughable to witness the races and maneuvering of parties in those days when men were

611

imprisoned for debt. If a man in Ontario County had a suspicion that an officer was on his track, he had only to step over the line into Genesee, to be beyond the power of an officer's precept.

A great deal of trouble as well as unpleasant feeling was engendered by the exercise of that law, which allowed the creditor so great advantage over the debtor. This, together with the fact that very many of the citizens of Rochester were men of small means, the more wealthy portion felt called upon to protect their interests, by forming themselves into what was called a "Shylock Society," the object of which was to obtain a list of all the names of persons who had been, or were then, on "the limits" for debt. This list of names was printed, and each member of the society furnished with a copy, which enabled him to decide whether or not to trust a man when he came to trade. The formation of this society gave rise to another, whose members pledged themselves to have no dealing with a member of the "Shylock Society," and also to publish all defaulters in "high life," which served to check these oppressive measures and restore harmony.

Among others who came to settle in the thriving village of Rochester, was a colored man named Daniel Furr, who came from the East. He soon became acquainted with a very respectable young white lady, of good family, who after a short acquaintance appeared to be perfectly enamored of her dusky swain; and notwithstanding the existing prejudice, she did not scruple to avow her affection for him,—a devotion which appeared to be as sincerely returned by the young "Othello." They resolved to marry; but to this, serious objections arose, and all that the lady's family and friends could do to break off the match was done, but without effect. They could, however, prevail on no one to perform the marriage ceremony in the village, and finally concluded to go to a magistrate in the town of Brighton, four miles distant. At this stage of the proceedings I was appealed to, to accompany them. I took the matter into consideration and came to the conclusion that I could take no active part in the affair, nor bear any responsible station in the unpleasant occurrence. Is it no sin in the sight of the Almighty, for Southern gentlemen(?) to mix blood and amalgamate the races? And if allowed to them, is it not equally justifiable when the commerce is prompted by affection rather than that of lust and force? But I at length consented to accompany them, after learning that all the mischief was already done that could be feared, and that the gallant lover desired to marry the lady as the only atonement he could make for the loss of her reputation.

We arrived at the house of the magistrate about one o'clock at night, and all were soundly sleeping. They were, however, aroused, and when our business was made known, an exciting scene followed. The magistrate refused at first to marry them; and the lady of the house took aside the intended bride, spending two hours in endeavoring to dissuade her from the contemplated union; assuring her that her house should be freely opened to her, that no attention should be spared during her expected confinement, &c.; but all to no purpose. They returned to the parlor where the magistrate again tried his power of persuasion, but with as little success as his lady had met: and then he reluctantly married them. The newly-made husband paid a liberal fee, and we took our leave. I returned to my home to reflect on the scenes of the past night, and Mr. and Mrs. Furr to the house of a friend of the bride in Penfield.

The report soon reached the village that the marriage had been consummated, which produced a great excitement. Threats of an alarming character were openly made against the "nigger" who had dared to marry a white woman, although at her own request. And there was also a class of persons who associated together, professing great friendship for the persecuted husband, and often drew him into their company, pretending to defend his cause while they were undoubtedly plotting his destruction.

One day, after Furr had been drinking rather freely with his pretended friends, he was taken so violently ill, that a physician was immediately called. I was with him when the doctor arrived.

He gazed upon the suffering man with an angry expression, and inquired in a tone of command, "Daniel, what have you been doing?" In vain the poor creature begged for relief, the doctor merely repeating his question. After looking at him for some time, he finally administered a potion and hastily left the room, saying as he did so, "that Furr was as sure to die as though his head had been cut off." And so it proved, though not so speedily as the medical man had predicted; nor did he ever visit him again, notwithstanding he lingered for several days in the most intense agony. It was a strong man grappling with disease and death, and the strife was a fearful one. But death at last ended the scene, with none of all his professed friends, except his faithful but heart-broken wife, to administer to his necessities. No sound save that of the moaning widow broke the stillness of his death-chamber. A few friends collected, who prepared the emaciated body for the grave; enclosing it in a rude board coffin it was conveyed to its last resting place, followed by three or four men, just as the shades of evening had fallen upon this sin-cursed world; there in darkness and silence we lowered his remains, and left the gloomy spot to return to his disconsolate wife, who had been too ill to join the meager procession.

It has ever been my conviction that Furr was poisoned, most likely by some of his false friends who must have mingled some deadly drug with his drinks or food; nor do I believe that the medicine administered by the physician was designed to save his life. But to Him who knoweth all things, we leave the matter.

His despised, forsaken, and bereaved wife soon followed him to the grave, where she sleeps quietly with her innocent babe by her side; and where probably this second Desdemonia finds the only refuge which would have been granted her by a heartless and persecuting world.

Oh, when will this nation "cease to do evil and learn to do well?" When will they judge character in accordance with its moral excellence, instead of the complexion a man unavoidably bears to the world?

CHAPTER XIV

INCIDENTS IN ROCHESTER AND VICINITY

After long petitioning, the inhabitants of that section succeeded in having the new county of Monroe set off from Genesee and Ontario Counties, in 1821, which gave a new impulse to the business interests of the already flourishing town, which had heretofore labored under some disadvantages in consequence of having all public business done at Canandaigua or Batavia.

About this time, too, was the Carthage bridge built by a company of enterprising gentlemen of that village which at that day was considered one of the wonders of the age; but as its history is well known to all interested in the enterprises of those days, it is only necessary to say, that the magnificent structure, so grand in its appearance, such a pattern of mechanical ingenuity, exhibiting in all its vast proportions, both strength and beauty, combined with utility and grandeur; and erected at such an enormous expense of time, labor, and cash, was destined soon to fall.

It had cost some ten thousand dollars; and had been warranted by the builders to stand one year. How great then must have been the loss and disappointment when in a little more than twenty-four hours after the time specified, the ruins of that beautiful structure were found floating on the broad bosom of the Genesee! And yet when we take into consideration the vast amount of human life which hourly passed over its solid surface, we can but wonder at the intervention of a kind Providence which prevented any loss of life at the time of its

615

fall. A child had but just passed over it, when with one general crash it sank to the waters below; mocking in its rapid flight, the wisdom of the architect and foresight of frail humanity. The fall of Carthage bridge was indeed a calamity felt by the public generally, and sounded the death-knell of all future greatness to Carthage, or at least for some years to come.

About this time the village was thrown into a state of excitement by the arrest of a colored woman named Ellen, who it was charged had escaped from service due to a Mr. D., south of Mason and Dixon's Line. She had been arrested in accordance with a law passed by Congress in 1793, which forbids persons owing service in one State to flee to another; and which also obliges those receiving such service, to render to the claimant any fugitive from labor due, &c. Poor Ellen! She had many friends and able counsel, but nothing short of an open violation of the law of the land, could prevent her return to the house of bondage. She was tried and given up to him who claimed dominion over her. Hopeless and heart-broken, she was escorted from the boasted land and village of freedom, by a company of the "Light Horse," under the command of Capt. Curtis. One poor, persecuted slave woman, upon whose heart had fallen a shadow darker than death's; driving every earthly hope of liberty from her wounded spirit; helpless and forlorn! She indeed must have required this military parade—this show of power! And that too, by men who throw up their caps with a shout for freedom and equal rights! Oh, "consistency, thou art a jewel!"

As I recollect but one other incident of the kind occurring in Rochester, I will now name it.

A colored man named Davis, generally known as "Doctor Davis," with a reputation unsullied for industry, truth and sobriety, was arrested as a fugitive from slave labor in Kentucky. Two men came on from that State, acting in the double capacity of agents for the claimant and witnesses against the slave. They employed Mr. L. as counsel, and hastened on the trial of the afflicted African. When it became generally known that Davis was arrested, and about to be tried, the excitement grew intense among all classes; but more particularly among the colored people. When the trial came on, the Court room was crowded to overflowing, and every avenue leading to it densely thronged with deeply anxious persons, assembled to witness the result. It became evident, however, that the poor man must be given up to his grasping master, unless some means were devised to rescue him from the power of an unjust law. His friends were on the alert, and as the trial proceeded, the colored men found an opportunity to get him into a corner of the crowded apartment; where, while the officers stood at the door, they dressed him in disguise, and otherwise so completely changed his personal appearance, that he passed out of the Court room, undetected by the officers, and as all supposed was safely pursuing his way to Canada.

The hawk-eyed counsel for the Kentuckians, however, too soon observed exultation written on every dusky countenance, to keep quiet. Starting to his feet in great alarm, he cried out "Where is Davis?" And oh, how that question startled every one present. Every eye gazed hither and thither, and every ear intently listened for the answer. After a moment of breathless silence, the excited counselor was assured that the "bird had flown," which announcement was received with a rapturous shout of joy by the audience, greatly, however, to the discomfiture of the gentlemen from Kentucky, who had thought themselves so sure of their prize. Nor would they be thwarted now. It was not yet too late to overtake their victim, and slavery required at their hands a sacrifice which they were ready to make. Hand-bills were in immediate circulation, offering a reward of fifty dollars for the apprehension of the flying fugitive. Fifty dollars, for the body and soul of a man to plunge into the degradation of Slavery! Fifty dollars for the ruin of a fellow being, for whom Christ gave his precious life! Yes, fifty dollars are offered to any human blood-hound who will hunt and worry the poor slave, who must fly from this boasted land of liberty, to seek protection in the dominion of England's Queen!

Unfortunately for Davis, some of these hand-bills were thrown on board the very packet on which he had embarked for Buffalo; nor was this all. The bills would have left him uninjured, but a scoundrel—an apology for a man—was there also, who, for the consideration of fifty dollars was willing to compromise all pretensions to manhood and humanity, and drag from the boat the panting slave, whom he cast beneath the heel of his oppressor. When Davis was finally retaken, those Kentucky dealers in human chattels, held him with a grasp that banished all hope of escape by flight; and then in his sorrow and despair the wretched, hopeless man cried out "Oh, my God, must I return to the hell of Slavery? Save me, Oh, dear Lord, save this, thy helpless, friendless servant, from a fate so dreadful! Oh, Christian friends and neighbors, I appeal to you to rescue me from a life far more terrible than death in any form! Oh, God, is there no protection for me in the laws of New York? I claim it, by all that is sacred in her past history! Give me liberty or death! or death!" he repeated, with a shudder; then casting one glance of hopeless agony on his persecutors, he secretly drew from his pocket a razor, and before he could be prevented he drew it across his throat, and fell gasping in the midst of his slave-hunting tormentors, while a collection of bystanders cried "Shame! shame! on the institution of Slavery!"

Poor Davis was not dead, but supposing he soon would be, these gentlemen were requested to give security, and indemnify the town for all expenses it might incur on Davis' account. But instead of giving their bond as requested, they took a sudden start for Kentucky, where it was very generally desired they might remain.

With good treatment, Davis, after a long time, recovered sufficiently to be removed by his friends to a place of safety; and when so far restored as to be able he returned to Rochester, where he received assistance which enabled him to reach Canada. I have often heard from him during his residence in that country, where no slaves exist and he has done well, having quite an extensive practice in medicine, and lives in the quiet enjoyment of that liberty which he struggled so hard to obtain and came so near losing; yet, to this day he prefers death to Slavery. And who does not? None, who have breathed the air of freedom after an experience of unrequited toil to enrich a brutal and selfish master. Truly is it said, "a contented slave is a degraded being."

THROUGH THE EYES OF A SLAVE

CHAPTER XV

SAD REVERSES OF CAPT HELM

I must again introduce to the kind reader my old master, Capt. Helm, who we left residing in Bath, several years ago. And as I have before intimated he had now become a very poor man; indeed so reduced was he now that he lived with one of his slave women, and was supported by public charity! Learning, too, that I had saved by my industry a few hundred dollars, it seemed very congenial with his avaricious habits to endeavor to obtain what I possessed. In accordance with his plan he employed a lawyer named Lewland to come to my place of business, which he did, and demanded of me to pay Capt. Helm two hundred dollars. He also left a notice, forbidding all persons to take or destroy any property in my possession; and then impudently inquired how I expected to gain my freedom; if I thought of applying for a writ of *habaeus corpus*; and many other questions; to which I replied that I should pay no money on the order of Capt. Helm; apply for no writ; but should continue to maintain my personal rights and enjoy the freedom which was already mine, and which I designed to keep, assuring him that the Captain had forfeited his claim, if he had any, to me or my services, when he hired me to Mr. Tower.

He hung about me for a day or two, and then left me to pursue my business —I saw no more of him. Some time afterward Mr. H.E. Rochester informed me that he had a *subpoena* for me, which I found was issued by the direction of Capt. Helm. By Mr. Rochester's counsel, I took it to Mr. A. Sampson, who assured me that my old master had commenced a suit against me in the Court of Equity, and the case would be tried before Wm. B. Rochester, Esq., who was one of the circuit judges. Capt. Helm claimed every particle of property I possessed; a claim that occasioned me great anxiety and some cost.

Mr. Sampson encouraged me to hope, however, that the case would be dismissed as two other cases of that kind had been.

I labored to the best of my ability to prepare myself for the trial, which was to decide whether I had a right to possess myself and command my own services and earnings, or whether all belonged to Capt. Helm. As I looked forward with anxious forebodings to the day appointed for the suit to commence, I was startled by the announcement of my old master's *death*! Yes, Capt. Helm was dead; and with him died the law suit. He who had so wronged me, who had occasioned me so much suffering and sorrow had gone to his account. He who had once been thought to be one of the wealthiest as well as one of the greatest men in the county, died a pauper—neglected and despised, and scarcely awarded a decent burial. Like his wife, who died such a horrid death, he had been reared in affluence and was an inheritor of vast possessions, but his home was in a slave State; he was raised on a plantation, and nurtured in the atmosphere of Slavery.

In his youth he had contracted the habit of drinking to excess, beside that of gambling, horse-racing and the like, which followed him through life. Forgotten and scorned in his poverty by many who had partaken of his abundance, sipped his wine, and rode his fast horses.

During the last war his princely mansion was ever open to the officers of the army, and many a wounded soldier has been cheered and comforted by his hospitality. But now he is regarded as no better than his poorest slave, and lies as lowly as they, in the narrow house appointed for all the living.

My old master had two brothers: the oldest, Thomas Helm, was a Captain in the United States Army, and had been in many hard-fought battles. His younger brother, William, was a Captain also; but Thomas was the man to awaken curiosity. I have lived with him, but never knew of his going unarmed for an hour, until he left Virginia and came to Steuben County, where he died. When at the South, I have seen strangers approach him, but they were invariably commanded to "stand" and to "approach him at their peril." He finally came to the State of New York, bringing with him his "woman" with whom he lived, and two children, with whom he settled on a piece of land given him by my old master, where the old soldier lived, died, and was buried on one of his small "clearings" under an old apple tree. He owned a few slaves, but at his death his "woman" collected every thing she could, and among the rest, two or three slave children, to whom she had no right or claim whatever, and made her way to Kentucky. About a year ago I visited the spot where the brave old defender of his country had been buried, but found very little to mark the resting place of the brother of my old master. They had passed away. Their wealth, power and bravery had come to nought; and no tribute was now paid to the memory of one of "Old Virginia's best families." The *blood* of which they were wont to boast, was now no more revered than that which commingled with the African and circulated in the veins of his despised and downtrodden slaves.

CHAPTER XVI

BRITISH EMANCIPATION OF SLAVERY

As time passed on I found myself progressing in a profitable business. I had paid for my house and lot, and purchased another adjoining, on which I had erected a valuable brick building. The Lord prospered all my undertakings and I felt grateful for my good fortune. I kept all kinds of groceries and grain, which met a ready sale; and now I began to look about me for a partner in life, to share my joys and sorrows, and to assist me on through the tempestuous scenes of a life-long voyage. Such a companion I found in the intelligent and amiable Miss B——, to whom I was married on the eleventh of May, 1825. She was the youngest daughter of a particular friend, who had traveled extensively and was noted for his honesty and intelligence.

About this time, too, "Sam Patch" made his last and fatal leap from a scaffold twenty five feet above the falls of Genesee, which are ninety-six feet in height. From thence he plunged into the foaming river to rise no more in life. The following spring the body of the foolish man was found and buried, after having lain several months in the turbulent waters of the Genesee.

This year was also rendered memorable by the efficient labors of Professor Finney, through whose faithful preaching of the gospel, many were brought to a saving knowledge of the truth.

The "Emancipation Act" had now been passed, and the happy time for it to take effect was drawing nigh. Slavery could no longer exist in the Empire State nor receive the protection of her laws. Would to God it had so continued to be what it professed—the refuge of the bondman and the home of the free.

But alas! Now the flying fugitive from Slavery finds no security within her borders; he must flee onward, to the dominion of Queen Victoria, ere he rests, lest the exaction of the odious "Fugitive Slave Law" return him to the house of bondage.

But the Emancipation Bill had been passed, and the colored people felt it to be a time fit for rejoicing. They met in different places and determined to evince their gratitude by a general celebration. In Rochester they convened in large numbers, and resolved to celebrate the glorious day of freedom at Johnson's Square, on the *fifth* day of July. This arrangement was made so as not to interfere with the white population who were everywhere celebrating the day of their independence—"the Glorious Fourth,"—for amid the general and joyous shout of liberty, prejudice had sneeringly raised the finger of scorn at the poor African, whose iron bands were loosed, not only from English oppression, but the more cruel and oppressive power of Slavery.

They met according to previous appointment, Mr. A. H——, having been chosen president, Mr. H. E——, marshal, and Mr. H. D——, reader of the "Act of Emancipation," and "The Declaration of Independence." A large audience of both white and colored people assembled, and the day which had been ushered in by the booming cannon, passed by in the joyous realization that we were indeed free men. To the music of the band the large procession marched from the square to the hotel, where ample provision was made for dinner, after listening to the following oration, which I had been requested to deliver.

I must not omit to mention that on the morning of that happy day, a committee of colored men waited upon the Hon. Matthew Brown, and in behalf of the citizens of Monroe County, presented their thanks for his noble exertions in the Legislature, in favor of the Act by which thousands were made free men.

They were received by that worthy gentleman with grateful and pleasing assurances of his continued labor in

624

behalf of freedom.

Now I will lay before the reader my address to the audience on that eventful day.

CHAPTER XVII

ORATION—TERMINATION OF SLAVERY

The age in which we live is characterised in no ordinary degree, by a certain boldness and rapidity in the march of intellectual and political improvements. Inventions the most surprising; revolutions the most extraordinary, are springing forth, and passing in quick succession before us,—all tending most clearly to the advancement of mankind towards that state of earthly perfection and happiness, from which they are yet so far distant, but of which their nature and that of the world they inhabit, are most certainly capable. It is at all times pleasing and instructive to look backward by the light of history, and forward by the light of analogical reasoning, to behold the gradual advancement of man from barbarism to civilization, from civilization toward the higher perfections of his nature; and to hope—nay, confidently believe, that the time is not far distant when liberty and equal rights being everywhere established, morality and the religion of the gospel everywhere diffused,— man shall no longer lift his hand for the oppression of his fellow man; but all, mutually assisting and assisted, shall move onward throughout the journey of human life, like the peaceful caravan across the burning sands of Arabia. And never, on this glorious anniversary, so often and so deservedly celebrated by millions of free men, but which we are to-day for the first time called to celebrate—never before, has the eye been able to survey the past with so much satisfaction, or the future with hopes and expectations so brilliant and so flattering; it is to us a day of two-fold joy. We are men, though the strong hand of prejudice

626

and oppression is upon us; we can, and we will rejoice in the advancement of the rapidly increasing happiness of mankind, and especially of our own race. We can, and we will rejoice in the growing power and glory of the country we inhabit. Although Almighty God has not permitted us to remain in the land of our forefathers and our own, the glories of national independence, and the sweets of civil and religious liberty, to their full extent; but the strong hand of the spoiler has borne us into a strange land, yet has He of His great goodness given us to behold those best and noblest of his gifts to man, in their fairest and loveliest forms; and not only have we beheld them, but we have already felt much of their benignant influence. Most of us have hitherto enjoyed many, very many of the dearest rights of freemen. Our lives and personal liberties have been held as sacred and inviolable; the rights of property have been extended to us, in this land of freedom; our industry has been, and still is, liberally rewarded; and so long as we live under a free and happy government which denies us not the protection of its laws, why should we fret and vex ourselves because we have had no part in framing them, nor anything to do with their administration. When the fruits of the earth are fully afforded us, we do not wantonly refuse them, nor ungratefully repine because we have done nothing towards the cultivation of the tree which produces them. No, we accept them with lively gratitude; and their sweetness is not embittered by reflecting upon the manner in which they were obtained. It is the dictate of sound wisdom, then, to enjoy without repining, the freedom, privileges, and immunities which wise and equal laws have awarded us—nay, proudly to rejoice and glory in their production, and stand ready at all times to defend them at the hazard of our lives, and of all that is most dear to us.

But are we alone shut out and excluded from any share in the administration of government? Are not the clergy, a class of men equally ineligible to office? A class of men almost idolized by their countrymen, ineligible to office! And are we alone excluded from what the world chooses to denominate polite society? And are not a vast majority of the polar race excluded? I know not why, but mankind of every age, nation, and complexion have had lower classes; and, as a distinction, they have chosen to arrange themselves in the grand spectacle of human life, like seats in a theater—rank above rank, with intervals between them. But if any suppose that happiness or contentment is confined to any single class, or that the high or more splendid order possesses any substantial advantage in those respects over their more lowly brethren, they must be wholly ignorant of all rational enjoyment. For what though the more humble orders cannot mingle with the higher on terms of equality. This, if rightly considered, is not a curse but a blessing. Look around you, my friends: what rational enjoyment is not within your reach? Your homes are in the noblest country in the world, and all of that country which your real happiness requires, may at any time be yours. Your industry can purchase it; and its righteous laws will secure you in its possession. But, to what, my friends, do you owe all these blessings? Let not the truth be concealed. You owe them to that curse, that bitter scourge of Africa, whose partial abolishment you are this day convened to celebrate. Slavery has been your curse, but it shall become your rejoicing. Like the people of God in Egypt, you have been afflicted; but like them too, you have been redeemed. You are henceforth free as the mountain winds. Why should we, on this day of congratulation and joy, turn our view upon the origin of African Slavery? Why should we harrow up our minds by dwelling on the deceit, the forcible fraud and treachery that have been so long practised on your hospitable and unsuspecting countrymen? Why speak of fathers torn from the bosom of their families, wives from the embraces of their husbands, children from the protection of their parents; in fine, of all the tender and endearing relations of life dissolved and trampled under foot, by the accursed traffic in human flesh? Why should we remember, in joy and exultation, the thousands of our countrymen who are to-day, in this land of gospel light, this boasted land of civil and religious liberty, writhing under the lash and groaning beneath the grinding weight of Slavery's chain? I ask, Almighty God, are they who do such things thy chosen and favorite people? But, away with such thoughts as these; we will rejoice, though sobs interrupt the songs of our rejoicing, and tears mingle in the cup we pledge to Freedom; our harps though they have long hung neglected upon the willows, shall this day be strung full high to the notes of gladness. On this day, in one member at least of this mighty Republic, the Slavery of our race has ceased forever! No more shall the insolent voice of a master be the main-spring of our actions, the sole guide of our conduct; no more shall their hands labor in degrading and profitless servitude. Their toils will henceforth be voluntary, and be crowned with the never failing reward of industry. Honors and dignities may perhaps never be ours; but wealth, virtue, and happiness are all within the compass of our moderate exertions. And how shall we employ a few moments better than in reflecting upon the means by which these are to be obtained. For what can be more proper and more profitable to one who has just gained an invaluable treasure, than to consider how he may use it to the best possible advantage? And here I need not tell you that a strict observance to all the precepts of the gospel ought to be your first and highest aim; for small will be the value of all that the present world can bestow, if the interests of the world to come are neglected and despised. None of you can be ignorant of what the gospel teaches. Bibles may easily be obtained; nor can there be a greater disgrace, or a more shameful neglect of duty than for a person of mature age, and much more, for any father of a family to be without that most precious of all books—the Bible. If, therefore, any of you are destitute of a Bible, hasten to procure one. Will any of you say that it can be of no use to you, or that you cannot read it? Look then to that noblest of all remedies for this evil, the Sunday School—that most useful of all institutions. There you may learn without loss of time or money, that of which none

629

should be ignorant—to read.

Let me exhort you with earnestness to give your most sincere attention to this matter. It is of the utmost importance to every one of you. Let your next object be to obtain as soon as may be, a competency of the good things of this world; immense wealth is not necessary for you, and would but diminish your real happiness. Abject poverty is and ought to be regarded as the greatest, most terrible of all possible evils. It should be shunned as a most deadly and damning sin. What then are the means by which so dreadful a calamity may be avoided? I will tell you, my friends, in these simple words—hear and ponder on them; write them upon the tablets of your memory; they are worthy to be inscribed in letters of gold upon every door-post—"industry, prudence, and economy." Oh! they are words of power to guide you to respectability and happiness. Attend, then, to some of the laws which industry impose, while you have health and strength. Let not the rising sun behold you sleeping or indolently lying upon your beds. Rise ever with the morning light; and, till sun-set, give not an hour to idleness. Say not human nature cannot endure it. It can—it almost requires it. Sober, diligent, and moderate labor does not diminish it, but on the contrary, greatly adds to the health, vigor, and duration of the human frame. Thousands of the human race have died prematurely of disease engendered by indolence and inactivity. Few, very few indeed, have suffered by the too long continuance of bodily exertion. As you give the day to labor, so devote the night to rest; for who that has drunk and reveled all night at a tippling shop, or wandered about in search of impious and stolen pleasures, has not by so doing not only committed a most heinous and damning sin in the sight of Heaven, but rendered himself wholly unfit for the proper discharge of the duties of the coming day. Nor think that industry or true happiness do not go hand in hand; and to him who is engaged in some useful avocation, time flies delightfully and rapidly away. He does not, like the idle and indolent man, number the slow hours with sighs—cursing both himself and them for the tardiness of their flight. Ah, my friends, it is utterly impossible for him who wastes time in idleness, ever to know anything of true happiness. Indolence, poverty, wretchedness, are inseparable companions,—fly them, shun idleness, as from eminent and inevitable destruction. In vain will you labor unless prudence and economy preside over and direct all your exertions. Remember at all times that money even in your own hands, is power; with it you may direct as you will the actions of your pale, proud brethren. Seek after and amass it then, by just and honorable means; and once in your hand never part with it but for a full and fair equivalent; nor let that equivalent be something which you do not want, and for which you cannot obtain more than it cost you. Be watchful and diligent and let your mind be fruitful in devises for the honest advancement of your worldly interest. So shall you continually rise in respectability, in rank and standing in this so late and so long the land of your captivity.

Above all things refrain from the excessive use of ardent spirits. There is no evil whose progress is so imperceptible; and at the same time so sure and deadly, as that of intemperance; and by slow degrees it undermines health, wealth, and happiness, till all at length tumble into one dreadful mass of ruin. If God has given you children, he has in so doing imposed upon you a most fearful responsibility; believe me, friends, you will answer to God for every misfortune suffered, and every crime committed by them which right education and example could have taught them to avoid. Teach them reverence and obedience to the laws both of God and man. Teach them sobriety, temperance, justice, and truth. Let their minds be rightly instructed—imbued with kindness and brotherly love, charity, and benevolence. Let them possess at least so much learning as is to be acquired in the common schools of the country. In short, let their welfare be dearer to you than any earthly enjoyment; so shall they be the richest of earthly blessings.

My countrymen, let us henceforth remember that we are men. Let us as one man, on this day resolve that henceforth, by continual endeavors to do good to all mankind, we will claim for ourselves the attention and respect which as men we should possess. So shall every good that can be the portion of man, be ours—this life shall be happy, and the life to come, glorious.

The opinion of the public regarding the celebration and performances of that day, together with the behavior of the colored people, will be seen by the following short extract from the *Rochester Daily Advertiser*, published soon after the occurrence of those events:

"ABOLITION OF SLAVERY

"The extinction of that curse by the laws of our State, was marked with appropriate rejoicings on the part of the African race in this neighborhood. A procession of considerable length and respectable appearance, preceded by a band of music, moved from Brown's Island through the principal streets to the public square, yesterday forenoon, where a stage and seats were erected, for the speakers and audience. The throne of Grace was addressed by the Rev. Mr. Allen, a colored clergyman. The act declaring all slaves free in this State, on the fourth day of July, 1827, was read, which was succeeded by the reading of the Declaration of Independence and delivery of an oration by Mr. Steward. We have heard but one opinion from several gentlemen who were present, and that was highly complimentary to the composition and delivery of the same.

"The exercises were concluded by a short discourse from the Rev. Mr. Allen, and the procession moved off to partake of an entertainment prepared for the occasion. The thing was got up in good order, and passed off remarkably well. The conduct of the emancipated race was exemplary throughout, and if their future enjoyment of freedom be tinctured with the prudence that characterised their celebration of its attainment, the country will have no reason to mourn the philanthropy that set them free."

* * * * *

Thus ended our first public celebration of our own and our country's freedom. All conducted themselves with the strictest propriety and decorum, retiring to their homes soberly and in proper season.

CHAPTER XVIII

CONDITION OF FREE COLORED PEOPLE

Pursuant to a call given in the summer of 1830, by the colored residents of Philadelphia, for a National Convention of their race, I started in company with a friend to attend it; having previously engaged seats inside Mr. Coe's stage-coach as far as Utica, N.Y., to which place we had paid our fare the same as other passengers.

We rode on to Auburn very pleasantly, but when at that place, we with others moved to resume our seats; we were met by a stern rebuke for presuming to seat ourselves on the inside, and were ordered to ride on the outside of the coach. In vain we expostulated; in vain we reminded the driver of the agreement, and of our having paid for an inside seat; we were told to take the outside of the coach or remain behind.

Desiring to attend the convention, we concluded to go on, submitting to this rank injustice and dishonesty, until our return, when we determined to sue the proprietor of that line of stages. An opportunity was offered soon after, when I commenced a suit for damages against Mr. Sherwood, who was the great stage proprietor of those days. He, however, cleared himself by declaring that he was in no way responsible for the failures of Mr. Coe, to whom I must look for remuneration. I never found it convenient to sue Mr. Coe, and so the matter ended.

We passed through New York City to the place of our destination, where we found many of our brethren already assembled.

Philadelphia, which I now saw for the first time, I thought the

634

most beautiful and regularly laid out city I ever beheld. Here had lived the peaceable, just, and merciful William Penn; and here many of his adherents still reside. Here, too, was the place where the Rt. Rev. Bishop Allen, the first colored American bishop in the United States, had labored so successfully. When the Methodists sought to crush by cruel prejudice the poor African, he stepped boldly forward in defence of their cause, which he sustained, with a zeal and talent ever to be revered.

Thousands were brought to a knowledge of the truth, and induced "to seek first the kingdom of heaven and its righteousness," through his instrumentality. Through the benign influence of this good man, friends and means were raised for his poor brethren, to build houses of worship, where they would no more be dragged from their knees when in prayer, and told to seat themselves by the door. Oh, how much good can one good and faithful man do, when devoted to the cause of humanity—following in the footsteps of the blessed Christ; doing unto others as they would be done by; and remembering those in bonds as bound with them. What though his skin be black as ebony, if the heart of a brother beats in his bosom? Oh, that man could judge of character as does our Heavenly Father; then would he judge righteous judgment, and cease to look haughtily down upon his afflicted fellow, because "his skin is colored not like his own."

We convened at the specified time, and organized by appointing Rev. R. Allen, president, A. Steward, vice-president, and J.C. Morrell, secretary. The convention which continued in session three days, was largely attended by all classes of people, and many interesting subjects were ably discussed; but the most prominent object was the elevation of our race. Resolutions were passed calculated to encourage our brethren to take some action on the subjects of education and mechanism. Agricultural pursuits were also recommended;—and here allow me to give my opinion in favor of the latter, as a means of sustenance and real happiness.

I knew many colored farmers, all of whom are well respected in the neighborhood of their residence. I wish I could count them by hundreds; but our people mostly flock to cities where they allow themselves to be made "hewers of wood and drawers of water;" barbers and waiters,—when, if they would but retire to the country and purchase a piece of land, cultivate and improve it, they would be far richer and happier than they can be in the crowded city. It is a mistaken idea that there is more prejudice against color in the country. True, it exists everywhere, but I regard it less potent in the country, where a farmer can live less dependant on his oppressors. The sun will shine, the rains descend, and the earth bring forth her increase, just as readily for the colored agriculturist as for his pale face neighbor. Yes, and our common mother Earth will, when life is ended, as readily open her bosom to receive your remains in a last embrace, as that of the haughty scorner of our rights.

In the city, however, there is no escape from the crushing weight of prejudice, to ramble over fields of your own cultivation; to forget your sorrows in the refreshing air that waves the loaded branches of an orchard of your own planting; nor to solace yourself with a gambol over the green meadow with your little ones. It is all toil, toil, with a burthened heart until shadows fall across the hearth-stone, and dismal forebodings darken the fireside, from whence the weary wife retires to refresh herself in broken slumber for the renewed toil of another day. Will not my friends think of these and many other advantages in favor of a country life, and practice accordingly?

After the close of the convention, I returned to my business in Rochester.

Until the discussion, which commenced about this time on the subject of temperance, I had been engaged, as most other grocers were at that time, in the sale of spirituous liquors somewhat extensively. My attention had never before been called especially to the subject, though I had witnessed some of its direst evils; but now, when I saw the matter in its true light,

I resolved to give it up. I was doing well and making handsome profits on the sale of alcoholic beverages. I had also experienced a good deal of trouble with it. My license allowed me to sell any quantity less than five gallons; but it was a fine of twenty-five dollars if drunk on the premises,—one half of the sum to go to the complainant. If a vicious man got out of funds it became both easy and common for him to give some person a sixpence, half of which was to be spent for whisky, which made him a witness for the other, who would make immediate complaint, and collect his share of the fine. Nor could I prevent men who came with bottles, and purchased whisky, from drinking it where they pleased; consequently I was often called to answer to such complaints.

One morning a man entered my store and called for liquor, which the clerk gave him. After drinking it, he went directly to the office of A. House, Esq., and entered a complaint against the clerk who had served him; then stepped out for consultation with his counsel. At that moment I arrived at the office of the magistrate to whom I immediately made complaint against myself, relating to him also just how the event happened. In a few minutes the original complainant returned, to whom 'Squire House explained that he should have arraigned the proprietor of the store, and not the clerk as he had done. Determined on making a speculation, however, he demanded a precept for myself. The 'Squire, laughing most heartily, informed him that he was too late,—that Mr. Steward had the start of him, having just entered a complaint against himself, by which he saves one half of the fine. The man walked out, looking rather "cheap," nor did he or others annoy me afterwards by making complaints of that kind.

But now I saw, as never before, the sin of selling that which would make beasts of men, and only stopped to inquire what was duty in the matter. All the arguments in favor of its sale were more forcible then than now. All classes of persons used and drank the article; and it required more moral courage,

637

to relinquish the business than it does now. Nevertheless, it appeared plain to my mind, that duty to God and my fellow-men required it, and I cheerfully gave it up forever.

I could not conscientiously, nor do I see how any man can, continue to traffic in this most fruitful source of pauperism and crime. No benefit whatever arises from its use as a beverage or from its sale. It is a curse to the drinker, to the seller, and to the community. Those who are licensed venders take from the government fifty dollars for every one put into the treasury. The money paid for licenses is a very meager compensation for the beggary, crime, and bloodshed which rum produces. All who have any knowledge of the statistics of the State, or of our prison and police records know, that intemperance has done more to fill the prisons, work-houses, alms-houses, and asylums of the State than all other influences combined; and yet men uphold the traffic. Their favors are for those who love its use and sale, and their anathemas for him, who is striving to save a nation of drunkards from swift destruction; yea, their own sires, sons, and brothers from the grave of the inebriate.

When in Rochester a short time since, soliciting subscribers for this work, I stepped into a distillery and asked a man to subscribe for it. He hesitated in his decision until he took a tumbler and filling it with brandy, invited me to drink. I thanked him, saying I never drink brandy. "Never drink!" he growled, "then I tell you, sir, that you stand a much better chance of being struck by lightning than of getting a subscriber here." Oh, very well; most likely had he agreed to take a copy, he would have been sorely displeased with my views of the liquor traffic, and perhaps with the compliment I have here paid him.

But in the foregoing remarks I have said but a tithe of what my heart feels, when I think of the sufferings occasioned by drunkenness.

Even the cup of the burthened slave, writhing in his chains and toiling under the lash, is not full of bitterness until the demon rum throws in its dregs and fills it to overflowing.

THROUGH THE EYES OF A SLAVE

How often does it occur that a passionate master, heated with wine,—mad with himself and all about him, pours out his vengeful ire on the head and back of some helpless slave, and leaves him weltering in his blood! How often may be heard the agonized wail of the slave mother, deploring the departure of some innocent child that has been lost in gambling, while the master was intoxicated!

How often do the shrieks of the poor but virtuous slave girl, ring through the midnight air, as she, pleading for death rather than life, rushes screaming away from a brutal master, infuriated and drunk! If it is a fact, and certainly it is, that the master is thus affected by his costly wine; what, think you, will be the temper and condition of the coarse and heartless overseer who drinks his miserable whisky or bad brandy? It is horrible, beyond description. I have often myself seen a drunken overseer, after pouring down dram after dram, mount his horse and ride furiously among the slaves, beating, bruising, mangling with his heavy cowhide every one he chanced to meet, until the ground presented the appearance of a battlefield.

CHAPTER XIX

PERSECUTION OF THE COLORED PEOPLE

While the colored population of New York were rejoicing in the measure of freedom allowed them by the more wholesome laws of that State, our brethren in Ohio were being oppressed and maltreated by the unjust and odious "black laws" of that professedly free State, enacted with special reference to the disposition of the colored race.

In Cincinnati, O., within sight of the slave land of Kentucky, a terrible persecution had commenced, and an effort was made to drive all colored persons from the place.

Our people had settled there in large numbers, but now a mob had assembled in that city with the determination to drive them, not only from their homes and city, but from the State. A bloody conflict ensued, in which the white and black man's blood mingled freely. So great had been the loss of property; and go horrid and fearful had been the scene, that our people chose to leave, rather than remain under such untoward circumstances. They lived in constant fear of the mob which had so abused and terrified them. Families seated at the fireside started at every breath of wind, and trembled at the sound of every approaching footstep. The father left his family in fear, lest on his return from his daily labor, he should find his wife and children butchered, and his house left desolate.

Meetings were held to devise plans and means for leaving the place where they had been so cruelly treated. But where should they go? And why should they be compelled to leave the State of Ohio? The fact is, that the African race there, as in all parts

640

THROUGH THE EYES OF A SLAVE

of this nominally free Republic, was looked down upon by the white population as being little above the brute creation; or, as belonging to some separate class of degraded beings, too deficient in intellect to provide for their own wants, and must therefore depend on the superior ability of their oppressors, to take care of them. Indeed, both the time and talents of eminent men have been wasted in unsuccessful research for the line of demarcation, between the African and the highest order of animals,—such for instance as the monkey or the ourang-outang. Some even, have advanced the absurd idea, that wicked Cain transmitted to them the "mark" which the Almighty set upon him for the murder of his brother; and that he, (who then must have survived the deluge), is the progenitor of that despised and inferior race—the negro slave of the United States of America!

If it be true, that the natural inferiority of the black man, connects him so closely with the animal creation, it looks passing strange to me that he should be made responsible for the violation of laws which he has been declared too imbecile to aid in framing or of comprehending. Nor is it less strange to see him enslaved and compelled by his labor to maintain both his master and himself, after having declared him incapable of doing either. Why not let him go then? Why hold with an unyielding grasp, so miserable and useless a piece of property? Is it benevolence that binds him with his master's chain? Judge ye. Stranger still is the fact of attaching such vast influence to his presence and so much concern regarding his movements, when in a state of freedom, if indeed, he is of so little worth and consequence, and so nearly related to the brutes that perish.

Surely, the Legislature of Ohio, or of any other State, would never feel called upon to sit in grave counsel, for the purpose of framing laws which would impose fine and imprisonment on a monkey, should one chance to locate within its jurisdiction; nor would they think it advisable for the court to assemble, or a jury to be empanelled, to drive from their midst an ourang-outang. And yet this and more must be done to get rid of the hated negro, who has been born in that State, or has fled to it for protection from the manstealer.

When strangers pass hastily through this country, and after a careless glance at the colored population, report them to be "an indolent, improvident, and vicious class of persons," they should consider some of the many obstacles thrown in the way of the most favored of that race. Knowing as they do, the rigor of the law, and feeling as they do, the oppressive power of prejudice, it becomes almost impossible for them to rise to that station they were designed to fill, and for which their natural abilities as certainly qualify them, as though they had never been robbed of their God-given rights. But let us return to our tried friends in Cincinnati.

They finally resolved to collect what they could of their possessions and establish a colony in Canada. In accordance with this resolution, they agreed to first send an agent to obtain liberty to settle there, and if successful to select and purchase a large tract of land, making such arrangements as he thought best for their speedy removal to their new home. Israel Lewis was their appointed agent, who departed immediately for Upper Canada to perform his mission; and there for the present we will leave him and return to Rochester.

Our more favored brethren in New York felt a deep sympathy for their outraged countrymen in Cincinnati; a sympathy equaled only by their indignation at the cause of such demand.

A meeting expressive of their views and feelings on that subject, was convened in the city of Rochester during which, the following preamble and resolutions were read and unanimously adopted:

Whereas, The city of Cincinnati has again become the scene of another dreadful mob and bloodshed, where nothing but terror and confusion reigned for a number of hours together.

And Whereas, Our brethren and fellow citizens were left exposed to the fury of an ungovernable mob, made up of the base, the ignorant, and vile, the very dregs of society; and probably led on by slaveholders, who of all men are the most execrable; while boasting of liberty, he tramples on the dearest rights of men and in the greatest robber of it on earth.

Resolved, That we deprecate an appeal to arms by any class of our fellow citizens, except in extreme cases, and we think that such a case has been presented in the late outrage at Cincinnati.

Resolved, That when a class of men so far forget the duty they owe to God, their fellow men, and their country, as to trample under their feet the very laws they have made, and are in duty bound to obey and execute, we believe it to be the duty of our brethren and fellow citizens, to protect their lives against such lawless mobs; and if in the conflict, any of the mobocrats perish, every good citizen should say Amen.

Resolved, That we do truly sympathize with the friends of God's poor; the friends of the oppressed, throughout this boasted land of liberty, in the losses they have sustained in consequence of the mob.

Resolved, That we believe the time is not far distant, when the *Queen City of the West*, shall be redeemed from the hateful influence of the slaveholder; redeemed from that cruel prejudice of caste which, hangs like a mill-stone around the neck of our people; redeemed from all those unequal laws, which have a tendency to make the strong stronger and the weak weaker; redeemed from their falsehearted friends, whose sarcastic smile is more to be feared than the frowns of an open enemy.

Resolved, That the untiring exertions of our friends, and the indefatigable industry of our brethren, are sure guarantees that the State of Ohio will not long be what she now is,—a hissing and by-word on account of her iniquitous laws; but that she will rise above every narrow minded prejudice, and raise up her sable sons and daughters and place them on an equality with the rest of her citizens.

Resolved, That we deeply deplore the loss our friends have sustained in the destruction of their printing press in Cincinnati.

Resolved, That we as an oppressed people, feel it our duty to give our undivided support to the press and the laborers in our cause.

Mr. Israel Lewis made his way to Canada, and having obtained permission to establish a colony, he bargained with the Canada Company for one township of land, for which he agreed to pay the money demanded, in a few days, and then returned to Cincinnati, by way of Rochester. The poor, persecuted colored people, had in the mean time made ready for their flight from their homes, their native land, and from this boasted free Republic, to seek a residence in the cold and dreary wilds of Canada; to claim that protection from the English government which had been denied them in the land of their birth; and like the overtasked Israelites, "they went out with their wives and their little ones," but with smaller possessions.

During the stay of Mr. Lewis in Rochester, he reported there and elsewhere, that eleven hundred persons were then in the dense woods of Canada in a state of actual starvation, and called upon the humane everywhere, to assist them in such extreme suffering.

To me he also told the story of their destitution, which affected me deeply. I had at that time just made a public profession of my faith in the Christian religion and my determination to be governed by its holy precepts, I felt for the distressed and suffering everywhere; but particularly for those who had fled, poor and destitute, from cruel task-masters, choosing rather the sufferings of cold and hunger, with liberty, than the meager necessities of life and Slavery. I concluded to go to Canada and try to do some good; to be of some little service in the great cause of humanity.

As soon as practicable therefore, I left Rochester for Toronto, the capital of Upper Canada, which I found quite a thriving town, and containing some fine brick buildings, and some I saw were built of mud, dried in the sun, wearing rather a poor than pretty appearance. At Toronto we hired a team to take us on to Ancaster, fifty miles distant. We traveled now through a new country; the roads were very bad, and the inhabitants few. We, however, reached Ancaster, a small village, where we remained one night and next morning pursued our journey to the settlement of the poor fugitives from Cincinnati. After some hard traveling, we finally arrived at the place where we found our brethren, it is true, but in quite destitute circumstances. Our fare was poor indeed, but as good as they could get. The township was one unbroken wilderness when purchased for the colony, and of course their lands must be cleared of the heavy timber before crops could be got in, hence, there was a great deal of destitution and suffering before their harvest could ripen after the land was prepared for the seed.

The day after I arrived at the settlement, which consisted of a few rude log cabins, a meeting was called to give the township a name. Several were suggested, but I at length motioned to name it in honor of the great philanthropist, Wilberforce. This was carried, and the township from that time has been known by that name. It is situated on what is known as the Huron Tract, Kent County, London District, and is the next north of the township of London. Our neighbors on the south, were a company of Irish people, who owned the township, and on the west side were a township of Welshmen, a hardy, industrious and enterprising people.

In Wilberforce there were no white inhabitants; the land appeared level and handsome, with but one stream of any magnitude running through it; this was the Oxsable, which was dry during a part of the year. All was one vast forest of heavy timber, that would compare well with that of Western New York. Beech, maple, ash, elm, oak, whitewood, bass, balm of gilead, &c. The soil was good for corn, wheat, rye, oats, and most kinds of the grain and vegetables raised in New York, and was a superior grazing country, about fifteen miles from London. This was a village containing perhaps thirty dwellings, and two hundred inhabitants; a court-house and jail all under one roof, built of stone and plastered; small doors and windows in the style of some of the old English castles. London was built in the forks, or between the east and west branches of the river Thames; hence, you would hear people speak of "going to the forks," instead of the village; it is about two hundred miles from Buffalo, and the nearest port between the two is Port Stanley, thirty miles from London.

I returned from Canada, where I had seen an oppressed people struggling with the hardships and privations of a new settlement; I had seen wretchedness in some places, but by no means sufficient to justify the report made by Mr. Lewis, and I determined I would remove there with my family, and do all in my power to assist the colored people in Canada.

I had witnessed a disposition on the part of some to prevent our brethren from settling in Wilberforce, while the colonizationists made a grand argument of it in favor of their wicked policy. All must see that it became a necessity with those who fled to Canada to save themselves from constant abuse or from Slavery, and in some instances their lives; and not because they admitted the justice of one portion of American citizens driving another from their native land; nor their right to colonize them anywhere on the habitable globe.

All these things taken into consideration, determined me to join them in the enterprize of building up an asylum for the oppressed, where our colored friends could obtain a home, and where, by their industry they could obtain a competency for themselves, besides providing a safe retreat for the weary fugitive from Slavery; guiding by its beacon light of liberty, the destitute and oppressed everywhere, to home and plenty.

I felt willing to make any sacrifice in my power to serve my Lord, by administering to the necessities of my down-trodden countrymen. How far my desire has been accomplished God only knows, but I do know that the purest motives influenced me, and an honest purpose directed my steps in removing to Wilberforce. Not so with all, however. Some there were,

646

Judas-like, who "cared not for the poor; but because he was a thief and had the bag, and bore what was put therein," made great exertions for a time in favor of the settlement. It too soon became apparent that to make money was the prominent object with by far too great a number of the colonists; hence, our future difficulties.

CHAPTER XX

REMOVAL TO CANADA

In 1830, I closed my business in Rochester, preparatory to leaving for Canada. Some of my friends thought I had better remain in the States and direct emigrants to Wilberforce; while others were certain I could benefit them more by going myself at once,—the latter I had determined to do; but as the time drew near for me to start, an unaccountable gloominess and forebodings of evil took possession of my mind. Doubts of the practicability of the undertaking began to arise, though nothing unfavorable had occurred. To the throne of grace, I often bore the subject and besought my Heavenly Father to enlighten my mind, and direct my steps in duty's path regarding it; but to confess the truth, I never received any great encouragement from that source, though it occupied my mind constantly. During the hours of slumber I was continually being startled by frightful dreams,—sometimes I thought I saw a monstrous serpent as large as a log stretched across the road between Rochester and the Genesee River; at another I thought myself in the air so high that I could have a full view of the shores of Lake Ontario, and they were alive with snakes; and then I saw a large bird like an eagle, rise up out of the water and fly toward the south.

Notwithstanding these omens, I turned my steps toward Wilberforce. In May, 1831, we bid adieu to our friends in Rochester, and taking passage to Buffalo on a canal boat, we arrived in due time, and from whence we sailed for Port Stanley, or as it is sometimes called, Kettle Creek. It took a week to make this trip, which, with favorable wind might have been made in two days. The mouth of the creek makes a safe harbor at that place, where there is also a dock, one ware-house and several farm houses. The place was then very wild and picturesque in its appearance; we did not stop long, however, to admire its beauty, but engaged a farmer to take us on to London.

Ten miles on our way, and we came to a newly laid out village, called St. Thomas, from whence we pursued our journey through a new country to London, where we arrived tired and hungry, and put up for the night with a Mr. Faden. There I purchased a span of horses for one hundred and fifty dollars, and putting them before a new lumber wagon brought on from Rochester, we started for our wild and new home in good spirits, at which we arrived in good time.

The colony was comprised of some fourteen or fifteen families, and numbered some over fifty persons in all. The first business done after my arrival, was to appoint a board of managers, to take the general oversight of all the public business of the colony. The board consisted of seven men, chosen by the settlers, and as I was now one of them, they gave me the office of President. It was also resolved by the board, to send out two agents for the purpose of soliciting aid for the erection of houses for worship, and for the maintenance of schools in the colony.

The Rev. N. Paul was chosen one of their agents, and he received from me a power of attorney, authorising him to collect funds for the above purposes in England, Ireland, and Scotland; the other, I. Lewis was empowered to solicit and collect funds for the same objects in the United States.

Preparations were immediately made to fit Mr. Paul out for his mission to England, from whence he was to remit any funds he might receive to Arthur Tappan, of New York City; first to pay for his outfit, and afterwards to the treasurer of the board of managers, for the support of schools in Wilberforce. Mr. Paul, however, still lacked money to proceed to England, and therefore went to Rochester, where he found my old and tried friend Everard Peck; who was ever known as the poor man's friend, and the support of the weak everywhere. To this good man, whose memory is still dear to thousands, Mr. Paul showed his power of attorney, at the same time informing him of the condition and wants of the colony; and as was ever his wont, when help was needed, his purse, (though not one of the heaviest), was at his service. Through the kind influence of Mr. Peck, and some of the colored friends in that city, a note for seven hundred dollars was drawn up, signed by Mr. P. and cashed at the Bank, which enabled the agent to make the voyage without further delay. He reached England, and collected quite large sums of money, but entirely failed in the remittance of any sums, either to Mr. Tappan or myself. When the note of seven hundred dollars became due, Mr. Peck was obliged to pay, and lose it. It was out of my power, nor had any of the friends the means to do any thing towards paying it, inasmuch as they had assisted Paul all they could and got nothing in return. There was one thing, however, that the reverend gentleman did do,—he wrote me from time to time, to keep me advised of the success of his mission, and once informed me that he had then twelve hundred dollars on hand; but not a farthing could we get. We wrote him again and again, reminding him of the bank debt, and the uneasiness of his friends on account of it, but all to no purpose,—the Atlantic was between us, and he was making money too easily, to like to be interrupted. He never paid one dollar.

Let us now look after the other agent, who had likewise been fitted out, to prosecute his mission in the States. That he collected money professedly for the assistance of the colony, is too well known to require proof, but how much, we could not determine; we had reason to believe, however, that he retained quite a large sum. He would neither pay it over to the board, nor give any account of his proceedings. Very little did he ever pay over to the aid of the colony as designed. He was frequently written to, and every means in our power used, to induce him to give some account of his mission, but in vain; he would do nothing of the kind. Things went on in this way for two years, when it became evident that he had no intention of satisfying the minds of the settlers; and farther, that he meant to collect what he could, and use it as he pleased. We learned too, that when abroad, he lived extravagantly,—putting up at the most expensive hotels, giving parties, and doing many things, not only beyond his means, but that brought dishonor on the cause and colony. When he returned to the settlement, he would, if he had funds, make presents to his particular friends instead of paying it to the treasurer, as he was pledged to do, until the majority of the colony became thoroughly disgusted with his heartlessness and dishonesty. It was also perceivable that Lewis and Paul both, were getting weary of the solicitations of the board and complaints of the settlers, and were anxious to be rid of them, and enjoy their ill gotten gains in their own way.

It was never intended by the managers, to send out agents to beg money to be divided among the colonists; but to support schools, &c. Most of the settlers were able to work and did so; and were now getting along quite pleasantly.

Finally, after we had tried every means in vain, to get a settlement with Lewis, and to obtain his papers, there was nothing more we could do, but to warn the public against him, by publishing the facts in the case; this we did in various newspapers of Canada and in the States. An article inserted in the "Rochester Observer," to that effect, was like throwing a lighted match into a keg of powder. The excitement was intense on the part of Lewis and his friends, who were joined by the friends of N. Paul, to destroy, if they could, the board of managers. I, however, being the only member of that devoted board, who happened to be extensively known in the States, their anathemas were all poured out on me, and all their energies brought forward to insure my destruction. They were few in number, it is true, but they had money, and I had little to spend in litigation; besides, Lewis was in debt, and his creditors did not like to see his means of paying them swept away. The Canadians seemed to think there was no harm done if Lewis did get money out of the "Yankees," as long as it came into their hands at last, and so, on the whole, they raised a tremendous storm, designed, however, to sweep nobody away but myself; and I have continued to this day, notwithstanding all their artful malignity. Nothing, I am persuaded, could have saved me from imprisonment at that time, had I not possessed a high reputation for truth and honesty during my previous sojourn in the colony.

Lewis had dealt somewhat extensively with Mr. Jones, who was the principal agent for the Canada Company; but failing to fulfil his agreement, regarding the payment for a large tract of land, it so exasperated Mr. Jones, that he declared he would have nothing to do with any of the colored people; and so when I wanted to buy a lot of land, he would not sell it to me because he so despised Lewis.

How much harm can one wicked man do! and yet it cannot be right to judge the character of a whole class or community by that of one person.

CHAPTER XXI

ROUGHING IT IN THE WILDS OF CANADA

The "Canada Company," of which I have so frequently spoken, was an association of wealthy gentlemen, residing in England; something like the East India Company, especially regarding the title of lands. They had sent on their agent and purchased a large tract of land known as the "Huron Tract," extending from London to Lake Huron, where they laid out a village, named Goderich, sixty miles distant from Wilberforce. With this company, Mr. Lewis had contracted for a township of land, as agent for the Cincinnati refugees; but failing to meet the demand, the company kindly extended the time of payment; but when that time also passed without receiving any thing from Lewis, the general agent, Mr. Jones became so indignant, that he utterly refused to sell a foot of land to any colored person whatever. This proved to be one of the greatest detriments to the prosperity of the colony it ever met.

The Society of Friends at this time, however, with commendable sympathy for the oppressed and abused colored residents of Cincinnati, and with their proverbial liberality, raised a sum of money sufficient to purchase eight hundred acres of land of the Canada Company for the benefit of the colony. The funds were placed in the hands of one of their number, Frederick Stover, who went to Canada as their agent, purchased the land, and settled colored people upon it, which comprised nearly all of the Wilberforce settlement. This occurred before I settled in Canada, and the consequence was, when I desired to purchase land, none could be obtained. At the time, however, of

653

which I am speaking, the Canada Company were constructing a road through their possessions, some seventy miles in length, and the principal contractor, Mr. Ingersoll, had agreed to take land in part payment for his services on the road. In accordance with this agreement, he accepted one lot of land situated within the Wilberforce settlement, which he agreed to sell to Mr. Lewis for twenty-five dollars. Mr. Lewis, knowing that I was anxious to purchase, accepted the offer, and then came and showed the contract, offering it to me on condition that I paid him the twenty-five dollars which he had just paid Mr. Ingersoll. This I was glad to do; I paid the demand; took an assignment on the back of the receipt, and passed into immediate possession of the land. He at the same time requested me to take up a note of twenty-five dollars for him; which I did, on his promising to refund the money in a short time.

I commenced laboring on the wild land I had purchased; cleared some ten acres, which in consequence of its being so heavily timbered, cost me at least twenty-five dollars per acre; built a house and barn—supposing myself its legal possessor,—until I chanced to meet Mr. Ingersoll, who informed me that Mr. Jones had refused to sell him the land to be disposed of to a colored person; that he had duly informed Lewis of the fact, and had returned to him the twenty-five dollars received. Not a word of this, had Lewis communicated to me, though he knew I was making expensive improvements, in the faith that I was its only owner. Instead of atoning for the wrong already done me, he made it the basis of a deeper injury.

After one year's residence in Wilberforce, I found it necessary to return to Rochester to settle some unfinished business; and when on my way thither I stopped at London, where I found Lewis, who had not only preceded me but had taken out a *capias*, for forty pounds currency. I was therefore obliged to get bail for my appearance at court, after which I pursued my journey.

On my arrival in Rochester, I found business at a stand; and the community in a state of excitement and alarm, on account of that fell destroyer, the cholera. This was its first visit to the United States, and the fearful havoc it was making, spread terror and consternation throughout the land. I returned to Canada; but found on my arrival at London, that "the pestilence that walketh at noon-day," had preceded me, and taken from that village my friend, Mr. Ingersoll, with several others. So great had been the alarm, that instead of my appearing at court as I expected to do, I found it adjourned, and the judge returned to his home.

I hastened on to Wilberforce, which had fortunately escaped the fearful scourge, with terrible apprehensions.

Having a little spare time, I went out with my rifle, in search of deer; but soon came upon a large wolf, which I wounded with the first shot; he, however, sprang aside and was gone. On looking about for him I espied another!—reloading my rifle, I fired, and he fell dead at my feet, while my dog at the same time I heard barking furiously. Having dispatched this second intruder, I saw that my dog had the first one, entangled in the branches of a fallen tree. I searched for my balls, and was vexed to find that I had left them at home. In this predicament I cut with my knife, a knot from a beech limb, put it in my rifle, and took deadly aim at the enraged wolf. The wooden ball struck him between the eyes and killed him on the spot.

The two dead animals, with their skins, I sold for nine dollars and a half,—making pretty good wages for a few hours labor.

Hunting was very generally pursued by the settlers, with great earnestness and considerable skill. The forest abounded with deer, wolves, bears, and other wild animals. Bears were plenty, and very troublesome because so dangerously tame. One day, our children had built for themselves a play-house, a few rods from the door, and were enjoying their play when they were called in to dinner. A moment after, I observed one of the settlers gazing intently at the play-house; I called to know what so attracted his attention, and he informed me that an old bear, with three cubs, had just then taken possession of the playhouse.

And sure enough there they were! knocking about among the dishes, and munching the crumbs of bread which the children had left. The man was supplied with a loaded rifle and urged to shoot them, but he begged to be excused from a pitched battle with so many; and the bears leisurely took their departure for the woods without molestation. The play-house, however, was soon deserted by the children after these unbidden guests had made so free with it; and we were ourselves somewhat alarmed for the safety of our children, who were accustomed to roam in the edge of the forest, and make swings of the luxuriant grape vines.

But such incidents are common in a new country, surrounded as we were by a dense wilderness.

CHAPTER XXII

NARROW ESCAPE OF A SMUGGLER

From the time I first settled in Wilberforce, my house had ever been open to travelers and strangers; but a conversation I happened to overhear, led me to take a course different from what I had at first intended. I was at a public house about twenty miles from home, when I heard the landlord advising his guest to eat heartily, for, said he, "you will find nothing more worthy of your attention, until you reach Wilberforce. When you arrive at that settlement, inquire for A. Steward, from the States, and he will give you a meal fit for a prince." I began to reflect on the subject and concluded, inasmuch as people would send company to me, it would be better to make some preparation for entertaining them. I had plenty of furniture, and all I needed was a larger supply of food, to commence keeping a tavern. This was easily obtained, and I opened a public house which was well patronized.

One day while I was absent from home, a man drove to the door the finest span of horses, I think I ever saw,—black as jet, with proudly arched necks, and glossy tails that nearly swept the ground. The gentleman sprang from his carriage, bounded through the open door, and in the most excited manner, began to inquire "who owns this establishment? When will he return? Can I be accommodated? Can I see your barn?" &c. The stable boy took him to the barn, from whence he soon returned; his face flushed, and breathing so heavily as to be heard all through the apartment; trembling so violently that he could scarcely speak at all,—but made out to inquire, "if there was not some

657

place besides the barn where he could put his horses?" He was told that there was a small shelter built for cows, in bad weather, and the next moment he was examining it. In a very short time he had his horses and carriage stowed away in the cow-shed. He acted like a crazy man; but when he had secured his horses, he re-entered the house and frankly apologized for his conduct. "I may as well tell you the truth," said he; "I am suspected of smuggling goods; a reward is offered for my arrest, and the constables are on my track, in pursuit of me. My name is Cannouse, and I am from M——, in Ontario County."

But perhaps they can not prove you guilty of smuggling, said I, in an after conversation.

"Ah," said he, "there is for me no such hope or probability; I have been engaged for the last few months in the sale of dress-goods and broad-cloths, and my exposure and flight is the consequence of my own folly. While in the village of St. Catharines, I took a young girl out to ride, after she had engaged to accompany another young fellow, which of course offended him; and he being too well posted up on my affairs, went directly to the custom house officer and informed against me. I was sitting in the parlor, perfectly at ease, when a young man, a relative of the young lady in question, burst into the room, shouting, 'Fly! fly! for your life! The officers are upon you!' And I did fly; with barely time to reach the woods, for as I sprang through the back door, the officers entered through the front door. My horses were my first consideration; they had been raised by my father, and should I lose them, I should never dare to meet him again. In my hasty flight, I engaged the young man to conceal them till night, and then to drive them to a certain place where I would meet him. This he did, and I kept on my flight until I came to the house of a friend, where I halted to make inquiries. The gentleman had just come from London, and had seen handbills at every conspicuous place, describing me and my horses. I asked him what I should do? He said, 'you are not safe a moment; there is no hope but in flight; avoid the main road, and get to the colony if you can; if you succeed, go to A. Steward; he is an upright man and will never betray you for money,' And here I am: if I am arrested, six months imprisonment, three hundred dollars fine, and the forfeiture of my father's valuable and favorite horses, will be my portion. I have had no regular meal for the last three days, and my head aches violently."

We gave him some refreshment, and conducted him to a room, assuring him that he should have it to himself. All remained quiet until midnight, when a man knocked cautiously at our door. I opened it myself, and a gentleman, looking carefully about the place, inquired,

"Are you full?"

"No," said I. — "Have you any travelers here to night?"

"Yes."

"How many?"

"Two."

"Where are they?"

"In this room; walk in, sir."

He took the light from my hand, and stepping lightly up to a bed, where two travelers were quietly sleeping, he closely examined their faces. He soon returned the light, and without further inquiry retired from the house. When his companions came up, I distinctly heard him tell them that the smuggler was not there.

"You may be mistaken," said the other, "and we must search the barn for his horses."

This they did thoroughly, after procuring a lantern; but without finding any thing to reward their diligent search; and they finally drove off.

When they had gone, Cannouse groaned most bitterly, and trembled from head to foot at the thought of his narrow escape. The next day an officer rode up to where the children were playing, with a handbill which he read, and inquired if they had seen a person bearing that description, pass *that day?*

They answered negatively, and he rode on. The poor frightened Cannouse stayed with us a week; and nearly every day during the time, the house and barn were searched for him. The children kept watch, and when they saw any one coming they would let him know, in time to take himself and horses into a thicket near by. When he thought pursuit was over, he started to leave; but when, in a half hour after, a *posse* of men drove up to my door, flourishing their handbills, I thought it all over with Cannouse. I told them that he was not there; but they chose to have another search, and when they found nothing, the officer sprang into his carriage, exclaiming, "come on, boys; we'll soon have him now; we have tracked him here, and he can't be far off."

Cannouse had left us, feeling quite secure; but he had traveled but a short distance, when he observed a horse shoe loose, and to get it fastened he drove down to a blacksmith's shop, which happened to stand at the foot of a hill; and between it and the highway there had been left standing a clump of trees which nearly hid it from view. While there, getting his horse shod, the officers passed him unobserved, and he finally escaped.

Some time after, a gentleman called on us who had seen Cannouse in Michigan, where he was doing well. He had succeeded in reaching Detroit, from whence he passed safely to his home; but probably learned a lesson not to be forgotten. He was a talented young man—one who would have felt deeply the disgrace of imprisonment,—and it was indeed a pleasure to me to do what I could, to effect his release from an unenviable position. I would never have betrayed him; but happily I was not asked directly for him, until he was gone from my house and protection.

CHAPTER XXIII

NARRATIVE OF TWO FUGITIVES FROM VIRGINIA

The settlers in Wilberforce, were in general, industrious and thrifty farmers: they cleared their land, sowed grain, planted orchards, raised cattle, and in short, showed to the world that they were in no way inferior to the white population, when given an equal chance with them. In proof of this let me say, that it was uniformly the practice of persons traveling from London to Goderich, to remain in our settlement over night, in preference to going on to find entertainment among their own class of people. And we believe that the whites are bound to admit, that the experiment of the Wilberforce colony proves that the colored man can not only take care of himself, but is capable of improvement; as industrious and intelligent as themselves, when the yoke is taken from off their necks, and a chance given them to exercise their abilities. True, many of them had just escaped from cruel task-masters; ignorant of almost every thing but the lash,—but the air of freedom so invigorated and put new life into their weary bodies, that they soon became intelligent and thrifty.

Among the settlers might be gathered many a thrilling narrative, of suffering and hair-breadth escapes from the slave-land,—one of which I will tell as 'twas told to me.

In a small rude cabin, belonging to one of the large plantations in Virginia, sat at a late hour of the night, an afflicted slave-man and his devoted wife, sad and weeping. At length the husband repeated what he before had been saying:

"I tell you, wife, we must flee from this place, without delay.

Oh, I cannot endure the idea of seeing you sold for the Southern market, to say nothing of myself; and we shall most likely be separated, which I can't bear! Oh, Rosa, the thought distracts me,—I can't bear it!"

"Are you sure," said Rosa, "that master thinks of such a frightful doom for us?"

"Oh yes, I know it; I heard master to-day making a bargain with the slave dealer that has been hanging about here so long; and when it was finished, I heard him reading over the list, and our names, wife, are the first on it."

"Oh, dear!" sobbed the wife, "we shall certainly be retaken and whipped to death; or else we shall starve in the wilderness! Oh, it is very hard to be compelled to leave all our friends and the old plantation where we were born!"

"Yes; it is both hard and unjust," said Joe, and an indignant frown contracted his brow,—"here is our birth-place, and here, for forty years have I toiled early and late to enrich my master; and you, my poor wife, a few years less; and now we are to be sold, separated, and all without a choice of our own. We must go, Rosa. If we die, let us die together!"

"It shall be as you say, Joe," she replied, "but it frightens me to think of the hardships of the way, and the danger of being recaptured."

"Courage, wife: no fate can be worse than the one designed for us; and we have no time to lose. Tomorrow night, then, we must make the first effort to gain our liberty, and leave all that is dear to us except each other!" And they retired to rest, but not to sleep.

The following night was very dark; and as soon as all was quiet on the plantation, they stole out of their cabin and stealthily crept over the ground until they reached the highway; and then, guided only by the north star, they made their way to the nearest woods. So fearful had they been of being suspected, that they took no provision of any kind with them. All night they plunged forward through the tangled thicket and underbrush, surrounded by thick darkness, glancing now and then upward to their only light,

"Star of the North! though night winds drift the fleecy
drapery of the sky,
Between thy lamp and thee, I lift, yea, lift with hope
my sleepless eye."

When day dawned they threw their weary bodies on the ground, famished and thirsty, and waited for the darkness to again conceal them while they pursued their journey. The second day of their flight, the pain of hunger became almost beyond endurance. They found a few roots which relieved them a little; but frequently they lost their way, and becoming bewildered, knew not which way to go; they pushed on, however, determined to keep as far from their pursuers as possible. Their shoes were soon worn out; but bare-footed, bare-headed, and famishing with hunger, they pressed forward, until the fourth day, when they found themselves too weak to proceed farther. Hope, the anchor of the soul, had failed them! They were starving in a dense forest! No track or path could they find, and even had they seen a human being, they would have been more terrified than at the sight of a wild beast!

Poor Rosa, could go no farther—her strength was all gone—and as her emaciated husband laid her on the cold earth, he exclaimed, "Oh, dear God! *must* we, after all our efforts, starve in this dark wilderness! Beside his fainting wife, he finally stretched himself, sheltered only by a few bushes, and tried to compose himself to die! but resting a few moments revived him, and he aroused himself, to make one more effort for life! Stay you here, wife, and I will try once more to find the highway; it cannot be far from here; and if I am taken, I will submit to my fate without a struggle; we can but die." So saying, he left her, and began to reconnoitre the country around them. Much sooner than he expected he emerged from the wood, and not far distant he saw a house in the direction from whence he came; being, however, as most of the slaves are, superstitious, he thought it would be a bad omen to turn backward, and so continued to look about him. It seemed, he said, that some unseen power held him, for though starving as he was, he could not take a step in that direction; and at last as he turned around, to his great joy, he saw another dwelling a little way off, and toward that he hastened his now lightened footsteps. With a palpitating heart, he approached the door and knocked cautiously. The man of the house opened it, and as soon as he saw him, he said, "You are a fugitive slave, but be not alarmed, come in; no harm shall befall you here; I shall not inquire from whence you came; it is enough for me to know that you are a human being in distress; consider me your friend, and let me know your wants."

"Bread! Oh, for a morsel of bread!" said the famished creature, while his hitherto wild and sunken eyes, began to distil grateful tears. The "good Samaritan" stepped to another apartment and brought him a piece of bread, which he expected to see him devour at once, but instead, he looked at it wistfully, literally devouring it with his eyes; turned it over and over, and at last stammered out, "my good master, without a piece of bread for my poor starving wife, I can never swallow this, tempting as it is."

"Poor man," said his benefactor, "can it be that you have a wife with you, wretched as yourself?" He brought out a loaf of bread, some cheese and meat, and while the fugitive was preparing to return, the kind gentleman said, "I am glad you came to me; had you called at the house you first saw, you would have been betrayed, and immediately arrested. You must remember," he continued, "that you are young and valuable slaves, and that your master will make every effort in his power to find you, especially since he has made a sale of you. To-day and to-night, remain in the woods, and the next morning you may come to me, if all is quiet; should I see danger approaching you, I will warn you of it by the crack my rifle. Go now, to your poor wife, and listen for the signal of danger; if you hear none, come to me at the appointed time." He returned, and after feeding his helpless Rosa, she revived, and soon felt quite comfortable and grateful.

When the morning came for them to leave their retreat, they listened intently, but hearing nothing, Joe started for the residence of his friend. He had been gone but a short time, when his wife, who lay in the bushes, thought she heard the tramp of horses,—she crept nearer the highway, and peeping through the bush—Oh, horror! what was her consternation and sickening fear, to find herself gazing upon the well-known features of her old master, and two of his neighbors, all armed to the teeth! Her heart seemed to stand still, and the blood to chill in her veins. Had she been discovered she would have been an easy prey, for she declared that she could not move a step. In the meantime her husband had got about half way to the residence of his preserver, when his quick ear detected the sound made by the feet of horses, and as he stopped to listen more intently, the sharp crack of a rifle sent him bounding back to his concealment in the forest.

The party of horsemen rode on to the dwelling of the kind hearted gentleman, and inquired whether he had seen any fugitive slaves pass that way.

"I saw," said he, "a man and woman passing rapidly along the road, but do not know whether they were fugitives, as I did not see their faces." The human blood-hound, thanked the gentleman for the information, and immediately set out in pursuit; but, just as the informant had intended, in a direction *opposite* to that the slaves had taken. That night, Joe and Rosa visited the house of their benefactor, where they were supplied with clothing and as much food as they could carry; and next day they went on their way rejoicing. They settled in Cincinnati, where they lived happily, until the mob drove them with others, to the Wilberforce settlement, where they are in no danger of the auction block, or of a Southern market; and are as much devoted to each other as ever.

CHAPTER XXIV

PLEASANT RE-UNION OF OLD AND TRIED FRIENDS

It is well known to those who have assisted in clearing land in a new country, that bears, who are not Jews, are very troublesome, and levy a heavy tax on the settlers, to supply themselves with pork-their favorite food. One old bear in particular, had for a long time annoyed the colonists, by robbing their hog-stys almost every night. We failed in all our plans to destroy his life, until a woman saw him one day, walking at ease through the settlement. A half dozen of us gave chase immediately, and came up with him after traveling two miles. So anxious was I to kill him, that I fired at first sight and missed him, which gave us another two miles chase. When, however, we came up, he was seated on a branch of a tree, leisurely surveying us and the dogs, with great complacency. The contents of my rifle brought him to the ground, and stirred his blood for battle. One blow from his powerful paw, sent my fine greyhound some yards distant, sprawling upon the ground, and when he renewed the attack, Bruin met him with extended jaws, taking and munching his head in his mouth. My rifle was now reloaded, and the second shot killed him on the spot. We tied his legs together, and lifting him on a pole, marched in triumph into the settlement, where guns were discharged and cheers given, in approbation of our success.

One winter's evening we had drawn closely around the blazing fire, for the air was piercing cold without, and the snow four feet deep on a level. Now and then, a traveler might be seen on snow-shoes; but though our cabin was situated on the king's highway, we seldom saw company on such a night as this. While the wind whistled, and the snow drifted about our dwelling, we piled the wood higher in our ample fire-place, and seated ourselves again, to resume the conversation, when I was startled by a loud and furious knocking at the door. I opened it to what I supposed to be three Indians. Their costume was that of the red man; but the voice of him who addressed me was not that of an Indian. "Can you keep three poor devils here to-night?" said he, and when I made farther inquiry, he repeated the same question; "we can sleep," he continued, "on the soft side of a board; only give us poor devils a shelter."

I told him we were not accustomed to turn away any one on such a night; that they were welcome to come in; and they were soon seated around our large and cheerful fire.

They had laid aside their snow-shoes and knapsacks, and the heat of the fire soon made their blankets uncomfortable; but as one of them made a move to throw it off, another was heard to whisper, "wait a little; we are among strangers, you know; so do not make a display of yourself." The fellow drew his blanket about him; but we had heard and seen enough to awaken curiosity, if not suspicion. In passing out of the room soon after, I heard one of these pretended Indians say to his companion, "I know these folks are from the States, for I smell coffee." When they finally sat down to table, and saw silver upon it, they cast surprised and knowing glances at each other, all of which we closely observed, and were convinced, that they were not red men of the forest, but belonged to that race who had so long looked haughtily down upon the colored people; that the least exhibition of comfort, or show of refinement astonished them beyond measure.

In the meantime, my wife had whispered to me that she was sure that the principal speaker was no other than the aristocratic Mr. G——, of Canandaigua. I could not believe it; I could not recognize in that savage costume, one who had been bred in affluence, and "the star" of genteel society. But my wife soon developed the affair to our mutual satisfaction: G——, on taking from her a cup of coffee, remarked, "this looks good; and I have had no good coffee since I left my mother's house."

"Does your mother still reside in C——?" asked Mrs. Steward.

"My mother! my mother! what do you know of my mother!" said he, looking sharply at her; but observing that they were recognized, they began to laugh, and we had a hearty congratulation all round; while G——, starting-up from table, exclaimed,

"Come, boys, off with this disguise; we are among friends now."

Our Indian guests, now appeared in costume more like "Broadway dandies," than savages. Dressed in the finest cloth, with gold chains and repeaters; and all that constituted the toilet of a gentleman. After tea they requested to dry some costly furs, which they took from their knapsacks and hung around the fire. The following day they took their leave, with many apologies and explanations, regarding their appearance and conduct. They were in the wilderness, they said, trading for very valuable furs; they had money, jewelry and rich goods, which they had taken that method to conceal.

During all this time, there had been another visitor in the house, who was sitting in a corner, absorbed in writing. Our mock Indians had noticed him, and not knowing who he was, expressed a determination "to quiz that deaf old devil," after supper. We all seated ourselves around the fire, and our Canandaigua friends, though no longer savages, had not forgotten the silent man in the corner; they began to question him, and he aroused himself for conversation; nor was it long before they forgot their design to quiz him, and found themselves charmed listeners to the brilliant conversation, of that world-renowned champion of humanity, Benjamin Lundy, for he it was.

On this particular evening, he gave us a sketch of his journey to Hayti; to accompany there and settle some emancipated slaves; which I thought very interesting, and as I have never seen

THROUGH THE EYES OF A SLAVE
it in print I will here relate it, as near as I can, in his own words:

In the State of Maryland, there lived a slaveholder the proprietor of some sixty slaves, and being somewhat advanced in years, he determined to free them, in accordance with the laws of that State, which required that they be sent out of it.

He had thought the matter over, but being undecided where to send them, he sent for Mr. Lundy to assist him in his proposed plan; who was only too glad to comply with a request calculated to carry out his own plans of philanthropy and equal rights.

When he had listened to the suggestions and expressed desires of the planter, he offered his arguments in favor of the West India Islands; and it was decided to send them to Hayti, as their future place of residence.

Six weeks were allowed for preparations; then Mr. Lundy was to return and take charge of them on the voyage, and see them settled in their new homes.

When the appointed time arrived, Mr. Lundy was there to accompany them on board a vessel bound for Hayti; on which was furnished as comfortable quarters, as the kindness of their conscientious master and his own benevolent heart could suggest. When all was ready, the Christian master came on board, to take leave of those faithful servants,—many of whom had served him from their childhood, and all of whom he had bound to his heart by kindness and Christian benevolence. It was a sad parting; not because the slaves did not love liberty, but because they appreciated their master's kind forbearance, and solicitude for their future welfare. He had ever been a humane and indulgent master; one who lightened the burthen of the poor slave, all in his power. A moment's reflection will show, that it is invariably this conscientious kind of slaveholders, who are induced to emancipate their slaves; and not the avaricious, cruel tyrant, who neither fears God nor regards his fellow man.

The master of the slaves had kindly informed them of his intentions,—of the probable length of the voyage, and the unavoidable sickness they would experience, &c.; but now, they were gazing up into his kind face for the last time, as he knelt in prayer, commending that numerous flock—raised on his own plantation—to the care and protection of Almighty God, beseeching Him to protect them in the storm and dangers of the ocean; to guide them through this life, and save them in the world to come; until the sobs and cries of the poor slaves drowned his utterance. He at length took his final leave of them, and of Mr. Lundy; and the ship sailed immediately. They, however, met storms and adverse winds, which detained them; and then the poor, ignorant slaves began to believe what they had before suspected: that this was only some wicked plan of Mr. Lundy's, laid to entice them away from a kind master, and to plunge them into some dreadful degradation and suffering. "Master" had not told them of the adverse winds, and they were certain that some mischief was intended; they grew sullen and disobedient; and notwithstanding the kindness of Mr. Lundy, they murmured and complained, until his kind heart sank within him; still he pursued the even tenor of his way, trusting in God for deliverance. He watched over them in sickness, and administered to all their wants; but his tender solicitude for their health and comfort, only excited suspicion, and increased their ungrateful ill humor.

One pleasant evening, Mr. Lundy paced the deck in deep thought. He was sad, and well nigh hopeless. He had seen enough in the fierce look and sullen scowl; and had heard enough of the bitterness, and threatening anger of the negroes, to know that a storm was gathering, which must soon burst in all its wild fury over his devoted head. He was a small, feeble man, compared with those who watched his every movement, and gnashed their teeth upon him so fiercely. None but the Almighty could save him now; and to Him who "rides upon the wings of the wind, and maketh the clouds His chariot," he drew near in fervent prayer; after which he retired in peace and confidence to his berth. During the night, a fine breeze sprang up; and when he went on deck the next morning, they were in

670

sight of the luxuriant shore of Hayti! The officers of the island boarded the ship; but their language was unintelligible to the negroes, who still looked daggers at every one who spoke. They landed; but the fearful, and ungrateful slaves continued sullen and forbidding. Mr. Lundy left them, however, and went into the country, where he selected their future residence; and made every preparation for their comfort and convenience in his power; saw them conveyed to their neat, pleasant homes, and all happily settled. This work was accomplished; and he merely called to bid adieu to his ungrateful charge, when he found that one of the slaves had been appointed to speak to him, in behalf of the whole number, and confess how deeply they had wronged him. While they were conversing, the others gathered around, with tears and prayers for forgiveness; and finally fell at his feet, imploring pardon for themselves, and blessings on the kind, patient and humane Benjamin Lundy. He hurried from the affecting scene, and soon after returned to America.

Thus that cold evening passed more pleasantly away in our rude cabin; and our Canandaigua gentlemen, after an agreeable acquaintance, and pleasant chat with Mr. Lundy, retired for the night—not like savages, but like gentlemen as they were; and I doubt not, with a more exalted opinion of "the deaf old devil in the corner"

CHAPTER XXV

PRIVATE LOSSES AND PRIVATE DIFFICULTIES

Soon after settling in Wilberforce, I found that the rumor I had heard in the States, concerning the refusal to sell land to colored persons, was literally correct, and my farm being too small to yield a support for my family, and knowing it would be useless to apply for more land, I engaged to carry packages for different merchants in the adjoining villages, as well as to and from the settlement. Possessing a pair of excellent horses and a good wagon, I found it a profitable business, and the only one I could well do, to eke out the proceeds of my farm, and meet my expenses.

One day as I was returning from the village, one of my horses was taken suddenly ill. I took him to a tavern near by, and as I could discover no cause for his illness, I concluded to leave him a few days, supposing rest would soon restore him. I accordingly hired another horse, and returned to the colony. In a day or two after, I collected my packages as usual, and started on my route, designing to leave the hired horse and take my own; but when I arrived at the tavern, I found some Indians engaged in taking off the hide and shoes of my poor, dead horse. This was indeed, a great loss to me; but I consoled myself with the thought that I had one good horse left, yet he would hardly be sufficient to accomplish alone, the labor I had engaged to perform; nor had I the means to spare, to purchase another. I therefore hired one, and commenced business again, with the determination to make up my loss by renewed diligence and perseverance.

I started in good spirits; but had proceeded but a few miles, when my remaining horse, which I had supposed perfectly sound, reeled and fell in the harness! And before I could relieve him of it, my noble animal and faithful servant, had breathed his last! Without a struggle or a movement he lay lifeless on the cold earth. I was sad. I deplored the loss of my good, and valuable team; but more the mystery and suspicion that hung over the event. I returned home and sat down to devise some plan of procedure. What could I do? Half the means of our support had been suddenly and mysteriously snatched from us. What could I do next? While thus ruminating, I arose to answer a summons at the door, and who should enter but Mr. B. Paul, a brother to our foreign agent, who had so long absented himself from our house, that I was indeed surprised to see him at this time. He, however, seated himself, with great apparent concern for my recent loss, which he soon made the subject of conversation and the object of his visit.

"There has been," said he, "a great deal of unpleasant feeling, and injudicious speaking on both sides, for which I am heartily sorry. The colony is too weak to sustain a division of feelings; and now, that your recent losses have left you in a far less favorable condition to sustain yourself and family, I have called to make a settlement of our former difficulties, and to offer you two hundred and fifty dollars out of the collections for the colony."

I saw through the plan at once, and considered it only a bribe, to prevent my exposing the iniquity of others. Should I consent to take a part of the ill-gotten spoils, with what confidence could I attempt to stay the hand of the spoiler. I wanted money very much, it is true; but after a moment's reflection, not enough to sanction the manner in which it had been obtained; and though I confess, the offer presented to me a strong temptation, I am thankful that I was enabled to resist it. I refused to accept the money; and after sending away the tempter and his offered gain, I felt my heart lighter, and my conscience more peaceful than is often the lot of sinful, erring man in this world of trial and conflict; and yet I could but feel that the mystery in which the death of my horses was involved, was partially at least, explained.

CHAPTER XXVI

INCIDENTS AND PECULIARITIES OF THE INDIANS

During our residence in Canada, we were often visited by the Indians, which gave us an opportunity to learn their character, habits and disposition; and some incidents illustrative of the peculiarities of that abused people, I will here mention.

I recollect one bitter cold night, about eleven o'clock, I happened to awake, and looking out toward the fire, I was surprised to see standing there, erect and quiet, a tall, brawny Indian, wrapped in his blanket; his long hunting knife and tomahawk dangling from his belt; and his rifle in his hand. Had he been in his own wigwam, he could not have looked about him with more satisfaction and independence. I instantly sprang to my feet, and demanded his errand.

"Me lost in the woods, and me come to stay all night," was his grave reply.

"Then," said I, "give me your weapons, and I will make no objection."

He disarmed himself, and gave his weapons to me, with an air of haughty disdain for my fears. I put them in a place of safety and then prepared his bed, which was nothing more than the floor, where they choose to sleep, with their head to the fire. My offer of anything different from this he proudly resented as an insult to his powers of endurance, and would say, "beds for pale faces and women; hard board for Indians." He threw himself down, drew his blanket about him, and was soon sleeping soundly. As soon as the day began to dawn, he was up, called for his arms, and after thanking me in the brief

Indian style of politeness, departed for the forest. He had found our doors all fastened, save a low back door, through which he entered, passing through a back room so full of miscellaneous articles, that it was difficult to go through it in the day time without upsetting something; but the Indian understood all this, he made no noise, nor would he have spoken at all, had I not awakened; and yet, he would have scorned to injure any one beneath the roof that gave him shelter, unless he had been intoxicated.

One sabbath afternoon, one of my children was sitting in the door, when a tall, emaciated Indian came up and said, "Will my little lady please to give me a drink of water?" While she went for it, I invited him to a seat within. There was something dignified and commanding in his appearance, and something in his voice and countenance, that won my confidence and respect at once. He remained in the place some time, and I learned his history.

In his younger days he had been a great warrior; and even now, when recounting, as he often did, the scenes of the battle field, his eye would burn with savage fire, lighting up his whole countenance with the fiercest kind of bravery, and often with a hideous yell that would startle our very souls, he would burst from the room and bound over the fields and forest, with the fleetness of a deer—making the woods ring with his frightful war-cry, until the blood seemed ready to curdle in our veins. He had also been one of the famous Tecumseh's braves; and had stood by him when he fell on the fifth of October, 1813. This old brave, whenever he called the name of Tecumseh, bowed his head reverently; and would often try to tell us how very deeply they mourned when it could no longer be doubted that the brave heart of Tecumseh, brother of the celebrated Wabash prophet, had ceased to beat.

"Had an arrow pierced the sun and brought it to my feet," said the old warrior, "I could not have been more astounded than at the fall of Tecumseh." Then he told us that once, after a great and victorious battle, Tecumseh, in his war paint and feathers, stood in the midst of his braves, when a little pale faced girl made her way weeping to him and said, "My mother is very ill, and your men are abusing her, and refuse to go away." "Never," said the Indian, "did I see a frown so terrible on the face of Tecumseh, as at that moment; when he with one hand clutched his tomahawk, and with the other led the little girl to the scene of riot. He approached the unruly savages with uplifted tomahawk, its edge glittering like silver, and with one shout of 'begone!' they scattered as though a thunderbolt had fallen in their midst."

But the old warrior at Wilberforce fought no more battles, except in imagination those of the past. After peace was declared he bought a valuable piece of land, with the intention of spending the remainder of his life more quietly; but unfortunately there lived not far from him a man who had once been the possessor of that farm, and had lost it in some way, and was now in reduced circumstances.

He was both envious and vicious; and because he could not himself buy the land, he was determined that the old Indian should not have it. After having tried many ways to get it from him, he finally complained of him, for fighting for the British and against the country where he now resided. This was successful; he was arrested and thrown into prison, and without a trial, removed from one prison to another, until he, with several others, was sent South to be tried as traitors. While on the way, the keeper of this Indian wished to call on his mother, who lived in a little cottage by the roadside, to bid her farewell. She was an aged woman, and when her son left her to join his companions, she followed him to the door weeping, wringing her hands in great distress, and imploring the widow's God to protect her only son. She had had four; all of whom went forth, with an American mother's blessing, to fight in defence of their country; and this one alone, returned alive from the field of battle. Now as he took his final departure for the South, she clasped her hands, raised her tearful eyes to heaven, and while large drops rolled over her wrinkled cheeks, she cried, "Oh, God, protect my only

677

one, and return him to me in safety, ere I die." This scene, the imprisoned, and as some supposed, heartless Indian, watched with interest; no part of it escaped his attention; but they passed on, and safely reached Detroit. The prisoners were conducted to a hotel and secured for the night; our Indian hero being consigned to an attic, which they supposed a safe place for him. There happened to be on that night, a company of showmen stopping at that hotel, and exhibiting wax-work; among the rest, was a figure of General Brock, who fell at Queenston Heights, and a costly cloak of fur, worn by the General previous to his death. Nothing of this escaped the eagle-eye and quick ear of the Indian. When all was quiet in the hotel, he commenced operations, for he had made up his mind to leave, which with the red man is paramount to an accomplishment of his design. He found no great difficulty in removing the window of his lofty apartment, out of which he clambered, and with the agility of a squirrel and the caution of a cat, he sprang for the conductor and on it he slid to the ground. He was now free to go where he pleased; but he had heard something about the cloak of Gen. Brock; he knew too, that the friends of the General had offered fifty guineas for it, and now he would just convey it to them.

With the sagacity of his race, he surveyed the hotel, and determined the exact location of the show-room. Stealthily and noiselessly, he entered it; found the cloak—took it and departed, chuckling at his good fortune. As he was creeping out of the apartment with his booty, a thought struck him, which not only arrested his footsteps, but nearly paralized his whole being. Would not his keeper be made to answer, and perhaps to suffer for his escape and theft? Of course he would. "Then in the darkness I saw again," said the old brave, "that old pale-faced mother, weeping for the loss of her only son," when he immediately returned the cloak to its place, and with far more difficulty than in his descent, he succeeded in reaching his attic prison, where he laid himself down, muttering to himself, "not yet,—poor old pale-face got but one."

They took him to Virginia, where, instead of a trial, they gave him about the same liberty they do their slaves. He staid one winter; but when the spring opened, the fire of the red man took possession of him, and when sent to the forest to chop wood, he took a bee-line for his former residence. But what was he to do for food? With a rifle, he could live happily in the woods, but he had none; so after considering the matter, he said to himself, "Me *must* get a rifle," and instantly started for the highway. The first cabin he saw, he entered in great apparent excitement, and told the woman of the house, that he had seen a "big deer in the woods, and wanted a rifle to shoot it. When you hear my gun," he said, "then you come and get big deer." She gave him her husband's excellent rifle and a few bullets; he looked at them, and said he must have more, for "it was a big deer;" so she gave him the bullet-mould and a piece of lead, with which he departed, after repeating his former injunction, to come when she heard the rifle; but, said he, "she no hear it yet."

He at length arrived at his own farm, from which he had been so cruelly driven, and concealed himself behind a log in sight of his own house, to watch the inmates. He soon learned that it was occupied by the man who had persecuted him in order to obtain it, his wife and one child. All day until midnight, he watched them from his hiding place, then assuming all the savage ferocity of his nature, and giving himself the most frightful appearance possible, he entered the house, and noiselessly passed to their sleeping room, where he placed himself before them with a long knife in his hand. Having assumed this frightful attitude, he commanded them in a voice of thunder, to get up and give him some supper. They were awake now. Oh, horror! what a sight for a guilty man, and a timid woman! "Me come to kill you!" said the Indian, as he watched their blanched cheeks and quivering lips. They tottered about on their trembling limbs to get everything he asked for, imploring him for God's sake to take all, but spare their lives. "Me will have scalps," he answered fiercely; but when he had eaten all he desired, he adjusted his blanket, and putting

679

on a savage look, he remarked as if to himself, "Me go now get my men and kill him, kill he wife, and kill he baby!" and left the house for his post of observation.

The frightened inmates lost no time, but hastily collecting some provisions, fled to the frontier, and were never heard of afterwards.

The Indian immediately took possession of his own and quite an addition left by the former tenants.

While the kind-hearted old Indian repeated to me the story of his wrongs, it reminded me of the injustice practised on myself, and the colored race generally. Does a colored man by hard labor and patient industry, acquire a good location, a fine farm, and comfortable dwelling, he is almost sure to be looked upon by the white man, as an usurper of *his* rights and territory; a robber of what he himself should possess, and too often does wrong the colored man out of,—yet, I am happy to acknowledge many honorable exceptions.

I have often wondered, when looking at the remnant of that once powerful race, whether the black man would become extinct and his race die out, as have the red men of the forest; whether they would wither in the presence of the enterprising Anglo-Saxon as have the natives of this country. But now I have no such wondering inquiries to make; being persuaded that the colored man has yet a prominent part to act in this highly-favored Republic,—of what description the future must determine.

CHAPTER XXVII

OUR DIFFICULTIES WITH ISRAEL LEWIS

Being under the necessity of referring again to the difficulties existing in the Wilberforce colony, I shall here introduce a circular, published in New York city, which will give the reader an understanding of the real cause of our embarrassments, and the character of our agent, Israel Lewis.

CIRCULAR

New York, May 9th, 1836.

The committee of colored citizens of the city of New York, as servants of the public, sincerely regret the necessity of bringing the within subject before the public. Their duty to God, to society, and to themselves, only actuates them in this matter.

The fact that many individuals in different sections of the country, have long suspected the integrity of Israel Lewis, but possessing no authentic documentary evidence, they have been prevented from making an effort, to counteract his too successful attempts and those of his agents, in the collection of funds from the public, has induced us to transmit this circular.

THEODORE S. WRIGHT, PETER OGDEN,
THOMAS DOWNING, GEORGE POTTS, CHARLES B. RAY,
DAVID RUGGLES, JOHN STANS, WILLIAM P. JOHNSON,
WILLIAM HAMILTON, SAMUEL E. CORNISH.

681

ISRAEL LEWIS.

Wilberforce, U.C., March 28th, 1836.

The board of managers of the Wilberforce settlement, met and passed unanimously the following resolutions—Present, Austin Steward, Philip Harris, Peter Butler, William Bell, John Whitehead, Samuel Peters.

Resolved, 1st. That we deeply regret the manner in which our friends in the States have been imposed upon by Israel Lewis; and that we hereby inform them, as a board of managers or otherwise, that we have received less than one hundred dollars of all the money borrowed and collected in the States.

Resolved, 2d. That although we have not received one hundred dollars from said Lewis, yet, when we shall have received the funds collected by our agent, the Rev. Nathan Paul, in England, we will refund as far as our abilities will allow and our friends may require, the money contributed for our supposed benefit, by them in the States.

Resolved, 3d. That we tender our sincere thanks to our beloved friends, Arthur Tappan and others, who have taken such deep interest in the welfare of our little colony.

Resolved, 4th. That the foregoing resolutions be signed by the whole board, and sent to the States to be published in the *New York Observer* and other papers.

AUSTIN STEWARD,
President,
PETER BUTLER,
Treasurer,
JOHN HALMES,
Secretary.
PHILIP HARRIS, WILLIAM BELL,
JOHN WHITEHEAD, SAMUEL PETERS,
Managers.

New York, April 25th, 1836.

At a public meeting of the colored citizens of New York city, held in Phoenix Hall, Thomas L. Jennings in the Chair, and Charles B. Ray, Secretary, the following resolutions were passed unanimously:

Resolved, That the thanks of this meeting be tendered to the Rev. Samuel E. Cornish, for the able and satisfactory report of his mission to Upper Canada, especially to the Wilberforce settlement.

Resolved, That this meeting deem it their imperative duty, to announce to the public, that in view of facts before them, Israel Lewis [7] has abused their confidence, wasted their benevolence, and forfeited all claim to their countenance and respect.

Resolved, That a committee of ten, be appointed to give publicity to the foregoing resolutions; also, to the communication from the managers of the Wilberforce settlement, as they may deem necessary in the case.

THOMAS L. JENNINGS,
Chairman,
CHARLES B. RAY,
Secretary.

It will now appear that I was not the only unfortunate individual who had difficulty with Mr. Lewis. Mr. Arthur Tappan made known through the press, about this time, that Israel Lewis was not a man to be fully relied upon in his statements regarding the Wilberforce colony; and also, if money was placed in his hands for the benefit of the sick and destitute among the settlers, it would be doubtful whether it was faithfully applied according to the wishes of the donors.

---

7 It necessarily follows that the public should withhold their money from his subordinate agents.

For this plain statement of facts, Mr. Lewis commenced a suit against Mr. Tappan, for defamation of character; laying the damages at the round sum of ten thousand dollars. It appeared that Lewis valued his reputation highly now that he had elevated himself sufficiently to commence a suit against one of the best and most respectable gentlemen in New York city; a whole souled abolitionist withal; one who had suffered his name to be cast out as evil, on account of his devotion to the colored man's cause— both of the enslaved and free; one who has, moreover, seen his own dwelling entered by an infuriated and pro-slavery mob; his expensive furniture thrown into the street as fuel for the torch of the black man's foe; and, amid the crackling flame which consumed it, to hear the vile vociferations of his base persecutors, whose only accusation was his defence of the colored man. This noble hearted, Christian philanthropist, who took "joyfully the spoiling of his goods" for the cause of the oppressed, was the chosen victim of Lewis' wrath and violent vituperation; and that too, where he was well known as a most honorable, humane gentleman; and all for naming facts which were quite generally known already.

Lewis returned to Wilberforce, flushed and swaggering with the idea of making his fortune in this speculation of a lawsuit against Mr. Tappan; and to remove all obstacles, he sent a man to me, to say that if I would publish nothing, and would abandon the interests of the colonists, he would give me a handsome sum of money. I soon gave him to understand that he had applied to the wrong person for anything of that kind; and he then laid a plan to accomplish by fraud and perjury, what he had failed to do by bribery.

I have before mentioned the fact of my having taken up a note of twenty-five dollars for Mr. Lewis, on condition that he would soon refund the money. I did it as a favor, and kept the note in my possession, until about a year afterward, when I sued him to recover my just due on the note. We had then began to differ in our public business, which led to other differences in our transaction of both public and private matters relating to the colony. He of course gave bail for his appearance at court, and it ran along for some time until he found he could not bribe me to enter into his interests, and then for the first time, he declared that I had stolen the note! And finally succeeded in getting me indicted before the grand jury!

In this I suppose Lewis and his confederates had two objects: first, to get rid of me; secondly, that they might have a chance to account for my continued hostility, by saying that it arose in consequence of a private quarrel, and not for any true interest I had in their collecting money deceptively.

Lewis appeared so bent on my destruction, that he forgot it was in my power to show how I came by the note. The Court of King's Bench met, but in consequence of the cholera, was adjourned, and of course, the case must lie over until another year.

When the time for the trial drew near, I was, in the midst of my preparations to attend it, counseled and advised by different persons to flee from the country, which I had labored so hard and so conscientiously to benefit, and received in return nothing but detraction and slander. But conscious of my innocence, I declared I would not leave; I knew I had committed no crime; I had violated no law of the land,—and I would do nothing to imply guilt. He who hath formed the heart, knoweth its intent and purpose, and to Him I felt willing to commit my cause. True, the court might convict, imprison, and transport me away from my helpless family of five small children; if so, I was determined they should punish an innocent man. Nevertheless, it was a dark time; I was not only saddened and perplexed, but my spirit was grieved, and I felt like one "wounded in the house of his friends,"—ready to cry out, "had it been an enemy I could have borne it," but to be arraigned, for the *first* time in my life, as a *criminal*, by one of the very people I had spent my substance to benefit, was extremely trying. Guiltless as I knew myself to be, still, I was aware that many incidents had transpired, which

685

my enemies could and would construe to my disadvantage; moreover, Lewis had money, which he would freely distribute to gain his point right or wrong, and to get me out of his way.

In due time the trial came on, and I was to be tried for *theft*! Lewis had reported all through the settlement that on a certain time I had called at his house, and from a bundle of papers which his wife showed me, I had purloined the note, which had caused me so much trouble. To prove this it was necessary to get his wife to corroborate the statement. This was not an easy matter. Mrs. Lewis, indignant and distressed by her husband's unkindness, had left him and taken up her abode in the family of a hospitable Englishman. After Lewis had been sent out as an agent for the colony, finding himself possessed of sufficient funds to cut a swell, he associated and was made a great deal of, by both ladies and gentlemen in high stations of life; the consequence of which was, he looked now with disdain upon his faithful, but illiterate wife, who like himself had been born a slave, and bred on a Southern plantation; and who had with him escaped from the cruel task-master, enduring with him the hardships and dangers of the flying fugitive.

Now her assistance was necessary to carry forward his plans, and he endeavored in various ways to induce her to return, but in vain. When he sent messengers to inform her how sorry he felt for his past abuse, she said she feared it was only some wicked plot to entice her away from the peaceable home she had found. Lewis saw that he must devise some other method to obtain her evidence. He therefore called on the brother of the Englishman in whose family Mrs. Lewis was, and in a threatening manner told him that he understood his brother was harboring his wife, and that he intended to make him pay dear for it. The brother, to save trouble, said he would assist him to get his wife, and that night conducted Lewis to her residence. No better proof can be given that Mrs. Lewis possessed the true heart of a woman, than that the moment her husband made humble concessions, and promised to love and protect her henceforth, she forgave him all his past infidelity and neglect, and looked with hope to a brighter future. In return Lewis presented her with a note, telling her to take it to a certain person and present it, and he would give her twenty dollars on it. This would, he doubtless thought, leave her in his power.

As Mrs. Lewis could not read, the unsuspecting wife presented the paper all in good faith. The gentleman looked at her sharply, suspiciously,—and then asked her, if she was not aware that she was presenting him a paper completely worthless! The poor woman was mortified and astonished; and instead of returning to her husband, fled to Wilberforce, and called at our house. Knowing how disastrous to me would be her false statement, and ignorant of her state of mind, I asked her if she had come to assist Mr. Lewis by swearing against me. I saw at once, that she had not yet been informed of her husband's design.

"Swear against you, Mr. Steward!" said she. "I know nothing to swear that would injure you; I have always known you as an honest, upright man, and you need not fear my turning against an innocent person, for the benefit of one I know to be guilty. Nor would I have left my place, had I known what I now do." So all help and fear was ended in that quarter.

When at length the appointed morning arrived, I arose early, but with a saddened heart. I looked upon my wife and helpless family, reflecting that possibly this might be the last time we should all assemble around the breakfast table in our hitherto quiet home, and I could scarcely refrain from weeping. I, however, took my leave, and a lad with me, to bring back a message of the result, if the court found sufficient cause to detain me for trial. But when I found that I must be tried, I felt too unhappy to make others so, and kept out of the lad's way. He returned without a message; and I took my seat in the prisoner's box. I had just taken a letter out of the post office, from Rochester, containing recommendations and attestations from the first men in the city, of my good character, which relieved

687

my feelings somewhat: nevertheless, my heart was heavy, and especially when, soon after I took my seat, a trap-door was opened and a murderer was brought up and seated by my side!

Chief Justice Robinson, made his appearance in great pomp—dressed in the English court style-then the crier, in a shrill voice, announced the opening of the court, and finished by exclaiming, "God save the King!" His lordship then called the attention of the jury to the law of the land; particularly to that portion relating to their present duty; and the grand jury presented me to the court, for feloniously taking a certain promissory note from the house of Israel Lewis. The King's Attorney had but one witness, and that was Lewis. He was called to the stand, permitted to relate his story, and retire without any cross-examination on the part of my Attorney; but that gentleman called up three respectable white men, all of whom swore that they would not believe Israel Lewis under oath! Then submitted the case to the jury without remark or comment, and the jury, without leaving their seats, brought in a verdict of "NOT GUILTY." Thus ended my first and last trial for theft! Oh, how my very soul revolted at the thought of being thus accused; but now that I stood justified before God and my fellow-men, I felt relieved and grateful; nor could I feel anything but pity for Lewis, who, like Hainan, had been so industriously engaged in erecting "a gallows fifty cubits high" for me, but found himself dangling upon it He raved like a madman, clutched the arm of the Judge and demanded a new trial, but he shook him off with contempt and indignation, as though he had been a viper. In his wild fury and reckless determination to destroy my character, he had cast a foul stain upon his own, never to be effaced. I had felt bound to preserve my reputation when unjustly assailed, but it had been to me a painful necessity to throw a fellow-being into the unenviable and disgraceful attitude in which Lewis now stood; and yet, he would not, and did not yield the point, notwithstanding his ignominious defeat.

He very soon began to gather his forces for another attack

upon me, and followed the same direction for his accusation,—the land purchase.

The reader will recollect without further repetition, that as I could purchase no land of the Canada Company, because of their indignation against Lewis, I was glad to accept of the contract he had made with Mr. Ingersoll, for lot number four in the colony; that I paid the sum demanded, and took his assignment on the back of the contract, and as we then were on good terms, it never occurred to me that a witness was necessary to attest to the transaction. But after his failure to prove me a thief; his next effort was to convict me of forgery! It will be remembered that Lewis after selling out to me, returned the contract to Mr. Ingersoll, and that I had lost by the means, the land, and at least five hundred dollars' worth of improvements. Then I brought a suit against Lewis, to recover the money I had paid him for the contract; and then it was that he asserted and attempted to prove, that I had forged the assignment, and therefore, had no just claim on him for the amount paid. But in this, as in the other case, he met a defeat and made an entire failure. I recovered all that I claimed, which, was only my just due. One would suppose that after so many unsuccessful attempts to ruin me, he would have left me alone,—but not so with Lewis: he had the ambition of a Bonaparte; and doubtless had he possessed the advantages of an education, instead of having been born and bred a slave, he might, like an Alexander or Napoleon, have astonished the world with his deeds of daring. I am, however, no admirer of what the world call "great men,"—one humble, self-sacrificing Christian, like Benjamin Lundy, has far greater claim on my respect and reverence.

Lewis, failing in his second attack, backed up as he had been in all his wicked course, by a friend wearing the sacred garb of a minister of the gospel, cooled off, and it became evident to all, that he was meditating some different mode of warfare. To this concealed confederate, I must attach great blame, on account of the influence his station and superior learning gave

689

him, not only over Mr. Lewis, but the colonists generally, and which should have been exerted for the good of all, in truth and honesty.

CHAPTER XXVIII

DESPERATION OF A FUGITIVE SLAVE

We had as yet received no funds from our foreign agent, N. Paul, and the board of managers had resolved to send a man after him. An Englishman and a white man named Nell, would gladly undertake the mission, leaving his wife and five children among the settlers. Again was I under the necessity of returning to New York, to obtain the funds required to send out Mr. Nell after our agent in England.

The night before I left home, I had a singular dream which I will briefly relate. I dreamed of journeying on a boat to Albany, and of stopping at a house to take tea. Several persons, I thought, were at the table, and as a cup of tea was handed me, I saw a woman slyly drop something into it. I, however, drank the tea, and dreamed that it made me very sick.

I found it difficult to drive from my mind the unpleasant impression this dream had made upon it, but finally succeeded in doing so, attributing it to the many and malicious threatenings which had been made by Lewis and his associates. They had boldly asserted, that "if I went to the States, I would never return alive," and several other threats equally malignant. I, however, started with Mr. Nell for Rochester, where we made an effort to raise money to aid in defraying the expenses of the voyage, and succeeded in collecting about a hundred dollars. From thence we passed on to Albany, where we fell in company with a number of Mr. Paul's friends, who appeared to be terribly indignant, and accused me of coming there to expose their friends,—Paul and Lewis. We had some warm words and unpleasant conversation,

691

after which they left me very unceremoniously, and appeared to be very angry. A short time after, one of them returned, and in the most friendly manner invited me to his house to tea. I was glad of an opportunity to show that I harbored no unpleasant feelings toward them, and immediately accompanied him home. The moment that we were all seated at the table, an unpleasant suspicion flashed through, my mind. The table, the company—all seemed familiar to me, and connected with some unpleasant occurrence which I could not then recall. But when the lady of the house poured out a cup of tea, and another was about to pass it, I heard her whisper, "I intended that for Mr. Steward," my dream for the first time, flashed through my mind, with all the vivid distinctness of a real incident. I endeavored to drive it from my thoughts, and did so. Pshaw! I said to myself; I will not be suspicious nor whimsical, and I swallowed the tea; then took my leave for the steamboat, on our way to New York city.

When we had passed a few miles out of Albany, the boat hove to, and there came on board four men—one of the number a colored man. The white men repaired to their state-rooms, leaving the colored man on deck, after the boat had returned to the channel. He attracted my attention, by his dejected appearance and apparent hopeless despair. He was, I judged, about forty years of age; his clothing coarse and very ragged; and the most friendless, sorrowful looking being I ever saw. He spake to no one, but silently paced the deck; his breast heaving with inaudible sighs; his brow contracted with a most terrible frown; his eyes dreamily fastened on the floor, and he appeared to be considering on some hopeless undertaking, I watched him attentively, as I walked to and fro on the same deck, and could clearly discover that some fearful conflict was taking place in his mind; but as I afterwards repassed him he looked up with a happy, patient smile, that lighted up his whole countenance, which seemed to say plainly, I see a way of escape, and have decided on my course of action. His whole appearance was changed; his heart that before had beat so wildly was quiet now as the broad bosom of the Hudson, and he gazed alter me with a look of calm deliberation, indicative of a settled, but desperate purpose. I walked hastily forward and turned around, when, Oh, my God! what a sight was there! Holding still the dripping knife, with which he had cut his throat! and while his life-blood oozed from the gaping wound and flowed over his tattered garments to the deck, the same exultant smile beamed on his ghastly features!

The history of the poor, dejected creature was now revealed: he had escaped from his cruel task-master in Maryland; but in the midst of his security and delightful enjoyment, he had been overtaken by the human blood-hound, and returned to his avaricious and tyrannical master, now conducting him back to a life of Slavery, to which he rightly thought death was far preferable.

The horrors of slave life, which he had so long endured, arose in all their hideous deformity in his mind, hence the conflict of feeling which I had observed,—and hence the change in his whole appearance, when he had resolved to endure a momentary pain, and escape a life-long scene of unrequited toil and degradation.

There happened to be on the boat at the time, several companies of citizen soldiers, who, shocked by the awful spectacle, expressed their decided abhorrence of the institution of Slavery, declaring that it was not for such peculiar villainy, that their fathers fought and bled on the battle field. So determined were they in their indignation; so loudly demanded they a cessation of such occurrences on board our boats, and the soil of a free State, that the slaveholders became greatly alarmed, and with all possible dispatch they hurriedly dragged the poor bleeding slave into a closet, and securely locked the door; nor have I ever been able to learn his final doom. Whether the kindly messenger of death released him from the clutches of the man-stealer, or whether he recovered to serve his brutal master, I have never been informed.

After this exciting scene had passed, I began to realize that I was feeling quite ill; an unusual load seemed to oppress my stomach, and by the time we had reached New York city, I was exceedingly distressed. I hastened to a boarding house, kept by a colored woman, who did everything in her power to relieve me; but I grew worse until I thought in reality, I must die. The lady supposed I was dying of cholera, sent to Brooklyn after Mr. Nell; but having previously administered an emetic, I began to feel better; and when I had finally emptied my stomach of its contents, *tea and all,* by vomiting, I felt into a profound sleep, from which I awoke greatly relieved. The kindness of that lady I shall not soon forget. She had a house full of boarders, who would have fled instantly, had they known that, as she supposed, I was suffering from cholera; and instead of sending me to the hospital, as she might have done, she kept all quiet until it was over, doing all she could for my relief and comfort; yet, it was a scene of distress which I hope may never be repeated.

On the following morning, I saw in the city papers, "A Card," inserted by the owner of the poor slave on board the steamboat, informing the public that he was returning South with a fugitive slave, who, when arrested, evinced great willingness to return; who had confessed also, that he had done very wrong in leaving his master, for which he was sorry,—but he supposed that the abolitionists had been tampering with him. That was all! Not a word about his attempt to take his life! Oh no, he merely wished to allay the excitement, that the horrid deed had produced on the minds of those present.

I was indignant at the publication of such a deliberate falsehood, and immediately wrote and published that I too was on board the same boat with the fugitive; that I had witnessed an exhibition of his willingness to return to Slavery, by seeing him cut his throat, and lay on the deck wallowing in his blood; that the scene had so excited the sympathies of the soldiers present, that his owner had been obliged to hurry him out of their sight, &c.

694

When this statement appeared in the newspapers, it so exasperated the friends of the slaveholder, that I was advised to flee from the city, lest I might be visited with personal violence; but I assured my advisers that it was only the wicked who "flee when no man pursueth, but the righteous are bold as a lion." I therefore commenced the business that brought me to that city. Messrs. Bloss, Nell, and myself, made an effort, and raised between three and four hundred dollars for the purpose of sending Mr. Nell after Rev. N. Paul.

Most of the funds collected, we gave to Mr. Nell, who sailed from New York, and arrived safely in England, just as N. Paul was boarding a vessel to return to New York.

Had Mr. Nell acted honorably, or in accordance with his instructions, he would have returned with the agent; but he remained in England, and for aught I know is there yet. He was sent expressly after Mr. Paul, and when he left that kingdom, Nell's mission was ended. He proved himself less worthy of confidence than the agent, for he *did* return when sent for, and he did account for the money he had collected, though he retained it all; but Mr. Nell accounted for nothing of the kind; and if he has ever returned, I have not seen him. Mr. N. Paul arrived in New York in the fall of 1834, and remained there through the winter, to the great disappointment and vexation of the colonists. I wrote him concerning our condition and wants, hoping it would induce him to visit us immediately; but he had married while in England, an English lady, who had accompanied aim to New York, where they were now living; nor did he appear to be in any haste about giving an account of himself to the board of managers who had employed him.

CHAPTER XXIX

A NARROW ESCAPE FROM MY ENEMIES

During my absence in New York city, Lewis and his confederates were prophesying that I would never trouble them more, and shaking their heads quite ominously at the happy riddance. One day, our hired man entered the house and inquired of my wife, when I was expected home. She told him she did not know, having received no intelligence from me. He assured her that a letter had been received by some one in the colony; that he had seen it, and had heard Mr. Lewis speak of conveying it to her,—but as it did not come, she gave it up, supposing some mistake had been made. I had, however, written, naming the time when she might expect me; but no letter of mine reached her, during my long absence, for which she could not account. A short time before that specified for my return, a woman, whose husband was an associate of Mr. Lewis, came to my house, and urged my wife "to leave word at the village of London, to have Mr. Steward detained there, should he arrive toward evening, and by no means allow him to start for the colony after dark." My family had so often been alarmed by such warnings, and had so frequently been annoyed by the violent threatenings of Lewis, that they ceased to regard them, and paid little attention, to this one.

I arrived at London on the day I had appointed for my return, but was detained there until a late hour; feeling anxious, however, to get home that night, supposing that I was expected,—I therefore hired a horse to ride the remaining fifteen miles to the settlement.

The road from London to Wilberforce led through a swamp,
known as "McConnell's Dismal Swamp," and it was indeed, one
of the most dreary places in all that section of country. I am
certain that a hundred men might conceal themselves within a
rod of the highway, without being discovered.

The horse I had engaged, was a high spirited animal, and to
that fact, I doubtless owe my life. The moon shone brightly, and
nothing broke the stillness of the night, as I rode onward, but
the clatter of my horse's hoofs, and an occasional "bow-wow" of
some faithful watch-dog.

When I reached the swamp and entered its darkened recesses,
the gloom and stillness was indeed fearful; my horse started at
every rustling leaf or crackling brush, until I attempted to pass
a dense thicket, when I was started by the sharp crack of a rifle,
and a bullet whizzed past me, close to my ear! The frightened
horse reared and plunged, and then springing as if for life, he
shot off like an arrow, amid the explosion of fire arms discharged
at me as I rode away. I lost my balance at first, and came near
falling, but recovering it I grasped the rein tightly, while my
fiery steed flew over the ground with lightning speed; nor did
I succeed in controlling him until he had run two miles, which
brought me to my own door.

I found my family well, and very grateful that I had arrived
safely after so fearful an encounter.

When morning came I sent a person out to inquire whether
any of the settlers were out the night previous, and the report
was, "Israel Lewis and two other men were out all night; that
they had been seen near the Dismal Swamp;" moreover, Lewis
was seen to come in that morning with his boots covered with
swamp mud,—these the Rev. Mr. Paul's boys cleaned for him, all
of which was evidence that he it was, who had way-laid me with
criminal intent.

I afterwards learned, that those three men left the settlement
at dusk, for the swamp; that they stationed themselves one rod
apart, all on one side of the road, each man with a loaded rifle,—

the poorest marksman was to fire first, and if he did not bring me down, probably the second would; but Lewis being the best shot of the three, was to reserve his fire until the last, which they supposed I could not escape. It was quite dark in the thicket, and my spirited horse plunged in every direction so furiously, that they could take no aim at me, until he had started to run, when we were soon beyond their reach.

We had already had so much difficulty in our little colony that we were getting heartily sick of it. I was well aware that Lewis was thirsting for revenge; that he wished to do me a great wrong; and yet I was thankful on his account, as well as on my own, that he had been prevented from imbruing his hands in the blood of a fellow being.

Had he succeeded in taking my life, as he undoubtedly intended to do, he would have been arrested immediately, and most likely punished as a murderer. He had boldly threatened my life, and the colonists were expecting something of the kind to take place. Had I not arrived at the colony, it was known at London that I had started for the settlement that night, and an immediate search would have been instituted; nor could the wicked deed have brought the least peace to the mind of Lewis or his companions,

> "No peace of mind does that man know,
> Who bears a guilty breast;
> His conscience drives him to and fro,
> And never lets him rest."

CHAPTER XXX

DEATH OF B PAUL,
AND RETURN OF HIS BROTHER

The bold and wicked attempt to take my life, recorded in the preceding chapter, aroused a feeling of indignation in the community against Lewis, and completely destroyed the little influence he had left; moreover, he had now been so extensively published as an impostor, that he could collect no more money on the false pretense of raising it for the benefit of the colony. As soon as his money was gone and his influence destroyed, —many who had been his firmest friends, turned against him, and among this class was the Rev. Benjamin Paul. He had ever professed the greatest friendship for, and interest in the success of Mr. Lewis. Heretofore, whenever he went to the States he was commissioned by that gentleman's family, to purchase a long list of expensive articles, which the poor colonists were seldom able to buy; and he generally returned to them richly laden with goods, purchased with, money given to the poor, sick, and destitute in the colony.

Mr. B. Paul had ever been a very proud man, but not a very healthy one. He was inclined to pulmonary diseases; but had kept up pretty well, until Lewis was effectually put down, and his own character involved in many of his notorious proceedings, together with the disappointment occasioned by his brother remaining so long in England, when his health failed, and he sank rapidly under accumulating disasters, to the grave.

The Welshmen had partially engaged him to preach for them the ensuing year, but something they had heard of him changed their minds, and they were about appointing a meeting to investigate his conduct, when they were informed of his illness, and concluded to let it pass. His son, with whom he lived, became deranged, and his oldest daughter on whom he was greatly dependent, had been dismissed from school, where she had been for some time engaged in teaching. All these unpleasant circumstances in his sickly state weighed heavily upon his proud heart; and he not only declined in health, but sank into a state of melancholy and remorse for his past course of living. As he lay pining and murmuring on his death bed, I could but reflect how different the scene from that of an apostle of the Lord Jesus Christ, who could exclaim, when about to be offered, "I have fought a good fight, I have finished my course, I have kept the faith; henceforth there is laid up for me a crown of righteousness."

I called to see him as he lay writhing in agony, his sunken eyes gleaming wildly, rolling and tossing from side to side, while great drops of perspiration stood upon his forehead, continually lamenting his misspent time, and the life he had led! He took my hand in his cold, bony fingers, thanking me that I did not so despise him, that I could not come to see him in his sorrow and affliction. Generally, however, when he raved and talked of his wicked life, his family excluded all persons from his room except his attendants.

Pride, which had ever been his besetting sin, displayed itself in his conduct to the last, for he had a lengthy will made, dispensing some sixteen hundred dollars to different individuals, when he must have known that his whole possessions would not amount to half that sum. As I looked upon him I could but reflect on the mysterious ways of Providence. Before me lay a man, who had for years arrayed himself against me, using all his influence as a man and a minister to injure me, by setting Lewis forward in his wickedness; his family living in extravagance and a style far beyond their means, while mine had labored hard and were sometimes destitute, often harassed and perplexed on every side by himself and party. And for what? Because I would not join hands with iniquity, and deeds of darkness. Notwithstanding the contrast, when I heard his bitter lamentations and self-reproaches, I could lift my heart to God, in gratitude for His protecting goodness, which had preserved me an *honest man*. I had often erred no doubt, but it had never been designedly; and never did I value a good conscience more than when standing by the death-bed of Benjamin Paul, who now had passed the Jordan of death; and it is enough to know that his future, whether of joy or woe, will be meted out to him, by a merciful and just God,— nevertheless, his last moments on earth were such as ought to arouse every professed Christian, to redoubled diligence in watchfulness and prayer, lest they fall into temptation,— lest they determine to become rich, and thereby fall into diverse and hurtful lusts, and pierce themselves through with many sorrows.

Soon after the event above narrated, a law was passed in the Province, allowing each township to elect three commissioners, whose duty it should be, to transact the public business pertaining to the township. Each township should also elect one township clerk, whose business it should be, to hold and keep all moneys, books, and papers belonging to said town; with power to administer oaths, and in fact, he, with the commissioners, were to constitute a board, possessing all the power of a court, in relation to township business.

In our colony, located in the township of Bidulph, the colored people were a large majority of the inhabitants, which gave us the power to elect commissioners from our own settlement, and therefore, three black men where duly chosen, who entered on the duties of their office, while your humble servant, A. Steward, was elected township clerk, with all the responsibility of the office resting upon him and the same power given him as though he had been born in Her Britannic Majesty's dominion, with a face as white as the driven snow. I felt the responsibility of my office, but not more deeply than I did this assurance of entire confidence, and respect shown me by my townsmen, after all the

701

cruel persecutions I had met; after all the accusations of theft, forgery, &c., that vicious person could bring against me.

The Rev. Nathaniel Paul, with his lady, arrived at Wilberforce in the spring of 1835, to the great joy of the colonists, to find that his brother had gone the way of all the earth, and his remains quietly resting on his own premises, where his afflicted family still resided.

In the colony there was a great deal of excitement regarding the course our agent would pursue, and all waited with anxious expectancy to see him enrich the treasury with his long-promised collections.

We had agreed, on sending him forth as an agent for the colony, to give him fifty dollars per month for his services, besides bearing his expenses.

The reverend gentleman, charged, on his return to the colony, the sum specified, for four years, three months and twenty days. We spent several days in auditing his account, with increased fearful forebodings. We found his receipts to be, in the United Kingdoms of Great Britain, one thousand six hundred and eighty-three pounds, nineteen shillings; or, eight thousand and fifteen dollars, eighty cents. His expenditures amounted to one thousand four hundred and three pounds, nineteen shillings; or, seven thousand and nineteen dollars, eighty cents. Then his wages for over four years, at fifty dollars per month, left a balance against the board of several hundred dollars, which we had no funds to cancel, inasmuch as the reverend gentleman had paid us nothing of all he had collected in Europe, nor even paid a farthing toward liquidating the debts incurred for his outfit and expenses.

There was also in Mr. Paul's charge against the board of managers, an item of two hundred dollars, which he had paid to Wm. Loyd Garrison, while that gentleman was also in England; but by whose authority he had paid or given it, it was hard to determine. We gave him no orders to make donations of any kind. To take the liberty to do so, and then to charge it to our poor and suffering colony, seemed hard to bear; still we allowed the charge. Had we, in our straitened and almost destitute circumstances, made a donation of that, to us, large sum of money to Mr. Garrison or any body else, certainly *we* should, at least, have had the credit of it; and as Mr. Garrison had made no acknowledgment of the receipt, I wrote him on the subject, and his answer will be found, heading our correspondence, in this volume.

Not a dollar did the treasurer ever receive of the Rev. N. Paul, unless we call the donations he had made without our permission, a payment. He did, it is true, award to the board, the sum of two hundred dollars, paid by him to Mr. Garrison, and fifty dollars more given by himself to Mr. Nell, on his departure from England. Not a farthing could we get of him; and in short, as far as the monied interest of the colony was concerned, his mission proved an entire failure. How much good the reverend gentleman may have done in spreading anti-slavery truth, during his stay in Europe, is not for me to say. The English, at that time held slaves; and report speaks well of his labors and endeavors to open the eyes of that nation to the sin of slavery and the injustice of the colonization scheme. It is said that he continually addressed crowded and deeply interested audiences, and that many after hearing him, firmly resolved to exert themselves, until every chain was broken and every bondman freed beneath the waving banner of the British Lion. Perhaps his arduous labors assisted in freeing the West India islands of the hateful curse of Slavery; if so, we shall not so much, regret the losses and severe trials, it was ours to bear at that time.

The indignant and disappointed colonists, however, took no such view of his mission; and knowing as they did, that he had paid not a cent of cash into the treasury, nor liquidated one debt incurred on his account, they became excited well nigh to fury,— so much so, that at one time we found it nearly impossible to restrain them from having recourse to Lynch law. They thought that the reverend gentleman must have large sums of money at his command somewhere—judging from his appearance and mode of living, and that a little wholesome punishment administered to his reverence, by grave Judge Lynch, enthroned upon a "cotton bale," might possibly bring him to terms, and induce him to disgorge some of his ill-gotten wealth, which he so freely lavished upon himself, and was withholding from those to whose wants it had been kindly contributed.

Just, as was their dissatisfaction, I was satisfied by the examination of his accounts, that he had spent nearly all of the money collected for us; his expenses had been considerable; beside, he had fallen in love, during his stay in England, with a white woman, and I suppose it must have required both time and money to woo and win so fine and fair an English lady, said also to possess quite a little sum of money, that is, several thousand dollars, all of which our poor, little suffering colony must pay for,—the reverend gentleman's statement to the contrary notwithstanding.

We succeeded at last, after a tedious effort, in satisfying the minds of the settlers to the extent, that a violent outbreak was no longer to be feared or dreaded. When all was quiet in the colony, I ventured to make my first call on the wife of N. Paul, who was then stopping with the widow of the late Rev. B. Paul, residing some three miles from us.

The houses of the colonists were generally built of logs, hewn on both sides, the spaces chinked with mortar, and the roof constructed of boards. The lower part was generally left in one large room, and when another apartment was desired, it was made by drawing a curtain across it. When we arrived at the residence of Mrs. Paul, we were immediately ushered into the presence of Mrs. Nathaniel Paul, whom we found in an inner apartment, made by drawn curtains, carpeted in an expensive style, where she was seated like a queen in state,—with a veil floating from her head to the floor; a gold chain encircling her neck, and attached to a gold watch in her girdle; her fingers and person sparkling with costly jewelry. Her manners were stiff and formal nor was she handsome, but a tolerably fair looking woman, of about thirty years of age: and this was the wife of our agent for the poor Wilberforce colony!

N. Paul had now settled his business with the colonists, and being about to leave for the States, we appealed to his honor as a man and a Christian, to call at Rochester and pay the seven hundred dollar bank debt, for which he was justly and legally holden, and relieve honorably, those kind gentlemen who had raised the money for him. He well knew the condition of our friend E. Peck, and that the names of some of our colored friends were also attached to the note; all of whom were relying implicitly on his or our honor to pay the obligation. That we had no funds in the treasury he was well aware; also, that all were deeply concerned about that debt. All this he knew; and in answer to our earnest and repeated injunction, he promised most faithfully and solemnly that he would call at Rochester, and take up the note. On those conditions he was allowed to leave the colony, and when parting with me, no more to meet in this life, his last assurance was, that he would cancel that obligation. What then could we think of his word, when we learned soon after that he passed Rochester, without calling, direct to Albany; nor did he ever return, or make any explanation of his conduct; nor give any reason why his promise was not redeemed and the money paid.

He preached in Albany until his health failed, then he was obliged to live the best way he could, and at last to depend on charity.

His disease was dropsy, from which he suffered deeply, being unable to lie down for some time previous to his death. I have been told that his domestic life was far from a peaceable or happy one, and that in poverty, sorrow and affliction, he lingered on a long time, till death at last closed the scene.

CHAPTER XXXI

MY FAMILY RETURN TO ROCHESTER

I was now seriously meditating a return to Rochester. My purpose in going to Canada, has already been made known to the reader, as well as some of the disappointments I met, and some of the trials and difficulties I had to encounter.

Now, after laboring, and suffering persecution for about five years, my way was comparatively clear; still I wished to leave the Province and return to the States, in which prospect my family greatly rejoiced. Doubtless most persons in the position I then occupied, would have chosen to remain; but for several reasons, I did not.

Notwithstanding I had been during my youth, a poor, friendless, and illiterate slave, I had, through the mercy of God and the kindness of friends, not only obtained my freedom, but I had by the industry and perseverance of a few years, acquired a tolerable English education, established a profitable business, built for myself a good and extensive business reputation, and had laid the foundation for increasing wealth and entire independence.

Indeed, so far as a competency is concerned, I possessed that when I left Rochester. My house and land was paid for; my store also, and the goods it contained were free from debt; beside, I had several hundred dollars in the bank for future use,—nor do I boast, when I say that the comfort and happiness of myself and family, required no further exertion on my part to better our worldly condition. We were living in one of the best countries on the earth, surrounded by friends,—good and intelligent society,

706

and some of the noblest specimens of Christian philanthropy in the world. My wife and children, had not only been accustomed to the comforts, if not the luxuries of life, but also to associate with persons of refinement and cultivation; and although they had willingly accompanied me to Canada, where they had experienced little less than care, labor and sorrow, it cannot be thought very strange that they should desire to return. We were colored people to be sure, and were too often made to feel the weight of that cruel prejudice, which small minds with a perverted education, know so well how to heap upon the best endeavors of our oppressed race. Yet truth and justice to my friends, compel me to say, that after a short acquaintance, I have usually been treated with all that kindness and confidence, which should exist between man and man.

At my house of entertainment in Canada, it was not uncommon for gentlemen of my former acquaintances, to stop for a friendly chat; merchants, journeying through our settlement, after goods, would frequently call, with their money, watches, and other valuables, carefully concealed about their persons; but when they learned our name, and had become acquainted a little, they would not only freely expose their wealth, but often place all their money and valuables in my hands, for safe keeping; nor was their confidence ever misplaced to my knowledge.

Another thing: when I went to Wilberforce, I supposed that the colonists would purchase the whole township of Bidulph, and pay for it, which might have been done, had they been fortunate enough to put forward better men. Then when we had a sufficient number of inhabitants, we could have sent a member to Parliament, one of our own race, to represent the interests of our colony. In all this we were disappointed. The Canada Company, in their unjust judgment of a whole people, by one dishonest man, had stopped the sale of lands to colored persons, which of course, put an end to the emigration of respectable and intelligent colored men to that place; nor was there any

707

prospect of a favorable change. Moreover, the persecutions which gave rise to the colony, had in a great measure ceased; anti-slavery truth was taking effect on the minds of the people, and God was raising up many a friend for the poor slave, to plead with eloquent speech and tears, the cause of the dumb and down-trodden.

These, with other considerations, influenced me in my decision to leave Canada. As soon, however, as my intentions were made known, I was importuned on all sides, by persons both in and out of the settlement, to remain awhile longer, at least. This will be seen by a reference to the appendix.

After due deliberation, I concluded to send my family to the States, and remain myself, until my year should terminate, for which I had been elected township clerk. In accordance with this determination, I made preparation to take my family to Port Stanley, forty miles distant. But what a contrast was there between our leaving Rochester, five years before, and our removing from the colony! Then, we had five two-horse wagon loads of goods and furniture, and seven in family; now, our possessions were only a few articles, in *a one-horse wagon*, with an addition of two members to our household! The settlers collected about us, to take an affectionate leave of my wife and children; but tears and sobs, prevented an utterance of more than a "God bless you," and a few like expressions. The scene was indeed an affecting one: all the weary days of our labor; all the trials and difficulties we had passed; all the sweet communion we had enjoyed in our religious and social meetings; all the acts of neighborly kindness, seemed now to be indelibly impressed on every memory, and we felt that a mutual regard and friendship had bound us closer to each other, in the endearing bonds of Christian brotherhood— bonds not to be broken by the adverse scenes incident to frail human life.

Arrived at Port Stanley, we were kindly entertained by a Mr. White, a fugitive slave from Virginia, who owned a snug little farm on the bank of Kettle Creek, and who appeared to be in a good and prosperous condition. Being detained there, waiting for a boat, on which I was anxious to see my family comfortably situated before I left them, I was aroused at an early hour on the second morning of our stay, by a loud rapping at the door; and hearing myself inquired for, I dressed myself immediately, and followed Mr. White into the sitting room, where I saw two strange men, armed with bludgeons! I soon learned, however, that one of them was the under-sheriff, who had come to arrest me for a debt of about forty dollars, and the other armed man had come to assist him, I assured them I was ready to accompany them back to London, which I was obliged to do, a prisoner, leaving my family among comparative strangers. The debt had become due to a man who had worked for us in the building of a saw-mill. I arranged the matter without going to jail, but before I could return to Port Stanley, my family, kindly assisted by Mr. White, had departed for Buffalo. The weather was cold and the lake very rough, but they safely arrived in Rochester, after a journey of three days. During their passage up the lake my oldest daughter took a severe cold, from which she never recovered.

I returned to the colony to attend to the duties of my office, and to close my business with the colony, preparatory to joining my family, who were now settled in Rochester, but in very different circumstances from those in which they had left it. I had deposited quite a sum of money in the Rochester Bank; but our continual expenditures at Wilberforce, in my journeyings for the benefit of the colony, and in the transacting of business pertaining to its interests, had left not one dollar for the support of my family, or to give me another start in business. Nevertheless, I felt willing to submit the case to Him who had known the purity of my intentions, and who had hitherto "led me through scenes dark and drear," believing he would not forsake me now, in this time of need.

Consoling myself with these reflections, I renewed my endeavors to do my best, leaving the event with my God.

CHAPTER XXXII

THE LAND AGENT AND THE SQUATTER

I have named, I believe, that all the colored people, who purchased lands of Lewis, could get no deed nor any remuneration for their improvements. This they thought hard and unfair. Some had built a house and barn, cleared land, &c.; but when they wished to pay for their farms, they could get no deed, and were obliged to lose all their labor.

This raised such a general complaint against the land agents, that they finally agreed to pay the squatters for their improvements, if they would leave their farms. An opportunity was soon offered to test their sincerity in this agreement. A shrewd fellow, who had been many years a sailor, named William Smith, had made valuable improvements on land, for which he could get no deed, and then he wished to leave it. His wife, also, died about this time, leaving him with eight children, which determined him to leave the colony, and after providing homes for his children, to return to his former occupation on the high seas; but he also determined not to leave without receiving the pay which the agents had agreed to give for his improvements.

"Oh yes," said they, in answer to his repeated solicitations, "you shall be paid, certainly, certainly; you shall be paid every farthing." But when the appointed day came for the pompous land agents to ride through the settlement, you might see Smith station himself at first one and then another conspicuous place on the road, hoping they would have the magnanimity to stop and pay him, especially, as he had informed them of his destitute and almost desperate condition, with eight young

710

children to maintain, and no means to do so, after giving up to them the farm. Before them as usual rode their body servant, of whom Smith would inquire at what hour the agents might be expected. And most blandly would he be informed of some particular hour, when perhaps, within the next ten minutes, the lordly agent would fly past him, on their foaming steeds, with the speed of a "lightning train." This course they repeated again and again. One day, when all of the land agents rode through the settlement in this manner, Smith followed them on foot over fifty miles. He at last intercepted them, and they promised with the coolest indifference, that on a certain day, not far distant, they would certainly pay him all he claimed, if he would meet them at a certain hotel in London. To this he agreed; and the poor fellow returned to the colony almost exhausted.

His funds were nearly all spent, and he wished to take his children to New York; yet his only hope was in the integrity and honor of the land agents.

On the day appointed, he was at London long before the hour to meet, had arrived. He entered the village with a determined air, and saw the agents just riding up to a hotel,—but not the one they had told him to call at. He, however, waited for no invitation, but entered the hotel and inquired of the servant for his master. He said his master was not there!

"I know he is," said Smith, "and I want to see him."

The servant withdrew, but soon returned to say that his master was engaged and could not see him that day. Smith followed the servant into the hall, calling out to him in the most boisterous manner, demanding to be told the reason *why* he could not see his master. The noise which Smith purposely made, soon brought into the hall one of the agents, a Mr. Longworth, a short, fat man,—weighing in the neighborhood of three hundred pounds! When he saw Smith, he strutted about, assuring him that this disgraceful uproar was quite uncalled for, and finally putting on a severe look, told him that he could not have anything for his improvements; of course not,— he really could not expect; certainly not, &c. Smith plainly assured the agent that his "blarney" would avail him nothing; he had come by their own appointment to get his pay, and that he certainly should *have*—if not in the way they themselves agreed upon, he would choose his own method of getting it! Thus saying, he stepped back, threw down his woolly head, and goat fashion, let drive into the fat Englishman's "bread basket!" He sprawled about and soon recovered his standing, but continued to scream and halloo with rage and mortification, more than with pain, until he had brought to the spot landlord, boarders, and servants, to witness the affray; but Smith, nothing daunted, administered two or three more effectual butts with his hard head into the lordly agent, when the subdued and now silent English gentleman, drew from his pocket book, and carefully counted out, every dollar Smith had at first demanded. Smith accepted it pleasantly, thanked him and withdrew, amid the shouts and jeers of the spectators, which the agent was more willing to avoid than he. That was the way the land agent paid the squatter.

It seemed, however, a little too bad, to make a fine English gentleman, feel as "flat" as Longworth appeared to feel; yet it was undoubtedly the only method by which Smith could recover a farthing. The agents, it was supposed, did not design to pay for any improvements; indeed, some very hard and unjust incidents occurred in connection with, that matter, and probably Smith was about the only one, who ever received the full value of his claim.

There was committed about this time, a most shocking murder, in the London district. A farmer who had a respectable family, consisting of a wife and several children, became so addicted to the use of spirituous liquors, that he neglected both his family and farm so much, that his friends felt called upon to request the distiller, who was his near neighbor, to furnish him with no more intoxicating drink. This, so exasperated the poor, ruined and besotted wretch, that he raved like a madman—such

712

as he undoubtedly was—crazed and infuriated, by the contents of the poisoned cup of liquid damnation, held to his lips by a neighboring distiller; a fellow-being, who for the consideration of a few shillings, could see his neighbor made a brute and his family left in destitution and sorrow. Perhaps, however, he did not anticipate a termination so fearful; yet that is but a poor excuse for one who lives by the sale of rum. When a rumseller gives that to a man, which he knows will "steal away his brains," and make him a maniac, how can he anticipate his future conduct? And who is responsible? Ah, who?

When Severin found he could get no more intoxicating beverage, he in his demoniacal rage, conceived the idea of despatching his whole family, and set about his purpose by first snatching the young babe and casting it into the fire! When the poor wife and mother came shrieking to the rescue of her darling infant, he with one furious blow, laid her a bleeding corpse at his feet! Two other young children he next murdered, and left them mingling their blood with that of their mother's, while he ran furiously after the two older ones, who were endeavoring to escape to a neighbor's for assistance; and overtaking, killed them both! When the miserable wretch had completed his hellish design, he started for his nearest neighbor, named Smith, and told him that there was a black and a white man at his house, murdering his family, requesting him to go to their assistance. Mrs. Smith, believing that Severin designed to murder her husband, insisted on his calling his young men to assist him, which he did; and on arriving at the scene of slaughter, a most horrid spectacle was before them: five dead bodies weltering in blood, aside from that of the innocent babe, whose little form lay roasted and charred, on the fatal and bloody hearthstone of the drunkard! Victims all, of an intoxicated husband and father! When the guilty man saw the mangled remains of his household, he only increased his depravity by trying to make others responsible for the wicked deed,—exclaiming in feigned anguish, "my dear wife! my poor children! I was afraid they would murder you! Oh, my lost family!" &c. Community was soon alarmed; Severin, arrested, tried, convicted, and sentenced to suffer the extreme penalty of the law.

It is sufficient for us to say, that the evidence was clear and conclusive, that he was the only murderer of his family; nor was it doubted that Mrs. Smith's suspicion was correct; yet, with all the array of positive testimony brought against him, he denied the commission of the crime to the last moment of his life! When brought out for execution, he was placed under the gallows, and the rope with its fatal noose adjusted around his neck, when one of the attorneys arose, and with great solemnity, addressed him, in the most impressive manner: "We have done," said he, "all in our power to save your life; but you are justly condemned, and in a few minutes more, will enter the presence of the All-seeing eye of Jehovah; now let me beseech you, in the name of God, to tell the truth, before you die." Severin declared himself innocent of the crime, for which he was about to suffer; but was consoled, he said, with the belief that he should, in a few short moments, meet in blissful re-union his dear, murdered wife and children in heaven, to part no more!

Prayers were read; and during the reading of the Lord's prayer, at the words "Thy will be done," the hardened wretch was launched into eternity.

No room was left to doubt the fact, that Severin with his own hand destroyed the life of his unhappy and abused wife, and also that of his helpless family. Yet in one sense, may we say with the murderer, it was not he who committed the awful and inhuman deed, but boldly and truthfully charge it to man's bitterest foe—Rum! What but the maddening effects of spirituous liquors, could so demoralize, so demonize a man, as to convert the once loving husband and proud father, into a reckless fiend, a heartless savage? Oh, Rum! earth contains not another so fell a foe!

Should any who may read these humble pages, find an effectual warning in the unhappy end of Severin, one which shall induce them to pause in their course, or at once and forever abandon the use of alcoholic drinks, I shall gratefully feel that I have not written this incident in vain.

Before I left Wilberforce, the Rev. S.E. Cornish, made a visit, and preached the Word of Life to the colony, greatly to the satisfaction and comfort of the settlers. After distributing liberally of his abundance, to his poor brethren, he departed for the States, attended by the prayers and blessings of the Wilberforce colonists.

CHAPTER XXXIII

CHARACTER AND DEATH OF I LEWIS

I have spoken in the preceding chapter, of a visit from the Rev. S.E. Cornish, to the colony. He had previously written me, concerning the object of his proposed visit, which was to obtain the depositions of the board of managers, relative to all the money received through their agents for the colony. He was sent to Canada then, and once afterwards, for and at the expense of A. Tappan, on business pertaining to the law-suit instituted by I. Lewis against that gentleman, for defamation of character. The depositions taken in the colony, with the expense of twice sending an agent to Canada, must have made a round sum for that kind gentleman to pay, merely for telling a truth already known!

Mr. Cornish had also been informed of my intention to leave the colony, and that my family were already gone. He, knowing something concerning the state of things, urged me to remain at least, until his arrival, as will be seen by a reference to his letter in the appendix.

As I look back on those scenes of labor and trial, I find cause for deep humiliation and gratitude to God, for His goodness and gracious protection, over my frail life, through unseen dangers of various kinds, and for his continued favors and unmerited blessings. Many of my fellow men have fallen in death's cold embrace since that time, while my health and life has been mercifully preserved.

Three of the leading characters of the Wilberforce colony are now dead. Rev. Benjamin Paul, lies in the silent grave-yard in

716

Wilberforce, C.W. His brother, Rev. Nathaniel Paul, also sleeps the dreamless sleep of death, and his dust rests in the beautiful cemetery in Albany, N.Y.

Israel Lewis has also finished his earthly career after robbing the poor of their just dues, and persecuting those who endeavored to defend them; after living in extravagance—"faring sumptuously every day,"—he became reduced in circumstances; despised and dishonored, his proud spirit was at last broken. His health gave way; when at length, unattended and alone, he found his way to a hospital in Montreal, where he soon after died, leaving not enough of all his gains to afford him a decent burial!

Oh, what a reward "for all his labor under the sun!" His fame, his wealth, and his law-suits, all have perished with his memory. Poor man!

Israel Lewis was born a slave, raised on a Southern plantation, and subjected to all the cruelties and deprivations of a bondman. His natural abilities were above mediocrity, but having never had the advantages of an education, or the privileges of a society calculated to cultivate and refine his natural aspiring intellect, and to direct his indomitable will in the acquirement of the more imperishable graces of the human heart, he had come to manhood with a determined, selfish disposition, to accomplish whatever gratified his vanity or administered to the wants of his animal nature.

And may we not, with propriety here inquire, whether our common Father, who has declared himself to be "no respecter of persons," has endowed men with enlarged capacities for the attainment of that knowledge and wisdom, so requisite to the elevation of character,—for the express purpose of seeing them made beasts of burden, and their superior faculties prostituted by the sensuality imposed by Slavery, and to be sold as chattels, with impunity? I tell you, nay. The day when Almighty God will avenge the work of his own hands, hasteth greatly! Were it not so, we might rejoice in the ignorance of the poor slaves, and pray that none of them may ever be endowed with a superior

717

intellect to that of the brutes they are made to resemble. Then would the proud spirit no longer chafe, and manhood writhe in the unbroken chain; but, like the ox to the yoke or the horse to the harness, they might submit, without a conscious violation of their dearest and God given rights. But we were speaking of Israel Lewis.

A natural energy and strength of character, he had inherited; a malicious, selfish, and consequently a deceptive disposition, his life as a slave had undoubtedly bestowed upon him. Intellect must have scope, and when nothing is left within its grasp but vice, can we wonder that the slave possessing the most talent, should generally prove the greatest villain.

Uneducated as was Lewis, his quick perception, his ungoverned passions, and his native independence, not only made him a dangerous slave, but an unfaithful and overbearing companion. He, however, took a wife—a slave like himself,— whose devotedness and good sense, cannot be made manifest, more than in her willingness to leave all that was dear to her on earth, and flee from their birth-place, she knew not whither; but confiding in the professed love and protection of her husband, she cheerfully followed him to the dense forest, in search of that freedom, denied them in their native country,—submitting herself gladly to all the hardships and fearful anxieties of a fugitive slave. What to her were horsemen, armed with dirk and rifle! What though the trained and inhuman blood-hound bayed upon their track! Was not he who had sworn a life-long allegiance to her by her side! Should he be killed or retaken, what could she desire, but to be his companion still! Slavery even, bitter as was the cup, might contain for her *one sweet drop*, while connubial love lighted up their rude cabin, and sweetened their daily toil; but the additional anticipation of LIBERTY, to their domestic happiness—oh blessed hope! How it quickened their weary footsteps, and, with fixed eyes upon the star of the North, they pressed forward through every difficulty, until they finally reached Cincinnati, O. There they lived quietly, and with others, suffered the terrors of the mob, where also he was chosen agent, to seek a more safe and quiet home for his afflicted and outcast countrymen. The office was accepted, and Lewis became the founder of the Wilberforce colony.

The personal appearance of Israel Lewis was prepossessing; his manner and address easy and commanding. To those unacquainted with his private life, his ungoverned passions, and his unprincipled, revengeful disposition, he could appear the gentleman, the philanthropist, and the Christian.

His education was limited; yet he had managed to gather a sufficient knowledge of the sciences to enable him to read and write, together with quite a fund of general information; and then his shrewdness and tact accomplished all the rest. To strangers he could appear a ripe scholar, if left unquestioned. He was a good speaker, and once spake with eloquence and marked effect before the Legislature, assembled in the Senate Chamber, at Albany, N.Y.

Had the childhood of Mr. Lewis been passed under more favorable auspices; had his intellectual faculties been so cultivated as to predominate over his animal propensities, and his towering aspirations directed toward the accomplishment of acts, lofty in their benevolence, noble in their sacrifice, high in their honorable purpose, and great in their purity; I can but believe that his powerful intellect would have achieved the fame of a Lundy, or would have bequeathed to his brethren a memory like that of a Clarkson. Instead, we have found him devoting his energies to the gratification of his avarice, pride, and ambition— characteristics directly opposed to the deportment of the humble Christian, and such as our Heavenly Father has never promised to prosper. How truly has "the wise man" said, "He that is greedy of gain troubleth his own house; but he that hateth gifts shall live." How strikingly has this passage been verified in the course of Lewis! For a few paltry sums of gain, could he consent, not alone to rob the poor, for whom it was kindly given as unto the Lord, but to turn scornfully away from that poor, illiterate, and humble slave wife, whom he had, in their mutual adversity, vowed to cherish in *prosperity* as well as in all other circumstances through life. That wife, who had borne with him the sorrows of Slavery—the humble choice of a bondman! She, who fled with him anticipating additional happiness in a life of freedom! Poor woman! Disappointment is of an earthly growth, yet God is merciful; notwithstanding we have the same authority as above, for saying that "Every one that is proud in heart is an abomination to the Lord: though hand join in hand, he shall not be unpunished."

In the hands of a righteous Judge we leave him, who, for the wealth that perisheth,—who, for worldly honor and selfish gratification, could barter his honesty and integrity, as "Esau, who sold his birth-right for a mess of pottage."

To me the lesson is an impressive one, and I am thinking it would be well for us all to examine the foundation on which we stand. If based upon the solid and broad foundation of christianity, doing to others in all things as we would they should do to us, sacrificing on all occasions our own ease, and worldly honor, for the benefit of our fellow-men, and the good of our country, then indeed, we need fear no evil; if the winds of adversity howl about our dwelling, we shall find it will stand, being founded on a ROCK. But if we build upon "the sands" of fame or self-aggrandizement, and, like the towering oak, lift our insignificant heads in proud defiance of the coming storm, we may expect that our superstruction will fall! "And great will be the fall of it!"

CHAPTER XXXIV

MY RETURN TO ROCHESTER

Having closed my business in Wilberforce, I prepared to leave on the expiration of my term of office as township clerk, which was now near at hand. Notwithstanding, I ever felt a sensation of relief and pleasure, when I thought of returning to my old home and friends in the States, yet as often as I look abroad over the settlement and remember all my glowing hopes,—all my delightful anticipations of a prosperous future for those poor, struggling colonists; when I recollected with what zeal and honest purpose, with what sincerity and sacrifice I had prosecuted my labor among them,—a dark shadow of disappointment would flit across my mind, however welcome it might be. That I had firm and tried friends in the colony, I had never the least reason to doubt, not to suppose their number less after a five years residence with them; but our expectations had not been realized. Our hope of settling a township, to be represented in Parliament by one of our own people, was now forever blasted. I remembered too, that many of the colonists had been unjustly incited against my course; but in the retrospect my heart did not condemn me. Errors many, no doubt I had committed; but I was grateful, when reviewing the whole ground, for a conscience void of offence toward God and man; and I finally took my leave of all, craving the choicest blessings of Heaven to rest upon that infant colony and its interests.

On the nineteenth day of January, 1837, I left Wilberforce, passing through Brantford, Hamilton, Queenston, Lewiston, and from thence to Rochester. During my journey, I could not avoid feeling sad and despondent, as my mind incessantly returned to the review of my mission, upon which I could look with no other decision than that of an entire failure. I had spent my time, wasted my substance for naught, and was now returning to my dependant family,—that, with myself, had been stripped of nearly every means of comfort and support.

What would my Rochester friends think of my conduct? Notwithstanding all my despondency and evil foreboding at that time, I am now well satisfied that my labor was not all in vain, but that some good did result from it.

As I drew near the city, a gloom like thick darkness overshadowed me: I thought of the unfavorable transactions which had occurred between the directors of the colony and my friends in Rochester, and fell to wondering how they would receive me.

On the twenty-third of January, 1837, I finally re-entered the city penniless; but as I soon found, not so friendless as my fears would have it. Among, the first to welcome me back to my old home, was that friend of "blessed memory," Everard Peck, who had been apprised of some of the losses I had met and the trials I had passed through. This gentleman was also one of the first to propose to be one of five men, who should loan me one hundred dollars each, for five years. Through the disinterested kindness of this worthy gentleman, I was in a few days after my arrival, well established in a store of provisions and groceries. The five kind gentlemen, to whom I was so deeply indebted for the loan, were: Everard Peck, George A. Avery, Samuel D. Porter, Levi W. Sibley, and Griffith, Brother & Co.

This noble act of generosity and kindness, on the part of my friends, to furnish me with the means to commence business, especially when their prospect was anything but flattering, regarding my ever being able to refund their well-timed and gracious liberality,—affected me more deeply than all the censure and persecution I had elsewhere received. Their frown and displeasure, I was better prepared to meet than this considerate act of Christian sympathy, which I am not ashamed to say melted me to tears, and I resolved to show my appreciation of their kindness by an industry and diligence in business hitherto unsurpassed.

E. Bardwell, then a merchant on Exchange Street, next laid me under a lasting obligation by offering to sell me goods on credit; others proffered assistance by promising their continual patronage, which was to me the same as cash,—and soon the store I had opened on Main Street, was doing an extensive business. My profits were small to be sure, and I had a heavy rent to pay for my store and dwelling, yet I was making a comfortable living for my family, and laying by something to reimburse the kind friends who had helped me in the time of need, when I found that the health of my family required more of my time and assistance than ever before. My oldest daughter, who, I have before mentioned, having taken a violent cold on Lake Erie, was now confined to her bed. All that could be done to save the life of a darling child—our first born—was done; and if we sometimes went beyond our means, it was a satisfaction to us to see her enjoy some of the comforts of life of which my mission to Canada had deprived her. One physician after another was employed to stay the approach of the destroyer: some said they could cure her, if paid in advance; to all of which I cheerfully acceded, but only to see our beloved sink lower, and patiently pine away.

No one but a parent who has watched the rapid decline of a darling child, and marked with a bursting heart the approaching footsteps of the spoiler, can imagine how powerless we felt at that time. The wealth of the Indias, had we possessed it, would have been freely given, although it would have been unavailing, to shield that loved and gentle form from pain, and we were obliged to look hopelessly on, while our little patient, suffering daughter sank lower and lower every day. In vain were our parental arms outstretched for her protection; from death we could not save her. She had long since ceased to glide about the house, and soothe with her silvery tones all the childish fears of the little ones. Helpless she now lay, burning with fever, and wasting from our sight, "till soft as the dew on the twilight descending," the cold damps of death gathered on her youthful brow. One pleasant morning after passing a restless night, I observed her to gaze earnestly upward, and a moment after I called her name but received no answer.

> "Her languishing head was at rest;
> Its thinkings and achings were o'er;
> Her quiet, immoveable breast,
> Was heaved by affliction no more."

On the fifteenth day of April, 1837, she sweetly fell asleep, aged eleven years. Sorrowfully we followed her remains to Mount Hope, where we laid her down to rest until the resurrection morning. Death had now made its first inroad in our family circle, and since then we have laid two other loved ones by her side. We sorrowed, but not without hope.

My business continued to prosper, and I concluded to buy a small variety store, containing some three or four hundred dollars worth of goods on the corner of Main and North Streets, formerly owned by Mr. Snow, but, having two stores on my hands, I did not make much by the trade.

The first summer after I returned to Rochester, the friends of temperance made a fine celebration, and gave me the privilege of providing the dinner.

I considered it not only a privilege, but an honor, and felt very grateful to the committee who conferred the favor upon me.

The celebration came off on the Fourth of July, and was indeed a splendid affair. The multitude were addressed on the public square, by some of the best speakers in the country. I laid in a large quantity of provisions of every available kind, built a bower, hired waiters, and prepared seats for five hundred to dine; but when the oration was over, and the multitude came to the table, I found that as many more seats were wanted. We, however, accommodated as many as we could, at one dollar each, and all passed off well, to the great satisfaction of all concerned.

When all was over, and the friends learned that I had on hand a large amount of cooked provision, they continued their kindness by purchasing it, thus preventing any loss on my part.

My store on the corner of Main and North Streets, was at the head of the market, and I was enabled to supply both of my stores with country produce on the best possible terms. I kept two clerks at each store, and all seemed prosperous for a time, when from some cause, which I could never understand, my business began to fail. My family had ever lived prudently, and I knew that was not the cause. I thought to better my circumstances by taking a store in the Rochester House, but that proved to be a bad stand for my business, and after one year, I removed to Buffalo Street, opposite the Court House. I ought to say, that as soon as I found that my income was getting less than my expenses, I went to the gentlemen who had loaned me the five hundred dollars, and showed them the true state of my affairs, and they kindly agreed to take fifty per cent., which I paid them.

After locating on Buffalo Street, I took in a partner, named John Lee, a young man, active and industrious, who paid into the firm three hundred dollars, with which we bought goods. With what I had on hand, this raised the joint stock to about a thousand dollars, on which we were making frequent additions, and on which we had an insurance of six hundred dollars. Our business was now more prosperous than at any previous time, and we began to look up with hope and confidence in our final success. One night I returned to my home as usual, leaving Lee in the store. About twelve o'clock, Mr. Morris awoke me with a few loud raps, and the announcement that my store was on fire and a part of my goods in the street! I hastened to the place, where I found, as he had said, what was saved from the fire piled up in the street and the fire extinguished. The building was greatly damaged and the goods they rescued were nearly ruined. Now we were thrown out of business, and the firm was dissolved. With the assistance of W.S. Bishop, a lawyer, we made out the amount of damage, which was readily paid by the agent for the insurance company.

When the Fourth of July came round again, the temperance men resolved on having another demonstration, and as before, I was requested to supply the dinner, which I did, after the same manner as the year previous.

Having been thrown out of business by the fire, I began to examine my pecuniary matters, and found that I was some three or four hundred dollars in debt, which I had no means of paying. True, I had met with a great misfortune, but I felt that to be an honest man I must meet all obligations, whether legally bound to do so or not; yet it was beyond my power at that time, and I finally concluded to leave the city, and try to better my condition by some other business, or at least to clear myself from debt.

CHAPTER XXXV

BISHOP BROWN—DEATH OF MY DAUGHTER

I removed with my family to the village of Canandaigua, where I commenced teaching a school for colored children, assisted by my daughter. The school was sustained partly by the liberality of the citizens of the village, and partly by donations from abroad. It was continued two years, and the children made rapid progress while they were under our tuition.

Soon after I left Rochester, I visited New York city, and while there, I joined "The African Methodist Episcopal Conference." Bishop Brown, of Philadelphia, presided over the deliberations of that body, and appeared to be a man of deep piety, as well as apt in business, and was a native of one of the Carolinas. I found a pleasing acquaintance also, with Bishop Walters of Baltimore, Md. He was small in stature; but a powerful speaker, and discharged every duty with "an eye single to the glory of God." He has now gone to give an account of his stewardship, and I pray that "his mantle may fall" upon one as capable of leading our people as he. The conference consisted of some sixty or seventy ministers of the gospel, with these two Bishops at their head. The conference continued its session ten days. When it was closed, Bishop Brown, with several others, started on a visit to the West. They called at Rochester, and then passed over to Canada, where a conference was to be holden. We arrived, after a pleasant journey, at Hamilton, where the English government have a regiment of black soldiers stationed. It was common, in passing through the streets of Hamilton, to meet every few rods, a colored man in uniform, with a sword at his side, marching

727

about in all the military pomp allowed only to white men in this *free republic.*

All being in readiness, Bishop Brown opened the conference under the authority of Her Britannic Majesty, with great solemnity, which seemed to be felt by the whole assembly. This meeting appeared to me far more interesting than the one we had attended in New York city. The colored people were much more numerous in Hamilton, and in far better circumstances than in New York. It is a hard case to be poor in any large city, but to be both poor and black, as was the condition of the majority of our friends in New York, was indeed a terrible calamity. Every class, no matter how worthless they might be, would be allowed to rent a house in preference to a colored man. The consequence was, our people were crowded back into the most unhealthy alleys, in old dilapidated tenements unfit for human beings to dwell in, and such as could not be disposed of to any other class of people. I am happy to say, however, that a favorable change has taken place in New York, since the time of which I am speaking. Capitalists have noted the good reputation of the colored people as tenants, and have of late erected good dwellings for their accommodation. In Hamilton there was none of that wretchedness and squalid poverty, nor any of that drunken rowdyism so common in Eastern cities, perceivable among the colored people.

Our conference was largely attended by all classes, both black and white, —many of the latter invited the Bishop with his associates to their dwellings to dine, indeed we seldom took a meal at our lodgings, so constantly were we solicited by friends to accompany them home.

We also found many fugitive slaves in that city, many of whom were intelligent mechanics. Some of them took us about the place, showing us the different buildings they were engaged in erecting; quite a number were employed in building a church which appeared to be done in a workman-like manner.

In the meantime our meeting was progressing in a very

interesting manner, and when the closing services were commenced, the house was filled to overflowing; still many could not be accommodated. The preaching was solemn and impressive, and it really seemed to me that the glory of God filled the house in which we worshipped; saints rejoiced and shouted "glory to God, in the highest," while sinners trembled and cried out, "what must we do to be saved from the wrath to come." There were several hopeful conversions during the session of conference; and after its close we spent one day in making social calls, and viewing the city and its surroundings.

Burlington Bay makes an excellent harbor for shipping, while Burlington Heights loom up on the north in all their wild and terrific grandeur. Near the bay resides Mr. McNab, so notorious in the history of the Canadian revolution. We went in a large company to look at his beautiful grounds and residence, over which we were politely conducted by his amiable lady.

It was indeed a lordly mansion, with its surroundings laid out in the English style of princely magnificence.

On our return to the city at evening, we were invited to attend a grand soiree, got up in honor of the Bishop's first visit to that place. Several families of colored people combined to provide the splendid entertainment, while one lady presided at the board. She was very beautiful and very dark; but a complete model of grace and elegance, conversing with perfect ease and intelligence with all, both black and white ministers, who surrounded the festive board, as well as our Irish friends, not a few of whom were present. One honest son of the Emerald Isle entered, and not understanding the matter, inquired of his brother "Pat," in rather a loud whisper, "What's all them nagurs setting to that table for?" He, however, soon satisfied himself, and all passed off quietly and in excellent order. At a late hour the company, after a benediction, withdrew and dispersed.

We left Hamilton the following morning, feeling grateful and pleased with our meeting and visit.

It was a beautiful morning; the lake was still, no sound was

729

heard but the rushing waves, as our boat moved on through its placid waters, toward our destination, then called Fort George, now Niagara, where we took stage for the Falls.

At that place of resort, we stopped to view the stupendous work of Almighty God, and listen to the ceaseless thundering of the cataract. How tame appear the works of art, and how insignificant the bearing of proud, puny man, compared with the awful grandeur of that natural curiosity. Yet there, the rich from all parts of the world, do congregate! There you will find the idle, swaggering slaveholder, blustering about in lordly style; boasting of his wealth; betting and gambling; ready to fight, if his slightest wish is not granted, and lavishing his cash on all who have the least claim upon him. Ah, well can he afford to be liberal,—well can he afford to spend thousands yearly at our Northern watering places; he has plenty of human chattels at home, toiling year after year for his benefit. The little hoe-cake he gives them, takes but a mill of the wealth with which they fill his purse; and should his extravagance lighten it somewhat, he has only to order his brutal overseer to sell—soul and body — some poor creature; perchance a husband, or a wife, or a child, and forward to him the proceeds of the sale. While the wretched slave marches South with a gang, under the lash, he lavishes his funds in extravagant living,—funds gathered from the tears and blood of a helpless human being. Have you, dear reader, ever watched the slaveholder at such places as I have, gliding through the shady groves, or riding in his splendid carriage, dressed in the richest attire, and with no wish ungratified that gold can purchase; and have you ever been guilty of envying him, or of wishing yourself in his condition? If so, think of the curse which rests on him who grinds the face of the poor. Think of his doom in the day of final retribution, when he shall receive at the bar of a righteous Judge, "according to the deeds done in the body," and not according to his wealth and power. Think you, that the prayers, cries, and pleadings of the down-trodden slave that for years have been ascending to the throne of a just God, will never be avenged? Yea, verily, the day of reckoning hastens on apace, and though, "He bear long with them; He will surely avenge them of their adversaries; and that speedily!"

As we pursued our journey to Buffalo, we passed Grand Island, from whence Mordecai Emanuel Noah, some years ago issued a proclamation, calling on the Jews to come and build on that island the "City of Refuge," but which I believe was not responded to, as I saw it remained in its native wildness. He had also a monument erected there at the time, which might be seen from the highway and canal, consisting of a white marble slab, six feet in height, with a suitable inscription upon it, to direct the poor Jew to the City of Refuge.

It was quite conspicuous, but not so magnificent as Gen. Brock's at Queenston Heights.

Arrived at Buffalo, we held several meetings which were very interesting. The colored people were then numerous in that city, and owned one of the largest churches in Western New York. We found a large and prosperous society under the superintendence of Elder Weir, who was a good and talented man, setting a godly example for his flock to imitate. At Buffalo I parted with my pleasant and instructive traveling companion, Bishop Brown, never to meet again on the shores of time. Soon after that pleasant journey he died, and passed from his labor to reward.

Buffalo was then, as now a great place for business. Vessels from all parts of the country crowded the docks, and I then thought that it must in time become one of the largest cities in the Union. After a pleasant visit with our people there, I returned to my home in Canandaigua, where I now began to feel quite settled.

I had been requested to act as agent for the "Anti-Slavery Standard," with which I complied, and leaving my daughter to teach the school, I spent the most of my time in traveling through the country to advance the interests of that paper.

When I returned from Buffalo, she was complaining of poor health, nor was it long before we saw that she was

731

rapidly declining.

This beloved daughter, I had spared no pains nor money to educate and qualify for teaching. I had encountered all the trials and difficulties that every colored man meets, in his exertions to educate his family. I had experienced enough to make me fear that I should not always be able to get my children, into good schools, and therefore determined at whatever cost, to educate this child thoroughly, that she might be able, not only to provide for her own wants, but to teach her younger brothers and sisters, should they be deprived of the advantages of a good school. Well had she rewarded my labor; well had she realized all my fondest hopes and expectations,—but alas! for human foresight and worldly wisdom! The accomplishments and qualifications of a teacher were attained; and proudly we looked for the achievement of our long-contemplated design. How hard to believe that the fell destroyer was upon her track! Her education had qualified her for teaching the sciences; but now I saw, that her faith in the religion of the blessed Christ, was assisting her to teach her own heart a lesson of patience, and quiet submission to the will of Him who holds the issues of life,—and Oh, how difficult for us to learn the solemn lesson, that her wasting form, her gradual sinking away, was hourly setting before us.

Slowly her strength failed; she, however, saw our sorrowful anxiety, and would try to relieve it with a cheerful appearance. One day perhaps she would be able to walk about, which would revive our wavering hope; the next she was prostrate and suffering; then hope died and we were sad! All the spring time she languished; the summer came, the roses bloomed, and the grain began to ripen, but she was wasting away. The orchard yielded its golden harvest; the birds sang merrily on the trees, but a dark shadow had fallen on our hearthstone, and a gloom, like the pall of death, rested on our household. Her place at table was already vacant; no longer she called the little ones about her to hear them repeat their tasks,—all of which admonished us, that soon the bed where we could now see her, would be vacated; and we should no longer witness her patient smile, and know that she was still with us. The pastor of the Baptist church often called to pray with, and for, the quiet sufferer, which she appreciated very highly, for she was a Christian in every sense of the word.

On the thirtieth day of August, at about eleven o'clock, A.M., without a struggle or a groan, her spirit returned to God who gave it. "Sweetly as babes sleep," she sank into the embrace of death. Happily, triumphantly, had she seen the grim messenger approach; but she knew whom she had believed, and that He was able to keep that which she had committed to Him, unto the resurrection of the just.

She had previously made a confession of her faith in Christ, and had been buried with Him in baptism. A few days after her demise, a long, sad train wound its way to the village church yard, where we deposited the remains of our beloved,—Patience Jane Steward, in the eighteenth year of her age; and then returned to our desolate house, to realize that she had left a world of pain and sorrow, where the fairest rose conceals a thorn, the sweetest cup a bitter drop, for a home where the flowers would never fade, and where pain, sorrow and death will never come. We all felt the solemn and impressive warning, "Be ye also ready, for in such an hour as ye think not, the Son of Man cometh."

As often as I recalled her triumphant, peaceful death, her firm reliance on God, and sweet submission to His will, I could not forbear contrasting her departure with that of Mrs. Helm, whose death I have elsewhere described; and could fervently pray, that I might live the life of the righteous, that my last end might be like hers.

"Behold the Western evening light,
It melts in deep'ning gloom;
So calmly Christians sink away,
Descending to the tomb.

The winds breathe low, the withering leaf
Scarce whispers from the tree,—
So gently flows the parting breath,
When good folks cease to be.

How beautiful on all the hills,
The crimson light is shed;
'Tis like the peace the Christian gives,
To mourners round his bed.

How mildly on the wandering cloud,
The sunset beam is cast,—
'Tis like the mem'ry left behind,
When loved ones breathe their last.

And now above the dews of night,
The yellow star appears;
So faith springs in the breast of those,
Whose eyes are bathed in tears.

But soon the morning's happier light,
Its glory shall restore;
And eyelids that are sealed in death,
Shall wake to close no more."

CHAPTER XXXVI

CELEBRATION OF THE FIRST OF AUGUST

The anti-slavery friends in Canandaigua, had resolved to celebrate the anniversary of the West India emancipation, in suitable manner in that village, for which funds had been unsparingly collected, to defray the expenses of the coming demonstration. The first of August, 1847, fell on Sunday, and our people concluded to devote that day to religious meetings, and the second to their proposed celebration.

Frederick Douglass and Mr. Van Loon, from Poughkeepsie, addressed the people on the Sabbath; and also, on the same evening, a large concourse at the Court House. The day following, there were not less than ten thousand people assembled on the beautiful grounds, belonging to the village Academy-attentive listeners all to the eloquent speeches delivered, and interested spectators of the imposing exercises.

When the vast multitude had convened, the exercises were commenced by the Rev. S.R. Ward, who addressed the throne of grace, after which, Mr. Frederick Douglass delivered an oration, in a style of eloquence which only Mr. Douglass himself can equal, followed by a song from the Geneva choir, and music by Barring's band. Rev. H.H. Garnet, editor of "The National Watchman," next spake, and with marked effect, followed by Messrs. Ward and Douglass; after which, the assemblage formed a procession, and marching to the Canandaigua Hotel, partook of a sumptuous dinner, provided by the proprietor of that house. At six P.M., they again assembled on the square, and were most eloquently addressed by both Ward and Garnet; at the close, they repaired to the ladies' fair, where they found everything in a condition which spake well for the enterprise and industry of our colored sisters. Their articles for sale, were of a choice and considerate selection, and such as sold rapidly and at fair prices. When all was pleasantly over, the ladies contributed twenty dollars toward paying the speakers present.

A most beautiful ode was composed by a warm and generous friend of the cause, which was sung in the grove, in a spirit which produced a thrilling interest. Gladly would I give the reader the whole composition, but its length makes it objectionable for this place, but should they happen to hear a soul-stirring and sublime ode, commencing with,

> "Hail! to this day returning;
> Let all to Heaven aspire," &c.,

they may know it is the one to which I refer.

It was indeed, a glorious day for the colored population generally; and many were the indications of a diminution of that prejudice so prevalent everywhere. Some, who had supposed the colored man so inferior to themselves as to be incapable of making an interesting speech, were convinced of their error, after hearing Messrs. Douglass, Ward and Garnet. Mr. Van Loon was a white clergyman, but a brother indeed; his soul illumined by the pure light of the gospel of peace; his heart full of sympathy for the oppressed; his tongue pleading eloquently for equal rights; and his hands busily engaged in breaking every yoke, resting on the necks of poor humanity. So vigorously, so zealously did he unfold the horrors of the slave system; so truthfully and faithfully did he expose the treachery of northern politicians, and so pathetically did he appeal to the humanity of every professed Christian to speak out boldly for the dumb; to shield, by the holy principles of their religion, the poor, bound, illiterate slave, from Southern cruelty and bondage,— that some of our aristocratic citizens, some of our white savans, repaid his truthful eloquence, by visiting upon him the bitterest maledictions. From the negro, said they, we will accept these statements as true,—from him, they are pertinent and forcible; but when such unpalatable truths are uttered by a white clergyman, we cannot abide, nor will we listen to them!

Let consistency blush, and justice hang down its head! Is not truth the same, whether proclaimed by black or white,— bond or free? Is a falsehood to be pardoned because uttered by a negro? If indeed, as was admitted, the sentiments expressed by our eloquent colored speakers, were *true*, could they be false, when enforced by our intellectual friend, Van Loon? Certainly not; nor would the case have been so decided by these Solons, in any other case: or where the prejudice against color had not warped and blinded their otherwise good judgments. Our speaker, however, performed his duty faithfully, and with great satisfaction to the colored people and their true friends present.

The remains of this fearless champion of liberty; this humble disciple of the despised Nazarene, now sleeps in death, beside the placid waters of the Hudson, while his cherished memory lives in the affections of thousands, who "are ready to perish," and is honored by the pure in heart, wherever his name has been known throughout the land. In the day of final reckoning, think you, he will regret having plead the cause of the bondman? Ah, no; nor can we doubt that to him will be rendered the welcome plaudits: "Well done, good and faithful servant; enter thou into the joy of thy Lord. Thou hast been faithful over a few things; I will make thee a ruler over many things." What then are the few light afflictions endured in this life, when compared with "an eternal weight of glory," awarded to the faithful in that which is to come?

Pleasant, happy, and beneficial, as had been the reunion of old and tried friends, to celebrate a glorious event, yet, like all earthly enjoyments, it was brought to a termination, reluctant as were the friends to separate. Since that day, many have been the demonstrations of grateful joy and gladness on the glorious anniversary of the emancipation of slaves on the West India Islands; and yet, in this boasted "land of the free, and home of the brave;" this famous and declared *free* Republic,—the American slave still clanks his heavy chain, and wears the galling yoke of the bondman!

CHAPTER XXXVII

CONCLUSION

For several years past, anti-slavery truth has been spreading, and in proportion as light has shone upon the "peculiar institution," exposing to the world its crimes and blood,— enstamping upon its frontlet, "THE SUM OF ALL VILLAINIES,"— has the wrath of the impious slaveholder been kindled, and his arm outstretched to strengthen the chain, and press closer the yoke upon the helpless slave, proving conclusively that he loves darkness because his deeds are evil. Nor is this all; he and his apologists will insolently tell you, that *you* are the guilty ones who have tightened the bonds of the slave, increased his hardships, and blighted his prospect of freedom, by your mistaken kindness, in showing the slaveholder the enormity of his sin! Can this be so? Have we any direct influence over his human chattels? None. Then who is it that rivets the chain and increases the already heavy burden of the crushed slave, but he who has the power to do with him as he wills? He it is, who has been thrust, unwillingly perhaps, into sufficient light to show him his moral corruption, and the character of the sin he is daily committing; he it is, whose avarice and idleness induces to hold fast that which is to him a source of wealth,— and by no means to allow the same light to fall in upon the darkened intellect of his slave property, lest his riches "take to themselves wings;" or, as may be more properly said, *take to themselves legs and run away.*

What stronger proof can we ask in favor of our position, than the intolerant spirit of the South? If the system and practice of Slavery is a righteous one, instituted by an All-wise God, certainly no human power— especially one so impotent and futile as the abolition power is said to be —can ever overthrow it. Why then are the mails so closely examined, and fines imposed on prohibited anti-slavery documents? Is it beyond their power to confute the arguments adduced, or are they fearful that a ray of Northern light may fall on the mind of some listening slave, and direct him to the depot of an under-ground railroad? Judge ye!

What but this same fearful and intolerant spirit,—this over-bearing, boasting spirit, was it, that cowardly attacked a Christian Senator, while seated unsuspectingly at his desk, and felled him to the floor, bleeding and senseless? Was not the villainous blow which fell upon the honored head of CHARLES SUMNER, dealt by the infamous Brooks of South Carolina, aimed at the free speech of the entire North? Was it, think you, a personal enmity that the cowardly scoundrel had toward our worthy Northern Senator, which induced the attack? No, no. Brooks spake for the South, and boldly has it responded—Amen!

It has said through its representatives, that you Northerners are becoming too bold in speaking of our sin, and we will use brute force to repel it— an argument with which we are familiar. You have told us that we ought not to hold slaves, nor extend slave territory, which will in a measure destroy our slave market, and prove injurious to our slave-breeding population. You have told us we have no right to usurp Kansas,—no right to murder "Free State men," and no right to sustain there, a set of "ruffians" to make Kansas a slave State. You have told us, that we have no right to live on the unrequited toil of our slaves; nor to sell them to the highest bidder; nor spend the proceeds of the sale in idle extravagance. Now know, all ye Northerners, by this cowardly blow on the devoted head of your honored and respected Senator, that we shall no longer permit you to tell us such unpalatable truths, nor allow you the privilege of free speech! We have too long held the balance of power in the government

740

to yield it now; and we give you to know, that whatever we ask of this government, we expect to obtain; nor will we hear any of your objections. When we desire you to turn blood-hound, and hunt for us our fugitive slaves, we expect you to do it, and to see them returned to their masters, without a murmur on your part. Should you object or dare refuse, we shall certainly *cane somebody*, or else do what we have threatened for the last quarter of a century,—"DISSOLVE THE UNION!" Bah!

My house has ever been open to the fugitive slaves; but more particularly when I resided in Rochester, did I have occasion to see and feel the distresses of that class of persons; and it appears to me, that the heart must be of adamant, that can turn coldly away from the pleadings of the poor, frightened, flying fugitive from Southern bondage.

For many years past, I have been a close and interested observer of my race, both free and enslaved. I have observed with great pleasure, the gradual improvement in intelligence and condition of the free colored people of the North. In proportion as prejudice has diminished, they have gradually advanced; nor can I believe that there is any other great impediment in the way to a higher state of improvement. That prejudice against color is not destroyed, we very well know. Its effects may be seen in our down-cast, discouraged, and groveling countrymen, if no where else. Notwithstanding the late diminution, it exists in many of our hotels: some of them would as soon admit the dog from his kennel, at table, as the colored man; nevertheless, he is sought as a waiter; allowed to prepare their choicest dishes, and permitted to serve the white man, who would sneer and scorn to eat beside him. Prejudice is found also, in many of our schools,—even in those to which colored children are admitted; there is so much distinction made by prejudice, that the poor, timid colored children might about as well stay at home, as go to a school where they feel that they are looked upon as inferior, however much they may try to excel.

Nor is that hateful prejudice—so injurious to the soul,

and all the best interests of the negro—excluded from the professed church of Christ. Oh, no; we often find it in the house of worship, in all its cruel rigor. Where people assemble to worship a pure and holy God, who can look upon no sin with allowance—the creator of all, both white and black,—and where people professing to walk in the footsteps of the meek and quiet Jesus, who has taught us to esteem others better than ourselves; we often see the lip of some professed saint, curled in scorn at a dusky face, or a scowl of disapprobation if a colored person sits elsewhere than by the door or on the stairs. How long, O Lord, must these things be!

Of my enslaved brethren, nothing so gratifies me, as to hear of their escape from bondage; and since the passage of that iniquitous "Fugitive Slave Bill," I have watched with renewed interest the movements of the fugitives, not only from Slavery direct, but those who have been compelled to flee from the nominally free States, and ask the protection of a monarchial government, to save them from their owners in a land of boasted liberty!

The knowledge I have of the colored men in Canada, their strength and condition, would cause me to tremble for these United States, should a war ever ensue between the English and American governments, which I pray may never occur. These fugitives may be thought to be a class of poor, thriftless, illiterate creatures, like the Southern slaves, but it is not so. They are no longer slaves; many of whom have been many years free men, and a large number were never slaves. They are a hardy, robust class of men; very many of them, men of superior intellect; and men who feel deeply the wrongs they have endured. Driven as they have been from their native land; unprotected by the government under which they were born, and would gladly have died,—they would in all probability, in case of a rupture, take up arms in defense of the government which has protected them and the country of their adoption. England could this day, very readily collect a regiment of stalwart colored men, who, having felt the oppression of our laws, would fight with a will not inferior to that which actuated our revolutionary forefathers.

And what inducement, I ask, have colored men to defend with their lives the United States in any case; and what is there to incite them to deeds of bravery?

Wherever men are called upon to take up arms in defense of a country, there is always a consciousness of approaching wrong and oppression, which arouses their patriotism and incites to deeds of daring. They look abroad over fields of their own cultivation; they behold too, churches, schools, and various institutions, provided by their labor, for generations yet to come; they see their homes, their cherished hearthstone, about to be desecrated, and their wives and little ones, with their aged sires, exposed to the oppression of a ruthless foe. Then, with what cheerful and thrilling enthusiasm, steps forward the husband, the father, the brother, and bares his bosom to the sword,—his head to the storm of the battle-field, in defence of his country's freedom, and the God-given rights of himself and family! But what sees the oppressed negro? He sees a proud and haughty nation, whose Congressmen yearly meet to plot his ruin and perpetuate his bondage! He beholds, it is true, a few Christ-like champions, who rise up with bleeding hearts to defend his cause; but while his eye kindles with grateful emotion, he sees the bludgeon of the South— already reeking in the blood of freemen—raised and ready to fall with murderous intent upon the head of any one, who, like the illustrious Sumner, dare open his mouth in defence of Freedom, or speak of the wrongs of the poor negro, and the sins of the Southern autocrat!

What inducement then, has the slave to shoulder his musket, when the American drum beats the call, "To Arms! To Arms!" Does he not remember that the wife of his bosom; the children,— "bone of his bone, and flesh of his flesh,"—and the rude hearth-stone they for a time are allowed to surround, belong not to himself, but to the tyrannical master, who claims dominion over all he possesses. As his property then, let the slave owner go forth in defence of his own, and lay down his life if he please; but the poor slave has no home, no family to protect; no country to defend; nor does he care to assist in sustaining a government that instead of offering him protection, drives him from the soil which has been cultivated by his own labor,—to beg at the hand of England's Queen, "life, liberty, and the pursuit of happiness."

Humiliating as it is for an American citizen to name these things, they are nevertheless true; and I would to God that America would arise in her native majesty, and divest herself of the foul stain, which Slavery has cast upon her otherwise pure drapery! Then would she be no longer a hissing and by-word among the nations; but indeed what she professes to be, "the land of the free, and the home of the brave;" an asylum for the oppressed of every clime.

But should the monarchial government of England call for the services of the colored man, freely would his heart's blood be poured out in her defence,—not because he has a particular preference for that form of government; not because he has ceased to love his native country,—but because she has acknowledged his manhood, and given him a home to defend. Beneath the floating banner of the British Lion, he finds inducements to lay down his life, if need be, in defence of his own broad acres, his family and fireside,—all of which were denied him under the Stars and Stripes of his fatherland. But a short time ago, the colored men of Cincinnati, O., were promptly denied the privilege they had solicited, to join with other citizens, in celebrating the anniversary of WASHINGTON'S Birth Day! Oh, no; there must be no colored man in the company, met to honor him who still lives in the heart of every American citizen,—"the father of his country,"—and yet, who scorned not to sleep beside his faithful negro! Nor did the nephew of the illustrious General, despise the command of the black regiment, which Gen. Jackson so proudly commended for their bravery, and bestowed upon it his personal thanks, for their services on the field of battle.

Do the Northern or Free States of the Union think to clear

their skirts of the abomination of Slavery, by saying that they own no slaves? Very true. But is the poor, flying fugitive from the house of bondage, safe one moment within your borders? Will he be welcomed to your homes, your tables, your firesides? Will your clergymen bid you clothe and feed him, or give him a cup of cold water, in the name of a disciple of that holy Christ, who has said,—"inasmuch as ye have done it unto one of the least of these little ones, ye have done it unto me?"—Or will your own miserable Fugitive Slave Law, close the mouth of your clergy; crush down the rising benevolence of your heart; and convert you into a human blood-hound, to hunt down the panting fugitive, and return him to the hell of Slavery? Oh, my God!—the fact is too horrible to acknowledge, and yet it is a stubborn one. Not on one foot of land under the broad folds of Columbia's banner, can the slave say, "I am free!" Hungry, naked, and forlorn, he must flee onward; nor stop short of the outstretched arms of an English Queen. Yet, thanks be to our Heavenly Father, that all have not bowed the knee to the Southern autocrat or slave power. A few noble souls, thank God, remain, who, in defiance of iniquitous laws, throw open wide their doors to the trembling, fleeing bondman, whose purses are freely emptied to supply his wants, and help him on in his flight to the British dominion. But can these out-gushings of a benevolent heart—the purest impulses of a noble nature—be permitted to flow out spontaneously, in open daylight? Alas, no! You must be quiet; make no noise, lest an United States' Marshal wrest from you the object of your Christian sympathy, and impose on you a heavy fine, for your daring to do to another as you would he should do to you.

Is not the necessity of an "*under ground railroad*," a disgrace to the laws of any country? Certainly it is; yet I thank God, that it does afford a means of escape to many, and I pray that the blessings of Heaven may ever rest upon those who willingly superintend its interests. Oh, my country! When will thy laws, just and equal, supersede this humiliating necessity!

745

Is my reader about to throw the blame of our nation's wrong on England, and accuse her of first tolerating Slavery? We admit it; but did she not repent of the evil she had done, and speedily break every yoke, and let the oppressed go free? Certainly; no slave now breathes in England's atmosphere. But, say you, her white poor are slaves to the aristocracy, from which sentiment I beg leave to differ. Oppressed they may be, and doubtless are, as the poor are apt to be in any and every country; but they are not sold in the market, to the highest bidder, like beasts of burden, as are the American slaves. No Englishman, however poor, destitute, or degraded he may be, but owns himself, his wife and children; nor does he fear that they be sold and torn from his embrace, while he is laboring for their support. Poverty, my friend, does not comprise the bitterness of Slavery, no more than "one swallow makes a summer,"—nor does it consist solely in ignorance and degradation. Its bitterness arises from a consciousness of wrong; a sense of the violation of every right God has given to man, and the uncertainty of his future, over which he has no control.

If the American people flatter themselves with the idea of getting rid of the hated negro race, by colonizing them on the sickly soil of Liberia, or any other country, they will surely find themselves mistaken. They are Americans; allied to this country by birth and by misfortune; and here will they remain,—not always as now, oppressed and degraded,—for all who have any interest in the matter, well know that the free colored people, are rapidly advancing in intelligence, and improving their condition in every respect. Men of learning and genius, are now found among those with fleecy locks, and good mechanics with dusky complexion.

This marked improvement in the condition and rapid advancement in intelligence among our people, seems to have alarmed the colonizationists, and made them fearful that those very down-trodden slaves, who have for years labored for nought; whose blood and tears have fertilized the Southern soil, may, perchance, become their equals in intelligence, and take vengeance on their oppressors for the wrongs done them; and lest they should do so, they would gladly remove them to some far-off country.

Yet here, in North America, will the colored race remain, and ere long in my opinion, become a great people, equal with the proud Anglo-Saxon in all things. The African has once been a powerful nation, before Christian Englishmen invaded her coasts with rum, and incited her chiefs to war, by purchasing with gaudy, but worthless trinkets, her conquered captives; and we have every reason to believe, that though her glory as a nation has departed, that her sons will yet be acknowledged free men by the white population of this country.

There have been black generals in the world before Napoleon was born, and there may be again; and to-day, notwithstanding all the prejudice against color, that everywhere exists in this guilty nation, there are men of talent among us, inferior to none on the earth; nor are their numbers few, though rapidly increasing.

Well may the South arouse herself, form societies, replenish its treasury with a tax imposed on the free colored people, to defray the expense of sending manumitted slaves to Liberia!

Listen a moment to the cant of the colonizationist. Hear him talk of the duty he owes to Africa, and how happy, how intelligent, how prosperous everything is in Liberia. But when that delightful country asks to be taken into fellowship with the United States, and to have her independence recognized—ah, then he lifts his hands in horror and begs to be excused from so close a relation.

This is all cant, in my humble opinion; and when I see men so anxious to send the negro out of their sight, I feel quite certain that they are conscious of having deeply wronged him, and think to remove him, to atone for their guilty consciences. Would they refuse to acknowledge the independence of Liberia, if their interest in the colored people was genuine, especially when several other nations had done so? Oh, no. But that is not "*the rub.*" How could one of our lordly nabobs of the South, sit in Congress with perhaps one of his own manumitted slaves as a representative from Liberia or Hayti! He would die of mortification. Very well then; but let him talk no more of sending colored men to that country to make them free men.

The colored people generally, I am happy to say, have a right conception of the colonization plan, and will never be induced to go to Africa, unless they go as missionaries to the heathen tribes, who certainly should have the gospel preached to them. Some, from a sense of duty, may go as teachers,—which is all well enough,—but certain it is, that no amount of prejudice or abuse, will ever induce the colored race to leave this country. Long have they been oppressed; but they are rising-coming up to an elevated standard, and are fast gathering strength and courage, for the great and coming conflict with their haughty oppressors.

That there must be ere long, a sharp contest between the friends of Freedom and the Southern oligarchy, I can no longer doubt.

When our worthy ministers of the gospel, are sent back to us from the South, clothed with a coat of tar and feathers; when our best and most sacrificing philanthropists are thrown into Southern dungeons; when our laboring men are shot down by haughty and idle Southern aristocrats, in the hotels of their employers, and under the very eye of Congress; when the press is muzzled, and every editor, who has the manliness to speak in defence of Freedom, and the wickedness of the slaveholder, is caned or otherwise insulted by some insignificant Southern bully; and when at last, our Mr. SUMNER is attacked from behind, by a Southern, cowardly scoundrel, and felled senseless on the floor of the Senate chamber, for his defence of Liberty,— then, indeed, may Northern men look about them! Well may they be aroused by the insolence and tyranny of the South!

And for what *is* all this? Do not our Southern men know, that if light and truth are permitted to reach the minds of the people, that Kansas will be lost to them as slave territory, wherein the Southern slave-breeder can dispose of his own flesh to the highest bidder! Hear them talk as they do, in their pious moments, with upturned faces, in solemn mockery, of returning the negro to his *native* Africa! How many pure Africans, think you, can be found in the whole slave population of the South, to say nothing of their nativity? Native Africa, indeed! Who does not know, that in three-fourths of the colored race, there runs the blood of the white master,—the breeder of his own chattels! Think you, that a righteous God will fail to judge a nation for such flagrant sins? Nay, verily. If the All-wise God, who has created of one blood all nations of the earth, has designed their blood to commingle until that of the African is absorbed in that of the European,—then is it right, and amalgamation of all the different races should be universally practiced and approved. If it be right for the Southern slaveholder, to cruelly enforce the mixture of the races, to gratify his lust, and swell the enormity of his gains, certainly it cannot be wrong to amalgamate from choice and affection. Let us ask then, why did our Omnipotent Creator make the marked distinction? Certainly not for the purpose that one race might enslave and triumph over another; but evidently, that each in his own proper sphere might glorify God, to whom their respective bodies and spirits belong. Why, indeed, was the black man created, if not to fulfil his destiny *as a negro*, to the glory of God?

Suffer me then to exhort you, my countrymen, to cease looking to the white man for example and imitation. Stand boldly up in your own national characteristics, and show by your perseverance and industry, your honor and purity, that you are men, colored men, but of no inferior quality. The greatest lack I see among you, is unity of action, pardonable, to be sure, in the eyes of those who have seen your oppression and limited advantages; but now that many of you have resolved to gain your rights or die in the struggle, let me entreat you to band yourselves together in one indissoluble bond of brotherhood, to stand shoulder to shoulder in the coming conflict, and let every blow of yours tell for Freedom and the elevation of your race throughout the land. Speak boldly out, for the dumb and enslaved of your unfortunate countrymen, regardless of the frowns and sneers of the haughty tyrants, who may dare lift their puny arm, to frustrate the design of the Almighty, in preserving you an unmixed and powerful race on the earth.

While I would not that you depend on any human agency, save your own unyielding exertion, in the elevation of our race; still, I would not have you unmindful of, nor ungrateful for, the noble exertions of those kind white friends, who have plead the cause of the bondman, and have done all in their power to aid you, for which, may the God of the oppressed abundantly bless them.

Let your attention be given to the careful training and education of the rising generation, that they may be useful, and justly command the respect of their fellow-men. Labor for a competency, but give not your whole attention to amassing the wealth that perishes; but seek to lay up for yourselves "treasures where moth doth not corrupt, nor thieves break through and steal."

Suppose not, my brethren, that your task is a light one, or one that can be performed without years of patient toil and unyielding perseverance. Our oppressors are not very ready to credit our exertion,—too often forgetting the effects of our long degradation, and vainly expecting to see us arise at once, to the highest standard of elevation, able to cope successfully with those who have known no such discouragements or disadvantages, as has been our lot to bear.

These and many other obstacles must be bravely met, and assiduously removed,—remembering that Slavery has robbed some of us, and prejudice many others, of that perseverance so necessary to the accomplishment of any enterprize; but in the elevation of ourselves and race, let us never falter and grow weary, until we have reached the elevated station God designed us to occupy, and have fitted the rising generation to fill and improve it after our earthly course is finished and we leave to them the stage of action.

Allow me, however, to entreat, that no success which may attend your determined efforts; no position which you may attain,—may ever so occupy your mind, as to cause you to forget for one moment, the afflictions of your countrymen, or to cease to remember the groaning millions in bonds, until every slave shall triumphantly chant the song of deliverance from Slavery's dark prison house.

Bear with me, my dear brethren, while I claim a friend's license, to say, that I would not that you place implicit confidence in any of the political organizations of the present time; but remember that the majority of those parties are diligently laboring for their own interest. Look you then to yours; are you less capable of securing your rights than they? Never was there a time when indolence and supineness among us, would be so unpardonable as now, nor when so much depended on our active and judicious exertions.

Let us not forget, that in the past, we could and did truthfully complain, that we had no helper,—bound and crushed beneath an overwhelming weight of prejudice and ignorance, we lay helpless at the feet of our political spoilers. A favorable change has since been effected in the public sentiment; and now that we see thousands who are willing to aid us, and as many more who will not hinder our labor,—shall we fold our hands in idleness?—or shall we renew our energies, in the cause of freedom and of our own advancement? Although we may not implicitly rely upon the political exertion of others, let us not fear to co-operate with the friends of liberty everywhere, as far as a good conscience will permit, and our limited privileges will allow, by our determined zeal for the right, make our influence felt in the nation. See what wrong and oppression our white brethren have met in Kansas, from the slave power; and let their noble deeds of patriotism; their liberal sacrifices for freedom, be not only our example, but an incentive to do our duty. Have they more at stake in that mighty struggle than we, that they should leave their homes of refinement and comfort, take their lives in their hands and bravely contend for their rights, surrounded by scenes of blood and carnage? Certainly not. No people on the earth can have greater incentives to arouse them to action, than the colored people of this country now have; I trust therefore, that our future independence and prosperity, will suffer nothing from the inactivity of our race.

Some may entertain the belief that the African slave trade is entirely abandoned. I think not. Often are seen strange, suspicious looking vessels, lying along the African coast, for no other purpose than that of kidnapping the poor, ignorant natives. Stealthily the slave-trader lands his wicked crew, in the vicinity of some negro village or cluster of huts, and when a favorable opportunity occurs, he and his men rush upon the frightened African, burn their huts, and amid the shrieks of the captives, and the groans of the helpless and aged, who have been trampled down in their rude haste to secure the young and able-bodied natives, bear them to the vessel, where they are stowed away in the hold of the ship, which bears them to Christian (?) America, where they are sold as slaves.

Some years ago, a woman engaged in washing clothes, near the sea coast, had a lad with her to take care of her two younger children—one a young babe—while she was at work. They wandered away a short distance, and while amusing themselves under some bushes, four men, to them strange looking creatures, with white faces, surrounded them; and when the lad attempted to run away, they threw the infant he held in his arms, on the ground, and seizing the other two children, bore them screaming with fear, to the ship. Frantic and inconsolable, they were borne to the American slave market, where they were sold to a Virginia planter, for whom they labored sorrowfully and in tears, until old age deprived them of farther exertion, when they were turned out, like an old horse, to die; and did die destitute and uncared for, in their aged infirmity, after a long life of unrequited toil. That lad, stolen from Africa's coast, was my grand-father.

It is not, however, necessary for us to look beyond our own country, to find all the horrors of the slave traffic! A tour through the Southern States will prove sufficient to satisfy any one of that fact; nor will they travel over one of them, before—if they have a heart of flesh—they will feel oppressed by the cruel outrage, daily inflicted on their fellow-beings. The tourist need not turn aside to seek evidences: he will very readily observe the red flag of the auctioneer floating over the slave pen, on which he may read in large letters, waving in the pure air of heaven, "SLAVES, HORSES, AND OTHER CATTLE, *in lots to suit purchasers!*" He may halt a moment, and look at the multitude, collecting under the folds of that infamous banner, where will be found a few gentlemanly appearing slave holding planters, superbly mounted, and perhaps with their servants in waiting; but the larger number he will find to be drunken, coarse, brutal looking men, swaggering about in the capacity of slave-traders.

Let him enter the low, dingy, filthy building, occupied by human merchandize, and he will there behold husbands and wives, parents and children, about to be sold, and perhaps separated forever! See the trader, as he examines with inhuman indifference the bones and sinews, the teeth and joints of the *articles* on hand, even of females, and hear him make inquiries concerning her capabilities, that would make a savage blush! And see the miserable woman lift her red and swollen eyes to the face of the heartless trader, and the next moment cast a despairing glance over the motley crowd, in search of a compassionate look—a pitying eye. Should she see one countenance wearing a kind, humane expression, it will most likely bring her frantically to his feet, where, kneeling, with uplifted hands, she pleads: "Oh, Massa, do buy me! Do buy me and little Sam! He be all of the chil'ens I got left! O, Lord! O, Lord! Do, Massa, buy me, and this one baby! Oh, do Massa!" But the weight of the cow-hide drives her to the auction block, where in mock solemnity she is represented as "an article of excellent breed, a good cook, a good seamstress, and withal a good Christian, a ra'al genewine lamb of the flock!"—and then she is struck off to the highest bidder, who declares that he "won't have the young'un any how, 'cause he's gwine to drive her down to Lousianny."

He may see, too, the wild, despairing look of some frightened young slave girl, passing under the lustful gaze of some lordly libertine, who declares himself "in search of a fancy article for his own use!"

One after another is taken from the block, until all are disposed of, amid the agonized wail of heartbroken wives and mothers, husbands and fathers, and the piercing screams of helpless children, torn from a parent's embrace, to be consigned to the care of strangers.

Nor need I inform our traveler of the inhuman method generally approved, in hunting with trained blood-hounds, kept and advertised for the purpose of recapturing any poor slave who may attempt to escape from this cruel bondage. He may perchance, come across the mangled and lifeless body of some fugitive, which has just been run down and torn in pieces by the dogs of the hunter! Should he stop a few moments, he will soon see a hole dug in the ground, and the remains of the slave pitched into it, covered sufficiently to hide the unsightly mass from view, and there will be an end of the whole matter! "Shall I not visit for these things? saith the Lord; and shall not my soul be avenged on such a nation as this?"

In giving to the public this unvarnished, but truthful narrative, of some of the occurrences of my humble and uneventful life, I have not been influenced by a vain desire for notoriety, but by a willingness to gratify a just and honorable request, repeatedly made by numerous and respected friends, to learn the truth concerning my connection with the Wilberforce colony; the events which there transpired during my stay, and the cause of my losing a hard-earned property. Regarding the affairs of the colony, I have, therefore, endeavored to be particular,—

believing that duty to myself and brethren, required me to give them the within information; but nothing have I set down in malice. Much more might have been said relative to some of the leading characters in that settlement, had I not been fearful of its assuming the character of a personal enmity or retaliation. He who knows and will judge the actions of men, will bear me witness, that I have cherished no such feelings toward any of those who then lived, but now sleep in death.

In justification, however, of my statements regarding the character of Mr. Lewis, I will call the attention of the reader to some of the many letters received from good and eminent men, to show that I was not alone in the low estimate of his virtues. Gladly I leave that unpleasant subject, hoping that nothing in our past history will serve to becloud the bright future beginning to dawn on the prospects of our disfranchised and oppressed countrymen.

Made in the USA
Las Vegas, NV
20 February 2023

67878629R00437